Una delle tendenze più evidenti della storiografia contemporanea è la riscoperta delle tradizioni e degli stili nazionali. Questa Collana vuole contribuire ad un'opera di ricostruzione e comprensione della cultura economica italiana. I volumi si articoleranno secondo tre coordinate. Una periodale, dal 1750 al secondo dopoguerra. Una monografica, dedicata agli economisti di maggior rilievo. Infine, una tematica (moneta, impresa, diffusione delle idee economiche, scelte di politica economica).

1. A. Magliulo, *Marco Fanno e la cultura economica italiana del Novecento*
2. Nicolò Bellanca e Nicola Giocoli, *Maffeo Pantaleoni, il Principe degli economisti italiani*
3. Luigino Bruni, *Vilfredo Pareto. Alle radici della scienza economica del Novecento*

Si ringrazia l'Ente Cassa di Risparmio di Firenze

Economisti Italiani
Collana diretta da Piero Barucci e Piero Roggi

4

In collaborazione con la rivista «Storia del pensiero economico»
del Dipartimento di Scienze Economiche dell'Università di Firenze

Via Santa Maria, 27/r - 50125 Firenze
Tel. 055.233.7702 - 055.229.410 - Fax 055.229.430
http: www.polistampa.com

I.S.B.N. 88-8304-352-9

From Economists to Economists

The International Spread of Italian Economic Thought, 1750-1950

Edited by
Pier Francesco Asso

Edizioni Polistampa

Contents

Introduction*

Pier Francesco Asso
University of Palermo

1. "Cross-fertilisation" of ideas has become a popular expression and a widely cultivated field of inquiry, particularly in the social sciences. Perhaps more than with other disciplines, in economics it can be an extremely difficult process to disentangle and represent. It requires widespread research of sources and textual evidence; it requires knowledge of how ideas are communicated and transmitted; it requires the understanding of how authors or books have been interpreted, readapted to meet some specific requirement, or introduced into different national contexts; it requires careful consideration of the historical, the political and the institutional setting of society; it requires extensive knowledge of biographical vicissitudes and environmental constraints; it might also require conjectural efforts, since some ideas may spread from one country to another, from one author to another without the latter's willingness or even awareness to actually recognise the former's specific influence. In brief, the diffusion of ideas in economics is a complex phenomenon that needs a rigorous definition of the object under investigation and an appropriate selection of methods, objectives and techniques of investigation.

In order to maximise the results of inquiries on "cross-fertilisation", historians of economic thought have often warned against possible dangers of dispersion. Concentration of efforts in one direction becomes an obvious methodological implication that is mainly driven by pragmatism and good sense: it just becomes a useful precaution to be followed. As a consequence, studies on the spread of economic ideas have been traditionally devoted to the analysis of specific authors, "classic" works, or well established schools of thought. To make it a useful exercise, also the object of inquiry needs to be precisely defined: "case studies" have been restricted to measure the impact of specific economic ideas within national or international contexts, within relevant economic or scientific institutions, within specific communities of potential users.

Therefore, to my knowledge, historians of economic thought have never attempted to investigate the process of international dissemination of a national

* I wish to express my gratitude to professors Piero Barucci and Piero Roggi, general editors of this series of volumes on Italian economic thought, and to Antonio Magliulo, for their continuous intellectual support in the preparation and realisation of this project.

group of economic thinkers from modern times to the inter-war years. The essays reproduced in this volume have the ambition to do so: they are all addressed to measure the fortune, the reputation and the influence which Italian economists had on the international community of economists between 1750 and 1940. This is why the papers in this volume deal with a rather novel theme and must be considered, to a large extent, exploratory. The volume contains 12 contributions that analyse the spread of Italian economic thought within different national contexts: Great Britain, the United States, France, Germany, Portugal, Spain, and Sweden.

2. How can the individual essays be related to the theme of the book and to each other? Most authors accept a very broad definition of "Italian economic thought". In fact, all essays are devoted to consider not only the small group of leaders and well-established innovators (such as Galiani or Pareto), but also the rank of average economists. Most authors, it must also be remarked, accept a very broad definition of what "diffusion" actually means. In so doing they have shared common objectives: first of all an attempt has been made to reconstruct the intellectual network in which Italian economic thought was transmitted and circulated. Secondly, great importance was attached to the "milieu" which imported the ideas and the direct or, even more often, indirect mechanisms which facilitated their movements.

All essays start with very simple questions. What was the degree of knowledge of Italian economic thought within different countries? How can it be measured and assessed? What explanations can be found for its capacity (or incapacity) to attract the attention of groups of economists living and working in different national contexts? However, studying the degree of knowledge also served to introduce more intriguing questions, which are related to the way this process of communication came about and to the results it managed to produce. In brief: what was the role of individuals or of the academic community at large? What were the more general connections with the process of institutionalisation and professionalisation of economics? In what degree did the foundation of the leading economic journals help to increase the interchange of ideas? Did learned societies or other relevant institutions create a favourable environment? Did civil society help to establish mutual relations at an international level? What was the part played by governments and politics? Finally, the process of "discovery" and reconstruction helped to introduce the most substantial question: in what degree has Italian economic thought been influential for the development of new economic ideas, the opening of scientific debates, or the refinement of new analytical instruments?

The determination of the **degree of knowledge** of Italian economics within different national contexts must then be considered, I believe, one first result produced by this project. Having established that, in many instances, the lines of direct or indirect communication between non-Italian and Italian economists existed and were wide open, the authors of the individual chapters have tried to measure and explain the **degree of influence**, understanding, reputation and interpretation. This collection of essays does not aim to address – unless in cursory form – such questions as the search for precursors or the identification of a national style of Italian economics. Rather, a common objective has been to establish whether and in what specific cases a difference existed between mutual knowledge and influence, between ordinary scholarly relationships and real productive exchanges of economic ideas. In other words, between the external and the internal history of "cross - fertilisation".

In this respect there are obvious national differences in the character and scale of penetration of Italian economic thought. The diffusion of Italian economic thought in 19th century Sweden or Portugal cannot be compared to the diffusion of Italian economic thought in, say, France, Spain, Germany, England or the United States. Quite expectedly, historical, political, economic and cultural ties did matter and constituted the natural background on which knowledge and mutual influence were established and transmitted from economists to economists. In fact, countries such as Spain or France, which were running neck to neck in the process of modernisation and industrialisation and which, at some stage or another, had with Italy strong political and economic connections, were definitely more open to the importation and discussion of our own domestic economic ideas and problems. Quite expectedly, all authors seem to agree that the late 19th century professionalisation of economics played a crucial role in the international spread of Italian economics. In the German area, for example, the academic environment was particularly favourable and open to Italian economists, who regularly established strong and mutual relations with their colleagues. After 1890 we record a remarkable presence of Italian economics in the Anglo-American, French and German journals, which is in striking contrast with the scattered references which have been found in the age of classical economics.

Therefore, in quite different cases and circumstances, it has been shown that the wealth of mutual contacts was absolutely remarkable and extremely articulated. It went from personal acquaintance and regular correspondence to the establishment of close intellectual ties through book reviews, book translations, specialised articles on Italian economic thought and frequent citations and discussions of Italian works which can be found also at the more "esoteric" level of textbooks or lecture notes. On all these features, the interested reader is referred to the individual chapters. In the remaining part of this *Introduction*, our main objective is to discern certain forms and patterns in the events that characterise the process of international diffusion of Italian economic thought.

3. Most authors have given some attention to the means by which the spread of economic ideas was actually worked out. Especially in the 18th century, for example, translations, direct communications, travels and personal acquaintances played an important part. We thus find confirmation to the fact that ideas circulated mainly because men circulated. In this regard, Italian economic thinkers were no exception to this rule: in the 18th century continental Europe, so Legris observes, Galiani's visits abroad, especially to France, as well as Beccaria's or Pietro Verri's, contributed to the setting of a cosmopolitan, literary republic and indirectly to the

diffusion of their own ideas. Just to name another example, the translation of Beccaria was a source of deep inspiration within intellectual circles in Paris and went through seven different editions in less than a year.

Particularly in the age of Enlightenment, also foreigners travelled and benefited in various degrees from their stay in Italy. Between 1750 and 1800, Cardoso and Astigarraga found that a host of political reformers, public servants, diplomats and intellectuals in exile wrote and conceived their works in Italy, sometimes under the direct influence of Italian economists. It was not a rare occurrence that Spanish and French intellectuals gained some acquaintance with economics through imported Italian books. Works by Galiani, Verri and Genovesi soon became "classics" to be re-exported: they were widely used to introduce economics in their own homeland and particularly to stress the difference between "scientific" economic truth and the state of economic statecraft. As it frequently occurred in those days, the German case is an interesting confirmation to the fact that Italian economic literature was imported only indirectly, mainly by reading J. B. Say, A. R. J. Turgot and A. J. Blanqui. As Gehrke and Kurz show in their paper, Thünen and List are just the two most distinguished authors who came to appreciate Italian economic doctrines by means of their "French connections".

Besides travels and politics, also education played no small part in developing new channels for the knowledge and dissemination of Italian economic thought. Throughout the 19th century, various continental reforms of the university system served to establish close institutional connections and greatly eased the process of international diffusion. For many countries, we have found out, Italy remained for quite a long time a successful model of the early institutionalisation of economics, with new chairs and the production of textbooks that other national contexts seemed eager to imitate. Many authors bring to light evidence of intense institutional influence and connections.

Thus, as Astigarraga and Zabalza show in their chapters, a growing number of Spanish economists took their university degrees in Italy and felt the influence of Italian teachers in a wide range of subjects, from agriculture to statistics, from public finance to applied economics. Spanish economic societies, Astigarraga notes, drew heavily on Italian sources in order to create suitable teaching methods of "the genuine laws of commerce". The establishment of new chairs in economics was also profoundly influenced by the Italian experience together with the way teaching methods and even syllabi were structured and designed. Verri's *Meditazioni* were recommended for classroom use and even in the formulation of Spanish economic policy. Italian books of "principles", from Genovesi to Cossa, from Filangeri to Supino, went through several editions and were occasionally adopted by local universities. Spain is also an interesting country-case with regards to the increased availability of Italian texts and monographs, particularly in the fields of public finance and applied economics. Both essays on Spain show that the number of translations as well as their promptness was quite impressive, and some of them were directly sponsored within official circles. Cardoso even discovered the interesting case of an Italian professor of economics in Portugal. Besides Universities, in the early 19th century, Parisi shows that Academies and learned societies contributed to the early spread of Italian economic thought in the United States. In fact, the first edition of the *Encyclopaedia Americana*, which was published in Philadelphia between 1829 and 1833, contained a good number of entries and quotations devoted to Italian economists and economics.

From this perspective, all essays provide new evidence that in the age of marginalism, the attractiveness of the Italian University system had almost vanished even for such relatively less developed contexts as Portugal or Spain. However, Zabalza has found that Italian authors continued to be influential, if only for their important role in introducing both marginalism and the German historical school in Spain. In this perspective, Boccardo's 3rd series of the *Biblioteca dell'economista* was an extremely successful enterprise and made available in Spain the translation of modern texts using marginalism and mathematical methods. Cusumano's writings provided secondary sources for the knowledge of German authors, while Nitti's works on public finance and catholic socialism proved to be a channel for the introduction of positivism in Spain. However, institutional connections were not limited to the case of Spain. It is not rare to find economists studying at foreign Universities who paid regular visits to Italian institutions during their sabbatical leaves. For example, in their paper, Asso and Fiorito recall the case of Frank Taussig and other distinguished North-American economists preparing their PhDs in Germany but actually writing their dissertation in Italy. Among textbooks, the most interesting and (perhaps) disappointing cases regard Cossa's and Pantaleoni's reception in England. Bruni has discovered unpublished sources to reconstruct the translation of Cossa's *Guide* and Pantaleoni's *Principles*: while Jevons played a crucial role for the success of the former, external circumstances significantly reduced the impact of Pantaleoni's volume on English economists.

Also the foundation of specialised journals or the publication of collections of volumes deeply contributed to the creation of intellectual networks. In the early period the Custodi collection was the most influential source for the spread of Italian economic doctrines within many Continental European countries. By the end of the 19th century most authors observe that the means for genuine professional interchange had greatly improved. The number of Italian book reviews which the leading economics journals (the *Economic Journal*, the *Journal of Political Economy*, the *Political Science Quarterly* and the *Revue d'Economie Politique*) hosted between 1890 and 1910 is quite impressive. In this perspective, Mornati gives an interesting case study on cross - fertilisation. He shows with great details how, ever since its foundation, the presence of Italian economists in the French *Revue d'Economie Politique* was quite outstanding. Italian economists participated as authors, as reviewers, and as the subject of articles and book reviews written by their French colleagues. Further research along the lines of

Mornati's piece is needed in order to provide a more comprehensive account of the relevance of Italian economics in France in the age of marginalism which, as Mornati suggests, was strong enough to deserve more than just one essay.

In terms of translations of Italian books, the German case is also very impressive. Apart from their number, Hagemann and Rösch show that some eminent economists – such as J.A. Schumpeter, F. Hayek, O. Morgenstern or J. Marshack – were directly responsible in the process of dissemination of Italian economic thought. In their paper – as well as in Asso-Fiorito's on the United States – a quantitative analysis based on the number of Italian book reviews significantly supports this conclusion.

As I already observed, all essays try to go beyond answering questions exclusively devoted to the "sociology of knowledge" domain. Also in matters of more analytical economics – and particularly in the assessment of the influence of Italian economists on specific points of theory or policy – there are strong national differences, which we leave to the interested reader to appreciate. In many cases – Raffaelli's study on British classical economists and Parisi's essay on American economic thought prior to the Civil war, being the two most outstanding – the lack of many explicit references to Italian works complicated the investigation and required the study of indirect sources or other methods.

However, again in Spain but also in France, for quite a long time Italy was perceived as the cradle of modern economic theory. Moreover, as Gehrke and Kurz show, in early 19th century German economic thought, Italian texts were deeply scrutinised and partly absorbed. Perhaps as a reaction to British cultural hegemony, Galiani, Verri, Beccaria and Ortes were often hailed as forerunners of Smith and Malthus on value, money, population and the general laws governing production and economic growth. Genovesi enjoyed some popularity in Portugal on matters of taxation, agriculture and economic policy: his *Lezioni* were the most received Italian text in Spain and, as Astigarraga mentions, were also very influential in the Spanish colonies of Latin America. On matters of land reform, Italian economics began to creep in even in the (almost) impenetrable community of British classical economists: as Raffaelli shows, via the "Italian" works of Sismondi, John Stuart Mill became a careful observer of the Italian agricultural system. And in his *Principles*, he wrote appreciative words on the merits of the metayer system as a form of joint production and profit-sharing.

Generally speaking, Italian economists were quoted and studied in connection with policy-oriented debates or with the way specific economic problems (population, land reform, taxation, trade policy and the business cycle) had been dealt with. In some cases, the publication of Italian works stirred analytical controversies and heated debates. Galiani's contributions to value and monetary theory had the most powerful and lasting impact on, particularly, French and German-speaking authors. In France, Legris shows how, particularly among French politicians, the circulation of Galiani's writings reached an intense degree, which "successfully reduced the spread of physiocratic ideas". Again in France,

Beccaria's writings played an important role in the reform of the justice system and the criminal law. While, at a more analytical level, Legris sees no strong French - Italian connection in the line of progress which runs from Galiani to Say, his essay shows that on methodological issues and the growing need for a more formal approach to economics, Verri, Beccaria and Galiani were the object of debate and criticism on the part of Condorcet, Turgot and Condillac.

However, with the only possible exception of Spain, Italian influences of any kind progressively disappeared at the beginning of the 19th century. Italian economic thought underwent an almost total eclipse, which approximately lasted until the 1880s. In the 19th century, for non-Italian economists, Italy's great 18th century economists maintained a merely historical interest, while the Italian economists of the Risorgimento were completely neglected. With little surprise, we have learnt that Francesco Ferrara remained almost completely unknown and is hardly ever mentioned in all these essays. The one and only exception remained the United States, where Ferrara had established close connections with the anti-Ricardian Henry Carey. As Parisi shows, their relationship was "complex, it underwent changes over the years, and was rich in controversial ideas and even profound misunderstanding". However, the fact that the golden age of classical political economy coincided with a period in which Italian economic thought languished, affected its fame and diffusion even in countries – such as Spain or France – which were relatively more open and receptive. For many economists Italy was a decaying or – at best – a "stationary" country lying at the very periphery of the new industrialised civilisation. Italian economists were absent from the international exchange of economic ideas mainly because – all authors seem to agree – Italy itself was absent as a producer of culture, scientific ideas or technical innovations.

Indeed, any application of strong determinism cannot provide a satisfactory, unique explanation of the collapse and subsequent recovery of Italian economics. In fact, the crisis of Italian economic thought – and in its international diffusion – ends suddenly after 1880 and never reappeared even in the dark times of the Inter-war years and the two decades of totalitarian dictatorship. To prove this statement, many authors have selected the two extremes of this new age: the historical school and the Italian corporativists. In this respect, Italian representatives of the historical school were well known and widely read in many countries. They were rather influential in Spain and the US for their conjunct criticism of laissez faire and British classical economic thought, particularly in matters of income distribution and economic growth. In the German area, Hagemann and Rösch found several instances of "strong parallels and issues of important mutual influences", particularly on methodology and socialism.

Similarly, corporativist authors enjoyed a considerable success in Spain and Portugal: in these two countries the political and economic ideology of corporativism influenced economists and politicians particularly for its destructive criticism of perfect competition and general equilibrium theory. On the other hand, also in the United States or Germany, Italian books on corporativism were widely read; even though American economists, almost by definition, systematically linked corporativism to Fascist ideology and politics, sometimes at the expense of a more productive interpretation of the many books which Italian economists published under the banner of "corporative economics".

One crucial question that is often addressed in many essays devoted to the post-1870s is whether we can talk of a limited knowledge or, more generally, of a scant international fortune of Pareto, Pantaleoni, De Viti de Marco and especially Barone. Most essays, for chronological reasons, do not consider the effects produced on the international diffusion of Italian economics which occurred after the rehabilitation by John Hicks, Joseph Schumpeter, Richard Musgrave, Maurice Allais, James Buchanan and many others mainly after the second World War. Nevertheless, Cardoso and Zabalza attribute the almost complete lack of references to the Italian leading marginalists to the delay with which marginalism itself was actually introduced in Portugal and Spain. There were again notable exceptions, such as the Portuguese mathematical economist Osorio who extensively followed Pareto's mathematical approach to general equilibrium and consumer choice. However, their conclusion seems plausible enough and receives indirect confirmation in the essays by Pålsson and Sandelin on Sweden, Bruni on Great Britain, Hagemann and Rösch on Germany and Austria, Asso and Fiorito on the United States. Where marginalism triumphed, Italian economists were read, translated, and often invited to contribute to journals, editorial initiatives or international conferences. In this respect, Pantaleoni's reputation in the Anglo-American world stands out: in 1898 he was invited by the British Economic Association while, ten years later, he was the first Continental economist to be honoured by the American Economic Association which organised an official symposium on his behalf to discuss his contributions to the field of economic dynamics. Hagemann and Rösch devote a paragraph to discuss the role of those "mediators" who gained great merits in the dissemination of Italian marginalist economists and to their entry in the North American market once the international academic framework collapsed as the Nazi regime rose to power.

More specifically the essay on Sweden by Pålsson and Sandelin shows that – despite strong linguistic and cultural barriers – the lessons of the Italian marginalists were well received in Sweden particularly in the domain of public finance. Bruni's research shows that Pareto was the only influential Italian economist within the British marginalists. Indeed, Pantaleoni had close connections with Edgeworth and even managed to influence the launching of the *Economic Journal*. However, apart from single episodes, Bruni generally dismisses Pantaleoni's case as a "missed occasion". The chapter by Hagemann and Rösch throws new light on the intense relations between Austrian economists – most particularly Schumpeter, Hayek, and Morgenstern – and some leading Italian colleagues in the Inter-war years. Active collaboration was established with Del Vecchio, Fanno and Bresciani Turroni on business cycle and monetary theory, public finance and economic dynamics. Conversely, Hagemann and Rösch observe that all efforts (and most notably, Schumpeter's and Weinberger's) to build up new studies after Pareto's *Manual* had been published, were rather unproductive "with the exception of personal income distribution and neoclassical demand curves".

Finally the essay by Asso and Fiorito – which also draws on an extensive archival research – provides new evidence on the reception of the leading figures of Italian neo-classical economics: apart from the rather exceptional case of E.R.A. Seligman, Pantaleoni's and De Viti de Marco's influence on American economic thought was limited and rather controversial. Pareto instead gained a strong reputation – indeed, Asso and Fiorito believe much stronger than Schumpeter and other more recent interpreters have generally admitted. This was particularly true with respect to Pareto's law of distribution and for his attempt to develop the formal conditions underlying the construction of the demand curve and the refinement of a theory of choice. Also Pareto's fame in America as a sociologist – albeit a rather explored subject – has been reassessed. New insights were found particularly with reference to Talcott Parson and his connections with American institutionalism and to the debate elicited by the many reviews which followed the publication of the American edition of Pareto's *Treatise*.

Asso and Fiorito's conclusions in the negative are also quite interesting and emblematic of the whole research project on the international diffusion of Italian economic thought: Barone's works on pure theory remained completely ignored while, despite the many potential areas of mutual interest, American institutionalists never showed any interest for what Italian economists were doing. On the German side, also Hagemann and Rösch assert that "it is unintelligible that the relationship between Weber and Pareto is characterised by mutual neglect", while it is even more surprising that, with very few exceptions, Bresciani Turroni's studies on the German inflation "went largely unnoticed in the contemporary German literature".

Therefore, at a more analytical level, the response of cross-fertilisation in the age of marginalism until the interwar years remains ambiguous. Apart from the ones just mentioned, all authors discuss several, contrasting episodes which shed "lights and shades" on the international spread of Italian economic thought. Hopefully, some of them will fascinate the reader as interesting milestones on which postwar, transnational economics was built. Even more so, some others will pave the way for further research on the history of intellectual exchanges in economics.

Palermo, July 2001

Italian influences on British classical political economy: a survey

Tiziano Raffaelli
University of Cagliari and University of Pisa

During the first half of the XIX century, while the Italians were fighting for their independence, studies in the history of Italian culture, politics and science were inspired by the quest for national identity. In the field of political economy the effort to build up a national tradition, helped by the timely and praiseworthy publication of the Custodi Collection of 'classical' Italian economists, was firstly undertaken by Gioia and then pursued by Pecchio (1829) and Bianchini (1845). Pecchio's book, 'written with a strong national bias' (McCulloch, 1845:31), maintained that Italian thinkers had anticipated most of the ideas later associated with English and French economists. McCulloch's reaction might have gone too far when he stated that 'there is an incomparably clearer appreciation of the grand source of wealth in the statement made by Locke, in the *Essay on Civil Government*, in illustration of the influence of labour in establishing a right of property than is to be found in all the writings of the Italian economists from Serra [i.e.: from 1613] down to the present day' (McCulloch, 1845:189), but it is certain that by the time these words were written Italian influences on British economists, if ever there were any, were completely forgotten.

After Smith's original and systematic synthesis of themes of the European Enlightenment, British political economy, from Ricardo to Mill, seems to have grown on its own, keeping some loose relationships only with French authors, Say in particular. The industrial revolution, even more than the Napoleonic wars, can explain why, for some decades, British economists were to follow a lonely path. Ricardo's *Principles of Political Economy and Taxation* was a comment on Smith, aimed at correcting the latter's theoretical mistakes, while Malthus's economic treatise was the result of his friendly discussions with Ricardo. Only John Stuart Mill's wider perspective brought English political economy back into contact with continental issues.

Moreover, the 'golden age' of classical political economy coincided with the period in which Italian economic analysis languished (Faucci, 2000). While Pietro Verri, Ferdinando Galiani and Cesare Beccaria were first-rank economists and social thinkers of the European Enlightenment, widely read and known abroad, Melchiorre Gioia and Giandomenico Romagnosi, the two main Italian economists of the first decades of the XIX century, were – and still are – almost unknown outside their own country. No original contribution to the theory of value and distribution can be attributed to Italian economists in the first decades of the XIX century (at least before Ferrara wrote his introductions to the series *Biblioteca dell'Economista*; see Faucci, 1995). Since this theory was the 'core' of British classical political economy, it is reasonable to think that Italian economists had almost no influence on its development, after Smith's work had established the 'canon' of economic discourse. The following brief survey confirms this impression. To make up for such deficiency, attention has been devoted to the Italian origin of some of Smith's and Mill's views on man and society.

A further and perhaps more promising subject of research would be Italian influences on 'applied economics' (agriculture, land tenure, irrigation, integration between small industrial activities and agriculture, saving banks). Though unoriginal in value and distribution theory, Italian economists of the first part of the XIX century were engaged in projects of social reforms along the lines laid down by their Enlightenment predecessors and delved into the connection between institutions, habits and economic activity with discernement and originality (Porta and Scazzieri, 1997). Some of the Italian issues had their echo in England, mainly for political reasons. Thus, the agriculture of Northern Italy, already praised by Arthur Young, was referred to in Parliamentary discussions about the Irish question[1] and both Lombardy's silk manufacture and Tuscany's metayer system were well known to many British social thinkers. However, such influences have been disregarded by historians of economic ideas and are outside the limits of this paper (and the competence of its author), except for a few remarks on their impact on Mill's work.

1. At a first glance, Smith does not appear to have been deeply influenced by Italian Enlightenment writers. In her detailed and thorough analysis, Lanaro (1980) points out that Smith shared the opinion of many British intellectuals of his age that the cradle of European Renaissance was a decaying country, where learning had become 'almost totally extinguished' (Smith, 1980:243). Criticisms of Italian economic and political conditions, expressed in *Wealth of Nations* (Smith, 1976b:347, 901-902 and 904), perhaps under the influence of the country's descriptions by British and French visitors, can explain Smith's lack of interest for contemporary Italian literature in these fields. Pietro Verri's *Meditazioni sull'economia politica* (two copies), Morellet's French translation of Beccaria's *Dei delitti e delle pene* and an early edition of his *Opere diverse* are the only books of Italian Enlightenment reformers in the catalogue of Smith's personal library[2].

---

[1] An English inquiry in 1847 pushed Cattaneo to write one of the masterpieces of Italian economic thought: answering a set of questions issued by Lord Ebrington, Cattaneo explained that the main difficulty of transplanting the model of Lombardy's irrigated agriculture did not lay in the Irish soil, orography, rainfall and temperature, but in differences of culture, custom and institutions that change slowly, silently and almost unconsciously (Cattaneo, 1847).

[2] Pilati's *Lettres sur l'Hollande* may be added to the list, but they bear witness to Smith's interest in the Netherlands more than in the author.

Galiani's *Dialogues sur les commerce des bleds* was certainly known to Smith through Morellet's refutation, which he possessed. It is also highly plausible that Smith met Galiani in 1766, while the two were in Paris, attending the same *salons*. However, given Morellet's and Hume's critiques of the Neapolitan abbot, it is probable that Smith had no strong interest in his work[3].

Verri deserves a closer look, since his affinities with Smith are striking. In 1790 the author of Smith's obituary in *The Times* noticed that 'Smith's system of political economy is not essentially different from that of Count Verri, Dean Tucker and Mister Hume' and in 1803 Say maintained that Verri, 'more than any other of Smith's predecessors', got near the laws of the production and consumption of wealth (Lanaro 1980:131). Though acknowledging the difficulty of tracing direct and personal influences for Enlightenment thinkers, Groenewegen (1999: 702-703) suggests that Verri's *Meditazioni* (§3) could be the source of Smith's views on the balance of production and consumption (Smith 1976b: 497-98)[4].

On the whole Lanaro's conclusion that Smith's economic culture was mainly British and French is convincing (Lanaro, 1980:137).

By contrast, Smith appears to have been well acquainted with earlier Italian authors, in particular with XVI, XVII, and early XVIII centuries political, juridical and historical writers. Works by Machiavel, Guicciardini, Giovio, Sidonio, Sarpi, Boccalini, Bentivoglio, Davila and Giannone are listed in Bonar's catalogue of Smith's library, together with many histories of Italian states – in particular of the republics of Venice (Contarini, Garzoni, Sandi and Sabellico's collection) and Genoa (Doria) and of formerly republican cities, like Florence (Varchi, Ammirato) and Siena (Malavolti). Smith's knowledge of Muratori's collections of documents and chronicles of Italian history is suggested by Smith (1978:156), which appears to refer to *Rerum Italicorum scriptores*, and by his ordering *Antiquitates Italicae medii aevi*, together with Graevius's *Thesaurus* of Italian histories, for the library of Glasgow University. This list is fairly long and significant, mainly for the attention paid to Italian republican thought and history, whose decisive influence on English and American political thought has been thoroughly investigated by Pocock (1975).

Smith's library also shelved Italian works on science (Galileo, Spallanzani, Malpighi, Borelli, Gorini Corio), the arts (Leonardo, Alberti, Palladio, Bellori) and poetics (Scaligero, Gravina, Ruscelli) together with books of literary prose

---

[3] Galiani's influence on British thought in general was scarcely relevant. Significantly, in Accademia Nazionale dei Lincei (1975) there are essays on 'Ferdinando Galiani et la culture allemande' and 'La fortune di l'Abbé Galiani en France au XIXe siècle', but none on Great Britain.

[4] Verri's and Smith's views on taxation were also similar (cfr. Del Vecchio, 1930), but they were shared by other thinkers of the period and Smith openly refers to Lord Kames for the principles of taxation (Smith 1976b: 827). The same can be said of some of their views on money. For Verri's Welsh connections see Venturi (1977). In Einaudi's opinion (1953:75), lack of quotations suggests that Smith was not influenced by Verri.

(Boccaccio, San Francesco, Caro, Castiglione, Ferrante Pallavicino, Forteguerri, Della Casa, Baretti, Boccalini, Famiano Strada) and poetry (Dante, Petrarca, Ariosto, Tasso, Tassoni, Boiardo, Berni, Chiabrera, Corsini, Guarini, Lippi, Maffei, Marino, Pulci, Sannazaro, Metastasio, Albergaro Capacelli and Zatta). Lanaro (1980:110) also notices that Vico's *Scienza Nuova* was indirectly known to Smith through Chastellux's *De la félicité publique* (1772), though both the analogy between Vico's 'storia ideale eterna' and Smith's 'conjectural history' and their similar views on the development of language do not imply any direct influence since such opinions were widely diffused in the European Enlightenment.

In general, given the lack of references usual at the time, it is difficult to assess the role that Italian authors played in Smith's works. Their impact is much clearer in his works on poetry, literary style and the history of science than in his writings on law and social history. *Lectures on Rhetoric and Belles Lettres*, with mentions of Ariosto, Sannazaro, Machiavel, Guicciardini and Boccalini, 'The history of astronomy', which refers to Galileo, Cassini and Fracassoro, and the essay 'Of the affinity between Italian and English verses', which discusses at length Metastasio, Tasso, Petrarca and Ariosto, showing Smith's good knowledge of the Italian language[5], are the works in which relatively more Italian authors are mentioned. In Smith (1976b), Machiavel, Guicciardini ('one of the most judicious and reserved of modern historians', p. 426), Baretti, Sandi, Marco Polo and the physician Ramazzini are explicitly referred to in the text. No indirect reference to other Italian authors has been provided by subsequent critical editions. Smith (1976a) mentions only Machiavel and Petrarch and Smith (1978) no Italian authors at all.

2. Among possible Italian influences on Smith, Machiavel stands out as by far the most relevant. Smith's judgments on the Florentine political writer are controversial. In Smith (1983:114-15) he refers to Machiavel and Guicciardini as 'the two most famous modern Italian historians', but takes notice of their striking differences. Guicciardini was more interested in petty Italian politics, 'subtle and refined', and 'his whole History is a criticall dissertation on the Schemes, the little and often crooked artifices of the time'. By contrast, Machiavel 'despised' such politics, giving them 'little attention' 'as of no great moment': 'Machiavel is of all Modern Historians the only one who contented himself with that which is the chief purpose of History, to relate Events and connect them with their causes without becoming a party on either side'.

Machiavel is also taken as an example of 'the Didactick Style': 'Aristotle amongst the ancients, and Matchiavel among the moderns are perhaps the only two writers who have adhered closely to this peculiar style of a didactick writer. They

[5] Smith possessed a French-Italian dictionary, an Italian grammar in French and the *Vocabolario della Crusca* (while for the library of Glasgow University he ordered Baretti's *New Italian Dictionary*).

trust solely to the strength of their arguments and the ingenuity and newness of their thoughts and discoveries to gain the assent of their readers' (Smith, 1983:36).

Smith was impressed by Machiavel's account of Cesare Borgia's assassination of his guests in Senigallia, written in 'that pure, elegant and simple language which distinguishes all his writings'. The coolness of Machiavel's description is explained by the fact that Italy was at the time a country 'where great crimes frequently pass unpunished, the most atrocious actions become almost familiar, and cease to impress the people with that horror which is universally felt in countries where an exact administration of justice takes place'. However, Machiavel's morality is even worse than that prevailing in such context since he is defined as 'not indeed a man of the nicest morality even for his own times'. Smith denounces lack of compassion for the young princes' 'miserable and untimely death' and absence of 'indignation at the cruelty and falsehood of their murderer' (Smith, 1976a:217). Finally, Smith indirectly criticizes Machiavel's admiration for Castruccio Castracani, *signore* of Lucca in the XIV century, whose politics, in the long run, damaged Lucca's economy by driving out of the town the silk artisans who were forced to migrate to Venice (1976b:407[6]). Smith's view of the 'uninteded social consequences' of human action appears to make fun of both Castruccio's plans and Machiavel's understanding.

Great historian and political writer, Machiavel seems to be neither a master of morality nor a careful interpreter of economic facts.

What can be said of Machiavel's influence on Smith in general? Smith's views on happiness[7] and fortune, 'which governs the world' (Smith, 1976a:104), though similar to Machiavel's, were rooted in classical and medieval thought[8]. The republican tradition, which was very influential (Winch, 1978 and Pocock, 1975), though stemming from Machiavel's writings, had been taken over by many English writers, from Harrington to Francis Hutcheson, the 'never to be forgotten' master of Adam Smith. Deep knowledge of this literature would be necessary before stating whether Smith's bits of republicanism are directly connected to Machiavel's similar views[9]. Ecclesiastical policy is another field where Machiavel exercised his influence and indeed Smith explicitly endorses Machiavel's views when he states that the

---

[6] The passage was added to the 2nd edn and probably suggested by Sandi's *History of Venice*.

[7] Bonar (1893:61) thought of an analogy between Smith's view that happiness is almost equally distributed between different classes and Machiavel's view that it is almost equally distributed between different centuries.

[8] Lanaro (1980:101) for example stresses that Smith's view of the providential role of fortune (Smith 1976a:105) could have been inspired by Dante Alighieri (*Inferno*, VII, verses 67-96). However, in Smith (1976b) and also in other sentences of Smith (1976a), fortune looks more like accidental lot, similar to the one described in Dante's *Convivium* (IV.xi.6) more than in his *Divina Commedia*.

[9] There are many examples of such possible connections. Thus, the respect for Hamburg where taxes are voluntarily paid by citizens 'with great fidelity', simply by declaring upon oath that what they pay is their due (Smith, 1976b:850), is almost similar to Machiavel's account and admiration (Machiavel, 1983:189-90, I.55.1). The lack of martial spirit in commercial countries (Smith, 1976b:697-98) is another instance, as it also is the discussion of the reasons why Alexander the Great did not meet with any resistance after he conquered the greatest part of Asia (Smith, 1978:157-58). Though obviously mediated by Montesquieu's dicussion of polygamy, the passage appears to show some direct reminiscences of Machiavel (1998:19-20, IV).

'mendicant orders ... revived, in the thirteenth and fourteenth centuries, the languishing faith of the catholick church' (Smith 1776b:790; Machiavelli 1983:361-62, III.1.5)

However, it is more in Smith's general view of man than in single aspects of his thought that Machiavel's influence is significant. Of course, these influences could have come indirectly through Hume, who was another admirer of the Italian political writer (Giarrizzo, 1962), or from Rousseau, but some Smithian themes are so close to Machiavel's views that a direct influence is plausible. One of Smith's favourite ideas is that powerful people, 'the rich and the great', tend to oppress the poor whenever they can. This is what happens in the labour market (Smith, 1976b: book I, chapter VIII) and in owner-slave and noble-serf relationships (Smith, 1976b: book III, chapter II). The chapter on wages, with Smith's defence of the poor labourer against the rich employer, appears to stem from Machiavel's opinion that 'senza dubbio, se si considerrà il fine de' nobili e degli ignobili, si vedrà in quelli desiderio grande di dominare ed in questi solo desiderio di non essere dominati' (Machiavelli, 1983:33, I.5.2). In a similar way, 'the pride of man' that 'makes him love to domineer', so much that 'wherever the law allows it, and the nature of the work can afford it, he will generally prefer the service of slaves to that of freemen' (Smith, 1976b:388) is an echo of the people's view that 'la superbia loro era tanta che non poserieno mai se non forzati' (Machiavelli, 1962:159, II.xiv). The rich and the noble oppress other people when the power they have allows them to do so without any danger. The same view applies to Smith's discussion of the exploitation of colonies by the servants of the East India Company: 'It is the system of government, the situation in which they are placed, that I mean to censure, not the character of those who have acted in it. They acted as their situation naturally directed, and they who have clamoured the loudest against them would, probably, not have acted better themselves' (Smith, 1976b:641). Once again, it is almost inevitable to think of Machiavel's well-known passage: 'è necessario a chi dispone una repubblica ed ordina leggi in quella, presupporre tutti gli uomini rei, e che li abbiano sempre a usare la malignità dello animo loro, qualunque volta ne abbiano libera occasione' (Machiavelli, 1983:27, I.3.1)[10]. These examples prove beyond doubt that Fay was right when he wrote that Smith (1976a) – and in general Smith's view of man – could be summarized as 'Hutcheson versus Mandeville', 'with the praise for Hutcheson and the argument from Mandeville' (Fay, 1956:24). They prove difficult to reconcile with any 'christianized' reading of Smith and with the idea that he placed

[10] The following passage could also have been inspired by Machiavel: 'All families are equally ancient; and the ancestors of the prince, though they may be better known, cannot well be more numerous than those of the beggar' (Smith, 1976b:713). One of the leader of the Ciompi rebellion harangued the revolutionary assembly with similar words: 'Né vi sbigottisca quella antichità del sangue che ei ci rimproverano; perché tutti gli uomini avendo avuto uno medesimo principio sono ugualmente antichi, e dalla natura sono stati fatti a uno modo' (Machiavelli, 1962:237-38; III.xiii).

'benevolence' amongst the prerequisites of a working society. They also suggest that Machiavellian influences were at work in shaping Smith's view of man and society.

3. Coming from Scotland to England and crossing the century borders, Italian influences almost disappear. From Sraffa's edition of Ricardo's works it seems that he did not owe much to Italian authors. Italian culture is referred to only in the letters written from Italy, in the Autumn of 1822 (IX, 221-28 and X, 291-339).

Malthus's *Principles of Political Economy* bear no traces of Italian authors, but his theory of population is a typical example of a doctrine that was 'in the air' and the list of forerunners includes many Italian authors. Following Cossa (1895), Reynad (1903) started with Botero's *Delle Cause della grandezza e magnificenza delle citta* (1598), mentioned by Schumpeter (1963:255-56; see also Jandelli, 1881) and then went on with other Italian books, among which Ortes's *Riflessioni sulla popolazione delle nazioni per rapporto all'economia nazionale* (1790), Beccaria's *Elementi di economia pubblica* (1769) and Filangieri's *Delle leggi politiche ed economiche* (1780).

However, none of these books is listed in Malthus's personal library and James (1979) does not refer to any Italian influences on the principle of population. For its closeness to Malthus's, Ortes's theory appears a possible forerunner, but it has to be discarded for lack of evidence, implausibility of direct influence and widespread acceptance of similar views. McCulloch's conclusions on the subject are worth quoting *in extenso*: 'This work (Ortes's *Riflessioni*) has been a good deal referred to by various foreign writers, from its anticipating in some respects the conclusions of Malthus. Ortes contends that population, were it not restricted by the difficulty of providing food and other accomodations, would increase in a geometrical proportion, doubling every thirty years; and he further contends that the difficulty of providing the means of subsistence, by operating on the reason of mankind, and restraining the principle of increase, keeps the latter within the necessary limits and prevents the extreme poverty and misery that would otherwise result from the tendency to increase. But notwithstanding the soundness of his conclusions, its obscurity and prolixity must have prevented the work of Ortes from having any practical influence. Most probably it was unknown to Malthus at the period when he published his *Essay* and besides, there is nothing in it that had not been stated by others' (McCulloch, 1845:265).

Italian books in Malthus's library, though less numerous than in Smith's, cover similar ground: poetry and literature (Ariosto, Boccaccio, Boiardo, Della Casa, Dante, Dovizi, Metastasio, Tasso, Alessandro Verri, Alfieri), science and the arts (Algarotti, Ficoroni, Malvasia), history and politics (Machiavel, Davila, Rossetti). The only Italian book referred to in Malthus's writings is Machiavel's *Historie fiorentine*. In the second edition of the *Essay*, Malthus (1986, II: 67-68) quotes the opening sentences of the first book of the *Historie*, already quoted by Gibbon, where the barbaric invasions are described as a kind of planned migration due to overpopulation. Not only Italian authors, but Italy itself is almost absent from Malthus's works. While Sweden, Switzerland, Russia and Spain, besides England and Ireland, provide statistical evidence to support the principle of population, the kingdom of Naples is the only Italian state referred to, and only once, in the first edition of the *Essay*.

Like his fellow countryman Smith, the Scottish McCulloch was able to read Italian. He was well acquainted with Italian economic literature, including the Custodi Collection, whose titles he reproduced in his *Literature of Political Economy*. In that book he included Italian authors under the headings 'Treatises on Political Economy' (Verri, Beccaria, Pecchio) 'Commerce in general' (Genovesi, Mengotti's *Del commercio dei Romani* and *Il Colbertismo*, Galiani's *Dialogues*, Verri's *Riflessioni sulle leggi vincolanti* and Contarini's *Dissertatio de re frumentaria*), 'Commercial Law' (Azuni, Fierli, Casaregis), 'Weights and Measures' (Cristiani), 'Book-keeping' (*Introduzione alla pratica del commercio*, Livorno, 1759), 'History of Commerce' (Formaleoni, Michele di Iorio, Contini, Marin and *Della decima*, Lucca and Lisboa, 1765-66), 'Money and Banks' (Serra, Turbolo, Galiani, Baldasseroni), 'Statistics' (Gioia's *Filosofia della statistica*, without any comment), 'Insurance' (Baldasseroni), 'Population' (Ortes, whose other economic works, McCulloch writes (p. 265), 'might have been advantageously omitted' from the Custodi Collection), 'Pauperism' (Ricci, Morichini, Petitti di Roreto), 'Revenue and Finance' (de Welz, Bianchini).

McCulloch praised Verri, whom he defined as 'by far the most distinguished of the Italian economists' (1845:27), for demonstrating 'the fallacy of the opinions of the French Economists respecting the superior productiveness of the labour employed in agriculture' (1825:35) and approvingly quoted Verri's opinion that knowledge of finance and trade was the best preparation for the undertaking of reforms (1975:10). He also appreciated Beccaria's *Elementi di economia pubblica*, the text of a course delivered in 1769 and firstly published in 1804, but found the 'Preliminary discourse', the only part that was translated into English and published in 1769, 'a very poor performance', 'neither worthy of the author, the subject, nor the course to which it was an introduction'. He considered Galiani a witty and brilliant author, but faulty with his critiques of free trade (1845:85), uninformed on navigation law and outperformed on this issue by Lampredi (1845:127), unoriginal in his view that labour ('fatica') is the source of wealth (1845:190), which McCulloch suggested he might have taken from Locke.

Nassau William Senior had strong links with Italy as shown by his *Journals*. Moreover, the Italian Arrivabene was the translator of Senior's *Outlines* into French in 1836. Charles Babbage owed much of his fame on the Continent to Menabrea's article on the *Bliothèque Universelle de Genève*, published in 1842. Though Babbage found in Turin, in 1840, an exciting environment which increased his powers of explanation and made his ideas 'clearer', as he himself acknowledged (Babbage, 1989), both are cases in which Italian intellectuals helped to spread ideas born on British soil but had no direct impact on their birth.

4. Also Mill's contacts with Italian intellectuals were wide. Pasquale Villari was among Mill's correspondents from the 1850s to the 1870s. His reformist activities in politics, social issues and education were openly inspired by Mill. The Italian tradition of 'civic humanism', to borrow Pocock's expression for the republican thought of the former period, took from Mill many of its values and proposals (Urbinati, 1990). Costantino Baer had an interesting correspondence with Mill on the taxation of interest (which Baer supported and Mill rejected, in the letters as well as in the review of Baer's book)[11]. Mill was also in contact with Giuseppe Mazzini, and the latter's view on liberty, his romantic eccentricism and 'love of solitude', admired by Mill (CW, XIII:378; XV:548; XVII:1759), could have inspired some of the ideas of *On Liberty*.

Knowledge of Italian culture was certainly part of Mill's education, but to a lesser extent than it was of Smith's. No Italian names are referred to in Mill's *Autobiography*. Acting on the principle of 'losing no time', his father made him learn Greek and arithmetics, than Latin and English poetry. Also history, one of the favourite readings of Mill's, was mainly classical and British (included British colonies). Logics, political economy, higher mathematics and experimental sciences could not be expected to need recourse to Italian sources. Neither did Mill's intellectual crisis, in 1826, change this picture: English romantic literature, French social thought and German writers were the main additions to his readings. Even his knowledge of Italian poetry was poor[12].

Like for Smith, Machiavel deserves a closer look. Mill took from the *Discorsi* a motto with strong 'republican' flavour for an article he wrote in 1826[13] and in 1854 in his diary he defended the Florentine writer from naif critiques (CW XXVII:650). He also showed interest in Villari's work on Machiavel, encouraging him to write on the subject (CW XV:531-32; XVII:1808).

However, where Italian influences show up in Mill's economic work is through his reading of Sismondi and Châteauvieux on the metayer system of Tuscany and Lombardy. Sismondi in particular had a great impact on Mill who often quoted with approval both *Nouveaux principes* and *Etudes sur l'economie politique*. Since the parts on the metayer system and especially the essay on Tuscan agriculture included in the last book were the result of Sismondi's Italian connections and in particular of his discussions with the 'campagnoli toscani' (Passerin d'Entreves, 1949), we find here a genuine influence of Italian economic culture on Mill.

Mill oscillates between two views of the metayer system. On the one hand it is considered a first approximation to the much better system of peasant ownership

---

[11] Baer's letters are in Urbinati (1990). Mill's review of Baer is in Mill (CW V:697-702).

[12] In 1854, in a letter to Harriet Taylor from Montpellier, while he was going to Italy, Mill writes: 'I have several times read a little of Tasso, to the benefit I hope of my Italian, for I do not seem likely to derive any other pleasure or profit from it. ... Fortunately the same volume contains Dante who with Filicaja and perhaps Alfieri seem to me as far as I know the only Italian poets' (CW XIV:258).

[13] 'L'opinione contra i popoli nasce, perché de' popoli ciascun dice male senza paura' (Machiavelli, 1983:203, I.58.3; Mill, CW XXVI:369)

(CW XXIV:1011), likewise capable of checking population growth (CW II:350, 369); on the other hand Mill stresses its own merits as a form of 'joint ownership', not dissimilar from 'profit-sharing' which Mill supported for reforming the modern system of industrial relations[14]. The first view is the more traditional one, associated with the names of Smith and Arthur Young, whom Mill quotes with approval in chapter VIII of book II of *Principles of Political Economy*, where however he also notices that they formed their judgment looking at the metayer system of England and France, where the metayer was at the landowner's mercy and was not protected by customary laws. The latter view creeps in when Mill looks at Lombardy and Tuscany. Thus for example in *The Claims of Labour* (1845) Mill writes that the metayer system of Tuscany and Lombardy 'affords to him [the metayer] considerable motives both to industry and produce ... the metayers are really partners with the landowners, and have the feelings of joint ownership' (CW IV:389). And in paragraph 3 of the above mentioned chapter of *Principles* he quotes Sismondi to the effect that 'the rights and obligations of the metayer being fixed by usage, and all taxes and rates being paid by the proprietor, "le métayer a les avantages de la proprieté sans l'inconvénient de la défendre" '.

Though Sismondi's quotations are no 'evidence of the intrinsic excellence of the metayer system', which has the disadvantages that 'the motives to exertion on the part of the tenant are only half as strong as if he farmed the land on the same footing of perpetuity under a money-rent', they prove that the system can work and should not be abolished 'on a mere *à priori* view of its disadvantages'. Even the substitution of the metayer system with money-rent tenures is not 'without alloy; for a metayer, though not himself a capitalist, has a capitalist for his partner, and has the use, in Italy at least, of a considerable capital' (CW II:310-11)[15].

Mill's last political writing, his *Chapters on Socialism*, is based on the concept that property laws are variable, and can be adjusted to human needs. In the last pages it significantly includes a positive judgment on the possibilities connected with the metayer system: 'in Tuscany, the *metayer* farmer is virtually co-proprietor with the landlord, since custom, though not law, guarantees to him a permanent possession and half the gross produce, so long as he fulfils the customary conditions of his tenure' (CW V:752).

This final remark proves how fertile the contact with Sismondi's description of the Tuscan metayer system was for Mill's wider social and economic perspectives[16].

---

[14] See the chapter on 'The probable future of the working classes' in *Principles of Political Economy*.

[15] Mill found evidence that confirmed Sismondi's remarks during his voyage from Pistoia to Modena, in 1855: 'I take the Tuscan peasantry to be on the whole the best off in the world. The little I could see quite agrees with Sismondi's account of them' (CW XIV:484).

[16] On Sismondi's influence on Mill, see Pappe (1976).

REFERENCES

ACCADEMIA NAZIONALE DEI LINCEI (1975), *Ferdinando Galiani*, Roma, Accademia Nazionale dei Lincei.

ALIGHIERI D. (1991), *La divina commedia*, Milano, Hoepli.

BABBAGE C. (1989), *Passages from the Life of a Philosopher, The Works of Charles Babbage*, vol. XI, London, W. Pickering.

BIANCHINI L. (1845), *Della scienza e del ben vivere sociale*, Palermo, Lao.

BONAR J. (1893), *Philosophy and Political Economy in some of their historical relations*, London, S. Sonnenschein; New York, Macmillan and Co.

BONAR J. (1932), *A Catalogue of the Library of Adam Smith*, London, Macmillan and Co. Reprint: New York, Kelley, 1966.

BOWLEY M. (1937), *Nassau Senior and Classical Economics*, London, George Allen & Unwin Ltd.

CATTANEO C. (1847), 'D'alcune istituzioni agrarie dell'Alta Italia applicabili a sollievo dell'Irlanda. Lettere a Roberto Campbell', in C. Cattaneo, *Saggi di economia rurale*, a cura di L. Einaudi, Torino, Einaudi, 1939.

COSSA L. (1895), *Il Principio di popolazione di T.R. Malthus*, Bologna.

DEL VECCHIO G. (1930), 'Osservazioni sopra le relazioni tra gli economisti italiani e gli economisti inglesi', *Annali di economia*, VIII, pp. 293-99.

EINAUDI L. (1953), 'Dei libri italiani posseduti da Adam Smith, di due sue lettere non ricordate e della sua prima fortuna in Italia', in *Saggi bibliografici e storici intorno alle dottrine economiche*, Roma, Edizioni di storia e letteratura.

FAUCCI R. (1995), *L'economista scomodo. Vita e opere di Francesco Ferrara*, Palermo, Sellerio.

FAUCCI R. (2000), *L'economia politica in Italia dal Cinquecento ai giorni nostri*, Torino, UTET Libreria.

FAY C.R. (1956), *Smith and the Scotland of his Day*, Cambridge, Cambridge University Press.

GALIANI F., *Dialogues sur le commerce des bleds*.

GIARRIZZO G. (1962), *David Hume, politico e storico*, Torino, Einaudi.

GIOLI G. ed. (1986), *Le teorie della popolazione prima di Malthus*, Milano, Franco Angeli.

GROENEWEGEN P.D. (1999), 'The significance of Verri's *Meditazioni* in the history of economic thought: the wider European influences', in *Pietro Verri e il suo tempo*, ed. by P. Capra, Bologna, Cisalpino-Monduzzi, vol. II, pp. 693-708.

JAMES P. (1979) *'Population' Malthus. His Life and Times*, London, Routledge and Kegan Paul.

JANDELLI G. (1881), "Il precursore di Malthus" in *La Filosofia delle scuole italiane* vol. XXIII, Roma.

LANARO SARTORI P. (1980), 'Echi della cultura italiana nel pensiero di Adam Smith', in G. Vivenza, P. Lanaro Sartori and M.L. Parolini, *Aspetti della formazione culturale di Adam Smith*, Verona, Quaderni della Facoltà di Economia e Commercio, pp. 83-141.

MACHIAVELLI N. (1962), *Istorie Fiorentine*, Milano, Feltrinelli.

MACHIAVELLI N. (1983), *Discorsi sopra la prima deca di Tito Livio*, Torino, Einaudi.

MACHIAVELLI N. (1998), *Il Principe*, Roma, Ed. Riuniti.

Malthus Library Collection. The personal collection of T. R. Malthus at Jesus College, Cambridge, New York, 1983.

MALTHUS T.R. (1986), *The Works of Thomas Robert Malthus*, 7 vls, London, Pickering.
MCCULLOCH J.R. (1825), *The Principles of Political Economy: with a sketch of the rise and progress of the science*, Edinburgh, W. And C. Tait.
MCCULLOCH J.R. (1845), *The Literature of Political Economy. A Classified Catalogue*, London, Longman, Brown, Green and Longmans. Reprint: London School of Economics and Political Science, 1938.
MCCULLOCH, J.R.(1975), *A Treatise on the Principles and Practical Influence of Taxation and the Funding System*, 3rd ed. (1863), ed. by D.P. O'Brien, Edinburgh and London, Scottish Academic Press.
MENABREA L.F. (1842), 'Sketch of the analytical engine invented by Charles Babbage', *Bibliothèque Universelle de Genève*.
MILL J.S. (1963-91), *Collected Works of John Stuart Mill*, ed. by J.M. Robson, Toronto, University of Toronto Press and London, Routledge and Kegan Paul, 32 vls.
MIZUTA A.H. (1967), *Adam Smith's Library. A Supplement to Bonar's Catalogue with a Checklist of the Whole Library*, New York, Kelley.
O'BRIEN D.P. (1970), *J.R. MacCulloch: a study in classical economics*, London, Allen & Unwin.
Pappe H.O. (1976), 'Sismondi et John Stuart Mill', *Economies et Sociétés*, pp. 1150-60.
PASSERIN D'ENTREVES E. (1949), 'L'anticapitalismo del Sismondi e i "campagnoli" toscani del Risorgimento', *Belfagor*, IV, pp. 283-99, 402-09.
PECCHIO G. (1829), *Storia dell'economia pubblica in Italia*, Lugano, Tipografia della Svizzera Italiana.
POCOCK J.G.A. (1975), *The Machiavellian Moment. Florentine Political Thought and the Atlantic Republican Tradition*, Princeton N. J., Princeton University Press.
PORTA P. e SCAZZIERI R. (1997), 'Concorrenza e società civile', in A. Quadrio Curzio (ed.), *Alle origini del pensiero economico in Italia. Economia e istituzioni: il paradigma lombardo tra i secoli XVIII e XIX*, Bologna, Il Mulino.
REYNAUD P. (1903), *La Theorie de la population en Italie. Du XVI au XVII siecle. Les precurseurs de Malthus*, Lyon, A. Rey.
RICARDO D. (1952-73), *The Works and Correspondence of David Ricardo*, ed. by P. Sraffa, Cambridge, Cambridge University Press.
SCHUMPETER, J.A. (1963), *History of Economic Analysis*, 5th edn, London, Allen and Unwin.
SENIOR W.N. (1871), *Journals Kept in France and Italy from 1848 to 1852*, 2 vls, ed. by M.C.M. Simpson, London, H.S. King.
SISMONDI J.C.L. (1827), *Nouveaux principes d'économie politique*, Paris, Treuttel et Würtz.
SISMONDI J.C.L. (1837), *Études sur l'économie politique*, Paris, Treuttel et Würtz.
SMITH A. (1976a), *The Theory of Moral Sentiments*, ed. by D.D. Raphael and A.L. Macfie, Oxford, Clarendon Press.
SMITH A. (1976b), *An Inquiry into the Nature and Causes of the Wealth of Nations*, 2 vls, ed. by R.H. Campbell and A.S. Skinner, Oxford, Clarendon Press.
SMITH A. (1978), *Lectures on Jurisprudence*, ed. by R.L. Meek, D.D. Raphael and P.G. Stein, Oxford, Clarendon Press.
SMITH A. (1980), *Essays on Philosophical Subjects*, ed. by W.P.D. Wightman, J.C. Brice and I.S. Ross, Oxford, Clarendon Press.
SMITH A. (1983), *Lectures on Rhethoric and Belles Lettres*, ed. by J.C. Brice, Oxford, Clarendon Press.

SMITH A. (1987), *Correspondence*, ed. by E.C. Mossner and I.S. Ross, 2nd edn (1st edn, 1977), Oxford, Clarendon Press.

URBINATI N. (1990), *Le civili libertà. Positivismo e liberalismo nell'Italia unita*, Venezia, Marsilio.

VENTURI F. (1977), *Le vite incrociate di Henry Lloyd e Pietro Verri*, Torino, Tirrenia-Stampatori.

VENTURI F. (1978), 'Le "Meditazioni sull'economia politica" di Pietro Verri, edizioni, echi e discussioni', *Rivista storica italiana*, XC, pp. 530-94.

VERRI P. (1804), *Meditazioni sull'economia politica*, Milano.

WINCH D. (1978), *Adam Smith's Politics. An Essay in Historiographic Revision*, Cambridge, Cambridge University Press.

Consents and Dissents
Moments of the Reception of Italian Economists in England: 1878-1938

*Luigino Bruni**
University of Milan - Bicocca

> Ideas are connected with each other much as prices are. Ideas form a system. They are all extremely complex functions of each other (Pantaleoni 1923, p. 582).

1. Introduction

This statement of Maffeo Pantaleoni, one of the main actors of the story I am narrating, is the outline of this study on the *reception* of Italian economists in England.

First of all, it can be worthwhile to specify that with reception we can understand two different concepts: reception as *influence*, or reception as *presence*.

We will see that the only Italian economist who has *influenced* English economic theory is Vilfredo Pareto, and in a different and surely minor way, Pantaleoni and Cossa.

Italian economic culture had a massive *presence* in England during the period at hand. From 1891 to 1899 the "Economic Journal" alone reviewed more than thirty books written by Italian economists on political economy. In the period between 1900 and 1910 the reviews were more than fifty.

Besides "The Economic Review" and "The Journal of Royal Statistic Society" with great attention followed the Italian economic literature.[1] In the main English libraries there are plenty of Italian books of economics. English Journals paid attention to the works of almost every Italian economist, and dozens of them wrote more than one paper in these journals – above all in the "Economic Journal".

But if we look through the volumes we discover that Achille Loria, an Italian scholar who was very much present in England between the XIX and the XX century, holds the primate of both reviews of his books, and original articles.

---

* *The author thanks Roger Backhouse, Nicolò Bellanca and Pierfrancesco Asso for their precious help in improving the paper. The usual disclaimers are applied. A special thank also to the librarians of the Archives of the London School of Economics, Manchester University, Nuffield College (Oxford), who allowed me to reproduce some unpublished manuscripts.*

[1] Interesting data on the Italian presence in England in the period (1915-1945) can be found in Magliulo (1993), Appendix.

Loria was in fact the Italian correspondent of the "Economic Journal" (an honour shared with Pareto and Pantaleoni in the '90's of the XIX century). His non-marginalist thought was present in the heterodox debate, but completely absent in the main English neoclassical economists.[2]

This paper is not an attempt of monitoring the *presence* of Italian economists in England in the period at hand. Given the richness and complexity of the fifty years I am examining, I do not believe that it is even possible to do such a work in a book, let alone in a paper.

On this topic there has been a previous research, that of Antonio Magliulo (1993) on *The Reception of Italian Economics in England*, who wrote a broad and detailed report for the period between 1915 and 1945. Apart from Pareto, Pantaleoni and other small points where I got new insights or new material, as far as the other Italian economists of 1915-1940 are concerned, I must turn the reader to this still unsurpassed research.

Because of Magliulo's research, only with the exception of Pareto, of whom I have followed the vicissitudes in England up to 1938 (the year in which John Hicks wrote *Value and Capital*, published in 1939), my research is centred on the period of the densest relationships between Italian economists and the *first* leading English marginalists: from 1878 (when Cossa wrote the first letter to Jevons) to 1910 (the date of publication of Wicksteed's *Commonsense*).

Therefore the core of this paper is the reconstruction of the encounters and scientific relationships between Pareto, Pantaleoni on the one hand, and Marshall, Edgeworth and Wicksteed on the other. Besides the relationship between Jevons and Cossa has a minor, but not irrelevant, importance in throwing light on the intellectual market among economists of these two countries.

The ways of organising a similar research are many. We could however outline two main ones: to choose the leading Italian economists of this period and then look at their presence/influence in England; or on the contrary: to organise the research around the pivotal English economists and to look at the Italian precence/influence. Given the general frame of the research (the reception of *Italian* economists in England), I have chosen the former.

In the next section I will sketch the *presence* of Italian economists in England through the interesting key-study of Luigi Cossa's relationship with Jevons (§ 2).

Then we look back at the Pantaleoni's story in England (§ 3), where I found a mixture of presence and (institutional) influence. Finally we analyse Pareto's *reception* in England, that of the *first* (§ 4) and the *second* Pareto (§ 5).

---

[2] The name of Loria doesn't appear in the index of names of Marshall's Correspondence. Having to avoid the analysis of Loria's presence and influence on non-marginalist English culture is a deficiency of this paper. I leave the task to fill the gap to some other colleague.

2. Cossa and Jevons: a "strange" encounter

The relationships between Stanley Jevons and Luigi Cossa was one of the main paths through which marginalism entered Italian economic milieu.

Jevons' *Theory of Political Economy* had already been translated in 1875 in the prestigious collection of foreign and Italian economists, *La Biblioteca dell'Economista*,[3] originally edited by Francesco Ferrara for the first two series.

Gerolamo Boccardo took the direction of the "Biblioteca" in 1874, and his aim was eclectic, an attempt to mediate between the opposite schools that in Italy and in the whole of Europe were in dispute.[4] Within this general cultural project, Boccardo introduced in Italy the recent developments of mathematics applied to economics, and the presence of translated marginalist economics in Italy began soon after the original publication.

In fact on the 9th of January 1875 the Italian economist and statistician Luigi Bodio wrote to Jevons: "Je crois que vous êtez déjà informé qu'on va traduire bientôt votre ouvrage dans la *Biblioteca dell'Economista*.[5] Sans doute on a du obtenir votre consentement pour cela. C'est une collection très intéressante et très répandue en Italie".[6,7]

Before the *Biblioteca dell'Economista* we have in Cossa one of the very first references in Italy to Jevons' *Theory of Political Economy*; and the translation of Jevons' *Primer of Political Economy* (1878), a sort of compendium of his *Theory of Political Economy*, *de facto* paved the way for the spreading of marginalism in Italy.

Luigi Cossa (1831-1896), studied in Germany with Roscher, and then became professor of Political Economy in Pavia (1858-1896), one of the leaders of the Italian economic movement in the second half of the XIXth century. Cossa cannot be defined a *marginalist*, and perhaps neither an *economist*. In today's academic classifications he would have been named a historian of economic thought: "He was the first modern full-time Professor of economics … He has elaborated just classificatory intellectual projects, based, however, on an erudition and philological rigour still enviable. Finally, he has promoted several and qualified research projects, finding financial, bibliographic and editorial resources, especially with the aim of edifying a grandiose reconstruction – only partly achieved – of Italian economic ideas from the middle-age to the Risorgimento" (Bellanca 2000, p. 195).

---

[3] Third series, II, pp. 175-311.

[4] See Barucci 1972, section 2.

[5] In fact in the 23th December 1874 Jevons wrote to J. D'Aulins: "I am informed by Professor Boccordo of Genoa that he proposes to translate my Theory into Italian" (in Jevons 1977, IV, p. 94). And on the 29th December he wrote to Boccardo, forwarding him a copy of his book (p. 95).

[6] In Jevons 1977, IV, p. 98.

[7] However, as Barucci (1972) underlined, this cultural operation by Boccardo missed the core message of marginalism (the final degree of utility). Only with the works of Pantaleoni (1883) did we have in Italy a scientific analysis built up on the marginal principle.

Thanks to his extraordinary knowledge of the past and current economic literature he met Jevons and other marginalists, but he had neither the age nor the mathematical tools to understand the new ideas which were being developed in economic theory after 1871-73: "The first is that the so-called 'marginal revolution' had made no impact on him whatsoever. He was aware of the work of Jevons and Walras, but he does not suggest that it offers anything that should be considered a radical break with the past" (Backhouse 2000, p. vii).

On his reputation in the Italian context still weighs a sarcastic and a rather nasty evaluation of his work pronounced by Pantaleoni, who in 1898, just after Cossa's death, wrote:

> There was no one abler than him in understanding books that he never would be able to write … He understood everything, but produced nothing. He had read everything … But he was affected by sterility up to the medulla (Pantaleoni 1898b [1925], I, p. 236).

Nevertheless, in the field of history and historiography of economics Cossa did an impressive amount of quantitative and qualitative work, and his books and essays were known and translated in all the main languages.

In particular both his "Guida allo Studio dell'economia politica" (1876) (*Guide to the Study of Political Economy*) and his "Introduzione all'economia politica" (1893) (*Introduction to the Study of Political Economy*) were translated in English, respectively in 1880 and in 1893.

In the translation of the *Guida* into the *Guide* Jevons played a crucial role, and consequently also in the translation of the *Introduction* in 1892, after Jevons' death:

> The favourable reception of the Author's *Guide to the Study of Political Economy*, translated and published in England and America at the suggestion and under the auspices of the late Professor Jevons, paved the way for an English version of what was begun as a third edition of that work, though it has finally shaped itself into a completely new book.[8]

How did Cossa meet Jevons?

Through Maggiorino Ferraris, a minor Italian economist, he knew that Jevons had a favourable impression of his *Guida*.[9] So, on the basis of this positive information, on the 3rd of April 1897 he wrote (in French[10]) to the English economist:

---

[8] Preface of the translator (Louis Dyner, Ballion College of Oxford) to Cossa 1893, p. v.

[9] Cf. Jevons (1977, IV, p. 41).

[10] I wonder whether Cossa had the command of the English language: in fact in the preface to the Italian translation to Jevons' Primer he acknowledged that the translation was made "thanks to the cooperation of my excellent pupil doctor Achille Loria" (Translator Preface, p. v).

> J'éspère que il puisse se présenter l'occasion de faire connaître mon travail au public anglais par quelque article de journals. Une citation seule de votre part me serait très utile. Si quelque jeune économiste de votre pays voulait par aventure le traduire, il serait bien facile de s'arranger pour le *copyright*.[11]

Later in the letter Cossa mentions his idea of translating Jevons' *Primer of Political Economy* (1878):

> Il vous fera peut-être agréable de savoir que dans le courent de l'année l'editeur milanais Hoepli publierà une *traduction italienne* de votre *Primer of Political Economy* qui paraître *sous ma direction*.[12]

It is worth noting that Cossa attached to his letter a list of names of ancient mathematical economists not present in Jevons' bibliography of the first edition of his *Theory* (1871).

In the second edition – not yet published in April 1879 – four names suggested by Cossa found a place in the new Jevons' bibliography: the German G. Von Falk, L. Brentano, H. Schumacher and the British H.H.E. Lloyd (1720-1783). For Lloyd, Cossa mentioned also the work (*An Essay on the Theory of Money*, 1771), and in the Preface to the second edition Jevons acknowledged his indebtedness to Cossa (p. XLI).

Cossa's hopes regarding the possibility of translating his *Guida* into English were crowned by success. In fact in the second letter dated 5th May 1879 he wrote to Jevons:

> Je vous prie d'employer *toute votre autorité* pour persuader votre éditor M. *Macmillan* à la pubblication d'une edition anglaise de ma *Guida*. … Il me tarde donc de savoir que l'affaire soit combinée. Une mention de mon ouvrage dans la préface de votre *Theory* (dont j'attends avec impatience l'exemplaire que vous me promettez!) rendra la chose encore plus facile.[13]

Jevons was very diligent and generous in following Cossa's "instructions". In fact, he not only mentioned Cossa's *Guida* in the Preface to the second edition of his *Theory of Political Economy*, but he personally wrote a very enthusiastic

---

[11] Letter published in Jevons (1977), V, pp. 41-43. The book "was translated by Margaret A. Macmillan (daughter of the publisher Alexander Macmillan), identified in the book simply as 'a former lady student in one of the excellent classes of Political Economy, conducted under the superintendence of the Cambridge Society for the Extension of University Teaching' (Backhouse 2000, p. i).

[12] In fact on the cover of the Italian edition of the *Primer* (Jevons 1880a), the Editor (Hoepli) put the double name: "Jevons-Cossa", and the role of Cossa in the book appeared in the eyes of the Italian economists as something more than a mere translation. It sounds not clear what Black writes in a footnote to this letter: "There is no record of this translation in the Bibliography of Jevons' writings" (Jevons 1977, V, p. 42, footnote 5).

[13] Letter published in Jevons (1977), V, pp. 59-60.

Preface to Cossa's *Guide*: "This book presents, in a compendious form, not only a general view of the bounds, divisions, and relations of the science, marked by great impartiality and breadth of treatment, but it also furnishes us with an historical sketch of the science, such as must be wholly new to English readers" (Jevons 1880b, p. vii).[14]

In the Preface to the second edition of his *Theory of Political Economy*, in 1879 Jevons wrote:

> Signor Cossa's excellent *Guida allo Studio dell'Economia Politica*, a concise but judiciously written texbook, is well qualified to open our eyes to the insular narrowness of our economic learning. It is a book of a kind much needed by our students of Economics, and I wish that it could be published in an English dress (Jevons 1879 [1871], p. XLI).

In fact he did convince Macmillan, for in his third letter dated 29th October 1880 Cossa wrote to Jevons:

> Je viens de recevoir les six copies de la traduction anglaise de mon petit ouvrage et je suis trés content de l'édition élégante et correcte de votre célébre *publisher* Macmillan. …
> Ce qui m'a fait un véritable plaisir c'est votre dotte et aimable Préface, dont j'apprécie avec une *reconnaissance sans bornes* la haute *porté*, et la bienveillante intention qui l'a dictée[15].

Therefore Cossa thanks Jevons for his "indulgente mention de ma *Guide* dans la Préface de votre *Theory* (1879)", which "dépasse le mérite bien modeste de mon écrit".

This last sentence is in line with Pantaleoni's conclusion of his profile of Cossa: "as he knew the others, likewise he knew himself. No ambition, no envy" (Pantaleoni 1898b [1925], I, p. 237).

The influence of both of Cossa's *Guide* and *Introduction* on English economists was very little. First of all this was due to the modest value of the book: "It is a book that can easily be criticised, for in large part it is a survey, approaching an annotated bibliography, of the literature on economics in which Cossa expresses blunt and unsubstantiated views on the works he discusses" (Backhouse 2000, p. v).[16] Secondly, Jevons died in 1882.

---

[14] It is interesting to note that in his *Preface* Jevons acknowledged the importance of the "historical method" even in pure economics: "One valuable result which will probably be derived from the reading of Professor Cossa's work is the conviction that the *historical method* must play a large part in economic science" (p. ix).

[15] This letter has mysteriously not been published by Black in Jevons' papers and correspondence (1977). The full text of the letter can be found in the Appendix.

[16] Later in his Introduction Backhouse adds: "Given all this, it is tempting to argue that the value of the book lies solely in its value as an extremely comprehensive bibliography of the literature on and about economics available in 1880. In this role is clearly very valuable, for Cossa reveals knowledge of a vast range of literature in English, German, French, Italian and other European languages" (p. 2). In fact the *Guide* has been considered worth of a reprint in the Collection of *Early Histories of Economic Thought* (Vol. 4).

No reference to Cossa's books can either be found in the Edgeworth's lectures in Oxford among the books for further readings, or in any Syllabus at the London School of Economics; let alone in Cambridge.

In Cannan's *History*, Cossa was not considered worth of reference.

The (little) economics contained in the book was far from the English marginalist's culture. Its strong points, i.e. the deep account of the different European national traditions, wasn't appealing enough in England. In the Marshallian era after the danger represented by the Continental Historical School was surmounted, English economics returned to be *the* economics.

However in 1886 Marshall answered to Edgeworth's request for good books of the history of Political Economy saying that Cossa's *Guide* was among the books he "must be most inclined to recommend" (1996, I, p. 209). And a few years later he sent to Cossa the second edition of his *Principles* (Groenewegen 1996, p. 427).

Cossa's *Introduction* stayed in Macmillan's page of publicity in the "Economic Journal" for almost three years: a longer presence than Pantaleoni's *Pure Economics*, which disappeared from that page after less than one year.

3. Pantaleoni's mediations

3.1. The most representative Italian marginalist in England

Maffeo Pantaleoni (1857-1924) is surely the Italian marginalist most present in the English economic milieu in the Marshallian era.

English was his native language (his mother was Irish), and this facilitated his knowledge of the English economic literature, in particular Cairnes' *Leading Principles of Political Economy*, and Jevons' *Theory of Political Economy*, that Pantaleoni came across at the very beginning of his studies at the "Sapienza" in Rome, at the end of 70's[17].

At the peak of his career as pure economist, the decade which goes from the preparation of his masterpiece, *Principii di economia pura* (1889), up to the publication of the English translation of the book, *Pure Economics* (1898a), he was in strict contact with Edgeworth and Marshall, the two leading English economists of the time.

Probably it was through Edgeworth that Pantaleoni came in possession of Marshall's lectures written in the 70's but published only "for private circulation".[18]

---

[17] Cf. De Viti de Marco (1925).

[18] I have found a copy of both *Pure Theory of Foreign Trade* and *Pure Theory of Domestic Values* in Edgeworth's paper in the Nuffied College of Oxford. The papers are instead absent in Pantaleoni's private library recently (June, 2000) opened to the public in the Biblioteca Comunale of Macerata: did Pantaleoni just borrow them from Edgeworth?

In fact, as it is well known, in his *Principii di economia pura* Pantaleoni reproduced some diagrams and formulas embodied in both Marshall's *Pure Theory of domestic values* and *Pure Theory of foreign trade*.[19]

In his *Money, Credit and Commerce* (pp. 331-32) Marshall wrote: "Some of the diagrams contained in the Appendix were reproduced, with my permission, by Prof. Pantaleoni in his *Principii di economia pura*". And in his Preface to *Pure Economics* T. Boston Bruce said: "The translator desires to acknowledge the kindness and courtesy of Professor A. Marshall of Cambridge in giving him access to some of his unpublished writings, to which reference is made in the text". Marshall's private relationship with Pantaleoni at that time is also proved by a letter from Marshall to J.N. Keynes of 15.1.1889:

> I think I spoke to you some time ago of Pantaleoni as seeming to me to have much truer mathematical instincts than Jevons, Walras, ... But I have not told him yet (in Marshall 1996, I, p. 283).

From this letter we can earn a couple of considerations. First, Pantaleoni's reputation in Cambridge was of a good mathematical economist – despite his feeling of inferiority with respect to mathematics.[20] Secondly, at that time Marshall was in private correspondence with Pantaleoni, a correspondence that, unfortunately, has been lost: "No correspondence has survived".[21]

By 1890 Pantaleoni had not yet met Marshall personally ("I only know English economists by their books"[22]). He only met him later. In fact now we know from Groenewegen's biography that Pantaleoni was guest in Marshall's house in 1895 (p. 244).

Furthermore Marshall was in possession of Pantaleoni's books. Referring to the *Principii di Economia pura,* in 1906 he wrote: "I had Pantaleoni's book for years of my shelf" (Marshall 1996, III, p. 141).[23] Only Luigi Cossa – the other Italian (non marginalist) economist very present in England – and Pantaleoni were present in the list of names that Marshall sent to Macmillan asking to send them a free copy of the second edition of his *Principles* (Groenewegen 1996, p. 427).

Pantaleoni reached the peak of his popularity in England when on the 24th of March of 1898 (thanks to Edgeworth?) he was invited to deliver a paper at the British Economic Association.[24] In the same year his *Principii* was translated into *Pure Economics*.

---

[19] See, for instance, Part One, section 3; Part Two, section 1.

[20] See in the Appendix the conclusion of his third letter to Edgeworth of 7.7.1995.

[21] Whitaker's annotation in Marshall 1996, I, p. 283.

[22] Letter from Pantaleoni to Edgeworth of 15.11.1890: see the Appendix.

[23] Pantaleoni's *Principii* are not present in Marshall's Library, then it has been lost. In the Library we have instead Pantaleoni's *Teoria della Pressione tributaria* (1882).

[24] The paper, "An attempt to analyse the concepts of "strong and weak" in their connections", a very interesting paper that anticipates current themes of neoinstitutional economics, was later published in "The Economic Journal" (Pantaleoni 1898b).

After this moment it seems that Pantaleoni attention towards English economists and economics diminished: we don't have any trace of other official invitations from the Royal Economic Society, or of letters to English economists – the last (by now rediscovered) letter to Edgeworth is dated 1895.

Despite the misunderstandings between Pareto and Edgeworth in the biennium 1895-1896 (we'll see how), and despite the natural fall of Pantaleoni's interest in pure economics, the relationship between Pantaleoni and English economists remained cordial to the end – as we can grasp from Edgeworth's obituary.

Over all, we can say that Pantaleoni's *presence* in England was significant. What about, however, the *reception* in England of his economic theory?

3.2. Pantaleoni's Pure Economics*: some reasons of a missed reception*

The reasons of the reception, or better, of the missed reception of Pantaleoni's economic theory in England are centred around *Pure Economics*.

The *Principii di economia pura*, Pantaleoni's "gem" (Edgeworth 1926a), was the fruit of his first years of teaching, and was written with an explicit didactic character, in line with his passion for teaching which has characterised his way of conceiving his scientific mission and work.

The main aim of the book was to give his students (and those of whole of Italy) an account of the new marginalist and hedonistic economic theory.[25]

Pure economics was Pantaleoni's *only manual*, and his *only book* translated into English. Therefore it deserves special attention in this paper, also on account of new documents I found regarding the vicissitudes of the translation.

The Italian *Principii* wasn't reviewed in British economics Journals, despite Pantaleoni's prevision: "I have heard of reviews that will be written in England".[26]

Marshall and Edgeworth surely knew the book, but I have not been able to find the first edition (1889) of the *Principii* in the main English libraries: even in the British Library of Economic and Social Sciences (LSE) there is only the second edition (1894).[27]

The story of the English translation of the *Principii* is linked with the narrative of the missed new edition of the book. Pantaleoni, in fact, never accepted the reiterated proposals of Barbera House (the *Principii*'s Publisher) of re-publishing a new edition of his *Manual* (Bruni, 1997b).

Why? What is surely true is the decisive role played in this story by Pareto, whom Pantaleoni met (1890) soon after having published his *Principii*.

---

[25] Pantaleoni's *Principii* is, mainly, the book of economics which has mostly influenced the training of Italian economists of XX century, from Einaudi to Ricci, from Amoroso to Sraffa, the book that "has been the most efficacious disseminator of the theory of utility in Italy as well as in other Latin countries" (Sraffa 1924, p. 651). Sraffa's reference to the "other Latin countries" lies in the Spanish translation of the book (1918).

[26] Letter to the Publisher Piero Barbera, dated 28.7.1889.

[27] The second edition was just a reprint of the first, with only the insert of a sheet of paper of *errata corrige*.

Pantaleoni was really impressed by Pareto's new theory, and when Pareto wrote the *Cours d'économie politique* (1896-7), the book convinced Pantaleoni that "economics had to be re-studied again". He saw the *Cours* as a masterpiece which "eliminates hundreds of previous works, and that will be the outline upon which other works will be built up for the next twenty years" (Pantaleoni 1897, p. 780).

The encounter with Pareto, and the publication of the *Cours*, is according to many scholars the reason which explains why Pantaleoni always denied to reprint his *Principii* (Amoroso 1925, Einaudi 1931).

Such a reading of the missed new edition, however, isn't coherent with Pantaleoni's resolution of translating his *Principii* into *Pure Economics*: why did he want to publish an English edition of his book *in 1898*, *after* Pareto's *Cours* (1896-7)?

The discovery of the correspondence between T. Boston Bruce,[28] the translator of *Pure Economics,* and Macmillan[29] the Publishing House, letters written from 1894 to 1898, has clarified Pantaleoni's strange choice.[30]

In fact this correspondence brings back Pantaleoni's project of translating the book before he met Pareto: the translation contract was in fact already settled in *October 1890.* The book was published eight years later because of Pantaleoni's drawbacks and delays, due also to the particularly stormy period in his private and professional life.

Pure Economics was ready to go in print only in February 1898, and Pantaleoni's gem entered the English economic milieu with a great delay with respect to the original project: a tremendously long delay, in particular in that period: "sometimes in the history of the progress of science, decades and even centuries do not count. However, at other times, single years or even months make a difference" (Pantaleoni 1904, p. 523). This delay surely didn't help Pantaleoni's reception in England, where the book arrived eight years after Marshall's *Principles*.[31]

---

[28] Thomas Boston Bruce (1857-1922), Englishman from New Castle, contemporary of Pantaleoni, was a barrister at the Court of London, member of the *Middle Temple* from the 22nd of January 1881, when he was still student at the Law faculty of Roma ("La Sapienza"), the same faculty of Pantaleoni. They became friends, probably thanks to the common knowledge of the English language. Also G. De Rosa, the editor of the correspondence between Pareto and Pantaleoni, wrote that Bruce was Pantaleoni's friend (Pareto 1960, II, p. 192). Probably he got this information from Luigi Amoroso (young colleague and friend of Pantaleoni), who helped De Rosa in the annotations of the letters. Bruce himself calls Pantaleoni "friend" (Bruni, 1997b, p. 167). Bruce's contribution to economic science is linked only to this translation, whilst he became a brilliant barrister. He was member of the "Ordine degli avvocati in Italia", consultant of the Italian Embassy in London, "Cavaliere dell'Ordine di Vittorio Emanuele" and LL.D. of the University of Rome.

[29] Bruce's letters are in the Macmillan's Archive, at the University of Reading (UK).

[30] The texts and the analysis of this correspondence can be found in Bruni (1997b).

[31] This great delay changed the perspectives of sale of the book, destined to be a "book for students of economics", as Macmillan wrote in the first publicity on the "Economic Journal" in June 1898. In the meantime Marshall's *Principles* (edited also by Macmillan) had reached the forth edition in 1894, and also Cossa's *Introduction* came out in 1893.

The "Economic Journal" reviewed *Pure Economics*, and the reception wasn't enthusiastic at all. Flux, a disciple of Marshall, the same reviewer of Pareto's *Cours*, made a criticism to the basic methodological foundations of the book:

> The author's conception of the considerations which come within the scope of pure theory seems to us unduly narrow. ... The title of "pure theory of value" ... would be more accurately descriptive" (Flux 1898, p. 356).

In particular Flux (as a loyal disciple of Marshall) didn't like the presence of the neologism "ophelimity" in Pantaleoni's book – only in the English edition, of course: Pareto had introduced the term in 1896 –, and probably this note was an indirect way of criticising Pareto too:

> In explaining Professor Pareto's new term 'ophelimity', our author says 'ophelimous is conformable to individual hedonism'... We presume that the inventor of the term may be allowed to be an authority on its meaning, unless the freedom to assign the most convenient meaning to a word is to be inordinately stretched, and the most careful study of Pareto's statements utterly fails to enable us to reconcile these with the definition just quoted. The contrast between useful and ophelimous is clearly non intended to be a contrast between what is a conformable to tribal and to individual hedonism respectively, unless every word in this definition of their difference be assigned a meaning other than that usually associated with it." (Flux 1898, pp. 357-58).

The only positive aspect of the book, "which will cause it to be of undoubted interest to many English students is that it will render available to them those studies of Professor Marshall" hardly available, i.e. the *Pure Theory of Foreign Trade* (p. 360).

What is the reason for such a negative welcome?[32]

Schumpeter singles out the reason on the absence of originality of the book: "The *Principii di economia pura* (1889) will serve as a landmark. Austrian or "Austro-Walrasian" in fundamentals, enriched by Marshall's apparatus of foreign and domestic trade (...), it gave an important lead away from the old and toward new things. In this consists its importance, for though it is brilliantly written – Edgeworth was not wrong when he called it a "gem" – and is still worth reading, there is nothing entirely original in it. Pantaleoni's original ideas are scattered in his papers and addresses. To mention but a few, he was one of the first theorists to

[32] An even more negative review was written by W.W. Carlile in the Economic Review. This is not surprising, given the anti-marginalist and socialist character of this Oxford Journal. The reviewer appreciates the "classical" part of the book (the quantitative theory of money, the theory of rent, the wage fund theory), but he regrets "the waste of useful energies involved in the barren disquisitions of the earlier part of the volume" (Carlile 1898, p. 558).

try his hand at the subject of price fixing (*prezzi politici*); he contributed to the theory of industrial combinations (*sindacati*)[33] … Nothing of this he carried very far" (Schumpeter 1954 [1994], p. 857).

Schumpeter's thesis that in the *Principii* there was "nothing entirely original" is too quick and a bit simplistic.

But Piero Sraffa was, symmetrically, too generous, when he instead stated that "an inattentive reader hardly realises the important original contributions by Pantaleoni which the book contains" (Sraffa 1924, p. 651).

In fact, if it is true, as Schumpeter underlines, that Pantaleoni's most original theories are scattered in papers which were never translated into English (apart from very few exceptions, such as the paper in the "Economic Journal" in 1898), I also agree with Sraffa in saying that *Pure Economics* is something more than a review of theories of classical and neoclassical economists.[34]

If we would look for the most profound reasons of the little impact of *Pure Economic* in the English economic theory, we must look deeper. It lies in the differences between Pantaleoni and the leader of English economics after 1890, Alfred Marshall, in the understanding of the nature and scope of pure economics.

Pantaleoni's *Pure Economics* was in fact a refinement of the hedonistic approach to economics, represented in England by Jevons and Edgeworth. When Pantaleoni's manual entered the English debate, the season of hedonism was already over: it was then the Marshallian era, where there was no place neither for hedonism nor for pure economics. Pantaleoni's failure was therefore the failure of the attempt of the first generation of English marginalists to build up economics on hedonism and on the methodology of the *homo oeconomicus*.

Marshall's approach to economics was completely different. To him the field of economics is determined by the *force* of man's motives "not the motives themselves", which "can be approximately measured by the sum of money" (Marshall 1890 [1946], p. 15) or "can be measured by a money price" (p. 33).

Therefore, it isn't the *motive* (to maximise utility, pleasure or self-interest) that delimits the field of economics, since the economist must deal with all the reasons for human action which must all be taken into consideration just as long as they can be expressed *in monetary prices*. Because of this, Marshall's economics does not study an abstract "economic man" but a man in "flesh and blood" (p. 27).

In doing so Marshall distances himself from the methodology of those like Jevons, Edgeworth, and mainly Pantaleoni, for whom the boundaries of economic science are determined by the *hedonistic* or *egotistic* principle.

---

[33] I would better translate "sindacati" with *trade unions*.

[34] This is not the place to analyse the topic of the originality (or not) of Pantaleoni's *Principii*, one *vexata questio* of the Italian historiography of economics (cf. Bini [1995], Bellanca [1995], Bellanca and Giocoli [1998]).

In fact the approach to pure economics based on *hedonism* and *self-interest* may be seen as the key to the whole reading of Pantaleoni's scientific approach, from the *Principii* to the *Erotemi di economia*.[35]

In *Pure Economics*, the analysis of the economic principle mainly examines the role which is carried out by hedonism in economics.

Either in Jevons or in Edgeworth we don't find such a radical hedonistic approach to economics. It cannot even be found in other marginalist works before the *Principii*, and perhaps for a long time later (see Einaudi 1931, p. 529).

The first two chapters of the book (in particular the first one, and the first four paragraphs of the second one) are completely dedicated to the attempt to base economics on a single *assumption or hedonistic premise*, that is the "economic principle", from where all the laws of economics can derive as on corollaries.

This principle opens the text as a "cornerstone" on which to construct his building:

> Economic science consists of the laws of wealth systematically deduced from the hypothesis that men are actuated exclusively by the desire to realise the fullest possible satisfaction of their wants, with the least possible individual sacrifice (1898a, p. 3)[36].

Piero Sraffa didn't miss this central point in his obituary:

> In the system of economics formulated by Pareto without having recourse to the psychology of the Hedonists, he recognised 'the most rigorous and also the most nicely constructed theory of economic equilibrium'; but he considered that generalisations had already been carried to the extreme limit, and that what was necessary was to discover the nature and actual form of functions with which economics deals. He thought that for this purpose the data furnished by psychological inquiry were of great value to the economist, and considered that to disregard them was a sterile act of aberration (Sraffa 1924, p. 651).

In fact, it is not just a case that the English economist with whom Pantaleoni had the strongest relationship was the "hedonist and psychologist" Edgeworth, who in his *Mathematical Psychics* (1881, p. 16) wrote that the "first principle of economics is that every agent is actuated only by *self-interest*".

---

[35] The "Erotemi di economia" (1925) are the book (two volumes) which collects the most important papers written by Pantaleoni after the *Principii di Economia Pura*.

[36] For a fuller English language account of Pantaleoni's approach to hedonism and egoism see Bruni (1999, section 3).

3.3. Pantaleoni's "recommendations" to Edgeworth

"You can't have forgotten that I come more than once for help to you, in some questions concerning chords which can be subtended to demand curves, or concerning the elasticity of demand curves and Marshall's theorem on the subject, &c, &c.".[37]

From this passage of a letter of reference that Pantaleoni wrote to Edgeworth, asked by the English friend for his professorship in Oxford, it is possible to understand that the relationship among the two economists started soon, at the very beginning of Pantaleoni's work as pure economist, most probably 1886-1887.

This letter, published by the *Journal of Political Economy*, is also interesting because Pantaleoni gives us an eloquent account of Pantaleoni's evaluation of the leading English economists of his time:

> I think and say you are the closest approximation of a match for Marshall living in England. You know that to my mind, Marshall is simply a new Ricardo who has appeared in the field, and to be second to him is as great an honour as a scientific man can wish look for, in our line (Pantaleoni [1890]).

Furthermore, it is worthwhile to note that Pantaleoni, together with Böhm Bawerk, was the only non-English economist to whom Edgeworth asked for a reference:[38] a sign of the high reputation of Pantaleoni and the Italian economics at that time in England, when "it was second to none" (Schumpeter 1954 [1994], p. 855).

We have trace of their relationships up to March 1898, when T.B. Bruce wrote to Macmillan about Pantaleoni: "He is guest of Prof. Edgeworth at Oxford" (in Bruni 1997b, p. 168).

This decade (1888-1898) was an intense period in the relationships between the two men – from the letters which survived one can deduce that most of the correspondence, from both sides, has been lost.

In particular, from 1890 to 1895, their relationship was very intense and productive: this is the period which saw both the launch of the "Economic Journal", and the publication of Egdeworth's papers in the Pantaleoni's "Giornale degli Economisti".

On 4.1.1891, Pantaleoni wrote a letter to the English colleague where he outlined how to plan the launch of the forthcoming "Economic Journal", of which Edgeworth was Editor.[39]

---

[37] Pantaleoni (1890) [1980].

[38] I got this information from a hand-written note by Edgeworth, in the Edgeworth Papers, at the Nuffield College, Oxford.

[39] The letter has been published by Bellanca (1992, pp. 13-14).

Pantaleoni's main suggestion to Edgeworth embodied in this letter was to orient the Journal towards pure theory, because the Economic Journal was based in a country "which can boast the largest group of first class economists" (in Bellanca 1992, p. 11). Then, the "publicity-work is much simplified. Scientific men look for *you*; so you need less to look for *them*" (p. 13). He also gave some suggestions about the names of economists and Journals to address the publicity, about the *text* of the publicity, etc., showing also an outstanding knowledge of the European institutional situation of Political Economy.

I have discovered another unpublished letter, which is the continuation of that of the 4.1.1891. This manuscript, more than the previous one, singles out the influence of Pantaleoni on the birth of the Journal.

The letter begins with his congratulations for Edgeworth's professorship, and soon he shifts to the theme, dealt with in the previous letter (and maybe in other letters that have been lost), that of the plan of launching "The Economic Journal".[40]

Pantaleoni is very convinced about what Edgeworth must do – as the reader can see in the text which has been transcript in the Appendix. Here I would just point out a rather curious recommendation: "As to the analysis of books and literature do all you can to shove off your shoulders that work, and put it on those of clever young people who have their way to make", because "you'll never have a friend after a bibliographical note". In the letter he explains why – and, at this point, I would rather not anticipate the niceties we can discover.

It is worth to note that during his professional activity Pantaleoni was very coherent with this approach, and wrote almost no book reviews, neither in the "Giornale" nor elsewhere. Edgeworth, on the contrary, did not follow this suggestion and reviewed an enormous amount of books and papers during his whole life.[41]

It is hard to single out how much Pantaleoni's suggestions have modified Edgeworth's strategies on launching the Journal; nevertheless what we can point out the high consideration and esteem that Pantaleoni had in Edgeworth's eyes, in that crucial era of the institutionalisation of Political Economy in England and in Europe.[42]

3.4. Pantaleoni, a bridge between Pareto and the English economists

The discovery of other two unpublished letters allowed me to know something about Pantaleoni's role as mediator, in a difficult moment, between Pareto and Edgeworth, and indirectly, Marshall.

---

[40] It is not easy at all to understand the subject of this letter without knowing the previous letter of the 4th of January.

[41] On Edgeworth as reviewer, see Newman (1991).

[42] The "Economic Journal" was the journal of the *British Economic Association,* founded in October 1890.

Edgeworth's *Mathematical Psychics* was one of the very first books of pure economics Pareto studied in his training as a marginalist economist.[43]

Through the intercession of Pantaleoni, for a short while (1891-2) Pareto was the Italian correspondent of the "Economic Journal". However, if we look through Pareto's correspondence, he never had an enthusiastic conception of English marginalist economists, viz. Marshall and Edgeworth.

The break-point in Pareto-Edgeworth's story is linked to Edgeworth's paper *The Pure Theory of International Trade* (1894).

In this article Edgeworth criticised Pareto's paper on international trade, "Teoria metematica dei cambi forestieri" (1894 [1982]), where Pareto made some criticisms to the theory of Marshall and Edgeworth, based mainly on the consideration that the English economists have missed the concept of the interdependence of all commodities and markets.

And, to Pareto, this is the reason why they criticise Walras's theory of *general* equilibrium: "Professor Edgeworth makes an objection to these formulae [of general equilibrium] which we admit do not understand" (Pareto 1894 [1982], p. 144).[44]

Furthermore, Pareto clearly stated in that article the great importance of mathematics for economics:

> As first thing we consider that is useful to utilise in its whole maximum power that wonderful tool of reasoning which we have in the mathematics. Its peculiar quality is the *generality*, and of that we want make advantages (p. 148).

From the letter Pantaleoni wrote to Edgeworth on 15.6.1895 we can deduce that Edgeworth, after having read Pareto's paper, wrote a "letter of complaints" to Pantaleoni.

Pantaleoni sent Edgeworth's letter to Pareto (or summarised it), and Pareto wrote to Pantaleoni on the 17th of June: "*It seems to me that Edgeworth is right in saying that there is a great difference between Cambridge and Lausanne Schools. Marshall has not yet managed to grasp the idea of economic equilibrium* … Marshall uses mathematics, and wants others to use it very little. For the use he makes of it, he uses it even too much" (Pareto 1960, I, p. 417).

In the 15th of June Pantaleoni, instead, had written to Edgeworth:

> I am very sorry to see you think such a thing as a School of Lausanne and a School of Cambridge exists. I am also sorry to see that mathematicians

---

[43] In January 1892 he wrote to Pantaleoni: "Now I am studying Edgeworth's *Mathematical Psychics*" (Pareto 1960, I, p. 173).

[44] The particular objection was about the "disutility of labour", that according to Edgeworth was not considered by Walras' formulae.

> think it is worth while to quarrel amongst themselves. … As to correcting a wrong appreciation of Pareto, you are in your right and I repeat that we are glad and proud to publish any scrap of your pen.
> Pareto is publishing a manual of political economy[45] of which I have read the mss. You will hardly see a formula in the whole book and, instead of mathematics, he has a most interesting series of inductive proofs of most economical theorems! He fully admits that this is the best way of treating the public.[46]

In September 1894 Edgeworth published his paper on international trade, and in his analysis of international trade (in the case of more than two nations, in the short run), when he enter "the more complicated part of the subject", Edgeworth:

a) Recalls Marshall's thesis on the use of mathematics in economic theory[47], an "implicit" dispute with the "Lausanne School" and Pareto's article on "Cambi Forestieri".
b) Bounds the analysis to the case of two commodities, and he adds: "I don't know that any fresh conclusions are presented by the case of many variables. Accordingly it may be left to the reader to elaborate that case" (Edgeworth 1894 [1970], II, p. 46). And in the footnote 2 he writes: "A statement of the general case is given by Professor Pareto in his able article … It may be observed that the formulae given by Professor Pareto, after Professor Walras, as proper to the case of industrial competition (domestic trade), are also applicable to that case of trade between "nations" (or "non-competitive groups") in which each commodity is produced by only one nation";
c) Indicates "how some of the concrete circumstances which have been abstracted may be restored". In particular, "the cost of production may be treated as varying with the amount produced by regarding a x (a2x, etc.) not as the product of x by a constant, but as a definite function of x" (p. 46).

On 16 December 1894 Edgeworth sent a letter and his article on international trade to Pareto. In that letter he recalls the theme of industrial competition (domestic) mentioned in the footnote 2 (see point b above), asking: "Can you refer me to passages in Prof. Walras' book [*Elements d'économie politique pure*] which form an answer to that note?" (Pareto 1962, p. 57).

From some hint present in Pareto-Pantaleoni's correspondence (see e.g. 1960, I, p. 421) one can conclude that the correspondence between the two economists

---

[45] The *Cours d'économie politique* (1896-1897).

[46] See the Appendix for the full transcription of the letter – where there is a very interesting statement on how Pantaleoni conceived the relation between business life and theory, in the light of his experience with the bankruptcy of the "Credito Mobiliare".

[47] "It seems doubtful whether anyone spends his time well in reading lengthy translations of economic doctrines into mathematics, that have not been made by himself" (Marshall, Preface to the *Principles*, in Edgeworth 1894 [1970], II, pp. 43-44).

went ahead. These letters have been lost. However in the nine of July 1895 Pareto went back to this dispute in a letter to Pantaleoni:

> That I am a porcupine is true. But Edgeworth's move disappoints me because of his will to be witty when there is no call for wit, and I am annoyed at losing time in such disputes which serve no useful purpose. Referring *exclusively* to the coefficients of production I never claimed a *substantial* difference from Marshall.
> As far as the point of *constant* coefficients production is concerned:
> 1°: There is bad faith in saying that Walras wants constant [coefficients of production]; (...)
> 2°: It is perfectly justifiable *to begin* with supposing coefficients of production constant; (...)
> 3°: Edgeworth continues to repeat like a parrot that our formulae don't account for "non-competitive groups". I have explained it particularly, and I have printed how we account for it. If he doesn't understand that means that he does not want understand" (Pareto 1960, I, p. 422-25).[48]

Edgeworth most probably sent to Pantaleoni the letter Pareto wrote to him. Even both these letters have been lost, but we can deduce the main message from the letter of 7th of July that Pantaleoni sent to Edgeworth.

This letter is probably the most interesting of the three unpublished letters to Edgeworth (see Appendix).

Pantaleoni goes through the points of the quarrel between the two (three) economists (i.e. the substantial accord in understanding the coefficients of production, the use of more or less mathematics in economics), with the attitude of mediation among them in order to support the spread of the new marginalist economics.

For Pantaleoni there is only *one* proper economic theory, with just differences in emphasising one aspect or another. But, deep down, the science is one.[49]

From that comes the "political" suggestion he gave to Edgeworth (and to Pareto):

> Now, if these people hear you, a leader in the field, a man exceptional for talent and brightness, say mathematics is *au fond* useless, we certainly have our ground very much spoilt. You would be made use of as an *argumentum ad hominem* against us; such arguments don't decide a question definitively, but they decide them for the masses for a long time. ... People won't discuss your reasons, or see the limits and conditions of your assertions, but take

---

[48] In his *Cours*, written more or less in the same period, Pareto wrote that "Edgeworth had studied, with respect to international trade, some unusual cases" (Pareto 1896-7, § 876).

[49] Pantaleoni's statement, pronounced in the opening lecture in Geneve in 1897, is well-known: in economic theory there are only *two* schools*: those who know economics and those who don't know it.*

> them in a broader sense and we will have to wait 20 years more before getting into clear waters.[50]

The continuation of the relationships between Pareto and Edgeworth shows that the English economist paid little attention to Pantaleoni's suggestions.

4. More wars than peace: the "first" Pareto and English economists

4.1. Did English economists know Pareto?

> He never appreciated Marshall fully - mainly because he objected on the principle to partial analysis. ...But he did appreciate Edgeworth and, many objections notwithstanding, Wicksteed (Schumpeter 1951 [1997], p. 126).

This statement will serve as landmark in our reconstruction of the relations of the "first" Pareto and the three English economists Schumpeter mentioned. We'll see that the story is much more complicated than the great Austrian economist thought.

Pareto's story in England perfectly fits T. Kuhn's theory of scientific revolutions. A theory, first marginalised in a given cultural climax (Marshall's era), years later became the fulcrum of the neo-positivistic revolution in microeconomics (Robbins' era).

Nicholas Georgescu Roegen, one of the first eminent Anglo-Saxon writers who discovered and greatly appreciated Pareto's economics, in 1975 wrote:

> There is no denying that Pareto's own ideas met with an incredible lack of attention from most economists during his life as well as during many years thereafter. In the last edition of Alfred Marshall's *Principles* (1920), Pareto is mentioned only once, as one of many who "have been inclined towards mathematical modes of thought" (1975, p. 223).

In 1913 W.E. Johnson wrote his important paper on utility (Johnson 1913), finding a solution regarding the measurability of utility in agreement with Pareto's, but did not quote Pareto. In 1929 E. Cannan wrote his *Review of Economic Theory* without mentioning Pareto or any other Italian. At that time, apart from a couple of papers published in American Journals, none of Pareto's works had been translated into English.[51]

---

[50] The full transcription is in the Appendix.

[51] In April 1898, Pareto tried, through Boston Bruce (the translator of Pantaleoni's *Principii*), to publish one book in English with Macmillan, which was to be more than just a translation of his *Cours* but something similar to what would then become a few years later the *Manuale* (cf. the "editorial project" that De Rosa published in

The Paretian Luigi Amoroso attributed Johnson's ignorance of the Paretian theory to a more general "lacuna of the area in which he lives" (Amoroso 1916, p. 410).

However, Pantaleoni in his obituary of Pareto in the "Economic Journal", an article that was not a translation but "written by Professor Pantaleoni direct into English"[52], he presented a slightly different thesis on the topic we are dealing with:

> His economic work is pretty well known to English readers, having been, incidentally at least, often quoted and discussed (Pantaleoni 1923, p. 586).

Who is right? I think that both are, because if it is undoubtedly true that, up to the 30's, Pareto theories, with the exception of his law of income distribution,[53] were not present in the English language debate on economics, it is nevertheless true that the English leading economists of his time did know Pareto's economics very well.[54]

How to rejoin these two elements that sound contradictory? Why, it is that in spite of the fact that leading English economists were aware of Pareto's theory, they almost ignored him in their theoretical works?

In order to answer this central question, which is more complex than simply accounting for the well known English insularity and Marshall's "dictatorship",[55] I shall try to show that the real reason of the missing reception of Pareto by English marginalist economists of his generation lies in a very profound, methodological difference in understanding the nature of economic science. This is particularly true in the case of three chief English economists with whom Pareto was most in contact: Marshall, Edgeworth and Wicksteed.

---

a footnote to a letter from Pareto to Pantaleoni: Pareto 1960, II, p. 192, footnote 3. The attempt was not crowned with success: "see, the English editor did not answer; I will go back to my dear Rouge and I will publish my book on sociology and economics with him" (Pareto 1960, II, p. 194). Actually he published both the *Manuale* and the *Trattato* in Italian – with great regrets: cf. Bruni (1996).

[52] "Note of the Editors" ... The note was most likely written by Edgeworth, in order to distinguish this article from the forthcoming obituary in the "Giornale degli Economisti" (1924), and to underline the perfect command of the English language by Pantaleoni: "the excellent English in which that memory is written" (Edgeworth 1926a, p. 710).

[53] On the presence of Pareto's law, of Corrado Gini and of other Italian statisticians in England, see Magliulo (1993).

[54] In fact, in an article in the "Economic Journal" of 1915, a review of the recent developments of mathematical economics, Edgeworth links Johnson's works to Pareto's and those of his school (Edgeworth 1915 [1970]). It is also worth noting that in the London School of Economics' *Prospectus* for the A.Y. 1898/99, in the notes for a course held by Edgeworth on "The Principles of International Trade" we find "General views will be tested by reference to the leading writers on international trade: especially Torrens, Ricardo, J.S. Mill, ... Marshall and Pareto" (London School of Economics, Arrangements for the Session 1898-1899, p. 10). No other reference to Italians in the other prospectuses up to 1930.

[55] See the classical interpretation of Schumpeter: 1954 [1994], pp. 829 seq.

4.2. *Pareto and Marshall: a missed encounter*

"If we consider the relative poverty of the Walrasian theory of industrial organisation and production; if we consider that twenty years of industrial management had led Pareto to give prominent importance to production and to corporate governance, and that this very experience was to lead him to a sort of *Marshallisation* of Walras' theory; if, lastly, we consider that upon his first reading of Principles, Pareto admired Marshall's concreteness, his refusal of theoretical excesses, we are led to conclude that, at the beginning of the Fiesole period [1890-1893] Pareto was more on Marshall's side than on Walras'" (Zanni 1999, p. 127).

This sharp and suggestive statement of Alberto Zanni is a good departure point in the analysis of the relationships between Pareto and Marshall.

Marshall's *Principles* had all the features to attract an economist like Pareto: why, then, did he prefer Walras? I agree with Zanni in saying that in order to explain Pareto's preference, it is not enough to call for the differences which Pareto himself had often pointed out.

At the beginning of his career, Pareto had a great consideration of Marshall's *Principles*. In 1892 he considered Marshall's analysis of the theory of productions "vraiment admirable" (Pareto 1892).

In October 1891 Pantaleoni sent the second edition of Marshall's *Principles* to Pareto: "Thanks for the Marshall. I have had a glimpse of what (I think) was the first edition. I will study the second one with pleasure. Walras is contrary to Marshall; I haven't understood why" (Pareto 1960, I, p. 67). The *Principles* surely was one of the main tests upon which Pareto studied pure economics.[56]

After 1893 Pareto's attitude towards Marshall changed drastically.

In the analysis of Pantaleoni's presence in England we have already seen that, around 1895, the relationships between Marshall and Pareto were over all quite bad.

I think there were three different reasons behind this shift of attitude: a) *environmental or academic,* b) *theoretical* and c) *methodological.*

These three reasons are obviously mixed-up together; nevertheless, it can be useful and clearer to analyse each of them one at a time.

a) Pareto's shift in his relationship with Marshall begins in 1893, *after his arrival in Lausanne.* In May, in the first letter he wrote to Pantaleoni from Lausanne, he said: "You should know that you are accused by him [Walras] of not having come out strongly enough against Marshall, and Auspitz and Lieben, ect." (1960, I, p. 371). And few days later: "On the quarrel with Marshall, Walras is right … *Mathematically* it cannot be held at all Marshall's thesis" (p. 373). From this moment onwards, all references we find in Pareto's correspondence and papers to Marshall's work are negative and even sarcastic – as one can

[56] On Marshall's presence in the first period of Pareto's study of pure economics see Zanni (1991).

easily note from the first volume of the letters to Pantaleoni (Pareto 1960, I). To become the heir of the Lausanne School, whose founder was in open contrast with Marshall (and Edgeworth), surely didn't help Pareto in his relationships with English economists, and surely contributed to the emergence of the theoretical and methodological differences which were present before.

b) As far as economic *theory* is concerned, differences between the two great economists were already present in Pareto's first theoretical papers (in particular the articles on the "Giornale degli Economisti" (1892-3)). In Lausanne the differences grew exponentially.
   In a letter to Pantaleoni in 1907 he wrote a synoptic table where, in polemic with Pantaleoni who in a paper had grouped Pareto together with Marshall, Edgeworth and other marginalists, Pareto summarised the theoretical differences with Marshall (the page numbers refer to the second edition of the *Principles*):

Marshall	**What Pareto says**
… p. 153: Demand schedule	… The demand of an individual is dependent on his income and on the prices of *all* the goods which he buys and sells. The use of mathematics makes it possible to take account of this very point; otherwise the use of mathematics *has no value*. I have said this over and over again, and still I am grouped with Marshall!
p. 154: Demand curve	This is ridiculous. Is it possible to make people understand that Pareto – whether he is right or wrong – says that this is rubbish?
… p. 180: The superior nobility of the collective over the private use of wealth.	… Sentimental proposition. It had its place in socialist novels which are the delight of English humanitarians. Anti-scientific stuff. The science of economics has no criterion with which to judge the *nobility* of the use of riches. People cannot do me greater wrong as a scientist than to put me in the same boat as someone who *thinks* that he is writing about science when he puts forward such propositions. (…)
The whole mathematical Appendix	Old stuff. It takes no account of interdependence (…)
Constant utility of money. See also Edgeworth "Teoria del Monopolio" in the *Giornale*.	*You cannot consider as constant* the utility of money. (…) The Marshalls and the Edgeworths persist in their error because they do not admit that in the debate with Walras they were in the wrong. These English believe that, outside of England and Germany, people are all donkeys. But I say that the English proposition of the constant utility of money is *asinine*.

Apart from the issues on the demand curve (where Pareto exaggerated: his pupil Barone too used this "ludicrous" tool)[57] and on the constant utility of money, the main differences have their origin in the problem of *interdependence*.

c) In fact, apart from these *theoretical* and "*sociological*" reasons, we must add a third *methodological* reason, where the most profound reasons for the progressive distance between the two economists lie.[58] Methodology is too broad a topic, and it can also sound a bit vague – also the theme of "interdependence" can also be considered a "methodological" difference. For this reason, in the analysis at hand with methodology I would refer to *the way of conceiving the relationship between economics and all the social sciences*, and consequently, the nature of *pure* economics.

   In the Introduction to his *Principles* Marshall wrote:

> Ethical forces are among those of which the economist has to take account. Attempts have indeed been made to construct an abstract science with regard to the actions of an "economic man", who is under non-ethical influences and who pursues pecuniary gain warily and energetically, but mechanically and selfishly. But they have not been successful, nor even thoroughly carried out. … In the present book normal action is taken to be that which may be expected, under certain conditions, from the members of an industrial group; and no attempt is made to exclude the influence of any motives, the action of which is regular, merely because they are altruistic (Marshall 1890 [1946], p. vi).[59]

This is a crucial passage in understanding Marshall's *methodology*.

Having defined economic science in this way, Marshall must say that the boundary between sociology and economics is very ill-defined, and the passage from one to the other is very easily made (*natura non fecit saltum*: it is written in the epigraph of the *Principles*).

The distance from Pareto is great. Already in May 1893 he wrote: "Pure economics is not banished by applied economics. Example: International trade: One does the pure theory, that is *not* that of Marshall" (1960, I, p. 387).

Both Pareto and Marshall went further with respect to the hedonistic and egoistic pure economics: but while Marshall went further by *broadening* (not only egoism but also altruism), Pareto *restricted* more and more the field of economic science.

---

[57] Pareto criticised the use of demand curve mainly to emphasise the superiority (because it is more experimental!) of the *indifference curves* approach to consumer theory.

[58] Zanni too singles out methodology as the main difference between Marshall and Pareto (Zanni 1999, pp. 127-8), and I have followed this path. A different interpretation can be found in Gallegati (1990), who, in line to Schumpeter's opinion (Schumpeter 1951 [1997], p. 126), singled out the main difference between the two economists on *partial* vs. *general* equilibrium.

[59] This statement on method brings Marshall even further apart from Pantaleoni than he is from Pareto, at least as far as the approach to the economic principle and the role of the premises in economic science are concerned.

In line with Mill's methodology,[60] for Pareto economics only studies a small part of the human behaviour. There is also another aspect, "born of non-logical actions, which also need to be studied. Here difficulties begin to arise" (Pareto 1900b, p. 162). In this assertion, we can find a synthesis of Pareto's approach to science.

A concrete action presents two main components:

a) the *logical* component, based on a *pure instrumental* reasoning, where the means are adequate to the end, subjectively and objectively;
b) the *non-logical* one, where *non*-logical does not mean *illogical* or irrational but just based on a different type of logic, as Pareto many times has specified.[61]

Economics deals with the *logical* part, and its work is simple. Sociology deals with the rest, and its work is very difficult. To study the non-logical part of an action, to understand the real phenomenon: this was the main challenge Pareto confronted for the rest of his life.[62]

This methodological attitude, by time, will become even wider and Pareto will have the tendency to circumscribe the field of economics and logical actions as much as possible.

In this framework it is possible to fully understand the reasons for the dissent between the two economists. Even Pareto was convinced of this.

In a letter to Vinci dated January 1912: "I am further away from Marshall than from many other economists who do not use mathematics", since "economics is but a part of the social sciences" (Pareto 1975, p. 757).

Another letter written later reiterates the same concept: "To completely separate economics from sociology. This is the characteristic I wished to give in the *Manuale*. In Marshall, the practical and especially the ethical considerations are very strong, making it difficult to make a distinction between economics and sociology" (Pareto 1975, p. 759).

Pareto's presence in Marshall's works is very little. As pointed out by Georgescu Roegen (1975), he mentioned Pareto only once in a footnote, describing him as good mathematician, and nothing more.

There is only one reference to Pareto in his correspondence: "I have failed in the attempt to have good books in French. I expect Pareto is the ablest: but he is very unreal & cranky, I think" (Marshall 1996, III, p. 42): a statement which is a perfect synthesis of this "missed encounter".

---

[60] On the strict methodological similarity between Pareto and Mill see Bruni and Guala (2000).

[61] The best and more complete definition of Pareto's theory of logical and non logical actions can be found in Pareto 1916, §§ 150-152.

[62] The method of analysis and synthesis may be found in the first chapter of his *Manual of Political Economy*: "abstraction is, for all the sciences, the preliminary and indispensable requirement for all research. (…) When we return to the concrete from the abstract, the parts which had been separated in order to study them better must be united again" (Pareto 1906 [1971], I, §§ 20; 26). In fact, the analysis of other kinds of social interactions, based on a non-instrumental rationality, is present in his Sociology. For example the "residues of the fourth class" (Residues in relation with sociality: Pareto 1916, §§ 113-1206), are entirely dedicated to "the want for sociality".

On the wave of this missed encounter can be also situated the missed dialogue between Pareto and Arthur Cecil Pigou, the heir of Marshall's chair in Cambridge, the father of Welfare Economics. He knew Pareto's works very well (in particular the *Cours* and the *Manual*), but when he wrote both his *Wealth and Welfare* (1912) and *Economics of Welfare* (1920) he completely ignored Paretian welfare economics, and criticised Pareto's law on income distribution. In particular, the more criticised aspect of Pareto's law (1920, Part IV, ch. II), was its implications for policy, namely, given the "naturalness" of the law, the inefficacy in the long run of any intervention tending to reduce inequalities: 'If, for example, the wealthiest citizen were deprived of all their income … the curve would not retain the [initial] form, but sooner or later would re-establish itself in a form similar to the initial curve' (*Manual*, Ch. VII, § 24). Pigou, follower of Marshall, had a vision of economics as a tool for improving the welfare of people, in particular of the poorest: nothing more far away from Pareto's.

4.3. Pareto and Edgeworth

4.3.1. A difficult beginning

In reconstructing Pantaleoni's relationships with Edgeworth, we have seen the first discrepancies between the author of *Mathematical Psychics* and Pareto, in the years 1891-1895, focused on the papers on international trade.[63]

The second, and deeper reason of conflict between them was offered by Pareto's article on income distribution. In 1896 Pareto published a paper (Pareto 1896a [1965]), where, based on empirical data, he presented a relation between the amount of income and the number of persons in receipt that or a higher amount.[64]

In 1896 in his "Supplementary notes on Statistics" Edgeworth reviewed Pareto's *La Courbe de la Répartition de la Richesse* (1896), where he said that the "formula appears at the first sight identical with that which Professor Karl Pearson ("Contribution", n. 11, *Transactions of the Royal Society*, p. 398) has given, in *pari materia*, for the statistics of house valuation … It is true no doubt that the difference

[63] A probable sign of the difficult relationship between Edgeworth and the Paretian School is Edgeworth's rejection in 1894 of a review written by Barone for the "Economic Journal" of Wicksteed's *Essay on the Coordination of the Laws of Distribution* (1894): on this matter see Jaffé (1964).

[64] The relation may be expressed by the equation: logN = LogA – aLogx (where x is an amount of income, N is the number of persons in receipt of that or higher income, A and a are constants). The ideological message behind this formula or law was to show the "constancy of the coefficient "a" under great variety of conditions that the causes of which the formula is the outcome are stable. Writers not usually partial to mathematical economics have welcomed Pareto's curve as evidencing that distribution is subject to law, not so readily modified as socialist assume" (Edgeworth 1926c, p. 713). With the passing years Pareto became more and more unsatisfied with his famous law, because of this ideological message it embodied, which, for the mature Pareto (after 1900), was a sign of no scientificity.

between the two curves was rather in form than in fact. Still I am not satisfied that the form preferred by Prof. Pearson is decidely preferable" (Edgeworth 1896, pp. 533-534).

On a more theoretical level, Edgeworth criticised Pareto's paper on two major points:

a) "a close fit of a curve to given statistics is not, *per se*, and apart from *à priori* reasons, a proof that the curve in question is *the* form proper to the matter in hand" (p. 533);
b) Pareto's formula "does not fit the phenomena at its lower extremity" (p. 533), for according to the formula there ought to be an infinite number of null incomes. In fact the formula gives $N = \infty$ when $x = 0$.

Edgeworth most probably sent the manuscript to Pareto already in June 1895. In fact on the 26th of June 1895 Pareto wrote to Pantaleoni: "Edgeworth can publish his article, and I will answer him with good ink, and without mathematics" (Pareto 1960, I, p. 420).

On the 4th of July 1895 Pareto wrote a letter to Pantaleoni:

> I am glad you too found Edgeworth's paper for … what it is. My reply will be just to make fun of him. If he writes for the *galleria* [the public] I will show him I too know how to write for the poor of spirits … I have sent you a copy of the letter I have written to Edgeworth, which I wrote only for loyalty's sake (Pareto 1960, I, p. 421).

Pareto saw in that review a "thinly veiled accusation of plagiarism" (Chipman 1976, p. 131).

Because of this review the already difficult relationships between the two economists became really hostile. Pareto replied in the "Giornale degli economisti" (Pareto 1896b [1965]), reiterating "a somewhat acrimonious explanation which is of interest as throwing light not only on the character of the curve, but also on that of its discoverer" (Edgeworth 1926c, p. 712):

> It seems, and we didn't know, that Prof. Pearson had found for the evaluation of houses a formula which, according to Prof. Edgeworth, would be almost $-dN/dx = A/x^{\alpha}\, 10^{-B\alpha}$. Mr. Edgeworth didn't like that I have hunted upon a ground which is reserved to Prof. Pearson, as political economy is reserved to Prof. Marshall. … I have found the law of **total** incomes, and I have found that it was almost the same for very different countries. Prof. Pearson has found for a **special** country the law of a **special** income. It seems to me that they are very different matters" (Pareto 1896b [1965], pp. 21-22).

Later in the paper Pareto, put aside "personal" matters, and entered the theoretical objections made by Edgeworth.

To (a) he said: "Who has never objected that? Before that in September Prof.

Edgeworth revealed this great truth, was there perhaps someone who confused empirical laws with rational laws?" (p. 22).[65]

To the second objection Pareto answered with two considerations: "1°. Those who have a total income equal to zero will be angels, since having zero of income they will also eat nothing. The formula doesn't account for angels. We agree. 2° Why do you want to apply a formula, valid within certain limits, outside these limits?" (p. 24).

And finally he concludes:

> Prof. Edgeworth has published works of great value, which we have often appreciated. ... When he will come back to the objective study of questions he will surely give a contribution to science and he will give us new and pleased occasion of greeting him as our master (p. 28).

Edgeworth replied to Pareto in the "Giornale degli Economisti" (1897), shifting the issue towards the curve of probability, and saying that "never has there been a more fallacious case, also called 'ignoratio elenchi'",[66] accusing Pareto of making just "a personal recrimination".

Pareto replied again in the "Giornale", despite the fact that Pantaleoni was trying hard to prevent him from breaking with English economists:[67] "Where are you going? I sell fish. This is the summary of Prof. Edgeworth's paper" (Pareto 1897 [1965], p. 41).

In these months his correspondence with Pantaleoni is full of references to this dispute:

> Edgeworth wrote only to demonstrate that Pearson did this matter before I did. If this were true, I wouldn't say anything: all the better! But here is an individual who finds for *houses*, for a country, a formula *completely different* from the one I found for *total income* and *for all countries*, and is it the same? But I don't worry about that. I only care about the enormous idiocies that Edgeworth comes out with. Therefore, rather, I say: whom must I answer? People who understand will read my book; people who do not understand, after my answer will know as much as before" (Pareto 1960, I, p. 473).

At the peak of this quarrel Pareto wrote two letters to Edgeworth (18th and 30th November 1896)[68]. In the first letter, an answer to a (lost) letter by Edgeworth dated 13.11.1896, he wrote:

---

[65] It is worth to note that in his first paper Pareto wasn't so precise in stating this methodological thesis. In fact he wrote: "La tendance des revenus à se grouper suivant une certaine loi pourrait bien dépendre, en grande partie, de la nature même des hommes" (1896a [1965], p. 7): a statement with a "naturalistic" and *à priori* flavour.

[66] Cf. also the letter to Pantaleoni dated February 1897, in Pareto 1960, II, p. 39.

[67] See also Pareto's letters to Pantaleoni letters dated 19.2.1897 and 3.3.1897.

[68] They are published in Pareto (1960, III, pp. 399 *seq.*).

> Il y a de cela quelques mois un conflit a dèja surgy entre nous. Je vous ai dit alors que quand on m'attaquait, je savais me défendre. Je ne désire rien tant que de rester en bons rapports avec un savant tel que vous, que j'estime et que j'honore. Ce ne sera donc jamais moi qui vous attaquera le premier. Mon rôle se bornera à la défense. … Je suis heureuex qu'elle se trouve erronée et que tout malentendu cesse nous à ce sujet (Pareto 1960, III, p. 400)

And in the second letter:

> Je vous remercie de vos explications et, pour ma part, je suis heureux que tout malentendu ait cessé subjectivement entre nous (p. 403).

Finally he wrote to Pantaleoni in 1901: "I am not at all anymore at war neither with him [Edgeworth], nor with Flux, nor with Sanger. With Edgeworth we made peace: with the others there has never been battle" (1960, II, p. 377).

4.3.2. Pareto's theory of choice: an escape from Edgeworth towards the "naked fact"

After this first vivacious period, mutual references became very few. We practically have to wait for the entry "Vilfredo Pareto" written by Edgeworth for the *Palgrave Dictionary of Political Economy* (1926b), to find an evaluation, on the whole positive, of Pareto's work.

From this item, it is possible to grasp the main methodological differences between the two great economists – a difference in which Edgeworth found in Pantaleoni (and Jevons) an ally.

Between the end of 1899 and early 1900, Pareto, after having written his *Cours d'économie politique* (1896-7), where he was in strict continuity with Walras, and not so far away from Pantaleoni and the hedonist economists, re-wrote his economic theory.

In these two very intense years he pursued two fundamental and distinct objectives, which were to be considered his main legacy to contemporary economic science:

a) *ordinalism*, or the replacement of a cardinal by an ordinal utility function, overturning Edgeworth's (cardinal and hedonist) indifference curves;
b) the interpretation of ophelimity as an index of preferences, or the emancipation of his theory of choice and equilibrium from hedonism. On the turning point of 1899 Pareto built up his economic theory on "the naked fact of choice", without having to resort to cardinal measuring and not even to the existence of utility (Pareto 1960, II, pp. 290-291).

Edgeworth's shadow was very present in this re-foundation of the theory of choice.

In a famous letter to Pantaleoni (December 1899) he answered some questions asked by Pantaleoni with respect to his forthcoming *Sunto di alcuni capitoli di un nuovo Trattato di Economia Politica* (1900a), a paper in which Pareto anticipated the new foundations of the theory of choice. One question was about Edgeworth:

> There is a footnote in which it is reminded that the name curve of *preference* has been given by Edgeworth. Another footnote is needed to say that also the name curve of *indifference* has been given by Edgeworth. That is enough (1960, II, pp. 287-88).

Most probably Pantaleoni's request was a major acknowledgement that the Paretian new theory of choice has its origin in Edgeworth's theory. But Pareto took this opportunity to reassert his profound differences with respect to Edgeworth:

> Edgeworth and others start from the concept of the final degree of utility and *arrive* at the determination of the curves of indifference (as in fact I have myself done in the article of the *Giornale*).[69] I now leave completely aside the final degree of utility and *start* from the curves of indifference. In this lies the whole novelty ... Up to now the principles of pure economics have been founded on the final degree of utility, the *rareté*, the ophelimity, etc. Well! This is unnecessary. One can start from the curves of indifference, *which are a direct result of experience* Pareto (1960, II, pp. 287-293). [70]

This is the new foundations on which the rational choice theory of the 30', thanks to Hicks, Allen and Samuelson, has been based.

Edgeworth was soon aware that between his and Pareto's system there was no bridge.[71]

In his item on Pareto in the *Palgrave Dictionary of Political Economy*, Edgeworth wrote:

> The *Manuale* is distinguished by the original idea of treating the laws of demand and supply, or rather the "curves of indifference", from which those may be deduced, as objective, capable of being ascertained by external observation without the psychological knowledge obtained through the

---

[69] Pareto refers to his first papers on pure economics and the demand theory that he published in the "Giornale degli Economisti" (Pareto 1892-93).

[70] I have here adopted Georgescu-Roegen's English translation (1975).

[71] The first paper in which Edgeworth showed that he had well understood Pareto's revolution in economics is his review to Pareto (1903): "As we understand Professor Pareto, these data [with which the mathematical economists have to deal] do not comprise measurement of utility: psychical quantity, unlike physical, cannot be expressed as the sum of so many units. The exercise of *choice*, the preference of the economic man for one combination of goods to another, results in a system of indifference-curves" (Edgeworth 1903 [1970], III, p. 44). This refutation of "psychical" dimensions in economics wouldn't have sounded so nice to the author of "Mathematics *psychics*".

> sympathy. In short, the economist may be a *solipsist*… The conception has been criticised (cf. Pantaleoni, *Giornale degli Economisti*, Jenuary-February 1924, p. 17 seq.) as a needless abandonment of one large source of information (Edgeworth 1926a, p. 711).

Of course, this criticism wasn't just Pantaleoni's.

Up to Pareto's shift, economists were psychologists too: not only Edgeworth, but also Jevons, Pantaleoni and all hedonist economists of the first generation of marginalists did renounce to psychological introspection in order to grasp the reality behind curves and formulas.

Pantaleoni, who more than anyone else understood the geniality of Pareto, never ever accepted to follow him in his theory of choice:

> How to distinguish economic acts from non economic ones looking at the sole choice, instead of the psychological motivation of choice, which is, like the choice, object of observation and experience? … From the choice we cannot trace the motivation back, but from the motivation we can descend to the choice. The two logical operations are like the direct operations with respect to the inverse ones. The former have many solutions, the latter only one (Pantaleoni 1924 [1938], pp. 355-56).

Then, the initial incident in the relationships between the two, even if it did not compromise this mutual respect on the scientific level, above all certainly contributed to Pareto's underlining the differences rather than the analogies (that existed) with the English economist, including the use of the "curves of indifference": "I am not at all with Marshall, and little with Edgeworth" (Pareto 1960, III, p. 61).[72] And the difference was much more deep-rooted than the interpretation of the law of income distribution.

Although Edgeworth was surely struck by Pareto's geniality, his economic theory remained far apart till the end of his life.[73]

4.4. P.H. Wicksteed: Pareto's first follower in England?

4.4.1. The review to the Manuale

The last contemporary English economist to Pareto we will take into consideration is H.P. Wicksteed. The analysis of his relationship with Pareto will also pave the way for the last section of this research.

---

[72] A reconstruction of the dialogue between Pareto and Edgeworth with regards to the curves of income is done by Busino in the introduction to the third volume of Pareto's *Oeuvres Complètes* (1965); Giacalone-Monaco (1961, pp. 136-39) also dealt with the same subject.

[73] See, f.i., his critical review of the *Manuale* of the Paretian Luigi Amoroso (Edgeworth 1922).

Pareto knew Wicksteed at least from 1895, when in his correspondence we find references of Wicksteed's article on the distribution of wealth (1894).

In the *Cours,* he mentions Wicksteed's *Alphabet of Political Economy (1888)* among the works to be consulted ("for those persons who have but an elementary knowledge of mathematics"); and he added that for a more in depth study of pure economics "it would be good to begin by reading this small book, which is very clear, which explains fairly well the nature of utility (ophelimity)".[74]

The most important moment in the dialogue between Wicksteed and Pareto is the review to the *Manuale* written by Wicksteed for the "Economic Journal" (1906) [1933].

Pareto mentions Wicksteed's review in a letter to Pantaleoni dated September 28th 1907, where he defines him as being a "bulldog" unleashed by Marshall to attack him, the economist from Cambridge not wanting to – at least according to Pareto – "give him too much honour" by intervening personally in the polemics on economic equilibrium and on method.

And then he adds: "Then, there is a certain Wicksteed whose speciality is publishing ill-will, malign and injurious reviews on everything I write. I have read the first ones, because one gathers a certain usefulness from enemies, that of knowing one's defects; but I found them vain and inconclusive" (Pareto 1960, III, p. 65).

Then he mentions of having known from his disciple Sensini that Wicksteed had just published a "nasty" review on the *Manuale*, and writes the following to Pantaleoni: "After what you have told me about Wicksteed, I no longer attack him, even if he speaks badly about me. I have always been upset, am upset and always will be upset at the powerful ones, but not with the weak ones. Rather, I will send the French edition of the *Manuale* to Wicksteed" (p. 66).[75]

Why was Pareto so disappointed with Wicksteed's review?

At first sight Wicksteed's note, centred on criticisms for the non ordinary language and for the unusual framework of the book, doesn't look so negative towards Pareto:

> we hear nothing of consumption or distribution, and very little of production, but in their place are led to examine the "balance of desires", the "obstacles" to their gratification, and the resultant equilibria. We find ourselves not exchanging and bargaining, but "ascending the hill of the pleasure" by a "path" and to a "point" prescribed by the "obstacles" (Wicksteed, 1906 [1933], p. 816).

But, in order to understand the profound criticism of Pareto embodied in Wicksteed's review we must explore his methodology.

---

[74] In his introduction to *Commonsense of Political Economy* (1933, p. ix), L. Robbins noted this reference, by the "great Pareto", to Wicksteed.

[75] It remains a curiosity to know what Pantaleoni said about Wicksteed!

4.4.2. Wicksteed's Non-tuism

Wicksteed, more than Jevons, and differently from Marshall, views marginalist economics as a "revolution" with respect to classical methodological foundations, which has re-founded economic science on completely different bases. The main pillar of his work is the *marginal principle*, seen as the key to explaining *any kind of choice*.

The most complete exposition of his thought may be found in *Commonsense of Political Economy* (1910 [1933]). Wicksteed Immediately asserts in the *Introduction* that the vast shift impressed by neoclassical economists on economic science is the consequence of having based economics on the "psychology of choice between alternatives" (Wicksteed, 1910 [1933], p. 2). It follows "that the general principles which regulate our conduct in business are identical with those that regulate our deliberations, our selection between alternatives, and our decisions, in all other branches of life" (p. 3). Then, economics has nothing to say about wants and motives.

The *Common Sense* contains a methodology already present in Gossen (1854 [1981], p. 54): Wicksteed starts from the behaviour of the individual, Robinson Crusoe alone. Later (in ch. IV) he introduces Friday: "Hitherto our examination of the administration of resources has been conducted purely from the personal or individual point of view... We must now turn, making the momentous transition from personal to communal economics" (Wicksteed, 1910[1933], p. 127).

The most interesting part of the story can be found in chap. V, entitled *Business and the economic nexus*: here, with the intent of definitively freeing economic science from egoism and hedonistic philosophy, he takes away *personalised* human interactions from economic science. The theoretical tool used was *non-tuism.*

Wicksteed defines the "economic motive" as one of the worst confusions that prevented science from evolving. The reason for this danger is that many economists limited their studies in economics to actions characterised by one particular motive, "the desire to possess wealth" (p. 163). This methodological approach does not work for Wicksteed, since it excludes altruism from the economic field, and this – for a clergyman – would be a very serious limitation. Economics seen as praxeology (to use Von Mises' expression) inserts altruism within the economists' city walls: "We are only concerned with the 'what' and the 'how', and not at all with the 'why'" (p. 165).

Wicksteed begins by examining the theme of "communal economics", where he introduces the concept of *non-tuism.* The economic relation is a positive-sum game: *alter* co-operates with *ego* because the relation is advantageous to both (p. 166). All positive sum types of relations, where the others' interests are seconded as an indirect way of reaching one's own "may be fitly called 'economic'" (p. 166). Then, having defined relations and economic conditions (pp. 168-9), Wicksteed emphasises that the methodological pillars on which his economics is built are substantially different from those present "in the current treatment of Political Economy" (p. 169).

The first column is "that the economic relation is entered into at the prompting of the whole range of human purposes and impulses, and rests in a no exclusive or specific way on an egoistic or self-regarding basis" (p. 169).[76]

Economic relations are like a game: "It would be absurd to call a man selfish for protecting his king in a game of chess… If you want to know whether he is selfish or unselfish you must consider the whole organisation of his life" (*ivi*, p. 181). He repeats this idea in even clearer terms:

> Once more, then, if *ego* and *tu* are engaged in any transaction, whether egoism or altruism furnishes my inspiring motive, or whether my thoughts at the moment are wholly impersonal, the economic nature of the action on my side remains undisturbed. It is only when tuism to some degree actuates my conduct that it ceases to be wholly economic. It is idle, therefore, to consider "egoism" as a characteristic mark of the economic life (p. 181).

The last two phrases summarise Wicksteed's methodological project. To save economics from the criticism of being a science founded on egoism, where there is no place for altruism, the price paid was leaving *personalised face to face* economic relations outside.[77]

4.4.3. A radical difference

Wicksteed's approach to economics was, like Pareto, an escape from egoism and hedonism, and he certainly didn't like to find in Pareto's *Manuale* these expressions with an hedonistic flavour – although some of them borrowed by Pareto from Wicksteed's "friend" Dante[78].

[76] Then, he goes back to the housewife he had already introduced in the first pages (p. 20), emphasising that she cannot use a different *set* of motives, a different rationality, when she is at home and when she goes to the market. Just as Saint Paul could not be inspired at first by altruistic motives when at Aquila and Priscilla's home, and then by egoism when he made tents, "the economic relation, then, or business nexus, is necessary alike for carrying on the life of the peasant and the prince, of the saint and the sinner" (p. 171). Saint Paul probably did not think about his interests but about those who would use his work. However, did not have *all the others* in mind but only those "at large", that is the generic ones, without faces. "In his attitude towards himself and 'others' at large, a man may be either selfish or unselfish without affecting the economic nature of any given relation, such as that of Paul to his customers" (pp. 173-174).

[77] In Robbins' work we cannot find the discussions on *non-tuism*; however we find them implicitly in his imprint and in his definition of rationality (Robbins 1933, p. xxii, note 2), where, for his calculating economic man, there is no room for sympathy in his choices.

[78] Wicksteed knew Italian from his early studies on Dante: the "hill of the pleasure" was a translation of the Dantian "dilettoso monte" (*Inferno*, I ch.).

Nevertheless, we must admit that Wicksteed was really impressed by the book: "it is a work which is likely to modify and stimulate economic thought to an extent quite disproportionate to the numbers of its readers. It will probably be understood by few, but every one who understands it will be influenced by it".

Given the technical difficulties of the book, he "looks forward to a long period of continued and intensified study, and probably to the exposition and comments of other students, before attempting to estimate its full significance" (p. 815). He had this lucky period: four years of study for writing his *Common Sense of Political Economy*, a work that "bears witness everywhere to the extent to which Wicksteed himself had been affected" by Pareto's *Manuale* (Robbins 1933, p. xviii).

In fact if we compare the theory of the *Common Sense* with the theory of the *Alphabet* "superficially, the two theories are the same ... But a closer inspection will reveal important points of difference" (*Ibid.*): differences in which it is too easy to single out Pareto's influence:

a) The *Alphabet* starts from the marginal utility; the Common Sense starts with the "relative scale of preferences";
b) In the *Alphabet*, utility is considered as something objective and measurable; in the Common Sense the idea of measurability gives place to the idea of "order of preferences".

More in general, "there is no feature of the presentation which does not bear evidence of reformulation and improvement. In all this, the influence of Pareto is very strongly discernible" (Robbins 1933, p. xix).

Despite this peremptory and authoritative thesis, in Wicksteed's *Common Sense* we find Pareto's name only to acknowledge the mutual dependence of the demand of commodities (1910 [1933], p. 479), and an account of the criticism Pareto (and Edgeworth) made to his paper on the theory of distribution (1894) which led him to change his mind (1910 [1933] p. 373, footnote).

In fact, in my opinion, Robbins' thesis is a bit excessive. The influence of Jevons and mainly that of the Austrians is much deeper if compared with that of Pareto. This emerges if we look at the methodological criticism that Wicksteed addressed to Pareto in the review of 1906, which despite the general appreciation was the main reason for Pareto's disappointment.

Wicksteed criticises his basic principle of his methodology, the method of analysis and synthesis.

To Wicksteed "it is its strength that it carries Pareto's own principle a notable step further; and it is its weakness that does not carry it far enough". The Paretian principle that "A in not a function of A alone, but a function of A, B, C, etc., and when this principle is driven through to its legitimate conclusion, we shall understand the impossibility of drawing a line between economic and non-economic phenomena; ... and it is impossible to raise the treatment of economic alternatives to any degree of abstraction, without perceiving that we are in reality dealing with a *psychology of choice*, the application of which extends far beyond economic problems" (p. 816).

We have here the *same criticisms* addressed to Pareto by the other English economists: Marshall (distinction between economic and non-economic) and Edgeworth (the psychology of choice).

Finally, Wicksteed criticised the book for having restricted the domain of economics too much, which, for Pareto, makes up "a very small part of the actual phenomena of the business" (Wicksteed 1906 [1933], p. 817). But above all, according to Wicksteed, Pareto does not realise that his "curves of indifference" can cover a much greater area of human behaviour. This is a reading of Pareto's theory of choice very close to those of the English economists of the 30', who were also influenced, through Robbins, by Wicksteed's interpretation of Pareto.

5. The "second" Pareto and the modern rational choice theory: which continuation?

In the thirties in the Anglo-Saxon world there was a real Paretian revival. During the period that Hicks was at the London School of Economics (he was appointed in 1928), he through Dalton discovered Pareto's *Manual* and his new theory of choice: "Hugh Dalton ... said to me 'you read Italian, you ought to read Pareto'. So it was reading the *Manuale* which started me off on economic theory. I was deep in Pareto, before I got much out of Marshall" (Hicks 1979, Introductory).[79]

In his Autobiography Robbins recalled that "the introduction of Walras and Pareto must be chiefly attributed to Hicks" (Robbins 1971, p. 129).[80]

The same discovery was made, independently, by R. Allen.

In the beginning of the 30s Pareto was the most influential foreign economist in the English new consumer theory. Pareto was seen as the father of both the new ordinalist and anti-utilitarian welfare economics (Hicks, Robbins), and the new microeconomics (Hicks, Allen). In England (and later in America) there was a veritable *Pareto's vogue*.

In the beginning of their pubblications, "Econometrica" and the "Review of Economic Studies" inserted as first articles respectively "Vilfredo Pareto", written by the Paretian Luigi Amoroso (1934), and "Pareto's Pure Economics" by Umberto Ricci (1938); and in the first number of the new series of "Economica"

[79] Cf. also Hicks (1981-83, III, chap. XVII). It is interesting to note that the knowledge of the Italian language was an essential element in the reception of Pareto's theory in England: Edgeworth, Wicksteed, Hicks, all knew Italian, and had the chance to read Pareto.

[80] On the glorious 30's at LSE see also Coase, 1994, pp. 208-214.

we can find the famous *A Reconsideration of the Theory of Value* by Hicks and Allen (1934).

In 1935, on the wave of discovery of Pareto, Hayek included Barone's *Ministro della Produzione* (1908) in the volume he edited on Collectivist Economic Planning. Barone's essay soon became a classic of this very central issue during the 30's and 40's. [81]

In a climate of behaviourism, operationalism and neo-positivism, Pareto was presented as the founder of a new economic science, based on the facts, free from unobservable metaphysical categories such as pleasure and utility[82].

This is a very well-known story. It is, however, only half of the whole story.

In fact, in the English reading of Pareto we can see how the image that comes forth is of an *uncertain, confused* and almost *schizophrenic* author. He was seen as a genial precursor, but who introduced a hybrid, remaining in the ford between the old and the new. This attitude is very well synthesised by Hicks:

> even after Pareto had established his great proposition, he continued to use concepts derived from the earlier set of ideas. The reason was, perhaps, that he did not take the trouble to rework his earlier conclusions in the light of a proposition, which he only reached at a rather late stage of his work in economics. However that may be, he missed an opportunity (Hicks 1939 [1946], p. 19).

Immediately Hicks and Allen began speaking about an *incomplete* Paretian revolution, basing their thesis on the many passages in which Pareto uses concepts which were still founded on cardinalist utilitarianism.

Many historians and economists have gone back to the viewpoint of Hicks during the following decades and by now continue to express the same evaluations.[83]

In other papers[84] I have analysed whether or not Pareto was inconsistent or confused in the theory of choice. Here I would just say that Hicks and Allen read Pareto's theory of choice separately from his methodology, and through their neo-positivistic perspectives, the picture which emerged was that of an "inconsistent" Pareto.

---

[81] After Hicks and Allen's 1934 paper, Paul Samuelson by means of a series of articles brought the ordinalist revolution to its extreme consequences with his theory of revealed preferences, and the mathematical economists finished their work during the forties and fifties.

[82] The rediscovery of "Pareto the sociologist", mainly through the American Henderson during the first years of the thirties, is a different story: cf. Chazel (1997).

[83] The same evaluation can be found in the Americans. Stigler felt that "Pareto was inconsistent" (Stigler 1950, p. 389); and even more clearly in Samuelson: "as it is well known, Pareto was inconsistent in espousing it [δ2U/ δq1δq2] *after* he had given up *cardinal* utility in favour of better-or-worse, *ordinal* utility" (Samuelson 1974, p. 1256).

[84] See, f.i., Bruni and Guala (2000), or Bruni (1999, ch. 6).

However, in this paper I would like to emphasise just one point: that there is a radical difference between Pareto's theory of action and that of Hicks and of contemporary microeconomics.[85]

In a 1934 paper written with Roy Allen, Hicks, under the influence of the neopositivistic philosophy, wrote: "The methodological implications of [the new] conception of utility [...] are far-reaching indeed. By transforming the subjective theory of value into a *general logic of choice, they extend its applicability over wide fields of human conduct* (Hicks e Allen 1934, p. 45, my italics).

The same concept is restated in *Value and Capital*:

> that there are a great many such extensions appears at once when we consider how wide is the variety of human choices which can be fitted into the framework of the Paretian scale of preference (Hicks 1939 [1946], p. 24).

It is a methodological attitude that is very close to that of Wicksteed.

Pareto had a completely different idea of action. He realised that economic laws explained a small part of human behaviour. The kinds of logic behind economic and non-economic actions are substantially different. To utilise the structure of the theory of choice in Pareto's approach presupposes that agents are performing logical actions. This is very clear in all his scientific work ("What everybody surely knows, *since here we are dealing with logical action*, is that ..." (Pareto 1898, p. 128, my italics).

In fact the theory of choice was introduced by Pareto in 1900, *after having developed his theory of logical and non-logical actions*... His theory of economic action before 1900 was still based on *pleasure*.[86]

In the *Manual*, Pareto clearly specifies that his whole economic theory is valid for "many logical, repeated actions which men perform to procure the things which satisfy their tastes" (1906 [1971], III, § 1). Therefore, it is not strange that we don't find indifference curves in his Sociology, or that he has devoted the second half of his life to study Sociology, to write his cyclopic Treatise on General Sociology, in order to understand the dynamics and laws of the different "kind of logic" which governs the great part of actions.

Only after having written a scientific sociology, a scientific analysis of the non-logical part of the action, would Pareto have completed his project, that is to write the synthesis, a "Treatise on synthetic economics", which would be able to combine the logical and non-logical elements present in every economic action. He never completed such a book, and nobody has followed Pareto in this project[87].

[85] For a broader analysis of the continuity or discontinuity between Pareto and the microeconomics of the thirties see Bruni and Guala (2000).

[86] See, for instance, the *Cours d'économie politique* (Pareto 1896-7), or the analysis of social imitation and emulation in Pareto (1897), pp. 46 and following.

[87] See Bruni (1997a).

Rational choice theory, that is most of today's economics has not only followed Pareto on the path indicated by him of a *synthetic* economics, but also resolved the problem of the complexity of action by making the field of application of economic logic coincide with that of intentional choice, in all fields: "contemporary economics provides models not just for the prices of the rights for off-shore oil drilling, where the market meets very nice conditions, but also for the effects of liberal abortion policies on teenage pregnancies, for whom we marry and when we divorce and for the rationale of political lobbies" (Cartwright 1999, p. 1).

At the basis of such a methodology lies the anthropological assumption that man "most of the time" is moved by rational calculations in pursuing his own individual goals. For Pareto instead, "most of the time" passions, feelings, ideals that cannot be analysed by the "logic" of economic science move the human person.

Pareto simply demonstrated "that the theory is true in its domain, not that its domain is universal" (Cartwright 1999, p. 27). Therefore from this point of view "much of the theorising we do in economics right now goes in exactly the opposite direction" (Ivi, p. 3).

Instead of working towards finding a "different logic" that moves in that type of action, the Twentieth Century economists have made a reducing simplification, in this way discarding, among other things, the most vivid part of Paretian inheritance.

Hicks, Allen, Samuelson, and after them the mainstream of the modern rational choice theory (from Becker's economic approach to human behaviour to standard game theory), took up *Pareto's theory of choice separating it from his theory of action*: they used a theory of choice born to explain the small and "simple" world of logical actions and also extended it to all kind of intentional actions. This is exactly the opposite of what Pareto did and intended to do.

A brief conclusion

After this long, maybe too long, trip through Italian and English economists who are at the root of contemporary economic theory, we can say that although the *presence* of the leading Italian economists in England was massive between 1878 to 1938, it is not improper to assert that there has been an *influence* of Italian economists in English Economics only for the case of Pareto.

The main character of this research was to focus on the *theoretical reasons* that lie behind the reception, or the *missed* reception, of Italian economists in England.

Therefore, the paper has dealt almost exclusively with Pantaleoni, Pareto and Cossa: the three Italian economists who had continuous relationships with the first generation of English marginalist economists; the only three Italians whose name appears in the index of Marshall's correspondence, and who wrote manuals that have been translated into English.

The paper has centred mainly on *influence*, and though dwelling particularly on the analysis of Cossa and Pantaleoni, I hope to have offered some new insights for a better understanding of the *presence* of the Italian economists in England. The combination of these partial analyses on influence and presence may have given an idea of the *reception* of Italian economists in England from 1878 to 1938.

Finally, I am aware that I have not covered all of the extent of the topic of this research, let alone to have given a full account of the relationships between the economists of these two countries at that time. Who will ever know the actual friendships, polemics, delusions and hopes that have taken place through letters and encounters among these great economists? We all know that this reality is lost for ever.

Nevertheless, I hope to have been able to produce a sketch, to recall some forgotten dialogues and stories, possibly to pass on the baton to other scholars who, with new material and new interpretations, would carry on writing, or re-writing, this story of scientific and human battles and encounters.

Appendix

A) Three letters from Pantaleoni to Edgeworth

1

Regia Scuola di Commercio in Bari – Direzione
Bari, 2/3/91

My Dear Edgeworth,

So I am: viz., glad that you got the Professorship! It is, morally considered, one of the highest scientific positions, and, I suppose, also financially a very valid factory one. You must only now make up your mind, not to feed any invitation if you occasionally meet some compatriots and brother in science, who can't restrain from showing he would not be very much displeased, if he heard you had been crushed in a railway accident; or swallowed up by a quick sand.

* * *

As to the analysis of books and literature do all you can to shove off your shoulders that work, and put it on those of clever young people who have their way to make. Me reasons are these:

I. You'll never have a friend after a bibliographical note:
   a) the author will in most cases think you have not praised him enough, if you have praised him; he will wonder you have not seen the point he most cared for, if you have done your best to be impartial; he will be furious if you have attacked him;
   b) every single reader who has read the book and read your note, will think you wrong somehow;
   c) authors of books on the same subject will read you only thinking of themselves and, you may imagine, how they will appreciate you.

II. You'll be overloaded with tedious work. Reading is a pleasure, writing a boar.[88] Gauss put it drastically: propagare iucundum, parturire molestum. You'll have to read, as it is, a lot of rubbish. You'll have to read proofs. You'll have to write letters. You'll fell the want of intellectual work. Ergo, don't overload yourself.

III. As to books, you'll always find young fellows ready to make a note on them, if you only make them a present of the book. As to reviews, let one man be paid for the work and do it on a systematic plan. If necessary, take two. For students this is a very instructive work. You must not change your men, if possible, because they get to know the scientific character of the staff of the

[88] Pantaleoni expressed a similar thesis in the introduction to one volume of his collected papers (1910).

different reviews and are less exposed to slip essential articles or to stop at the foolish ones and give a right weight (proportional) to the articles. All this under your supervision. Not a line ought to be printed, you have not read.

IV. As to your plan of inviting authors to furnish abstracts, it presents some dangers. Very few authors will make an impartial abstract and not too long abstract of their own writing; some, on the other hand, wont make any, refusing to any thing in their own favour, out of dignity; publishers will often furnish you with quite unreliable notes and abstracts. I can give you just a case in point.

I include in this letter two sheets of notes. Now look at what the Times says of Prof. James and look at what it says of Prof. Baldwin! Evidently both notes were furnished by a clerk of Macmillan and he has damaged both books and discredited the Times in the opinion of some people who may have noticed the matter.

What will be very useful, is a post-card attracting notice to the topics which are thought worth a mention. As the Italian reviews, you ought to ask to exchange with the Nuova Antologia, which is our largest review.

It is published every 15 days in a volume like the *Revue de II mondes*, and, unfortunately for me, it can pay much better and get the best articles. There are never abstracts scientific, but have nevertheless a general importance when the arguments roll on topics which mutatis mutandis start up everywhere. It is not strictly economical; it is a political & literary review, but continuously has economical articles. The editor is a man called Protonotari – brother to the late Prof. Protonotari, who lectured on Pol. Economy in the University of Rome, was my master, and taught me <u>nothing</u> not knowing himself anything. His nickname was Protosomari[89] among the students.

The Nuova Antologia has 2,400 subscribers and has a commercial value of 400 thousand francs. Having a long standing and enormous diffusion (for Italian conditions) it is confident to have a sort of monopoly and when Protonatori died, its netto rent was multiplied by 10, as a basis for sale and division among heirs. As a criterion for the enormousness of this factor I'll add, that my associees and I bought the "Giornale"[90] multiplying by 4 its rent, and that the factor I would (and, in general, commerce would) agree too in the case of a good, safe review is 6. This is a sort of empirical integral.

In one of your last letters[91] you wrote to me that you have sent the Manifesto to the Neapolitan address I gave you. I don't remember a Neapolitan address. On the other hand I am sure I mentioned the "Economista" of Florence, directed by Prof. De Johannis, Via Cavour n. 1. This is a paper like the *Economiste* française. Don't I perhaps remember correctly, or have I made a *lapsus talami*? I received your copies and ordered the publisher to put one in every copy, as far as they went. But

[89] The nikcname plays with the suffix "notari" changed into "somari" (donkeys)

[90] The "Giornale degli Economisti", of that Pantaleoni was one of the Editors.

[91] No Edgeworth's letters to Pantaleoni has survived (to my present knowledge).

I would need about a 1000 copies. I am now discussing the plan with my friends of backing the "Giornale" by a weekly commercial paper, like the Economista. If I succeed to change my residence, as I hope, I think we'll do the thing. The principal difficulty lies in my objecting to shareholders: *eis kouranos esto*,[92] if I still remember Homer. In business a republic is an unmanageable thing and my nerves are too much overworked to stand long discussion.
This letter having ruled 24 hours on my table has given the Giornale time to be issued. You we'll find in it your article and two other ones.[93] The one by Imperatori will be followed by two more on the same subject.[94] Its general interest lies in this, that is shows how medical doctrines are not to be made a base for legislation before being certain – while it is not the case of most of them – and that hygiene is the pretext for an enormous mass of socialistic plunder and political home bug.
The other one furnishes a model of logismographic account Keeping for Communal and Provincial finances, which by law will have now to be kept on logismographical[95] principles.

Your affect. M. Pantaleoni

2

Giornale degli Economisti
Roma, Via Nazionale n. 87

15/6/1895

My dear Edgeworth,

I am very sorry to see you think such a thing as a School of Lausanne and a School of Cambridge exists. I am also sorry to see that mathematicians think it worth while to quarrel amongst themselves, instead of turning against the common host of Exoterics or Arosmatics.

Without the mathematicians the economists would not have had a true theory of equilibrium; they central idea which is perfectly clear and evident, as well is Walras' equations as in Marshall, is an unexhausted source of theorems and has corrected a series of fallacies of verbal economics, particularly all "residual theories".

---

[92] "Be the unique executive": in the original it is written in Greek letters.
[93] Edgeworth's article was Edgeworth (1891).
[94] The article was "La Nuova Politica sanitaria in Italia" (March 1891, pp. 246-290)
[95] *Logismographics* was a technique of accounting.

Of course economics is not rendered popular by mathematics. But besides and above the work of popularisation, you have the work of invention and of communication amongst *sebastikoi*.

As to correcting a wrong appreciation of Pareto, you are in your right and I repeat that we are glad and proud to publish any scrap of your pen.

Pareto is publishing a manual of political economy[96] of which I have read the mss. you w'll hardly see a formula in the whole book and, instead of mathematics, he has a most interesting series of inductive proofs of most economical theorems! He fully admits that this is the best way of treating the public. I have never before seen such a collection of inductive demonstrations as he has collected in his treatise.

* * *

You are very kind to wish to say anything of my articles on the Credito Mobiliare. They are not finished. I still have an article on the subject and I had to make place for other subjects. I'll give it in the number for the 1th of August. But, my things don't merit any particular mention. Having been one of the liquidators of the Credito Mobiliare I thought I would not let the occasion pass to make the post mortem examination, because economists rarely have similar occasions of looking into business. Economists are generally professors and don't see business. Businessmen see business, but are not economists, don't reflect, and when they do, don't tell the tale. I consequently amused myself for my own pleasure.

* * *

On the question of the Tax on exportation of sulphur. I could ask Ricca Salerno, professor at Palermo, to write to you. Ricca Salerno is a name probably known to you. He is a good economist. No genius, but correct good studies, no inventive talent.

I have written him a line, telling him to send you a line if he accepts and otherwise to send me a line, if he does not. If he cant write the note, La Loggia can; so could Colajanni. You only have *l'embarasse the choix*.

Barone will write in prose and only add mathematical notes, for those who like them.

My friend De Viti de Marco has married an american girl and will come soon to England. If he does, may I give him a letter for you?

Yours truly

M. Pantaleoni

---

[96] It is the *Cours d'èconomie politique*, 1896-1897.

3

Giornale degli Economisti
Roma, Via Nazionale n. 87

7/7/95

My Dear Edgeworth,

I answer your last letter within a couple of days only, because I have been very busy.

I have had your article returned me and if you desire it to be sent back to you, I'll do so immediately. Else it will sleeps in my archives.

As to controversy, Marshall's proposition that life is too short for it, my as a rule be correct. I would only suggest a distinction, limited at some 2600 years ago by our common friend Hesiod:

> Eris was not born, one alone; on earth
> There are two of them; one of these may be praised by the sage;
> damnation merits the other one; they have a different spirit, etc.

in the beginning of his *Erga kai emerai*[97]. The latter *Eris*[98] is very rare and degenerates as easily as certain chemical compositions which one hardly knows how to keep as they are, as anything will destroy their equilibrium.
I really think that you and Pareto have to take a lent (magnifying glass) to find out discrepancy. I even deny, that, as far as I understand you, him and Marshall, there is any difference as to coefficients of production. The whole matter seems to me be this. If L, K, T are the quantities of ingredients of a produce, Marshall and you put Produce = Φ (L, K, T),[99] id est you consider the quantity as varying with the amount to be produced. And this is really the law of real commerce. It is even <u>more complicated</u>.
Now Pareto, instead, speaks of coefficients – what are coefficients is not the same quantity in a unit of produce, *id est*, L/P = l, K/P = k, T/P = t. Consequently his equations come to be P = Φ (l, k, t), or a θ function of l, k, t and P, θ (l, k, t, P) = 0.[100] Is not that exactly the same? Can't coefficients be put subject to variations, when P varies, put like total quantity? Problems may be easier to handle in one way or another, according to circumstances, just like curves having unit prices on the ordinates may sometimes, or often, be preferable to curves having total price drown out on ordinates; but the substance is the same.

---

[97] "Works and Days": written in Greek letters in the original.
[98] "Eris" means "dispute", controversy, battle.
[99] Cf. his paper on International Trade (Edgeworth 1894, p. 45).
[100] Cf. Pareto's *Cours* (1896-7, § 104, footnote 1).

The only point at issue was a misrepresentation by Pareto of what you had written and that was easily corrected.
Your discourse about more or less mathematics would have been most damaging for the progress of the science. The fact is that it is a wonder when we can get an economist to undergo a course of mathematics or a mathematician to read economics. We, I mean the Giornale, is trying as hard as it can to get people to interest itself in mathematical economics. And we are object of great attach, from Loria, from Nitti, from Cossa, from Ferraris, Rabbeno, Supino, and have now and then to put some of them down. Now, if these people hear you, a leader in the field, a man exceptional for talent and brightness, say mathematics is *au fond* useless, we certainly have our ground very much spoilt. You would be made use of as an argumentum ad hominem against us; such arguments don't decide a question definitively, but they decide them for the masses for a long time. And you must consider that the people who wont read Walras, or Pareto, or Barone, wont either read Marshall, or you, but will keep to … and good chats like Wagner, or Schäffle, or Leroy-Bealieu, can have them, or to history, like Schmoller, Brentano, etc. People wont discuss your reasons, or see the limits and conditions of your assertions, but take them in a broader sense and we will have to wait 20 years more before getting into clear waters.
I am competing for the chair of Naples[101], vacant since the death of Ciccone, id est, since 4 o 5 years and I hope, if I gain the place, to get every year at the ears of some 500 students, giving the new doctrines and methods an impulse which will put Loria, Cognetti, Nitti, Rabbeno into despair. In my case you need not fear too much mathematics, because I can only stumble laboriously through differentials!

Yours affectionately

M. Pantaleoni

[101] Pantaleoni in 1895 did gain the place in Naples, where he taught up to 1897, when he left for a chair in Geneva.

B) ONE LETTER FROM L. COSSA TO S. JEVONS[102]

Monsieur et très honoré Collègue

Pavia (Italie) 29 Octobre 1880

Je viens de recevoir les six copies de la traduction anglaise de mon petit ouvrage et je suis trés content de l'édition élégante et correcte de votre célébre *publisher* Macmillan.

La version est fidèle et bien faite; j'approuve les notes adjointes et nécessaires pour le lecteur anglais. Comme il était inévitable, quelques fautes, pariculièrment dans les noms des auteurs non anglais, se sont glissées ça et la. Mais, elles ne sont que rares et ôtent bien peu aux mérites de l'édition.

Ce qui m'a fait un véritable plaisir c'est votre dotte et aimable Préface, dont j'apprécie avec une *reconnaissance sans bornes* la haute *porté*, et la bienveillante intention qui l'a dictée. Si mon livre pourra être utile à la jeunesse anglaise qui désire connaître l'histoire abrégée de l'économie politique, qu'elle peut étudier dans vos grands auteurs, j'en serai trés flatté; et je n'oublierai jamais que c'est à Vous et à votre indulgente mention de ma *Guide* dans la Préface de votre *Theory* (1879) qui est du l'initiative d'un succés qui dépasse le mérite bien modeste de mon écrit.

Je serai très reconnaissant et à Vous et à M. Macmillan si je receverai les principaux *articles critiques* qui paraîtront éventuellement sur ma *Guide* dans les journaux anglais.

Je vous prie d'avoir la bonté de faire remettre la lettre ci-jointe à Ms. Macmillan.

Presentez mes compliments à M.me Jevons, et croyez moi touyours avec les sentiments de ma profonde reconnaissance et sincère amitié.

Votre dévoué Collège
Prof. Louis Cossa

[102] The original manuscript is at the "J. Rylands University Library", University of Manchester, Jevons Papers.

REFERENCES

AMOROSO L. (1916), "Sulle teorie delle curve di utilità", *Giornale degli Economisti*, 52, pp. 409-12.

AMOROSO L. (1921), *Lezioni di economia matematica*, Zanichelli, Bologna.

AMOROSO L. (1934), "Vilfredo Pareto", *Econometrica*, 1, pp. 1-21.

BACKHOUSE R.E. (2000), "Introduction" to the reprint of Cossa (1880), 4th Volume of *Early Histories of Economic Thought*, Routledge, London.

BARONE E. (1935) [1908], "Il Ministro della Produzione nello stato collettivista", *Giornale degli Economisti,* September-October. Republished in "Le Opere Economiche", Zanichelli, Bologna, 1936, Vol. I, pp. 231-297.

BARUCCI P. (1972), "The Spread of Marginalism in Italy (1871-1890)", *History of Political Economy*, IV, pp. 512-531.

BECKER G. (1996), *Accounting for Tastes*, Harvard University Press, Cambridge Mass.

BELLANCA N. (1992), "The liberalist political economy of Maffeo Pantaleoni", *Economists' Archives* (supplement to the n. 22 of the *Bollettino di storia del pensiero economico*), pp. 5-14.

BELLANCA N. (1995), "From Principii to Erotemi. An Organic Interpretation", *Rivista di Politica economica,* March, pp. 97-153.

BELLANCA N. (2000), *Dinamica economica e istituzioni. Aspetti dell'economia politica italiana tra Ottocento e Novecento*, Franco Angeli, Milan.

BELLANCA N., GIOCOLI N. (1898), *Maffeo Pantaleoni. Il principe degli economisti italiani*, Edizioni Polistampa, Firenze.

BINI P. (1995), "When Economics Talked to Society: The Life, Thought and Works", *Rivista di politica economica*, March, pp. 11-46.

BRUNI L. (1996), "Gli anelli mancanti. La genesi del Trattato di sociologia generale di Pareto alla luce di lettere e manoscritti inediti", *Il Pensiero Economico Italiano*, 1/9, pp. 93-135.

BRUNI L. (1997a), "The "Unwritten" Second Edition of Pareto's *Cours d'économie politique* and its Italian Translation", *History of Economic Ideas*", 3/1997, pp. 103-126.

BRUNI L. (1997b), "La nascita, le vicende e la traduzione inglese dei Principii di economia pura di Maffeo Pantaleoni (Lettere 1888-1921)", *Storia del pensiero economico*, 36, pp. 135-177.

BRUNI L. (1999), "The Historical School Taken Seriously. The Debate on the "Economic Principle" According to De Viti, Pantaleoni and Pareto", *Revue Européenne des Sciences Sociales*, XXXVII, pp. 149-172.

BRUNI L., Guala F. (2000), "Pareto and the Epistemological Foundations of Rational Choice", forthcoming in *History of Political Economy* (Spring 2001).

CANNAN E. (1929), *Review of Economic Theory,* Kings and Son, London.

CARLILE W.W. (1898), "Review" to Pantaleoni (1898), *Economic Review*, VIII, pp. 554-558.

CARTWRIGHT N. (1999), *The Dappled World. A Study of the Boudaries of Science*, CUP, Cambridge.

CHAZEL F. (1997), "L'entrée de Pareto dans la sociologie américaine et son appropriation sélective par T. Parson et George Homans", in *Pareto Aujourd'hui*, ed. by A. Bouvier, PUF, Paris, pp. 129-153.

CHIPMAN J.S. (1976), "The Paretian Heritage", *Cahiers Vilfredo Pareto. Revue européenne des sciences sociales*, 14, pp. 65-173.

COASE R.H. (1994), Essays on Economics and Economists, Chicago University Press, Chicago.
COSSA L. (1876), *Guida allo studio dell'economia politica*, Hoepli, Milan.
COSSA L. (1880), *Guide to the Study of Political Economy*, Macmillan, London.
COSSA L. (1893), *Introduction to the Political Economy*, Macmillan, London.
DE VITI DE MARCO A. (1925), "Maffeo Pantaleoni", *Giornale egli Economisti*, 25, pp. 165-77.
EDGEWORTH F.Y. (1881), *Mathematical Psychics,* Kegan, London.
EDGEWORTH F.Y. (1891), "Osservazioni sulla teoria matematica dell'Economia Politica con riferimento speciale ai Principiii di Economia di Alfredo Marshall", *Giornale degli Economisti*, March, pp. 233-245.
EDGEWORTH F.Y. (1894) [1970], "The pure theory of international values", *The Economic Journal*. Reprinted in Egdeworth (1970), II, pp. 3-60.
EDGEWORTH F.Y. (1896), "Supplementary Notes on Statistics", *Journal of the Royal Statistical Society*, 59, pp. 529-539.
EDGEWORTH F.Y. (1897), "La curva delle entrate e la curva delle probabilità", *Giornale degli Economisti*, 19, pp. 215-220.
EDGEWORTH F.Y. (1903) [1970], "Review" to Pareto (1903), *The Economic Journal*. Reprinted in Edgeworth (1970), III, pp. 43-47.
EDGEWORTH F.I. (1915) [1970], "On some theories due to Pareto, Zawadski, W.E. Johnson and others", *Economic Journal*, March-June. Reprinted in Edgeworth (1970), II, pp. 450-491.
EDGEWORTH F.Y. (1922), "The Mathematical Economics of Professor Amoroso", *Economic Journal*, XXXII, pp. 400-407.
EDGEWORTH F.Y. (1926a), ad vocem "Pantaleoni", *Palgrave Dictionary of Political Economy*, Vol. 3, pp. 709-10.
EDGEWORTH F.Y. (1926b), ad vocem "Pareto", *Palgrave Dictionary of Political Economy*, Vol. 3, pp. 711-12, Macmillan, London.
EDGEWORTH F.Y. (1926c), ad vocem "Pareto's Law*", Palgrave Dictionary of Political Economy,* Vol. 3, pp. 712-13, Macmillan, London.
EDGEWORTH F.Y. (1970), Papers Related to Political Economy, 3 Voll., Burt Franklin, New York. Reprint of the original edition, 1925.
EINAUDI L. (1931), "Review" to Pantaleoni (1889), Reprinted Treves (1931), *La Riforma Sociale*, 42, pp. 527-29.
FISHER I. (1898), "Review" to Pantaleoni (1898a), *Annals of the American Association*, July-December, pp. 294-297.
FLUX A.W. (1898), "Review" to Pantaleoni (1898a), *The Economic Journal*, 8, pp. 355-60.
GALLEGATI M. (1990), "The Spread of Alfred Marshall's Economics in Italy", 1885-1925, in McWilliams Tullberg (1990), pp. 512-32.
GEORGESCU-ROEGEN N. (1975), "Vilfredo Pareto and his Theory of Ophelimity", *Atti dei Convegni Lincei: Convegno internazionale Vilfredo Pareto*, Accademia Nazionale dei Lincei, Rome, pp. 223-265.
GIACALONE MONACO T. (1961), *Pareto e Sorel. Rilfessioni e ricerche*, Cedam, Padova.
GROENEWEGEN P. (1996), *A Soaring Eagle: Alfred Marshall 1842-1924*, E. Elgar, Cheltenham.
HAYEK F. ed. (1935), *Collectivist Economic Planning*, Routledge and Kegan, London.
HEY J.D., WINCH D. (1991), *A Century of Economics. 100 Years of the Royal Economic Society and the Economic Journal*, ed. by, Blackwell, Oxford.

HICKS J.R. (1932), *Marginal Productivity and the Lausanne School: A Reply*, "Economica", 12, pp. 297-300.
HICKS J.R. (1946), *Value and Capital*, Oxford University Press, Oxford.
HICKS J.R. (1979), "The formation of an economist", *Banca Nazionale del Lavoro Quarterly Review*, pp. 355-364.
HICKS J.R. (1981-83), *Collected Essays on Economic Theory*, Voll. 3, Clarendon Press, Oxford.
HICKS J., R. ALLEN (1934), "A Reconsideration of the Theory of Value", *Economica*, 1, pp. 52-76; 196-219.
JAFFÉ W. (1964), *Barone's Unpublished Review of Wicksteed's Essay on the Coordination of Laws of Distribution and Related Documents*, Cahiers Vilfredo Pareto, n. 3, pp. 61-102.
JEVONS S.H. (1878), *Primer of Political Economy*, Macmillan, London.
JEVONS S.H. (1871) [1879], *The Theory of Political Economy*, Macmillan, London.
JEVONS S.H. (1880a), *Economia Politica*, Italian Translation of the *Primer of Political Economy*, edited by Luigi Cossa, Hoepli, Milan.
JEVONS S.H. (1880b), *Preface* to the English Translation of Cossa (1876), pp. vii-xii.
JEVONS S.H. (1977), *Papers and correspondence of William Stanley Jevons*, ed. by R.D. Collison Black, voll. 7, Macmillan, London.
JOHNSON W.E. (1913), "The Pure Thoery of Utility Curves", *The Economic Journal*, 23, pp. 483-513.
MAGLIULO A. (1993), "The reception of Italian economics in England (1915-1945)", *Il Pensiero Economico Italiano*, I, pp. 7-53.
MARSHALL A. (1890) [1946], *Principles of Economics*, Macmillan, London.
MARSHALL A. (1996), *The Correspondence of Alfred Marshall, Economist (1868-1924)*, ed. by Whitaker, Cambridge University Press, Cambridge.
MCWILLIAMS TULLBERG R. (1990), *Alfred Marshall in Restospect*, E. Elgar, Cheltenham.
MILL J.S. (1862), *System of Logic, Ratiocinative and Inductive*, Parker, Son, And Bourn, London.
NEWMAN P. (1991), "Reviews by Edgeworth", in Hei and Winch (1991), pp. 109-141.
PANTALEONI M. (1882), *Teoria della traslazione dei Tributi. Definizioni, dinamica e ubiquità della traslazione*, Paolini, Rome.
PANTALEONI M. (1883), "Contributo alla teoria del riparto delle spese pubbliche", *La Rassegna Italiana*, 15 ottobre, pp. 25-60. Reprinted in Pantaleoni (1904), pp. 49-110.
PANTALEONI M. (1889), *Principii di economia pura*, Barbera, Florence.
PANTALEONI M. (1897), Review of Pareto (1896-7), *Rivista popolare*, pp. 726-730.
PANTALEONI M. (1898a), *Pure Economics*, English translation of Pantaleoni (1889), Macmillan, London.
PANTALEONI M. (1898b), "Dei criteri che debbono informare la storia delle dottrine", *Giornale degli Economisti*, IX, pp. 407-31. Reprinted in Pantaleoni (1925), I, pp. 223-47.
PANTALEONI M. (1904), *Scritti vari di economia*, First Series, Sandron, Palermo.
PANTALEONI M. (1910), *Scritti vari di economia*, Third Series, Castellani, Rome.
PANTALEONI M. (1923), "Vilfredo Pareto. Obituary", *The Economic Journal*, XXXIII, pp. 582-590.
PANTALEONI M. (1924) [1938], "In occasione della morte di Pareto. Riflessioni", *Giornale degli Economisti*, 64, pp. 1-19. Republished in Pantaleoni (1938).
PANTALEONI M. (1925), *Erotemi di economia*, Voll. 2, Laterza, Bari.

PANTALEONI M. (1938), *Studi di finanza e statistica*, Zanichelli, Bologna.

PANTALEONI M. (1890) [1980], "An Edgeworthly letter of Recommendation", *Journal of Political Economy*, 88 (in the forth of cover).

PARETO V. (1892) [1966], "Les nouvelles théories économiques", *Le Monde Economique*, July-August-September-October. Reprinted in *Oeuvres Complètes*, Vol. IX, *Marxisme et Economie pure*.

PARETO V. (1892-93), "Considerazioni sui principi fondamentali dell'economia pura", *Giornale degli Economisti*, May, pp. 390-420; June, pp. 485-512; August pp. 119-157. Republished in *Oeuvres complètes,* vol. 26, Droz, Genève.

PARETO V. (1894) [1982], "Teoria matematica dei cambi forestieri", *Giornale degli Economisti*, pp. 143-73. Republished in *Ecrits d'économie politique pure, Oeuvres Complètes*, Vol. XXVI, ed. by G. Busino, Droz, Genève.

PARETO V. (1896a) [1965], "La Courbe de laRépartition de la Richesse", *Universitè de Lausanne, Recueil Publié par la Faculté de Droit à l'occasion de l'Exposition nationale Suisse, Genève 1896,* in Pareto (1965), pp. 5-15.

PARETO V. (1896b) [1965], "La curva delle entrate e le osservazioni del Professor Edgeworth", *Giornale degli Economisti*, November 1896, in Pareto (1965), pp. 19-28.

PARETO V. (1897) [1965], "Ultima risposta al Prof. Edgeworth", *Giornale degli Economisti*, March 1897, pp. 219-220, in Pareto (1965), pp. 41-42.

PARETO V. (1896-97), *Cours d'économie politique professé à l'Univérsité de Lausanne*, 2 voll., Rouge, Lausanne. Republished in *Oeuvres complètes,* Vol. 1, Droz, Genève.

PARETO V. (1898), *Comment se pose le problème de l'économie pure*, Mémoire présenté en decembre 1898 à la Societé "Stella" par le professeur V' P', Lausanne (chez l'auteur). Republished in *Cahiers Vilfredo Pareto*, 1, 1963, pp. 121-130, and in *Oeuvres Complètes*, Vol. 9, Droz, Genève.

PARETO V. (1900a), "Sunto di alcuni capitoli di un nuovo trattato di economia politica del prof. Pareto", *Giornale degli Economisti*, vol. X, March, pp. 216-235; June, pp. 511-549.

PARETO V. (1900b), "Sul fenomeno economico. Lettera a Benedetto Croce", *Giornale degli Economisti*, 21, pp. 139-162.

PARETO V. (1903), "Anwendungen der Mathematik auf Nationalökonomie", *Encyklopädie der mathematischen Wissenschaften mit Einschluss ihrer Anwendungen*, Leipzig, Vol. I, n. 7, pp. 1094-1120.

PARETO V. (1906) [1971], *Manual of Political Economy*, Kelley, New York. English translation of *Manuale d'economia politica con una introduzione alla scienza sociale*, Società Editrice Libraria, Milan. French Edition, 1909, republished in *Oeuvres complètes*, Vol. 7, Droz, Genève.

PARETO V. (1916), *Trattato di sociologia generale*, Barbera, Florence. English translation, *The Mind and the Society: a Treatise on general Sociology*, New York, Dover, 1963.

PARETO V. (1960), *Lettere a Maffeo Pantaleoni*, a cura di G. De Rosa, voll. 3, Banca Nazionale del Lavoro, Rome.

PARETO V. (1962), *Carteggi paretiani*, a cura di G. de Rosa, Banca Nazionale del Lavoro, Rome.

PARETO V. (1965), *Ecrit sur la curve de ripartition de la richesse*, *Oeuvres Complètes*, vol. III, Droz, Genève.

PARETO V. (1975), *Corrispondance: 1890-1923*, ed. by G. Busino, *Oeuvres Complètes*, vol. XIX, Droz, Géneve.

PARETO V. (1982), *Ecrits d'économie politique pure*, ed. by G. Busino, Oeuvres Complètes, tome XXVI, Droz, Genève.

PIGOU A. C. (1912), *Wealth and Welfare*, Macmillan, London.

PIGOU A. C. (1920), *Economics of Welfare*, Macmillan, London.

RICCI U. (1924), "Pareto e l'economia pura", *Giornale degli Economisti*, 64, reprinted in Ricci (1939).

RICCI U. (1938), "Pareto on Pure Economics", *Review of economic studies*, 1, pp. 3-21.

RICCI U. (1939), *Tre economisti italiani. Pantaleoni Pareto Loria*, Laterza, Bari.

ROBBINS L. (1933), "Introduction" to Wicksteed (1933).

ROBBINS L. (1971), *Autobiography of an economist*, Macmillan, London.

SAMUELSON P.A. (1974), "Complementarity. An Essay on the 40th Anniversary of the Hicks and Allen Revolution in Demand Theory", *Journal of Economic Literature*, 12, pp. 1255-89.

SCHUMPETER J.A. (1949), "Vilfredo Pareto (1848-1923)", *Quarterly Journal of Economics*, 63, pp. 147-173.

SCHUMPETER J.A. (1954) [1994], *History of Economic Analysis,* Routledge, London.

SCHUMPETER J.A. (1951) [1997], *Ten great economists*, Routeledge, London.

SRAFFA P. (1924), "Maffeo Pantaleoni Obituary", *The Economic Journal*, 34, pp. 648-53.

STIGLER G. J. (1950), "The Developement of Utility Theory: I, II", *Journal of Political Economy*, 58, pp. 307-327; 373-396.

WICKSTEED H. P. (1906) [1933], "Review" to Pareto (1971) [1906], *The Economic Journal*, 16, pp. 553-57.

WICKSTEED H.P. (1888), *The Alphabet of Political Economy*, Mcmillan, London.

WICKSTEED H.P. (1910) [1933], *The Common Sense of Political Economy*, Routledge, London.

ZANNI A. (1991), "Pareto's monologue with Marshall", *Quaderni di storia dell'economia politica*, IX, pp. 399-423.

ZANNI A. (1999), "Pareto in Tuscany. Discontinuities and Premonitory signs of an Economist and Sociologist", *Révue Internationale des Sciences Sociales*, XXXVII, pp. 119-140.

The spread of Italian economic thought in France (1750-1850)*

*André Legris***
University of Nice-Sophia Antipolis and CNRS

If Voltaire is to be believed, "il faut écrire ou en français, ou n'être pas lu." (Voltaire, *Correspondance*, vol. 33, p. 128). Such a succinct statement would have given little opportunity for Italian economic literature to spread in France without it having been translated, or without its authors having journeyed across the border to diffuse their ideas in person. It could be argued that the above opinion does not sufficiently take into account the sociology of the Europe during the Age of the Enlightenment, where such a spreading of ideas in the intellectual community led to it being described as a "literary republic". It is therefore useful to discuss the means by which such a spreading works: through travelling, meeting places, writings translated or read by notable linguists, and cultured circles with a shared interest in certain topics. It is in this way that, according to Voltaire once again, "vers 1750, la nation rassasiée de vers, de tragédies, de comédies, d'opéras, de romans, d'histoires romanesques, de réflexions morales plus romanesques encore, et de disputes théologiques sur la grâce et sur les convulsions, se mit à raisonner sur les blés."[1 2].

The second half of the eighteenth century would therefore mark in France, and in Europe in general, an interest in economic matters among an enlightened public. Paris was becoming an important centre for what was emerging as a serious discipline in its own right. Authors' ideas and publications were being discussed in the *salons*, which were brimming with great minds of the period. These salons were often the creations of *ladies* from the aristocratic intelligentsia, where almost all of the great influential figures in the movement of ideas could be seen. One of the most famous was the salon of Julie de Lespinasse.

Of course, other factors were involved in the fairly rapid spread of ideas and discussions (M.M. Augello [1994], p. 10 and note 9). The publishing of satirical tracts and opuscules, often in the form of a didactic dialogue, and other writings seem to have been equally important. In France such works included the

---

* The author has benefitted from the comments made by Philippe Steiner about the quotations of Italian economists in Say's writings, and from the comments made by James Webb, undergraduate of Oriel College, Oxford, for the English version of the text. Usual caveats apply.

** The author is a member of the Department "Institutions, Organization and Economic Dynamics".

[1] Voltaire, *Blé*, in *Dictionnaire Philosophique* [1770], "Questions sur l'Encyclopédie".

[2] See Larrère [1992], pp. 221-222.

Encyclopédie, the *Ephémérides du citoyen*, the *Nouvelles Ephémérides* and the *Décade philosophique littéraire et politique* [3]. Correspondence reflected the spread of ideas. Academic departments, such as that at the *Collège de France* headed originally by J.-B. Say and then by P. Rossi, and specialist periodicals like le *Journal des Economistes* founded in 1841[4], were to ensure a certain spreading of economic thought, but unlike in countries where public finance was studied, like Italy, the institutionalization of the discipline was disputed and late in coming, which considerably limited the discussion and development of ideas (L. Le Van-Lemesle [1991], p. 355). The study of public finance, which was flourishing in Italy and linked to the teaching of economics, was confined to the law faculties[5].

In Italy the spread of economic ideas was carried out in a more academic fashion from the 1750s. Large cultural centres, spread far and wide and often with strong links to university education [6] [7], were expanding. They gave rise to a certain diversity and ideas circulated via specific channels. The foundation of other specialist periodicals and reviews, both scientific and literary, attested the growing interest in social sciences[8]. These included *Il Caffè* (1764-1766), *Estratto della Letteratura Europea* (1766-1770) and later the *Biblioteca Italiana* and the *Conciliatore* (1818-1819) in the Milan area alone (M. Guidi [1996], pp. 21-36).

There are several consequences of these particular sociocultural circumstances. Indeed, it seems difficult to assert the existence of well-established national traditions, especially in Italy in the second half of the eighteenth century, all the more so since economic thought was developing in several geographical centres [9]. It seems better to imagine a sort of European community of ideas, the "Literary Republic of Enlightenment Europe", where economic matters were discussed. Debates and discussions among individuals and small groups were the basis for the construction of theories as well as for suggestions for economic policy.

However, the aim of this chapter is to study the spread of Italian economic thought in France in the period 1750-1850.

---

[3] See Steiner [1991], pp. 174-178 on J.-B. Say and the reviews in Faccarello-Steiner [1991].

[4] Rossi was one of the five founders of the *Journal*.

[5] See the papers of the Conference in Florence [March 1986], the *Institutionnalisation of Political Economy in the World.*

[6] Such teaching of economics arrived very late in France. In the middle of the revolutionary period a public chair of political economy was created at the *Ecole Normale* [1795] held by Alexandre Vandermonde. J.-B. Say taught from 1819, under the Bourbon restoration, at the *Conservatoire des Arts et Métiers*, and from 1831 he taught industrial economics at the *Collège de France*. The chair was later taken away during the tenure of Michel Chevalier for a few months, and then re-established after the intervention of Guizot, who subsequently handed it to Rossi. However, it was not until the end of the nineteenth century that the university chairs were created under the aegis of the law faculties. After the Second World War, the faculties – now UFRs – of economics gained their independance.

[7] For instance at Milan with C. Beccaria and P. Verri, Bologna with L.M. Valeriani, tutor of P. Rossi and Catania with S. Scuderi and P. De Luca.

[8] See Angello, Bianchini Guidi [1996].

[9] These centres are identified in the publication in review form contained in Augello, Bianchini and Guidi [1996].

If we limit ourselves to describing the actual spread of ideas itself, our account could be clarified by presenting it in terms of periods, inasmuch as Italian economic thought tended to spread in France during particular periods of history. We can, for instance, eliminate the revolutionary period. We can mark the first period from 1750 to 1789. The second period ran from 1803, which saw the first edition of J.B. Say's *Traité d'économie politique*, until 1848 which saw Joseph Garnier publish the second edition of *Les Eléments d'économie politique*. The two periods both reflected certain themes like the question of freedom of trade, a certain idea of justice, debates on method to expand research in the social sciences, and the defence of economical liberalism.

The decision to limit this work to the spread of ideas itself runs the risk of it becoming a descriptive piece which, although enriching, would overshadow its impact and influence on french economists. We would therefore be unable to gauge whether an idea has been correctly interpreted, whether it has led to further reflection on the work of other writers, whether it has provoked debate and whether it has added to the sum of knowledge.

That is why I have chosen to devote the first part of this chapter to the study of the spreading of Italian economic thought in France, so as to gauge, in the second part, the influence of this thought on certain authors from a theoretical point of view.

Yet we must not underestimate the difficulty of such an undertaking, given the importance of the period studied and the usual constraints on space. On one hand, certain topics and certain economists have to be given preference to others due to the author's own subjective opinions.

On the other hand, the material published during this period did not always conform to the practice to which we are accustomed today, particularly in that references to other works were not always made explicit and quotations were sometimes re-worded while their origins remained somewhat dubious.

It should also be pointed out that this study in no way claims to be exhaustive. It does not attempt to trace every single connection which there may have been between French and Italian economists, but rather to underline the most fundamental ones. We are therefore bound to limit ourselves to those economists generally regarded as important according to international criteria. Public finance is not dealt with due to the reasons which I mentioned earlier.

1. The spread of ideas or a study by networks. Actors, institutions and economic sociology

The main aim of this first part of the chapter is to analyse not the impact of Italian economic theory in France, but the conditions in which its spreading took place. In France, Paris was unchallenged as the centre for culture and the *salons* were to play a vital role in the creation of networks, the welcoming of foreign economists, the discussion of ideas and even in the decision-making of the editors of economic literature.

The salons

The function of the Paris salons, considered as one of the institutions of the eighteenth century (A. Lebeau [1902], p. 6), is explained by, among others, La Harpe: "C'étaient de véritables petits parlements qui connaissaient de tout en toute matière, où le talent de bien dire autorisait à tout dire et qui parfois gouvernaient les ministres en un temps où les ministres gouvernaient le roi." ([1795], vol. 1, p. 386).

The salons of Mme d'Epinay, the Holbachs, the Helvétius, the Marquise de Choiseul, Sophie de Grouchy, the wife of the Marquis de Condorcet, Mme de Staël and the daughter of Necker were each of great importance.

Sophie de Grouchy's salon, for example, was set up at the *Hôtel des Monnaies, quai de Conti*, in the official residence occupied by Condorcet since he was appointed *Inspecteur des Monnaies* by Turgot in 1775. Figures who frequented the salon included Adam Smith, who already knew Turgot and Condorcet[10], as well as Beccaria, Jefferson, Etienne Dumont, La Fayette and Beaumarchais. In the salon of Julie de Lespinasse (1732-1776) and d'Alembert in the *rue de Bellechasse*, no doubt the most popular among economists between 1760 and 1775, regular visitors included Quesnay, Du Pont, Trudaine, Marmontel, Condorcet, Morellet, Galiani, Condillac, Diderot and Turgot, *Intendant du Limousin* at the time, whenever he was in Paris. Thus, at Mme de Lespinasse's salon, "le fait d'être reçu était presque un titre de considération" and "l'on était sûr de trouver, depuis cinq heures du soir jusqu'à dix, l'élite de tous les états, hommes de cour, hommes de lettres, ambassadeurs, seigneurs étrangers, femmes de qualité." (*ibid.*, p. 386). Marmontel[11] gives us an insider's view of the salons:

> A l'exception de quelques amis de d'Alembert, comme le chevalier de Chastellux, l'abbé Morellet, Saint-Lambert et moi, ce cercle était formé de gens qui n'étaient point liés ensemble. Elle les avait pris ça et là dans le monde, mais si bien assortis que, lorsqu'ils étaient là, ils s'y trouvaient en harmonie comme les cordes d'un instrument monté par une habile main. [...] Et remarquez bien que les têtes qu'elle remuait à son gré n'étaient ni faibles, ni légères: les Condillac et les Turgot étaient du nombre; d'Alembert était auprès d'elle comme un simple et docile enfant. Elle avait le talent de jeter en avant la pensée, et de donner à débattre à des hommes de cette classe.

---

[10] Sophie de Condorcet translated *The Theory of Moral Sentiments* [1759] into French and had it published in 1795.

[11] *Mémoires*, vol. 1, critical edition by John Renwick in the " Ecrivains d'Auvergne " collection, Clermont-Ferrand [1972].

While they were staying in Paris in 1766, Beccaria, A. Verri and P. Verri all visited the salon in the *rue de Bellechasse*[12]. We know that Ferdinando Galiani, after his arrival in Paris in 1759 as Embassy secretary, made himself known in enlightened circles by frequenting the salons of Mme d'Epinay (1726-1783), Julie de Lespinasse, Mme Geoffrin and the Duchess of Choiseul. Moreover he became a close friend of Mme d'Epinay and their correspondence after his return to Naples provides us with precious information. The *Dialogues sur le commerce des bleds*, written between 1768 and 1769, was later to be discussed line by line by Diderot and Mme d'Epinay.

So, in this particular period, the Abbé Galiani exercised unquestionable influence during his time in Paris, but as a skilful stirrer of ideas rather than as a master theorist. Galiani's presence in certain Paris salons and the circulation of the *Dialogues* stimulated the debate which had already started[13], and caused the thinkers to reflect further on a number of topics. The resulting opinions focused on the analytical quality of the themes developed as well as the quality of interpersonal relationships. For instance, we are aware of Turgot's strong opposition to the arguments presented in the *Dialogues*. It was with some reservation that Turgot judged the clarity and verve of the Abbé's reasoning when he wrote to Du Pont:

> L'ouvrage est très amusant et il sera donc très difficile d'y répondre de façon à dissiper la séduction de ce qu'il y a de spécieux dans le raisonnement. (Turgot [1773], letter to Du Pont de Neumours in G. Schelle, *Œuvres de Turgot et documents le concernant*).

At the same time, Galiani did admire the honesty of Turgot; although he also considered him naïve for having taken on responsibilities in order to push his ideas forward:

> Enfin M. Turgot est contrôleur général. Il restera trop peu de temps en place pour exécuter les systèmes. [...] Il punira les coquins, il pestera, se fâchera, voudra faire le bien, rencontrera des épines, des difficultés, des coquins partout. Son crédit diminuera; on le détestera... Il se retirera ou on le renverra. (Galiani, letter to Mme d'Epinay, *Correspondance*, vol. 2)

The problem of grain and the spreading of Frederico Galiani's thought.

Between 1750 and 1789 France seems mainly to have been preoccupied, from an economic point of view, by agricultural matters. Thus, questions

[12] On their journey to Paris, see E. Morato [1993], pp. 93-95 in Augello, Bianchini and Guidi.

[13] An earlier debate, also on the general problem of regulation versus freedom of enterprise, remains known as *L'affaire des toiles peintes*. See Larrère [1992], pp. 138-144.

concerning methods of production led to debates on economic policy. It should be emphasized that the *Edits*, promulgated between 1763 and 1764[14] in order to progressively achieve the freedom of the corn trade, were the direct consequence of the physiocrats' polemic against the prohibitionist measures, early introduced by Laffemas from 1600 under the reign of Henri IV, which were followed up by Colbert's policies. Debates on the corn trade provided much material for economic literature. Veron de Forbonnais [1768] was in favour of France exporting its corn in the event of a surplus on the condition that the consumption within the kingdom be protected and evened out through a hoarding policy. He thereby contradicted the Physiocrats and their allies who wanted the free trade measures to include the city of Paris where old practices were still in force. In fact, the French people and some Parliaments such as those in Paris and Rouen did everything they could to oppose the *Edits*, which they regarded as harmful and responsible for the high price of bread. Opinions were getting extreme on both sides. Figures sympathetic with the physiocrats' cause included Abeille, Turgot, Condorcet, d'Alembert, the Abbé Morellet and Voltaire, while the opponents of the *Edits* in addition to Forbonnais and the Abbé Galiani included Diderot, d'Holbach, Necker, Grimm and the Abbé Terray.

The Physiocrats thought they had most of France on their side, given their campaign of persuasion bolstered by Turgot, and it was their influence which prompted Bertin, the *Contrôleur général*, to make a declaration in the Paris Parliament confirming certain provisional measures which had been decided on since 1754. The physiocrats, who were in favour of introducing further measures against prohibition, used periodicals to spread their propaganda: first the *Gazette du Commerce* and then the *Journal de l'Agriculture, du Commerce et des Finances*, edited by Du Pont de Neumours until 1766, the year their opponents took control of the publication. The Abbé Baudeau, convinced by the arguments for the freedom of the corn trade, gave the Physiocrats access to the columns of his *Ephémérides du citoyen*, which he had just founded and whose editorship he entrusted to Du Pont[15]. When the prices rose following the poor harvests from 1766 to 1768, opinion turned against the *Edits*. The Marquis de Mirabeau, the Abbé Baudeau, Du Pont and the Abbé Roubaud took responsibility for their defence in the face of violent attacks, and Du Pont de Neumours in the *Journal Oeconomique* ([1770], p. 326)[16] believed the battle was won when he wrote: "la question de la liberté du commerce des grains est finie". Du Pont was of course mistaken since the vast

---

[14] To be more precise, it was from 1759 that Contrôleur Général Machault authorized the unrestricted trade of corn. This decision was backedup by the decrees of 1763 and 1754 due to the resistance to the changes which this decision provoked.

[15] The *Sociétés daAgriculture,* founded in France with the support of Bertin, devoted most of their meetings to commentaries on texts by Quesnay, Du Pont de Neumours, Marcier de la Rivière and Le Trosne.

[16] The articles appeared with the title *Observations sur les effets de la liberté du commerce des grains et sur ceux des prohibitions.*

majority of the public and even certain intellectuals were in favour of the return of prohibition. The *Contrôleur général* Terray, relying on the support of key figures such as Diderot, d'Holbach, Grimm[17] and Mme d'Epinay, ignored the seven letters sent to him by Turgot between October and December1770 and welcomed the wide circulation of Galiani's work. Indeed, in the same year, Galiani decided to get his *Dialogues sur le commerce des bleds* published and turn public opinion for the removal of the *Edits*. In that way, he attacked the opinions of the Physiocrats and Turgot. A few years ago, the decline in popularity of the physiocrats' views on economic policy caused the Marquis de Mirabeau to try to extend the group's sphere of influence abroad[18]. But Galiani's writing steel reduces the spread of physiocratic ideas.

We know that the *Dialogues* had been circulating in the salons[19] for at least a year. Even Voltaire and d'Alembert were momentarily impressed by the style (see E. Badinter & R. Badinter [1988], p. 65, footnote 3). The *Dialogues* were of course later condemned in circles which preferred the arguments of the *Economistes*, but if their arguments would not seriously affect the theoretical reasoning, they were to provide material for an important French debate.

First of all, the spreading of the *Dialogues* had consequences for the press. In 1772 the *Ephémérides du citoyen*, which attacked the arguments in favour of regulation, was banned by the authorities[20]. When Turgot came to power, the arguments for the freedom of the corn trade were listened to once again and the Abbé Baudeau relaunched the *Ephémérides* under the new name *Nouvelles Ephémérides - Bibliothèque raisonnée de l'histoire, de la morale et de la politique*, and it appeared until Turgot's fall from power. Literature about the *Dialogues*, whether for or against them, can assist us in our description of the arguments. For example, Du Pont, Roubaud, the Abbé Baudeau and most notably the Abbé Morellet[21], published pieces which opposed the arguments put forward by Galiani. Necker was on Galiani's side with his *Législation et le commerce des grains* which he wanted Turgot to read and to permit its publication. Despite allowing it to be published, Turgot refused to read it. Diderot published his *Apologie de l'abbé Galiani*.

Then, if the corn issue was still burning away by the time the Revolution came, bubbling under the surface of the debate were other matters such as whether it was the right time to educate the people, the nature of freedom, and the philosophical

---

[17] Grimm *Correspondance*, letter on 1st Junuary 1770) wrote: "Tandis que le peuple criait faim et misère de tous côtés, les Physiocrates ont eu la courageuse imbécilité de continuer leurs criallereries pour l'exportation illimitée." in Edition Tourneux, Paris [1848], p. 418.

[18] See A. Alimento [1994], *Il pensiero economico italiano*, uno, pp. 37-53.

[19] On editions of the *Dialogues*, see Luigi de Rosa, Introduction, in Galiani [1987], pp. XXVIII-XXXV.

[20] "C'est ce Bertrand (*le Censeur royal*) et le Gardaine qui voulaient escroquer de votre ami Du Pont une pension de 100 pistoles pour Marin et qui ont fait supprimer les *Ephémérides*", in *Oeuvres de Condorcet*, letter to Turgot on 2nd December 1773.

[21] In *Réfutation de l'ouvrage qui a pour titre "Dialogues sur le commerce des bleds"*.

grounds for the exercising of justice. As Larrère noted ([1992], p. 222), the corn controversy broke the unity which characterized the Age of Enlightenment and encyclopaedists found that they could not agree. The nature of the events would only exacerbate a debate which was strongly influenced by Galiani when in 1770 the Abbé Terray, then *Contrôleur Général des Finances* imposed regulation of trade against the wishes of Turgot. Turgot urged Terray to reconsider his decision, writing him seven letters between October and November 1770, which caused d'Alembert and Voltaire to defend the arguments of the *Intendant du Limousin*. When Turgot was appointed *Contrôleur Général des Finances* by Louis XVI on 24th August 1774, controversy blew up once more. Indeed, the first act of the *ex-Intendant du Limousin* was the ruling of 13th September of the same year which re-established the freedom of the corn and flour trades within the domestic economy. We know that Turgot thought such freedom as "l'unique moyen de prévenir, autant qu'il est possible, les inégalités excessives dans les prix." (Turgot [1774], *Préambule de l'arrêt du 13 septembre*). Galiani believed that agricultural concerns should not be dealt with by such radical intervention which risked destroying the equilibrium and hindering development of industry. We know the end of the story. Bad harvests, the *Guerre des Farines* and the undermining of Necker backed up by the spread of Galiani's writings caused the experiment to fail. On 12th May 1776 the king dismissed Turgot, who took refuge at the *Duchesse d'Enville* home in La Roche-Guyon, and renounced all responsibility.

From economics to freedom and justice: the spread of Cesare Beccaria's thought

In the second half of the eighteenth century in France, debates on the easing of trade restrictions on grain had to be considered alongside debates on the power of the monarchy, the status of the people, and the status of justice. The desire to see the end of the prohibitions on the trade and distribution of goods led to a questionning of one of the essential ties between the king and "his" people – the covenant of subsistence. Royal power was based on the tacit moral obligation to provide food for the people, who in return submit to his will. The king must "pourvoir à la subsistance des peuples, sans quoi il n'y a pas de loi ni de force qui puisse le contenir." (Bossuet in *Politique tirée des propres paroles de l'Ecriture sainte*). The power of the state and its representatives was measured by its capacity to keep the nation free from the threat of famine (Larrère [1992], p. 231). The debate on the lifting of trade restrictions on corn not only challenged the workings of the traditional French monarchial society and the equilibrium between central power, Parliaments and people, but it also created suitable conditions for the reception of a different philosophy of justice. Old practices such as judgment without trial, taxation, forced selling and appropriation of foodstuffs were replaced in the new Enlightened age by a right to defence, freedom of trade and the assertion of property as a right which could not be forfeited. The need to defend property led to the conception of an "état policé où la violence se convertit en droit et le besoin en titre de propriété." (Abeille [1768], *Principe sur la liberté du commerce des grains*, p. 12). On this fertile ground, the spread of the *Illuministi milanesi's* ideas could be discerned. The summer of 1764 saw the appearance of *Dei delitti e delle pene*, a work first published anonymously in Livorno. We know that *Dei delitti e delle pene* was the fruit of discussions by the small group of Italian enlighted figures who linked up again for the review *Il Caffè* (1764-1766), and that Beccaria and Verri brothers were main members of its editorial staff. As soon as it became well known, the text inspired Parisian intellectuals. In his *Mémoires*, the Abbé Morellet recalls that: "En 1766 [...] M. de Malesherbes nous donnait à dîner, à M. Turgot, M. d'Alembert. Il venait de recevoir l'ouvrage d'Italie [...] Essayez, me dit-il, de le traduire. Je passai dans la bibliothèque, et j'en revins avec cette phrase comme elle est aujourd'hui. On fut content, on me pressait de continuer. J'emportais le livre et je le publiais en français au bout de six semaines." (vol. 1, p. 163). We know that the Abbé Morellet, as the private tutor to the Duc de La Galaisière, was travelling in Italy between 1758 and 1759[22]. During his stay he met Cesare Beccaria and therefore knew the identity of the author from the moment *Dei delitti* were published. The anecdote also informs us that Morellet had mastered the Italian language. The translation of *Dei delitti* spread rapidly[23], as the Abbé pointed out that "cette traduction eut sept éditions en six mois." (Morellet, *op. cit.*). The Abbé Morellet invited Beccaria and Verri brothers to Paris where they stayed from mid-October until the end of November, 1766. A. Verri returned the following year from February to mid-March (Condorcet [1994], p. 24). Beccaria got on particularly well with Condorcet, and explains how he felt for him "l'amitié tendre et le respect que l'on doit à un illustre bienfaiteur de l'humanité." (Beccaria [1910], p. 179).

We can begin by basing the spread of Beccaria's thought on a piece of indisputable evidence provided by two letters addressed to him in 1770. The first came from Count Giovanni-Maria Mazzuchelli and the second from Count Giuseppe Gorani (*Correspondence and related documents*, D 16668 and D 17075). The two counts were witness to certain discussions which took place while d'Alembert and Condorcet were visiting Voltaire in Ferney (25th September - 10th

[22] Simone Meyssonnier hypothesizes that it was during this journey that the Abbé Morellet brought back Galiani's writing [1751] to Vincent de Gournay (Meyssonnier [1989], p. 238). Indeed, we known that *Della Moneta* was in the Gournay's library from 1760 and that Turgot read it and then consulted it while writing his article *Valeurs et Monnaies*, which was left unfinished ans never published. *Valeurs et Monnaies* was intended, on Morellet's request, to be included in the *Dictionnaire du Commerce* swhich was never completed either, but the project for which we can read about in the *Prospectus* of 1769.

[23] The Abbé Morellet's translation to the *Tratatto dei delitti* into French was often regarded as a totally accurate one. For instance, F.B. de Felice, editor of the Yverdon *Encyclopédie*, wrote to Pietro Verri about plans to tranlate the *Meditazioni* into French: "Puisque M. Morellet veut traduire votre ouvrage qu'il le traduise. Votre ouvrage y gagnera pourvu qu'il ne le mette pas en capillotade comme il a fait du Traité des délits. Je me charge de l'impression." (C. Donato [1992], pp. 108-110). Morellet's tranlation never apparead in print.

October 1770)[24]. The content of the letters confirms the important role played by Beccaria's writings on reform of the French justice system. We know that at this time, Condorcet, d'Alembert and Voltaire agreed not only to support one another's ideas, but also to defend the arguments of Turgot in favour of the unrestricted trade of grain, against the measures imposed by the finance minister Terray, but most of all against the juries, judgment by the Parliaments without trial, and sentencing. Thus Condorcet played an essential role as his correspondence with the *Intendant du Limousin*[25] testifies. This correspondence stretched between February and July 1771 and allows us to assess the considerable power which the ideas developed in the treatise *Dei delitti e delle pene* had on the French mathematician with regard to criminal justice. Moreover, Turgot was persuaded by several of the document's arguments concerning the abolition of torture, public access to trials and defence of the accused. Yet, as far as abolition of the death penalty was concerned, whereas Condorcet seems to have been convinced, Turgot still had his doubts: "Bornée au petit nombre de cas où elle doit avoir lieu, c'est une autre matière à discussion sur laquelle, malgré mon penchant, je trouve bien des difficultés à adopter l'opinion de Beccaria"[26]. In an unfinished and undated piece, Condorcet wrote about the criminal laws in France: "En composant cet écrit je n'envisage d'autre avantage que celui d'être utile. L'amour de l'humanité a pu seul me faire surmonter le dégoût d'un pareil travail, je n'y ai pas été soutenu par l'espérance de la gloire. Plein des principes lumineux qui brillent dans les ouvrages de Montesquieu et de Rousseau, ayant à côté de moi *le traité des délits et des peines*, je ne fais que me traîner sur leurs traces, et appliquer aux lois françaises les principes généraux qu'ils ont puisés dans la nature de l'homme et dans la Constitution des Etats." (Condorcet, *Manuscrits Inédits*, [1994], p. 231). Having read Beccaria's work, Condorcet drew up with Voltaire, d'Alembert and Turgot a list of necessary reforms in criminal justice.

The wide spread of Beccaria's thought can be confirmed by many historiographic facts. The problem then lies in gauging the limits of such an influence and thinking about what conclusions we can draw for a proper economic analysis. If Beccaria's influence on French intellectuals is not in doubt, it still has to be considered beyond Turgot's reservations about the abolition of the death penalty alone.

First of all, the teaching in Beccaria's work, read by the eyes of an economist, seem to have escaped French readers who were unaware of his economic writings, except J.B. Say. Beccaria appears only to have been an expert on criminal law, and

---

[24] On this journey, see E. And R. Badinter [1998], pp. 64-67, Fayard, Paris.

[25] For example, this is what Condorcet said of Beccaria's work to Turgot in 1770: "Connaissez-vous un livre italien de M. Beccaria sur le style? On va le traduire en français, mais si vous le vouliez en italien, je vous enverrais mon exemplaire." in *Correspondance* by C. Henry, XXIX p. 41, letter on Tuesday 19 February 1771). The book in question was *Richerche intorno alla natura delle stile.*

[26] Letter from Turgot to Condorcet on 17th May 1771 in *Oeuvres de Turgot et documents le concernant*, ed. Schelle, vol. 3, p. 517.

in France more than elsewhere (Schumpeter [1954], vol. 1, p. 256). It must be added that writings such as the *Elementi di economia pubblica*, published in Italy in 1804, were only translated into French in 1852 at the Bouchard-Huzard publishing house.

Then Beccaria and his circle from Milan insisted on the important role that applied mathematics could play in questions of law and economics[27]. He opposed the views of d'Alembert, who was not convinced by the potential use of real sciences to deal with social sciences (letter on 3rd January 1766). This criticism also appears in Condorcet's work and must not be underestimated. It is expressed even better in the criticisms of the *Meditazioni sulla economia politica* sent by Condorcet to Count P. Verri (letters from 1771 and 1772).

Formalization and social sciences

Pietro Verri received two letters from the Marquis de Condorcet in 1771 and 1772 concerning a passage from the *Meditazioni sulla economia politica*, a work largely the result of discussions and articles from the review *Il Caffè* and probably written in October and November 1770. During this time, he was a rival of Beccaria who had held the chair of public finance at the Scuola Palatina in Milan from 1769. The text appeared in Livorno in April 1771. According to F. Venturi ([1978], p. 535 onward), the *Meditazioni* were also inspired by discussions with Henry Lloyd on the problem of using mathematical calculations in social and political science. From 18th April, Italian copies reached Trudaine, Diderot, Holbach, d'Alembert, Helvétius, Marmontel, Condorcet and Morellet (*ibid.*, p. 532)[28]. In Condorcet's letters mentioned above, he argued against the use of algebra (or *géométrie* as it was known at the time) in representing human behaviour in social science and the laws which are supposed to result from it. The passage in the *Meditazioni* brought under attack from the first letter dated 7th November 1771 corresponds to the statement: "Il prezzo delle cose è la ragione diretta del numero de' compratori, e inversa del numero de' venditori"[29]. Condorcet wrote :

> Pardonnez, Monsieur, si un géomètre a osé vous faire une observation à un endroit de votre livre où vous employez le langage de la géométrie. Vous dites que le prix est en raison inverse du nombre des vendeurs, et en raison

---

[27] For instance, see *Tentativo analitico su i contrabbandi* (Beccaria, *Il Caffè*, vol. 1, p. 15).

[28] From October 1771, F.B. De Felice wanted to publish a Frech translation of the *Meditazioni* (letter on 3rd October to Verri in F. Venturi [1978]). He discovered that the Abbé Morellet had a similar intention, and wrote told Verri in a letter on 24th October. There was then going to be a translation by de Keralo and Suard which was revised by Condorcet at the end of 1772 (F. Venturi [1978], p. 589). These efforts failed and the first French translation, taken from the seventh Italian edition, was published by Jules Henri Pott in Lausanne and put on sale in 1773. From this historiographic information we can surmise that Condorcet had a full understanding of Verri's text [1771] from the first edition in Italian (see Condorcet [1994], pp. 68-69).

[29] The passage was set out in this form in the first edition of the Italian text in chapter IV.

directe de celui des acheteurs. Je sais bien que le prix augmente quand le nombre des acheteurs augmente, et qu'il diminue quand celui des vendeurs s'accroît; mais est-ce dans le même rapport? C'est ce que je ne crois pas. (Condorcet [1994], pp. 70-71).

Condorcet interpreted P. Verri's text literally since he credits the Milanese economist with the idea of using mathematical functions. Condorcet said the same thing in a second letter, the date of which is uncertain but which was probably sent at the start of 1772. In this letter, written before the sixth edition of the *Meditazioni*, the French mathematician wrote: "Je ne puis être de votre avis sur la manière dont vous faites dépendre le prix du nombre des acheteurs et des vendeurs." (*ibid.*, p. 72)[30]. With these comments, Condorcet distanced himself from the development of a formalization of social sciences with whose philosophy he did not agree. The criticisms levelled at P. Verri by the mathematician mainly interest us, because they were shared by a large number of French enlightened figures of the period like d'Alembert and Turgot[31].

Of course, for Condorcet, political arithmetic could serve a useful purpose when used to determine which methods to apply in economic policy. But apart from this econometric approach[32] to social phenomena built from a macroeconomic point of view, human behaviour seemed to unpredictable to be successfully understood by a mathematical function, let alone by feeding it into an equation. At the very most, "dans les problèmes économiques où il s'agit de quantités, devons-nous nous estimer très heureux quand nous savons que l'une augmente et l'autre diminue." (Condorcet [1994], p. 73). Perhaps these criticisms were the beginning of an important distrust throughout the nineteenth century of the use of mathematics in political economy on the part of the "recognized" economists in the French academic world. That would partly explain why Cournot and Dupuit were to continue their work in secret and this same attitude led to add to the refusal on admitting L. Walras into the scientific community which meant he became an exile in Lausanne.

The epistemological position present in Condorcet's criticisms hardened even in the time of J.-B. Say. This explains the rejection of the hypothetical deductive approach, symbolized by Ricardo, which was considered too abstract, and therefore the scepticism which made Say and his closest followers shift to some of Pelegrino Rossi's teachings, particularly after the latter's split from utilitarism which he

---

[30] On how Verri reacted to Condorcet's remarks, see F. Venturi ([1978], p. 577).

[31] On 12th November 1771 (letter in Schelle, vol. 3, pp. 512-513), Turgot wrote to Caillard: "J'ai reçu, mon cher Caillard, vos critiques et le livre du comte Verri, dont je vous remercie bien [...] Je vous parlerai également du comte Verri dont je suis très peu content [...]." There is however a letter written by Voltaire in support of P. Verri with regard to the *Meditazioni* and the passage which was criticised by Condorcet, "L'interesse è sempre in ragione diretta dalle ricerche e inversa dalla offerta". The letter has no date and no addresses, but some believe it was sent in 1762 to Beccaria (D. Best 10557) or even to P. Verri (E. Bouvy [1889], p. 170).

[32] See Schumpeter [1954], vol. 1 on Turgot.

had defended with Etienne Dumont following his embracing of Victor Cousin's philosophy around 1829[33]. For instance, Joseph Garnier [1846] whom we know was an important academic figure on Say's side, cites Rossi no less than thirty times. But Rossi's analyses were praised when they reinforced Say's own, but were criticized for being too abstract as soon as they went against the official doctrine. Generally, the French orthodox liberals reproached P. Rossi not only for his references to the Ricardian theory, but also for the attempts at formalization in his *Cours* which he taught at the *Collège de France* during the academic year 1837-1838. Rossi used the teaching which he had been given in Bologna by Valeriani with his famous formula p = i/o (see Pucci [1989], p. 91). Moreover, we know that Gioia's philosophia naturalis were very distinct from Valeriani's arguments (P. Barucci [1964], A. Macchioro [1989] and T. Maccabelli [1996], pp. 143-145). If, like the *New Palgrave*, we regard P. Rossi as an Italian economist, his teaching spread a certain aspect of Italian thinking which led him to develop a theory of the monopoly price which Vatin suggests inspired Dupuit and perhaps Cournot as well (F. Vatin [1998], pp. 125-127). Likewise, the debate between Say and Gioia[34] on the role of statistics in studying social phenomena can be partly explained by Say's fidelity to a French tradition against economic formalization which continued up until the work of Léon Walras and which Say helped to strengthen.

The importance of J.-B. Say's thought and liberal thinking

The first half of the nineteenth century shows us that spreading occurred mainly from France in the direction of Italy, as testified by the reception of French economic works in the Italian peninsular (P. Travigliante [1996] - T. Maccabelli [1996] - M. Guidi [1996]). French liberal thought in particular crossed the Italian border by way of translations of the books of J.-B. Say, on the one hand (See Steiner [1996b], pp. 9-35) and the efforts of Ferrara[35]. The revolutionary period in France, on the other hand, was characterized by the implementation of legislative and statutory reform. Theoretical innovation was therefore largely absent and I agree with the interpretation of this period given by G. Faccarello and P. Steiner ([1990], pp. 9-56). Of course, the exceptional events of the period provided a wealth of material to discuss. But as far as analysis was concerned, any new theoretical advances had to wait for the work of J.-B. Say[36]. Say appears to have

[33] On the links between Rossi's thought and utilitarianism see Vatin [1998], pp. 109-111.

[34] See P. Travigliante [1996], pp. 183-187 in Augello, Bianchini and Guidi.

[35] See P.F. Asso, P. Barucci and M. Ganci (ed.), *F. Ferrara e il suo tempo*, Bancaria editrice, pp. 205-213.

[36] On the links between Say's writings from 1789-1802 and the *Traité d'économie politique*, see Steiner [1990], pp. 173-193.

been at the time an enlightened witness to economic revolution in France and Europe. As such, he discusses the economic and social changes in his work. He was the undisputed leader of a specifically French school of thought, orthodox liberalism, which was to wholly dominate the doctrine and diffusion of political economy throughout the nineteenth century[37]. The propagation of the doctrine was carried out through the press, and it was the British model which influenced the French orthodox liberals with periodicals such as *The Edinburgh Review*, founded in 1802, the *Quarterly Review* [1809] and the *Westminster Review* founded in 1824 by Jeremy Bentham (Laurent-Marco [1996], p. 79)[38].

However, J.-B. Say and his brother had been educated in their childhood by two Italian teachers, Giro and the Abbé Gorati. For that reason, Jean-Baptiste mastered the Italian language and cites Italian authors in his work. In this way one could carry out a search of the quotations of Italian authors in the French economist's work.

In the first edition of the *Traité d'économie politique* [1803], we find references to P. Verri (twice) and Villani (once). The number of references increases in the second edition [1814] and thereafter, and for the most part can be found in the *Discours Préliminaire*. Few changes were made up to the fifth edition of 1826, where the references included Algoratti (2), Beccaria (5), Beloni (1), Carli (1), Davanzati (1), Filangieri (1), Galiani (8), Genovesi (1), Gorani (1), Intieri (1), Rinuccini (1), Serra (1), Verri (7) and Villani (1). The *Cours complet* (1828-1829) revealed a noticeable decrease in the number of references to Italian authors, but the name Gioia continued to appear. So, two preliminary conclusions can be drawn from this rapid quantitative analysis[39]. Firstly, comparing it to other statistics of references to authors in Say (see Steiner [1999]), no one Italian author is continuously and principally mentioned in any of his works. The highest number of references are to Galiani (8), Verri (7) and Beccaria (5); and then the references to Beccaria were not only concerned with the legal side of the Milanese author's work and are accompanied by commentaries on Montesquieu, Voltaire, Turgot and Smith on capital products and division of labour (see 4th edition of *Traité*, *Discours preliminaire*). On the other hand, references to Galiani and Verri are concerned with the analysis of value, markets and economic freedom, and it is these analysises which we will deal with in the next part of our problematic.

---

[37] See Yves Breton and Lutfalla [1991], *Introduction.*

[38] After numerous editorial failures, in 1841 the French liberal movement found a medium worthy of spreading their ideas in the *Journal des Economistes*, nearly ten years after the death of J.-B. Say.

[39] The conclusions drawn from the data provided are consistent with the recent more general presentation by Steiner [1999].

II. Influences and economic analysis

Throughout the studied period, the principal topics for analysis were those questions of value and market. However, these theoretical reflections gave rise to an epistemological questioning of the bases on which an increasingly independent discipline must lie. Let us start with the general reflections which established links between the conditions of individual freedom of the distinctive economic sociology in the Age of Enlightenment, and the theoretical processes made possible by these conditions.

Mechanical analogy and political economy

The Enlightenment period was crucial for a further two sets of reasons which are worth being elaborated on here. The first set has its roots in events and is principally the result of the circulation of Galiani's work in 1770 about the corn trade. Opposing Quesnay and his followers, Turgot and Condillac all at once, Galiani appeared to be the main enemy of J.-B. Say's utilitarian liberalism movement. But the situation was more complex than that, and the opinion that the French Lights had of Galiani was passed down to their successors and focused on Italian economists in general in the nineteenth century, with the notable exception of Ferrara. In the work of Italian economists, the French liberal economists would see an extension of the ideas proposed in Galiani's *Dialogues* only concerning interventionist economic policy. First, that partly explains just how little influence these Italian economists from the first half of the nineteenth century had on their French counterparts between 1803 and 1850, with the exception of Pelegrino Rossi, if we consider Rossi, who wrote in French, as a typical economist in the Italian tradition. Secondly, we can see, due to the significant legacy left by Galiani's intervention, a sort of caricatured opposition between the freedom-seeking economists whose arguments were based in the work of Quesnay, Turgot, Condillac, Smith and Say on one side, and on the other side those like Sismondi who questioned the efficiency of self-regulatory mechanisms and who considered most of their Italian counterparts as objective allies. Yet putting such considerations into perspective enables us to assess the extent of influence inasmuch as the Italian economists no longer appeared to be tuned into the wave of theoretical innovation[40]. For instance, an author like Sismonde de Sismondi, who had the cultural and historical means to draw inspiration from the work of the Italian economists, seems to have been considerably lacking from their sources of influence, as is confirmed by P. Barucci's introduction to Sismondi's work in the recent edition of the *Nuovi Principi* in Italian.

[40] In a comprehensive presentation on nineteenth century economic thought and the sub-period in question here, Umberto Meoli [1968] mentions no Italian economist.

But as far as economic analysis is concerned, the approaches of Galiani and Turgot were not so different from each other as supporters of conflicting economic policy would have had us believe. More generally, the analogy with Newtonian physics has been standard in sciences in general and in the social sciences in the second half of the eighteenth century. Mechanics had been a regular source of economic inspiration since scientists became aware of Newtonian concepts. The gravitation of physical bodies around an equilibrium led to the idea of a social body whose laws organize themselves automatically. This perception of equilibrium as in the movement of forces of nature largely underlies the economic analysis of Galiani [1751 & 1770]. This aspect of his work would be an important source of inspiration for most French economists who directly or indirectly knew his writings but who rarely cited him on this topic. In *Della Moneta*, the analogy with Newtonian physics is clear:

> Quello, che la gravità è nella fisica, è il desiderio di guadagnare, o sia di viver felice, nell'uomo, e, ciò posto, tutte le leggi fisiche de' corpi possono perfettamente, da chi sa meditarlo, nel morale di nostra vita verificare. (Galiani [1751], p. 54)

Galiani then compares economic organization with the workings of a machine in the *Dialogues*. Here it is easier to discern the analogy with the major principles of applied economics which were the origin of prescriptions for economic policy because "dans cette machine immense de l'état politique tout se tient ensemble, tout est lié, tout est enchaîné; rien ne doit sortir de l'équilibre, si on ne veut pas voir toute la machine renversée. [...] Voilà pourquoi la science politique est si difficile; voilà pourquoi je ne recommande rien tant que d'éviter les secousses et les mouvements subits. Les secousses cassent les liens et les ressorts et la machine est détruite." (Galiani [1770], p. 142). According to Galiani, whoever decides what reforms are made must adopt a pragmatic attitude, accounting for the current situation and proceeding with the reforms while taking care not to cut corners to achieve them. His attitude towards the upheaval caused by the *Edits*, and then his comments on the failure of Turgot's policies, went against the prevailing view which had spread throughout France.

Turgot used the same analogy and Perrot [1998] lists six examples of it in Turgot's work. For instance, regarding agricultural workers' salaries and the upper and lower limits between which those salaries varied, Turgot wrote to the *Contrôleur Général* Terray[41]: "Mais c'est cette espèce de *superflu* surtout que l'on peut dire qu'il est *chose très nécessaire*; il faut qu'il y en ait, comme il faut qu'il y ait *du jeu* dans toutes les machines. Une horloge dont toutes les roues

[41] This is the fifth of seven letters sent from Saint-Angel on 14th November 1770 during a tour of his *Intendance du Limousin.*

engrèneraient les unes dans les autres avec une exactitude mathématique, sans le moindre intervalle, cesserait bientôt d'aller." (in Ravix-Romani [1997], p. 304). Three years earlier, in an often quoted letter[42] to Hume, Turgot expressed the same view: "Il y a un degré de relâchement nécessaire dans toute machine, sans lequel elle courrait le risque de se briser à tout moment.".

But even if we accept that Galiani, using the analogy with Newtonian mechanics, was breaking new ground in the construction of political economy modelling, we should nonetheless put into perspective the influence that he may have had on his readers, such as Turgot. In fact, in Turgot's work from l'*Eloge de Vincent de Gournay* [1759] (*ibid.*, pp. 123-153) onward, we find a natural and mechanical phraseology when he explains how we must "reconnaître ces lois universelles et primitives, fondées sur la nature même, par lesquelles toutes les valeurs existant dans le commerce se balancent entre elles et se fixent à une valeur déterminée, comme les corps abandonnés à leur propre pesanteur s'arrangent d'eux mêmes suivant l'ordre de leur gravité spécifique." (*ibid.*, p. 124). We could always assume the hypothesis that Turgot had already read Galiani and used him without referring to. But the mechanical analogy was so common, particularly among the Physiocrats, that it was virtually a requirement for most economists to use it, on the one hand. On the other hand, as Vatin put it so finely: "si la référence à la machine permet à Turgot comme à Galiani de formuler l'opposition entre théorie économique "pure" et son application [...], il (*Turgot*) en tire des conclusions diamétralement opposées à celles de l'économiste italien." ([1998], p. 92). For Turgot, the need for the clock to operate less than perfectly justified the pursuit of the maximum freedom in the economic policies to be implemented, whereas in Galiani's work the fear of disturbing the fragile mechanism meant accounting for the state of affairs as fashioned by history and avoiding any sudden changes.

Value, market and price

Authors who have studied the writings of the French and Italian economists of this particular period tend to underline the presence of a main analytical theme which was handed down from Galiani to J.-B. Say and is also present in the work of Turgot, P. Verri and Condillac. Due to the dates of publication of their works, the influence of *Della Moneta* was either suggested implicitly or in some cases made explicit. Schumpeter's authority is regularly referred to, even though, strictly speaking, the author of the *History of Economic Analysis* didn't write about the role of influences but rather on the link between the instant a theoretical innovation was born and the need for analytical progress often achieved by several authors.

[42] Letter on 25th March 1767 in Ravix-Romani [1997], pp. 217-274. On this theme see Vatin [1998], pp. 90-92.

According to Schumpeter, there was an analytical line of progress which ran from Galiani to J.-B. Say and also passed through Quesnay, Beccaria, Turgot, Verri and Condillac ([1954], pp. 421-422). Schumpeter stressed the importance of this line, since he saw in it the path which led to Léon Walras, whose *Eléments d'économie pure* are the "carta magna" of the economics. Now the virtues of an analysis in retrospect which when completed presents the theoretical solutions, and notably the developments on value, of preclassical – Galiani, Beccaria, Verri, Condillac and Turgot – or Classical – Say – authors as the precursors of the marginalist revolution in general, and the Walrasian economic model in particular, are not apparent for the whole scientific community[43]. Independently from Schumpeter's argument, other works have contributed to the suggestion or the assertion of the influence of the Italian authors on their French counterparts. For example, A. Dubois [1897] developed the idea of a common approach towards the so-called psychological theories on value in the works of Galiani, Turgot and Condillac. In his doctorate thesis submitted in Poitiers in 1903, Auguste Lebeau upholds, in careful terms, the influence of the approaches of Galiani and P. Verri on Condillac:

> Il n'est point téméraire de penser que Condillac connut les œuvres des principaux économistes italiens, car il semble que l'on peut relever dans *Le Commerce et le Gouvernement* la trace de quelques idées du comte Pierre Verri et de quelques unes de celles émises par l'abbé Galiani dans son traité *Della Moneta*. (A. Lebeau [1903], p. 10).

More recently, Simone Meyssonnier ([1989], pp. 242-243) accepted the influence of Galiani's theory on value and price on Morellet and especially on Turgot. F. Vatin [1998] uses Meyssonnier's writing to confirm the role allegedly played by Galiani in Turgot's work. Groenewegen ([1987], p. 564) hypothesizes that some of Condillac's theoretical developments had Italian origins: "It is, however, possible to detect some influence from the economies of Turgot, Galiani and Verri on the theory of value, price and competition (cf. Spengler, 1968, p. 212)." (Groenewegen, *The New Palgrave*, p. 565). The reference to Spengler prompts us to consult the *Encyclopedia of Social Sciences*: "Condillac's views reflect mainly those of Cantillon and some of those of Galiani, Verri, Turgot and the physiocrats." For the confirmation, the author consults A. Lebeau. The traces of Italian sources in J.-B. Say's analytical thought have been upheld and discussed by André Tiran [1990]. In this article, Tiran shows with the aid of the texts the similarity between the thinking in Say's theory on value and the law of markets and P. Verri's developments.

With all these supposed influences we must be careful since it is always difficult to prove for certain the degree of influence when it is not explicitly

---

[43] For instance, see the interpretations of Arena [2000] on Say, Ravix-Romani [1998] on Turgot, those of Legris [1996] on Galiani.

recognized by the author. In the period which concerns us, the economists did not conform to modern practice and rarely gave their sources; when references to particular works did appear, they were sometimes quoted or interpreted extremely inaccurately. As a result, we can only formulate assumptions which are backed up by conjecture rather than certainty.

F. Quesnay and his closest followers do not seem to have been influenced by the writings of the Italian economists in the construction of their main original ideas. The theory on value and price found in *Della Moneta*, published roughly ten years before the *Tableau économique,* was apparently unknown to F. Quesnay. No reliable document or reference proves that Quesnay had read Galiani's work on these topics, or even that the two met in Paris[44]. But, the influence of *Della Moneta* can be discussed in Turgot or Condillac.

Turgot and the Italian influences

It could be argued that Turgot used a copy of *Della Moneta*, the one left in de Gournay's library by the Abbé Morellet, as I mentioned before (refer to footnote 22). We also are aware that Turgot could read Italian and that he could have had direct access to the text. Yet Turgot mentions Galiani on just one occasion in *Valeurs et monnaies* [1769], a text which included the plan of an article for a *Dictionnaire de Commerce* requested by Morellet but never published:

> C'est cette vérité (*i.e. the question of a general theory of value*) que M. l'abbé Galiani énonçait, il y a vingt ans, dans son traité *della Moneta*, avec tant de clarté et d'énergie, mais presque sans développement, en disant que la commune mesure de toute valeur est l'homme. (Turgot [1997], p. 286).

The citation seems to allude too much to Galiani's text for it not to require an interpretation. One of Galiani's innovations regards the analysis of value as a starting point in economics. Two remarks can be said about this.

Firstly, it would be helpful to underline the fact that another theme was explored by economists, a theme which put the analysis of commerce at the heart of their reasoning. The importance given to the *doux principes du commerce* by authors such as Forbonnais and de Gournay is testament to that[45].

Secondly, we can recall that ideas on value underlay all economic thought before the eighteenth century. But the theme of value appeared through concerns other than those which made it, as in Galiani, the starting point for independent reflection on economics.

---

[44] See Legris [1996], pp. 71-73.
[45] See Larrère [1992], pp. 135-172.

We know that, for Galiani, value first appeared as a concept which came before exchange, and therefore also the price of goods. So the concept of value became eminently subjective since "il valore, è una idea di proporzione tra 'l ossesso d'una cosa e quello d'un'altra nel concetto d'un uomo." (Galiani [1751], p. 39). Value is therefore treated as a ratio, said by Galiani to constitute two other ratios relative to the complementary notions of *utilità* and *rarità* (*ibid.* p. 39)[46]. Utility is defined as the capacity of something to give pleasure. Scarcity is defined as "la proporzione che è fra la quantità d'una cosa e l'uso che n'è è fatto" (*ibid.*, pp. 45-46)[47]. But human labour also gives value to the good which has been fashioned for consumption since "Io stimo che il valore de'talenti degli uomini si apprezzi in quella stessima guisa che si fa di quello delle cose inanime, e che sopra i medesimi principi di rarità e utilità, congiunti insieme, si regga." (*ibid.*, p. 48). So Galiani introduced a concept of value which on one hand attributed the origin of something's value to the utility expected from it, and on the other hand, established a method of measurement which takes labour and scarcity into account and which can be converted into price.

> Having defined value as a relationship of subjective equivalence between a quantity of one commodity and a quantity of another, Galiani argues that the value depends on utility (utilità) and scarcity (rarità). [...] Scarcity refers to the quantity of goods available in the market. Although the interdependence between price and quantity in the determination of market equilibrium is clearly explained by Galiani [...], he states that the value of commodities is given by the quantity of labour. (F. Cesarano [1987], p. 456).

In the same way, there is a clear relationship between the utility of a good and the quantity of that good when Galiani writes "quando crede l'utilità primaria (di una cosa), tanto si trova più abbondanza, e perciò non può esser grande il valore." (*ibid.*, p. 44)[48]. Then, starting with the distinction between the *stati permanenti e fissi* and the *primi movimenti* (*ibid.*, p. 54), Galiani developed a process of market prices adjustment leading to natural prices. In so far as "poichè è da stabilirsi per certo che, siccome la rarità ed il valore dipendono dal consumo, così il consumo secondo il valore si conforma e si varia." (*ibid.*, p. 51), the problem seems to have

---

[46] Such an analytical advance would be taken up in part by P. Verri some twenty years later (P. Verri [1771] section 4).

[47] In this context the author satisfactorily resolves the "*paradoxe de la valeur*".

[48] Starting from such an analysis, certain economists have seen in Galiani an early form of marginalist principles, particularly G. Rossetti who established a close parallel between the Italian author and J. Dupuit (*De l'influence des péages* [1849]). The Italian origin of such a hypothesis can no doubt be found in M. Pantaleoni who having cited Galiani in his *Principi di economia pura* [1889] marks him as the precursor of the law of decreasing scale of marginal utility. As we have just noted, it is true that Galiani explains that utility depends on the quantity of the good possessed. He does this by studying first the starving man and then the satisfied man (ibid., pp. 40-41). But between the two situations the notion of continuity is hardly noticeable at all. There is not a total understanding in Galiani's work of a continuous demand function, nor even a decreasing scale of marginal utilities.

no solution. But, "da questa concatenazione nasce il grande ed utilissimo effetto dell'equilibrio del tutto." (*ibid.*, p. 53)[49]. General equilibrium seems comparable to the principle of gravity in Newtonian physics since "quello, che la gravità è nella fisica, è il desiderio di guadagnare, o sia di viver felice, nell'uomo; e, ciò posto, tutte le leggi fisiche de' corpi si possono perfettamente, da chi sa meditarlo, nel morale di nostra vita verificare." (*ibid.*, p. 54).

So, the conception of the individual (Legris [1996]) which naturally leads to this moral equilibrium is also specified unambiguously by Galiani when he writes: "E questo equilibrio alla giusta abbondanza de' commodi della vita ed alla terrena felicità maravigliosamente confà, quantunque non dall'umana prudenza o virtù, ma del vilissimo stimolo di sordido lucro derivi." (*ibid.*, p. 53).

As for Turgot, he tackled the question of value and price for the first time in his *Plan d'un ouvrage sur le commerce* [1754], which was never completed. The essential aspects of his economic thinking can be found in the *Réflexions sur la formation et la distribution des richesses* written in 1766, but published later. *Valeurs et Monnaies* was written in 1769. According to more or less reliable dating, Turgot could only have read Galiani [1751] from 1760 onwards. But as the *Réflexions* never mention the work of the Italian author, it seems that his knowledge of *Della Moneta* was only used for the citation in *Valeurs et Monnaies* [1769], as hypothesized by S. Meyssonnier ([1989], p. 238). Such a statement limits, of course, the extent of the influence of the Italian work on Turgot's thought, which goes against the numerous interpretations that we have mentioned, since Turgot's ideas on price were already partly formed (J.-T. Ravix - P.-M. Romani [1997], p. 42). We know that Turgot, on one hand, distinguished between two types of value: the *valeur estimative ou appréciative* and the *valeur échangeable,* and on the other, that he introduced the concept of subjective value as "le degré d'estime que l'homme attache aux différents objets de ses désirs." ([1766], p. 284). The *valeur estimative* depends, as it does in Galiani, on subjective utility and scarcity of goods capable of satisfying human needs, but this concept in Turgot only applies to the isolated individual. Utility and scarcity are essentially subjective since, when the exchange of a good is carried out between two people, the subjective value "n'a d'existence que dans l'esprit de chacun d'eux pris séparement." (*ibid.*, p. 290). But the subjective value does not entirely determine the exchange value. That can be clearly seen in Turgot's text: "il suit de notre définition de la valeur appréciative qu'elle n'est point le rapport entre les deux choses échangées, ou entre le prix et la chose vendue." (*ibid.*, pp. 291-292). It therefore appeared impossible for Turgot to deduce the exchange value – in the sense of current price – starting from utility and scarcity. This interpretation of *Valeurs* is confirmed by the *Réflexions* and most of all by the *Plan*. Indeed, if the text of the *Valeurs* limits the

[49] There we can also see link with P. Verri's earlier work (Schumpeter [1954], p. 254 and F. Venturi [1978]).

analysis to the exchange of two goods between two people, in the general case where there are many people exchanging, the venal value, rendered by the current price, results from the supply and the demand which are governed by competition (Turgot [1754], p. 383). Furthermore, "lorsque la concurrence a réduit le profit des vendeurs à ce point, les denrées sont au prix le plus bas qu'il soit possible."[50]. The market price can therefore not sink below a floor value which is equivalent to a fundamental value[51]. Moreover Turgot [1767][52] states that "la valeur fondamentale est ce que la chose coûte à celui qui la vend, c'est-à-dire les frais des matières premières, intérêts des avances, salaires du travail et de l'industrie." In other words, the fundamental value for Turgot could be interpreted analytically as a lowest price[53].

We can now gauge the limits of the influence of *Della Moneta* on Turgot's theory of value. The *Intendant du Limousin* cut his approach into two sequences. In the first, "nous n'en sommes pas encore à l'échange, et voilà déjà la *rareté*, un des éléments de l'évaluation." (Turgot [1769], p. 284). And the *évaluation* is nothing other than "le compte qu'il [*l'homme isolé*] se rend à lui-même de la portion de la peine et de son temps, [...] de la portion de ses facultés qu'il peut employer à la recherche de l'objet évalué." (*ibid.*, p. 285). In these conditions, "la *valeur estimative* d'un objet, pour l'homme isolé, est précisément la portion totale de ses facultés qui répond au désir qu'il a de cet objet." (*ibid.*, p. 285). In this context, Turgot accorded to Galiani the merit for having discovered the clearly subjective nature of the *valeur estimative*, which is based on the utility and scarcity experienced by the isolated man. But beyond this definition which is integrated into the historical philosophy of our author as can be seen in the *Plan d'un premier discours sur l'histoire universelle* [1751] (G. Schelle, vol. 1), Turgot went his own way and distanced himself from Galiani's solutions when he developed his analysis of exchange value and the theory of price which follows from it. More precisely, it is clear that in the *Réflexions*[54], which appeared after *Valeurs*, Turgot does not postulate his theory on value as a starting point, but instead puts into perspective the division of work, and thereby gives pre-eminence to production versus exchange.

Finally, the conception of the individual which appears in Turgot differs completely from the *sordido lucro* seen clearly in Galiani and then in the Smithian tradition. In Turgot, any sensible being capable of reason must "acquérir des idées morales qui ne sont pas arbitraires, mais découlent de notre nature." (Letter to Hume on 25th March 1767, in *Œuvres*, vol. 2, p. 660). Human nature in Turgot is not identified with the physical nature of phenomena which constantly renew

---

[50] The lowest price is equivalent to a production cost incorporating subsistences, advances and interest paid on borrowings to finance those advances occasioned by the activity of vendors.

[51] Letter from Turgot to D. Hume on 25th March 1767 in *Œuvres*, pp. 272-273.

[52] *Observations sur l'impôt indirect* in *Œuvres*, vol. 2, p. 266.

[53] See J.-T. Ravix - P.-M. Romani [1997], p. 46.

[54] The first two parts of the *Réflexions sur la formation et la distribution des richesses* appeared in volumes XI and XII of the *Ephémérides du citoyen* in 1769. The third part appeared in 1770 in volume I of the same review.

themselves in that Turgot defends, along with Condorcet, the theory according to which human nature can be improved with the aid of reason, and therefore with the aid of education (Turgot [1770], in Ravix-Romani [1997], p. 22 - Condorcet [1998], p. 71).

As far as the role played by Verri's work in Turgot's analytical reasoning is concerned, an examination of the dates relative to the spread of the Milanese count's work seems to prove an absence of influence since the *Meditazioni*, the only one of Verri's works known by Turgot, were written after the latter's main works were published.

Condillac and Italian influences

According to P. Groenewegen, "The impetus for Condillac's writing *Le Commerce et le Gouvernement* has been ascribed to a desire to assist his friend Turgot in the difficulties he faced in 1775 as finance minister over the grain riots induced by his restoration of the free trade in grain." ([1987], p. 565). This argument, already put forward by G. Le Roy [1947] and F. Knight [1968], allows us to account for Condillac's argument in favour of the freedom of commerce, but does not give us any information about the sources he used. Groenewegen then refers to J. Spengler [1968], according to whom "Condillac's views reflect mainly those of Cantillon and some of Galiani, Verri, Turgot and the physiocrats". In particular, 'he (*Condillac*) describes value as depending upon utility and as varying inversely with supply, as does price'." (p. 212).

The study of *Le Commerce et le Gouvernement, Considérés relativement l'un à l'autre*[55] seems to confirm these hypotheses. Indeed, as in Galiani [1751], the construction of theory starts with "Les fondements de la valeur des choses." (title of Part 1, Chapter 1). As in Verri [1760], scarcity, accumulation of wealth and commerce are part of a logical system, "*la chaîne d'opulence*", which had already been analysed by Boisguilbert, but which found a new meaning in the subjective notion of value. The philosophical background can be made clearer by the utilitarianism of the *Illuministi milanesi* which led to Jeremy Bentham, as well as by sensualism[56]. For Condillac the concept of value therefore appears eminently subjective since "La valeur des choses, ou l'estime que nous en faisons, fondée sur l'utilité, est en proportion avec nos besoins." (Condillac [1776], p. 221)[57]. Value is

---

[55] *Le Commerce et le Gouvernement, Considérés relativement l'un à l'autre - Ouvrage élémentaire par m l'Abbé de Condillac de l'Académie Française et membre de la Société royale de l'Agriculture d'Orléans* was printed for the first time with this very title in February in Amsterdam and published by Joubert et Caillot, *Libraires rue Dauphine* in Paris. On the first edition, see A. Lebeau ([1903], p. 25).

[56] See A. Lebeau [1903], pp. 83-101 on the links between *Le traité des sensations* [1754] and Condillac's economics.

[57] Quotations from *Le Commerce et le Gouvernement* are taken from the 1795 edition republished by G. Romeyer-Dherby [1980], chosen because of the text's faithfulness to the 1776 original.

therefore treated as a subjective ratio in accordance with Galiani. Condillac then states that "la valeur de ces choses, en proportion avec leur rareté et leur abondance, varie encore suivant l'opinion vraie ou fausse que nous avons de cette rareté et de cette abondance." (*ibid.*, p. 221). This sort of analytical choice can also be seen in P. Verri ([1971], section 4).

We can follow the analogies with the texts of Galiani [1751] and Verri [1771], especially on the concepts of utility, price, and most of all luxuries. Thus in Condillac as in Verri, prosperity co-exists with need and abundance (Condillac, chapter 7, part 1 and Verri [1771], pp. 11-19). As in Verri (*ibid.* p. 37) and Galiani (Cesarano [1987], p. 456), Condillac derives the price of a good directly from its value since "ces valeurs, estimées par comparaison, sont ce que l'on nomme le prix des choses." (*Le Commerce*, p. 221). On the question of price, Condillac, with his concept of "vrai prix" (see Heyne [1999], p. 94), seems closer to Verri than to Galiani when he states that "comme la concurrence est plus grande, moins grande ou nulle, tantôt d'un côté, tantôt de l'autre, il arrive que les prix haussent et baissent alternativement. De cette variation, il en résulte qu'il n'y a point de prix absolus." (*ibid.*, p. 18). We know that Verri introduced the concept of *prezzo commune*, a true price which is a market price, as opposed to Galiani who distinguished between the *primi movimenti* and the *stati permanenti e fissi* (Galiani [1751], pp. 53-54) and suggested a theory of gravitation of market price around a fundamental one. The accumulation of wealth depends not only on field labour, but also on manufacturing labour (Verri [1771], pp. 21-23) and on commerce as a forum where buyers and sellers meet (*ibid.*, p. 36). For Condillac, "tous, colons (*agriculteurs*), marchands, artisans, concourent à augmenter la masse des richesses." (Condillac, *Commerce,* p. 39) and "les commerçants sont comme des canaux de communication entre les producteurs et les consommateurs." (*ibid.*, p. 222). The issue on accumulation of wealth by the artisans and traders meant a break with the Physiocrats who since the publication of Condillac's work replied through the Abbé Baudeau (*Nouvelles Ephémérides* [April-May 1776])[58]. By rejecting the principle of the exclusive productivity of agriculture, Condillac put himself in the same tradition as Galiani, P. Verri and Turgot. The ideas which emerged from this crucial debate were directed towards creation of the concept of industry in its modern sense, a sense which evolved from *savoir-faire* or *industria* into that of *sterile* activity in the physiocratic sense. As P. Fontaine notes ([1992], p. 9), "cette remontée vers la tradition *commerciale* incarnée par Condillac, Galiani et Graslin n'est pas sans résultat: dotée d'un pouvoir civilisateur, l'industrie se voit dépouillée de ses dernières composantes antisociales". The celebration of industrial virtues in the first half of the nineteenth century owes much to J.-B. Say, and the

[58] *Observations économistes à M. L'abbé de Condillac par M. L'abbé Baudeau, Les Nouvelles Ephémérides Economiques*, in A. Lebeau [1903], pp. 422-445.

developments of Galiani [1770][59] and then Condillac [1776] opened up the way to a deeper understanding of economic activity.

We could carry on listing the similarities between the text of the *Commerce* and the writings of the two Italian economists. Apart from the comparative analysis of the texts, other factors speak in favour of the of the Italian influence on the works of Condillac.

Firstly, Condillac became interested in political economy thanks to Turgot, who knew the Italian works, and whom he met in Mme de Lespinasse's salon (Le Roy [1947], p. IX).

Secondly, Condillac lived in Parma from 1758-1767, where he was the Duke of Parma's private tutor. In that time he met Beccaria and Gherardò (F. Knight [1968], pp. 231-232). It seems probable that such an intellectual would have become interested in Italian economic literature during his stay.

Yet Condillac never confirms these influences. Indeed, the *Commerce* makes no reference to Galiani or to Verri. It must be noted that the French economist cited very few authors and usually just alluded to them. Take for example his defence of Turgot's policies without naming him: "Sourd à tous ces propos, le nouveau ministre montrait du courage." (*Commerce*, p. 331) or "Il y a un gouvernement qui voit les abus, qui songe aux moyens d'y remédier." (*ibid.*, p. 375). The only work mentioned several times, without its author being named, is *Essai sur la nature du commerce* by Cantillon [1755][60], and Condillac writes: "C'est sur cette matière (*La circulation de l'argent et le commerce*) un des meilleurs ouvrages que je connaisse; mais je ne les connais pas tous, à beaucoup près."

Even if we make the hypothesis without written proof that there are Italian influences in the thought of Condillac, the consequences on the period concerned remain limited due since the author's work was not well known in France. Auguste Lebeau, who up until very recently was considered the foremost specialist of Condillac, and whose thesis submitted in Poitiers is used in this work, recognizes that "il n'en reste pas moins certain que *Le Commerce et le Gouvernement* tomba, presque dès son apparition, dans le plus complet oubli." (Lebeau [1903], p. 49) Then, that is before 1850, Say criticized Condillac in his *Traité d'économie politique* with respect to the productivity of commerce when he writes: "Condillac s'égare aussi lorsqu'il veut expliquer de quelle manière le commerce produit." It was not until A. Dubois's article [1898] that Condillac, via his theory on value, regained prestige in national economic thought. We should also note that, according to Dubois ([1898], p. 863), "Sa doctrine ne renferme rien d'original, sauf une erreur. Elle est superficielle et bien inférieure aux analyses de Turgot et surtout de Galiani."

[59] "Vous n'avez aucun exemple de pays libres où les manufactures n'aient été florissantes." the Chevalier said to the Président in the *Dialogues*.

[60] In chapter XVI of the first part (footnote 1, p. 92).

Two remarks can be made about Dubois's statement. On one hand, the error was that Condillac "ne distingue pas le prix de la valeur en échange." (*ibid.*, p. 863). On the other, Galiani's influence shows through in the author's comment on the *Revue d'économie politique*[61].

The weak impact of Condillac's[62] writings on French economics up until 1850 (Heyne [1999], p. 94) does not, however, shut the door on the role of Italian influences. In the first half of the nineteenth century, the power of J.-B. Say's analytical developments became hegemonic and if it is seen in terms of a critical version of Adam Smith's thought as expressed in *The Wealth of Nations*, it was not lacking in references to Italian economists' ideas.

Say and the Italian influences

It is clear that J.-B. Say had access to Italian literature, for the reasons I mentioned at the end of the first part of this chapter. Moreover, Say is one of the few French economists from the first half of the nineteenth century to cite Italian authors. For instance, Say cites Galiani with respect to the theory of value in his *Préliminaires* to the second edition of the *Traité d'économie politique* in terms which have, however, surprised several specialists of the French economist[63]: "Ce que cet ouvrage (*Della Moneta*) a de singulier, c'est qu'on y trouve quelques uns des fondements de la doctrine de Smith, et entre autres que le travail est le seul créateur de la valeur des choses, c'est-à-dire la richesse." (Say [1814], *Préliminaires*, 5th book). To explain this erroneous interpretation by Say, I propose that he had not deeply analysed Galiani's text, and that he cites it perhaps via Turgot's commentary in *Valeurs et Monnaies*. Say probably confused *homme* and *travail humain*.

Unfortunately for Galiani's theory on value, and due to the authority of Say, the error was reproduced in the commentaries of other French economists. Take for example this passage from Auguste Walras, who writes: "... des économistes sont survenus qui ont placé dans le *travail* l'origine de la richesse... [...] Cette opinion, dont le germe se trouve dans les écrits de *Galiani*, s'est principalement dévéloppée en Angleterre..." (A. Walras [1849], p. 320).

Here is a good example of the reproduction of an error about an author, and it proves that it is not enough for an idea to be well spread in order for it to be correctly interpreted and be a positive influence on the reader. A. Walras is probably making the mistake of assessing the theme of value in Galiani simply by reading

[61] At the time the *Revue d'économie politique* published articles which competed against the orthodox French liberal thought and its main periodical voice, le *Journal des économistes*.

[62] Described by A. Walras [1849] as the theorist of value utility before Say (pp. 329-326).

[63] Including André Tiran himself who classed Say's comment as a severe error.

Say, and probably also trying to play down the ancients, who introduced the concept of scarcity in the theory of value, in order to make himself out to be its precursor. We also know that L. Walras gave the credit for this to his father[64].

The issue of the the influence of Italian authors on the intellectual reasoning of J.-B. Say therefore remains open for discussion. In an article on the issue, Tiran [1993] develops an argument based on a comparative analysis of texts to determine, in his view, the influence of *Meditazioni sulla economia politica* on J.-B. Say's thinking.

Such argumentation could be surprising, since usual economic thought presents the French economist in the light of the project he pursued since the publication of the first edition of the *Traité* [1803]. This interpretation has it that Say planned to circulate a corrected version of the so-called errors of Adam Smith which he believed he saw in *The Wealth of Nations*. If we were to accept A. Tiran's argument, its consequences on the evolution of French economic thinking would be important, given the great impact which Say's teaching was to have. To forget the role played by P. Verri's writings would seem an historiographic injustice and could justify the attitude of M. Gioia[65] who, from 1826, reproached J.-B. Say for having underestimated the contribution by Italian economists in the development of the economics.

In the first volume of *Encyclopédie progressive* of 1826, Say wrote an article[66] on the history of political economy, in which he attributes to himself the discovery of the law of markets. Gioia responded through several texts, the first of which was published in the *Annali universali di statistica*, and the others in *Biblioteca Italiana*[67]. In particular Gioia accuses Say of attributing to French or English economists theoretical innovations which had in fact been discovered by Italians since the eighteenth century (A. Macchioro [1989], p. 82). We can however point out the partly unjust nature of Gioia's words since Say was one of the few who knew Italian literature. In l'*Histoire abrégée de la pensée économique*, Say wrote: "Verri est un des auteurs les plus judicieux qui aient écrit sur l'économie politique." (*Cours* [1828-1829], p. 395), perhaps after Gioia's criticisms. But, from the 1826 edition of the *Traité* we read that "Le Comte de Verri compatriote et ami de Beccaria, et digne de l'être, à la fois grand administrateur et bon écrivain, dans ses *Meditazioni sull'economia politica* publiées en 1771, s'est approché plus que personne, avant Smith, des véritables lois qui dirigent la production et la

---

[64] "Il y a, dans la science, trois solutions principales du problème de l'origine de la valeur. La première est celle d'A. Smith, De Ricardo, de MacCulloch [...]. La seconde est celle de Condillac et de J.-B. Say [...]. Enfin, la troisième, qui est la bonne, est celle de Burlamaqui et de mon père, A-A. Walras : elle met l'origine de la valeur dans la rareté." (L. Walras [1874], *Eléments d'économie pure*, first edition).

[65] On Gioia's general attitude, see P. Barucci [1964], pp. 140-148.

[66] Article from the fifth edition of the *Cours* of 1826.

[67] See M. Gioia, *Encyclopédie progressive..., Articolo Economico di G. B. Say, "Biblioteca Italiana"* [1826], XLIV, pp. 200-226 for the first article in the review.

consommation des richesses." (Say [1826], p. 16). More generally, Gioia denounces the whole community of French economists, and notably, apart from Say, Sismondi who wrote the *Nouveaux Principes* for having used Italian works without acknowledging them (T. Maccabelli [1996], pp. 158-163).

Due to the importance of the problem, after having summarized the arguments in Tiran's article, I will attempt to gauge its impact. According to Tiran, the influence of P. Verri [1771] on the Say's theoretical constructions is definite on two levels. The first concerns the theory of value and the second the Say's law.

As far as the theory of value is concerned, Verri is said to have given Say a theory of value-utility, of which Say only retained the first term (Tiran [1993], p. 446). One of the other alleged borrowings concerns the definition of production, a definiton which would permit an approach to the question of supply and demand and would also permit not only the dismissal of the Smithian distinction between productive and unproductive activities, but also the provision of the most essential ingredients enabling Say to formulate the law of markets (Tiran [1993], pp. 459-467). We must however put Tiran's argument into perspective on several points, even if the comparison of the textual analyses leaves us with virtually no doubts about what Say borrowed from the *Meditazioni*.

First of all, P. Verri's theory on value fits comfortably into the tradition founded by Galiani, that of subjective theory leading, among other destinations, to the learned utilitarianism tradition taken up again a little later by Jeremy Bentham.

Now, for Say, wealth is defined as the complete set of "choses que nous possédons et qui ont une valeur." ([1819], p. 16). The reference to private property enabled our economist to establish a difference between "*les richesses naturelles* non produites et gratuites" and "celles qui ont une *valeur échangeable*, que nous nommerons *richesses sociales*, parce qu'elles ne peuvent exister que parmi les hommes en société." (*ibid.*, p. 98). Therefore, the exchange is understood as a social institution and "la valeur que nous possédons n'est plus arbitraire". So "il faut être en société non seulement pour que ces richesses soient contradictoirement évaluées, mais encore pour que la possession en soit reconnue, sanctionnée par la société." (*ibid.*, p. 98).

The result is an objective idea of value, very different from that developed by Galiani, Verri or Condillac. Say belongs, from an analytical point of view, to the Classical tradition despite his choice of retaining utility in place of work as the source of value, unlike the subjective pre-classical tradition that some would believe was reproduced in H.H. Gossen's work, then in the work of the fathers of marginalism.

This interpretation also explains why he rejected the concept of scarcity in his definition of value, and this is backed up buy A. Walras [1848], who established a dividing line between what he presents as his personal contribution, the theory of value-scarcity, the ideas for which he acknowledges Burlamaqui only, and the theory developed by Say.

That did not prevent Say from copying his definition of production from that of P. Verri (Tiran [1993], p. 459) and from subsequently being able to develop an approach to supply and demand close to that of the Milanese economist. If value only derives from utility, production must be understood as production of wealth and therefore of utility, due to the *industrieux* human labour and the necessary productive services. In this context, "la production est une espèce d'échange dans lequel on donne les services productifs, ou leur valeur, quand on les achète, pour obtenir en retour les produits." (Say [1821], p. 337).

In P. Verri's work, only the exchangeable quantity of production can act on prices, that is to say on value by modifying the supply-demand ratio (*Meditazioni*, p. 36). Say therefore evolved in the same theoretical tradition since economic activity depends on a number of exchanges and the supply of a good is "la quantité d'une marchandise que ses possesseurs actuels sont disposés à céder en échange d'une autre." (Say [1841], p. 319). As in Verri and Condillac, for Say demand is a function of need since "le motif qui détermine les hommes à faire un sacrifice quelconque pour se rendre possesseurs d'un produit est le besoin que ce produit peut satisfaire." (*ibid.*). But, adds Say, consumers "ne peuvent acquérir les produits dont ils ont envie qu'en offrant d'autres produits de leur propre création." (*ibid.*). We therefore find ourselves in an economy where the current value of a good can only be equal to the value of the productive services necessary for its appearance on the market. There is therefore, in Say and Verri, application of a common price to adjust simultaneously the value of supply and the value of demand on the market.

If in Verri demand creates production ([1771], pp. 37-39), in Say supply creates outlets and therefore real demand. But in treating production as a particular form of exchange, Say and Verri make supply and demand play symmetrical roles. In these conditions, Say's law is already implicitly included in the theory of production developed by P. Verri. Furthermore, Verri even had the idea of reversing the roles of supply and demand suggesting that the greater the number of producers, the greater the number of buyers and sellers ([1771], p. 56).

Tiran's proposition therefore seems feasible if we limit it to the considerable contribution that is the Say's law. Yet there are still some doubts. Firstly we could ask ourselves why Say does not acknowledge what he borrowed from the Italian economist, when he does not hesitate to mention Smith or French sources (P. Steiner [1999]). We recall Say's desire to create a specifically French tradition in the face of British hegemony, hence the justified reaction of M. Gioia [1826]. But we can also defend the hypothesis, accepted by Tiran ([1993], p. 465), according to which the law of markets was already floating around and Say was just the first one to state clearly what was already implicitly present in a number of theoretical constructions at the time (see Schumpeter [1954], vol. 2; Spengler [1945] and Sowell [1972, 1977]).

Concluding remarks

At the end of this study, it must be acknowledged that Voltaire was not altogether wrong when he underlined the importance of the French language as a vehicle of diffusion during the second half of the eighteenth century. Indeed, the best known works of the Italian economists were those which had been translated into French as *Des délits et des peines* and *Réflexions sur l'économie politique* by the Abbé Morellet and at the J.H. Pott publishing house respectively, or those written directly into good French such as the *Dialogues sur le commerce des bleds*. The precocious knowledge seen in *Della Moneta*, due to the Abbé Morellet's journey to Italy and Turgot's reading of it in Vincent de Gournay's library, did not lead to a correct interpretation of the theories developed by the young Galiani and it was not until the marginalist revolution, and then the translations propsosed by G. H. Bousquet, that French economists understood its meaning and drew from it pertinent conclusions. We can therefore confirm the hypothesis according to which, at the birth of political economy as a self contained discipline, Italian was no longer a language sufficiently capable of spreading ideas, and this contributed to a kind of *provincialismo* which followed (R. Faucci [1990], p. 10).

In the first half of the eighteenth century, the works of economists such as Gioia, P. de Luca, Scialoja, Romagnosi or Valeriani would undoubtedly have merited a wider spread beyond the cultural zone covered by the Italian language, but the desire of Say and his French followers to found a national tradition on the basis of the liberal doctrine was not conducive to the reading of the works of the authors mentioned above. It was not until 1867 that Ferrara, the *cousin libéral*, published an article in the *Journal des Economistes* and not until 1891 that Pareto for it became the Italian correspondent (Laurent-Marco [1996], pp. 97-109).

If we enlarge the notion of spread to gauge the influence of certain authors, we can mainly limit ourselves to just Galiani and P. Verri, in that Beccaria was only read as a public law specialist. Galiani's stimulating influence can be seen in the work of Turgot [1769], and especially in that of Condillac [1776], and Count Verri's influence can also be seen in Condillac and certainly in Say. It seems clear that if Say had ben inspired by Verri as much as Tiran [1993] claims, then the circulation of the *Meditazioni* would have played just as great a role in France as *The Wealth of Nations*. But as we know, history has it a different way.

References

Alimento A. (1994), *La ricezione del pensiero fisiocratico nelle traduzion settecentesche: il caso toscano e quello veneto*, "Il pensiero economico italiano", II-1, pp. 37-53.

Augello M.-M. (1994), *L'evoluzione della letteratura economica in Italia: 1861-1900*, "Il pensiero economico italiano", II-1, pp. 7-36.

Augello M.-M., Bianchini M., Guidi M.-E.L. (edited by) (1996), *Le Riviste di Economia in Italia (1700-1900), Dai giornali scientifico-lettarari ai periodici specialistici*, Franco Angeli, Milan.

Barucci P. (1964), *Il pensiero economico di Melchiorre Gioia,* Giuffré, Milan.

Barucci P. (1975), *Introduzione* a J.C.L. Sismonde de Sismondi, *Nuovi Principi di economia politica*, Isedi, Milano.

Beccaria C. (1764), *Dei deletti e delle pene*, directed by F. Venturi [1981], G. Einaudi, Torino and A. Morellet [1766], Philadelphia & co.

Beccaria C (1910), *Lettere e Scritti inediti*, directed by Eugenio Landry, Milan.

Bouvy Eugène (1889), *Le comte Pietro Verri (1728-1797)*, Hachette, Paris.

Breton Y. et Lutfalla M. (1991), *L'Economie politique en France au 19e siècle*, Economica, Paris.

Cesarano F. (1976), *Monetary theory in Ferdinando Galiani's Della Moneta*, "History of Political Economy", 8 (3), pp. 380-399.

Cesarano F. (1987), Galiani Ferdinando (1728-1787), in "The New Palgrave. A Dictionnary of Economics", vol. 2, pp. 456-457.

Condillac (1776), *Le commerce et le gouvernement, Considérés relativement l'un à l'autre*, in Ressources, Genève-Paris [1980], nouvelle édition de An III [1795], Letellier et Maradan, Paris, *Présentation* by G. Romeyer-Dherbey.

Condillac, Etienne Bonnot, Abbé de, *Commerce and Government Considered in Their Mutual Relationship*,Translated by Shelagh Eltis, Edward Elgar Pubished Limited, Northampton.

Condorcet, *Arithmétique politique. Textes rares ou inédits (1767-1789)*, Edition critique commentée par Bernard Bru et Pierre Crepel, [1994], INED, PUF, Paris.

Diderot. (1770), *Apologie de l'abbé Galiani*, in *Oeuvres Politiques*, P. Vernière, Paris [1963], Garnier.

Donato C. (1992), *The letters of Fortunato Bartolomeo De Felice to Pietro Verri,* "Modern Language Notes", 107, pp. 74-111.

Dubois A. (1897), *Les théories psychologiques de la valeur au XVIII siècle*, "Revue d'économie politique", 11, pp. 849-864.

Eltis S. & W. (1997), *Introduction* to a Translation by Shelagh Eltis of Condillac's *Commerce and Government Considered in Their Mutual Relationship*, Edward Elgar Pubished Limited, Northampton.

Faccarello G. - Steiner P. (1991), (directed by), *La pensée économique pendant la Révolution française*, Pug, Paris-Grenoble.

Faccarello G. (1994), *Nil Repente': Galiani and Necker on economic reforms,* "The European Journal of the History of Economic Thought", vol. 1, n° 3, pp. 519-550.

Faucci R. (1990), *Un'epoca di transizione? Le coordinate teirico-instituzionali del periodo*, in "Quaderni di Storia dell'Economia Politica", VIII/2-3", pp. 3-22.

Fontaine P. (1992), *Le concept d'industrie au XVIIIe siècle: A la recherche d'une acceptation oubliée.* In "Economies et Sociétés, série Oeconomia", PE n. 16, 3, pp. 7-33.

FORBONNAIS F. V. (de) (1768),. *Examen du livre de Paul Abeille intitulé: Principes sur la liberté du commerce des grains*, "Journal d'agriculture, du commerce et des finances", Paris.

GALIANI F. (1751), *Della Moneta*, Banco di Napoli, Naples, Edizione speciale per il bicentenario della morte dell'Autore, [1987].

GALIANI F. (1770), *Dialogues sur le commerce des bleds*, Banco di Napoli, Naples, Edizione speciale per il bicentenario della morte dell'Autore, *Introduzione* di Luigi del Rosa [1987].

GALIANI F. (1885), *Correspondance*, edn Pery et Maugras, 2 t., Calmann-Lévy, Paris.

GARNIER J. (1846), *Eléments de l'économie politique*, 2° edn de 1848, Guillaumin & Cie, Paris.

GROENEWEGEN P. (1987), *Beccaria, Cesare Bonsana, Marchese di (1738-1794),* in "The New Palgrave. A Dictionnary of Economics", vol. 1, pp. 218-219.

GROENEWEGEN P. (1987), *Condillac, Etienne Bonnot de, l'Abbé Mureau de (1714-1780),* in "The New Palgrave. A Dictionnary of Economics", vol. 4, p. 807.

GROENEWEGEN P. (1987), *Verri, Pietro (1728-1797),* in "The New Palgrave. A Dictionnary of Economics", vol. 4, p. 807.

GUIDI M. (1991), *Il sovrano e l'imprenditore, Utilitarismo ed economia politica in Jeremy Bentham*, Gius. Laterza & Figli, Bari.

GUIDI M. (1996), *Economia politica ed economia sociale nelle riviste moderate piemontesi di metà ottocento (1838-1860)*, in Augello, Bianchini, Guidi [1996], pp. 233-263.

HEYNE P. (1999), *Book Reviews* on *Commerce and Government Considered in Their Mutual Relationship*, Edward Elgar Pubished Limited, Northampton, in "Journal of the History of Economic Thought", Volume 21, Number 1, pp. 93-95.

KNIGHT I.F. (1968), *The Geometric Spirit. The Abbé de Condillac and the French Enlightnment*, Yale University Press, New Haven & London.

LA HARPE J.F. (1801-1807), *Correspondance littéraire adressée au grand-duc de Russie et au comte de Schowalow depuis 1774 jusqu'en 1789*, 6 t., Migneret, Paris.

LARRERE C. (1992), *L'invention de l'économie au XVIIIe siècle*, Léviathan, puf, Paris.

LAURENT E. & L. MARCO, (1996), *Le "Journal des Economistes" ou l'apologie du libéralisme*, in Marco [1996], pp. 79-120.

LEBEAU A. (1903), *Condillac économiste*, *Thèse de Doctorat* at Poitiers, Guillaumin & Cie, Paris.

LEGRIS A. 1993), *L'analyse économique en Italie pendant l'entre-deux-guerres*, Thèse de Doctorat, Latapses-Cnrs, Nice.

LEGRIS A. (1996), *Galiani et Quesnay : deux conceptions de l'individu*, "Il pensiero economico italiano", IV-1, pp. 71-91.

LE ROY G. (1947-51), *Editions des oeuvres philosophiques de Condillac*, puf, Paris.

LE VAN-LEMESLE L. (1991), *L'Institutionnalisation de l'économie politique en France*, in Breton-Lutfalla [1991], pp. 355-388.

MACCABELLI T. (1996), *La "biblioteca italiana" e il "conciliatore" nella Milano della restaurazione: il dibatto economico*, in Augello, Bianchini, Guidi [1996], pp. 129-169.

MACCHIORO A. (1989), *La "philosophia naturalis" gioiana dell'economia*, "Quaderni di Storia dell'Economia Politica", VII, 2-3, pp. 69-93.

MARCO L. (1996], (directed by) *Les revues d'économie en France (1751-1994)*, Association Charles Gide pour l'Histoire de la Pensée Economique, L'Harmattan, Paris.

MEOLI U. (1961), *Il pensiero economico del Condillac,* Instituto Editoriale Cisalpina, Milano.

MEOLI U. (1968), *Il pensiero economico del secolo XIX*, in *Storia delle idee politiche, economiche e sociali*, (directed by L. Firpo), Utet, Torino.

MEYSSONNIER S. (1989), *La Balance et l'Horloge - la genèse de la pensée libérale en France au XVIIIe siècle*, Les éditions de la passion, Paris.

MORELLET (abbé), *Mémoires inédites sur le XVIIIè siècle et sur la Révolution*, 2 volumes, Slaltkine Reprints [1967], Genève.

PERROT J.-C. (1988), *Equilibre économique et déterminisme, étude d'un cas*, "Bulletin de l'Institut d'histoire économique et sociale de l'Université de Paris 1", 17, pp. 15-43.

PUCCI L. ((1989), *Luigi Valeriani Molinari (1758-1828): un economista della restaurazione*, "Quaderni di Storia dell'Economia Politica", VII, 2-3, pp. 75-95.

RAVIX J.-T. (1999), *La pensée économique classique*, Topos, Dunod, Paris.

ROSSETTI G. (1942), *Galiani e la teoria dei gradi finali di utilità,* "Rivista di Storia Economica", n° 3-4, pp. 111-116.

SAY J.-B. (1819), *Cours d'économie politique et autres essais*, "Cours à l'Athénée", GF-Flammarion [1996], Paris.

SAY J.-B. (1821), *Cours d'économie politique et autres essais*, "Catéchisme d'économie politique", GF-Flammarion [1996], Paris.

SAY J.-B. (1841), *Traité d'économie politique*, 5th edn., in E. Duire, *Collection des principaux économistes*, t. 9, Guillaumin, Paris.

SCHELLE G. (1913-1932), *Oeuvres de Turgot et documents le concernant*, G. Schelle edn., 5 vol., Alcan, 1913-1923, Paris.

SOWELL T. (1972), *Say's Law: An Historical Analysis*, Princeton, Princeton University Press.

SOWELL T. (1977), *Classical Economics Reconsidered*, New Jersey, Princeton University Press, pp. 35-52.

SPENGLER J.J. (1945), *The physiocrats and Say's Law of markets*, "Journal of Political Economy", 53, pp. 193-211; 317-47.

SPENGLER J.J. (1968), *Condillac, Etienne Bonnot de*, in *Encyclopedia of the Social Sciences*, 2nd edn, vol. 3, Chicago University Press, Chicago.

STEINER P. (1996 a), *Les revues économiques de langue française au XVIIIème siècle (1751-1776),* in Marco [1996], pp. 33-778.

STEINER (1996 b), *L'économie politique comme science de la modernité*, pp. 9-46, Introduction à *J.-B. Say-Cours d'économie politique et autres essais*, GF-Flammarion, Paris.

STEINER P. (1998), *La "science nouvelle de l'économie politique"*, puf, Paris.

STEINER P. (1999), *J-B.Say ans the political economy of his time: a quantitative approach*, "Journal of the History of Economic Thought", vol. 21, n° 4, pp. 349-368.

TIRAN A. (1993), *Pietro Verri, aux origines de la théorie de la valeur et de la loi des débouchés de Jean-Baptiste Say - Pietro Verri, Values and Law of markets*, "Revue d'économie politique", 103-3, pp. 445-471.

TRAVAGLIANTE P. (1996), *Cultura economica e dibattito nei periodici palermitani degli anni trenta-quaranta*, in Augello, Bianchini, Guidi [1996], pp. 171-208.

TURGOT A.R.J, *Oeuvres de Turgot et documents le concernant*, G. Schelle éd., 5 vol., Alcan, 1913-1923, Paris.

TURGOT (1997), *Formation & distribution des richesses* - directed by Joël-Thomas Ravix & Paul-Marie Romani, GF-Flammarion, Paris.

VATIN F. (1998), *Economie politique et économie naturelle chez Antoine-Augustin* Cournot, puf, Paris.

VENTURI F. (1978), *Le Meditazioni sullla economia politica di Pietro Verri, edizioni, echi e discussioni,* "Rivisti storica italiano", XC-3, pp. 530-594.

VERRI P. (1760), *Degli elementi di commercio*, in *Scritorri classici italiani di economia politica*, parte moderna, edn P. Custodi, [1804], Milan.

VERRI P. (1771), *Meditazioni sulla economia politica, Scrittori Classici Italiani di economia politica*, parte moderna, edn P. Custodi, [1804], Milan.

VOLTAIRE F.M, Arrouet de, *Correspondance*, directed by T. Besterman, 1953-1965, Institut et Musée Voltaire, Genève.

WALRAS A. (1849), *MEMOIRE sur l'origine de la valeur d'échange* ou *Exposition critique et réfutations des opinions les plus accréditées, chez les économistes, sur cette question.* Lu par l'auteur à l'Académie des Sciences morales et politiques (Séance du 15 septembre 1849), in ANNEXE n° 2, pp. 316-339, *De la nature de la richesse et de l'origine de la valeur* [1938], Félix Alcan, Paris.

Italian economic thought in the "Revue d'économie politique" from 1887 to 1950: a bibliographical survey

Fiorenzo Mornati
Université de Lausanne, Centre Walras-Pareto

The spread of Italian economic thought in France from the second half of the 19th century to the years following the Second World War may be documented with reference to four types of contemporary Transalpine sources: textbooks and monographs of the history of economic theories, textbooks and monographs of political economy, the archives of economists and the journals of political economy and history of economic theories.

Since we consider that the study of these sources is still in large part to be done, we aim here to make a contribution through a survey of the most significant journals. For reasons of time we have had to concentrate on the "Revue d'économie politique" (founded in 1887, hereafter REP [1]), since its eclectic approach afforded the widest resonance to the Italian economic literature[2] of the period. Our research, therefore, did not investigate, inter alia, the "Journal des Economistes"[3], the "Monde économique"[4], the "Economiste français" (organs of various expressions of French liberalism) or "Reforme sociale" (expression of the significant Le Play school of social sciences). While these journals are certainly important in the reconstruction of the spread of Italian economic thought in France, however their stated affiliation to particular schools is likely to have meant that they did not pay the same disinterested attention to the international literature as we believe can be said of REP.

What is lost in breadth of coverage is, we believe, more than compensated for in the variety and richness of the data obtained. The abundant material surveyed will be presented (for the most part in chronological order) in three broad categories: the most widely covered authors, textbooks and monographs. In the conclusion, we shall attempt to sketch the types of interest shown by REP in different features of Italian economic thought.

---

[1] On the history of the REP, see Penin (1996).

[2] We have, therefore, decided not to survey the several references made by REP to Italian works on economic history, sociology and economic statistics. The journal also published occasional summaries of Italian economic journals.

[3] Pareto's contributions to this journal are in any case in Pareto (1965).

[4] Pareto's contributions to this journal are in any case in Pareto (1987, 2002).

THE MOST WIDELY COVERED AUTHORS

This section will cover those Italian economists to whom REP gave the greatest attention. In line with the well-known critical orientations that the journal had towards liberal economic thought, at least until after the Second World War, and the preference it showed for various forms of heterodoxy, the first Italian scholars to feature consistently in Gide's journal were Loria (undoubtedly the Italian economist to receive the greatest attention), Rabbeno and Nitti, with Pantaleoni and Pareto, who were at first observed with interest and respect but without agreement with their views. They were gradually rediscovered after the First World War, in the context of a more open attitude towards liberal views. Thus, considerable space was dedicated to Ricci, a liberal (but, according to REP, not an uncritical one), and the heretical socialists Rignano and Graziadei while, among other prominent writers, Einaudi and Del Vecchio were featured less regularly. We shall see that it was only in the period following the Second World War that REP followed the mainstream assessment of Pareto.

Achille Loria

As mentioned, the Italian economist most featured in REP was clearly Achille Loria. He wrote articles for the journal, his publications were reviewed and once (see the second section) he published a review himself, over more than forty years. He appeared in REP for the first time in 1892, with the French translation (pp. 692-712) of his Padua lecture of 21 November 1891, entitled *La terre et le système*. In the lecture, Loria criticised those theories which explain economic phenomena in terms of human nature or the technical organization of production, and instead proposed his fundamental idea of the crucial importance of the type of land ownership and illustrated the necessity, for human development, of ensuring the availability of free land for workers. The first reaction to Loria's views from the founder, editor and deus ex machina of REP, Charles Gide, appeared on the occasion of the appearance of *Les bases économiques de la constitution sociale* (Paris, Alcan, 1893). In his review (1894, 87-94), Gide appreciated the intellectual power with which Loria explained the entire history of humanity on the basis of the history of land ownership, but also noted that his theory had the same claim to a mono-causal explanation as the hedonistic school, and observes that Loria's free association, Gide's cooperation and anarchy were different ways of achieving the common objective of a society without conflicts of interests among persons.

Loria's next book, *Problemi sociali contemporanei* (Milan, 1895), was praised by Carlo Angelo Conegliani (1895, 182-185) for its ability to set out, in a rigorous but accessible way, the author's critical discussion of social institutions on the basis of his hypothesis that they have an economic foundation: however, the reviewer noted that Loria denied the possibility of a collective solution to the social question and asked him to indicate the concrete solution he supported. And Auguste

Souchon, in his review (1897, 418-240) of the French edition (*Problèmes sociaux contemporaines*, Paris, Giard et Brière, 1897), noted Loria's unusual socialist rereading of Smith and Darwin.

Gide returned to Loria's theory in his review (1895, 526-527) of the Modena lecture by the "Lorian" Ugo Rabbeno *L'odierna crisi nella scienza economica* (Turin, 1894). Here he noted how Rabbeno criticised various economic schools and their treatment of several questions for falling short of the mark, but he did not accept Rabbeno's claim that the way out was Loria. And in his review (1897, 768-770) of the volume by Carlo Francesco Ferraris *Il materialismo storico e lo Stato* (Palermo, 1897), Gide identified the antidote to Loria's thesis in Ferraris' view (which he hoped, in vain, would be translated into French) that the economic factor, important though it was, did not in itself explain all social phenomena. And in his review of *La proprietà fondiaria e la questione sociale* (Padova, 1897), Gide (1897, 351-354) recognised that Loria distinguished himself from those advocating land nationalization and agreed with his aim of a world where every worker (thanks to free land) would receive the whole product of his labour, but asked whether the Italian author was not in fact an enemy of land ownership.

Gide showed the same critical admiration for Loria's *Costituzione economica odierna* (Turin, 1899) (1900, 410-412), his *Sociologia* (Padua, 1900) (1901, 418), *Verso la giustizia sociale* (Milan, 1904) (1905, 660 – in a review of the second edition he asked, 1909, 75, whether Loria's insistence on the equality between price and cost of production was similar to the ideal of the hedonistic school), *La morphologie sociale* (Bruxelles, Larcier, 1905) (1906, 678-679), *La sintesi economica* (Milan, 1909) (1909, 722-724 and wrote a comment, 1913, 534-535, on its French translation *La synthèse economique*, Paris, Giard et Brière, 1911) and *Malthus* (Modena, 1909) (1910, 477 – he also expressed a positive judgement on the occasion of the publication of the third edition and emphasised, 1919, 349-350, its treatment of Malthus' economic thought). In the same period Loria was also reviewed in REP by Adolphe Landry, who discussed (1902, 843-846) the volumes *Il capitalismo e la scienza, studi e polemiche* (Turin, 1901) and *Le basi economiche della costituzione sociale* (Turin, 1902).

Loria's familiarity with REP is also shown by the appearance of his articles *Des méthodes pour régulariser la valeur de la monnaie* (1902, 109-124) and *Quelques remarques sur la rente du sol* (1913, 149-163). The latter gave rise to a brief debate with Georges Turgeon who, in *Comment expliquer les mouvements de la population humaine* (1913, 432-449, 555-577), had criticized Loria for his reduction of the entire economy to the system of land ownership, which led Loria to publish in 1914 his *Réponse aux critiques de M.Turgeon* (1-12). In 1915, Loria also published *De l'influence du chomage sur le taux du salaire* (101-113).

Loria continued to feature prominently in REP in the years following the First World War. Gide criticized his *Corso di economia politica* (Milano, 1919) for its arbitrary exclusion of a specific treatment of consumption (1920, 503-504), but shortly after (1922, 383-384) assessed the volume *Aspetti sociali ed economici della guerra mondiale* (Milano, 1921) as "l'étude la plus scientifique qui ait été faite des perturbations causées par la guerre dans les relations économiques entre nations", stating that he preferred it to Keynes and was sorry that Keynes did not share its basic arguments.

Gaëtan Pirou (1925, 950-951) saw the volume *I fondamenti scientifici della riforma economica* (Turin, 1922) as an attempt to bridge the gap between economists and reformers by means of the study of suboptimal production, which had to be eliminated as the necessary point of departure for any social reform. In reviewing the monograph *Davide Ricardo* (Rome, 1926), Pirou (1926, 158-159) praised the way in which Ricardo's thought was linked with contemporary thought and the emphasis on the fundamental link between Ricardo's theory of return and Loria's economic theory. Pirou also (1928, 1022-1023) wrote a long presentation of the third edition of the *Corso di economia politica* (Turin, 1927). He criticized Loria's choice to explain the theory of distribution before the theory of circulation but appreciated his ability to continue to present the discipline while avoiding the approach of general economic equilibrium and his interpretation of economic imperialism as an English disease, which he too hoped Italy would be able to avoid. And in his note on the fourth edition of the *Corso* (Turin, 1934), Pirou (1936, 1219) drew attention to the two new pages on cooperative organization, which he considered worthy of note for their sense of moderation which, on this topic, "on n'est plus accoutumé à trouver dans la littérature économique italienne".

Finally René Courtin (1937, 165-167) wrote on *Dinamica economica. Studio sulle leggi delle variazioni* (Turin, 1935). After noting the methodological weakness of the study of dynamics as discontinuous variations, Courtin spoke positively of the broad bibliographical updating undertaken by the author and, while he noted that the doctrine of free land continued to be unconfirmed, he appreciated the power and anticonformism of Loria's use of this doctrine to explain the Soviet revolution and identify Lenin as a sort of new Prometheus.

Ugo Rabbeno

In order of appearance, the first time Italian economic thought featured in REP was a short but favourable review by Gide (1887, 216-219) of the three volumes on cooperation recently published by Ugo Rabbeno (*La cooperazione in Inghilterra*, Milano, 1885; *La cooperazione in Italia*, Milano, 1886; *Un preteso precursore della cooperazione in Francia*, Milano, 1886). This economist of the Loria school was given the title, by Gide, of successor to Francesco Viganò as leader of the Italian cooperative movement. The REP editor expected contributions of theoretical importance from Rabbeno, starting with the non-inevitability of the transformation of consumption cooperation into production cooperation.

Rabbeno was to continue his international survey of cooperation in REP, publishing *Le mouvement coopératif aux Etats-Unis* (1887, 590-620; 1888, 45-91), a long essay in which he surveyed the American economic situation and described the USA cooperative movement. REP reveals Rabbeno's persistent interest in the United States with his review (1891, 303-309) of Edwin Seligman's two volumes *The general property tax* and *The taxation of corporations* (New York, 1890). Rabbeno praised these volumes for their clear exposition of a complex subject but insisted that Seligman's hope, to contribute to the reorganization of the fragile public finance system of his country through theoretical reflections and not with detailed studies of reality, was an illusion. Gide wrote (1893, 1075-1078) on Rabbeno's volume *Protezionismo americano* (Milan, 1893), praising the accurate documentation, but did not accept the distinction between factual description and theoretical interpretation of the phenomenon, since it was likely to produce confusion and repetition.

The principal meeting ground between Rabbeno and REP was however the study of cooperation. Gide (1890, 87-92) wrote favourably on Rabbeno's new volume *Le società cooperative di produzione* (Milano, 1889), defining it as one of the most important volumes on the subject. He praised the accuracy of its data, particularly for the French situation, but disputed the conclusions that called into question the spread of cooperation (in view of the serious difficulties existing in the cooperative production societies). Gide countered with the need to give the appropriate importance to the production activity carried out in the more established consumption companies. And in his necrology for the young Italian scholar (1897, 1066), Gide described Rabbeno as one of the earliest collaborators of REP and recalled his disappointment with cooperation, but drew attention to the generosity of this ideals and also to the contradiction inherent in Rabbeno's criticism of the dogmatism of classical economy and the new abstract school and, on the other hand, the dogmatism of his own adherence to empiricism.

Rabbeno's intense collaboration with REP also took the form of a series of reviews which began with a positive critique of Leone Wollemborg's *La teoria della cooperazione* (Bologna, 1887), which was the first contribution by an Italian to the journal (1887, 531-537). Rabbeno also reviewed (1890, 86-88) *Sull'assicurazione in generale e in particolare sull'assicurazione contro i danni della mortalità del bestiame* (Udine, 1889) by the same author, and emphasized the conceptual clarity and ability with which the Venetian scholar indicated the contribution which cooperation can make to the reform of the livestock sector. Worthy of note is also his analysis (1897, 525-530) of *La base agronomica della teoria della rendita* by Ghino Valenti (Bologna, 1896), which Rabbeno defined as one of the best Italian studies of economics since, by applying the historical and positive method, it showed how the theory of diminishing returns belonged to the time of Ricardo and not to the contemporary era, in which agriculture produced evidence of growing returns.

Francesco Saverio Nitti

The REP also paid considerable attention to the long, complex and fragmentary career of the scholar and column writer, Francesco Saverio Nitti. Gide gave a very favourable reception to Nitti's volume on *Il Socialismo cristiano* (Turin, 1891). He considered it singularly significant in those times in which much was written on this subject but an overall survey was still lacking. However, while he agreed with Nitti, whom he saw as both "socialist" and "Catholic", that socialism and Catholicism could fight together against current social institutions, Gide, who was a Protestant, doubted that the aspirations of modern socialism could be achieved in the new society which Nitti called for, in which socialism would be achieved under the rule of Catholic authoritarianism. Nitti responded to this objection in a letter (1891, 669-672), saying that he was neither socialist nor catholic but simply a positivist and that as such he had felt the need to analyse both Catholicism and Protestantism objectively, and had found the former (despite his persistent scientific obscurantism) more inclined to socialism that Protestant individualism (in which he found many other things to praise).

This cordial difference of views did not prevent an ever more constant presence by Nitti in the pages of REP. He published (1892, 774-803) a long essay on *La législation sociale en Italie. Difficultés que rencontre son établissement*, in which he reflected critically on the causes of the backward nature of Italian social legislation, which he identified not so much in the strength of the intransigent liberal school as in the conservative character of the political institutions and in the centuries-old political and social weakness of the peasant class, which was still numerically superior to the working class. Nitti illustrated the features lacking in labour legislation, and observed that an improvement in the public finances would not make it possible to introduce measures to improve the condition of Italian workers, since positive change would only be possible by following Loria's implicit indications and facing the issue of land holding.

Nitti's brilliant presence with REP continued with a positive review by Gide (1893, 1078-1081) of his treatise on demography *La popolazione e il sistema sociale* (Turin, 1893). Gide appreciated the erudition (especially in the first part on the history of theories) and clear exposition which, he observed, was accompanied by a certain haste in the argument which led the author to claim, somewhat unpersuasively, that socialism was the root of the development of individualism which Nitti saw as giving the lie to Malthus' pessimism. There is also evidence in REP of Nitti's concurrent interest in monetary issues. Gide (1896, 400-402) in a review of Nitti's volume *La misura delle variazioni di valore della moneta* (Turin, 1895) noted the conclusion that, if it is not possible to measure the variations in currency value, it is socially just to make that value constant, and this objective can only be achieved through State issue, with international approval, of sufficient paper money to satisfy demand. Nitti himself published his *Essai sur les variations du taux de l'escompte* (1898, 367-398, 793-826; 1899, 278-320), a long statistical and interpretative study of the problems of the emission of paper money.

Nitti's progressive involvement in the highest circles of Italian politics reduced his scientific production but REP continued to follow his work closely. Gide

(1902, 94-95) wrote a warm review of *L'Italia all'alba del secolo* (Rome, 1901) and acknowledged the educational usefulness of the textbook *Scienza delle finanze* (Naples, 1903), whose French translation (*Principes de la science des finances*, Paris, Giard et Brière, 1904) received praise from H.-E. Barrault (1905, 572-574). Gide also wrote positively about Nitti's volume *Il capitale straniero in Italia* (Bari, 1915) and agreed with the view that Germany's capitalistic colonization would allow Italy to conquer new markets after the war (1915, 409). Gide did not forget his former Italian collaborator when he was in exile in Paris. He defined (1928, 1690-1691) the new edition of the *Principes des sciences des finances* (Paris, Giard, 1928) one of the fundamental texts of finance literature in French, on account of its theoretical and comparative approach. Finally, the original testimonies of Nitti's tortured thought of the 1930s were presented with interest. Marc Aucuy (1934, 1386-1387) reviewed *L'inquiétude du monde (la guerre, la crise, L'Etat)* (Paris, Denoël et Steel, 1934) and explained how the renewal of Nitti's liberal thinking saw financial capitalism as the preparation for statism, the inefficiency of which lay at the origin of the crisis and of war. Henri Hauser (1938, 898-899) presented *La désagregation de l'Europe. Essai sur des vérités impopulaires* (Paris, Spes, 1938) and emphasized the clear but contentious nature of Nitti's theory that the imminent disaster in Europe was due to the success of totalitarian regimes which, though of opposite political colour, were all derived from Marxian thought.

Maffeo Pantaleoni

The attitude of REP towards Pantaloni is introduced by the brief but not anodyne presentation (1890, 552) of the second series of the *Giornale degli Economisti*. The note ascribes this review to the liberal and classical school but also points out the limitations the review is prepared to concede to free competition and emphasizes that the works of the editor guarantee that the journal will be edited "dans un esprit hautement scientifique".

In line with these international good-neighbourly intentions, Gide produced a long review (1890, 323-326) of *Principi di economia pura* (Florence, 1889). This volume, he said, was of great importance in that it relaunched classical economics in the face of the new historical school and freed the former of that optimistic and conservative aspect that has been inappropriately imposed on it. It is noteworthy that Gide identified the "purity" of the book in the absence of applications and in the author's ability to establish a series of theorems, based on the hedonistic hypothesis, which treat all aspects of the theory of value and place production persuasively within it. The *homo oeconomicus* outlined here is the skeleton of real man but knowledge of him is as important to the reformer as knowledge of the human skeleton is to the doctor. Gide also stressed the breadth of Pantaleoni's bibliographical knowledge but questions his excessive tendency to accuse others of plagiarism and to forget the fact that in the history of the sciences it is typical to encounter simultaneous discoveries or genuine rediscoveries, since they are based on the ignorance of one's predecessors. He concluded by noting that Pantaleoni is unusually harsh on German economists and thanks him for the even more unusual rediscovery of the French mathematical economists, such as Cournot and Dupuit. In response to this initial cordial relationship, Pantaleoni then published his important monograph on economic statistics *Observations sur la sémiologie économique* (1892, 1067-1096).

But interest in Pantaleoni by REP was only resumed after the First World War, with the exception of Gide's review (1910, 847-848) of *Scritti vari di economia* (Milan, 1910), which spoke positively only of the first part, on the origin of exchange. In 1922 Roberto Michels reviewed (674-675) *Bolscevismo italiano* (Bari, 1922), stressing the book's nature as a scientific apologia for fascism as the suppressor of socialism. But Pantaleoni's economic thought was also to reawaken attention from REP, particularly Pirou who welcomed (1924, 718-719) Pantaleoni and Broglio d'Ajano's set of exercises *Temi, tesi, problemi e quesiti di economia politica teorica e applicata* (Bari, 1925). He then presented (1925, 949-950) *Erotemi di economia* (Bari, 1925) as the evidence of an approach that was questionable (especially with respect to the conception of the history of economic thought and the critique of cooperation), but also so brilliant as to be worthy of study and, at least in theoretical terms, less intransigent as it appeared. And in 1926 Pirou reported (1404-1405) on the republication of *La crisi del 1905-1907* (Milano, 1925) and then published (1144-1165) *M. Pantaleoni et la théorie économique* where he critically analyzed Pantaleoni's economic thought and identified his methodological individualism as both his theoretical strong point and his applicational weakness since it led him to ignore how far the reality was from the individualistic-hedonistic hypothesis. Finally the publication of *Studi storici di economia* (Bologna, 1936) gave Pirou (1938, 451-452) the opportunity to speak favourably of the openness of all Pantaleoni's work. He cited the study, in this volume, of exchange and compared it with Mauss' study of gifts, reaching the conclusion that Pantaleoni had not demonstrated that in primitive times there was the same exchange mentality as today.

Vilfredo Pareto

The way REP treated Pareto – it only published his favourable review (1902, 90-93) of the *Essai sur la théorie générale de la monnaie* by Albert Aupetit (Paris, 1901) – is perhaps representative of the history of the critical fortune of Pareto, which was mostly posthumous.

In fact, when Gide wrote one of the few reviews (1897, 189-194) of *Cours d'économie politique* (Lausanne, Rouge, 1896-1897), he noted its methodological pluralism and agreed with its positivist scientific intentions, but drew attention to Pareto's efforts at terminological innovation which Gide judged not new and manifestly pointless, his theoretical liberalism (which opposes Pareto to Walras though he shared his representation of the economy as general economic equilibrium), the arbitrary nature of his eugenic explanation of the constancy of the distribution of incomes and the illusion of discouraging those who hope for less inequality in social conditions. In a similar fashion Gide (1902, 168-171) gave a friendly but critical review of the first volume of *Systèmes sociales* (Paris, Giard et Brière, 1902), commenting favourably on the book's brilliance and the idea that the bourgeoisie had to regenerate itself or else disappear, but disagreeing with the claim that Pareto was not attempting to persuade anyone and stressing the untidy organisation of the book which had already harmed the success of the *Cours*, but was also the *felix culpa* of an author with too many ideas, which inevitably spilled over. Gide reviewed (1907, 231-233) the *Manuale di economia politica* (Milan, 1906 and stressed the difficult graphic appearance of the text, and noted that it contained three textbooks, one on logic, one on pure mathematics (while he was not a mathematician, Gide recognised that this discipline taught students to think and to showed how the complexity of reality can never totally be grasped), and one on applied economics – in this case he commented on the disorganised, but acute and brilliantly pleasing exposition, even though it rested firmly on an implacable individualism.

Gide's attitude of critical admiration towards Pareto was confirmed in the speech he gave at Pareto's Jubilee in 1917 (430-433), where he drew a distinction between Pareto and Walras in terms of the fact that Pareto occupied himself only with science and not with social action. And the sociologist Maurice Halbwachs adopted Gide's critical line in his long review of the French edition of the Treatise (*Traité de sociologie générale*, Paris, Payot, 1917) where he noted the suggestive but enigmatic character of the work (1918, 578-585).

The attitude of REP towards Pareto began to change in 1923 with the necrology of Pareto entrusted to the engineer-economist Jacques Moret who (712-718) praised the interdisciplinary nature of Pareto's work and noted the capital importance, in the construction of general economic equilibrium, of the move from the cardinal theory to the ordinal theory of utility. In 1928 (1026-1027), the historian of economic theories René Gonnard presented *Vilfredo Pareto, sa vie et son oeuvre* (Paris, Payot, 1928) by Georges Henri Bousquet as an important introduction to Pareto's thought, and noted however that it was possible to disagree with Pareto's view that mathematical economics has exhausted its theoretical possibilities. In 1932 (1321-1346), François Bompaire offered a synthesis of his doctoral thesis *Du principe de la liberté é conomique dans l'oeuvre de cournot et dans celle de l'Ecole de Lausanne (Walras, Pareto)* (Paris, Recueil Sirey, 1931) which François Divisia (1932, 1181-1182) praised for the breadth and accuracy of its documentation. But in his review of Pirou's fundamental volume *Les théories de l'equilibre économique: L.Walras et V.Pareto* (Paris, Ed. Domat-Montchrestien, 1934), Charles Rist (1936, 1793-1794) stated his belief that Pareto had contributed to the development of the theory of general economic equilibrium less than was claimed and had remained for too long under the influence of de Molinari's liberal absolutism.

It was only after the Second World War that REP toned down its reserves about Pareto and dedicated to him, in 1949 (just after the centenary of his birth), a special issue with articles by Giovanni Demaria *L'oeuvre économique de Vilfredo Pareto* (517-544), Bousquet, *Pareto sociologue* (545-554), René Roy, *Pareto statisticien: la distribution des revenus* (555-577), John Hicks, *Courbes d'indifférence collective* (578-584), Eraldo Fossati, *Pareto dans son et notre temps* (585-599) and of the young Debreu, *Les fins du système économique* (600-615), a review of the nature and limitations of the economics of well-being. The issue attempted to give an account of the scientific directions which were believed to have inspired directly or indirectly by Pareto, by also publishing articles by Justman, *La théorie des jeux. Une nouvelle théorie de l'équilibre économique* (616-633), Gehrard Tintner, *La position de l'économetrie dans hierarchie des sciences sociales* (634-641) and Jan Tinbergen, *Du système de Pareto aux modèles modernes* (642-562).

Umberto Ricci

The author of the next generation who was most interesting to REP was Umberto Ricci, who made his debut in 1908 (180-187) with a report of the proceedings of the statistics and political economy section of the Parma congress of the Italian Society for the Advancement of Science. The report stressed the significance of the fact that the participants adhered to both the theory of economic equilibrium and statistical correlation theory. Rist (1912, 389-390) dedicated a favourable review to the volume *Il capitale. Saggio di economia teoretica* (Turin, 1910). He appreciated the distinction between consumer goods and production goods (in opposition to Fischer's stock-flow opposition) but noted that Ricci's position, unlike Fischer's, was not supported by the fundamental reasons of facilitating theoretical developments. Pirou (1922, 386-387) wrote of the volume *Protezionisti e liberisti italiani* (Bari, 1920) that Ricci's liberalism no longer seemed intent on persuasion and that Ricci seemed to be considering theoretical studies oriented towards a deeper understanding of reality. Writing on the volume *Il fallimento della politica economica* (Florence, 1921), Pirou (1924, 1121-1122) noted the breadth of the documentation and the brilliance of his criticism of the woes of regulatory policies. However, at the same time as he credited Ricci with a non-extreme liberalism, Pirou lamented the absence of a discussion of the effects of a liberal war economy. From Ricci's intense work after the War as a column writer, Pirou (1926, 159-160) also presented *Dal protezionismo al sindacalismo* (Bari, 1926) and noted the book's thesis that the defence of free exchange was conditional on its utility to Italy and its fear that Fascist inter-class syndicalism was too weak to prevent workers returning to their traditional class-based organizations. REP's interest in Ricci's scientific work culminated in the publication of a substantial series of articles by the Roman economist. The series opened with *La loi de la demande individuelle et la rente de consommateur*, a study of the history of analysis but containing certain theoretical innovations (1926, 5-24). This was followed by *La Taxation de l'epargne* (1927, 860-883) and, most notably, *La pression fiscale* (1937, 249-272), a complete exposition of Ricci's financial theory which was completed in 1939 by the original article on the *Idées de N. F. Canard sur l'impôt* (820-827) which developed Canard's theory of the spread of impost. After a reference by Bousquet (1939, 115) to the importance of the *Tre economisti italiani: Pantaleoni, Pareto, Loria* (Bari, 1939), Ricci's collaboration with REP came to an end with his article, dated April 1940, *Les dépenses militaires sont-elles productives?* (1940-1945, 3-5-319). Here Ricci's economic analysis of war concludes that war must be avoided by means of an international organization which can prevent conflicts, while guaranteeing respect for the non-aggressive qualities of individual countries.

Luigi Einaudi, Eugenio Rignano, Antonio Graziadei, Gustavo Del Vecchio

There is, finally, a group of authors followed by REP for a limited period of their scientific activity.

Luigi Einaudi was cited, as an economist, by REP for the first time in André Andréades' review (1921, 787) of the *Relazione della Commissione parlamentare consultiva per l'applicazione della legge 24 settembre 1920 sull'avocazione dei profitti di guerra allo Stato* (Roma, 1920), which was presented as proof of how useful it is to have professors of economics in Parliament. Michels (1922, 674) reviewed *Gli ideali di un economista* (Florence, 1921), remarking on his Anglophilia and questioning his aversion for the German historical school, and also (1925, 634) *Le lotte del lavoro* (Turin, 1924) in which he highlighted the liberal leanings. In the same period, Pirou (1924, 162-163) presented *La terra e l'imposta* (Milan, 1924) as a useful contribution to the debates in France at the same time on the taxation of agricultural incomes (an opinion repeated by Michel Augé-Laribé, 1928, 1033-1034). In 1936, REP, over the signature of Pirou (1436) expressed regret at the end of *Riforma Sociale*, which was known as less conformist that the *Giornale degli Economisti* and had a growing readership abroad, and wished better luck to the *Rivista di Storia Economica*. This latter journal was appreciated for its interest in economic ideas and facts and for some of its early articles. REP also published the article *Morale et économique* (289-311) in which Einaudi replied to the long essay *Droit et économie* (1935, 1457-1494) in which Giorgio Del Vecchio had claimed that it was necessary to subordinate study of the political economy to study of the law. Finally, in 1949, Gerard Dehove (223-227) reviewed *Lezioni di politica sociale* (Turin, 1949) and paid homage to the author as scholar and stateman. Dehove shared the message of trust in freedom that the volume wished to send out to the whole of Europe but questioned its persuasiveness in defending free competition.

REP paid particular interest to Eugenio Rignano, the original theorist of liberal juridical socialism. In 1904 (425-427), Landry reviewed the French edition

(*Un socialisme en harmonie avec la doctrine économique libérale*, Giard et Brière, 1904) of the volume *Di un socialismo in accordo colla dottrina economica liberale* (Turin, 1904). He enthusiastically supported the guidelines of respect for private property, as a necessary stimulus for work and saving, and of a practical (in opposition to collective millenarianism) and pacific passage to socialism through taxing succession with rates rising according to the distance of family relationship between testator and heir. In 1920 Gide (760-761) wrote on Rignano's new book *Per una riforma socialista del diritto successorio* (Bologna, 1920), stating that the juridical socialism outlined in it can be applied to land property. In 1921 (1-10) he accepted the article *Un programme socialiste libérale* in which Rignano again presented his socialist plan as a way to rebuild the unity of the socialist party and to bring about socialism through peace, as an alternative to the Bolshevik violence. This plan was heard again in 1924 in the interesting study by Giovanni De Francisci Gerbino on the *Situation financière de la France et un nouveau projet d'amortissement del dettes publiques* (674-684), which stresses how Rignano's socialism, if applied, could facilitate financial reform in France. In 1930 REP, through the pen of William Oualid (1456), commemorated its Italian friend and remembered, along with his socialist program, his encyclopedic spirit which was so original in a time dedicated to specialization.

The interest of the journal for contemporary critiques of socialism can also be seen in the attention paid to the publications in French of Graziadei. Gide (1932, 468-469), who considered Graziadei's forced return to economic studies as an unexpected benefit of Fascism, presented *Rente et la propriété de la terre. Critiques aux théories de Marx* (Paris, Rivière, 1931). He agreed with the fundamental thesis that the theory of labour-value was irreconcilable with the theory of land rent but doubted that Marxist theory could stand up without the former. Pierre Fromont (1935, 1423) praised the clear exposition in the volumes *Les variations de la rente et la propriété de la terre* and *La rente de la terre (critiques aux théories de Marx)* (Paris, Rieder, 1933, 1934) but commented it was not original to show, as the volumes did, that the Ricardo-Marxian thesis had failed to explain price variation purely in terms of cost variation. Landry (1936, 556-557) reviewed *Le capital et l'intéret (critiques aux théories de Marx)* (Paris, Rieder, 1935) and agreed with the criticism of modern interest rate theories and noted that the book offered ideas for a new theory on the subject.

Gustavo Del Vecchio appeared in REP for the first time in 1913 when Jean Lescure (541) reviewed *Relazioni fra entrata e consumo* (Rome, 1912), applauding the attempt at a monographic study of mathematical economics with a statistical basis, although the quality of the statistics still seemed weak to the reviewer. This economist was cited again in 1932 when Bousquet reviewed (461-462) *Grundlinien der Geldtheorie* (Tübingen, Mohr, 1930) and emphasized its theoretical depth, particularly with respect to discount rate dynamics, but drew attention to the unclear exposition and gaps in the bibliography. In the following year, REP published the critical review of *Les nouvelles théories économiques de la monnaie* (1265-1274) and Louis Baudin (1264) presented *Cronache della lira in pace e in guerra* (Milan, 1932) with positive words for the clear interpretation of Italian monetary policy and the emphasis given to psychological factors in its success.

TEXTBOOKS

As mentioned above, one sector of the Italian literature in economics that was followed with particular interest by REP was the field of textbooks (manuals) in political economy. This clearly reflects how important the synthetic organization of the discipline was for Gide[5], author of the famous *Principes d'économie politique*[6] and, for Charles Rist, author of *Histoire des doctrines économiques*[7]. The material surveyed here will be presented in chronological order, while certain information on textbooks in financial science, history of economic thought and methodological statistics is contained in the following note[8].

---

[5] For a recent intellectual and scientific biography of Gide, cf. Penin (1991).

[6] From its first edition in 1884, this volume ran to twenty-six editions, the last in 1931.

[7] From its first edition in 1909, this volume ran to five editions, the last in 1926.

[8] With respect to the presence in REP of textbooks of public finance, one must mention, alongside the texts by Cossa and Nitti (cited *infra* and *supra*), Flora (1893) which made a favourable impression on Gide (1893, 1089-1091). Gide noted the clarity of its exposition of new Italian and German financial theories and its demonstration of the greater fiscal burden borne by Italians, but only agreed in part with Flora's aversion to progressive taxation and noted the incomplete treatment of public debt. André Andréades (1921, 509-511) reviewed its third edition (Livorno, 1921), praising the completeness of its theoretical and applied aspects, as well as the author's originality, which made him "le Gide de la science des finances". REP also followed the editorial fortunes of Graziani (1911, 1929). Gide (1912, 117-118) criticized its first edition (1911) for being too complex for teaching purposes and unappreciative of French writers but, in reviewing its third edition (1929), Louis Trotabas (1929, 1451-1452) stressed how it showed the many substantial similarities between the different national financial systems. Trotobas also presented (1929, 1452) Tivaroni (1929), emphasizing its educational usefulness and the up-to-date treatment of the financial features of corporativism, and also Griziotti (1929) which he praised for its original political-legal approach and its conception of the difference between fiscal system and the economic system. In his review (1930, 1026-1027) of Gangemi (1929), Trotobas observed that its originality and accuracy made it an excellent introduction to the study of public finance, to be preferred to Griziotti (1930) which Trotobas (1931, 434) did however recognise as making a strong case for the quality and wealth of this sector of Italian economic literature.

Italian textbooks on the history of economic thought first appeared with Gide's positive review (1892, 1252-1253) of Cossa (1892). Gide observed that the volume's erudition and impartiality would make it "le vademecum de tout professeur d'économie politique", and would make its author well-known as the leader of his school. Auguste Souchon later (1900, 329-330) reviewed its French translation (Cossa 1899) and praised the meticulous search of the sources while disagreeing with the tendency to consider ideas as the children of ideas rather than of facts. This current was subsequently reduced to the quotations which Gonnard offered from Mauri (1924), which was praised for its exhaustive bibliography (1925, 770), and especially from Gangemi (1932) which, Souchon claimed (1934, 1052), had the task of updating Cossa's earlier classic, cited above and hoping for a wider readership not only in Italy but also abroad where Italian economists still enjoyed little recognition among treatises on the history of economic thought.

It is worth noting the very favourable treatment which REP gave, in the years after the First World War, to texts on methodological statistics. Rist (1919, 101-102) reviewed Niceforo (1919), acknowledging its rigour and the clear section on methodology as well as the breadth of its applications. A few years later (1925, 626) Rist also reviewed (1925, 626) Niceforo (1925), the French translation of Niceforo (1923) and called it the textbook "le plus commode et le plus clair de statistique en langue française". For the same reasons, Pirou (1925, 1099) considered Mortara (1922) an indication of a university culture which, unlike the French situation, had given statistics its rightful academic autonomy.

The Italian author of textbooks who received the most admiration from REP was certainly Luigi Cossa, in whose necrology (1896, 696) Gide remembered him as a friend of the journal, though he only published one review[9].

Christian de Boeck praised Cossa's *Premiers éléments d'économie politique* (Paris, Larose, 1889) and *Premiers éléments de la science de finances* (Paris, Larose, 1891) (first French translations of, respectively *Principi di economia politica*, Milan, 1888, and *Principi di scienza della finanze*, Milan, 1890). He stated that both were useful for teachers and students, and expressed regret in the first of the volumes had omitted the bibliography which could however be consulted in the Italian edition ("qui est sur le rayons de toutes nos Facultés"). De Boeck observed that the fact that the first text did not take a position on the theoretical differences that were shaking political economics would make it attractive to all and that the second text treated all the fundamental subjects (from taxation, to the description of the different types of public expenditure, to public debt) in the discipline which was about to enter French Faculties. Traces of Cossa's prestige[10] are also to be found after the First World War, when Pirou (1923, 874-875) and Henry Truchy (1924, 435) spoke of *Premiers éléments d'économie politique* (Paris, Giard, 1922, French translation of the 14th edition of *Primi elementi di economia sociale*, Milan, 1920). Pirou appreciated the synthetic exposition of the subject of economics and the enduring usefulness of the famous bibliographies (which did need, however, some updating to include the new and original French literature on the crises), while Truchy considered the volume one of the best introductions to political economy.

REP did not ignore the rest of the considerable Italian literature in this period.

De Boeck (1891, 667-668) reviewed Giuseppe Majorana Calatabiano's *Le leggi naturali dell'economia politica* (Rome, 1891) and praised the clear treatment of the various subjects of economic theory (production, exchange, distribution and consumption of wealth) in the light of the view that they are governed by natural laws but without excessive regard to the positions of the liberal school. Gide (1900, 1043) reviewed the French translation (*Principes d'économie politique*, Paris, Oudin, 1899) of Matteo Liberatore's *Principi di economia politica* (Naples, 1899) noting the involuntary slide towards communist ideas. He criticized (1903, 96) Arnaldo Agnelli's *Nozioni di economia politica per le università popolari* (Milan, 1902) but praised (1903, 861-862) the similar volume by Alberto Giovannini, *Lezioni di economia politica* (Parma, 1903). Another important collaborator of REP who followed Italian texts of political economy in this period was Landry, whose first review in this sector (1905, 266-267) criticized Augusto

---

[9] This was a notice (1893, 78-79) concerning Feilbogen (1892). The professor from Pavia agreed with the opposition between the dogmatic nature of the concept of economic freedom in Turgot and its practical nature in Smith, as well as the emphasis given to Smith's support for the labour theory of value.

[10] This prestige reverberated to some extent on his son Emilio, whose Cossa (1889) was reviewed by Rabbeno (1890, 98-100), with positive comment on its novelty and on the author's ability to treat the subject with the lucidity and bibliographical richness that characterized his father.

Graziani's *Istituzioni di economia politica* (Turin, 1904) for its complicated explanations. The fourth edition (Turin, 1925) was praised by Pirou (1926, 1237-1238), who singled out for praise the sections on the theory of value and distribution. Landry later (1909, 845-846) praised the original exposition in Ghino Valenti's *Principi di scienza economica* (Florence, 1909) and the clarity of Camillo Supino's *Principii di economia politica* (Naples, 1908). The fourth edition of Supino's text was reviewed favourably by Jean Lescure (1914, 714-715), who asked for a chapter on the crises and updating of the French bibliography.

The new season of textbooks in pure economics also received immediate attention. While William Oualid (1910, 492) claimed that pervasive hermeticism reduced the educational value of Pasquale Boninsegni's *Précis d'économie politique* (Lausanne, Rouge, 1910), Rist (1910, 578-579) considered Enrico Barone's *Principi di economia politica* (Rome, 1908) an excellent proof that the graphic method could be used with rigour and with clarity to explain pure economics. He considered the most original chapters of the volume to be those on the crises and on trusts, while the most questionable were those on demography and on the theory of interest, where Pareto (who inspired the author) was less successful. And Jacques Moret (1929, 147-148) reviewed the German translation (*Grundzuge der theoretischen nationalokonomie*, Bonn, 1927) remembering Schumpeter's positive appraisal. Moret emphasized the educational value of the volume and noted the appendix with its new subjects.

Italian textbooks in the period following the First World War made their first appearance with Landry (1919, 782), who reviewed the first part of Ulisse Gobbi's *Trattato di economia* (Milan, 1919). He praised the clarity of the explanations but criticized the complicated organization of the materials. Pirou (1924, 717-718) covered the second part of Gobbi's treatise (Milan, 1923) and also noted the original structure but doubted its educational value, because of the fragmentary nature of the exposition and because it started with theory rather than with a description of economic reality. Pirou had already hinted at this "realistic" preference of him in his positive review (1920, 95-97) of Arturo Labriola's *Manuale di economia politica* (Naples, 1919) and the way it gave greater importance to the most significant political phenomena.

Jacques Moret, meanwhile, was the principal reviewer of texts of pure economics. He harshly criticized (1921, 99-100) the French translation (*Leçons d'économie politique suivant la doctrine de l'Ecole de Lausanne*, Paris, Payot, 1920) of Roberto Murray's *Lezioni di economia politica* (Florence, 1912) as a useless paraphrase of Pareto's economic theory, made worse by the hostile attitude of Murray and his co-translator (the Paretian Pierre Boven, from Lausanne) towards Gide who, despite what they claimed, was the main supporter of mathematical economics. Maurice Byé, on the other hand, in a review (1931, 193-194) of Boninsegni's *Manuel élémentaire d'économie politique* (Paris, Payot, 1930), acknowledged the rigour, clarity and methodological pluralism of its exposition.

REP's treatment of corporative economics textbooks opened with an interesting five minutes of infamy for Gaetano Napolitano, whose *Corso di economia politica svolto sui principi della Carta del Lavoro* (Rome, 1928) was reviewed by Gide (1928, 1173-1174). Gide took issue with its infantile claim that fascism was the first to criticise liberal economics, rejected the statement that the regime had found the definitive solution to the difficult relations between capital and labour and observed that the author's ideological obsession weakened the section on consumption theory and also led him to a biased justification of Italian economic imperialism. REP allowed Napolitano to clarify his ideas through an article *Principes économiques du corporatisme fasciste* (1929, 1257-1292) in which he attempted to justify his theoretical choices via anti-deductivist and anti-individualist methodological options. Gide (1930, 1689-1690) was to review Napolitano's later work *Principi di economia corporativa* (Rome, 1930) as an economic study of Fascism which seemed to him to be a form of forced solidarity, unlike the version proposed by French solidarity. The young Italian scholar replied to this review with a booklet *Saggio di economia corporativa* (Rome, 1932) which was reviewed by François Perroux (1933, 1628), who disputed the idea that economic science could be usefully reconstructed on the basis of *homo corporativus* and stated that the originality of corporatism lay in its actual capacity, which was yet to be proved, to solve the conflict between business owners and employees and between producers and consumers.

It was Pirou, on the other hand, who reviewed the less militant texts *Lezioni di economia generale e corporativa* by Giuseppe Ugo Papi (Padua, 1935) e *Principi di economia corporativa* by Luigi Amoroso (Bologna, 1938). The review of the former (1935, 1814) noted that, compared to French texts of political economy, more space was devoted to theory than to practice and that the text defended the need to provide a deductive treatment of corporativism, until it achieved its aim of diminishing costs through increasing quantities of production. The review of the latter (1938, 1022-1023) appreciated the dynamic and taxonomic generalization provided of general economic equilibrium but disapproved of the juxtaposition of pure economics and corporativism (which was ideologically claimed to be a synthesis of the best of previous theories).

The increasingly difficult political climate did not distract REP from taking note of the first volume of *Principi di scienza economica* by Riccardo Bachi (Turin, 1937), an author already praised by the journal for his yearbooks of Italian economic statistics. Pirou (1938, 451) wrote that this latest publication proceeded from exchange theory to production theory (unlike French texts which moved from the concrete to the abstract) and included a useful series of questions aimed at easier learning.

In the early years after the Second World War, Italian textbooks of political economy featured the rapid emergence of new texts of mathematical economics. Henri Bartoli (1948, 657-658) favourably reviewed Arrigo Bordin's *I principi di scienza economica* (Turin, 1947). He praised the methodological development represented, in the textbook structure, by the passage from partial equilibrium to general equilibrium, which was explained first in static and then in dynamic terms, and was then illustrated in the hypotheses of determinacy and stochasticity. This helped to demonstrate the importance, for France, of the applied study of the question of a State which wished to modernize the national economic system. In his remarks on Felice Vinci's *Breve introduzione all'economia* (Milan, 1948) Bartoli (1949, 387-388) hoped that this volume would stimulate its readers to get to know the more demanding *Ordinamenti economici* (Milan, 1944-1945) by the same author (a follower of Pareto). Bartoli described (1950, 555-556) *Elementi di economia razionale* by Eraldo Fossati (Padua, 1947) as an important formulation of the probabilistic nature of dynamic equilibrium, which contained useful formal appendices. Finally he reviewed (1950, 342-343) *Introduzione all'economia* by Giuseppe Palomba (Naples, 1950) and claimed that between the encyclopedic-ideological economics of this author (which was not necessary for identifying the crisis of capitalism) and rational economics, there was a *neo-Gidean* space for the development of an economic science that was "pleinement humaine".

MONOGRAPHS

The presence of Italian economic thought in REP also took another form, that of monographic studies by authors who received less attention from the journal. We shall attempt here to present this body of work in the least fragmented way possible by discussing them in (mostly) chronological order according to the following categories: *theoretical economics* (broadly defined), *theory of public finance*, *history of economic thought* (with reference to the methodology of economic science too) and *economic and social policy*.

Theoretical economics[11]

In the time span from the foundation of the journal to the First World War, Italian monographic studies of theoretical economics published in REP dealt mainly with the theory of value and of distribution[12].

[11] Works of applied economics in the strict sense of the term also appear. Thus, Gide (1914, 508-509) praised the completeness of information in Marconcini (1914) but questioned its claim that this type of industry [paid domestic work] had a future. Michel Augé-Laribé presented (1928, 1034-1035) Tassinari (1926) as an example of a new line of research which ought to be followed in France as well. In the same way, in his review (1947, 347-348) of Medici (1946) he welcomed the regional analysis of Italian agricultural problems, an approach which ought to be introduced into France. On this topic, Lucien Brocard (1935, 1826) had noted the theoretical originality of Bachi (1933).

[12] There are, however, also references to studies on the theory of production. Rabbeno wrote a rather critical review (1888, 228-230) of Cossa (1888), questioning whether the company could be given an abstract definition, since it always had to be explained in terms of elements such as the aim, the risk-taking capacity and the juridical personality of the company owner. René Maunier wrote a brief note (1911, 420) on Arias (1911). Oualid wrote a positive review (1919, 606-607) of Garino-Canina (1916) and recommended it be updated to include the current wartime situation.

Gide (1887, 547-548) gave a benign presentation of Graziani's volume *Sulla teoria generale del profitto* (Milan, 1887), with words of praise for its bibliographical rigour and critical acumen but stressing the absence of any reference to Walras' theory of the businessman with its innovative idea of cancelling profit. Loria (1892, 832-834) reviewed Graziani's next book *La teoria economica delle macchine* (Turin, 1891) and praised its interesting critique of the Marxian theory of capital but stressed that the book gave a purely implicit demonstration that the Böhm-Bawerk theory of capital was only a useful corollary of utility theory.

Conigliani (1895, 1042-1044) reviewed Vincenzo Tangorra's volume *Per la teoria del fondo salari* (Roma, 1894) and questioned its claim that it was restoring the scientific destiny of wages fund theory since it was irredeemably compromised by tautology. Gide, in his review (1899, 564-566) of Adolfo Musco's *La dottrina del salario* (Naples, 1898), saw this book as the confirmation of how good Italians were in producing bibliographically complete monographic studies. He emphasized the original explanation of work productivity as a function of pay, but considered the categorization of the various theories to be forced and the treatment of certain of them to be questionable.

In this period, the editor of REP did not miss the opportunity to report on Vincenzo Giuffrida's *III volume del "Capitale" di Karl Marx: esposizione critica* (Catania, 1899) and judged it (1899, 1043) particularly useful for French readers, who still did not even have access to the second volume of Marx's trilogy. Another young Italian socialist scholar noted by Gide was Giovanni Montemartini in a review (1896, 932-934) of his volume *Il risparmio nell'economia pura* (Milan, 1896), in which he particularly appreciated the idea of the economical or anti-economical nature of saving depending on whether future earnings (on the savings) would be greater or lesser than the present sacrifices (involved in the saving). He also reviewed (1901, 94-95) *La teorica delle produttività marginali* (Pavia, 1899) with criticism of its expositional complexity[13].

This appreciation of the ability of young Italian economists in the field of textbook writing is a common theme running through a number of subsequent reviews by Gide: first (1901, 92) of Emilio Cossa's *Consumo delle ricchezze* (Bologna, 1898) though he did note a lack of theoretical creativity; then (1908, 466-467) of Costantino Ottolenghi's *I profitti industriali nella costituzione economica odierna* (Turin, 1907), but here he noted the omission of the law of decrease of profits as a result of perfect competition and cooperation. The period in question was closed by Rist's review (1913, 413) of Guido Sensini's *Teoria della rendita* (Bologna, 1912), which he praised for tracing the history of rent theory clearly from Ricardo to Pareto though the exposition was complicated by pointless personal polemics.

---

[13] Another work by this Lombard scholar which was received positively by REP, over the signature of Emile Bouvier (1919, 785-786), was the new edition of Montemartini (1916).

In the following period the monographies in theoretical economics presented by REP cover a wider range of the topics.

On the theory of value and distribution, Pirou (1925, 626-627) reviewed Roberto Cossa's *Legge di formazione del valor fisso e comune misura dei valori* (Naples, 1924) as an ingenious attempt to fix the value of a currency in terms of quantities of purchasable goods. Bousquet (1929, 346) commented on the clarity but also the superficiality of Bruno Foà's short volume *Di alcune influenze del tempo sul valore* (Milan, 1928) while Baudin (1929, 143) praised the analytical acumen and theoretical completeness shown by the same young author in *Influenze monetarie sulla distribuzione delle ricchezze. L'inflazione* (Milan, 1927). Another young author who received some attention in this period was Mario De Luca, whose volumes *La legge dei rendimenti decrescenti nei suoi presupposti e nella sua portata* (Naples, 1933) and *Gli aspetti ciclici della distribuzione dei redditi* (Naples, 1939) received substantially positive reviews from Byé (1936, 558-559) and Giuseppe Ugo Papi (1940-1945, 422-423).

On international and domestic economic organization, one can begin by noting a review by Byé (1935, 1206) of Carlo Bucci's *Nuovo equilibrio economico (Origine, decorso e sbocco della crisi mondiale)* (Milan, 1933), which was described as very interesting from the statistical point of view but somewhat superficial from the theoretical perspective. On the real and monetary international economy, Baudin (1930, 175) praised Attilio Cabiati's *Scambi internazionali e politica bancaria in regime di moneta sana ed avariata* (Turin, 1929) for its persuasive and up-to-date thesis of the lasting validity of the theory of comparative costs but noted the limited nature of the English-language bibliographical choices. Dehove (1949, 102-103) reviewed Amedeo Gambino's *Gli ammodernamenti della teoria degli scambi internazionali* (Padua, 1946) and emphasized the discussion of the recent modifications to the theory of international commerce and the presentation of Gambino's own theoretical contributions.

On industrial organization, Pirou (1935, 1420-1421) reviewed volume VII of *Nuova collana di economisti stranieri e italiani* (1934) and noted Masci's interesting interpretation of the new organization of the machine industry on monopolistic lines (thus requiring public intervention). Similarly, Bartoli (1950, 555) reviewed De Luca's *Diffusione dei costi di produzione* (Naples, 1950) and praised the deep analysis of the question of the influence that public intervention has on the costs of production for businesses.

There were also mentions of works on the subject of general economic equilibrium. Byé (1937, 170-171) reviewed Giorgio Tagliacozzo's *Economia e massimo edonistico collettivo. Saggio sul problema del massimo benessere collettivo nella scienza economica* (Padua, 1933) and appreciated the use of the Pigou doctrine for a criticism of the theories of collective maximization. Moret (1939, 601) reviewed Giulio La Volpe's *Studi sulla teoria dell'equilibrio economico dinamico generale* (Naples, 1936) and noted the in-depth analysis of the issue and the way in the discussion of the dynamic equilibrium of single agents and of the economic system was followed by a discussion that extended the ideas to certain general observations: while this made for a most interesting contribution, it would probably restrict its readership to mathematical economists. Bartoli reviewed La Volpe's next volume *Convenienza economica collettiva* (Padua, 1948) and praised its reconstructive criticism of the economy of well-being in terms of a collective re-evaluation of well-being (which received an important analytical discussion), and went so far as to suggest that the work be included in a possible collection of French translations of the most important foreign authors.

Monographic studies on corporativism in REP will be discussed in the section on economic and social policies. However, we will mention here Papi's review (1939, 427-428)[14] of Massimo Fovel's *L'identité des actions économiques de l'individu et de l'Etat dans l'économie corporative* (Ferrara, 1938), in which he claims Fovel's central idea is that the pure corporative economy will only be able to be created when there is compatibility between the exchange actions of the individual and the supervisory action of the State. As a curious reflection of the times, he adds that the complex expository style of the author did not mean that he could not be included among the best scholars of contemporary economic thought, particularly if he was compared to the anaemic writing of many studies claiming to deal with pure economics.

THEORY OF PUBLIC FINANCE

During the entire period under consideration, REP showed great interest in monographic publications on public finance.

From its beginning up to the First World War, the journal carried news of volumes of a more economic slant but also reported volumes of a juridical approach. Thus the Austrian economist Emile Loew (1891, 116-119) reviewed Amilcare Puviani's two volumes *Questioni preliminari ad uno studio dell'imposta sui fabbricati* (Bologna, 1889) and *Il contenuto dell'imposta seconda la scienza delle finanze ed il diritto finanziario* (Perugia, 1890), with some criticism of the theoretical pretensions of the former but words of praise for the acute discussion in the latter of the various legislative solutions that had been proposed for the problem of levels of taxation.

Gide (1890, 338) reviewed Ugo Mazzola's *I dati scientifici della finanza pubblica* (Rome, 1890) and appreciated its application of the new science of optimizing economics to issues of public finance and also emphasized the importance, for French readers, of the exposition of the finance theories of Wagner,

[14] The Roman professor later took on the task of producing Papi (1946), an interesting survey of Italian economic writing during the period of the war, when the journal had practically suspended its activity.

Sax, Stein and Schaffle as well as of the public finance studies by such Italian authors as Ricca-Salerno, Ferrara, Pantaleoni, "qui, malheureusement, sont fort peu connus en France". Emile Massa (1893, 622-623) reviewed Emilio Cossa's *I fenomeni della finanza pubblica e i loro rapporti con l'economia sociale* (Milan, 1892) and appreciated the development of the concept of the State as a supplier of services freely requested by individuals. Gide (1898, 356-357) also reviewed Flora's *La finanza e la questione sociale* (Turin, 1897), which he considered more literary than scientific in view of its argument that the solution to the social question could only be religious and not political and financial.

This coincided with a short period of intense attention by Gide to the finance studies of Alessandro Garelli. First Gide (1897, 93-94) reviewed *L'imposta successoria* (Turin, 1896) and, as well as agreeing with inheritance tax, he praised the volume for its comprehensive information which made it of interest for the debate then taking place in the French parliament. He then (1898, 473-475) placed *La proprietà sociale* (Hoepli, 1898) within the solidarity school and praised its attempt to explain taxation on the basis of sharing in common property but criticized the overly nebulous definition of the boundaries between public and private property. In reviewing (1899, 730-731) *Filosofia del monopolio* (Milan, 1899), he noted the original but contradictory idea that price differentiation according to individual utilities may increase social utility, which he considered an argument in favour of progressive taxation. Lastly, he reviewed (1900, 920-921) *Diritto internazionale tributario* (Turin, 1899) while it was Landry (1904, 421-424) who reviewed the first volume of the treatise on *Le imposte nello stato moderno* dedicated to *L'imposizione personale secondo il diritto finanziario positivo* (Milan, 1903).This was followed by reviews by Réné Gonnard (1901, 212-213) of Federico Flora's study of international comparison of federal financial systems *Le finanze degli stati composti* (Turin, 1900), by Marcel Porte (1904, 167-169) of Ivanoe Bonomi's *La finanza locale e i suoi problemi* (Milan, 1903), by Dalla Volta (1904, 151-153) of Achille Plebano's *Storia della finanza italiana dalla costituzione del nuovo Regno alla fine del secolo XIX* (Turin, 1899-1902) and Luigi Nina's *L'imposta di successione nella scienza, nella storia e nel diritto italiano* (Turin, 1902). Landry wrote a positive review (1909, 641-643, 842-843) of Fabrizio Natoli's *L'imposta sull'incremento di valore del suolo urbano* (Palermo, 1908) and *Studi sugli effetti economici dell'imposta* (Palermo, 1909).

The period following the First World War reflected the gradual affirmation of the political-legal public finance school and opened with an interesting article *L'état actuel de la science des finances en Italie* (1919, 432-454), in which Pirou gave an accurate account of Italian finance literature and emphasized its vitality in contrast with the crisis afflicting the same sector in France. Pirou remained the reviewer in this sector up to the 1920s. He first reviewed (1921, 511-513) Ettore Lolini's *Dell'attività finanziaria nella dottrina e nella realtà. Saggio di una sistemazione scientifica dei fenomeni finanziari* (Rome, 1920) and appreciated its original political approach to the study of financial problems but disagreed with its absolute nature which in particular ignored social psychology variables. Subsequently Pirou reviewed (1922, 103) Aldo Contento's *Per una teoria induttiva dei dazi sul grano e sulla farina* (Florence-Rome, 1919) and emphasized its empirical result that grain and wheat taxes are transferred not only to national consumers but also to foreign exporters; he then reviewed (1924, 1128-1129) Antonio Calandra's *La ripercussione dell'imposta sul reddito* (Turin, 1923) and appreciated the doubt it raised as to whether a tax on income increases the taxpayer's activity but he looked forward to this idea being tested against reality; he also reviewed (1924, 719) Gangemi's *La politica economica e finanziaria del governo fascista nel periodo dei pieni poteri* (Bologna, 1924) and appreciated its comprehensive information but also noted the author's unconditional approval for Mussolini's writings.

Pirou later handed over the role of public finance reviewer to Trotabas whose first review (1931, 1511) was a positive one of Ernesto d'Albergo's *La crisi dell'imposta personale sul reddito. La riforma dell'imposta nel Belgio* (Padua, 1931) which supported the view that direct income tax should be replaced by indirect taxation. He then reviewed (1931, 1150-1151) Gangemi's short volume *La politica finanziaria del governo fascista* (Palermo, 1929) judging it as simply descriptive but with a rich bibliography, following Lescure's review (1926, 1099-1100) of Benvenuto Griziotti's *La politica finanziaria italiana* (Milan, 1926). Trotabas (1932, 1201-1202) later wrote a long review of *Le tasse nella scienza e nel diritto positivo italiano* and *L'imposizione delle imprese di carattere internazionale* (Padua, 1930) by Mario Pugliese (a follower of Griziotti). He agreed with their legal-political approach and appreciated their analytical acumen but noted, particularly for the latter volume, that the proposed solutions were insufficient in practice. He appreciated (1940-1945, 137-138) Pugliese's *La Finanza e i suoi compiti extra-fiscali negli Stati moderni* (Padua, 1932) for the same reasons. Griziotti's *Vecchi e nuovi indirizzi nella scienza delle finanze* (Padova, 1935) was greeted by Trotabas (1938, 1674-1675) as the history of the shift of Italian public finance from the economistic trend of De Viti De Marco to the legal-political trend of Griziotti which had made an impact in France as well as in Italy. But, in his review (1938, 212-213) of Barone's *Opere economiche* (Bologna 1936), Pirou commented on the presence, in the collection, of essays in financial economics and on the different theoretical presentation of this discipline compared to the juridical form then in vogue in France;

On the other hand, in 1946 Dehove published (249-291, 436-456) a long essay *Oeuvre financière d'Antonio De Viti De Marco* presenting a theoretical analysis of De Viti's theory of public finance. And lastly, Bartoli reviewed (1948, 658-659) Aldo Scotto's *Gli aspetti economici e finanziari della durata degli impianti produttivi* and *Sulla pressione comparata dell'imposta sul reddito e dell'imposta sul consumo* (Genoa, 1947) and emphasized the originality and formal rigour of the former (and looked forward to French development of the theme) and the theoretical brilliance of the latter.

History of economic thought and economic methodology

During the period from its foundation to the First World War, REP seems to have paid limited attention to Italian studies of history of economic thought.

The first monographic study of the history of Italian economic thought cited in REP was Hermann von Schullern-Scrattenhofen's, *Die theoretische Nationalökonomie Italiens in neuester Zeit*, (Leipzig, Duncker und Humboldt, 1891), which Conigliani described (1892, 214-216) as an excellent way to present the work of contemporary Italian economists to a foreign readership. These economists were in fact producing publications which deserved to be better known outside Italy, thanks in part to a better knowledge of foreign languages among Italian economists. Von Schullern-Scrattenhofen had applied Cossa's method and gathered together the views of Italian economists on the major economic issues (method, production, circulation, distribution, consumption, history of theories and statistics). However, because of the amount of material covered, he had failed to distinguish sufficiently between the great writers (the theoretical importance of Loria was overlooked) and the less important, and had eschewed the perhaps more effective method of monographic studies of specific topics (for example, the Cossa school, the new classical school, cooperation and popular banks, university socialism, the theory of Loria, etc)[15]. Conigliani (1894, 813-814) also reviewed Tangorra's *Teoria economica della produzione* (Roma, 1893) and judged its treatment of the issue to be complete from the point of view of history of ideas but bemoaned the lack of any comparison with the new Austrian theory of value.

For his part, Gide (1896, 834-837) reviewed the publications by Emilio Cossa - *Il metodo degli economisti classici nelle sue relazioni col progresso della scienza economica* (Bologna, 1895) and *Il principio di popolazione di Tommaso Roberto Malthus* (Bologna, 1895). He appreciated the bibliographical richness (typical of Italian scholarship and already praised previously) and gave a positive assessment of the attempt to reconcile the classical and historical schools in their interest for reality, as well as the accurate exposition of the thought of Malthus, of which the author seemed to be a supporter. In his review of Arturo Labriola's *Le dottrine economiche di Quesnay* (Naples, 1897), Gide (1899, 471-473) appreciated the bibliographical fullness, the clear representation of the Tableau économique and the emphasis given to the theoretical originality of the physiocrats, but deplored the excessive harshness of the criticism of Smith. Moreover, the REP editor also reviewed (1910, 414-415, 688-690) Labriola's subsequent volumes *Il capitalismo* (Turin, 1910) and *Karl Marx, l'économiste, le socialiste* (Paris, Rivière, 1910) and noted the original treatment of a subject on which the journal had published *Sur l'interprétation économique de l'histoire*

[15] Bousquet (1929, 1680-1681) later followed the same critical line in his brief presentation of Kühne (1928). He emphasized that the volume was a novelty for German-language literature but criticized the choice to give a detailed presentation, rather than a synthetic and critical one, of the thought of the various authors.

(1904, 111-132), a long essay in which Dalla Volta had discussed the reasons for the success of materialism in historical studies.

Interesting references to Italian discussions of economic methodology also appear in this period. Conigliani (1895, 285-287) appreciated the lucid and balanced exposition that characterized Supino's *Il metodo induttivo nell'economia politica* (Turin, 1894) but also noted that the application of the inductive method was rarely possible, which lent support to the legitimacy of the continued, though not a-critical, use of the deductive method. The *Introduzione all'economia matematica* by Filippo Virgili and Cesare Garibaldi (Milan, 1899) was included by Gide (1899, 831) among the attempts to make it possible for economists to understand mathematical economics. Gide however judged himself to be too incompetent to assess whether or not the attempt had been successful, but did express the opinion that in order to practice mathematical economics one had to possess not only the language but also the spirit of mathematics. Landry (1906, 414-415) reviewed *Disarmonie economiche e disarmonie morali* by Mario Calderoni (Firenze, 1906) with a positive assessment of the attempt to clarify what ideas the economist could contribute to the moralist.

The impact of Italian historical studies was without doubt more lively in the period following the First World War, a period ushered in by the lecture by Arias (1919, 261-277) on *Les idées économiques et sociales de Giuseppe Mazzini.* Michels (1921, 639-640) presented *La teoria dei cambi esteri di Bernardo Davanzati* by Giuseppe Candido Noaro (Rome, 1921) as an important contribution to the history of economic thought, since it showed how Davanzati's monetary theory was an important step from scholasticism to early mercantilism. This subject was developed further by Arias in his 1922 article *Les precurseurs de l'économie monetaire en Italie: Davanzati et Montanari* (733-750).

As for studies of the classic writers, Pirou (1922, 677) emphasized the clear exposition (though lacking in originality) of Graziani's *Ricardo e J.S. Mill* (Bari, 1921). Jean Boudon (1922, 677) reviewed *Teoria di Carlo Marx sulla miseria crescente e le sue origini. Contributo alla storia delle dottrine economiche* by Arturo Labriola (Turin, 1922) and appreciated the attempt to show that Marx's theory of growing poverty originated in the 17th century and also to identify Marx's contribution to this subject.[16] Thereafter Pirou (1925, 625) presented Jacopo Mazzei's study *La politica economica internazionale inglese prima di Adamo Smith* (Milan, 1924) and Albert Aftalion (1927, 173-174) reviewed Adolfo Crosara's *Saggio sulle teorie dello scambio e della capitalizzazione* (Bologna, 1926), commenting on the accurate exposition of Smith's ideas and of

[16] Labriola continued to feature in REP. Pirou's (1923, 875-877) review of Labriola (1922) pointed Labriola's aversion for methodological individualism and his move towards Loria's materialism. The last review of Labriola was by Emile James (1935, 1212-1213), of Labriola (1933), which praised the originality of the volume, which showed how all explanations of economic crisis had failed, and proposed a physiological description of crisis.

contemporary ideas, but pointing out the lack of any reference to the work of Böhm-Bawerk, which he considered to be crucial.

Subsequently Michels (who in 1924, 855-868 had published a learned article *Quelques propos sur le role de la terminologie dans la science économique* in which he supported a unified terminology for economics and sociology) did not enjoy unqualified acceptance from REP [17]. *La teoria demografica del Malthus nella storia delle dottrine economiche* (Naples, 1929) was reviewed by Gonnard (1930, 383) who pointed out that the bibliography was not completely up to date and that Michels' support for Fascist anti-migration policy allowed the reviewer to state that, if this policy was not accompanied by a recovery of the Italian national economy, it would lead to a drop in birth rate. Gonnard (1932, 1183-1184) also reviewed *Introduzione alla storia delle dottrine economiche e politiche, con un saggio sulla economia classica italiana e la sua influenza sulla scienza economica* (Bologna, 1932) and noted that it was not suitable as a textbook and that its international bibliography was incomplete, but supported the call by Michels for studies of Italian economists of the past (of which Michels gave some examples) and also of the present. Gonnard also (1933, 200-201) reviewed Filippo Carli's *Studi di storia delle dottrine economiche* (Padua, 1932), with words of praise for its elegant ability to synthesize (even if the bibliography was incomplete), and then (1934, 1052-1053) Modestino Manfra's study of *Pietro Verri e i problemi economici del tempo suo* (Milano, 1932) with praise for its clear and simple exposition.

In the mid-1930s, REP showed considerable interest in the work of Francesco Ferrara. The Sicilian economist had previously received some attention, in a long study by Dalla Volta, *Francesco Ferrara et son oeuvre économique* (1902, 377-421, which described Ferrara's work as a page in the history of economic ideas that was important beyond Italy), in the mention by Virgilio Gayda (1909, 153-154) of *Scritti monetari di Francesco Ferrara e di Angelo Messedaglia* (Padua, 1908), and in the review by Michels (1925, 770) of the monograph by Carlo Battistella *Francesco Ferrara nella scienza e nella politica economica* (Rome, 1924). The publication in 1935 of *Lezioni di economia politica di Francesco Ferrara* (Bologna, 1934) led Bousquet (1403-1404) to praise Ferrara as the greatest exponent of Italian liberalism, and to describe him as "à bien des égards, très supérieur à Stuart Mill". Bousquet remarked on the importance of the rediscovery of Ferrara, especially in an era of dominant Statalism, and called for the translation into French of his famous prefaces and claimed that the time had come for a general study of Ferrara's work. The translation was carried out by Bousquet himself (with the assistance of J. Crisafulli) and the volume *Oeuvres économiques choisies* (Paris, Rivière, 1938) was reviewed by Georges Bourgin (1938, 1025-

[17] The journal did, however, dedicate a necrology to its faithful collaborator in 1936 (1416-1417), under the pen of Oualid, who praised Michels' cultural pluralism and his longstanding friendship with France, notwithstanding his personal support for Fascism.

1026). The reviewer described Ferrara's liberalism as even more intransigent as Guyot's and de Molinari's and concentrated on the theory of cost of reproduction, interpreting this not as an early version of marginalistic economics but as a more precise reformulation of the classical theory of value.

The end of the 1930s saw the final, rich season of reviews by Pirou. The review (1935, 1824-1825) of Giuseppe Santonastaso's *Georges Sorel* (Bari, 1932) e *Proudhon* (Bari, 1935) praised the bibliographical completeness and the interpretative depth of the former but noted the lack of originality of the latter, at least for a French readership. Pirou (1936, 1433-1434) praised *Saggi critici di teoria e metodologia economica* by Guglielmo Masci (Catania, 1934) for the clear methodological discussion in favour of the deductive and marginalistic method and, in his review of Francesco Vito's *Economia politica corporativa. Parte generale* (Milano, 1938), he (1939, 890) commented favourably on the author's courage in maintaining his interest for English-language economic thought (which had recently earned him criticism from Arias) and praised the perceptive methodological discussion, even if this meant further criticism of him from the nationalistic Italian academy.

The last Italian historical writings were reviewed by Gonnard. He described (1940-1945, 114-115) *I problemi metodologici nella storia delle dottrine politiche ed economiche* by Felice Battaglia and Alberto Bertolino (Rome, 1939) as an interesting introduction to the history of economic ideas. He praised (1945, 209-210) *Dal naturalismo al Neo-Volontarismo. La dottrina economica di J.C.L. Sismondo de Sismondi* by Armando Belleri (Milan, 1940) (despite some non-negligible gaps in the bibliography) as one of the best studies of Sismondi, in the Fanfani line (and here Gonnard recalled Fanfani's distinction between voluntaristic theories, naturalistic theories and neo-voluntaristic, i.e. anti-naturalistic theories). Finally, in his review (1950, 554-555) of *La terza via nelle teorie di Menegazzi, Keynes, Beveridge e Röpke* (Lecce, 1950) by Alfredo Aiello, Gonnard commented on the argument that the most complete treatment of the "third way" had been written by Guido Menegazzi.

Themes and problems of social and economic policy

This section covers one of the sectors of Italian scientific publication that was probably of greatest interest to REP, given the applied orientation of the journal up to the Second World War. The issues covered can be grouped around the following topics: cooperation, emigration and colonization, the war economy and the reconstruction economy, the monetary crisis (national and international) and corporativism.

The writings by Ugo Rabbeno on cooperatives mentioned above were complemented, initially, by an essay by Vincenzo Meneghelli *Le mouvement coopératif en Italie* (1892, 855-889), a long (and passionately critical) review of the issues of Italian cooperation, which was later completed by an article by Luigi

Sbrojavacca *Des sociétés cooperatives en Italie autres que les sociétés de crédit* (1892, 1268-1286)[18]. At the beginning of the new century, Georges Blondel (1902, 368-370) and Gide (1903, 286-288) discussed the monographic volume by Giovanni Lorenzoni *La cooperazione agraria nella Germania Moderna* (Trent, 1902). In 1907, in his review (72-74) of *Il fatto cooperativo nell'evoluzione sociale* (Bologna, 1906) by Mariano Mariani, Gide recognised Italy as the country that had most studied the phenomenon of cooperation and acknowledged that this volume had compensated, with its theoretical dimension, for the empirical tendency of cooperation studies. Gide detected this same tendency again, with approval, in the book by Angelo Mariotti *Della intermediazione e dei suoi rapporti con la cooperazione e la concentrazione capitalistica nel commercio al minuto* (Naples, 1914). Gide did not hesitate to describe (1923, 590-592) the volume by Giovanni Preziosi *Cooperativismo rosso. Piovra dello Stato* (Bari, 1922) as a testimony of the type of aggression that Fascism was by this time carrying out against Italian cooperation. The last reference to cooperation is found in Vakhan Totomianz's review (1931, 1138-1139) of the booklet by Ernesto Lama entitled *Cooperazione* (Lanciano, 1930), in which Lama's respectful attitude towards the cooperative tradition is noted but at the same time Fascist cooperation is no longer seen as an alternative, but simply as a correction, to capitalism.

Studies on emigration and colonization received fragmentary but not insignificant attention. This began with the publication of the essay by Pietro Sitta *Le problème de l'immigration dans les Etats-Unis de l'Amérique* (1893, 815-832), which claimed that European emigration to the USA would continue as long as Europe had greater demographic density, and hence lesser well-being, that the USA, and another by Dalla Volta *L'emigration anglaise* (1898, 311-327), which showed the fundamental role of private assistance in the success of English emigration. This idea was developed more fully by Dalla Volta in his study on *Bienfaisance au point de vue sociologique* (1906, 185-208). In 1907 Gide (152-154) wrote a detailed review of Marco Fanno's volumes *Il regime e la concessione delle terre nelle colonie moderne* (Padua, 1905) and *L'espansione commerciale e coloniale degli Stati moderni* (Turin, 1906), and concluded that the author's youth had led him to transform political economy into an epic poem. Gide and Lescure (1915, 98) wrote a brief review of Carlo Grilli's *Gli esperimenti coloniali nell'Africa neolatina* (Roma, 1914) with special approval

[18] It is interesting to note how much space Gide reserved, during this period, to the echoes in Italy of the rival school of Le Play. He published two articles by Santangelo-Spoto (1893), which proposed a long critical examination of the conflict over the issues of private property which, at the 18th Italian Workers Congress, had set the republican and collectivist wings against each other. Santangelo-Spoto, too, defended the concept of a renewed individualism, a concept he also elaborated in his Santangelo-Spoto (1894). In his review (1893, 1092-1094), Gide appreciated the book's value as source of information but commented ironically on the author's proposal that the solution to Italian social problems lay in the conservation of the integrity of agricultural property.

for the arguments in favour of Franco-Italian colonial cooperation. Again on the migration question, Blondel (1912, 657) made reference to *Protectionnisme ouvrier* by Giuseppe Prato (Paris, Rivière, 1912), and emphasized the completeness of the investigation and the support for a liberal solution to the issue of immigration. On the other hand Oualid (1929, 342), in his review of Filippo Virgili's volume *Emigrazione* (Rome, 1928), spoke highly of the new Italian policy in this sector.

One also finds references to the Italian literature on the war economy and the problems of reconstruction. Most references on the former topic are found following the First World War, and on the latter following the Second World War. Oualid (1918, 316) refers to the lectures on the war economy given by Graziani and Mariotti and published in the collective volume *La legislazione di guerra* (Naples, 1916). He applauded (1919, 606-607) Francesco Gallina's monographic volume *Sull'economia di guerra* (Palermo, 1918) as a useful summary on the international literature on the topic, to which German writings needed to be added. Gide (1918, 634-636), in a review of Franco Savorgnan's volume *La guerra e la popolazione* (Bologna, 1918), took issue with the thesis that war ensures the suppression of the worst elements of the population. In the same spirit, in his review (1919, 348-349) of Lanfranco Maroi's *I fattori demografici del conflitto europeo* (Rome, 1919), he rejected its central thesis that war may be explained with sole reference to demographic imbalances. Furthermore, in reviewing Carlo Grilli's *Il protezionismo dopo la guerra* (Rome, 1921), Gide commented (1922, 385-386) on the choice of liberalism but questioned the thesis that economic freedom guarantees peace, and instead agreed (1923, 605) with the thesis of the volume by Angelo Fraccacreta *Sicurezza ed insicurezza economica* (Naples, 1923) that stressed the importance of economic security for world reconstruction.

In 1947 Dehove reviewed (503-504) *L'economia e la guerra* by Federico Chessa (Turin, 1946), and applauded the author's attempt to explain the methodological reasons that allow an economic analysis of war with costs and benefits, as well as the author's examination of the conditions for the achievement of peaceful collaboration between countries. He also reviewed (504-506) *La ricostruzione economica e il suo finanziamento* by Francesco Coppola d'Anna (Milan, 1946) and analyzed the conditions for the economic reconstruction of Italy and the role of the State and of international loans. Lastly, Baudin reviewed (1947, 173-174) Papi's I*ntroduction to post-war reconstruction programmes* (Rome, 1944) noting the macro-economic analysis of the conditions for reconstruction in a free regime.

The attention paid by REP to Italian studies of monetary issues began with Christian de Boeck , mentioned above, who (1893, 742-743) discussed an article by Carlo Francesco Ferraris *La riorganizzazione delle banche di emissione* ("Nuova Antologia", 16 April 1891) and applauded the author's support for the creation of an issue monopoly in Italy, a position he considered worthy of consideration for the added reason that the renewal of the monopoly of the Bank of France was being considered at the same time[19].

This attention resumed with great intensity after the First World War. Pirou (1922, 819) gave a positive presentation of the study by Camillo Supino *La carta moneta in Italia* (Bologna, 1921) and paid particular attention to the part on post-war inflation. In 1926 Louis Baudin analyzed (1241-1242) the study by Giulio Alessio *La rivalutazione della lira* (Milan, 1926) and agreed with the importance accorded by the author to moral factors in the success of currency stabilization policy. In 1928 (1632-1633) Baudin gives a brief account of *Saggi di riporto e di deporto della lira italiana a Londra dal 1921 al 1928* by Giovanni Demaria (Milan, 1928). Baudin reviewed (1936, 275-276) *Evolution monétaire dans le monde depuis la guerre de 1914* di Griziotti (Paris, Sirey, 1935) and applauded the synthesis of fifteen years of international monetary turbulence and disagreed with the political postulates of the analysis, such as the claim that world political power should be violently redistributed or the need for the monetary sovereignty of the State. Similarly, in his review (1937, 196) of *Poincaré, La stabilizzazione del franco e gli ammassamenti d'oro in Francia* by Mario Alberti (Milan, 1932), Baudin found the analysis correct but took issue with the bias inherent in the under-evaluation of the political responsibilities for the World War and for the present protectionism. Baudin also reviewed (1937, 1641-1642, 1938,1031-1032) the double-volume set by the same author *Guerra delle monete, t.1 La lotta dell'oro contro l'argento e della carta contro l'oro, t.II Schieramenti e battaglie fra le valute* (Como, 1937), and highlighted the brilliant exposition and the clear demonstration of what responsibilities the British bore for the current monetary quagmire and how the French were failing to assert their gold orthodoxy on the world stage. Jean Saint-Germès reviewed (1936, 1442) *Problema del trend secolare nelle fluttuazioni dei prezzi* by Jenny Griziotti Kretschmann (Pavia, 1935) and praised her ability to explain seven centuries of price variations by referring not only to the variable of currency but also to changes in economic organization. But in his review of *Dell'autarchia economica e finanziaria ed economia mondiale* (Padua, 1937) by the same author, Landry (1939, 623-624) questioned the claim that autarchy aimed to maximize the well-being and not the power of a country that practised it. Similarly, in his review of Cabiati's *Fisiologia e patologia economica negli scambi della ricchezza fra gli stati* (Turin, 1937), Pirou (1939, 635-636) welcomed the political analysis that the world economic crisis was due to the choice, made during the First World War, to turn away from the beneficial laws of rational economics, which humanity no longer seemed to want to accept.

---

[19] Mention must be made of the review (1894, 618-619) by Emile Massa of Marjorana (1894), which highlighted the author's pessimism regarding how effective the constitution of the Banca d'Italia would be as a solution to the question of emission.

Finally, Bresciani Turroni was remembered at the end of the 1930s. Baudin (1938, 1288) took his cue from the publication of the English edition of *Vicende del Marco tedesco* (*The economics of inflation. A study of currency depreciation in post-war Germany*, New York, 1938) and recalled the author's conclusions (depreciation of the mark was unfavourable to the German economy and caused by internal monetary policy). In 1939, Moret wrote a note (601-602) on the booklet *Inductive verification of the theory of international payments* (Cairo, 1933) and agreed with the analysis of the well-known German case but regretted the fact that the eternal problems of balance of payments were presented from time to time as if they were new.

Lastly, the interest of REP in the issues of corporativism seems to us to have begun with the attention paid to the booklet by Ulisse Gobbi *La scienza economica e la crisi sociale* (Milan, 1921). In his review Pirou (1924, 413) observed that the author looked favourably on the workers' control of factories as a means to solve the conflict between capital and labour. Pirou also reviewed (1926, 1250-1251) the volume by Supino *Le basi economiche del movimento operaio* (Milan, 1925) and noted the argument that Fascism had acted properly in reorienting the trade union movement in a patriotic direction and was wrong when it denied the conflict of interest between capital and labour and attempted to reunite them in the same organization.

While we must remember the attention paid by REP to Gaetano Napolitano at the beginning of the 1930s, the first review of literature on corporation is, strictly speaking, Roger Picard's review (1930, 159) of the volume by Gangemi, *Il problema della durata del lavoro* (Florence, 1929). Picard noted Gangemi's broad knowledge of the international literature and his support for the Fascist solution, that is to make individual needs conditional on those of the State. Michels (1930, 1021) described the volume by Arias *L'economia nazionale corporativa* (Rome, 1929) as a useful synthesis of corporative theory and stressed that the author did not see corporations as a panacea but as one way of taking the heat out of social conflicts. In his review (1935, 1209-1210) of *Capitalismo e Corporativismo* by Ugo Spirito (Florence, 1934), Byé saw a conception of corporativism that was very close to socialism. However when François Perroux (1933, 1627-1629) reviewed Gangemi's volumes *Lineamenti di politica economica corporativa* (Catania, 1932) and *Le società anonime miste* (Florence, 1933), he agreed with the interpretation of corporativism, in the former, as an economic policy correction of capitalism and praised the latter for its bibliographical breadth but lamented the absence of any theoretical analysis of mixed property companies. In an article of 1934, *La politique économique du corporatisme fasciste* (1537-1574), Gerolamo Bassani reported on the way corporativism was attempting to organize the Italian economy. Bousquet then gave the first empirical assessment of this experience in his review (1938, 1644) of the booklet by Eugenio Cacace *I sindacati industriali e la distribuzione del reddito* (Rome, 1934), where he noted the argument that Fascist economic policy could modify Pareto's income curve towards less inequality but also noted that there was no proof that this was actually happening.

CONCLUSIONS

The view that REP had of Italian economic thought was the result not only of the nature of Italian scientific publication but also of the very particular choices made by the journal. From its foundation up to the Second World War, the journal had always been outside the mainstream of Parisian *économistes* and, later, of mathematical economists. For this reason, while the journal was aware of the varied spectrum of Italian economists on this period, it ended up paying greatest attention to non-liberal literary economists, especially those who proposed new interpretations of economic phenomena and new solutions to their problematic features.

In line with this approach, the writer given most attention was Loria, even if his theory of free land was attacked for being largely arbitrary in nature and having uncertain political consequences, at the same time as he was admired because of the intellectual energy with which he was used it to explain all economic reality. The cooperativist Rabbeno and the reformist Nitti were, on the other hand, followed affectionately because of their interest in the political applications of economics.

However, the attitude of REP towards Italian pure economics, under both Gide and Pirou, was one of respectful attention but not agreement. Thus, Gide praised Pantaleoni's *Principii* for their innovative conception and exposition, which made them a scientific tool in the battle against the *économistes* and the German historical school. But it was not until the mid 1920s that the journal turned again to Pantaleoni's economic thought and praised its provocative intelligence but questioned the dogmatic persistence of its hedonistic hypothesis. In the same way, Gide praised the originality of Pareto's research but criticized the dispersive nature of its presentation and, above all, its claim that it was not intended as persuasion. For this reason, while Pareto's mathematical economics was not rejected by Gide, it was not praised by the journal until after the First World War (even with criticism for Pareto's claim that his economics was like the Pillars of Hercules of the discipline) and was only recognised as one of the fundamental components of the discipline after the Second World War.

Between the two wars, REP seemed to prefer Ricci's version of mathematical economics, because it was no longer heavily conditioned by liberal ideology and because of its attempt to explain certain, particular aspects of reality (Del Vecchio was later considered in a similar way). The free-trade orientation was constantly criticized in citations in REP of the work of Einaudi, while his political liberalism was always appreciated. Another indication of the militant but not extremist reforming character of the journal was the interest always shown for the work of Rignano and Graziadei, two heretics of Italian socialism.

Also worthy of note is the attention paid by REP to the Italian publication of textbooks and manuals during this period. The greatest praise seems to have been reserved for Luigi Cossa (he was still being praised after the First World War), while texts in pure economics took longer to gain approval, either because they initially attempted to paraphrase Pareto's *Manuel* or because of the corporative influence of the volumes by Amoroso and Papi (which were, however, praised on other counts). After the Second World War, only texts of mathematical economics drew praise from the journal (which remained, however, sceptical towards the complex proposal developed by Palomba).

Lastly, we have brought to light the considerable attention paid by REP to the publication of monographs by many authors who were not particularly closely followed by the journal (and who, in many cases, were in fact less important). These authors did however deal with economic applications to which REP gave primary importance: so, alongside cooperation, we have registered significant interest for Italian studies of emigration and colonialization, the economics of war and reconstruction, the monetary crisis and corporativism.

Many of the reviewers of the work of Italian economists were of considerable importance in the history of French economic thought (including Gide, Landry, Pirou, Bartoli, Baudin, Gonnard, Lescure and Perroux). A deeper understanding of the role of the Italian texts discussed above in the construction of the thought of these authors is one of the possible future avenues for this complex investigation which aims to reconstruct the fortune of modern Italian economic thought in the country which, it seems reasonable to state, gave it the greatest attention.

References

Arias G. (1911), *Forme moderne dell'impresa industriale e commerciale*, Rome.

Bachi R. (1933), *Le regioni nell'economia nazionale*, Rome.

Cossa E. (1888), *Concetto e forma dell'impresa industriale*, Milan.

Cossa E. (1889), *Primi elementi di economia agricola*, Milan.

Cossa L. (1892), *Introduzione allo studio dell'economia politica*, Milan.

Cossa L. (1899), *Histoire des doctrines économiques*, Giard et Brière, Paris.

Feilbogen S. (1892), *Smith und Turgot*, Vienna.

Flora F. (1893), *Manuale di Scienza delle Finanze*, Livorno.

Gangemi L. (1929), *Lineamenti di letteratura finanziaria*, Milan.

Gangemi L. (1932), *Svolgimento del pensiero economico*, Milan.

Garino-Canina A. (1916), *Intorno al concetto di industria naturale nella letteratura economica*, Turin.

Graziani A. (1911-1929), *Istituzioni di scienza delle finanze*, Turin.

Griziotti B. (1929), *Principii di politica, diritto e scienza delle finanze*, Padua.

Griziotti B. (1930), *Primi lineamenti delle dottrine finanziarie in Italia nell'ultimo cinquantennio*, Padua.

Kühne O. (1928), *Die mathematische schule der Nationalökonomie: die italienische Schüle*, Berlin.

Labriola A. (1922), *Il valore della scienza economica*, Naples.

Labriola A. (1933), *L'Etat et la crise*, Rivière, Paris.

Majorana G. (1894), *I dati statistici nella questione bancaria*, Rome.

Marconcini F. (1914), *L'industria domestica salariata nei rapporti interni ed internazionali*, Naples.

Mauri A. (1924), *La storia delle dottrine nell'economia sociale*, Rome.

Medici G. (1946), *L'agricoltura e la riforma agraria*, Milan.

Montemartini G. (1916), *Municipalizzazione dei pubblici servizi*, Milan.

Mortara G. (1922), *Lezioni di statistica metodologica*, Città di Castello.

Niceforo A. (1919), *La misura della vita*, Turin.

Niceforo A. (1923), *La misura della vita*, Messina.

Niceforo A. (1923), *Metodo statistico*, Messina.

Niceforo A. (1925), *La méthode statistique et ses applications aux sciences naturelles, aux sciences sociales et à l'art*, Giard, Paris.

Papi G.U. (1946), *Bibliographie des ouvrages et articles en langue italienne publiés depuis 1940*, «Revue d'économie politique», pp. 227-236.

Pareto V. (1965), *Libre-échangisme, protectionnisme et socialisme*, Œvres Complètes, vol. 4, Droz, Genève.

Pareto V. (1987), *Marxisme et Economie pure*, Œvres Complètes, vol. 9, 2nd ed., Droz, Genève.

Pareto V. (2002), *Nouvelles pages retrouvées*, Œvres Complètes, vol. 32, Droz, Genève (in preparation).

Penin M. (1996), *La Revue d'économie politique ou l'essor d'une grande devancière (1887-1936)*, in L. Marco (ed.), *Les revues d'économie en France (1751-1994)*, Paris, L'Hartmattan, pp. 157-196.

Penin M. (1991), *Charles Gide, l'hétérodoxie bien tempérée*, in Y. Breton and M. Lutfalla (eds), *L'économie politique en France au XIX siècle*, Economica, Paris, pp. 303-334.

SANTANGELO-SPOTO I. (1893), *La propriété et le collectivisme* and *Individualisme et collectivisme*, «Revue d'économie politique», pp. 133-145, 444-452.
SANTANGELO-SPOTO I. (1894), *I beni di famiglia*, Caserta.
TASSINARI G. (1926), *Saggio intorno alla distribuzione del reddito nell'agricoltura italiana*, Piacenza.
TIVARONI J. (1929), *Compendio di scienza delle finanze*, Bari.

The Spread of Italian Economics in the German Language Area: 1750-1890

Christian Gehrke and Heinz D. Kurz
University of Graz

1. Introduction

To write about the spread of Italian economics in Europe presupposes, first, an elaboration of a concept of 'Italian economics' and, secondly, an elaboration of a measure how to assess its reception abroad. These are intrinsically difficult tasks which cannot be expected to be tackled other than in pragmatic terms in a short paper like this. The terms employed here are the following. We do not understand the title of the project as implying a simple leader-follower model with a superior Italian economics exporting her ideas and the inferior English, French or German economics in the role of importers. To assume such a national division with one innovater and several imitators would involve a travesty of historical facts. What can be said is that Italian economists in the period under consideration contributed to the development of important ideas and concepts and their achievements were acknowledged and occasionally even praised by their European colleagues. Conversely, Italian economics was not formed *ab ovo* but emerged in a productive discourse within the context of a European-wide scientific community of philosophers and political economists.

Studying the intellectual exchanges in the period exhibits indeed a remarkable fact: there were intensive transnational discussions with a swift diffusion of ideas across Europe, temporarily interrupted perhaps by wars and its consequences and by social and political turmoil. This communication was possible because authors generally were able to read several languages and therefore did not have to wait for translations in order to have access to new publications. It was not at all uncommon that scholars would have a sufficient command of three or even more languages in addition to their mother language (some even published in more than one language). A few examples must suffice: Jean-Baptiste Say read English, Italian and Spanish; Friedrich Benedikt Wilhelm Hermann read English, French and Italian; Karl Marx was fluent in English and French and read Italian and Spanish; Carl Menger read English, French and Italian. Moreover, it should be kept in mind that in the time period under consideration the political boundaries of the different nation states in Central Europe have changed several times. For a subperiod some regions of northern Italy were a part of the Austrian Empire, so that some of the 'Italian' economists became Austrian citizens. Pietro Verri, for instance, was temporarily an officer in the Austrian administration of Milan, and Cesare

Beccaria was appointed to a chair of economics in Milan in 1768 by the Austrian government.

Given this fertile exchange it would be difficult, if not impossible, to speak of a genuinely 'Italian economics'. If there was ever such a thing as a well defined entity, it certainly no longer existed in the period under discussion. What can at most be said is that some Italian economists deserve credit for having put forward certain important ideas or concepts in a particularly compelling way or for having contributed in significant ways to their further elaboration and sophistication. This concerned first and foremost Ferdinando Galiani and his contributions to value and monetary theory. It should also be clear that ideas developed elsewhere that get adopted do so hardly ever without some significant adaptation. And ideas that get rejected are seldomly done so without leaving traces in the writings of their critics. Intellectual victories as well as defeats are reflected in the economics literature and shape the future development of doctrines. This holds also true with regard to the issue at hand.

These considerations show that our aim in this paper of necessity has to be modest. What we intend to do is to illustrate the impact of the doctrines of some Italian authors on some German-speaking authors. On both sides it appears to make sense to focus attention on the better known authors and touch upon authors that are not so well known only in passing. More precisely, we shall especially attempt to trace the impact of the writings of Italian authors on two 'schools' of thought which are associated mainly, although not exclusively, with German-speaking economists: Marxist economics, on the one hand, and Austrian economics, on the other. Interestingly, Italian scholars were influential in both regards: their ideas were scrutinized and partly absorbed both by Karl Marx and by Carl Menger and their respective followers.

The composition of the paper is the following. In section 2 we distinguish between direct and indirect routes in the dissemination of 'Italian economics' and exemplify both routes with regard to the writings of particular authors. In section 3 we document Karl Marx's reception of the contributions of the Italian economists, and in section 4 we turn to the influence of Italian contributions in the major works of Carl Menger and Eugen von Böhm-Bawerk.

2. Direct and indirect routes

The ideas of Italian economists were either directly absorbed by their German-speaking colleagues, who read the original writings, or they learned about these ideas indirectly, that is, via the writings of some other scholars who had studied the Italian economics literature.

In the following we shall exemplify the first route with regard to Friedrich Benedikt Wilhelm Hermann and Karl-Heinrich Rau. Hermann's *Staatswirthschaftliche Untersuchungen*, published in 1832, are generally considered one of the most important contributions to economic theory stemming from a German author in the 19th century. Rau wrote a very successful and highly influential textbook that went through several editions. It should be noted that both authors referred to Custodi's collection of *Scrittori classici italiani di economia politica*, which was published in altogether fifty volumes in the period from 1803-1816, and which was of enormous importance for the international spread of 'Italian economics'.[1]

With regard to the second route it seems appropriate to distinguish between at least two main transmission channels. The first of these consists in the spread of 'Italian economics' through the writings of important non-Italian authors who were widely read in the German-speaking countries. The second channel for an indirect transmission of the ideas of the Italian authors are surveys and reviews of the Italian economic literature, which became available in the early 19th century. Those interested in Italian economics could consult, for instance, J. A. Müller's *Chronologische Darstellung der italienischen Klassiker über Nationalökonomie* (1820), which provided such a survey in German, Pecchio's *Storia della economia pubblica in Italia*, which was available in the original Italian version (see Pecchio 1829) and in a French translation (see Pecchio 1830), or Blanqui's *Histoire d'Economie politique en Europe* (1837), which was also translated into German some years later.

The indirect route will be exemplified by the writings of three non-Italian authors who were widely read in the German-speaking world and who can be said to have probably drawn the attention of many German and Austrian economists to the Italian literature: the authors under consideration are the Scotsman Adam Smith and the two Frenchmen Anne-Robert Jacques Turgot and Jean-Baptiste Say.

Indirect route: via Smith, Turgot and Say

The importance of Smith and Say for the dissemination of economic ideas in the German-speaking countries is unrivalled by that of any other author. Second in importance with regard to the indirect spreading of Italian economics are perhaps Turgot and Condillac, who were both influenced by Galiani with regard to the theory of value and interest (see Pribram, 1983, pp. 115-20, and Eltis, 1997, pp. 49-50). Smith's *Wealth of Nations* was the most important source of inspiration for German-speaking economists in the nineteenth century. While Smith had undoubtedly absorbed much of the earlier economics literature, it is not fully clear how much he knew of the Italian contributions to economics. It is

[1] While most German scholars studied, or at any rate cited, the original Italian versions, it should nevertheless be mentioned that some of the Italian works in political economy were available in German translations. Thus Genovesi's *Lezzione di commercio o sia d'economia civile*, for instance, was translated by A. Witzmann as *Grundsätze der bürgerlichen Ökonomie* (Leipzig 1776), and Verri's *Meditazioni* was published in a German translation by M. Schmidt as *Betrachtungen über Staatswirthschaft* in 1785.

known that a copy of Verri's *Meditazioni* was in Adam Smith's library, and he may have used it in the preparation of the *WN*, although he did not acknowledge Verri directly as a source. Whether or not he was familiar with the contributions of Galiani is not clear, although the latter's *Dialogues* can hardly have escaped his attention (see Hutchison, 1988, p. 270). That Galiani was influential with regard to Anne-Robert Jacques Turgot is much easier to establish. Galiani's influence is perhaps less visible in Turgot's *Réflexions* than in his lesser-known unfinished essay on *Value and Money* (1973 [1808]), which was written around 1769 but published only posthumously in 1808 in Dupont's edition of Turgot's *Œuvres*. In this essay Turgot attempted an explanation of value in terms of the interaction between 'scarcity' and 'utility'. Following Galiani, the former concept was seen as including not only the varying degrees in which the commodities under consideration are provided by nature but also the varying quantities of resources (or amounts of 'labour') required to produce them. As Ronald Meek aptly observed, in his essay Turgot in effect 'attempts to incorporate "scarcity" into "utility" – or putting it another way, to reduce the former to the latter – and by this means to base exchange value primarily on utility' (Meek, 1973, p. 79). In Turgot's essay on *Value and Money*, as in Galiani's *Della Moneta*, we thus find the germs of a utility-based theory of value and simultaneously those of the alternative approach to the theory of value – via the quantity of resources (or 'labour') required to produce the commodities. Turgot indeed explicitly referred to Galiani in connection with his statement that 'the *esteem value* of an object, for a man in isolation, is precisely that portion of the total of his resources which corresponds to the desire he has for this object, or that portion which he is willing to employ to satisfy this desire' (Turgot 1973 [1808], p. 89). With this proposition Turgot claims

> to have come into reach of one of the newest and most profound truths which the general theory of value contains. It was this truth which M. the abbé Galiani put forward, twenty years ago, in his treatise *Della Moneta*, with so much clarity and force, but with scarcely any amplification, when he said that *the common measure of all values is man*. (ibid., p. 89)

In an attempt to elaborate a pedigree for his own views, Jean-Baptiste Say screened the writings of earlier authors. In the fourth edition of his *Traité* which was translated into English as *A Treatise on Political Economy* (Say, 1971 [1821]) he provides in the introduction a summary account of his views on the history of the subject. There he states:

> In every branch of knowledge, example has preceded precept. The fortunate enterprises of the Portuguese and Spaniards during the fifteenth century, the active industry of Venice, Genoa, Florence, Pisa, the provinces of Flanders, and the free cities of Germany at this same epoch, gradually directed the attention of some philosophers to the theory of wealth.

He adds:

> These inquiries, like almost every other in the arts and sciences, after the revival of letters, originated in Italy. As far back as the sixteenth century, *Botero* was engaged in investigating the real sources of public prosperity. In the year 1613, *Antonio Serra* composed a treatise, in which he particularly noticed the productive power of industry: but the title of his work sufficiently indicates its errors. Wealth, according to his hypothesis, consisted only of gold and silver. [In a footnote the title of Serra's book is mentioned: *Breve Trattato delle cause che possono far abondare li regni d'oro et d'argento dove non sono miniere.*] *Davanzati* wrote upon money and upon exchange; and at the beginning of the eighteenth century fifty years before the time of Quesnay, *Bandini* of Sienna had shown, both from reasoning and experience, that there never had been a scarcity of food, except in those countries where the government had itself interfered to supply the people. *Belloni*, a banker at Rome, in the year 1750, published a dissertation on commerce, evincing his intimate acquaintance with the nature of money and exchanges, although at the same time infected with the theory of the balance of trade. ... *Carli*, before Dr. Smith, demonstrated that the balance of trade neither taught nor proved any thing. *Algarotti* ... wrote also upon the science of political economy; and the little he has left exhibits the accuracy and extent of his knowledge, as well as his acuteness. He confines himself so strictly to facts, and so uniformly founds his speculations on the nature of things, that although he did not get possession of the proof of his principles, and of their relation to each other, he has, nevertheless, guarded himself against every thing like hypothesis and system. In 1764, *Genovesi* commenced a course of public lectures on political economy, in the chair founded at Naples by the care of the highly esteemed and learned *Intieri*. (ibid., pp. xxix-xxx)

Say continues:

> In 1750, the abbé *Galiani*, so well known since from his connexion with many of the French philosophers, and by his Dialogues on the Corn Trade, although at that time a very young man, published a Treatise on Money, which discovered such uncommon talents and information, as to induce a belief that he had been assisted in the composition of his work by the abbé *Intieri* and the Marquess of *Rinuccini*. Its merits, however, appear to be of a description similar to those the author's writings always afterwards displayed [the reference is to Adam Smith]; genius united with erudition, carefulness in uniformly ascending to the nature of things; and an animated and elegant style. (ibid., pp. xxx-xxxi)

Say takes issue with three views put forward by Galiani. The *first* is said to contain 'some of the rudiments of the doctrine of Adam Smith'; namely, 'that labour is the sole creator of the value of things or of wealth.' The reference is to a passage in *Della Moneta* (book I, chap. 2), in which Galiani states that the 'value of things' is greater or smaller in proportion 'as it requires more or less labour' to produce them (ibid., p. xxxi, n*). According to Say this is a principle which, 'although not rigorously true, as will be made manifest in the course of this work, but which, pushed to its ultimate consequences, would have put *Galiani* in the way of discovering and completely unfolding the phenomena of production' (ibid., p. xxxi). Therefore, this discovery is said to belong no less to Galiani than to Smith. The *second* difference of opinion concerns Galiani's related view 'that man, that is to say his labour, is the only correct measure of value. This, also, according to Dr. Smith, is a principle; although considered by me as an error' (ibid., n*). *Thirdly*, Say opposes Galiani's view 'that whatever is gained by some must necessarily be lost by others; in this way proving, that a very ingenious writer may not even know how to deduce the most simple conclusions, and may pass by the truth without perceiving it.' Say goes on: 'For, if wealth can be *created* by labour, there may then be a new description of wealth in the world, not taken from anybody' (ibid., n ; Say's emphasis).

Say also stresses that several of the Italian writers of the late eighteenth century were themselves influenced by the Physiocrats:

> The economists [i.e. the Physiocrats] not only exercised a particular sway over French writers, but also had a very remarkable influence over many Italian authors, who even went beyond them. *Beccaria*, in a course of public lectures at Milan [in a footnote the reference is to the Custodi collection], first analysed the true functions of productive capital. The Count de *Verri*, the countryman and friend of Beccaria, … both a man of business and an accomplished scholar, in his *Meditazion[i] sull' Economia politica*, published in 1771, approached nearer than any other writer, before Dr. Smith, to the real laws wich regulate the production and consumption of wealth. *Filangieri*, whose treatise on political and economical laws was not given to the public until the year 1780, appears not to have been acquainted with the work of Dr. Smith, published four years before. The principles de Verri laid down are followed by Filangieri, and even received from him more complete development; but although guided by the torch of analysis and deduction, he did not proceed from the most fortunate premises to the immediate consequences which confirm them, at the same time that they exhibit their application and utility. (ibid., pp. xxxvi-xxxvii)

Several other principles established by Smith are said to have been anticipated by earlier authors. Thus, '*De Verri* had observed … that *reproduction was nothing more than the reproduction of value*, and that *the value of things constituted wealth*' (ibid., p. xxxiii, n; Say's emphases).

In the context of a discussion of the laws of production and his view that 'industry is nothing more or less than the human employment of natural agents', Say refers to Algarotti's *Opuscula*, in which the innovation of spiral springs that check the balance-wheels of watches is discussed (ibid., p. 65, n*). Say is of the opinion that such innovations add to the values of products, which is perhaps true in the short run, that is, as regards market prices, whereas in the long run the value of the product with regard to which the innovation took place will tend to fall.

In the context of a discussion of transport activities Say refers to the Napolitan political economist Genovesi who defined commerce as 'the exchange of superfluities for necessaries' (see ibid., p. 66, n*). Say disagrees. According to Genovesi 'in every transaction of exchange, the article received appears to each of the contracting parties more necessary than that given. This is a far-fetched notion, which I think myself called on to notice, because it has obtained considerable currency.' Hence Say explicitly denies that there are gains from trade. In support of his view he expounds: 'It would be difficult to prove, that a poor labourer, who goes to the alehouse on a Sunday, exchanges there his superfluity for a necessary. In all fair traffic, there occurs a mutual exchange of two things, which are worth one the other, at the time and place of exchange. Commercial production, that is to say, the value added by commerce to the things exchanged, is not operated by the act of exchange, but by the commercial operations that precede it' (ibid., pp. 66-7, n*).

While he criticizes Genovesi, he praises Verri, who is said to be 'the only writer within my knowledge, who has explained the true principle and ground-work of commerce. In the year 1771, he thus expressed himself: "Commerce is in fact nothing more than the transport of goods from one place to another." (*Meditazioni sulla economica politica*, § 4.)' (ibid.). In this regard Verri is said to be superior to Smith, who 'merely discards the opinion, that there is any production of value in the act of exchange' (ibid.). Verri is criticized, however, for having excluded 'the occupations of the sovereign, the magistrate, the soldier, and the priest' from 'the cognizance of political economy. (*Meditazioni sulla Economia Politica*, § 24.)' (ibid., p. 120, n*).

In the context of a discussion of the effects of the division of labour Say refers to Beccaria, who, 'in a public course of lectures on political economy, delivered at Milan in the year 1769, and before the publication of Smith's work, had remarked the favourable influence of the division of labour upon the multiplication of products.' To this Say quotes a passage from Beccaria and then continues: 'However, I have given Smith the credit of originality in his ideas of the division of labour; first, because, in all probability, he had published his opinions from his chair of professor of philosophy at Glasgow before Beccaria, as it is well known he did the principles that form the ground-work of his book; but chiefly because he has the merit of having deduced from them the most important conclusions' (ibid., pp. 91-2, n*). Say enunciates the 'general maxim, that the population of a state is always proportionate to the sum of its production in every kind.' He adds: 'This is a truth acknowledged by most writers on political economy, however various and discordant their opinions on most other points.' Among many others he mentions explicitly Verri and Beccaria (ibid., p. 374 and n).

Finally, in the context of a discussion of the influence of taxation on the habits of a nation, Say mentions Beccaria (ibid., p. 458, n*): 'The efficacy of the characteristics of punishment has been placed beyond all doubt by Beccaria, in his tract, *Dei delitti e delle pene*.'

Indirect route: via surveys of the Italian economic writings

The second channel for the indirect transmission of 'Italian economics', via surveys of the Italian economic literature and histories of political economy, can be exemplified with regard to two well-known German economists. Johann Heinrich von Thünen is widely considered as the best German economic theorist of the early nineteenth century. In his famous *Der isolirte Staat* (1826; part II: 1850) no Italian author is cited or mentioned. However, an unpublished manuscript on political economy by Thünen contains excerpts from the German edition of Blanqui's *Histoire d'economie politique en Europe*, to which the German translator had appended some extracts from Pecchio's *Storia della economia pubblica in Italia*. From the latter Thünen excerpted two short passages, which in turn are citations from Ortes' *Economia nazionale*, and which apparently interested Thünen, because Pecchio maintained that Ortes had anticipated the Malthusian law of population.[2] Apart from this short manuscript note there is no evidence that the ideas of the Italian economists were in any way influential with regard to von Thünen.

The second author is Friedrich List, a particularly famous and politically influential German economist, although not regarded highly in academic circles. The third part, titled 'Systems of political economy', of List's treatise *Das nationale System der politischen Ökonomie* opens with a brief chapter on 'The Italian political economists' (see List, 1982 [1841], ch. 28). The reason for the inclusion of this chapter is that in List's view 'Italy has been the first of all modern nations in both the practice and the theory of political economy' (ibid., p. 337). List in particular discusses at some length the main ideas of Macchiavelli's *Principe* of 1513 and Antonio Serra's *Breve trattato* of 1613. Serra's work, which in List's view is much superior to Say's, obtains the highest praise because Serra 'had a correct view of the role of political institutions for the wealth and prosperity of nations' (ibid., p. 341). While he entertained a wrong notion of wealth, which to him is given by a country's surplus of gold and silver, he held a correct view with regard to the sources of wealth: agriculture, manufacturing, and foreign trade are seen as the main sources of prosperity, together with a stable, trustworthy administration that guarantees personal freedom and individual property rights. Beccaria is credited with having introduced the principle of the division of labour 'prior to or at least simultaneously with Adam Smith' (ibid., p. 344), but his general outlook

[2] We are indebted to Heinz Rieter (University of Hamburg) for having provided us with the information on Thünen's unpublished manuscript.

is said to be shaped by the mistaken ideas of the Physiocrats. Filangieri's views are characterised as being 'the least satisfactory', while Verri, according to List, 'acknowledged the necessity of protecting the domestic industry against foreign competitors, but did not see or was not allowed to see that such a policy is conditioned by the size and the unity of the nation' (ibid.). List's discussion of the Italian authors is based – without acknowledgement – on the account given in Pecchio's history of Italian economics (see Pecchio, 1830). As Marx (1982 [1845], pp. 446-7) pointed out and documented in great detail, List's account of the early Italian political economists is indeed nothing else but an (unfaithful) copy of some passages in Pecchio's book.

Direct influence: the cases of Hermann and Rau

Hermann's knowledge of early and contemporary English and continental European economic literature was remarkable. He read the authors in their mother languages, English, French and Italian. His *Habilitation* thesis submitted in 1823 to the University of Erlangen was written in Latin and deals with economic concepts and analyses in early Roman authors (cf. Hermann 1823). The dissertation foreshadows several of the concerns and ideas of the *Untersuchungen*. In the latter Hermann generally premises his own discussion on a summary of the received views on a particular problem. While his emphasis is on British (Steuart, Smith, Ricardo, Malthus, McCulloch, Torrens, James Mill), French and French-speaking (the Physiocrats, Jean-Baptiste Say, Louis Say, Ganilh, Simonde de Sismondi) and German authors (Rau, Hufeland, Jakob, Storch, Lotz), he also refers to Italians. For example, in the context of a discussion of the factors affecting the productivity of labour Hermann writes: 'Amongst the Italians we have to mention in particular Gioja, who on the whole advocates J. B. Say's view (*Nuovo prospetto delle scienze economiche*, Milano I, 1818)' (Hermann, 1832, p. 20). To this he adds in a footnote: 'If it applies to any book, then what Buffon says in the famous speech about the style of writings in which the division and systematization is carried too far certainly applies to this one: *le livre parait clair aux yeux, mais le sens de l'auteur demeure obscur*' (ibid., footnote).

Rau's *Grundsätze*, the first edition of which was published in 1826, contains a reading list at the end of each chapter. In the opening chapter Rau pointed out that 'the Italian writers, not sufficiently recognized by the other Europeans, have made original and painstaking contributions to political economy' (Rau, 1837 [1826], p. 34). Rau then mentions in particular: Scaruffi, Davanzati, Turbolo, Serra, Belloni and Genovesi; and Galiani, Pagnini, Beccaria, Ortes and Verri as precursors of Adam Smith. However, Rau was not only important for the dissemination of economic ideas from the French, British, and Italian writers in the German-speaking countries by means of his textbook. He was also influenced in the development of his own contributions to economics by the attempts of Canard, Verri, Gioja and Fuoco to apply algebraic expressions in political economy. In the fourth edition of the

Grundsätze (1841 [1826]), Rau provided a list of political economists who had made use of mathematics, and mentioned among others the Italian economists Ortes and Fuoco (see Rau, 1841 [1826], pp. 7 and 31-2). According to Baloglou (1995, p. 355), Rau's graphical exposition of supply and demand schedules in the fourth edition of his *Grundsätze* (1841) was directly inspired by the contributions of the Italian authors. Rau knew, in particular, Frisi's notes in the sixth edition of Verri's *Meditazioni* (1772), as well as Gioja's and Fuoco's accounts of Canard's price theory (see Gioja, 1815; and Fuoco, 1827). Rau's introduction of the graphical method in the exposition of his price theory, in which cost of production is seen as the main determinant of price on the supply side, giving the lower limit of the price, and utility ('Wertschätzung') is seen as the major determinant on the demand side, giving the upper limit of the price, thus owed much to the contributions of the Italian economists, even if Canard must be regarded as the major source of inspiration for Rau.

Before we go on to document in detail the reception of 'Italian economics' by Marx, Menger and Böhm-Bawerk, we should briefly mention a few references to Italian writers that can be found in the works of other authors from the German-language area. At the Austrian universities, Sonnenfels' *Grundsätze der Polizey, Handlung und Finanz* (1765) remained the standard textbook for students of law, public administration and political economy until the mid-nineteenth century (see Pribram 1983, p. 96). There is no indication in this cameralistic treatise that Sonnenfels was particularly influenced by 'Italian economics'; he at any rate did not quote any Italian author. Sonnenfels' textbook was eventually superseded at the Austrian universities by Joseph Kudler's *Grundlehren der Volkswirtschaft* (1846), a book which was studied, for instance, by the young Carl Menger when the latter was a law student in Vienna. In his first chapter Kudler provides a discussion of different systems of political economy, and refers to the Italian 'mercantilists' Serra, Davanzati, Belloni, and Genovesi, to the 'Smithians' Gioja, Bosellini and Agazzini, and to the Italian 'opponents of physiocracy', Verri and Galiani (ibid., pp. 27-35).[3]

Occasional references to Italian economists can also be found in the writings of the group of German economists who were mainly influenced by Adam Smith, that is, authors like Sartorius, Lüder, Kraus, Schlözer, Jakob, Soden, Hufeland, Lotz and Storch. Volume 1 of Lotz's *Handbuch der Staatswirthschaftslehre* (1821), for instance, contains a brief chapter on the history of political economy, in which Genovesi's *Lezzione di commercio* and Serra's *Breve trattato* are mentioned, and volume 3 of Riedel's *Handbuch der National-Oekonomie oder Volkswirthschaftslehre* (1838-41) contains a survey of the international economic literature. And Karl Steinlein wrote in the Preface of his *Handbuch der Volkswirtschaftslehre* (1831):

[3] Kudler's references are to the Custodi collection.

> The attentive reader will surely recognize that the author of the present book has variously made use of the very thoughtful and still not sufficiently known treatise of the Italian Melchiorre Gioja (*Nuovo prospetto di Scienze economiche* ...), and that he has adopted several of his views. (Steinlein, 1831, p. vii)

Steinlein indeed stresses with special reference to Gioja (and Ganilh) the productivity of immaterial services (ibid., pp. xix ff. and 224), the importance of the combination of labour (rather than its division), and the role of nature as a factor of production (ibid., p. 317). With regard to Schmitthenner's *Zwölf Bücher vom Staate* (1839), in which a plea for a competitive industrial system is combined with a strong opposition to the liberalization of international trade, Julius Kautz observed: 'That the writings of a Gioja, Ganilh, Sismondi had some influence on Schmitthenner ... cannot be doubted' (Kautz, 1860, p. 641 n.). And Kosegarten, who was strongly influenced by Smith's economic liberalism as well as by medieval-theological ideas, is said to have attempted 'a synthesis of the ideas of Ortes and Gioja ... with those of Adam Müller and Adam Smith' (ibid., p. 669).

A significant influence of Italian economics cannot be discerned in the contributions of the so-called 'German-Russian school', which comprises a rather heterodox group of authors, including Storch, Cancrin, Schlözer, and Bernhardi, among others. Bernhardi's critique of Ricardian economics in *Versuch einer Kritik der Gründe* (1849), for instance, contains no references to the contributions of Italian economists, although Bernhardi had spent several years in Italy and was generally very widely read. Notable Italian influence can be detected only in the 'Instruction ... für ein neues Gesetzbuch' (1768) of Catherina II, which was primarily inspired by Montesquieu and Beccaria (see Roscher, 1874, p. 793). Significant Italian influences are also missing from the works of the group of authors known as the 'German historical school', like Hildebrandt, Knies, and above all Roscher. These economists, whose encyclopedic knowledge comprised of course also the works of the major Italian economists, do not seem to have drawn significant inspiration from them, and specifically either develop or refute doctrines of the Italian economists. Wilhelm Roscher's voluminous history of political economy in Germany includes only a handful of references to Italian economists. While Galiani (ibid., pp. 411 and 746), Verri (ibid., pp. 230, 231, 411), and Beccaria (ibid., p. 478 and 793) are mentioned, there is no indication that Roscher was particularly impressed with their contributions. And it is surprising that Carl Knies also does not acknowledge any debts to Italian economists in his voluminous treatise *Geld und Credit* (1873-79).

3. Marx's reception of Italian economics

Karl Marx's knowledge of the contributions of the major Italian economists was based on a first-hand study of their works from the Custodi collection. Marx apparently only studied this collection after he had written the *Economic and Philosophic Manuscripts of 1844*, in which no Italian economist is mentioned. However, in the economic manuscript of 1857-58 (the first rough draft of *Capital*, also known as the *Grundrisse*) Marx referred to Verri, Galiani, and Rossi. And in *A Contribution to the Critique of Political Economy*, which was published in 1859, he remarked on the Custodi collection:[4]

> The entire history of the Monetary System from the early Middle Ages until well into the eighteenth century is a history of such bilateral and antagonistic counterfeiting, and Custodi's voluminous collection of works of Italian economists is largely concerned with this subject. (Marx, 1970 [1859], pp. 109-110)

Galiani is cited several times, mainly in connection with money and monetary theory (see ibid., pp. 34, 57, 72, 89, 104, and 153), but also as a precursor of the labour theory of value. In a historical note Marx wrote: 'We shall now leave the Physiocrats and disregard a whole series of Italian economists, whose more or less pertinent ideas come close to a correct analysis of the commodity' (ibid., p. 57). To this statement he added in a footnote: 'See for instance Galiani, *Della Moneta* … He says: "It is only toil" (*fatica*) "which gives value to things"' (ibid., p. 57 n.).

As regards the contributions of the Italian economists to the theory of money, Marx quoted approvingly, and adopted, Galiani's distinction between nominal money and real money (ibid., p. 89); his statement that the velocity of circulation rather than the amount of metal determines whether much or little money is available (ibid., p. 104); and his statements on the peculiar qualities of gold and silver that render these metals especially fit to serve as money (ibid., p. 153). Apart from Galiani's *Della Moneta*, Marx also cited from Genovesi's *Lezione di economia civile* (ibid., p. 124) and from Verri's *Meditazioni* (ibid.), and he acknowledged that the term 'universal commodity' favoured by him had been introduced before him by Genovesi and Verri (ibid., p. 48).

In the economic manuscript of 1861-1863 (the second rough draft of *Capital*) Marx cited approvingly Galiani's statement in *Della Moneta* that an exchange involves the exchange of equivalents: 'Where there is equality there is no gain' (Marx, 1975a [1861-3], p. 23). He also cited from Galiani's *Della Moneta* and from Ortes' *Economia Nazionale* in connection with a discussion of the Malthusian law of population, noting that Ortes' *Della Economia Nazionale* of 1774 'is much more

[4] Marx's citations are all in Italian.

ingenious than Malthus' (ibid., p. 205). And under the heading 'Replacement of labour' Marx cited the following statement from Galiani: 'Perfection of the crafts means nothing other than the discovery of new ways of making a product *with fewer people*, or (which is the same thing) in *less time than previously*. (Galiani, *Della Moneta, Parte Moderna*, p. 158)' (ibid., p. 344). Marx noted: 'This is true as much for simple cooperation or the division of labour as it is for machinery – *fewer people* and *less time* for the manufacture of a product are identical. … Therefore every means of reducing the necessary labour time of an individual worker implies at the same time a reduction in the number of workers required to bring about the same effect' (ibid.). In the economic manuscript of 1861-1863 Marx also disputed Rossi's views on the role of wage labour in capitalistic production (ibid., pp. 141-151), and cited a passage from Beccaria's *Elementi di economia pubblica* on the division of labour (ibid., p. 286), as well as a note by Carli on Verri's *Meditazioni* (ibid., p. 258). The most interesting citation is a passage from Verri's *Meditazioni*:

> The value reproduced is that part of the price of an agricultural or industrial product which exceeds the original value of the material and the outlay on consumption incurred while it is being produced. In agriculture the seed and the consumption of the peasant must be deducted: equally in manufacture one must deduct the raw material and the worker's consumption; and so every year a reproduced value is created, to the amount of the part that remains (P. Verri, *Meditazioni sulla economia politica* … . (Ibid., pp. 155-6).

Marx commented:

> The extent to which the concept of capital implies not only the preservation and reproduction of value but *its valorisation*, i.e. the multiplication of value, the positing of surplus value, can be seen from … the earlier Italian political economists, who applied the term *reproduction of value* only to this production of surplus value. (Ibid.)

In the manuscript of *Theories of Surplus Value*, which Marx wrote in 1861-63, no separate chapter was devoted to the Italian economists. However, Italian writers are variously cited by Marx in the other chapters. In the chapter on the Physiocrats, for instance, Marx quoted a passage from Ferdinando Paoletti's *I veri mezzi di render felici le società* as well as some passages from Verri's *Meditazioni*, 'against the superstition of the Physiocrats' (Marx, 1975a [1861-3], pp. 375-6). And in the chapter on Adam Smith there is a critical discussion of Rossi's distinction between productive and unproductive labour (Marx, 1975b [1861-3], pp. 189-95), while in the chapter on the dissolution of the Ricardian school Galiani is cited in the context of a discussion of Hodgskin's pamphlets (Marx, 1975c [1861-63], p. 400). However, overall Marx had surprisingly little to say on the contributions of the Italian economists in his *Theories of Surplus Value*.

In volume I of *Capital* he made several references to Italian economists, and in particular to Galiani.[5] In the first chapter Marx quoted Galiani's statement 'Value is a relation between two persons', and commented: 'He ought to have added: a relation between persons expressed as a relation between things' (ibid., p. 74 n.). (Marx seems to misunderstand Galiani's statement, as he quotes it in connection with his own statement: 'whenever, by an exchange, we equate as values our different products, by that very act, we also equate, as human labour, the different kinds of labour expended upon them' (ibid., p. 74).) Marx expounded:

> So far ... as the circulation of commodities ... is free from disturbing influences, it must be the exchange of equivalents. Little as Vulgar-Economy knows about the nature of value, yet whenever it wishes to consider the phenomena of circulation in their purity, it assumes that supply and demand are equal, ... If therefore, as regards the use-values exchanged, both buyer and seller may gain something, this is not the case as regards the exchange-values. Here we must rather say: "Where equality exists there can be no gain" [Galiani, *Della Moneta*, Custodi ed., p. 244]. ... the exchange of commodities ... in its normal state is an exchange of equivalents, consequently, no method for increasing value' (ibid, pp. 158-9).

Marx also cited Galiani in the section 'Production of relative surplus value', where he stated that 'by an increase in the productiveness of labour, we mean, generally, an alteration in the labour-process, of such a kind as to shorten the labour-time socially necessary for the production of a commodity, and to endow a given quantity of labour with the power of producing a greater quantity of use-value' (ibid., p. 314). In connection with the theory of money, Galiani's statement that 'although gold and silver are not by Nature money, money is by Nature gold and silver' is cited approvingly (ibid., p. 89); similarly his statement on the separation of the money name from the money weight that is caused by debasing.

Verri's *Meditazioni* are quoted approvingly by Marx on three counts. First, Marx referred to Verri's statement that use-value is produced by labour in combination with nature (ibid., p. 43); secondly, he acknowledged, and indeed adopted, Verri's notion of money as 'the universal equivalent' (ibid., p. 89); thirdly, he approved of Verri's ideas on hoarding (ibid., pp. 133-4). In volume 2 of *Capital* no Italian author is mentioned, while in volume 3 Marx criticized Verri for confounding commerce with the transportation industry; see Marx (1959 [1894], p. 274 n.). Our reading thus confirms Groenewegen's assessment (1999, p. 699) that Verri's work is recognized but is not to any extent influential with respect to Marx. Rossi is criticized for his views on means of subsistence and productive

---

[5] See Marx (1954 [1867], pp. 74, 89, 90, 100, 153, 158, 314, 643).

consumption (ibid., pp. 173 and 572). In a note on the Malthusian theory of population Marx referred to Ortes as 'an original and clever writer' (ibid., p. 616 n.). According to Marx, the 'antagonistic character of capitalistic accumulation is enunciated in various forms by political economists, although by them it is confounded with phenomena ... belonging to precapitalistic modes of production. The Venetian monk Ortes, one of the great economic writers of the 18th century, regards the antagonism of capitalistic production as the general natural law of social wealth. "In the economy of a nation, advantages and evils always balance one another ...: the abundance of wealth with some people, is always equal to the want of it with others ...: the great riches of a small number are always acccompanied by the absolute privation of the first necessaries of life for many others. The wealth of a nation corresponds with its population, and its misery corresponds with its wealth"' (ibid., p. 646). Marx apparently thought highly of Ortes, even if he criticized him on this account.[6]

There is no evidence that Johann Karl Rodbertus, who came close to anticipating the main elements of Marx's theory of value and surplus value (see Rodbertus, 1837 and 1842), was influenced by the writings of the Italian economists. Although he had studied economics during his stay in France and Switzerland and may thus very likely have come across the writings of Beccaria, Verri, or Galiani, he does not mention any of these writers in his own publications.

4. The influence of Italian economists on the development of marginal utility theory in Germany and Austria

Galiani,Verri, and Rossi have often been mentioned as important precursors of marginal utility theory, and in particular of the Austrian school. According to Schumpeter (1954, pp. 300 and 302), it was in particular Galiani who 'foreshadowed much later development (marginal utility theory)' and 'carried this analysis to its 18th-century peak.' Friedrich August Hayek (1973, p. 3) maintained that the 'source of inspiration' of Jevons, Menger, and Walras 'seems to have been an intellectual tradition which, at least since Ferdinando Galiani in the eighteenth century, had run side by side with the labour and cost theories deriving from John Locke and Adam Smith'.[7] And the Russian mathematical economist V. K. Dmitriev remarked:

[6] Marx also cited Pagnini and Genovesi (ibid., pp. 91 and 153), as well as a note by Carli on Verri regarding the effects of cooperation of labour (ibid., p. 329 n.), and Beccaria is said to follow the ancient writers with regard to the divison of labour (ibid., p. 365).

[7] Edgar Salin (1951, p. 65) also stressed the importance of especially the doctrine of Galiani for the 'psychological' theories of value. He added that Galiani, the abbé, and Turgot, the student at the Jesuit seminar of Saint-Sulpice, can be assumed to have received a major inspiration in their writings by the works of Antonin (ibid., p. 47).

> An impartial analysis must lead to the conclusion that *the Austrian school* as such (Menger, Böhm-Bawerk, von Wieser and others) *added very little* (unless much significance is given to the introduction of new terms) *to what had been done before them for the solution of the problem.* Quite apart from such nineteenth-century writers as Senior, Rossi, Dupuit and some others, in whose works the main elements of marginal utility theory are quite clearly shown (we do not include Gossen, since the 'founders of the school' of marginal utility themselves acknowledge him as their forerunner), we find *all the information* needed for the construction of a *finished* theory of marginal utility in the work of such an 'old' economist as Galiani (the first 'positivist' in political economy who hitherto has not been properly appreciated in the literature). (Dmitriev, 1974 [1902], pp. 181-2)

According to Salin (1951, p. 76) the point of view expressed by Galiani in his *Dialogues sur le commerce des bleds* (1770) foreshadowed the confrontation between advocates of pure theory, on the one hand, and those of the historical method, on the other, in the *Methodenstreit*, with Menger and Gustav Schmoller as the main protagonists.

Carl Menger

In the Preface to the *Grundsätze*[8] Carl Menger pointed out: 'It was a special pleasure to me that the field here treated, comprising the most general principles of our science, is in no small degree so truly the product of recent development in German political economy, and that the reform of the most important principles of our science here attempted is therefore built upon a foundation laid by previous work that was produced almost entirely by the industry of German scholars' (Menger, 1981 [1871], p. 49). According to Kauder, who checked the books in Menger's library[9] for annotations and unpublished notes, Menger had read several Italian authors but did not think all that highly of their contributions: 'He examined, but not too carefully, Montanari, Galiani, Turgot, and Condillac. He dismissed the achievements of the earlier French and Italian writers with the remark that the German economists offer a more profound treatment of the subject. Besides Aristotle, the German economists of the first half of the nineteenth century were his main teachers' (Kauder, 1965, p. 83).[10] Friedrich von Wieser also stressed the indebtedness of the Austrian school to German predecessors: 'It may be said that, in great part, the German school long ago formulated the conceptions, leaving for

[8] In the following all citations from Menger's book will be taken from the English translation by James Dingwall and Bert F. Hoselitz; see Menger (1981).

[9] As is well-known, Carl Menger was a great book-collector. In 1911 Menger estimated his collection to consist of 25.000 volumes and considered it the most complete collection on economics in private hands.

[10] See also Howey (1960, p. 26).

us only the task of filling them out by adequate observation. In this it has laid up a treasure from which all succeeding economic effort may draw indefinitely … The new value theory is in truth the fulfilment of what German theory had long demanded' (Wieser, 1893, p. xxxiv). More recently, Streissler (1990, pp. 154-8) has also emphasized the importance of the German "use value" tradition for the development of Menger's ideas.

Emil Kauder claimed that 'before he wrote his *Principles*, Menger knew neither Gossen nor Mangoldt nor the greatest part of the older marginalist literature. Most works which he perused for the publication of his *Principles* are quoted in two lengthy footnotes [see Menger, 1871, pp. 78-80, 108-113][11] which read like a history of the value-in-use theories from Aristotle to Albert Schäffle' (Kauder, 1965, p. 83). In the chapter on the *theory of value* Menger listed seven articles, all written by German or Austrian authors, which are said to be concerned with the 'central theme' of the *Grundsätze* (Menger, 1871, pp. 78-80 n. [1981, pp. 292-5): Eberhard Friedländer (1852), A. E. F. Schäffle (1885-6), Hermann Roesler (1868; 1869), Otto Michaelis (1863), Arnold Lindwurm (1865), Karl Knies (1855), and Johann von Komorzynski (1869). Menger continued: 'Among earlier attempts to define the general concept of value I wish also to mention those of: Geminiano Montanari (*Della moneta*, in *Scrittori classici Italiani di economia politica*, Milano 1803-5, II, 43); A. R. J. Turgot ("Valeurs et Monnaies" in *Ouevres de Turgot*, ed. by G. Schelle, Paris, 1913-23, III, 79 ff.); E. B. de Condillac (*Le commerce et le gouvernement*, reprinted in E. Daire, [ed.] *Mélanges d'économie politique*, Paris, 1847, I, 251 ff.); G. Garnier (in the Preface to his French translation of A. Smith's *Wealth of Nations* under the title *La Richesse des Nations*, Paris, 1843, I, xlvi ff.); and H. Storch (*op. cit.*, I, 56 ff.). Among these, it is Condillac's definition of value in particular that bears no small resemblance to the recent developments of the theory of value in Germany' (Menger, 1981, p. 295). While Galiani's *Della Moneta* is not mentioned, it may still be considered as a major source of ideas, given its influence on Turgot and Condillac. And in the long footnote in the section 'The Original Measure of Value' of chapter III, 'The Theory of Value', Menger writes: 'As early as Aristotle we find an attempt to discover a measure of the use value of goods and to represent use value as the foundation of exchange value. … In the same spirit Ferdinando Galiani (*Della moneta* in *Scrittori classici Italiani di economia politica*, Milano 1803-5, X, 58) writes "ch'essendo varie le disposizioni degli animi umani e vario i bisogni, vario è il valor delle cose"' (ibid., p. 296). Menger then cites from Turgot and Condillac, and concludes: 'A deeper treatment of the problem of the measure of use value is to be found only among the German writers' (ibid., p. 297). This remark is followed by references to Hildebrand, Friedländer, Knies, Rau, Schäffle and Lorenz von Stein.

[11] In the English translation these footnotes are put in an appendix; see Menger (1981, pp. 292-5 and 295-302).

In the chapter on the *theory of price* Menger refers to Montanari (*Della moneta*, ed. Custodi, p.a. III, pp. 119-20) as one of the many authors who, following Aristotle, wrongly supposed that in the market an exchange of equivalents takes place, and that the problem of price determination therefore consists in demonstrating the equivalence of two bundles of commodities (see Menger, 1981, p. 305.). There is no reference to any Italian author in the chapter on 'Use Value and Exchange Value', but in the chapter on 'The Commodity Concept' he maintains that 'With few exceptions, the theory of the commodity has not been independently treated by English, French, and Italian writers' (Menger, 1981, p. 309).

The chapter on *money* contains a long footnote on the history of theories of the origin of money (ibid., pp. 315-20). Menger mentions Bernardo Davanzati (1588) and Montanari (*Delle moneta*) as strict followers of Aristotle and Paulus's view that the origin if money is to be traced back to the authority of the state (ibid., pp. 317-8). Antonio Genovesi (ibid., p. 318) is said to follow John Law in opposing the theory that traces the origin of money to a contract between men. And Beccaria is credited with having 'taken up and admirably accomplished in part' Law's attempt 'to explain the genesis of the money character of the precious metals from their special nature' (ibid.); in this context he mentions also Verri. Among more recent writers in the same tradition is said to be Melchiorre Gioja (ibid., p. 319). In a footnote on money as the measure of value, Menger refers to Carlo Antonio Broggia (1743), Pompeo Neri (1751), Galiani (1750), and Genovesi (ibid., p. 277 n.). Finally, there is a footnote in connection with the idea that money can serve as a store of value (with which Menger does not agree). This idea can be traced back to Aristotle, Menger notes, and was then adopted and developed by Italian authors such as Sallustio Antonio Bandini, Giammaria Ortes, Gian-Rinaldo Carli and Giambattista Coriani (ibid., p. 279 n.).

Eugen von Böhm-Bawerk

According to Hennings, all the major ideas of Eugen von Böhm-Bawerk's theory of interest 'had been expressed by earlier writers. Böhm himself referred to Galiani and Turgot as early instances of the insight that differences in time find a reflection in differences in the value of commodities' (Hennings, 1997, p. 177). Böhm-Bawerk indeed discusses the interest theory of Galiani at some length in chapter 3 of his *Geschichte und Kritik* (Böhm-Bawerk, 1921, I, pp. 41-4). He introduces his discussion with the observation that 'Italy was directly under the eyes of the Roman church. However, Italy was also that country in Europe, which was the earliest one to arrive at a rich blossoming of commerce and business, and which therefore was bound to feel the pressure of the Canonical prohibition of interest taking as unbearable.' He adds: 'The way, in which one went about the latter took into account both facts: nowhere in Europe remained the prohibition of interest more ineffective, and nowhere in Europe dared the economic theorists to openly challenge the church's dogma later.' Therefore, it should come as no surprise that 'no Italian author appears to have launched an open frontal assault at the Canonical doctrine before the 18th century' (ibid., p. 41).[12]

Then Böhm-Bawerk turns to Galiani who, in 1750, cites Salmasius as the first author to have put forward a doctrine that was favourable to interest taking.[13] This triggered a debate in Italy between advocates and opponents of the usury law. Galiani's own theory of interest Böhm-Bawerk calls 'peculiar' (ibid., p. 42) and summarizes its content in the following way. Galiani subscribes to the conventional view that if interest were to constitute a gain or advantage obtained by the lender of a sum of money, then interest would indeed be despicable. However, Galiani contends, interest is not a true gain, but rather a complement that is needed in order to arrive at the equivalence between service and return service. Clearly, there ought to be an exchange of equivalents. Since value represents the relation between things and our needs and wants, it would be futile to try to find that equivalence in the equality of the weight, the outer appearance etc. of two things that are exchanged for one another: what matters is rather the equality of utility. 'In this regard present and future sums of money of the same size are not of the same value in the same way as in the trading of bills equivalent amounts of money in different locations are not of equal value. And in the same way in which the gain of a bill (cambio) despite its appearance as an agio (soprapiù) is in truth a compensation …, the money rate of interest is nothing but a compensation of the different values of sums of money available at present or at some date in the future' (ibid.).

This idea, while according to Böhm-Bawerk not entirely new – he refers to Petty and Rice Vaughan –, provides the basis for an entirely new way of justifying interest on loans. Alas, Böhm-Bawerk continues, Galiani did not consequently go down the road opened by him. According to him the fact that present sums of money are ordinarily of greater value than future sums of the same size resides exclusively in their different degrees of security. Hence, Galiani considered interest to be a variant of a risk or a security premium. 'Galiani gives this view a drastic expression when in one place he declares the "so-called fruit of money" to be the price of the "palpitation of the heart" (prezzo del batticuore)' (ibid., p. 43). Böhm-Bawerk concludes: 'This, however, implied to fundamentally mistake the essence of the money rate of interest' (ibid.).

What can be said about the contributions of the other Italian authors of the eighteenth century to elaborating 'the very first germ of an idea, from which … the modern theory of interest, the so-called "agio theory", has developed' (ibid., p. 38)? With the possible exceptions of Genovesi and Beccaria, these writers are said to have not really advanced the subject. Genovesi (*Lezione di economia civile*) and

[12] Translations from the German original are ours.

[13] The French Claudius Salmasius published a set of pamphlets against the usury laws: in 1638 *De usuris*, in 1639 *De modo usurarum*, and in 1640 *De foenore trapezitico* (see Böhm-Bawerk, ibid., p. 29).

Vasco (*Usura libera*) are said to have adopted the teachings of Salmasius without adding anything of importance (ibid., p. 43). Most important, according to Böhm-Bawerk, are perhaps Beccaria's considerations. He distinguishes sharply between interest and interest rate (usura), the former being the direct utility of a thing and the latter the '"utility of a utility" (l'utilità dell'utilità)' (ibid.). A direct utility is provided by all goods. In the case of money its direct utility consists of it being the general equivalent of all other goods and thus of the utility provided by those goods. More specifically, since a sum of money can represent a particular piece of land, the interest of that sum of money is given by the yearly yield of the land. Hence the average rate of money interest equals the average rate of yield of the different qualities of cultivated land.

In Beccaria's argument, Böhm-Bawerk observes, the word 'interest' apparently means the same thing as the rate of return on capital. Therefore Beccaria's attempt to explain the existence and level of the 'original return of capital' in terms of the possibility of buying land and pocketing rent may be considered 'a primitive expression' of a point of view developed already a few years earlier by authors such as Turgot (ibid., p. 44). In a chapter which is devoted to 'eclectic explanations' of interest Böhm-Bawerk discusses briefly the ideas of Rossi and Cossa. Rossi's theory (*Cours d'economie politique*, 4th ed., 1865) is described as an incoherent mixture of an 'abstinence theory' and a 'productivity theory' of interest.

Interestingly, there is no mention of Galiani, or of any other Italian economist, in Böhm-Bawerk's *Positive Theorie des Kapitales*. Böhm-Bawerk only referred to Galiani as an important precursor in the *Geschichte und Kritik*, in a footnote to a passage in which he briefly stated the so-called 'agio theory': 'The germs of this theory, which I consider to be the only correct one, can be found already in *Galiani* and *Turgot*, then in *Bentham* and *John Rae*, and recently also in *Knies*, who however has later explicitly withdrawn it' (ibid., p. 232).[14] Galiani and Turgot are mentioned again as precursors in his discussion of Bentham's and John Rae's theory of interest (ibid., p. 299). There can be little doubt, then, that Galiani's theory of interest was an important source of inspiration in the development of Böhm-Bawerk's theory of interest.

[14] According to Böhm-Bawerk, Knies adopted Galiani's idea of explaining interest on loans from the different use values of present and future commodities in an essay titled 'Erörterungen über den Kredit' (1859). However, in his voluminous treatise *Geld und Credit* (1880) Knies then withdrew his former theory and instead adopted what Böhm-Bawerk called a 'Use theory' ('Nutzungstheorie') (see Böhm-Bawerk, 1921, I, p. 191). In *Geld und Credit* Knies indeed made no reference to Galiani at all (apart from a footnote appended in the second edition, in which he responded to Böhm-Bawerk's account of his interest theory; see Knies, 1885, p. 106 n.). The only Italian economist mentioned is Genovesi (*Nuovo prospetto della scienze economiche*) (ibid., p. 29). There is thus no direct evidence that Galiani's *Della Moneta*, with which he was certainly familiar, was in any significant way influential with regard to Knies' theory of money.

REFERENCES

BALOGLOU C. (1995), *Die Vertreter der mathematischen Nationalökonomie in Deutschland zwischen 1838 und 1871*, Marburg: Metropolis.

BECCARIA C. (1804), *Elementi di economia pubblica*. In: *Scrittori classici italiani di economia politica. Parte Moderna*, vol. XI, Milan.

BERNHARDI T. (1849), *Versuch einer Kritik der Gründe, die für großes und kleines Grundeigentum angeführt werden*. Second edition 1924, Leipzig: Ernst Wiegandt.

BLANQUI J.A. (1838), *Histoire de l'économie politique en Europe depuis les anciens jusqu'à nos jours*, Bruxelles.

BÖHM-BAWERK E. von (1921 [1884] [1889]), *Kapital und Kapitalzins*, 4th edition in 3 vols, Part 1: *Geschichte und Kritik der Kapitalzinstheorien*, first ed. 1884, Part 2, vol. 1: *Positive Theorie des Kapitals*, first ed. 1889, Part 2, vol. 2: *Positive Theorie des Kapitals*, Exkurse, Jena: Gustav Fischer.

BRANDT K. (1992), *Geschichte der deutschen Volkswirtschaftslehre, Vol. 1: Von der Scholastik bis zur klassischen Nationalökonomie*, Freiburg: Rudolf Haufe.

BÜLAU F. (1835), *Handbuch der Staatswirtschaftslehre*, Leipzig.

CUSTODI (ed.) (1803-1816), *Scrittori classici italiani di economia politica*, Milan.

DMITRIEV V.K. (1974 [1902]), The Theory of Marginal Utility, in D.M. Nuti (ed.), V.K. Dmitriev, *Economic Essays on Value, Competition and Utility*, Cambridge: Cambridge University Press, pp. 179-91.

ELTIS W. (1997), 'Introduction' to Etienne Bonnot de Condillac. *Commerce and Government considered in their mutual Relationship*, edited and translated by Shelagh Eltis and Walter Eltis, Cheltenham: Edward Elgar.

FUOCO F. (1827), *Saggi economici*, vol. 2, Pisa.

GALIANI F. (1751), *Della Moneta*. In: *Scrittori classici italiani di economia politica. Parte Moderna*, vols III and IV, Milan 1803.

GALIANI F. (1769), *Dialogues sur le commerce des bléds*.

GIOJA M. (1815), *Nuovo Prospetto delle Scienze Economiche*, Milan.

GROENEWEGEN P. (1986), Introduction, in Pietro Verri. *Reflections on Political Economy*, Fairfield, NJ: A.M. Kelly, pp. vii-xxix.

GROENEWEGEN P. (1999), 'The Significance of Verri's *Meditazioni* in the History of Economic Thought: The Wider European Influences', in C. Capra (ed.), *Pietro Verri e il suo tempo*, vol. II, pp. 693-708.

HAYEK F.A. (1973). 'The Place of Menger's *Grundsätze* in the History of Economic Thought', in J.R. Hicks and W. Weber (eds), *Carl Menger and the Austrian School of Economics*, Oxford: Clarendon Press, pp. 1-14.

HENNINGS K.H. (1997), *The Austrian Theory of Value and Capital. Studies in the Life and Work of Eugen von Böhm-Bawerk*, Cheltenham: Edward Elgar.

HERMANN F.B.W. (1832), *Staatswirthschaftliche Untersuchungen*, Munich: Anton Weber.

HOWEY R.S. (1960), *The Rise of the Marginal Utility School*, New York: Columbia University Press.

HUTCHISON T.W. (1988), *Before Adam Smith. The Emergence of Political Economy, 1662-1776*, New York: Basil Blackwell.

KAUDER E. (1965), *A History of Marginal Utility Theory*, Princeton: Princeton University Press.

KAUTZ J. (1860), *Die geschichtliche Entwickelung der National-Oekonomik und ihrer Literatur*, Vienna. Reprint 1970, Glashütten: Auvermann.

KNIES C. (1873-79), *Das Geld. Darlegung der Grundlehren von dem Gelde* (Geld und Credit, Erste Abtheilung), Berlin 1873: Weidmann. *Der Credit. Erste Hälfte* (Geld und Credit. Zweite Abtheilung), Berlin 1876: Weidmann. *Der Credit. Zweite Hälfte* (Geld und Credit. Zweite Abtheilung), Berlin 1879: Weidmann.

KUDLER J. (1846), *Die Grundlehren der Volkswirtschaftslehre*, 2 vols, Vienna.

KURZ H.D. (1998), 'Classical Economics in German-speaking Countries', in H.D. Kurz and N. Salvadori (eds), *The Elgar Companion to Classical Economics*, vol. I, pp. 128-135, Cheltenham: Edward Elgar.

LIST F. (1982 [1841]), *Das nationale System der politischen Ökonomie*, Stuttgart and Tuebingen: Cotta. Reprint 1982, Berlin: Akademie Verlag.

LOTZ J.F.E. (1821), *Handbuch der Staatswirtschaftslehre*, vols 1-3, Erlangen.

MARX K. (1954 [1867]), *Capital*, vol. I, Moscow: Foreign Languages Publishing House. English translation of *Das Kapital*, vol. I, Hamburg, 1867: Meissner.

MARX K. (1957 [1885]), *Capital*, vol. II, Moscow: Foreign Languages Publishing House. English translation of *Das Kapital*, vol. II, Hamburg, 1885: Meissner.

MARX K. (1959 [1894]), *Capital*, vol. III, Moscow: Foreign Languages Publishing House. English translation of *Das Kapital*, vol. III, Hamburg, 1894: Meissner.

MARX K. (1970 [1859]), *A Contribution to the Critique of Political Economy*, Moscow: Progress Publishers.

MARX K. (1975a [1861-3]), *Economic Manuscript of 1861-63*, Part I, Volume 30 of Karl Marx and Frederick Engels, *Collected Works*, New York: International Publishers.

MARX K. (1975b [1861-3]), *Economic Manuscript of 1861-63*, Part II, Volume 31 of Karl Marx and Frederick Engels, *Collected Works*, New York: International Publishers.

MARX K. (1975c [1861-3]), *Economic Manuscript of 1861-63*, Part III, Volume 32 of Karl Marx and Frederick Engels, *Collected Works*, New York: International Publishers.

MARX K. (1982 [1845]), Über Friedrich Lists Buch 'Das nationale System der politischen Ökonomie', in List (1982), pp. 440-77.

MEEK R.L. (1973), Introduction to 'Value and Money', in R.L. Meek (ed.), *Precursors of Adam Smith*, London: Dent, pp. 77-9.

MENGER C. (1871), *Grundsätze der Volkswirthschaftslehre*, Vienna: Wilhelm Braumüller.

MENGER C. (1981 [1871]), *Principles of Economics*, New York: New York University Press. English translation by J. Dingwall and B.F. Hoselitz of the second edition (1923) of *Grundsätze der Volkswirtschaftslehre*.

MÜLLER J.A. (1820), *Chronologische Darstellung der italienischen Klassiker über National-Ökonomie ...*, Pest.

ORTES G. (1774), *Della economia nazionale*, Venice.

PECCHIO G. (1829), *Storia della economia pubblica in Italia*, Lugano.

PECCHIO G. (1830), *Histoire de l'économie politique en Italie, ou Abrégé critique des économistes italiens*, translated by L. Gallois, Paris.

PRIBRAM K. (1983), *A History of Economic Reasoning*, Baltimore and London: The Johns Hopkins University Press.

RAU K.H. (1826-37), *Lehrbuch der Politischen Ökonomie*. Vol. I: *Grundsätze der Volkswirtschaftslehre*, Heidelberg 1826 (second ed. 1833, third ed. 1837, fourth ed. 1841, fifth ed. 1847). Vol. II: *Grundsätze der Volkswirtschaftspflege*, Heidelberg 1828, Vol. III: *Grundsätze der Finanzwissenschaft*, Heidelberg 1832-37.

RODBERTUS C. (1837), *Die Forderungen der arbeitenden Klassen*. In: Rodbertus (1972), *Gesammelte Werke und Briefe*, Abteilung I, Osnabrück.

RODBERTUS C. (1842), *Zur Erkenntnis unserer staatswirtschaftlichen Zustände. Heft 1: Fünf Theoreme*. In: Rodbertus (1972), *Gesammelte Werke und Briefe*, Abteilung I, Osnabrück.

ROSCHER W. (1874), *Geschichte der National-Oekonomik in Deutschland*, Munich and Berlin: Oldenbourg.

ROSSI P. (1843), *Cours d'économie politique*, Bruxelles.

SALIN E. (1951), *Geschichte der Volkswirtschaftslehre*, 4th edn, Tübingen: J.C.B. Mohr.

SAY J.-B. (1971 [1821]), *A Treatise on Political Economy*. English translation by C.R. Prinsep of the fourth edition (1819) of *Traité d'économie politique*, Philadelphia: Claxton, Remsen and Haffelfinger. Reprint 1971, New York: A.M. Kelley.

SAY J.-B. (1818), *Darstellung der Nationalökonomie und der Staatswirtschaft*, 2 vols, Heidelberg.

SAY J.-B. (1829-30), *Vollständiges Handbuch der Nationalökonomie*, 6 vols, Stuttgart.

SCHUMPETER J.A. (1914), 'Epochen der Dogmen- und Methodengeschichte', in: *Grundriß der Sozialökonomik*, I. Abteilung, Tübingen: Mohr, pp. 19-124.

SCHUMPETER J.A. (1954), *History of Economic Analysis*, New York: Oxford University Press.

SONNENFELS J. VON (1765), *Grundsätze der Polizey, Handlung und Finanzwissenschaft*.

STEINLEIN K. (1831), *Handbuch der Volkswirtschaftslehre*, vol. 1, Munich.

STREISSLER E. (1990), 'Menger, Böhm-Bawerk, and Wieser: The Origins of the Austrian School', in: K.H. Hennings and W.J. Samuels (eds) (1990), *Neoclassical Economic Theory 1870-1930*, Boston, Dordrecht, London: Kluwer.

THÜNEN J.H. von (1826 and 1850), *Der isolirte Staat in Beziehung auf Landwirtschaft und Nationalökonomie*. Part 1, Hamburg 1826, Part 2, Rostock 1850.

TURGOT A.R.J. (1971 [1770]), *Reflections on the Formation and the Distribution of Riches*, English translation by W.J. Ashley of *Réflexions sur la formation et la distribution des richesses*, Paris, 1770.

TURGOT A.R.J. (1973 [1808]), Value and Money, in R. L. Meek (ed.), *Precursors of Adam Smith*, London: Dent, pp. 79-100. English translation of 'Valeurs et monnaie', in *Œuvres*, ed. by Dupont de Nemours, 1808-1811.

VERRI P. (1760), *Elementi del commercio*.

VERRI P. (1771), *Meditazioni sulla economia politica ... con annotazioni di Gian-Rinaldo Carli*. In: *Scrittori classici italiani di economia politica*. Parte Moderna, vol. XV, Milano 1804.

VERRI P. (1986), *Reflections on Political Economy*, English translation of *Meditazioni sull'economia politica*. Fairfield, NJ: A.M. Kelly

WIESER F. (1893 [1889]), *Natural Value*, London. English translation (by W. Smart) of *Der natürliche Wert*, Vienna, 1889.

The reception of Italian economic thought in Germany and Austria from 1900 to the Second World War

Harald Hagemann and Matthias Rösch
University of Hohenheim*

> *"The most benevolent observer could not have paid any compliments to Italian economics in the early 1870's; the most malevolent observer could not have denied that it was second to none by 1914."*[1]
>
> Joseph Alois Schumpeter

1. Introduction

> *"... the great turning point was given by World War I. Before the war, Italian culture life had strong and regular connections with Germany. Practically all educated people in Italy could read German, most of them had visited Germany and studied there."*[2]
>
> Augusto Graziani

In a splendid paper Gioia (1999) has recently given a well-informed survey on the exchange and mutual stimulation between German and Italian economists in the period from 1861 to the 1930s. He rightly emphasizes that "[t]here is no doubt that in the period from the Unification of Italy to the outbreak of the Great War, there was a wealth of contacts between Italian and German scholars that is unequalled in the recent history of the two countries."[3] Although the "German model" had an enormous impact on the modernization process in Italy, and the Humboldt type of university in general had also a decisive influence on Italian culture and institutions, in economics there emerged a rather strange anomaly in the 1870s shortly after German

* The authors like to thank Pier Francesco Asso, Riccardo Faucci, Augusto Graziani, Marco Guidi, and Riccardo Realfonzo for most valuable comments.

[1] Schumpeter (1954, p. 855).

[2] Graziani (1989, pp. 58-59).

[3] Gioia (1999, p. 17).

unification. On the one hand, the Historical School influenced Italian economists, who early on took a strong interest in the activities of the *Verein für Sozialpolitik.* Vito Cusumano (Palermo), for example, was a participant in the 1872-73 foundation meetings in Eisenach and shortly afterwards published a book on the German historical school and the social question.[4] On the other hand, Francesco Ferrara's critical response and early attacks against "economic Germanism" initiated a fierce debate in Italy which in many respects parallelled the debate on method between Menger and Schmoller which occupied German-speaking economists until World War I.

There are further strong parallels and issues of important mutual influences, as, for example, an extensive debate between German and Italian authors on Marxian economics and socialism.[5] Throughout more than six decades from its foundation until its dissolution in 1936 problems of trade policy were much more at the centre of repeated controversies between academic members of the Verein für Socialpolitik than problems of social policy. This parallelled the struggle between free-traders and protectionists in the decades after Italian political unification.[6]

After decades of strong exchange it is therefore not surprising to find at the beginning of our period under closer consideration that the young Schumpeter in his early essay on the mathematical method of theoretical economics does not only mention Pareto as the successor of Walras but also explicitly refers to Barone, Antonelli and Rossi as representatives of mathematical economics in Italy.[7] It might be more surprising to find among the eighteen contributions included in the Festschrift dedicated to Adolph Wagner on the occasion of his seventieth birthday (Adler 1905), besides ten contributions in German, eight other papers not only written by Italian colleagues but also published in Italian, thereby indicating that the linguistic barriers must have been lower than today. The list of Italian authors includes Cusumano, Carlo F. Ferraris who had studied in Germany in 1873 and as the minister for public works was responsible for the nationalization of the Italian railway system in the year the Wagner Festschrift was published, Achille Loria and Costantino Bresciani who had attended Wagner's courses and seminars in 1881 and 1902/3 respectively, Camillo Supino, Fedele Lampertico, Rodolfo Benini and Augusto Graziani.

In the following we concentrate on the reception of Italian economic ideas in the German language area between the beginning of last century and World War II. In s*ection II* we present the outcome of the systematic analysis of the leading scholarly journals with regard to contributions by Italian authors or

---

[4] See Cusumano (1875) and Faucci (1999).

[5] See, e.g., the more recent contributions by Groenewegen (2000) and Kurz (1995, 1999).

[6] See Augello (1989) and Hagemann (2001).

[7] See Schumpeter (1906, p. 49).

reviews and surveys informing the readers on the development of economic thought in Italy. Our results show that the direct routes were so numerous, but also important with regard to quality, that, in contrast to the contribution on the spread of Italian economics in the German language area in the earlier period by Gehrke and Kurz, we don't have to rely on indirect routes in the dissemination of Italian economics via foreign authors. The material is already much richer than can be dealt with in a single paper. We therefore will focus our attention on some authors, topics and streams of dissemination we find important.

Section III will deal with the resonance of the ideas of the leading representatives of the Italian School of marginalism in the German language area. Issues of monetary theory (including the analysis of inflation) and business cycle theory were among the major topics in the interwar period. Although Italo-German relations overall decreased in this phase, compared to pre World War I standards, nevertheless in this field the exchange of ideas remained on a very high level until the Nazis' rise to power, as is shown in *section IV*. In *section V* we discuss the dissemination of the main ideas of the Italian school of Public Finance in Austria and Germany, where their importance was recognized much earlier than in the Anglo-Saxon world. For the dissemination of ideas educated, enlightened and internationally-oriented scholars are indispensable. In *section VI*, besides some more prominent cases, we put emphasis on the work and achievements of two economists whose contributions deserve merits but who are hardly known anymore to a young generation of economists today. This signals the strong internationalization of economics in the post-1945 period. In *section VII* we draw some conclusions on the era of a strong exchange of ideas between economics in Italy and in the German language area which basically came to an end with the fascist period.

2. Italian Economic Thought in German and Austrian Learned Journals

> *No, Italian economics need to be ashamed of its performance during the fifty years of Croce's period. For the sake of our country let us pass over the false and deliberately false things that were written about the so-called corporative economy. These misguided efforts are expiated by the resistance of the majority. Two journals were suppressed - the Riforma Sociale in 1935 and the Giornale degli Economisti in 1943.*
>
> Luigi Einaudi[8]

[8] Einaudi (1955, pp. 22-23).

At a time when different national styles of economic research were prevailing and internationalization was in an infant state publications in learned journals were very important for the information on theoretical developments abroad and an exchange of ideas between scholars in different countries. We therefore have examined leading journals for articles and reviews on works by Italian economists in the relevant period.[9] We focused our analysis on the following six journals

- the *Zeitschrift für die gesamte Staatswissenschaft*, the oldest scholarly journal in the German language area which was edited by Karl Bücher since 1904 and by Georg Brodnitz from 1924 until 1933;

- the *Jahrbücher für Nationalökonomie und Statistik*, founded in 1863 by Bruno Hildebrand and edited by Johannes Conrad since 1879 and by Ludwig Elster from 1915 to 1933;

- *Schmollers Jahrbuch für Gesetzgebung, Verwaltung und Volkswirtschaft im Deutschen Reiche*, founded in 1871, edited by Gustav Schmoller from 1881 until his death in 1917, thereafter by Hermann Schumacher and from 1923 until 1938 by Arthur Spiethoff;

- the *Finanzarchiv,* founded in 1884 and edited until his death in 1931 by Georg von Schanz, followed by Hans Teschemacher;

- the *Weltwirtschaftliches Archiv*, founded in 1913 by Bernhard Harms as a new specialized journal to focus on international trade and the world economy as the object of economic research. In the two decades of Harms's editorship the journal also published important theoretical papers and soon gained international reputation, and

- the Austrian *Zeitschrift für Nationalökonomie*, founded in 1930 and edited by Hans Mayer, which particularly because of the activities and connections of the managing editor Oskar Morgenstern became the leading scholarly journal in the German language area in the 1930s.

---

[9] For a detailed analysis of the role of learned journals in the professionalization process of economics in the German language area see Hagemann (1991).

Our analysis shows the following results.

Title	Reviews		Articles	
Zeitschrift für die gesamte Staatswissenschaft	1900-1909:	2	1900-1909:	1
	1910-1919:	0	1910-1919:	0
	1920-1929:	12	1920-1929:	1
	1930-1939:	15	1930-1939:	0
	1900-1939:	**29**	**1900-1939:**	**2**
Jahrbücher für Nationalökonomie und Statistik	1900-1909:	65	1900-1909:	5
	1910-1919:	37	1910-1919:	0
	1920-1929:	21	1920-1929:	1
	1930-1939:	84	1930-1939:	14
	1900-1939:	**207**	**1900-1939:**	**20**
Schmollers Jahrbuch für Gesetzgebung, Verwaltung und Volkswirtschaft im Deutschen Reiche	1900-1909:	14	1900-1910:	0
	1910-1919:	12	1910-1919:	0
	1920-1929:	12	1920-1929:	2
	1930-1939:	46	1930-1939:	0
	1900-1939:	**84**	**1900-1939:**	**2**
Finanzarchiv	1900-1909:	3	1900-1909:	4
	1910-1919:	8	1910-1919:	0
	1920-1929:	5	1920-1929:	0
	1930-1939:	17	1930-1939:	2
	1900-1939:	**33**	**1900-1939:**	**6**
Weltwirtschaftliches Archiv	1913-1919:	33	1913-1919:	5
	1920-1929:	20	1920-1929:	2
	1930-1939:	84	1930-1939:	14
	1913-1939:	**137**	**1913-1939:**	**21**
Zeitschrift für Nationalökonomie	**1930-1939:**	**80**	**1930-1939:**	**24**

With regard to our key question *Schmollers Jahrbuch*, the *Finanzarchiv* and the *Zeitschrift für die gesamte Staatswissenschaft* are the least interesting of the inspected journals. This is particularly disappointing in the case of *Schmollers Jahrbuch* since so many Italian economists until World War I had a stronger orientation towards the Historical School. However, this is not reflected in substantial contributions but only in numerous book reviews, among them several by prominent economists like Achille Loria, Augusto Graziani, Francesco Vito and Amintore Fanfani. The situation is not better with the *Finanzarchiv* despite the high quality of the Italian contributions to public finance which has been recognized rather early in Germany. The problem was that in the journal for a very long time the archive character dominated and the quality and reputation increased significantly only after Fritz Neumark took over editorial responsibility in 1955. So it is not surprising that three out of six articles in our period are reports by Bresciani on the development of the financial system in Italy between 1902 and 1908. In four decades the *Zeitschrift für die gesamte Staatswissenschaft* included only two articles by Luigi Nina (1900) and Robert Davidsohn (1928). One paper and 27 of 29 reviews (among them two by Gustavo Del Vecchio and one each by Enrico Barone, Benedetto Croce and Antonio De Viti de Marco) were published in the decade after Georg Brodnitz became the sole editor at the end of 1923. After the Nazis' rise to power Brodnitz was dismissed from his position at the University of Halle and also forced to resign as the editor of the journal (and later killed in the Holocaust in Lodz 1941-42). With the new editors publications by Italian authors ebbed completely.

The most important article published in the *Jahrbücher für Nationalökonomie und Statistik* by an Italian author is perhaps the article on the methods of income distribution statistics by the young Costantino Bresciani (1907) who assumed also the family name of his mother in the following year.[10] Bresciani's early work on personal income distribution focusses on "Pareto's law". Although crediting Pareto for his innovative application of exact mathematical methods to income statistics he criticizes that the Pareto distribution is valid only for high incomes whereas for lower incomes other methods are better suited as a measure of inequality. Bresciani thereby followed Ladislaus von Bortkiewicz who had proposed the mean deviation as a measure of inequality and had evoked his life-long interest in statistical methods and statistical tests of theoretical propositions when he had been his teacher at the University of Berlin a few years before. Interestingly, in the year of his death Bortkiewicz (1931), when discussing disparity measures in income statistics, paid tribute to Bresciani Turroni. His former student, on the other hand, had defended his teacher against the critique raised by Corrado Gini against Bortkiewicz's contribution on the 'law of small numbers' with which he had made his name in statistics only a few years before when he recognized the importance of the Poisson distribution which he applied to the analysis of the frequency of deaths from horse-kicks among Prussian cavalrymen. This debate which took place in the *Giornale degli Economisti*, mainly in 1908/9, is another good indicator of the strong exchange and mutual influence between German and Italian economists before the war.

In the following two decades the *Jahrbücher* published only reviews with the notable exception of a paper by Umberto Ricci (1931a) on the static theory of rent. The strong increase in the number of articles and reviews in the 1930s seems to be mainly caused by political reasons. This is made explicit by the new editors (since 1934) Otto von Zwiedineck-Südenhorst and Gerhard Albrecht who published an article by Giorgio Del Vecchio on 'economics and jurisprudence' in 1936 to which they added an introductory footnote in which they emphasized the importance to argue against the dominant position of the relationship between law and economics in the Romanic literature from the viewpoint of fascism (p. 274 n.). The prevailing political publishing motive is even better indicated by the 'boom year' 1938 in

[10] See Bini (1992) for a detailed study of Bresciani Turroni's life and work.

which no less than ten papers by Italian authors focussing on economic problems of the corporate state are included. However, despite some contributions by some staunch promoters of corporative economics, such as Gino Arias or Giuseppe Bottai, we also find articles by Giovanni Demaria, Giuseppe Ugo Papi and by Marco Fanno on the structure of the corporative economy (Fanno 1938b). In this paper the author distinguishes the corporate from the collectivist economy but also emphasizes the necessary complementarity of the corporate state and the corporate economy and the three main functions of the latter: the leading, the incentive and the production-stimulating function. Furthermore, the author who had made his main contributions in business-cycle theory finally emphasizes the welfare-enhancing nature of the corporate economy compared to a liberal economic system by an elimination of economic fluctuations. Knowing that the author was forced to resign from his professorship at the University of Padova soon afterwards because of the racial legislation issued in 1938 and that his academic career was interrupted until 1945, it is quite puzzling to read some of the passages of this article published in a German journal in 1938.[11]

The situation was quite different with the *Weltwirtschaftliches Archiv* which from the very beginning published articles and reviews by Italian economists as well as reviews on their works on a regular basis. International scientific standards were mainly kept even in the Nazi period when, after a short interplay by Jens Jessen, Andreas Predöhl as the new Director of the Kiel Institute was also the editor of the journal from 1934 to 1945. Gustavo Del Vecchio, for example, gave a detailed theoretical analysis of the world economic crisis (1932) based on his earlier theory of economic dynamics[12], and a survey on new problems in international trade theory (1935) in which, amidst a period of increasing political pressure towards autarky and protectionism, by admitting some inadequacies of the classical theory of international trade, the author argues to avoid the worst 'mercantilist failures' by skillfully referring to 'dynamic issues' such as retaliatory tariffs and 'practical experiences' that those countries which are most liberal in their foreign trade policy will be granted the most favourable conditions by other countries.

Corrado Gini, the great statistician who joined the fascist movement, against the background of Italy's conquest of Ethiopia and Nazi Germany's claim for getting back the former colonies, on the other hand, came to the result that "trade follows the flag", i.e. the dependence of international trade upon territorial

[11] However, Fanno is the only contributor besides Arias, who is not included in a volume on 'Corporative Economic Theory', edited by Eraldo Fossati, and published also by Gustav Fischer in Jena. Besides Bottai, Demaria and Papi, Gino Borgatta, Giovanni de Francisci Gerbino, Agostino Lanzillo, Guglielmo Masci and Arrigo Serpieri are present in both collections to which contributions by Benito Mussolini, Federico Chessa and Mario Marsili-Libelli are added in the book collection.

It should also be recalled that Demaria was the only one who in 1941, during a meeting held in Pisa, launched a courageous attack against the Fascist policy of national self-sufficiency and advocated a policy of free exchange.

[12] For a detailed study on Del Vecchio as the most important Italian advocator of the Austrian business cycle theory see Realfonzo (2002).

sovereignty which had become greater since World War I particularly with regard to exports (Gini 1938). In an earlier article in which he analyzed the 'consequences of extreme forms of inflation on the economic organism' Gini (1934) pointed out the function of inflation as one of the "most efficient and bloodless means" to counteract the tendency of capital to overgrow and the 'beneficial' effects of the hyperinflation for Germany to exempt herself from greater parts of the reparation payments. His organic interpretation of the German inflation is not only strongly at odds with the careful theoretical analysis by his Italian colleague Bresciani Turroni (see section IV) but his emphasis on the great trust of foreigners into the efficiency of the German economy which led to greater capital imports after the end of inflation also neglects the fact that these capital imports basically came to an end with the greater electoral successes of the Nazi party since the election to the *Reichstag* in September 1930 which led to a substantially higher political risk premium in the interest rate.

Bresciani Turroni, himself a well-known author in the German language area who lectured at the newly established University of Cairo from 1927 to 1940, contributed three papers on 'The Elasticity of Consumption of Egyptian cotton' (1931), 'Egypt in the world economic crisis' (1933) and 'The Structure of the Egyptian Economy' (1943) which were published in the *Weltwirtschaftliches Archiv*. Most interesting, however, is his long article on 'Current Trends in Italian Economics', submitted already in October 1942 but published only shortly before the end of the war (Bresciani Turroni 1944). The article is a masterly example of keeping scholarly standards under difficult political circumstances. The author never attacked explicitly the corporatist views of the fascists but nevertheless gave an elaborated implicit critique in which he sticked to his liberal convictions and his theoretical preferences. Bowing to the great German economists Gossen and Thünen, emphasizing that all great Italian economists hold the view that there is only one unifying economic theory which is the classical one, and emphasizing parallels between the classical doctrines and the Austrian School at the start, Bresciani Turroni takes the critique by the Vienna economist Hans Mayer (1932) against the theory of general economic equilibrium as the strawman to introduce that very same theory as his standard of reference, in particular for corporatist economics. Referring to logical conclusions and necessities, such as the correspondence of the number of equations with the number of unknowns, the author stresses that governmental intervention, for example by price-setting or the introduction of rationing schemes, makes the solution of the equilibrium problem in a system of interventionism impossible.[13] In the same way the conditions of bilateral equalization of all trade balances is deemed to failure in a multilateral world. Economic laws such as those of production or the distribution of income by

[13] See Bresciani Turroni (1944, p. 195).

consumers on different goods according to their preferences, also hold in the corporate state which may change distribution "within certain boundaries" by way of taxation or subsidies *after* prices of factors of production are fixed according to the economic laws of production. Corporate interventions thus cannot escape the validity of economic laws. Bresciani Turroni (p. 209) comes to the final conclusion that the transformation to a corporative economy in Italy has no major consequences for pure economic theory and that with regard to this main result of his investigation he is in line with the great majority of his Italian colleagues, in particular with such an important theorist like Fanno who had written one of the best books on corporatism.[14]

Although Hans Mayer was officially the main editor (until 1938 together with Richard Reisch and Richard Schüller), it was basically the work of Oskar Morgenstern as the managing editor (until 1934 in collaboration with Paul Rosenstein-Rodan) who made the *Zeitschrift für Nationalökonomie* the outstanding learned journal in the German language area in the 1930s. In the three years of his Rockefeller Foundation fellowship from 1925 to 1928, of which he spent the first two in the United States and the final year in France and Italy, Morgenstern had built up an enormous range and depth of contacts to the world's leading economists. In the eight years until the 'Anschluss' in 1938 the journal published not only papers by the best Austrian and German scholars, such as Haberler, Hayek, Machlup, Karl Menger, Mises, Morgenstern, Röpke, Schneider and Stackelberg, but also by eminent international economists, among them Aftalion, Åkerman, Ellis, Frisch, Hicks, Hutchison, Knight, Lange, Leontief, Marget, Myrdal, Ohlin, Opie, Joan Robinson, Henry Schultz, Tinbergen, Viner, Wald and Zeuthen. It is the more remarkable that in one decade no less than 24 articles by Italian economists were included. The 'leaders' were Umberto Ricci and Eraldo Fossati with six articles each, followed by Attilio Cabiati with four. Mauro Fasiani contributed a long article on 'The current state of the pure theory of public finance in Italy' which was published in three parts. Whereas Luigi Einaudi, Benvenuto Griziotti and Giuseppe Ugo Papi published one article, Marco Fanno contributed two important papers on 'The elasticity of demand for replacement goods' (1930) and 'Errors over time as causes of economic fluctuations' (1933b), a different version of his 1931 Italian article[15] which, although keeping the core of the analysis, stresses more Hayekian elements of the time-structure of production as equilibrium conditions whereas in the Italian version greater emphasis is on

---

[14] In contrast to Bresciani Turroni who based his statement on general equilibrium theory in the tradition of Walras, Pareto and Pantaleoni, Fanno (1938) based his similar reduction of the problems of a corporative economy to a special case of applied economics on the Marshallian partial equilibrium approach. For a more detailed discussion of Italian economics in the interwar period and the different blends of corporativist theory see Faucci (1990) and Bini, Guidi and Magliulo (2000).

[15] The Italian article 'Production Cycles, Credit Cycles and Industrial Fluctuations' was published in an English translation only in 1993 with an excellent introduction by Augusto Graziani.

Wicksell's monetary theory distinguishing between the monetary and natural rates of interest and on some Cambridge contributions like Keynes's *Treatise*.

It is also quite interesting to have a closer look at the translators. Here we do not only find Oskar Morgenstern himself as the translator of the first three articles delivered by Ricci in 1930-31 but also Rosenstein-Rodan and the young Privatdozent from the University of Cracow Oskar Lange as the translators of parts I and II of Fasiani's contribution respectively. Louise Sommer translated the first Fanno paper and Martha Stephanie Braun (later Browne) another paper by Ricci. Furthermore, if one also includes the long list of Italian books in economics, reviewed by Italian and non-Italian colleagues, then clearly an overall picture emerges of a rather good knowledge of Italian among contemporary Austrian economists in particular which comes to a close second to the knowledge of German among contemporary Italian economists.

3. The Italian School of Marginalism

> *"No other country erected a similar pedestal for his statue, and in the Anglo-American world both the man and the thinker have remained strangers to this day."*[16]
>
> Joseph A. Schumpeter about Vilfredo Pareto

Piero Barucci has convincingly shown that "by 1890 marginalism in Italy had already reached its maturity; by this time it had completed its first steps", and this despite the fact "that during the twenty years from 1865 to 1885 (the interim between Francesco Ferrara and Maffeo Pantaleoni) Italian economic thought did not succeed in producing any really outstanding theoretician" (Barucci 1972, pp. 512-513). The decisive breakthrough came with the early work of *Maffeo Pantaleoni* (1857-1924), in particular his 'Contribution to the Theory of the Distribution of Public Expenditure', with which he applied the new theory of marginal utility to the public domain and which also became the starting point of the great Italian tradition in public finance, and his textbook *Principii di economia pura* (1889), which, quite uncommon at the time, less than a decade later had already been translated into English. Barucci therefore regards the publication year of the article as "the entrance date of marginalism into Italy" (p. 522) and Schumpeter (1954, p. 857) speaks of *Pure Economics* as a "landmark", paving the way to new developments, although he adds not without ambiguity that "there is nothing entirely original in it" and concluding, what at the reader's impression might be seen as Pantaleoni's greatest achievement, namely that "he introduced Pareto to the work of Walras" (p. 858).

[16] Schumpeter (1949, p. 147).

There can be no doubt that the evolution of modern Italian economic thought originated from Pantaleoni who had a very cosmopolitan education and was well versed in the contemporary economic literature in the most important language areas. His mother an English lady, his father a physician, political writer and friend of Cavour, Pantaleoni got his early education in Berlin. He attributed his new theory to Jevons and Walras but he was also influenced by Gossen and later instrumental for the Italian translation of Menger's *Grundsätze* which were first published as a supplement to the *Giornale degli Economisti* in 1906/1907. Nevertheless Pantaleoni was rather critical of Menger and also of Böhm-Bawerk (very much to the dislike of Schumpeter), but more appreciative for Friedrich von Wieser.

Among the leading economists in the German language area it was undoubtedly Schumpeter who displayed the greatest interest for the development of Italian economic thought. Being himself fluent in Italian and having a great inclination for Italian culture in general, his affection was greatly enhanced by his admiration for the theory of general economic equilibrium as it had been formulated by Walras who for Schumpeter remained the greatest of all economists during his whole life. This explains that he regarded Pareto as the most eminent of all the Italian economists to whom he sent a copy of his Vienna habilitation thesis *Das Wesen und der Hauptinhalt der theoretischen Nationalökonomie (The Essence and the Main Content of Theoretical Economics,* 1908) immediately after publication. To his disappointment Pareto, who was deeply embedded in French and Italian culture, had a great admiration for the ancient Greek and Roman ones but was disinterested in the German one, and, in contrast to most of his Italian contemporary colleagues was unable to read German, passed the book forward to Pantaleoni.

It should be emphasized that for Schumpeter the two books, *Wesen* and *The Theory of Economic Development* published three years later, formed a unity. He saw economic processes falling into two different and clearly distinguishable classes, *static* and *dynamic* ones and regarded economic development as essentially a disturbance of the static equilibrium of the economy. In *Wesen* first the strict equilibrium conditions and their logical implications had to be worked out. According to Schumpeter Walras had provided the required pure logic of the interdependence between economic quantities whereas it was Marx whose vision of economic evolution as a distinct process generated by the economy itself formed the main challenge for the complementary *Theory of Economic Development.* The basic ideas of that book are already formulated in his 1910 article 'On the Essence of Economic Crises' which was soon notified in Italy where Grilli published a synthesis of the paper in the same year.[17]

---

[17] See Graziani (1989) for an excellent and more detailed analysis of the reciprocity of Schumpeter and the Italian economists' thought.

During his German years when he was Professor at the University of Bonn, Schumpeter made some attempts to launch a German translation of Pareto's *Manuale*. In a letter to the publisher Oskar Siebeck in Tübingen from 3 June 1929 he stresses the importance of Pareto's book and particularly of the mathematical appendix. However, in typical Schumpeterian ambiguity he emphasizes that Pareto's appendix comprises small errors wherefore it has to be checked carefully by a competent mathematician. For that considerable and expensive work he recommended Erich Schneider (1900-1970), at that time a high school teacher for mathematics and physics, who three years later finished his habilitation with Schumpeter. Next Schumpeter recommends more strongly a translation of Pigou's *Study in Public Finance* and comes to the conclusion: "From the viewpoint of the publisher I could recommend this translation even more than that of Pareto although being a theoretician myself naturally I would be much happier with the latter since thereby the knowledge of one of the most important works on economics would be disseminated."[18] Can it be surprising that until today no publisher had taken the risk and we are still lacking a German translation of the *Manuale*?

Despite all the efforts of Schumpeter and in particular Weinberger, in whose 1930 introduction to mathematical economics Pareto figures prominently, his work, with the exceptions of the analyses of personal income distribution and neoclassical demand curves, became not well known in Germany and Austria. Gottfried Eisermann, in his famous essay on Pareto as an economist *and* sociologist which stresses the complementarity for a deeper understanding of his work, in 1961 therefore had to diagnose that Pareto is still "underrated"[19] in Germany, a statement which comes very close to Schumpeter's diagnosis for the Anglo-American world quoted above. In this centennial article Schumpeter certainly reveals a close affinity for Pareto which may be rooted also in some close parallels between the two. Although they were both theoretical economists with a deep appreciation for the theory of general equilibrium based on rational individual behaviour, they both had also a great interest on sociology and politics which centered on irrational collective behaviour. It would be an understatement to stress that they were not great believers in democracy.

This was different with the great German sociologist and economist Max Weber (1864-1920) who was among the intellectual founders of the Weimar Republic. Weber and Pareto were contemporaries and there were some strong similarities, such as their emphasis that scientific work had to be 'objective', i.e. free of personal values, and the preferences and prejudices of researchers should not be allowed to interfere with theoretical analysis, the collection of empirical data and its 'objective' evaluation. However, they both conflicted with their own

[18] Schumpeter (2000, pp. 166-167).

[19] See Eisermann (1961, pp. 22-23) who is critical of Schumpeter's "excessive overestimation" of Walras and ambivalence towards Pareto.

conception from time to time.[20] In particular Pareto transcended the concept of a value-free science at characteristic places. It is unintelligible that the relationship between Weber and Pareto is characterized by mutual neglect.

The most able follower of Pantaleoni and particularly Pareto was *Enrico Barone* (1859-1924). While he has become famous for his paper on the collectivist state his textbook *Principi di economia politica* (1908) is a brilliant, clearly written introduction into the major contributions and key ideas of the members of the Lausanne school. It was Schumpeter who initiated the German translation of Barone's *Principles* (1927), excellently done by Hans Staehle (1902-1961), son of an Italian mother and at that time Lecturer at Schumpeter's faculty at the University of Bonn, and also an able econometrician who was Visiting Lecturer at Harvard University from 1939 to 1945 and in 1947 became the Director of the Statistic Section of the Research Division of the UN's Economic Commission for Europe in Geneva. Schumpeter himself wrote the introduction to Barone's *Grundzüge* in which he points out the qualities of the book and the complementarity with Gustav Cassel's textbook *Theoretische Sozialökonomie*, very successful in Germany in the 1920s, with which it had in common the descent from Walras. Schumpeter (p. 8) saw advantages of Cassel's exposition in the areas of monetary and business-cycle theory but found Barone's textbook superior in the theoretical foundations and particularly with regard to the monopoly problem. The book was soon widely recognized. Among the great resonance Barone's book received two longer reviews are worth mentioning: by Schumpeter's former fellow student from Vienna Emil Lederer[21] and by Friedrich August Hayek[22] who, in contrast to Schumpeter, praises the chapter on crises and agrees with Staehle that it anticipates the major ideas of modern research on business cycles.

It was Hayek himself who in the heated British debate on the economics of socialism in the 1930s took Barone's paper on 'The Ministry of Production in the Collectivist State' in his collection (Hayek 1935) and made it known to the English-speaking world, when so-called 'neoclassical socialists', like H.D. Dickinson, Oskar Lange and Abba Lerner, dominated the debate. In contrast to this debate on collectivist economic planning and the earlier heated debate in Germany which had been launched by Ludwig von Mises's article 'Economic Calculation in the Socialist Commonwealth' (1920), ideological motivations had been excluded from Barone's article. Like Pareto earlier, whose "contribution has been overshadowed by that of Barone" (Schumpeter 1954, p. 987), he showed that the conditions for a collective maximum in a socialist economy are equivalent with the conditions for general equilibrium in a fully competitive economy. Barone

[20] Due to the greater interest of sociologists a selection of his writings was published in German in the 1970s. See Pareto (1975). Shortened German versions of his *Trattato di Sociologia Generale* (1916), which have been translated and edited by Carl Brinkmann and Gottfried Eisermann, have been published already in 1955 and 1962.

[21] *Archiv für Sozialwissenschaft und Sozialpolitik*, 58, 1927, pp. 655-658.

[22] *Zeitschrift für die gesamte Staatswissenschaft*, 85, 1928, pp. 178-181.

dismissed the concepts of utility and indifference curves entirely and based it completely on observable data on prices and quantities, thus striving for a theory of revealed preference. However, it took until the publication of Samuelson's *Foundations* (1947, p. 214ff.) to give a full proof of the Paretian conditions of optimum as they relate to the planning of production under collectivism and a thorough assessment of Barone's achievements.

4. Monetary Theory and Business Cycle Theory

> "*... it seems significant that in connection with business cycle theory, there was an expansion and a consolidation of relations between Italian economists and the Austrian school, not only with reference to the general vision of the economy and economic relations, but also with reference to certain explanations of the business cycle.*"[23]
>
> Vitantonio Gioia

Since the mid-nineteenth century the study of crises and economic fluctuations became a major issue in German economics. This holds for the Historical School as well as for Marx for whom crises and cycles were the very essence of the evolution of capitalist economics. At the beginning of the twentieth century we can find leading economists like Arthur Spiethoff and Werner Sombart in this area. Shortly afterwards Schumpeter published his *Theory of Economic Development* and in the late 1920s a new generation of excellent young theoreticians is working in this field.[24] In Italy the situation was quite different. Due to the dominance of an approach that considered equilibrium, or at least a tendency towards equilibrium, as the normal state of affairs and crises as something "pathological"[25], economic fluctuations were regarded as of some practical importance but of no greater significance for theoretical analysis, and even Pantaleoni's call for economic dynamics went largely unanswered. Nevertheless there was some dissemination of economic ideas also in this area and when business-cycle theory and monetary theory took on greater weight in the interwar period some important collaborations between Italian economists and their colleagues in the German language area developed.

An integral part of the latter was Knut Wicksell whose distinction between the money and the natural rates of interest later became an important element as the

[23] Gioia (1999, p. 42).
[24] For a more detailed analysis see Hagemann (1999).
[25] See, for example, Supino (1907, pp. 1-14).

propagation mechanism in Austrian approaches to business-cycle theory as they were developed by Hayek and Mises. Although his original aim was to extend the quantity theory of money and his own theory of the business cycle remained a fragment, he essentially regarded (an unsteady stream of) technical inventions and improvements as the deepest cause of cyclical fluctuations, treated the cycle as fundamentally a real phenomenon on which monetary disorders may indeed be superimposed. This is made clear in his article 'A new theory of crises', written in 1907 but published only recently (Wicksell 1998). In that article we find Wicksell also commenting on Supino's attempt to restate the significance of the theory of economic equilibrium.

> Finding a satisfactory explanation for *general* crises has hitherto been as difficult as finding one for partial or local crises has been easy. It has therefore been tempting to interpret a general crisis as simply the sum, the chance conjunction, of a number of partial crises. An attempt along these lines can be found, for example, in Camillo Supino's book *Le crisi economiche*, which, although not very original, is certainly worth reading. However, that is probably a false view. The relationship of a general crisis to ones that are only partial is, if I am not mistaken, precisely like that of a change in the general price level to movements in the prices of particular types of goods, because the characteristic feature of a *partial* crisis is that the depression affecting one type of good or one location is *offset* by an upswing in other types of goods or other locations. (Wicksell, 1998, p. 260)

At that time Italian economists had not so much to say on the subject. A little bit more than two decades later we find Hayek whose *Geldtheorie und Konjunkturtheorie* (1929) was strongly influenced by Wicksell's distinction between the two rates of interest and the cumulative process analysis repeatedly in high praise of another Italian economist, namely Marco Fanno. In the German edition of *Prices and Production* Hayek (1931, p. 24, n. 1) writes concerning Fanno's book on *Banks and the Money Market*:

> After I have tried in vain for a long time to get this extremely rare work and therefore neither in my earlier works nor in the English edition of this book could refer on it finally the author himself was so generous to borrow me his copy for examination while I finalize the German edition for printing. I very much regret that this extremely clear and careful investigation so far was not only inaccessible for me but also otherwise seemingly had become rarely known outside Italy and therefore could not exert the influence it would have deserved in the interest of the development of monetary theory. Unfortunately, even now my insufficient knowledge of the Italian language and the only temporary possession of this extensive work have prevented to realize all the benefits which a corresponding study must offer.

These benefits then must have been greater when Fanno's 1933 paper was published in the *Zeitschrift für Nationalökonomie* and particularly when Fanno's new version of his 1912 essay on banking, 'The pure theory of the money market', came out in a collection edited by Hayek himself in the same year (Fanno 1933a).[26] Hayek's high praise for Fanno was not surprising since the Italian colleague's views were strongly shaped by Wicksell's *Interest and Prices*, published in 1898 and for a long time available only in the German original. According to the leading Italian expert on Fanno, in the 1920s and early 1930s "Fanno was the only Italian author who had fully appreciated the Wicksellian doctrine of the monetary and natural rates of interest as well as the doctrine of forced saving, first formulated by Ludwig von Mises" (Graziani 1993, p, 395).

Gustavo Del Vecchio's research on monetary theory was strongly influenced by the theory of money Walras had developed in the fourth edition of *Elements d'economie pure* (1900). In a series of papers, which were published from 1909 onwards, Del Vecchio (1883-1972) applied the marginal principle to money and incorporated the special case of the value of money into the general structure built upon the law of marginal utility. Del Vecchio's work is clearly distinct from that of Marco Fanno. Whereas the latter is 'Austrian' in character, Del Vecchio is more closely associated with Schumpeter's interest in the interplay between pure economics and economic history. Del Vecchio came also significantly near to a Schumpeterian approach in his 1928 Vienna paper 'Untersuchungen zur Theorie des Unternehmergewinnes' in which he regarded profits as the most evident expression of the dynamic character of the economy and problems of equilibrium as only special cases in the study of dynamic theory.

In his *History of Economic Analysis* Schumpeter (1954) not only praises Albert Aupetit and Karl Schlesinger as two excellent followers of Walras in the creation of the modern theory of money but also refers "to the original work of Del Vecchio" (p. 1082) which was "summed up in his *Grundlinien der Geldtheorie* and more completely in his *Ricerche sopra la teoria generale della moneta* (1932)". The German book on money was an outline of Del Vecchio's theory which was largely based on his earlier Italian papers but for the first time made the attempt of forming a concise theoretical unity, in which also problems of bank credits and the determination of and effects of changes in the discount rate were in the centre of his analysis. Although Schumpeter, in collaboration with Emil Lederer, was the general editor of the series *Beiträge zur ökonomischen Theorie*, in which Del Vecchio's book was the first volume to be published, interestingly in the German edition, contrary to the later Italian one, most of the historical explanations, as well as case illustrations, statistical data and critical discussions of other authors' viewpoints, were eliminated in order to concentrate on the theoretical core. This

[26] In this collection of essays Gunnar Myrdal's German edition of his 1931 series of lectures on Wicksell's monetary theory was also published (Myrdal 1933).

procedure had caused several troubles for the translator and editor, which was openly admitted in the foreword by Otto Weinberger who himself had been one of a few exceptions to the widespread neglect of Walras's contributions to monetary theory.

Del Vecchio, who had completed his postgraduate studies in Berlin before World War I, was forced to resign from his academic activities in 1938 at the Bocconi University in Milan when the Italian fascist government adopted anti-semitic measures. His German contributions (like those of Fanno) can be regarded as an instance of the existence of an (academic) international civil society which during the Weimar Republic – although less intensively than before World War I, when, e.g., Wicksell had published his *Geldzins und Güterpreise* (1898) – still expressed itself in German as an international medium. During the Nazi years this academic framework collapsed under the impact of the same factors which forced many scholars to emigrate from Germany and Austria.

The most active Italian economist in Germany undoubtedly was Bresciani Turroni since he had started to publish quite regularly in scholarly journals in his postgraduate student phase in Berlin between 1903 and 1905. His long experience with and deep knowledge of the German economy qualified him to become a member of the Italian delegation at the Reparations Commission in fall 1920 and financial adviser to the Berlin office of the Allied Reparations Commission in 1924. So he had first-hand observations and professional experience with the early Weimar Republic's hyperinflation which formed the basis of his brilliant masterpiece *Le vicende del marco tedesco* (1931). In a modern reference work on the German inflation the following assessment is given:

> Three standard works, namely, those by Frank D. Graham, Costantino Bresciani-Turroni, and Karsten Laursen and Jørgen Pedersen, reflect the character of existing research on the course, causes and consequences of the German inflation of 1914-1923. They have the following in common:
>
> 1 They were all written by non-Germans, were published outside Germany and have not been translated into German. Despite the extraordinary importance of the inflation in German history, and the long shadow it has cast over subsequent events, the literature generated by German economic historians about the period is, to date, rather slight.
> 2 They all confine their attention to the period following the First World War, without due regard to the fact that the origins of the postwar inflation lay in the financial policy of the Reich during the War itself.
> 3 They were all written by economists with primarily theoretical interests.
> 4 Historical and archival source material that could provide information concerning the intentions of contemporary makers of economic policy, and the process of decision-making, was either not consulted by these authors, or was not then available for them to consult. (Holtfrerich, 1986, p. 1)

However, in the contemporary German literature the Italian original went largely unnoticed. One of the few exceptions was Emil Kauder who in his review correctly noted that Bresciani Turroni understands to apply the basic ideas of the quantity theory to the special circumstances of the German monetary system from 1914 to 1923.[27] Therefore, it is no greater surprise that until today the book never has been translated into German, with the exception of a shortened version of chapter 10 on capital shortage and currency stabilisation (Bresciani-Turroni 1932). However, it was Hayek who, attracted by the Austrian component of Bresciani Turroni's business-cycle theory, initiated the English translation of the text which was published in 1937 with an introduction by Lionel Robbins.[28] In the third of his 1931 LSE lectures on 'The working of the price mechanism in the course of the credit cycle' Hayek had added a longer note on the history of the doctrines in which he gave the following assessment:[29]

> Another contemporary author who is evidently indebted to the same strand of thought and whose views on these problems are even more closely related to those taken in these lectures, but with whose work on this point I have unfortunately only became acquainted since he has collected his earlier scattered articles in book-form, is Professor C. Bresciani-Turroni. His monumental study of the German inflation (*Le Vicende del Marco Tedesco*, Milano, 1931) appears to me to be one of the most important contributions to the study of money which have appeared in recent years. Particularly the chapters on the influence of inflation on production and on the scarcity of capital after the stabilisation … seem to me of extraordinary interest and to contain a wealth of concrete illustrations of these difficult theoretical questions which is not to be found elsewhere. Few other foreign books on economic problems would equally deserve being made available in an English translation. (Hayek 1935, p. 103)

After the publication of the English translation Bresciani Turroni's book was increasingly noticed also in Germany, as is shown, for example, by Rudolf Stucken's favourable review.[30] Internationally it became the standard reference work on the German inflation for decades. It soon outcompeted Graham's 1930 work as the classic study. Whereas Graham's interpretation was based on the balance of payments theory approach, widely held at the Reichsbank and dominant among German economists as well as among German political elites, according to which the reparation claims by the victorious powers were the major cause for the

---

[27] *Zeitschrift für Nationalökonomie*, 5, 1934, pp. 270-271.

[28] Robbins also invited Bresciani-Turroni to London where in May 1935 he gave two lectures on 'The Theory of Saving' at the LSE (see Bresciani Turroni 1936).

[29] The Appendix is missing in the German version of *Prices and Production*..

[30] *Weltwirtschaftliches Archiv*, 50, 1939, pp. 94*-95*.

depreciation of the mark which led to domestic price inflation, Bresciani Turroni based his analysis on the quantity theory approach and put the blame on the irresponsible fiscal and monetary policies of the German authorities. In contrast to Graham and later Gini (1934) who stressed the beneficial effects of the inflationary process to the German economy, Bresciani Turroni rightly advocated the view that on balance the implications were clearly negative, particularly because inflation led to distortions in relative prices and subsequently in the structure of production and thereby became a source for later stabilisation crises, a conclusion which made his analysis very attractive for Hayek.

It is a widely overlooked fact that Bresciani Turroni's former mentor Bortkiewicz, himself a close friend of Knut Wicksell, who kept the author of *Interest and Prices* informed on the development in German economics and at the Berlin faculty, made some important contributions to monetary theory inspired by the Swede's critical examination of the quantity theory of money and the inflationary processes in Germany. Bortkiewicz, like the banker Ludwig Albert Hahn and Ludwig von Mises, belonged to the minority group of economists, who examined the role of inflationary expectations, to reconcile the root cause of inflation in quantity theory, namely the excessive creation of money, with the key stylized facts, the extraordinary increase in the price level running well ahead of the increase in money supply from mid-1921 onward, the much greater rate of depreciation in the exchange rate compared to the increase of the domestic inflation rate and the widely noticed shortage of money. In his contributions to the 1924 Stuttgart meeting of the Verein für Sozialpolitik which focussed on issues of trade policy and the currency question Bortkiewicz made pretty clear that the enormous rise in the velocity of money is not the cause of the higher inflation rate but the effect of a great mistrust in the monetary authorities leading to elastic expectations concerning the further fall in the value of money as the consequence of the actual inflation caused by misguided monetary and fiscal policies and thereby strengthening the impact of the actual increase in money supply. Although intensively discussing Bortkiewicz's contribution, Bresciani Turroni (1937, pp. 175-182) misinterprets his former teacher's position as being an opponent of an inflation-expectations augmented version of the quantity theory whereas in fact Bortkiewicz gave a very early and innovative discussion of the role of destabilizing expectations which explained key features of the German hyperinflation.[31]

[31] See Bortkiewicz (1924), in particular pp. 266-268, and Laidler and Stadler (1998) for a very thorough and knowledgeable treatment of the issues involved from a modern theoretical perspective.

5. The Italian School of Public Finance

> *"Now that the important early Swedish contributions on monetary and cycle theory have been made available, it may be asserted that the single most important national body of doctrine which remains largely unknown to and unappreciated by English-language economists is the Italian work in fiscal theory."*[32]
>
> James M. Buchanan

With the exception of Pareto almost all leading Italian economists since Ferrara have made important contributions to the glorious Italian school of public finance.[33] In contrasts to the English language area this has been perceived much earlier in the German language area which was not exclusively conquered by a tradition of *Staatswissenschaft*, integrating legal, political and administrative with economic aspects. Starting with Emil Sax's *Foundations* (1887) important theoretical contributions to modern public finance were made, the most outstanding ones of Swedish origin: Wicksell's *Finanztheoretische Untersuchungen* (1896) and Erik Lindahl's *Die Gerechtigkeit der Besteuerung* (1919). The relevance of the contribution by Sax was soon recognized in Italy where in the 1880s the "Scienza delle Finance" started to flourish and was the main door by which marginalism entered Italy. What is surprising from a modern neoclassical point of view is that Pantaleoni first applied the marginal calculus to the theory of public expenditure rather than to the incentive problem in the theory of taxation.

In his contribution on the development of public finance outside Germany to the *Handbuch der Finanzwissenschaft* Edwin Seligman (1926), gives a detailed survey on the Italian literature[34], mentions Augusto Graziani's *Istituzioni di scienza della finanze* (1897) as the most thoughtful of all and comes to the final conclusion that "the newer Italian literature on public finance surpasses those of all other European countries as to versatility, erudition and wealth of stimulations" (p. 308). The *Archiv für Sozialwissenschaft und Sozialpolitik* published an extensive review article by Umberto Ricci (1930) soon after the third edition of Graziani's book was published. Graziani[35] was a former student of Ricca Salerno who in 1888 had summarized the science of public finance in a *Manuale* which appeared in a collection including also the classic paper 'Il carattere teorico dell'economia finanziaria' by Antonio De Viti de Marco (1888), in which parallel

[32] Buchanan (1960, p. 24).

[33] For a detailed survey see Buchanan (1960).

[34] In the new edition of the *Handbuch der Finanzwissenschaft*, which was published after World War II, the history of Italian Public Finance got an own contribution written by Emanuele Morselli (1952).

[35] Graziani (1927) wrote the contribution on Italy to the comprehensive project *The Economic Theory of the Present*, edited by Hans Mayer in Vienna.

to Sax the author developed ideas on the application of the new value theory to public finance.

De Viti de Marco is also the author of a major textbook on the Foundations of Public Finance whose earlier version circulated since 1888 but which was not published until 1928. Although the book was later also translated into Spanish and English it was the German edition which came out first in 1932, due to the joint efforts of his friend Oskar Morgenstern and De Viti de Marco's most eminent student Luigi Einaudi who contributed a substantial introduction, specifically written for the German edition, in which the *Grundlehren der Finanzwirtschaft* are properly integrated into the Italian school of public finance. In a preliminary note Oskar Morgenstern expresses his hope and expectation for a great benefit for German public finance by the translation of Marchese De Viti de Marco's book and directs the reader's attention to the fact that in the preceding year the author had resigned from his chair at the University of Rome because he refused to take an oath to Mussolini's regime endorsing the education of the Italian youth according to the fascist ideas. Among the economists it was Wilhelm Röpke who stood out in his acquaintance with the work of Einaudi with whom he shared strong liberal beliefs. Röpke, who had emigrated from Nazi Germany in 1933 and stayed in Switzerland after the war, in 1952 became the first non-Italian receiving the Premio Cremisini, an important prize in literature.

Among the scholars who were in opposition and had many difficulties during the fascist era was also Einaudi who finally in 1943 was forced into exile which he spent in Switzerland. Shortly after the war he became governor of the Bank of Italy and made an outstanding political career culminating in the Presidency of the Italian Republic from 1948 to 1955 for which, at least outside Italy and a narrow circle of specialists, he is better remembered today than for his contributions to public finance. In postwar Germany Einaudi got a high reputation for his early conceiving the idea of the United States of Europe.

One of the reasons for the lack of reception of Einaudi's work on a broader scale is the fact that his main treatise *Principii di Scienza della finanza*, which was published in several editions, has never been translated into German. Buchanan (1960, p. 73) recommends the book but adds that "his best work has appeared in his essays". One of the most important essays was his contribution to the Festschrift for Georg von Schanz, the founder of the *Finanzarchiv*, on the occasion of his 75th birthday: 'On the Methodology of the Theory of Tax Capitalization' (1928). However, the article was published in Italian (and only three decades later translated into English), and only a limited number of readers could understand the text, and not all who were able to read and write Italian were enthusiastic about Einaudi's work as is shown, for example, by Schumpeter's rather restricted approval.[36] On the other hand, Louise Sommer, a member of the Subcommittee on Public Finance of the Verein für Sozialpolitik in her reviewing Einaudi's 1929 article 'Contributo alla

[36] See Schumpeter (1954, pp. 206 and 855f.).

ricerca dell'ottima imposta' comes to the conclusion: "The work of Einaudi is an extraordinary important contribution on the problem of influencing economic equilibrium via taxation. It is full of fruitful suggestions for the theory of taxation, yet also tax practice is shown new ways by reference to interrelations existing between the level of taxation, the interest rate and the capital market."[37]

Richard Musgrave who in his own scientific career benefited from the 'crossing of traditions' (see Musgrave 1997), took up four Italian contributions when he edited the *Classics in the Theory of Public Finance* (1958) together with Alan Peacock: by Barone, Montemartini and the two founders of the Italian school of public finance, Pantaleoni and Ugo Mazzola (1890). The latter's contribution is an important stepping stone in the application of the marginal utility analysis to the theory of public goods as it was started by Sax. In retrospect Musgrave comes to the following conclusion with regard to the situation in Germany where he had begun his studies from 1930 to 1933:

> "The state-oriented view of the fiscal process, offered in the works of v. Stein, Schäffle and Wagner, blossomed during the very period when Austrian, Italian and Swedish economists set out to refine the individualistic approach by applying the newly developed tools of marginal utility analysis to the public sector. This literature largely appeared in the German language, so that its message could not be overlooked as easily as had been the case with English authors. The new approach was not welcomed, however, by mainstream Finanzwissenschaft since it did not fit that tradition. Nevertheless, German scholars made a central contribution to the new school, setting the frame of what was to blossom later into modern expenditure theory, English language style." (Musgrave 1996, p. 158).

6. Economic Thought in Italy and the reception in the German Language Area: The Role of Mediators

> *"In the meantime, my Italian friends: Gustavo Del Vecchio, Luigi Einaudi, and Bresciani Turroni, write me letters according to which they want me – and only me – to make the Pareto translation."*[38]
>
> Louise Sommer

With the First World War and the death of Schmoller and Wagner in 1917 the cultural atmosphere in Italy became unfavourable to German and Austrian influence,

[37] *Weltwirtschaftliches Archiv*, 1932, p. 268*.

[38] Louise Sommer (Washington), letter to Fritz Machlup (Johns Hopkins University, Baltimore), March 10, 1958. Fritz Machlup Papers, Box 65, Folder 7, Hoover Archives, Stanford, CA.

and the Historical School lost its followers, in Italy even more so than in Germany. Nevertheless, a relatively high level of mutual exchange of ideas continued in the interwar period. Schumpeter, in particular, had an enormous influence on Italian economic thought in this phase (see Graziani 1989), but he also played a central role in the reception of Italian economic ideas in the German language area. The same holds for Morgenstern and to some lesser extent for Hayek. In an article on 'Open problems in the theory of costs and returns' Morgenstern (1931), for example, also recognized rather early the importance of Sraffa's 1925 essay on the relationship between costs and quantities produced and basically shared Sraffa's criticism of the neoclassical, predominantly Marshallian theory of cost. In this section we want to supplement our foregoing analysis with reflections on the role of another prominent economist and two less-known scholars as mediators for the reception of Italian economic thought in Germany and Austria until World War II.

When *Jacob Marschak* (1898-1977) died he was President Elect of the American Economic Association and prominent economists like Kenneth J. Arrow and Tjalling C. Koopmans wrote obituaries in which understandably Marschak's work at the Cowles Commission and his contributions to the economics of decision and uncertainty were at the centre of the analysis. Having been the founding director of the Oxford Institute of Statistics since 1935 Marschak was in the US as a Rockefeller Foundation Fellow when the Second World War broke out. He stayed there and spent the first three years at the New School for Social Research (1939-1942), running also a seminar on econometrics and mathematical economics on behalf of the National Bureau of Economic Research in New York. In this period the young Franco Modigliani, who had left Italy because of the racial measures adopted by the fascist regime in 1938, became the doctoral student of Marschak which he later remembered in the following way: "I had the fortune to meet Jacob Marschak. He took me in his hands. There were other good people there, but he was very instrumental in giving me a style … He was a wonderful teacher" (Modigliani 1984, p. 115).

Born in Kiew Marschak started to study economics at the university there in fall 1915. The teacher who left the greatest impression on him was Eugen Slutsky who only a few months before had published his famous paper 'On the theory of the budget of the consumer' in the *Giornale degli Economisti e Rivista di Statistica* which, building on earlier work of Pareto, showed that the effect of a price change on the quantity demanded can be divided into two effects, a compensated variation of price and the income effect. It took almost two decades before Slutsky's achievements, due to the work of Hicks and Allen, became known to a wider international audience. During that time Marschak had been Minister for Labour in a regional government in the Northern Caucasus for some months in 1918 before he came to Germany in January 1919 from where he had to emigrate a second time after the Nazis' rise to power. In his German period Marschak not only wrote his habilitation thesis on 'The Elasticity of Demand' (1931) which he submitted to the University of Heidelberg, but was also watching closely the

Italian literature and political development. Besides several book reviews he published two long articles on 'The corporative and hierarchical idea in Fascism' in the *Archiv für Sozialwissenschaft und Sozialpolitik* which gave an early and deep theoretical analysis of Italian developments.

Marschak also was the translator of Umberto Ricci's article 'Classification of demand curves on the basis of the elasticity concept' which was published in the *Archiv* in 1931. When the journal had to terminate publication in 1933 it had been the leading one in the social sciences in Germany for almost three decades since Werner Sombart, Max Weber and Edgar Jaffé had taken over editorship in 1904. From 1922 onwards Emil Lederer was the editor together with Joseph Schumpeter and Alfred Weber as coeditors. In this period the only other articles, besides the Ricci paper, which were submitted from Italy were numerous papers by the important political sociologist Robert Michels, once a social democrat (which was the main barrier for an academic career in Imperial Germany) and a close friend of Max Weber, who in the 1920s showed some sympathies for the fascist movement and in 1928 became professor of economics at the University of Perugia.

Perhaps the most active mediator of Italian economic thought in the German linguistic area in the interwar period was the Austrian *Otto Weinberger* (1882-1958), a renowned jurist and expert for commerce and sea law, who acquired a PhD degree in law at the University of Vienna in 1905[39] and a third PhD in theology with a thesis on the economic philosophy of the old testament in 1946. Already inspired as a young student by the lectures and seminars of Carl Menger and Eugen von Böhm-Bawerk Weinberger made his PhD in economics with a work on Jevons in 1923 (and later in 1945 his habilitation which was the basis for a short extraordinary professorship at the University of Vienna for two years until his retirement in 1952), followed by a book on the marginal utility school (1926), in which he already attempted to trace the origins of the subjective theory of value in the older Italian literature. The next book was his theoretical opus magnum on mathematical economics (1930), which made explicit that Weinberger did not share the aversions of several members of the Austrian school against modern mathematical methods. Appraising the work of Gossen and Thünen, Cournot and Walras, Jevons, Edgeworth and Marshall, and emphasizing the common elements and not the differences between the variants of the marginalist school Weinberger felt, that in contrast to the Anglo-Saxon and the French contributions, in the German language area only insufficient attention was paid to the works of the great Italian scholars. This made him an untiring fighter against a lack of knowledge of the Italian literature and led to various activities. Weinberger contributed numerous reviews on the Italian literature to almost all leading scholarly journals and became a very engaged translator, most importantly of Del Vecchio's *Grundlinien der*

[39] Thereafter Weinberger spent some time as a junior barrister in Trieste where he learnt his perfect Italian and met his Italian wife.

Geldtheorie based on the series of articles published in the *Giornale degli Economisti* between 1909 and 1917. Above all he wrote many analytical articles, in particular on Vilfredo Pareto and Maffeo Pantaleoni's achievements. In March 1938 Weinberger was dismissed as the President of the Court of Commerce in Vienna for racial reasons. He did not emigrate from Austria and was shortly afterwards sentenced to two years compulsory labour. In that period his article on 'The Importance of Francesco Ferrara in the History of Economic Thought' (1940) was published in the *Journal of Political Economy*. Weinberger's great merits for the dissemination of Italian economic thought led to some honours like the membership in the Royal Academy of Sciences (Società Reale) in Naples and the Accademia Virgiliana in Mantova.

A very active mediator of Italian and French economic thought in the German language area was *Louise Sommer*. Born in 1889 in Vienna where she also studied at the University, under the influence of Carl Grünberg and Karl Pribram she wrote an outstanding PhD thesis on Austrian cameralism which she submitted to the University of Basle in 1919. Spending most of the time in the interwar period in Switzerland, where she became a Privatdozent at the University of Geneva in 1927, she moved to the United States in 1947 where she continued to be active as a translator and active book reviewer. For example, she translated Bernoulli's classical paper on subjective probabilities from Latin into English, which was published in *Econometrica* (Bernoulli 1954) and continued to review books of Italian economists, like Gustavo Del Vecchio's *La Sintesi Economica e la Teoria del Reddito* and Luigi Einaudi's *Saggi bibliografici e storici intorno alle dottrine economiche*.[40] The *Essays in European Economic Thought* (1960), which she translated and edited also contain Luigi Einaudi's 'The Doctrine of Original Sin and the Theory of the Elite in the Writings of Frédéric Le Play'.

Being an engaged reviewer, translator and disseminator of the Italian literature since the mid-1920s Sommer also developed friendships with leading Italian scholars, such as Bresciani Turroni, Del Vecchio and Einaudi. In her own works she made some important contributions on the *Methodenstreit*. Most interesting in our context is her analysis of 'Abbé Galiani and the physiocratic system' (1927) in which she puts forward a decisive methodological difference between Galiani's positivistic method and the normative economic doctrines of the physiocrats which, influenced by natural law, are of a more ideal type nature. According to Sommer it would be too simplistic to reduce Galiani's opposition against the Physiocrats to the mere alternative mercantilism versus physiocracy or free trade against protective tariffs, because Galiani is not an opponent of free trade per se but only against the full liberalisation of corn trade under the prevailing historical and political circumstances and France's economic stage of development. Thus the differences are more of a methodological nature, reflecting a precursor of the

---

[40] See *American Economic Review*, 41, 1951, pp. 676-678 and 46, 1956, pp. 421-422.

later dispute on method between Schmoller and Menger where Galiani plays the Schmollerian part and the Physiocrats are the advocates of pure theory.

Interestingly in 1957 Louise Sommer and Fritz Machlup took joint efforts to translate Pareto's *Manuale* into English for which Sommer would have been the right person able to make careful annotations of the differences between the French and Italian editions. However, finally the Committee on Research and Publications at Yale University lost interest and it took fourteen more years before an English translation came out (Pareto 1971). The 'German situation' is described in a letter by Sommer to Machlup on April 4, 1957: "Professor F.K. Mann has just told me that there exists a German translation of Pareto's *Manuale* which has been made by Professor Brinkmann, but owing to Brinkmann's death this translation remained a fragment." [41]

7. The Post-1945 Internationalization of Economics or the End of an Era

"For the times they are a-changin"
Bob Dylan

As is well known, the post-1945 development of economics is characterized by a growing process of internationalization combined with an increasing dominance of American economics. This holds for Italy as well as for Germany and Austria. Whilst there are important similarities, such as the delayed rise of Keynesian economics after the Second World War, there are also some notable differences, such as the greater importance of the Sraffian debate for Italy or the much greater loss of leading economists due to emigration for Germany and Austria in the fascist period. English has become the dominant language and Italian as well as German or Austrian economists of the younger generation have become similar to their American, British, Dutch or Scandinavian counterparts. Thus there is not so much to 'discover' in the modern contributions made in other countries and foreign languages. The period of bilateral fruitful exchange has come almost to an end except for historians of economic thought.

[41] Fritz Machlup Papers, Box 65, Folder 7, Hoover Archives, Stanford, CA. Carl Brinkmann (1885-1954) succeeded Emil Lederer as Professor at the University of Heidelberg in 1932, was Professor at the University of Berlin from 1942-45 and in Tübingen from 1947-53. His 1950 contribution on Pareto was the very first article in the new journal *Jahrbuch für Sozialwissenschaft*. So far we were not able to trace the state of the manuscript of the German translation mentioned in Sommer's letter.

REFERENCES

ADLER G. et al. (1905), *Festgaben für Adolph Wagner zur siebenzigsten Wiederkehr seines Geburtstages*, Leipzig: C.F. Winter'sche Verlagsbuchhandlung.

AUGELLO M.M. (1989), 'The Societies of Political Economy in Italy and the Professionalization of Economists (1860-1900)', *History of Economics Society Bulletin*, 11, pp. 99-112.

BARONE E. (1908), 'Il Ministro della produzione nello stato collettivista', *Giornale degli Economisti*, 37, pp. 267-293 and 391-414, Engl. transl. as 'The Ministry of Production in the Collectivist State', in F.A. Hayek (1935), pp. 245-290.

BARONE E. (1927), *Grundzüge der Theoretischen Nationalökonomie*, translated by H. Staehle and introduced by J. Schumpeter, Berlin and Bonn: Ferd. Dümmlers Verlag.

BARUCCI P. (1972), 'The Spread of Marginalism in Italy (1871-1890)', *History of Political Economy*, 2, pp. 512-532.

BERNOULLI D. (1738), 'Exposition of a New Theory on the Measurement of Risk', *Econometrica*, 22, 1954, pp. 23-36.

BINI P. (1992), *Costantino Bresciani Turroni. Ciclo, moneta e sviluppo*, Civitanova Marche: Otium Edizioni.

BINI P., GUIDI M.E.L. and MAGLIULO A. (2000), 'Italian Economics in the Inter-war Period', ms., University of Macerata.

BORTKIEWICZ L.V. (1924), 'Die Ursachen einer potenzierten Wirkung des vermehrten Geldumlaufs auf das Preisniveau', in *Verein für Sozialpolitik: Schriften. Vol. 170*, Munich and Leipzig: Duncker & Humblot, pp. 256-274.

BORTKIEWICZ L.V. (1931), 'Die Disparitätsmaße der Einkommensstatistik', *Bulletin de l'Institut International de Statistique*, 25, The Hague, pp. 189-298.

BRESCIANI C. (1907), 'Über die Methoden der Einkommensverteilungsstatistik', *Jahrbücher für Nationalökonomie und Statistik*, 88, pp. 577-600.

BRESCIANI TURRONI C. (1929), 'The Movement of Wages in Germany During the Depreciation of the Mark and After Stabilization', *Journal of the Royal Statistical Society*, 92, pp. 374-414.

BRESCIANI TURRONI C. (1931), 'Le Vicende del Marco Tedesco', *Annali di Economia*, 7, Milano: Università Bocconi Editrice, revised English translation as *The Economics of Inflation. A Study of Currency Depreciation in Post-War Germany 1914-1923*, London 1937: Allen & Unwin.

BRESCIANI TURRONI C. (1932), 'Kapitalmangel und Währungsstabilisierung', in H.Mayer (ed.), *Die Wirtschaftstheorie der Gegenwart. Vol. II: Wert, Preis, Produktion, Geld und Kredit*, Vienna: Julius Springer, pp. 391-403.

BRESCIANI TURRONI C. (1936), 'The Theory of Saving', *Economica*, 3, pp. 1-23 and 162-181.

BRESCIANI TURRONI C. (1944), 'Gegenwärtige Strömungen in der italienischen Wirtschaftswissenschaft', *Weltwirtschaftliches Archiv*, 59, pp. 173-211.

BRINKMANN C. (1950), 'Über Vilfredo Pareto', *Jahrbuch für Sozialwissenschaft*, 1, pp. 1-11.

BUCHANAN J.M. (1960), '"La Scienza delle Finanze": The Italian Tradition in Fiscal Theory', in J.M. Buchanan, *Fiscal Theory and Political Economy. Selected Essays*, Chapel Hill: The University of North Carolina Press, pp. 24-74.

CASSEL G. (1918), *Theoretische Sozialökonomie*, Leipzig: C.F. Winter; Engl. transl. *Theory of Social Economy*, London 1923: T.F. Unwin.

CUSUMANO V. (1875), *Le scuole economiche della Germania in rapporto alla quistione sociale*, Naples: Marghieri.

DEL VECCHIO GIORGIO (1936), 'Volkswirtschaftslehre und Rechtswissenschaft', *Jahrbücher für Nationalökonomie und Statistik*,143, pp. 274-304.

DEL VECCHIO GUSTAVO (1928), 'Untersuchungen zur Theorie des Unternehmergewinnes', in H. Mayer (ed.), *Die Wirtschaftstheorie der Gegenwart, Vol. III: Einkommensbildung*, Wien: Julius Springer, pp. 281-292.

DEL VECCHIO GUSTAVO (1930), *Grundlinien der Geldtheorie*, Tübingen: Mohr.

DEL VECCHIO GUSTAVO (1932), 'Zur theoretischen Analyse der Weltwirtschaftskrisis', *Weltwirtschaftliches Archiv*, 36, pp. 322-355.

DEL VECCHIO GUSTAVO (1935), 'Neue Probleme der Außenhandelstheorie', *Weltwirtschaftliches Archiv*, 41, pp. 316-331.

DE VITI DE MARCO A. (1888), *Il carattere teorico dell'economia finanziaria*, Rome: Pasqualucci.

DE VITI DE MARCO A. (1928), *I primi principii dell'economia finanziaria*, Rome: Sampaolesi; German transl. as *Grundlehren der Finanzwirtschaft* with an introduction by Luigi Einaudi, Tübingen 1932: J.C.B. Mohr (Paul Siebeck); Engl. transl. *First Principles of Public Finance*, London 1936: Jonathan Cape.

EINAUDI L. (1928), 'Intorno alla metodologia della teoria della capitalizzazione dell'imposta', in H. Teschemacher (ed.), *Beiträge zur Finanzwissenschaft, Festgabe für Georg von Schanz zum 75*. Geburtstag, Bd. II, Tübingen: Mohr Siebeck; Engl. transl. as 'On the Methodology of the Theory of Tax Capitalization', *International Economic Papers*, 7, 1957, pp. 40-52.

EINAUDI L. (1955), 'Fifty Years of Italian Economic Thought: 1896-1946. Reminiscences', *International Economic Papers*, 5, pp. 7-25.

EISERMANN G. (1961), *Vilfredo Pareto als Nationalökonom und Soziologe*, Tübingen: J.C.B. Mohr (Paul Siebeck).

FANNO M. (1912), *Le banche e il mercato monetario*, Rome: Athenaeum; partly translated into English as *The Money Market*, London 1995: Macmillan.

FANNO M. (1930), 'Die Elastizität der Nachfrage nach Ersatzgütern', *Zeitschrift für Nationalökonomie*, 1, pp. 51-74, revised Engl. transl. 'The Elasticity of Demand of Substitute Goods', in L.L. Pasinetti (ed.) (1997), *Italian Economic Papers III*, Bologna: Il Mulino - Oxford University Press, pp. 99-116.

FANNO M. (1931), 'Cicli di produzione, cicli del credito e fluttuazioni industriali', *Giornale degli Economisti*, pp. 329-369, English translation 'Production Cycles, Credit Cycles and Industrial Fluctuations', *Structural Change and Economic Dynamics*, 4, 1993, pp. 403-437.

FANNO M. (1933a), 'Die reine Theorie des Geldmarktes', in F.A: Hayek (ed.), *Beiträge zur Geldtheorie*, Vienna: Julius Springer, pp. 1-113.

FANNO M. (1933b), 'Irrtümer in der Zeit als Ursachen wirtschaftlicher Schwankungen', *Zeitschrift für Nationalökonomie*, 4, pp. 25-51.

FANNO M. (1938a), *Principii di scienza economica. Vol. VII: Introduzione allo studio della teoria economica del corporativismo*, 3rd ed., Padova: Cedam.

FANNO M. (1938b), 'Die Struktur der korporativen Wirtschaft', *Jahrbücher für Nationalökonomie und Statistik*, 148, pp. 317-330.

FASIANI M. (1932-33), 'Der gegenwärtige Stand der reinen Theorie der Finanzwissenschaft in Italien' I+II+III, *Zeitschrift für Nationalökonomie*, 3, pp. 651-691, 4, pp. 79-107 and 357-388.

FAUCCI R. (1999), 'Notes on the Influence of German Economic Thought in Italy', *Storia del Pensiero Economico*, 37, pp. 73-86.

FOSSATI E. (ed.) (1938), *Korporative Wirtschaftstheorie*, Jena: Gustav Fischer.

GINI C. (1934), 'Wirkungen der extremen Formen der Inflation auf den Wirtschaftsorganismus', *Weltwirtschaftliches Archiv*, 40, pp. 399-436.

GINI C. (1938), '"Trade follows the Flag"', *Weltwirtschaftliches Archiv*, 47, pp. 181-227.

GIOIA V. (1999), 'German and Italian Economists between 1861 and 1930: Some Points to Consider', *Storia del Pensiero Economico*. 37, pp. 17-52.

GRAHAM F.D. (1930), *Exchange, Prices and Production in Hyper-Inflation: Germany, 1920-1923,* Princeton: Princeton University Press.

GRAZIANI A. (1927), 'Italien', in H. Mayer (ed.), *Die Wirtschaftstheorie der Gegenwart, Vol. I: Gesamtbild der Forschung in den einzelnen Ländern*, Wien: Julius Springer, pp. 100-121.

GRAZIANI A. (1989), 'Schumpeter and Italian Economic Thought in the Interwar Period', *Studi Economici*, 44, pp. 41-83.

GRAZIANI A. (1993), ' M. Fanno's 'Production Cycles, Credit Cycles and Industrial Fluctuations: An Introduction', *Structural Change and Economic Dynamics*, 4, pp. 393-402.

GROENEWEGEN P. (2000), 'German Political Economy, History, and the Law of Value: Marx and Engels contra Achille Loria', in V. Gioia and H.D. Kurz (eds.), *Science, Institutions and Economic Development. The Contribution of "German" Economists and the Reception in Italy (1860-1930)*, Milano: Dott. A. Giuffrè Editore, pp. 623-646.

HAGEMANN H. (1991), 'Learned Journals and the Professionalization of Economics: The German Language Area', *Economic Notes*, 20, pp. 33-57.

HAGEMANN H. (1999), 'The Development of Business-Cycle Theory in the German language area 1900-1930', *Storia del pensiero economico*, 37, pp. 87-122.

HAGEMANN H. (2001), 'The Verein für Sozialpolitik from its foundation (1872) until World War I', in M.M. Augello and M.E.L. Guidi (eds.), *The Spread of Political Economy and the Professionalisation of Economists. Economic societies in Europe, America and Japan in the nineteenth century*, London and New York: Routledge, pp. 152-175.

HAYEK F.A. (1929), *Geldtheorie und Konjunkturtheorie*, Vienna: Hölder-Pichler-Tempski; Engl. transl. *Monetary Theory and the Trade Cycle*, London 1933: J. Cape.

HAYEK F.A. (1931), *Preise und Produktion*, Vienna: Julius Springer; Engl. transl. *Prices and Production*, second revised and enlarged edition, London: Routledge and Kegan Paul.

HAYEK F.A. (ed.) (1935), *Collectivist Economic Planning*, London 1935: Routledge and Kegan Paul.

HOLTFRERICH C.-L. (1980), *Die deutsche Inflation 1914-1923. Ursachen und Folgen in internationaler Perspektive,* Berlin and New York: de Gruyter, Engl. translation as *The German Inflation 1914-1923*, Berlin and New York 1986: de Gruyter.

KURZ H.D. (1995), 'Marginalism, Classicism and Socialism in German-speaking Countries: 1871-1932, in I. Steedman (ed.), *Socialism and Marginalism in Economics 1870-1930*, London and New York: Routledge, pp. 7-86.

KURZ H.D. (1999), 'Sraffa's Reception of the German Economics Literature: A Few Examples', *Storia del Pensiero Economico*, 37, pp. 53-72.

LAIDLER D.E.W. and STADLER G.W. (1998), 'Monetary Explanations of the Weimar Republic's Hyperinflation: Some Neglected Contributions in Contemporary German Literature', *Journal of Money, Credit and Banking*, 30, pp. 816-831.

LINDAHL E. (1919), *Die Gerechtigkeit der Besteuerung. Eine Analyse der Steuerprinzipien auf der Grundlage der Grenznutzentheorie*, Lund: Gleerup and H. Ohlsson.

MARSCHAK J. (1924), Der korporative und der hierarchische Gedanke im Fascismus I+II', *Archiv für Sozialwissenschaft und Sozialpolitik*, 52, pp. 695-728 and 53, pp. 81-140.

MARSCHAK J. (1931), *Elastizität der Nachfrage*, Tübingen: Mohr.

MAYER H. (1932), 'Der Erkenntniswert der funktionellen Preistheorien. Kritische und positive Untersuchungen zum Preisproblem', in H. Mayer (ed.), *Die Wirtschaftstheorie der Gegenwart, Vol. II: Wert, Preis, Produktion, Geld und Kredit*, Vienna: Julius Springer, pp. 147-239b; enlarged Italian translation *Il concetto di equilibrio nella teoria economica*, Nuova collana di economisti stranieri e italiani, 4, Torino 1937.

MAZZOLA U. (1890), *I dati scientifici della finanza pubblica*, Roma: Loescher; in part translated as 'The Formation of the Prices of Public Goods', in R.A. Musgrave and A.T. Peacock (eds.) (1958), pp. 37-47.

MEACCI F. (1998), *Italian Economists of the 20th Century*, Cheltenham, UK and Northhampton, MA, USA: Edward Elgar.

MISES L.v. (1920), 'Die Wirtschaftsrechnung im sozialistischen Gemeinwesen', *Archiv für Sozialwissenschaft und Sozialpolitik*, 47, pp. 86-121; Engl. transl. 'Economic Calculation in the Socialist Commonwealth', in F.A. Hayek (1935), pp. 87-130.

MODIGLIANI F. (1984), in A. Klamer (ed.), *The New Classical Macroeconomics. Conversations with New Classical Economists and Their Opponents*. Brighton: Wheatsheaf, pp. 114-126.

MORGENSTERN O. (1931), 'Offene Probleme der Kosten- und Ertragstheorie', *Zeitschrift für Nationalökonomie*, 2, pp. 481-522.

MORSELLI E. (1952), 'Geschichte der italienischen Finanzwissenschaft', in W. Gerloff and F. Neumark (eds.), *Handbuch der Finanzwissenschaft*, Vol. I., 2nd ed., Tübingen: Mohr-Siebeck, pp. 499-513.

MUSGRAVE R.A. (1996), 'Public Finance and Finanzwissenschaft Traditions Compared', *Finanzarchiv* N.S., 53, pp. 145-193.

MUSGRAVE R.A. (1997), 'Crossing Traditions', in H. Hagemann (ed.), *Zur deutschsprachigen wirtschaftswissenschaftlichen Emigration nach 1933*, Marburg: Metropolis, pp. 63-79.

MUSGRAVE R.A. and PEACOCK A.T. (eds.) (1958), *Classics in the Theory of Public Finance*, London: Macmillan.

MYDRAL G. (1933), 'Der Gleichgewichtsbegriff als Instrument der geldtheoretischen Analyse', in F.A. Hayek (ed.), *Beiträge zur Geldtheorie*, Vienna: Julius Springer, pp. 361-507; revised English transl. *Monetary Equilibrium*, London 1939: Hodge.

PANTALEONI M. (1883), 'Contributo alla teoria del riparto delle spese pubbliche', *Rassegna Italiana*, 15 Oct.; Engl. transl. as 'Contribution to the Theory of the Distribution of Public Expenditure', in R.A. Musgrave and A.T. Peacock (eds.) (1958), pp. 16-27.

PANTALEONI M. (1889), *Principii di economia pura*, Florence: Barbera; Engl. transl. as *Pure Economics*, London 1898: Macmillan.

PARETO V. (1896), *Cours d'Economie Politique, 2 Vls.*, Lausanne: Librairie de l'Université.

PARETO V. (1927 [1971]), *Manual of Political Economy*, edited and translated from third French edition by A.S. Schwier, New York: A.M. Kelley.

PARETO V. (1975), *Ausgewählte Schriften*, edited and introduced by C. Mongardini, Frankfurt/Berlin/Vienna: Ullstein.

REALFONZO R. (2002), 'Gustavo Del Vecchio. Critical Conscience of the Italian Neoclassical School', in W. Samuels (ed.), *Neglected Continental Economists. Vol. II*, Cheltenham, UK and Northhampton, MA, USA: Edward Elgar.

RICCI U. (1930), 'Diskussion finanztheoretischer Fragen', in: *Archiv für Sozialwissenschaft und Sozialpolitik*, 64, pp. 368-379.

RICCI U. (1931a), 'Die statische Theorie der Grundrente', *Jahrbücher für Nationalökonomie und Statistik*, 135, pp. 641-655.

RICCI U. (1931b), 'Klassifikation der Nachfragekurven auf Grund des Elastizitätsbegriffes', *Archiv für Sozialwissenschaft und Sozialpolitik*, 66, pp. 36-61.

SAMUELSON P.A. (1947), *Foundations of Economic Analysis*, Cambridge, Mass.: Harvard University Press.

SAX E. (1887), *Grundlegung der theoretischen Staatswirthschaft*, Vienna: Hölder.

SCHUMPETER J.A. (1906), 'Über die mathematische Methode der theoretischen Ökonomie', *Zeitschrift für Volkswirtschaft, Sozialpolitik und Verwaltung*, 15, pp. 30-49.

SCHUMPETER J.A. (1908), *Das Wesen und der Hauptinhalt der theoretischen Nationalökonomie*, Munich and Leipzig: Duncker & Humblot.

SCHUMPETER J.A. (1910), 'Über das Wesen der Wirtschaftskrisen', *Zeischrift für Volkswirtschaft, Sozialpolitik und Verwaltung*, 19, pp. 271-325.

SCHUMPETER J.A. (1911), *Theorie der wirtschaftlichen Entwicklung*, 2nd rev. ed. Munich and Leipzig 1926: Duncker & Humblot; Engl. transl. *The Theory of Economic Development*, Cambridge, Mass., 1934: Harvard University Press.

SCHUMPETER J.A. (1949), 'Vilfredo Pareto (1848-1923)', *Quarterly Journal of Economics*, 63, pp. 147-173.

SCHUMPETER J.A. (1954), *History of Economic Analysis*, London: Allen & Unwin.

SCHUMPETER J.A. (2000), *Briefe/Letters*, selected and edited by Ulrich Hedtke and Richard Swedberg, Tübingen: Mohr Siebeck.

SELIGMAN E. (1926), Geschichte der Finanzwissenschaft außerhalb Deutschlands, insbesondere seit Beginn des 19. Jahrhunderts, in W. Gerloff, and F. Meisel (eds.) *Handbuch der Finanzwissenschaft*, Vol. 1, Tübingen: J.C.B. Mohr (Paul Siebeck).

SLUTSKY E. (1915), 'Sulla teoria del bilancio del consumatore', *Giornale degli Economisti e Rivista di Statistica*, 51, pp. 1-26.

SOMMER L. (1927), 'Abbé Galiani und das physiokratische System', *Zeitschrift für Volkswirtschaft und Sozialpolitik*, N.S., 5, pp. 318-341.

SOMMER L. (1960), *Essays in European Economic Thought*. Princeton, N.J.: Van Nostrand.

SRAFFA P. (1925), 'Sulle relazioni fra costo e quantità prodotta', *Annali di Economia*, 2, pp. 277-328.

SUPINO C. (1907), *Le crisi economiche*, Milano: Ulrico Hoepli.

WEINBERGER O. (1926), *Die Grenznutzenschule*, Halberstadt: H. Meyer.

WEINBERGER O. (1928), 'Vilfredo Pareto', *Zeitschrift für die gesamte Staatswissenschaft*, 85, pp. 521-542.

WEINBERGER O. (1930), *Mathematische Volkswirtschaftslehre. Eine Einführung*, Leipzig and Berlin: B.G. Teubner.

WEINBERGER O. (1939), 'Zur Erinnerung an Maffeo Pantaleoni', *Schmollers Jahrbuch für Gesetzgebung, Verwaltung und Volkswirtschaft im Deutschen Reiche*, 63, pp. 331-338.

WEINBERGER O. (1940), 'The Importance of Francesco Ferrara in the History of Economic Thought', *Journal of Political Economy*, 48, pp. 91-104.

WICKSELL K. (1896), *Finanztheoretische Untersuchungen*, Jena: Gustav Fischer.

WICKSELL K. (1898), *Geldzins und Güterpreise*, Jena: Gustav Fischer; Engl. transl. *Interest and Prices*, London 1936: Macmillan.

WICKSELL K. (1998), 'Eine neue Krisentheorie', in E.W. Streissler (ed.), *Studien zur Entwicklung der ökonomischen Theorie. Vol. XVIII: Knut Wicksell als Ökonom*. Berlin: Duncker & Humblot, pp. 259-268.

Italian influences in Portuguese Economic Thought (1750-1950)

José Luís Cardoso
ISEG, Technical University of Lisbon

One of the least investigated, but certainly most interesting, areas in the study of the history of economic thought in a given country is the process by which doctrine and theory are imported and assimilated either through the reading of, or through direct contact with, foreign authors. In the Portuguese case, this line of research is the key that enables us to unlock and understand an immense store of experiences and interchanges that, in one way or another, have contributed towards the formation of the different elements shaping the economic thought produced in our country[1].

When compared with the influences coming from other countries, it cannot be said that the winds of political economy and economics that came from Italy blew with any notably greater force. Nonetheless, the marks that were left by Italian authors throughout the particular period under analysis are clearly visible. This chapter seeks to document the most significant moments in the spread of this influence and its effects on the formation of economic discourse in Portugal, an influence that was particularly notable towards both the beginning and the end of the period under consideration (1750-1950).

1. The Italian presence during the Enlightenment in Portugal

The reform of the Statutes of Coimbra University in 1772, a process that was set in motion and controlled by D. José's powerful chief minister – the Marquis of Pombal – was one of the main factors behind the development of a new enlightened mentality and culture in Portugal.

Besides the new teaching methods and practices that were introduced by this reform, subjects that had previously not existed were also placed on the curriculum and incorporated into entirely new courses. A particularly symptomatic example of this spirit of renewal was the restructuring that took place in the teaching of both law and the exact and natural sciences. In the first case, because of the political

[1] This point has already been discussed at some length in Almodovar and Cardoso 1998.

implications arising from the attention thus given to the concrete study of Portuguese legislation and to the social universe that was regulated thereby. In the second case, because of the new perspectives that such restructuring provided for the development of an empirical and cognitive relationship with the surrounding material world, stimulating greater interest in in-depth studies of social and economic life.

For the implementation of his plan of reform, the Marquis of Pombal enjoyed the valuable support of a number of foreigners who, imbued with the enlightened ideas of European culture at that time, offered greater guarantees that the new courses and programmes would be endowed with both the form and contents needed to challenge the scholastic routine that had prevailed until then at the only university in existence in Portugal. And amongst these foreigners were a particularly important group of authors from Italy, whose importance derives not only from their actual number, but also from the quality and merit of the activities that they developed at Coimbra University.

The presence of Italian teachers in Portugal dated back to the beginning of the 1760s, when they were summoned by the Marquis of Pombal to lecture in scientific subjects at the *Colégio Real dos Nobres de Lisboa* (Royal College of the Nobles of Lisbon)[2]. Amongst these teachers were Michiele Antonio Ciera (the College Prefect), Giovanni Angelo Brunelli (responsible for the teaching of arithmetic and geometry), Michiele Franzini (responsible for the teaching of algebra) and Giovanni Antonio Dalla Bella (responsible for the teaching of physics). This attempt to modernise the education given to the sons of the most important Portuguese aristocratic families did not produce the expected results, so that in 1772 the Marquis of Pombal was able to set these Italian teachers to work on another no less noble mission: the already-mentioned reform of the Statutes of Coimbra University.

Thus, Ciera and Franzini were to play an active role in drawing up the part of the statutes dealing specifically with the course of mathematics and began to direct the teaching of subjects in this area. Dalla Bella was appointed to the chair of physics at the Faculty of Philosophy. These teachers were also joined by Domenico Vandelli, who was responsible for directing the teaching of chemistry and natural history, subjects that were now included in the new philosophy course. The great influence of these Italian teachers was also to be noted in the teaching manuals that were used.

Of all the authors that have so far been mentioned, undoubtedly the most important and influential in relation to the area that is of interest to us here was Domenico Vandelli. In fact, in addition to his direct involvement and active participation in the reform of Coimbra University (from 1772 onwards), Vandelli also played an important part in the setting up of the *Real Academia das Ciências de Lisboa* (Lisbon Royal Academy of Sciences, founded in 1779) and in the

[2] For a brief account of the Italian presence at this College, cf. Carvalho 1959.

realisation of economic studies that were undertaken under his auspices, as we shall now see in the following section.

2. Vandelli: an Italian in Lisbon

If we take as our frame of reference the subjects that were taught by the various Italians who came to settle in Portugal under the auspices of the Marquis of Pombal, it is not very clear how any of these might have played a particularly important role in the formation of Portuguese economic thought at the end of the eighteenth century. It is, however, essential to remember that political economy was at that time beginning to take its first steps towards gaining the status of an autonomous subject and that the scientific interest in problems and matters relating to economic life resulted from the coming together of different contributions from such distinct fields of knowledge as law, ethics, politics and the natural sciences. From this latter area, it borrowed the particular methodological procedures and the desire for a knowledge that was based on observation and experience; from the former areas, it drew the normative features that were indispensable for identifying problems and defining the most suitable solutions, taking into account the particular model of society that was being constructed. It was not therefore surprising that reflections of an economic nature should be undertaken by authors who operated within a polysemic scientific space, in which encyclopedism and the universality of knowledge were predominant characteristics. This was, after all, both the spirit and the *raison d'être* of the Enlightenment.

The work of the Italian author Vandelli (1735-1816) fits perfectly within this set of characteristics. The texts that he published in the collection of *Memórias Económicas*, produced by the Real Academia das Ciências de Lisboa, as well as the various manuscripts that he left us, make it possible to confirm the unique role that he played in the development of economic and financial doctrines and policies in Portugal at the end of the eighteenth century. A previous question that may be posed is that of deciding whether this author can be considered a "false Italian", given that *Domenico* Vandelli remained in Portugal almost uninterruptedly for more than 50 years of his long life. But there is no doubt that the "Portuguesified" *Domingos* Vandelli offers us a safe pretext for increasing our knowledge of the history of the relations between the two countries, as well as for learning more about the cultural and scientific exchanges taking place between them, particularly with regard to the spread of political economy[3].

---

[3] The Italian bibliography on Vandelli is extremely limited and is only concerned with his work as a naturalist and botanist, cf. Battelli 1929, Longo 1940 and Melli 1966. For a general appraisal of his economic writings, see Cardoso 1988 and Serrão 1994.

Vandelli's writings stand out in the midst of the abundant literature produced on economic subjects under the auspices of the Real Academia das Ciências. He was the author of texts that served as programmes and guidelines in what was later to become one of the most important collections of documents for the study of political economy and Portuguese economic thought towards the end of the *ancien régime*[4].

His basic concern was to encourage the preparation of a rigorous inventory (a process in which he himself also participated) of the existing natural resources that were potentially usable for productive and commercial purposes, both in the metropolis and in the overseas territories. The proposals that he made for the undertaking of philosophical journeys, or the incentives that he sought to create through the Real Academia das Ciências for the preparation of local and regional descriptive memoirs, were instruments that were specifically designed for this purpose and had the aim of creating diagnostic elements that would make it possible to define a strategy for the optimal allocation of available resources.

Sometimes, he adopted a merely descriptive and naturalistic approach to the subject, limiting himself to making classifying annotations based on the system designed by Lineu, with whom he had in fact corresponded during the earlier stages of his career in Italy. On other occasions, however, Vandelli went beyond this simple naturalistic description and centred his analysis on the physical or moral (i.e. natural or social) obstacles to the development of the agricultural sector, or further on the conditions that would permit an efficient and waste-free use of natural, human and technical resources, both in terms of production and in the circulation of products and raw materials. This diagnostic component of his work was coherently accompanied by proposals for reform and improvement that helped to fashion a strategic option for the economic development of the country, based on agriculture.

Such a strategy was outlined by Vandelli in one of his most famous dissertations, with the suggestive title of "*Memória sobre a preferência que em Portugal se deve dar à agricultura sobre as fábricas*" (Memoir on the preference that should be given in Portugal to agriculture over factories), published in Volume I of the *Memórias Económicas* (1789-1815) of the Real Academia das Ciências. In this text, Vandelli criticised the system of manufacturing protectionism followed in France by Colbert, a criticism which should also be read as a negative appraisal of the similar economic policy being pursued by Pombal. He also presented his arguments in favour of greater freedom in domestic and foreign trade as a means of guaranteeing a reduction in the price of agricultural goods. But what best characterises his text is the unequivocal enthusiasm shown for an economic policy based on the principles of agrarianism, to which the process of manufacturing development would be subjugated (Vandelli 1770-1804, 143-152).

---

[4] The most important of Vandelli's economic and financial writings are collected in Vandelli 1770-1804.

Vandelli's agrarianism bears certain similarities to the economic discourse produced by the French physiocrats. At certain moments, Vandelli even went so far as to advocate the idea of the exclusive productivity of agriculture and came very close to the physiocratic concept of *bon prix*. But this was as far as his incursions were to go into the theoretical territory being cultivated by the disciples of François Quesnay, which serves only to demonstrate his receptiveness towards this view of economic activity that regarded the agricultural sector as its main axis and driving force.

The importance of Vandelli's texts does not derive only from the great clarity with which the author expounds his guidelines with regard to economic doctrine and policy. They are also valuable for the way in which they further reflect the object of research and the programme for reforms that had inspired the series of texts published in the collection of *Memórias Económicas* by the Real Academia das Ciências de Lisboa. We can therefore conclude that the configuration of Portuguese economic thought at the end of the eighteenth century was largely the result of the gradual maturation of an enlightened mentality that had originated from the writings of authors coming from Italy.

3. Incomplete readings and translations

In his writings, Vandelli never quotes any of the Italian economists that were his contemporaries. In view of the nature of his particular legacy and the approaches that he adopted for the discovery of economic territories, one might also question whether he would in fact have had the opportunity to acquaint himself fully with the most significant economic works that were being produced in Italy in the second half of the eighteenth century. We should, for example, consider the cases of authors such as Galiani or Genovesi: although they might have provided useful reading material for Vandelli to reinforce his arguments in favour of free trade, or to stress the advantages of a process of economic development centred upon agriculture, or even to defend a reform of the property and taxation systems, we never find any explicit evidence in the writings of this Portuguese-based Italian author to suggest that he might ever have been enriched by such hypothetical readings.

Any speculation as to whether the presence in Portugal of Vandelli and other Italian scientists might have proved useful as a vehicle for the spread of Italian economic thought therefore requires empirical proof. However, there are some indications that the works of a number of Italian economists were read and known in Portugal, although they seem to have had a very limited impact.

This was certainly the case with Genovesi, whose *Lezioni di Economia Civile* were used by José Veríssimo Álvares da Silva (1744-1811) to write a historical memoir on Portuguese agriculture (Silva 1782).

The Portuguese author begins by quoting Genovesi in order to justify the principle according to which the nation's annual income depends on the number of men employed in productive labour, namely in agriculture (ibid., 171). This principle is used by him as an argument against parasitism and the immobility that is inherent in the system of bestowing estates upon the first-born or eldest son and the consequent entailment of the ownership of the land. Similar concerns are a pretext for making a further reference to Genovesi on the subject of the sovereign's income and the difficulties caused by the system existing for the endowment of the crown's assets (173). His criticism of the privileges enjoyed by nobles and the clergy within the *ancien régime* and the obstacles that these raised for the development of agriculture do, in fact, represent one of the most important ideas expressed in the writing of Álvares da Silva, who once again drew upon the ideas of Genovesi when the latter claimed that the ecclesiastical orders were responsible for the lack of improvement in scientific knowledge in Naples (184). One final reference that he makes to the Neapolitan author arises from a brief analysis undertaken of the negative effects of high taxation on the price of agricultural and industrial products and the consequent decline in the competitiveness of such goods abroad (191).

Álvares da Silva was not the only Portuguese author to be interested in Genovesi's economic writings. The possibility of making a translation of the *Lezioni* began to be aired by António Ribeiro dos Santos (1745-1818), an important figure in Portuguese political and economic thought at the end of the eighteenth century. The knowledge that he had of the experience of teaching political economy, enjoyed firstly by Genovesi in Naples, and then by Beccaria in Milan and by Sonnenfels in Vienna, led him to defend the implementation of an identical system in Portugal so that "the science of legislation may be taught and treated, together with the application of the general principles of political economy to the nature of government and to the customs and circumstances of the nation" (Santos 1789, fl. 124). In order to achieve this, he proposed the translation of Genovesi's *Lezioni*, a task which was partially accomplished by Ricardo Raimundo Nogueira. In fact, Nogueira's translation covers only chapters I to VIII and X of Part I of the *Lezioni*. The incomplete translation never enjoyed any public visibility and still remains available only in manuscript form in the Lisbon National Library (Nogueira 179?).

The interest shown by António Ribeiro dos Santos in Genovesi's work derived from the powerful influence that the Neapolitan master had exerted upon his development as a philosopher and jurist. After the university reform of 1772, the teaching of logic and metaphysics followed the textbooks produced by Genovesi, which were published by Coimbra University in a special edition (Genovesi 1808), with Ribeiro dos Santos becoming one of the teachers that most faithfully followed Genovesi's guidelines in such matters as the insufficiency of natural religion, the transcendent foundations of being and the subjection of reason and the senses to divine revelation[5].

---

[5] On the influence of Genovesi's philosophical system in Portugal, particularly on the work of Ribeiro dos Santos, cf. Pereira 1983. See also Vaz 1999.

Further evidence of the Portuguese assimilation of Italian texts was provided by D. Rodrigo de Souza Coutinho (1755-1812), during the period that he spent as a diplomat in Turin, as the Portuguese representative to the court of Sardinia. In one of the informative official letters that he sent from Turin to Lisbon, Souza Coutinho referred to the legislation in force at that time in the region of Lombardy that was inspired by Galiani's work and which he described as "pleasant and profound" (Coutinho 1787, 69). Referring explicitly to the *Dialogues sur le Commerce des Blés*, Coutinho applauded the policies being pursued for the total liberalisation of domestic trade and demonstrated his approval of the levying of a slight tax on foreign trade in cereals, both on imports (to avoid a sharp fall in less competitive internal prices) and exports (to prevent hoarding and speculation). Equally positive views of Galiani's work, namely about the precursory nature of his work in relation to Adam Smith, were to be expressed later by José Acúrsio das Neves (1814-1817, 476), José da Silva Lisboa (1819, 64) and Manuel de Almeida (1821, 6).

During his stay in Piedmont, D. Rodrigo de Souza Coutinho was to have the opportunity to engage in a close study of the commercial relations between Portugal and Italy, expressing his support for a greater openness and liberalisation of trade between the two countries. He also had occasion to encourage Italian craftsmen specialising in silk manufactures to work in Portugal. Generally speaking, he was an attentive observer and admirer of the Italian reality. The diplomatic apprenticeship that he served in Turin (where he was to remain for a period of 17 years) was of major importance for his development as a statesman with a special vocation for dealing with matters relating to economic and financial administration. He returned to Portugal in 1796, where he began to perform the ministerial duties that were to make him famous as one of the most highly regarded reformers of the Portuguese Enlightenment.

With the exception of the already-mentioned Álvares da Silva, Ribeiro dos Santos and Souza Coutinho, we could safely admit that the influence of Italian economic literature in Portugal at the end of the eighteenth century was really quite discreet. The odd reference that was made to Beccaria, Filangieri or Verri, without any real appreciation being attempted of the contents of the respective works, does not alter this overall impression of a fairly scanty influence, a situation which certainly led José da Silva Lisboa to summarise the progress of political economy in Italy in the following terms: "After the middle of the last century [eighteenth century], there appeared a number of Italian authors of merit writing upon the subject; however, their works are much more demonstrations of the irregular political economy predominating in the respective nations than sources of solid instruction for somebody desirous of discovering the truth" (Lisboa 1819, 64).

This opinion, which was expressed by a fervent and unconditional supporter of Adam Smith, should not encourage us to conclude that the lesser Italian presence was the result of a blindness imposed by the greater brilliance of the influences coming from other European countries. Even if it may be admitted that the spread of physiocracy and the work of Adam Smith had a much greater impact[6], it is also essential to bear in mind that the process of the assimilation and spread of political economy in Portugal has always been noted for the absence of any unequivocal claim as to the foreign sources used.

The relative lack of attention paid to theoretical and analytical aspects (where it would be possible to detect substantial differences depending on the foreign authors that were used) and the consequent importance attached to doctrinal messages that had an impact on the way in which economic policy was conducted, together created an environment that sewed the seeds of an immense eclecticism in the reception afforded to the discourse of political economy. Such eclecticism was in turn encouraged by an attitude of healthy cosmopolitanism, which had always characterised the development of Portuguese economic thought.

The lack of translations of Italian works published in Portugal should similarly not be regarded as a negative aspect, since the same situation occurred with regard to works written in other languages. Foreign authors were generally read in the original language, which substantially reduced their respective spread, given the tiny number of potentially interested readers. In this context, the incomplete translation of Genovesi that has remained until the present day as a manuscript still represents a remarkable feat.

Despite the limitations that have just been mentioned, the conclusion that must be drawn from this section is that the impact of political economy originating from the Italian Enlightenment resulted in the conception and execution of a programme of economic reforms and a moderate liberalisation of the economic system in force in Portugal at the end of the eighteenth century.

4. The decline of the Italian presence in nineteenth-century Portuguese textbooks

The references made by Portuguese authors to the pioneering experiments being conducted in Italy by Beccaria and Genovesi in the teaching of political economy led to an insistence in Portugal on the advantages of institutionalising this subject, with the aim of creating a genuine science of legislation and government. In this context, the work of Filangieri, which was read in Portugal both in its original edition and through its French translation, proved to be particularly important and useful. The authors who quoted this work showed how political economy should be considered an integral part of a process of instruction leading to the acquisition of full citizenship, with the ultimate responsibility for this process belonging to the government itself. The discreet preference shown for the constitutional cause and the open praise that he lavished upon measures tending

[6] On this particular point, cf. Cardoso 1990.

towards economic liberalisation made Filangieri a particularly interesting author from the viewpoint of the economic and political changes that were thereafter to be carried out in a gradual fashion. One of his most attentive readers was José Acúrsio das Neves, who, despite remaining faithful to the system of political absolutism, found in Filangieri the inspiration for one of his favourite mottoes: "The whole science of government lies in the art of knowing in which cases one must give orders and in which cases one should allow people to act according to their own interests" (Neves 1814-1817, 227). For Acúrsio das Neves, the cases that concerned him were essentially ones of an economic nature.

The debate on the institutionalisation of the teaching of political economy gained momentum after the liberal revolution of 1820, or, in other words, in a political context that was more propitious to the exercise of the rights of full citizenship. The reading of the work of Filangieri was now to acquire its fullest possible meaning. One of the first Portuguese authors to become interested in this subject was Manuel de Almeida, who was in fact directly commissioned by parliament to study this matter (Almeida 1821). In the preface to his book, he presents the reader with a brief list of the sources that he will follow most closely in the preparation of his textbook, referring explicitly to Beccaria, Galiani, Genovesi and Filangieri. He also includes in his list Verri's *Meditazioni sull'Economia Politica*, which he quotes once again in the main body of his work.

At the beginning of the 1830s, the debate on the teaching of political economy was to take a new turn and now involved consideration of its institutionalisation as a university subject. The progress already made by this science made it much easier to compile a relevant archive upon the subject, with a view to drawing up textbooks and teaching manuals [7]. In this particular area, the Italian authors clearly lost out to some extent, largely in view of the great attention that was then being paid in Portugal to the work of Jean-Baptiste Say. In order to provide a symbolic picture of this decline in the Italian influence, it is sufficient to say that amongst the 20 works of reference that were included by José Ferreira Borges in the book that was initially adopted for the teaching of political economy at the Faculty of Law at Coimbra University, there is not one single book included that was written by an Italian author (Borges 1834).

There was no notable improvement in the situation when new textbooks were produced by A. Forjaz de Sampaio that would then be used almost uninterruptedly between 1839 and 1874 for the teaching of political economy at Coimbra. References were once again made to Italian authors, although the authors that were now recommended were those who had already served the purposes of economic and political reformism the century before: Beccaria, Genovesi and Filangieri. The works of these authors could still be considered relevant and up-to-date, particularly from the

[7] On the process of the gradual institutionalisation of the teaching of classical political economy in Portugal throughout this period, cf. Almodovar 1995.

viewpoint of justifying the learning of political economy by law students. However, there was a total absence of any Italian authors who could be considered representative of nineteenth-century classical and liberal economic thought. There was a fleeting reference to Giovanni D. Romagnosi, as well as evidence that the Portuguese teacher had recommended that his work be purchased in Italian for the Faculty library (Sampaio 1853, 141), but this is not sufficient to suggest that there was any real reversal in the trend towards the progressive disappearance of Italian authors. One of the authors that was most abundantly quoted and widely used by Forjaz de Sampaio was Pellegrino Rossi. But his work belonged in its own right to the tradition of the French liberal school that enjoyed such a significant influence in Portugal[8].

By the end of the nineteenth century, the disappearance of Italian economic literature in Portugal was a consummate and incontrovertible fact. However, something was shortly to happen in the design of the curricular structure at the Faculty of Law at Coimbra University that would cause this situation to be altered.

5. The rediscovery of Italian sources

At the turn of the century, there was one particular figure who stood out from the rest of the teachers at the Faculty of Law at Coimbra University: J. F. Marnoco e Sousa (1870-1916). Although his teaching career was relatively short, due to his untimely death at the age of 46, he still had time to publish various manuals on the different subjects taught as part of the degree in law, namely ecclesiastical law, public law, commercial law, the history of law, colonial administration, political economy and public finance[9]. He played an active role in all of these areas, for which he promoted the respective curricular reorganisation. And, although it must be admitted that his greatest impact was undoubtedly in the teaching of political economy, one must not overlook the importance of his integral and integrating vision of the training of jurists, bearing in mind certain background elements that should be taken into consideration.

First of all, the idea that legal phenomena are social phenomena that may be seen as subjects for positive study, as is the case within the field of the natural sciences. In other words, it is possible to establish relationships of cause and effect and propound laws that express observable regularities. Secondly, the principle that the social nature of legal phenomena requires that they be studied from the broader perspective of the characteristics of the social fabric and the needs that are associated with its maintenance or transformation; or, in other words, that the study of law must be understood as an integral part of the study of society.

---

[8] Cf. Cardoso 2000.

[9] One of the most complete of his texbooks in economics is Sousa 1910.

Thirdly, the defence of economics as the social science that is specifically geared towards understanding the workings of the legal systems of modern societies, namely as far as the study of the systems of property, labour, capital, credit, circulation, taxation, etc. is concerned.

In view of this ambitious plan of action, it is quite easy to understand the wide-ranging scope of the readings and bibliographical references that Marnoco e Sousa made use of. As we read through his economics manuals, we can see that his comprehensive work resulted in the compilation of an updated inventory of the works produced in different European countries. And there is no doubt that, amongst the readings assimilated and recommended by Marnoco e Sousa, it was the Italian books and reviews that were clearly the most prevalent. His programme of action had found solid bibliographical support there.

It would certainly be far too laborious to enumerate here the scores of Italian books and articles (especially those published in *Giornale degli Economisti*) quoted by the Portuguese teacher. It should, however, be noted that he permanently made use of Italian authors in such different fields as the history and philosophy of law (Andreani, Cavagnari, Lilla and Morasso), commercial law (Vidari and Vidanti), property law (Manara and Nazzani), industrial organisation (Bozzini and Cassola), population (Arduino, De Lucca and Raggi), social economy (Cossa, D'Ippoliti and Loria) and public finance (Cossa, Einaudi, Graziani, Lorini, Mazzola, Nitti and Ricca-Salerno, amongst others). Amongst the most frequently quoted works of a general nature, the most important are perhaps those by Luigi Cossa, Augusto Graziani, Lo Savio, Achile Loria, Camillo Supino and Ghino Valenti.

As far as these latter works are concerned, they are a fairly miscellaneous group, exhibiting notable differences in regard to their overall conception of the economic problems and phenomena that they seek to interpret and control. Marnoco e Sousa does not openly admit to sharing the opinion of any of the Italian authors that he quotes, which is not in fact surprising in view of the diversity of concepts that set either the socialism of Loria and Labriola or the incipient marginalism favoured by Graziani and Valenti[10]. Common to almost all the Italian authors was the division of economics into *individual economics* (centred on the questions of utility and choice) and *social economics* (centred on the questions of trade and the market), a division that is generally accepted by Marnoco e Sousa in the structure of his textbooks.

The eclectic encyclopedism of Marnoco e Sousa sometimes caused the use of his vast archive of authors to degenerate into an amalgam of unconnected references that it seemed difficult to render compatible with one another. However, the author had clearly made an effort to offer his readers a wide-ranging and multidisciplinary framework to guide themselves by, in which economic and legal

---

[10] On the joint development of socialism and marginalism in Italy in this period, cf. Faucci and Perri 1995.

themes were defined through references of a historical and sociological nature. In addition to providing a broad spectrum of pedagogical objectives, Marnoco e Sousa also sought to direct his readers towards a recognition of the disadvantages of political and economic systems that were based on individualism and socialism, preferring instead to adopt the intermediate solution of a "socialism of cathedra" in which the state would be called upon to perform certain non-transferable duties as a guarantee of harmony and social welfare.

The great triumph of this view of social and economic problems that was successfully imposed as a model for teaching at the Faculty of Law at Coimbra University was only made possible by the extreme fragility of the theoretical and analytical economic discourse that was prevalent at that time in Portugal. The echoes that were being heard of the "marginalist revolution" and the neoclassical economics were no more than simplified reports being aired of barely understood advances in theory. The erudition shown by Marnoco e Sousa, who was capable of identifying and recognising the innovations that had been introduced with the discovery of the principle of decreasing marginal utility, as well as recognising the respective mentors of these innovations, was not in itself sufficient to allow his name to become associated with this new torrent of ideas that was now leading the science of economics down paths of analysis that had never before been explored.

Marnoco e Sousa's activity as a teacher and compiler of textbooks was to prove crucial for the development of the economic doctrines of corporatism, for which the ground was largely prepared by the great receptiveness to be found in Portuguese university and political circles towards the ideas of Italian authors. This aspect will be touched upon in the next section. First of all, however, it is worth analysing an exceptional case that occurred within the broad panorama of Portuguese economic thought at the beginning of the twentieth century and which was not at all favourable to the theoretical digressions of a largely abstract nature that would be evident to an attentive reader of Walras and Pareto.

António Horta Osório was the author of this remarkable feat consisting of the publication of a work designed to justify the importance of the mathematical method in economics, in the context of the general equilibrium theories of the Lausanne School (Osório 1911). Two years later he had the honour of seeing his book translated and published in France, with an introduction by Vilfredo Pareto (1913).

Although somewhat wary of the alleged comprehensive utility of mathematics in economic reasoning, Pareto maintains that the book by Osório is not only "bien ordonné, sachant allier la simplicité de la forme à la profondeur de la pensée", but also that "il pourra rendre de grands services aux personnes qui veulent étudier la science" (1913, 288). The same credit would later be given by Schumpeter, by including Osório in a small list of books designed to encourage and disclose the use of mathematics in economic matters, which were published throughout the 1910s (Schumpeter 1954, 957).

We are not dealing here with an original work. Osório follows very closely the works by Walras and Pareto, presenting and discussing them as a whole, but also giving particular emphasis to their conceptions of pure economics as a particular branch of political economy. Besides, some importance is given to historical and methodological problems, mainly in order to provide an impressive explanation of the importance and necessity of the use of mathematics in economic analysis. Walras and Pareto are also used as a starting point for the specific development of a general equilibrium model applied to the analysis of the market for final goods.

From all the concepts and theories that are presented to the readers, we think that special emphasis should be given to the way in which the Paretian distinction between utility and ophelimity is discussed, for these concepts are used by Osório as the foundation to his view of economic science – as a disciplinary field restricted to the study of a small part of human behaviour, a kind of "rational mechanics of desire" (1911, 72), while psychology is portrayed as the global science pertaining to the study of human action. Consequently, economics would be no more than one of the branches of the general study of mankind. There is no doubt that the publication of this book in the Portugal of 1911 was a bold accomplishment. One may say about this book that it was quite out of place and time, defying conventional wisdom and mainstream reasoning.

Yet, regardless of the peculiar characteristics of Portuguese mainstream economic thought when the book was published, it is important to notice that the topics of Osório's analysis were somewhat troublesome even for the marginalist and neoclassical economists. It is quite different to accept the importance and usefulness of mathematical concepts as a means of systematising economic reasoning, and to claim, as Osório did, that the scientific character of pure economics in itself demanded the presence of mathematics not only as a language, but also as a logical device for the development of hypotheses, and as a procedure for expressing conclusions. For him, pure economics was an abstract and experimental science which had to evaluate its scientific character, like all the exact sciences, not through the practical utility of its conclusions but chiefly by establishing the exactness of its formal internal logic. Therefore, it took a lot of courage – at least as great as his devotion to pure science – to warn his readers that "in the present work we will not deal with any practical topic nor find a solution to any concrete problem. Here we will only deal with the abstract relationships among human desires, and between them and the obstacles to their satisfaction" (1911, 3).

When Osório was writing, the perceptiveness of this methodological attitude was weak, even for those learned in economic matters. It should also be stressed that Osório lived in a country whose academic elite, albeit with a certain degree of economic education, was either maladjusted or openly hostile towards the analytical contents of his book.

In an environment that was clearly hostile to pure theory, Osório was condemned to oblivion and his book was dismissed. This may explain his attempt to spread his ideas outside Portugal, by publishing a French translation of the book under the implicit patronage of Vilfredo Pareto.

6. The Italian foundations for the economic doctrine of corporatism

Osório's enforced silence basically meant a devaluation of pure economics in favour of economic concepts and programmes that were geared more towards providing an ethical, social and political framework for economic agents. In fact, Portuguese economic thought had always been more prodigal in importing and producing normative guidelines that could be assimilated by a broader public than in developing theoretical reflections of an abstract nature that were only accessible to a restricted intellectual elite. The reading of Pareto could not be compared to the reading of other Italian texts, such as those which were proposed by Marnoco e Sousa in his textbooks compiled for the education of jurists at Coimbra University.

One of Marnoco e Sousa's pupils, and later a continuator of his pedagogical activities, was António de Oliveira Salazar. In the first years of his public career, before he became a minister and later the head of government of a dictatorial political regime implanted in 1926, Salazar lectured in the subjects of political economy and public finance at the Faculty of Law at Coimbra University. And it was there that he had the opportunity to witness the emergence of the economic and political ideology of corporatism and to keep abreast of its increasing impact at the level of doctrinal innovation.

For the main ideologists of the *Estado Novo* (New State), corporative organisation ought to fully embody objectives of social equilibrium and harmony, with the state being entrusted with the fundamental task of leading the whole process, with a view to establishing its effective control over the nation's social and economic life. Thus the institutionalisation of the *Estado Novo* – achieved through the approval of a coherent set of programmatic documents that would serve as guidelines for economic, social and political life – respected the essence of the corporatist ideology, which was based on the subjection of the individual to the superior interests of the nation and on the defence of the state's permanent moral and spiritual integrity, taking account of the supreme interests of maintaining law and order and social stability.

In the design and development of the corporative programme in Portugal, a crucial role was played by the influences originating from Italy, both with regard to the models of legislation adopted (such as, for example, the adaptation made of the *Carta del Lavoro* into the Portuguese *Estatuto do Trabalho Nacional*) and in terms of the readings that served as the source of its inspiration.

Gino Arias and, above all, Ugo Spirito, whose work was translated into Portuguese only a year after its original publication (Spirito 1934), were the most influential authors. But many others were read and quoted in the main works of reference used for the teaching of the economic, political and legal doctrine of Portuguese corporatism[11].

[11] Such as Amoroso, Arena, Biaggi, Fanno, Lanzillo, Micelli, Sforza, Vella, etc.

As was explicitly recognised by Teixeira Ribeiro, it was not surprising that there should be such frequent recourse to Italian authors, "for it is in Italy – as everyone knows – that the economic theory of corporatism has so far been subjected to the broadest and most profound study" (Ribeiro 1939, 3).

Spirito's influence was to be noted particularly in the criticism that was made of neoclassical economic theory and its presuppositions of free competition, the spontaneous equilibrium of markets and the absence of state interventionism. As staunch opponents of *laissez-faire*, the ideologists of corporatism extolled the notion of a self-directed economy, which did, however, have nothing to do with the mechanisms leading to the spontaneous equilibrium of the market that were so much to the liking of neoclassical economics. The following excerpt from Teixeira Ribeiro clearly illustrates this distinction:

"Corporations therefore collaborate in the performance of a normative role. And this is why the activities of individuals and companies are now subjected to a form of discipline or, better still, are conditioned by certain initial positions that are implied by this discipline.

We are far removed from automatic equilibrium: instead of this, we have a directed economy. But, in this case, such direction does not belong directly to the state, for it is the industries that, through their corporation, take the initiative of drawing up the rules and regulations. Afterwards, it is the task of the government, as the representative of the national interest, to decide upon these rules in the last instance, either approving them or rejecting them. Now, since the industries collaborate in their own discipline, it is said that we have instead a *self-directed economy*" (1939, 61-62).

The self-directed economy thus presupposed a high degree of state intervention at the time when the corporative organisation was first founded, which thereafter would be followed by a gradual decline in such protagonism.

The incentive for the creation of corporations embodied a logic of social and economic organisation in which the realisation of the general interest was previously measured by harmonising the interests of the different agents and groups of agents operating in a market that was overseen by the state. The fixing of prices, the entry of new firms into the market, the regulation of working conditions, the determination of wage levels, the analysis of production costs and, generally speaking, all operations that involved the use of economic calculation, which, under a system of free competition, represent elementary procedures in the choices that can be made within the context of scarcity of available resources – i.e. the typical framework for the decision-making of the *homo economicus* enshrined in the neoclassical economic literature – all these features would be the privileged area for the corporations and the employers' federative organisations (guilds) to decide upon. The guilds would afford corporations greater national representativity and, above all, provide a horizontal control of the activities associated with a particular product (wheat, rice, olive-oil, wool, wine, just to mention the main ones).

The teaching of Portuguese corporative doctrine was directly influenced by Italian theory in many other aspects: the replacement of the notion of individual utility by the notion of social utility provided by the corporations; the acceptance of the concept of the corporative just price as a normative alternative for subjective or speculative calculations of utility and costs; the defence of a controlled organisation of individual interests in contrast to the unconditional acceptance of the search for self-interest; the primacy given to the ideals of cooperation and solidarity that make it difficult for the market to operate according to the self-regulatory system of free competition; the call for a voluntary association between labour and capital; the encouragement of economic cartelisation for the representation of the main companies in each sector, thereby guaranteeing the coordination and effective control of all activities relating to a product (production, industrial processing, distribution) with the power to control prices, collective bargaining, technical auditing and the fixing of quotas for market transactions.

The strong influence of Italian corporatism in Portugal throughout the 1930s and 1940s was also visible at the level of the historiography of economic thought, as can be seen from the translation of a series of essays by Alberto Bertolino (1941). The corporatist theses were therefore not restricted to influencing the development of economic policy and doctrine in Portugal. Their effects were also felt in the consolidation of a methodological framework for the interpretation of the history of economic thought, according to which corporatism was seen as a higher synthesis of a coherent reflection on economic life and phenomena.

* * *

The translations of the works of Spirito and Bertolino proved to be extremely rare exceptions in a process of cultural and scientific exchange that did not need linguistic familiarities to make its impact felt. In fact, it was not because of the lack of translations that Italian authors ceased to have an influence on Portuguese economists.

Throughout the extensive period under consideration here, we have uncovered the influence of Italian authors and Italian sources in the formation of economic thought in Portugal. Sometimes, such a presence was discreet and hard to discern, as was almost always the case throughout the nineteenth century; but, on other occasions, it could also be observed operating in a markedly open fashion, as was the case in the second half of the eighteenth century and in the first half of the twentieth century. The testimonies that have been gathered together here are clear evidence of how a national history is made up of multiple contacts and cross fertilisations that, regardless of their intensity, show themselves to be indispensable not only for the identification of problems, but also for the presentation of the solutions that are considered to be most suitable and opportune in each period.

REFERENCES

ALMEIDA M. (1821), *Compêndio de Economia Política*. Lisboa (New edition, Lisboa: Banco de Portugal, 1993, Series of Portuguese Economic Classics, edited with an introduction by Maria de Fátima Brandão).

ALMODOVAR A. (1995), *A Institucionalização da Economia Política Clássica em Portugal*. Porto: Edições Afrontamento.

ALMODOVAR A. and CARDOSO J.L. (1998), *A History of Portuguese Economic Thought*. London & New York: Routledge.

BATTELLI G. (1929), *Domenico Vandelli e il Giardino Botanico di Coimbra*. Coimbra: Biblos (offprint).

BERTOLINO A. (1941), *Orientações Metodológicas na História do Pensamento Económico*. Lisboa: ISCEF (Translation of *Problemi Metodologici nella Storia delle Dottrine Politiche ed Economiche*, 1939)

BORGES J.F. (1834), *Instituições de Economia Política*. Lisboa: Imprensa Nacional (New edition, Lisboa: Banco de Portugal, 1995, Series of Portuguese Economic Classics, edited with an introduction by A. Sousa Franco).

CARDOSO J.L. (1988), Os escritos económicos e financeiros de Domingos Vandelli. *Ler História*, nº 13, 31-51.

CARDOSO J.L. (1990), Economic thought in late eighteenth-century Portugal: physiocratic and Smithian influences. *History of Political Economy*, 22:3.

CARDOSO J.L. (2000), French "traditions" and economic thought in Portugal (1850-1910). In: *Actes du Colloque 'La tradition économique française 1848-1939'*. Lyon: Editions CNRS, 939-953.

CARVALHO R. (1959), *História da Fundação do Colégio Real dos Nobres de Lisboa (1761-1772)*. Coimbra: Imprensa da Universidade.

COUTINHO D.R. DE SOUZA (1787), Recopilação dos ofícios expedidos de Turim no ano de 1796. In: *Textos Políticos, Económicos e Financeiros (1783-1811)*. Lisboa: Banco de Portugal, 1993, Vol. 2, 34-93 (Series of Portuguese Economic Classics, edited with an introduction by A. Dinis Silva).

FAUCCI R. and PERRI S. (1995), Socialism and Marginalism in Italy, 1880-1910. In: Steedman, Ian (ed.), 1995. *Socialism and Marginalism in Economics, 1870-1930*. London & New York: Routledge, 116-169.

GENOVESI A. (1808), *Institutiones Logicae et Metaphisicae in Usum Tironum Scriptae*. Coimbra: Imprensa da Universidade.

LISBOA J. DA SILVA (1819-1820), *Estudos do Bem Comum e Economia Política*. Rio de Janeiro: Impressão Régia, Vol. I (1819) and Vol. II (1820) (New edition, *Escritos Económicos Escolhidos, II*, Lisboa: Banco de Portugal, 1993, Series of Portuguese Economic Classics, edited with an Introduction by António Almodovar).

LONGO B. (1940), Domenico Vandelli e la fondazione del primo Orto Botanico nel Portogallo. In: *Relazione Storiche fra l'Italia e il Portogallo*. Roma: Reale Accademia d'Italia, 403-408.

MELLI G. FRANCHI (1966), Un italiano in Portogallo – Domenico Vandelli. *Estudos Italianos em Portugal*, nº 26.

Memórias Económicas da Academia Real das Ciências de Lisboa para o Adiantamento da Agricultura, das Artes e da Indústria em Portugal e suas Conquistas, 1789-1815. Lisboa: Academia Real das Ciências (New edition, Lisboa: Banco de Portugal, 1990-

1991, Series of Portuguese Economic Classics, edited with an introduction by José Luís Cardoso).

NEVES J.A. (1814-1817), *Variedades sobre Objectos Relativos às Artes, Comércio e Manufacturas, Consideradas Segundo os Princípios da Economia Política*. Lisboa: Impressão Régia (New edition in: José Acúrsio das Neves, *Obras Completas*. Porto: Edições Afrontamento, 1983-1989, Vol.3, edited by António Almodovar and Armando Castro).

NOGUEIRA R.R. (179?), *Lições de Economia Civil e Política Traduzidas das que Escreveu em Italiano a Abade António Genovesi*. National Library of Lisbon, manuscripts, Cod. 2168.

OSÓRIO A. HORTA (1911), *A Matemática na Economia Pura: a Troca*. Lisboa: Centro Tipográfico Colonial (New edition, Lisboa: Banco de Portugal, 1996, Series of Portuguese Economic Classics, edited with an Introduction by Manuel Farto).

OSÓRIO A. HORTA (1913), *Théorie Mathématique de l'Échange*. Paris: Girard & Brière.

PEREIRA J.E. (1983), *O Pensamento Político em Portugal no Século XVIII: António Ribeiro dos Santos*. Lisboa: Imprensa Nacional-Casa da Moeda.

RIBEIRO J. J. TEIXEIRA (1939), *Princípio e Fins do Sistema Corporativo Português*. Coimbra: Coimbra Editora.

SAMPAIO A.F. (1853), *Estudos de Economia Política ou Breve Explicação dos Elementos desta Ciência*. Coimbra: Imprensa da Universidade (New edition in: *Estudos e Elementos de Economia Política (1839-1874)*. Lisboa: Banco de Portugal, Vols. I and II, Series of Portuguese Economic Classics, edited with an introduction by Alcino Pedrosa).

SANTOS A.R. (1789), *Apontamentos e Refexões sobre Alguns Artigos de Economia Civil Necessários na Legislação*. National Library of Lisbon, manuscripts, Cod. 4676.

SCHUMPETER J.A. (1954), *History of Economic Analysis*. Oxford: Oxford University Press.

SERRÃO J.V. (1994), Introduction to Domingos Vandelli, *Aritmética Política, Economia e Finanças (1770-1804)*. Lisboa: Banco de Portugal (Series of Portuguese Economic Classics).

SILVA J.V.Á. (1782), Memória histórica sobre a agricultura portuguesa considerada desde o tempo dos romanos até ao presente. In: *Memórias Económicas da Academia Real das Ciências de Lisboa para o Adiantamento da Agricultura, das Artes e da Indústria em Portugal e suas Conquistas (1789-1815)*, Vol. 5, 149-196.

SOUSA J.F.M. (1910), *Ciência Económica*. Coimbra: F. França Amado (New edition, Lisboa: Banco de Portugal, 1997, Series of Portuguese Economic Classics, edited with an introduction by Maria de Fátima Brandão).

SPIRITO U. (1934), *Princípios Fundamentais da Economia Corporativa*. Lisboa: Livraria Clássica Editora (Translation of *I Fondamenti dell'Economia Corporativa*, 1932).

VANDELLI D. (1770-1804), *Aritmética Política, Economia e Finanças*. Lisboa: Banco de Portugal, 1994. (Series of Portuguese Economic Classics, edited with an introduction by José Vicente Serrão).

VAZ F.L. (1999), A difusão das ideias económicas de António Genovesi em Portugal. *Cultura - Revista de História e Teoria das Ideias*, Vol. XI (2ª série), 553-576.

The Light and Shade of Italian Economic Thought in Spain (1750-1850)*

Jesús Astigarraga
Departamento de Estructura, Historia Económica y Económia Pública
(University of Zaragoza)

Introduction

There are two distinct phases in the history of Italian political economy in Spain between 1750 and 1850. During the second half of the eighteenth century, and specially between 1770 and 1800, Italy played an active role as an export centre of economic ideas to Spain and emitted a constant stream of brilliant light, illuminating the advance of the economic thought and the economic reform of the Spanish Enlightenment. After 1800 this brilliance was dulled and the intensity of Italian economic thought and its influence gradually faded. It was obscured by the dazzling ray of clarity that the British Classical School and its French disciples began to direct at Spain.

The Brilliance of Italian Political Economy in Spain between 1760 and 1800

Carlos the Third's Reign: "libertad, luces y auxilios"

Carlos the Third's ascent to the Spanish throne (1759) marked the beginning of a fruitful and sustained period of development, propagation and application of economic ideas. During this period the volume of available publications on economics increased considerably and, even more importantly, Spain immersed itself in the vigorous international flow of economic ideas. It always remained a late comer on the scene, and principally an importer of ideas, but the quantity, quality and variety of the literature on economics invalidates the caricature of Spain as a country of little intellectual depth and dominated by the priesthood [Smith 1968]. Whilst it is true that enlightened Spanish thinkers made no original contributions to economic theory, it is hardly fair to dismiss their efforts out of

* The completion of this work was made possible by a research residency in the Dipartimento di Scienze Economiche at the Università of Firenze from April to August of 1998 financed by a grant from the C.A.I. under the *Programa Europa*. I also wish to express my gratitude to Professor A. Magliulo.

hand. They were certainly aware that economics, as the principal "science of government", was "invaluable" for the prosperity of the nation and its people; their readiness to put theories into practice made them into outstanding applied economists; finally, being politicians and senior public servants, they were able to sustain one of the most fruitful economic reform of the entire eighteenth century in Europe between 1760 and 1790 [Llombart 1992]. As Jovellanos [1795] suggested, there were three important factors in this process: "freedom", "lights" and "aids" ("*libertad, luces y auxilios*"), that it is to say: an intellectual climate unfettered by the old political and religious restrictions, small cells of enlightened thinkers and *Sociedades Económicas* actively involved in the propagation of the economics ideas and a regime that safeguarded and encouraged the whole process. However, this period cannot be fully understood without examining the flood of foreign economic literature that inundated Spain from 1760 onwards and kept the country in touch with the latest findings of global economic science[1].

Venturi's Penetrating Evaluation of Italo-Spanish Relations

Analysing Italo-Spanish relations in the eighteenth century means following the path opened by Venturi[2], developing, enlarging and, in some cases, modificating his analysis. Relations between these two countries cannot be understood without taking into account the political climate created by the return of the Spanish Bourbons to southern Italy in 1734 and also the future Carlos the Third's reign in the *Regno delle due Sicilie* during the preceeding twenty-five years. Venturi [1969-1984, II, 44ss.] has analysed the Italian influence in Spanish reformist politics during the Enlightenment and the creation of a "political and intellectual" tie between the two countries. Behind this process were, initially, Squillace, "*il grossolano*", and Grimaldi, "*il colto*" – these Italian ministers played crucial roles in Spanish politics between 1759 and 1766 –; afterwards, Muniain, Roda, Azara and Floridablanca – all were important representatives of the Spanish diplomatic corps in Italy –; and, everywhere, Tanucci, who, as well as keeping Naples under the Spanish Crown's control, made a lasting contribution to national politics, particularly in the regalistic struggle. Nevertheless, in order to avoid an overly political interpretation, we stress – as does Venturi [1973-4, 7-8] – that the Spanish presence in the Italian *Mezzogiorno* was not accompanied by any kind of intellectual and cultural *rispagnolizzazione*. In addition to this, eighteenth century Spanish economists, unlike their predecessors, had no desire to expand the national

[1] See, amongst others: on Physiocracy, Lluch-Argemí [1985]; on Cameralism, Lluch [1999]; on the early days of the Classical School, Smith [1957]; and as an overview, covering the various national neo-mercantilist currents, Llombart [at press].

[2] See, especially, Venturi [1962; 1973-4; 1969-1984, II, 44-64, IV, 239-328].

market to include the Italian possessions; thus the exchange of ideas between Spain and Italy, including Naples, represented a genuine dialogue between two quite different interlocutors.

As Venturi [1962, 204-205] has indeed noted, the great majority of enlightened thinkers in Spain, right from the "mercantilist" Uztáriz through to the "liberal" Foronda, saw Italy as a model for progress in their own country. They correctly pointed to its flourishing population and economy – especially in the North – and likewise to the status that economics had achieved throughout the country; this was particulary apparent in the increased availability of texts and its introduction as a discipline in educational institutions and Chairs. Italy also enjoyed a more vigorous "intellectual and social climate" than Spain during the eighteenth century [Venturi 1962, 250]. This was partly due to the flair for analytical innovation of some Italian economists (something nobody now questions, especially after Schumpeter's exhaustive study [1954, 203, 218]) and to the vigorous intellectual dynamics that traditional Italian regionalism produced. As Schumpeter [1954, 219n] has so perspicaciously pointed out, only in Spain an Italy do we find regionalism used as a starting point for economic analysis. However, it would be pure pariochialism to suggest that the Spanish Enlightenment produced schools as authorative as the Neapolitan or the Milanese or economists as outstanding as Galiani, Verri or Beccaria[3]. However, there is one important point on which we disagree with Venturi: he maintains that Italian economists' influence in Spain throughout the eighteeenth century was "isolated or lacked continuity" in comparison with the "more far-reaching" influence that the Spaniards exerted in Italy [Venturi 1962, 250]. Uztáriz, Ulloa, Campomanes, Sisternes, Foronda, Conca and Sempere were some of the authors whose ideas found their way from Spain to Italy; their works aroused considerable interest in the *Mezzogiorno* whilst in the North, most of the times, they "failed to excite a response"[4]. Nevertheless the flow in the opposite direction was just as strong (Venturi highlights the names of Galiani, Beccaria, Genovesi, Carli and Filangieri). The intellectual exchange between the two nations in the eighteenth century was genuinely mutual; it amounted to much more than just the fascinating lessons that Zanoby presented to Roquemare.

---

[3] If there is something we have learnt from Venturi, it is that any sort of patriotic bias "è stato tanto nocivo alla comprensione di un'epoca storica quanto il giorno in cui esso venne applicato al nostro Settecento" [Venturi, 1957]. We wish to dedicate this work to his memory, as a token of our appreciation for his immense intellectual legacy.

[4] All too often the influence of Spanish Scholastics on the work of Galiani – and perhaps Beccaria – on a subjective value theory is overlooked [Grice-Hutchinson 1982, 149-151]. On the other hand, Guasti's [1996, 1998] recent research confirms Uztáriz as the most successful and enduring Spanish economist in Italy. His influence was supported in the critical translation in French of his book due to Forbonnais and can be detected in the output of the Neapolitans (Genovesi, Filangieri, etc.), the Milanese (Beccaria, Verri, etc.) and subsequent economists as well.

The Propagation of Italian Economics: Translating and Institutionalizing Political Economy

The Spanish were well aware of the broad-based Italian economic tradition. The nine authors to be translated were from Naples (Galiani, Genovesi, Filangieri), Milan (Beccaria, Griselini, Carli), Veneto (Donato), Modena (Muratori) and the Papal State (Belloni)[5]. Notwithstanding this, the bulk of translations were of Neapolitan and Milanese economists. Muratori's [1782, 1790, 1794] wide-ranging and multifaceted works went way beyond pure economics[6] and the translations of Belloni [1788] and Donato [1789], as well as arriving fairly late on the scene, received poor circulation and made little impact[7]. All these translations were done between 1774 and 1794.

Campomanes, *Fiscal* for the *Consejo de Castilla* and the real force behind Carlos the Third's government, sponsored the translations of Beccaria's *Dei Delitti* [1774] and Galiani's *Dialogues* [1775]; the translator was probably the same person – a priest, De las Casas –. The translation of Galiani's work was fairly faithful if slightly condensed. It was also rather more conservative: it appeared "purged of various oversights" not in keeping with "our censors' critique and severity" and "the serious nature of our nation"[8]. Of course, Beccaria's writing was translated with a great deal of restraint and healthy respect for the Government, the Church and Spanish Law[9]. Despite this the Inquisition banned it in 1777 and renewed its ruling in 1790 and 1803. Only the constant protection of the *Consejo de Castilla* ensured that its importance was not entirely overloooked.

The principal publisher of translation of Italian works on economics during the Enlightenment in Spain was the *Sociedad Económica Aragonesa*. This fact was inseparably linked to the foundation in Zaragoza in 1784 of the Chair of Civil Economics and Commerce, the first of its kind in Spanish history. The *Sociedad* subsequently embarked on an ambitious preliminary publishing programme to create suitable teaching materials. They drew heavily on Italian sources. Between 1784 and 1788 the organization took delivery of a translation of Griselini [1784]

---

[5] Reeder [1973], Aguilar Piñal [1981-1995] and original research.

[6] The reference to the three translations of Muratori's work represent one small example of just how well received this sophisticated expression of enlightened Italian Catholicism was in Spain until 1790 (this question is still in need of indepth research). His ideas were presents at the very beginnings of the Spanish Enlightenment. His influence can be perceived in the pioneering work of Mayans and in the training of people of the stature of Campomanes and Capmany [Mestre 1976; Llombart 1992].

[7] Both translations followed the French version, which explains their late appearance. Labrada, a Galician, did the translation of *Della moneta* in order to set out the basic laws of commerce -"an honourable and useful art"- for the members of the then recently founded *Consulado* of La Coruña [Belloni 1788, translator's note]. The version of *L'uomo di governo* by a Valencian, Arbuxech, formed part of a series of translations related to cameralist thought, but it appeared out of date and was superseded by Bielfeld and Justi.

[8] Galiani [1775, translator's note]. This involved the omission of various observations critical of the clergy and sophisticated political terminology. The translation was dedicated to Campomanes.

[9] Beccaria [1774, Prologue].

by J. Amar, a member of the Society, and others of Filangieri [1784], Genovesi [1785-6] and Carli [1788] by V. de Villava, Professor at the University of Huesca. Nevertheless the programme did not live up to expectations. The translations of Griselini, Filangeri and Carli were either of little interest, incomplete or just extracts. The economic content of the discourse by the Secretary of the *Accademia dei Georgofili* was minimal[10]; the translation of Filangeri was merely an extract from the *Scienza* – the chapter about the grain trade [Astigarraga, 1997] –; and the translation of Carli, peppered with uninteresting notes, was from two short pieces: *Sull'impiego del denaro al Sig. Marchese Scipione Maffei* and *Breve Ragionamento sopra i bilanci economici delle nazioni*[11].

The conspicuous exception was the translation of the Genovesi's *Lezioni*, without doubt the most polished piece of work in the *Sociedad's* entire catalogue. It was intended primarily for the classroom. Once the Chair of Economics had been set up, Floridablanca, *Secretario de Estado* and the man in charge of overseeing its activities, requested the *Sociedad* to devise "a political economy syllabus". The *Sociedad* chose the *Lezioni* and entrusted its translation to Villava, who supported the choice of text on two grounds: the work's originality and the fact that it was directed at students[12]. Villava did not simply confine himself to translating the work, but incorporated extensive "translator's notes"; as well as explaining Genovesi's ideas, they also brought them up to date, adapted and expanded them [Usoz 1996, 414-422]. The *Lezioni* were already twenty years old when Villava translated them, so that he was obliged to update the bibliography which in turn led him to refer readers to the works of Necker, the Physiocrats, Galiani, Beccaria and Filangeri. Likewise, the adaptation of the Neapolitan's ideas to Spanish and Aragonese economic conditions led him to include a large amount of information about the Spanish economy and law; in addition, he drew on the ideas of various seventeenth and eighteenth century Spanish and Aragonese economists (mainly Uztáritz, Ulloa and Campomanes). However, the most unusual aspect of this translation lies in the "shortcomings" and "mistakes" that Villava found in Genovesi's text. The most serious ones related to certain "political errors" and religious ideas which he felt obliged to correct. Villava toned down certain of the Neapolitan's criticisms of theologians and religious bodies, as well as his arguments in favour of luxury, and voiced his reluctance to the implement his

---

[10] The discourse advocated the participation of rural clergy in the propagation of agricultural techniques. The translation included a state ordinance that facilitated their participation (this is evidence of how the influence of the Austrian interventionist model of María Teresa and Giuseppe II was felt in Spain).

[11] The complete work of this cameralist politician began with these two pieces [Carli 1784-1794]; this suggests that Villava's intention was in fact to translate it entirely. His work was interrupted by his subsequent transfer to America as a public servant with the Department of Justice. Carli's *Lettere americane* and *Elementi morali* were also translated into Spanish and published in 1792 after rigorous censorship by the Inquisition.

[12] Genovesi [1785-6, Introductory Discourse, v, xvi]. Various Spanish universities had already slowly begun to adopt his Antischolastic works on physics and metaphysics published prior to 1753-4 [Venturi 1969-1984, I, 535-6]; this facilited the subsequent acceptance of his economic work.

proposal for the reform of primogeniture in Spain. There is, therefore, no doubt that Villava was "more conservative, more moderate and more admiring of the Spanish Catholic monarchic tradition" than Genovesi [Venturi 1969-1984, I, 639].

Filangeri's published output in eighteenth century Spain was not restricted to the extract translated by Villava. Three years after its publication, a translation of a legal pamphlet by the Neapolitan author appeared [Filangieri 1787]; at the same time, J. Rubio, a Valencian lawyer, was making the first attempt at translating the whole of the *Scienza* [Filangieri 1787-9]; eight years later, another lawyer, F. Paula [1792], published various sections of the work with a detailed critical commentary on Filangieri's ideas about monetary policy and luxury. The reason for the broad selection of material available goes beyond the purely economic, gived the wide variety of issues dealt with in the work. It is however unquestionable that his ideas on "political and economic laws", collected in volume II, were of just as much interest to enlightened thinkers here as those on legal, educational or criminal matters [Astigarraga 1997]. Likewise, for a better insight into the propagation of this material, we must stress that it was done in conjunction with a massive advertising campaign that presented the *Scienza* to the Spanish public as "the most perfect of works" in the field of legislation and as a highpoint in the European Enlightenment[13]. It comes as no surprise that the powerful enemies of the Enlightenment soon began preparing to attack it. In 1790 the *Scienza* was banned by the Inquisition. Subsequently the publishing of J. Rubio's translation was suspended in midstream; it was to have included the second volume, although the quality of his work was not up to standard[14].

Teaching was the second medium for the propagation of Italian economic thought in Spain. The pioneering experiments in economics teaching in Italy during the second half of the century [Gioli 1988, 387-393] were well known in Spain, especially the ones in Naples and Milan. In 1774 the influential Campomanes [1774, 92] acclaimed these two institutions as models for the teaching of "the genuine laws of commerce". Ten years later the *Sociedad Aragonesa* urged the government to set up an institution "to recreate the Naples Chair directed by the celebrated Genovesi". In other words, they proposed doing in Spain what Carlos the Third had permitted B. Intieri to do thirty years before in Naples. The government not only took up the proposal at once, but also offered it official protection, anticipating the antipathy that it would attract. It was also expected that this pilot scheme would in time spread to other *Sociedades*

---

[13] We find substantial evidence of this publicity campaign in periodicals of the time: *Memorial literario*, *Correo literario de la Europa* or *Espíritu de los mejores diarios literarios*. *Scienza* was by far the most reviewed work in these publications. We have discovered a dozen such articles on it. There are also five on various works by Carli and three on Genovesi's *Lezioni*.

[14] Rubio mixed up works, authors and economic concepts quoted by Filangieri, changed his stance on ecclesiastical matters and, what is even worse, left out numerous passages from the original, especially those that questioned Spanish commercial and colonial strength.

Económicas. This, the first Chair in Spanish history therefore represented official support for these *Sociedades*, which were to participate in this initial phase of economics teaching. In addition, it was a victory for the members of the Spanish Enlightenment: it satisfied their demands that the propagation of economic ideas be stimulated in institutions devoted to its teaching.

The Chair in Zaragoza was conceived along the same lines as the Chair of *Commercio e Meccanica* in Naples. It was funded privately; teaching was done in the vernacular; it was free of charge and open to students from all walks of life – gentlemen, aristocrats and businessmen –, although it was especially targeted at law students and future public servants. At the same time, the major part of the courses' material reveals the heavy influence of Genovesi's thought, at least during the first twenty years, when the Chair was directed by L. Normante, a young Aragonese lawyer. From 1784 to 1786 the course text book was the Valencian Danvila's *Lecciones* [1779]. This book is regarded as the first economics teaching handbook written in Spain and its author used it in his moral philosophy classes at the *Seminario de Nobles* in Madrid. His sources were varied: Cantillon, Condillac and Genovesi, the last being by far the most important [Cervera 1998]. Villava's translation of the *Lezioni*, published in 1786, whilst not replacing Danvila's text altogether, certainly acquired greater importance and was also used in conjunction with the works of other Spanish economists of the eighteenth century. The teaching materials that Normante prepared also reveal an enormous respect for the ideas of Genovesi, the "immortal" teacher from "Intieri's Chair" in Naples. He favoured the use of J. Cary's translation of the two Genovesi brothers, discovered Antonio's *Elementi del commercio* and drew extensively on his *Lezioni* in two of the three works he prepared for the classroom, one of them was a concise and selective summary of the *Lezioni* [Normante 1784; 1785]. It is more than likely that he based his syllabus on Genovesi's model (demographics, agriculture, etc.) and there is no doubt that it was directed more at the technical and applied aspects of economics than at the theoretical ones.

But, apart from the Chair in Zaragoza, we can detect Genovesi's influence in the only other two economics teaching experiments carried out in Spain before the end of the eighteenth century. R. De Salas of the Faculty of Law at the University of Salamanca (1787 to 1792) was responsible for the first and J. A. Mon of the Academy of Political Economy of the *Sociedad Económica* of Mallorca (1793 to 1800) for the second. Both based their syllabuses on the *Lezioni*. Unfortunately, the success of these pioneering attempts was limited and short-lived. This was due, above all, to the virulent opposition that a range of social groups directed at the projects from their very beginnings. In 1793 the University of Salamanca suspended Salas from teaching (he was denounced by the Inquisition for spreading "suspicious" ideas). The Chair in Zaragoza was never actually closed down, mainly because of constant government protection. However, the bitter campaign conducted by a priest, D. de Cádiz, against its professor, L. Normante, minimized the possibilities of the concept spreading to other *Sociedades* (amongst other things, he accused him of encouraging usury and luxury and questioning clerical celibacy). At the turn of the century the only institution still teaching economics in Spain was the Chair in Zaragoza. Its history, together with that of Salamanca and Majorca, reveals the complete dominance of the Neapolitan model during the early stages of economics education in Spain. Its presence goes beyond just the syllabus and the teaching methods, and should rightly be regarded as an example of intense institutional influence[15].

The overall analysis of the spread of Italian economic thought in translation and through teaching reveals that, whilst Spain may not have been unreceptive to the Milanese economists, it certainly accepted the Neapolitans' in a more universal way[16]. Proofs of this are the eight translations, plagiarized versions or adaptations of the works of Galiani (1), Genovesi (3) and Filangieri (4), and the "Genovesian" character of the Chair in Zaragoza[17]. Added to this, was the interest that the "applied" treatises aroused at the expense of more worthwhile works on economic analysis. The treatment that Galiani's work received in Spain is illustrative of this: his *Dialogues* was translated and widely read, whilst *Della moneta* remained unknown. The contrast is even more striking when we look at the Milanese school. Whilst Carli's "unorthodox, narrow minded and outdated" approach [Venturi 1958, 428ss.] attracted attention in Spain, the work of Verri and Beccaria, the economist, did not[18]. We can explain the ostracism of the *Il Caffè* economists as a kind of defence mechanism against the interpretation, shared by Verri, that blame to the many years of "poor government" by Spain the economic collapse of Lombardy [Venturi 1969-1984, I, 691], or as well as an eloquent silence in response to an economic agenda seen as utilitarian, hedonistic and egalitarian, to sum up, just too radical for an Enlightenment that had found it necessary to dilute the Neapolitans' economic thought and had seen the only "unprotected" work

[15] This view obliges us to extend the limits of the Chair at Naples' area of influence beyond the Italian *Mezzogiorno*. The enlightened Italian Academies constitute the second example of institutional influence. Without doubt the best known example in Spain was the *Accademia dei Georgofili*; its foundation was received very positively at an very early date [Società economica 1791, 6-7, 33], although its role in the shaping of the Spanish *Sociedades Económicas* was somewhat overshadowed by the Societies in Dublin, Brittany and Berne [Astigarraga 1990, 162ss.].

[16] We are adamant that authors from the Kingdom of Aragon played the leading role in the propagation of Italian economic thought. Amongst them were Villava, Arbuxech, Amar, Sempere and Rubio, as well as the Duke of Villahermosa, the Spanish Ambassador in Paris, who corresponded with Galiani. The deep-rooted political and cultural relations between the Kingdom of Aragon and Italy became stronger and stronger throughout the eighteenth century, especially because of the numerous Aragonese, Valencians and Catalans who were educated there.

[17] This meant that, except for Filangieri, most of the members of the brilliant Genovesian economic school that formed around the Chair in Naples were little known in Spain, and likewise the economic writings of the Neapolitan "fringe" (Puglia, Calabria and Sicily) [Di Battista 1983].

[18] Beccaria's monetary opuscules and his contributions to *Il Caffè* sank without a trace. On the other hand, Verri's work, which in Italy was compared to that of Campomanes –without much foundation-, circulated in private circles. It is possible that Foronda was familiar with it and Jovellanos certainly read it and made summaries of it for his personal use. Nevertheless, we still lack an indepth study of the Milanese economist's influence on Jovellanos.

– Filangieri's – fail to pass the censors[19]. However the ostracism also had a lot to do with the nature of the channels through which these ideas entered Spain from Italy. The decisive roles of Campomanes and Floridablanca and the official protection that the Chair in Zaragoza received indicate that these channels enjoyed a "semi-official" status. All this was a result of the considerable importance that public servants acquired during the Spanish Enlightenment (Venturi) and of how much the affinity between the Neapolian economists and Tanucci and the Bourbon authorities facilitated the introduction of their ideas in Spain. Always thinking to the practical application of these ideas. It is no coincidence that the Italian economic thought received maximum exposure in Spain between 1770 and 1800, the most vigorous period of enlightened reform in the country.

Italian Influences in Spanish Economics Literature

Compared to Italy [Hutchinson 1988, 254-270, 298-307; Bianchini 1989], very little work was done on pure analysis in the Spain of the seventeen hundreds. As far as value and price theory are concerned, Foronda's [1789-1794] is the only comparable contemporary study: he was able to draw on Italian sources (Galiani), but more frequently on French ones (Condillac, Graslin), in formulating a value theory based on utility and scarcity [Barrenechea 1984, 199-221]. Other innovative issue that originated in Italy, the foundations of hedonistic utilitarianism and its consequence in the principle of the self-interest, was known in Spain, even the celebrated normative law "the greatest happiness for the the greatest number" was familiar. However, their main medium, as well as Helvetius, was Beccaria's *Dei delitti*, and consequently its first effects were not felt in economic areas but rather in legal ones[20]. Something similar happened with monetary analysis: Spanish economists did not devote much time to it either. The vigorous monetary debate that raged in Italy during the fifties reached Spain quite late, so by the time Belloni's [1788] theories on international trade and Carli's [1788] hypotheses in support of usury and against the exagerated importance attached to the impact of the balance of payments on the economy were propagated in Spain at the end of the eighties, they offered very little that was new. In addition, some of the conclusions of this debate entered the country, instead of leading figures (Galiani), through indirect channels (Genovesi, Filangieri). We find a good example of this

---

[19] It is also true that we can never be completely sure if the cautious approach employed by Villava, De las Casas and Rubio in translating was due to the fear of the Inquisition, the conservatism of their patrons or, quite simply, self-censorship.

[20] Once again we must refer to Foronda [1789-1794; 1801] on this point; he based his sophisticated proposal for the reform of the Spanish penal laws on the utilitarian principles of Beccaria and Filangieri and the criminal code of Pietro Leopoldo of Toscana [Barrenechea 1984; 1994; 1998]. Extracts from his work were translated into Italian by Fabbroni. Vasco regarded him as an example of "the advances made by Spain in political science, rhetoric and publishing."

in the most important contribution to monetary theory of the century: it was a "Smithian monetarist" piece by J. Alonso [1796], that it showed only one Italian influence – Genovesi's – [Fernández-Schwartz 1978]. Finally there is no reference in Spanish texts to the pioneering Italian innovation of applying mathematics to economics [Bianchini 1982].

As far as methodology is concerned, Galiani's relativist and pragmatic approach received, together with that of the Necker, a most sympathetic hearing [Astigarraga, at press]. It was the dominant one in Spain from 1770 to 1800, even partly accepted by authors more inclined towards abstract and deductive methodologies, like Foronda and Jovellanos, and created a climate for the rise of Neapolitan economics as a whole. All this goes to show that the Galiani's criticism of the "spirit of system" of the *économistes* could not help but meet with a warm reception in Spain, given the country's underdevelopment. And indeed Galiani's "science of details" was interpreted in Spain as a proposal that each nation seek its own means of economic development. This approach turned out to be indispensible in the analysis of the grain market. Spanish economists returned repeatedly to Galiani's ideas and repute to demonstrate that in this particular area, more than in any other, there were no universally valid practical principles nor was it possible to generalize the foreign experiences (Jovellanos [1795], Anzano [1795], Calomarde [1800]).

As can be imagined, the economic policy debates generated the strongest influx of Italian economic thought. There were six particularly important issues: population, land property, the size of rural holdings, guilds, luxury and the grain trade. As far as the first was concerned, Genovesi and his idea of an "ottima o giusta" population, and, to a lesser extent, Filangieri, helped to consolidate an already existing opinion which supported a moderate populationist attitude; it also acknowledged the existence of ceilings to the population growth and related them to other economic factors [Finoia 1995]. In second place, the movement attacking primogeniture and the immense *"mano muerta"* of the Church, especially active after 1780, received encouragement from Italy as simultaneous expression of the anti-curial struggle and the rise of agrarian liberalism. The condemnation of this practice by the principal Italian economists had a considerable influence on the issue, as did the widespread awareness – mainly due to Campomanes [Llombart 1992, 204] – of the prohibitory legislation proclaimed in various Italian states and the support Tanucci extended to the *Consejo de Castilla* from Naples. Nevertheless, Spanish economists were generally more favorable than the Italians to support regulatory measures of the primogeniture instead of expressly prohibitives. Thirdly, there was a very favourable reaction to the proposals by Genovesi and Filangieri to avoid demographic concentration in the cities and to redistribute the large agricultural property, although, despite Genovesi, Spanish economists put a great deal of effort into the drafting of an Agrarian Law. Fourthly, the measures decreed by Leopoldo of Toscana abolishing the guilds were well known in Spain, and even acclaimed (Campomanes, Foronda), but, except for a small minority, Spanish economists showed preference to the gradual and progressive reform of the guilds. Fifthly, the ideas of Genovesi and Filangieri consolidate a body of opinion, already disposed, in favor of a moderated luxury and, as in Italy, this hindered the acceptance of the opposite position, concerned about the effects of luxury on accumulation [Perrotta 1982]; nevertheless, Filangieri's idea of "passive" luxury and its potential application in the Spanish economy received a sceptical hearing [Paula 1792][21].

As far as grain trade is concerned, Galiani, Genovesi and Filangieri, in that order, were the principal sources of reference. This is a good indication of the theoretical diversity that typified this crucial controversy of the Spanish Enlightenment. We must not read the sympathetic reception afforded the *Dialogues* as just a reaction against Physiocracy: its economic agenda, although well known in Spain, had hardly any adherents and had never been applied [Lluch-Argemí 1985]. On the contrary, its concept of grain as a strategic commodity that demanded clear distinction between its "political" and "commercial" roles, sat well with a broad sector of writers sympathetic to liberal reforms in the grain trade with an approach less dogmatic and more cautious than the Physiocrats', especially with regard to foreign trade. Nevertheless, as usual, opinions varied enormously within this current. Campomanes was the most influential of the authors. Being the idealogue behind the official liberal reform programmme, begun in 1765, he did not share Galiani's Antiphysiocratic pragmatism in all its extremes [Llombart 1992, 171], because he was much closer to Herbert's liberal agrarianism, and therefore to Genovesi's position [Venturi 1969-1984, I, 620], regarding the response that the tragic agricultural crises of the mid-seventies demanded. It was necessary to wait for a change in the agricultural cycle and a slackening in the pace of liberal reforms so that Galiani's ideas, which were strengthened by the simultaneous arrival of those of Necker, could achieve a higher profile in Spain. The *Dialogues* influenced the two most important works on agriculture in the closing years of the century: one by Jovellanos [1795], who was very close to Galiani and Necker in his position on foreign grain trade [Llombart 1996, 140-1; Astigarraga 1998]; the other was by Anzano [1795], who was even closer to the Neapolitan in his reasoned defence of a "restricted" grain trade which would eliminate the danger of shortages and would serve both the consumer and industrial interests [Usoz 1996, 436-457]. On the other hand, the difficult conditions at the end of the century would close the door to a genuine hearing for Filangieri's liberal agrarian and partly Physiocratic ideas, which were then starting to circulate in Spain.

Two works of the Spanish Enlightenment require special mention, because they were conceived and written in Italy. The first was due to Gándara [1811], a

[21] In our opinion more indepth research on the mark that Genovesi left on Sempere's [1788] work is still required; it constitutes Spain's major contribution to the international debate on luxury.

public servant in the Papal State and lived in Naples between 1758-9, where he wrote it under orders from Tanucci[22]. His work is more interesting from a political standpoint than an economic one. Gándara is closer to the old Spanish "*arbitrista*" economic movement than the innovative ideas of "political economy" that he encountered in Naples. Nevertheless, its substantial anticlerical content, its advocacy for the foundation in Spain of a Chair of Agriculture, Manufacturing and Commerce and its defence of the reduction of the privileges of the clergy link it had with the Naples of Tanucci's reforms, although it seems a bit far-fetched to suggest it, as indeed has been done, Genovesi's influence is discernable. The second work was a treatise with a subject matter more substantially economic. Its author was Generés [1793], an Aragonese Jesuit and theology teacher in exile in Bologna, where he wrote it in 1793. Despite having been conceived at such a distance, the work's objective was to analyse the Aragonese economy and its growth possibilities. Generés fully subscribes to the reformist agenda identified with the *Sociedad Aragonesa* -he was later to become a member- [Usoz 1997]. However he also introduces some interesting innovations. Generés adds his enthusiasm for Bologna and Emilia to the Aragoneses' traditional admiration for Catalonia, and he presents these two as complementary models for overcoming the social and economic backwardness of Aragon. The almost ever present Italian influence in Generés' work had two sources[23]: certain innovative reforms, but conservatively structured, developed by Pietro Leopoldo of Toscana and a mixture of ideas, unique in the Spanish Enlightenment, worked up by various economists from the north and south of Italy (Griselini, Sapetti, Genovesi…), that revolved around an analytical and reformist agenda not entirely compatible with Genovesi's work.

All this confirms two things: the Spanish were more interested in the "applied" and "practical" ideas of Italian economics and the Neapolitan authors had by far the most impact. At the same time, all this demonstrates that Genovesi's *Lezioni* was the best received Italian text of the Spanish Enlightenment. Its was read right throughout the period from 1770 to 1800 and its public can be described as varied and broad: varied, because, as well as stimulating the study and teaching of economics, the work was associated with the very first modern empirical researches into the Spanish economy (carried out by Larruga, an Aragonese, and the Zaragoza Chair's first students, amongst them, Calomarde and Polo); it was also broad, because of the impressive list of authors that made use of it (Alonso, San Adrián, Jovellanos, Calomarde, Sempere, Generés, Anzano…). This gives an idea of the

---

[22] His work was banned and subsequently circulated in manuscript until published in 1804.

[23] In addition to what has already been suggested by Lluch-Sánchez [1996], an analysis of Generés' work reveals the readily identifiable Italian influence in at least the following areas: the reasons for the decline in population growth in Spain and Aragon; the debate over its distribution; the controversy over the use of animal power in agricultural labour; his support for agrarian liberalism; his approach to luxury and its relationship with the development of the arts; the incisive consideration to the passions and private interest as the driving force behind economic activity; and the reform proposals for the clergy's incomes, the guilds, primogeniture and criminal justice.

extent to which the Neapolitan's ideas, after first establishing themselves at Court and in Aragon, ended up meeting with acceptance all over the country (Valencia, Navarre, Majorca, etc.).

It is highly likely that Genovesi's "civil" economics – a commonly used term in the Spanish Enlightenment – offered enlightened Spaniards certain advantages compared to Galiani and Filangieri. These three Neapolitans shared the idea that all the productive sectors were mutually dependent, but Genovesi's answer was probably the most viable from the Spanish interests point of view. Filangieri's proposal "to protect the arts and manufacturing without jeopardizing agriculture" was tainted with a pronounced agrarian liberalism, even Physiocratic on some critical issues – private property, the grain trade and tax policy [Cotta 1954, 153ss.; Nuccio 1971, 213ss., 237ss.] –, that this impregnated the whole of the *Scienza* with a radicalism that exceeded the normal limits of reform acceptable by Spanish economists. The *Dialogues* suffered from the opposite problem. This book was normally used to argue that agriculture and manufacturing should be developed simultaneously [Campomanes 1774, ix; Sisternes 1786, 129], but it was framed in terms that emphasized the complementary nature of these two sectors rather than the greater importance of manufacturing, just as Galiani had maintained so insistently [Porta 1995, 131-2]. In other words, the Physiocrats' economic policies were just as impractical in Naples as in Spain, but just as Galiani's proposals for Naples proved inappropiate for Spain: that the country abandoned its heavy agricultural bias to regain its previously strong manufacturing base. Spain's lack of economic development needs an alternative solution. This solution did not question the fundamental role of agriculture in economic development nor did it regard industry as the driving force behind such development. All these aspirations were much more readily reflected in Genovesi's œuvre: he advocated a certain protectionism to achieve industrial progress and, without adopting a Physiocratic stance, he defended the primacy of agriculture, the strategic value of exporting its surpluses and the superiority of rural life. But, notwithstanding their differences, the Neapolitans economists must be seen, as Lluch [1999, 147] argues, as forming part of a bright "constellation of theorists" (Forbonnais, Steuart, Necker, etc.) which contributed to the consolidation of the dominant economic approach of the Spanish Enlightenment; its influence, as was the case in Italy [Gioli 1972, 44], endured longer than Smith's work.

We find even more evidence of the dominance of the Neapolitan school in the Spanish colonies in America. It constituted the principal vehicle for the propagation of the Italian economic ideas that reached the colonies from Spain during the final decades prior to the emergence of the various movements of independence. This can be observed in already well analysed examples, such as that of the River Plate and M. Belgrano [Chiaramonte, 1964], a father of the Argentine nation and Secretary at the *Consulado* in Buenos Aires: Galiani and Genovesi occupied a central position both in the economics training he received and in everything he wrote [Gondra 1927]. Genovesi's ideas also made an impact in Cuba and, through

Villava, they became known in Bolivia and Peru. In Chile two people were responsible for propagating his principles: A de la Cruz, Secretary at the *Consulado* in Santiago, and M. De Salas, founder of the independence movement in this country. The latter used the *Lezioni* as a teaching handbook for political economy courses given at the *Instituto Nacional* from 1813 onwards (these are regarded as the first experiments in economics education on American soil). Finally, in Argentina, as well as influencing Belgrano and numerous others, Genovesi made a considerable impression on M. Moreno, a distinguished politician and writer. Moreno was also mainly responsible for the enormous reputation that Filangieri acquired in this country after 1810. We do not propose to conduct an exhaustive examination of an area that is as yet inaccessible given the limited amount of published material available. We merely wish to draw attention to the fact that the consistency between economic thought in the colonies and on the peninsular during the final decades of the century prolonged the influence of Italian economic thought in Latin America. Despite the considerable displeasure that it would have caused F. Ferrara, it is highly probable that it was Neapolitan school that occupied a central position in this interesing case of transmission of economic ideas mediating the metropolis [Chiaramonte 1979, xxiv-xxv].

The Eclipse of Italian Political Economy in Spain (1800 to 1850)

The Ups and Downs in the Academic Consolidation of Economics

The impact of the French Revolution and the change of century marked a new era in the history of economic thought in Spain. Despite the climate of political instability and the disruptive changes of power, first (1795 to 1814) between the conservative Anti-Enlightenment group and the liberal "Frenchified" group, inheritor of the Enlightenment's legacy, and later (1814 to 1854) between the absolutists and the liberals, moderate and progressive, economics continued to consolidate itself as an academic discipline. More economics books were published, the first specialist magazines began to appear and the range of institutions committed to the propagation and teaching of economic knowledge broadened (the decisive step would be the promulgation of a law in 1857 by the minister Moyano), all this in turn produced a significant increase in the number of teaching texts available. Whilst not directly proportional, there is some relation between the government of the moment and the academic coming of age of economics. The liberals facilitated the process: they permitted a high degree of freedom of speech, of the press and of assembly and actively promoted the teaching of economics in universities (especially in Law faculties); on the other hand, the absolutists hindered any progress: they encouraged the suspension of economics teaching, the exiling of prestigious economists, especially in Great

Britain and France, and a return to censorship. However, the fact that the censors were stricter with Spanish economics texts than foreign ones meant that the inflow and assimilation of ideas from outside was not significantly disrupted. There were four main periods in the assimilation of classical economic thought. The most important figures of each period were: Smith (1790 to 1820), Say (1810 to 1840), the disciples of Say and Rau (1839 to 1846), and Bastiat and his school, who were to dominate the third quarter of the century. During the period in which Say enjoyed greatest influence, the works of Malthus, Sismondi, Bentham and, to a lesser extent, those of Ricardo and the Ricardians began to circulate, either in original or alternative form[24]. This sequence gives us advance warning of the central intellectual position that French and, to a lesser extent, Bristish economic thought would occupy in Spain, subsequently commanding greater attention than the Italian scholars.

The Propagation of Italian Economics: Translating and Institutionalizing Political Economy

During the first half of the nineteenth century, three complementary ways contributed to the propagation of Italian economic thought in Spain: the continuing existence of the eighteenth century Italian economists, the rediscovery of some of its forgotten figures and the appearance of diverse works from its classical period.

Verri was the only eighteenth century economist to be rediscovered through translation[25]. His *Meditazioni* first appeared in Spanish in 1820, no less than fifty years after the original had been published[26]. In addition, this version, by F. Rodríguez, a lawyer, was done with a very specific purpose in mind: the Milanese economist was presented to the Spanish public as a direct forerunner of Smith and Say; his work – that was compared to the latter's *Cathéchisme* – was recommended for classroom use and in the formulation of the Spanish economic policy [Verri 1820, x-xi]. Along with Verri, the eighteenth century legacy survived through Genovesi and, above all, Filangieri. The former's *Lezioni* were republished in 1804. The latter's *Scienza* received extensive exposure between 1813 and 1839: J. Rubio's initial translation, suspended by the Inquisition in 1789, was finally completed in 1813-14; another lawyer, J. Ribera, brought out a new translation in 1821-2, which, as was his intention, substantially improved the quality of Rubio's rather unsatisfactory version; a new anonymous translation appeared in 1836, it was

---

[24] The best overview of the period is by Lluch-Almenar [1992], notwithstanding not nearly as well known as the previous one; references to less thorough studies can be found in it. Likewise those by Smith [1957; 1968] and Almenar [1976; 1980] come highly recommended.

[25] Surely, this discovery is inseparably tied to the distribution of the Custodi Collection in Spain.

[26] The Spanish translation was extremely good, although it was slightly condensed and did not include Carli's critical notes (the translation was the 1781 edition of the *Meditazioni* published in Milan).

based on B. Constant's annotated edition; finally, in 1839, another lawyer, B. de la Torre, published a brief synopsis of Filangieri's economic and penal theories [Filangieri 1787-9; 1813; 1821-2; 1836; 1839][27]. This intensive exposure demonstrates just how long it took for economics to achieve professional status in Spain and occupy its own space free from legislation. It also reveals the extraordinary lengths to which enlightened Spaniards and liberals were obliged to resort in order to avert the intellectual isolation of their country: more than thirty years went by before there was a complete version of the *Scienza* available in Spain. The persecution of this work by the Inquisition was by no means its only problem. It was banned by the absolutists (they were aware of the vitriolic arguments in favour of the constitutionalist cause), so the work could only be published whilst the liberals were in power. All this is confirmation of how much nineteenth century liberals owed to thinkers of the eighteenth century: Filangieri's economic ideas were generally faithfully reproduced by his translators, although they contrived to include extensive notes which rendered his writings more relevant to the liberal cause. They enlarged on his ideas or even reworked them using classical precepts, drawing heavily on Say and Bentham.

As for "classical" Italian economic texts[28], there were by and large very few translations done. In addition, some were of minor works [Chitti 1847; Mastrofini 1859][29], whilst others of far greater interest entered Spain in radically abridged versions (Fuoco-De Welz's – or G. Velzi's – controversial work [De Weltz 1838]). None of the important Italians economists of the period were translated – this includes the "Lombardic-Venetian" schools (Romagnosi, Bosellini, Cattaneo and Messedaglia) and the Neapolitan school (Cagnazzi, Fuoco, Di Augustinis and Scialoja) –, although there are two exceptions: Rossi and Gioia. An incomplete translation was made of Rossi's lengthy *Cours* [1840][30], but the Spanish considered him more "French" than "Italian": his book reached Spain on the same wave that brought handbooks by other disciples of Say, it was claimed that his was "the only work capable of rescuing the science from lethargy into which it had sunk since Say's death" [Rossi 1840, xxxii] and it did not contain any additional notes which may have confronted his ideas with the Italians'. The case of Gioia was unusual too, although for different reasons. There is a Spanish version of his Benthamite treatise *Del merito e delle ricompense* [Gioia 1840] and quite a number of the historico-literary *Nuovo Galateo* (1866, 1868, 1875…), but *Il Nuovo Prospetto* was

[27] In addition, as was the practice in Italy, some of these versions incorporated translations of Filangieri's *Riflessioni politiche su … la riforma … della giustizia* and the *Elogio* that D. Tommasi dedicated to him; that is why Spaniards were so familiar with the Neapolitan's career and œuvre.

[28] Cabrillo [1978] and original research.

[29] Mastrofini's restrained work still inspired reply from very conservative quarters [Corral 1864].

[30] Only his theories on value, prices and production were translated. It seems that their translator, P. Madrazo, attended Rossi's lectures at the *College de France*. E. M. del Valle's Spanish translation of Malthus' *Essai*, published in 1846, was also based on the French version by Rossi.

never formally translated. Nevertheless, M. Torrente [1835], a liberal economist who worked in the Department of public finance in Cuba, compensated for this serious oversight. His book, published precisely in Cuba, amounted to little more than a concealed "literal translation for the most part" of *Il Nouvo Prospetto*, "although some sections were summarized and others reworked" [Lluch-Almenar 1992, 118-9] [31]. It was thanks to Torrente that the "sublime" Gioia and his "fuori misura" work became the principal vehicle for the dissemination of Italian economic thought both on the Spanish peninsular and in the colonies for the first half of the nineteenth century.

The gradual formalizing of the discipline's teaching in Spain during those years contributed little to a fuller understanding of Italian economics [Martín 1989]. At the beginning of the nineteenth century, there was a change of texts at the Chair in Zaragoza: Danvila and Genovesi (his *Lezioni* was then considered to be "riddled with mistakes and far too academic") gave way briefly to Garnier and Smith. This signalled a change in the direction that had been established by the teachers of the Enlightenment. Say quickly took their place on a much more permanent basis: his *Traité* commanded a pre-eminent position in Spanish Chairs between 1807 and 1835, and from 1836 to 1850 a number of different handbooks were used (amongst the authors were disciples of Say and Spanish economists). It was in this climate that books by Rossi and Torrente-Gioia appeared in Spanish teaching circles. They were officially adopted as textbooks in 1841 and 1848 respectively and constituted the only Italian treatises used in economics teaching in Spain during the first half of the nineteenth century.

Italian Influences in Spanish Economics Literature

As we have seen, nineteenth century Spanish liberalism was more receptive to the enlightened agenda than is generally thought. Thus, the ideas of eighteenth century Italian economists continued to receive "ample" application during the first decades of the eighteen hundreds. The use of the term "civil" economics continued as well, even amongst economists under Say's and other classical authors influence (Jaumeandreu, a Catalan, is one example) [Lluch 1973, 307-308]. Various factors explain these circumstances: the translations of Genovesi, Filangieri and Verri, the

[31] Torrente had spent time in Italy. His version was intended for use in teaching. As indicated by Lluch-Almenar, its principal innovations related to two matters: modifications in the formal structure of the work (the separate treatment given to production, distribution and consumption in the original was retained but a specific study of the effect of the State's role was included in each section) and changes in the weighting of each subject area (the sections on public finance were expanded but issues related to agriculture and technology were omitted). It is also worth mentioning differences in approach to certain issues (population and interest fixing policy) and the considerable enlargement of the detailed sources contained in the original (numerous references to Spanish economists were added on two issues in particular: public finance and luxury, stressing the perspective of the demand).

"hardy perennial" nature of the Spanish mercantilism [Smith 1971] and the kind of impact the first classical authors made in the country: their ideas were interpreted according to a pre-Smithian model, generally compatible with the political and social structure of the Ancien Régime [Almenar 1976; Lluch-Almenar 1992, 140ss.]. Two important examples are R. de Dou and J. Canga. The former is known for his translation of A. Smith's work, published in 1817. Far from accepting the Scot's conceptual structure, this Catalan economist embraced the "mercantile" system and made quite considerable use of the eighteenth century economists, including Galiani, the foreign author who most influenced him [Lluch 1973, 189-201]. J. Canga's work was the most important of the period in the area of public finance. Despite the marked influence of the early classical authors, this work drew on a wider variety of sources, including Verri and Filangieri[32]. But, apart from public finance, the Filangieri's *Scienza* continued to act as a source of reference in Spain for rural land redistribution programs. This movement also turned to Ricci and the emphyteutic reforms put forward by Pietro Leopoldo of Toscana; they were very favourably evaluated by Flórez Estrada and he advocated them as a means of stimulating Spanish agricultural development [Almenar 1980, ci-ciii].

The enduring nature of the enlightened agenda assumed a new dimension during the forties: it was vigorously revived, but this time with the benefit of hindsight. Pecchio's ideas on the supposed "italianità" of political economy and the distinctive nature of the Italian economics tradition compared to the British one [Parisi 1984, 141-5] were enthusiastically received in Spain (also partly due to Blanqui [1837, 410ss.]). The Spanish perceived Italy as the cradle of "modern" economics; they reinstated Beccaria as the inventor of the division of labour and Ortés as the forerunner of Malthus; they acknowledged the enlightened Italians as the first critics of the theory of the balance of trade and as the pioneers of free trade [Paso 1841; Mora 1843; Colmeiro 1845; Borrego 1844; Bona 1850; etc.].

There are five "classical" authors that come under consideration when evaluating the impact of Italian economists on Spanish economic literature in the first half of the nineteenth century: Mengotti, Romagnosi, Scialoja, Gioia and Rossi. Almenar argues Mengotti's influence in the views expressed in Flórez Estrada's very early economic writings [Almenar 1976, 80-1]. He also regained influence halfway through the forties in relation to the debate over protectionism and free trade. More than anything else, *Il Colbertismo* was used repeatedly to explain French "Colbertism", as the archetype of the "mercantile" system, to

[32] Canga took up the Filangieri's pioneering support for free trade, his opposition to the concession of tax collection rights and his belief that all social classes payed tax on the net income from land. He did the same with Verri's ideas on defining the science of public finance, his advocacy of free trade and gradual reform for public finance and his stance in favour of reducing the cost of tax collection [Canga 1833, 5, 205; 1834, I, 11, 188, 368; II, 59, 291, 325, 433, 522; 1840, 53, 54].

criticize it and to point out the damage inflicted by a restrictive trade system [e.g.: Borrego 1844; Mora 1843]. Romagnosi's work was used in this debate as well. His ideas were taken up by a prominent Catalan protectionist, Borrego [1844, 52-4], to point out the "demonstrable errors in Say" and to support the hypothesis, very characteristic of Romagnosi [Finoia 1996, 110-112], that the government should guarantee public interest over private and create and tutelary, through the legal system, conditions suitable for competition. Borrego himself [1844, 301] was one of the first Spanish authors to recommend Scialoja's work in the study of the rent of land. As for Gioia, it is difficult to demonstrate exactly how his ideas were used. He is mentioned in the defence of economics as a science in its own right, as the father of modern day statistics and as the author of an erroneous theory of credit [Bona 1850; Canga 1834; Colmeiro 1845]. His interest in tying the development of "emerging" industry and "mass production" to a protectionist tariffs policy [Barucci 1965, 124-129] received an understandably positive reception in Spain. This proposal, which Torrente had already received, was taken up by moderately protectionist Spanish economists, like Valle; he also made reference to Gioia's debate with Sismondi and his theories on money and work association [Valle 1842, 40, 50, 143-4, 434]. Finally, we come to Rossi. His stature increased rapidly in the forties after the translation of his handbook. He was acknowledged by Colmeiro [1842; 1845] as the leading exponent of an "eclectic" economics that sought to avoid the supremacy of the "absolute" theories and the "disruption of the spirit of the system".

This brief analysis should not overlook one significant fact: no work specifically based on the Italian economic thought was written in Spain during the first half of the nineteenth century. The few ideas that did seep into the country were more closely related to "political" economic than economic "analysis", surely in keeping with the nature of Italian economic literature of the period [Porta 1993], and they did contribute to correcting liberalism in its purest form, following the Gioia's modernization of the Lombardan economic tradition and Romagnosi's quite traditional paternalism an moralism [Barucci 1965, 141, 181-3; Romani 1994, 88ss.].

Conclusions

Between 1770 and 1800 Italy, and especially Naples, played an active role as an export centre for economics ideas to Spain. This confirms Italy's position as a scientific forum of international standing during the Enlightenment and the Neapolitan economists as the creators of an economic agenda that would prove particularly appealing to underdeveloped countries (Venturi, Iraci…). Spain and Naples had a great issues in common: a similar past (the "tragic" decadence inherited from the seventeeth century), a shared present (the economic backwardness, due as much to their own past as to the current might of the northern European nations) and the same yearning future (to overcome their current state of economic dependence to achieve one of economic autonomy). All this combined to create a neo-mercantlism of similar nature in each country; meanwhile, the already existing close political ties created ideal conditions for maintaining a dialogue on the fringe of Europe[33]. Two additional factors facilitated it: the Neapolitan writers openly questioned to the Spaniards (Spain always had a place in the wide cosmopolitan *collages* of experiences and ideas that their writings covered) and their brand of liberalism sat perfectly with the moderate nature of the Spanish Enlightenment.

The success that Neapolitan thought experienced in Spain reflects the great affinity that existed between the national "styles" of economics. In this sense, Genovesi's "civil" economics epitomized the dominant approach during this period in Spain: it was an analytical "quasi-system" with a profound normative root and especially oriented to increase the social wealth and the *felicità pubblica*, in other words, to the economic growth [Schumpeter 1954, 172, 218-9]. (It eventually came to represent an alternative to "mainstream" economics analysis [Perrotta 1985]). The *Lezioni*, whilst providing an excellent overview of the economic debate of the forties and fifties, failed to introduce significant theoretical innovations in contemporary Spanish economic thought. They did, however, provide an appealing example of how the principles of pre-Physiocratic neo-mercantilism and liberalism developed in Great Britain and France had been finally applied in a depressed, still notably feudal and dependent economic environment in order, in Genovesi's words, "to populate, enrich and civilize the nation" [Iraci 1967, 63-5; Venturi 1969-1984, I, 567ss.; Pii 1985, 50ss, 84ss, 168ss.]. Cardoso and Lluch [1999, 478-9] would say that Spain was wide open to be "contaminated" by the Neapolitans' ideas, since they were scientifically outstanding and useful for appliying to the reality. As we have seen, the effects of this "contamination" were so far-reaching that we are forced to reject Venturi's proposition that the influence of Italian political economy in Spain was "isolated or lacked continuity". It was in fact the other way round: Naples emitted a constant stream of economic ideas that were amongst the most incisives in the Hispanic world during the Enlightenment. We can also extrapolate this conclusion to the entire period between 1750 and 1850: Genovesi's was the most influential Italian text of the period and Filangieri's the most translated.

The way these economic ideas circulated changed as the nineteenth century advanced. At first, the eighteenth century Italian economic agenda survived in

[33] In the same way, future parallels between the reform programmes undertaken by Tanucci in Naples and Carlos the Third's ministers in Spain were to become more apparent as were the potentially striking similarities that we sense in the foreign economic doctrines that were propagated in each economic environment (Herbert, Melon, Mirabeau…).

Spain and even experienced a minor revival. Nevertheless, as the nation began to abandon the rich and widespread doctrinal and national plurality generated by the Enlightenment and conform to the standard of the new classical orthodoxy demanded, these ideas ceased to be a living force, and those proposed by the Italian economists whose treatises appeared between the collections compiled by Custodi and Ferrara did not move in to fill their place. This phenomenon reveals much more than just the significant decline in political relations between Spain and the Italian *Mezzogiorno*. The problems do not appear to have their origin in Spain, since the country, between 1800 and 1850, not only maintained its interest in importing foreign economic ideas, but the slow pace of academic progress in the field of economics during those years actually created a more favourable climate for this process. Meanwhile, we observe a fascinating paradox in Italy. At the same time as it became a unique area for intellectual activity [Romani 1994, 25], its role as an exporter of ideas to Spain fell into decline. It is reasonable to assume that this was just one more consequence of the process of "modernization" of economic thought prior to *l'Unità*. This process was, in the words of Di Battista [1983, 7-14; 1990, 197-213], "reflected and not autonomous". In addition, in order to be acknowledged as "*netto, semplificato e ridotto all'osso*", Italy was obliged to transform itself into yet another forum for the lively Anglo-French economic debate, even though this entailed the slow destruction of its own intellectual tradition and a decline in the standard of scientific inventiveness, which was only regained with the appeareance of works by Pantaleoni and Pareto [Schumpeter 1954, 571]. Given the nature and the end result of this modernizing process, the Spanish economists' choice was clear: they preferred the "original" to the "imitation". Nevertheless, it is also true that they identified with some of the distinguishing features of the Italian authors who were active during the slow transition from neo-mercantalism to classicism, such as Gioia's protectionism or Romagnosi's anachronistic interventionism. Venturi would have said that the wide open spaces that were occupied by "Italy outside Italy" in Enlightenment Spain became smaller and smaller as the nineteenth century advanced.

References

I. Translations

BECCARIA C. (1774), *De los delitos y de las penas*, Madrid. Trans: J. A. de las Casas.

BELLONI G. (1788), *Disertación sobre la naturaleza, y utilidades del comercio: escrita en italiano por el Marqués de Belloni*, Santiago, I. Aguayo. Trans.: J. Labrada.

CARLI G. R. (1788), *Carta del Conde Carli al Marqués de Maffei sobre el empleo del dinero y Discurso del mismo sobre los balances económicos de las naciones, al cual van añadidas las Reflexiones del Marqués de Casaux sobre este mismo asunto*, Madrid, Viuda de Ibarra, hijos y compañía. Trans.: V. de Villava.

CHITTI L. (1847), *De la crisis de la Hacienda y de la reforma del sistema monetario*, Madrid, Viuda e hijos de A. Calleja. Trans.: P. de Madrazo.

DE WELTZ G. (1838), *Del crédito y los empréstitos públicos*, Madrid, Miguel de Burgos. Trans.: P. Pita.

DONATO N. (1789), *El Hombre de Estado*, Madrid, Cano; 2nd ed.: Madrid, Imprenta Real, 1790-1791. Trans.: P. Arbuxech.

FILANGIERI G. (1784), *Reflexiones sobre la libertad de comercio de frutos del Señor Gaetano Filangieri, Caballero del Orden de S. Juan*, Madrid, J. Ibarra. Trans.: V. de Villava?

— (1787), *Reflexiones políticas sobre la ley de Fernando IV*, Madrid, Cano. Trans.: anonymous.

— (1787-1789), *Ciencia de la legislación*, Madrid, M. González, 6 vols; 2nd ed.: Madrid, Ibarra, 1813-1814, 10 vols.; 3th ed.: Madrid, Núñez, 1822, 10 vols. Trans.: J. Rubio.

— (1813), *Ciencia de la legislación*, Madrid, Imprentas de Ibarra, Fuentenebro y Alvárez, 10 vols. Trans.: anonymous.

— (1821-1822), *Ciencia de la legislación*, Madrid, Fermín Villalpando, 6 vols; 2nd ed.: Burdeos, P. Beaume, 1823, 6 vols. Trans.: J. Ribera.

— (1836), *Ciencia de la legislación, por G. Filangieri, ilustrada en comentarios por Benjamin Constant*, París, Librería americana de Lecointe, 10 vols. Trans.: anonymus.

— (1839), *Comprendio de la obra que escribió el Caballero Gaetano Filangieri, titulada Ciencia de la legislación, con notas de los autores más clásicos, redactado en el año 1834*, Madrid, I. Boix. Trans.: B. La Torre.

GALIANI F. (1775), *Diálogos sobre el comercio de trigo, atribuidos al abate Galiani*, Madrid, J. Ibarra. Trans.: J. A. D. L. C (J. A. de las Casas?).

GENOVESI A. (1785-6), *Lecciones de Comercio o bien de Economía civil*, Madrid, J. Ibarra, 3 vols.; 2nd ed.: Madrid, J. Collado, 1804. Trans.: V. de Villava.

GIOIA M. (1840), *La ciencia del hombre de bien*, Madrid, T. Jordán. Trans.: J. M.

— (1868): *La ciencia del querer y de ser querido en la Sociedad por cortesía, por respeto y por amor*, Madrid, Librería D. Leocadio López.

GRISELINI F. (1784), *Discurso sobre el problema de si corresponde a los párrocos y curas de las aldeas el instruir a los labradores en los buenos elementos de la economía campestre*, Blas Miedes. Trans.: J. Amar.

MASTROFINI M. (1859), *Tratado de la usura*, Barcelona, Pablo Riera; 2nd ed.: Barcelona, Librería religiosa, 1891. Trans.: J. de Ibargüengoitia.

MURATORI L. A. (1782), *Reflexiones sobre el buen gusto en las ciencias y en las artes*, Madrid, A. de Sancha. Trans.: J. Sempere.

— (1790), *Tratado de la pública felicidad, objeto de los buenos príncipes*, Madrid, Imprenta Real. Trans.: P. Arbuxech.

— (1794), *Defectos de la jurisprudencia, tratado utilísimo para todos los que se dedican al estudio de esta facultad y llegan al honor de actuar como abogados, ó decidir como jueces en los tribunales*, Madrid, J. Ibarra. Trans.: V. Mª de Tercilla.

ROSSI P. (1840), *Curso de Economía Política*, Madrid, Boix. Trans.: P. de Madrazo.

VERRI P. (1820), *Tratado elemental de la Economía Política, dirigido a los Ministros de la Gobernación y de la Hacienda Nacional*, Madrid, Imprenta de Espinosa. Trans.: F. Rodríguez de Ledesma.

II. Primary Sources

ALONSO J. (1796), *Ensayo económico sobre el sistema de la moneda-papel y sobre el crédito público*, Madrid, Imprenta Real.

ANZANO T. (1795), *Ensayo sobre la policía general de los granos, sobre sus precios, y sobre los efectos de la agricultura*, Madrid, Antonio Espinosa.

BLANQUI A. (1837), *Histoire de l'Économie Politique despuis les anciens jusqu'aux nos jours*, París (Spanish trans.: *Historia de la Economía Política en Europa desde los tiempos antiguos hasta nuestros días*, Madrid, Imprenta de Nicolás Azara, 1839).

BONA J. E. (1850), *Clave de los economistas en el poder y en la oposición*, Madrid, Francisco García Arias.

BORREGO A. (1844), *Principios de Economía Política con aplicación a la reforma de Aranceles de aduana, a la situación de la industria fabril de Cataluña, y al mayor y más rápido incremento de la riqueza nacional*, Madrid, Imprenta de la Sociedad de Operarios.

CALOMARDE T. (1800), *Discurso económico-político*, Madrid, Gerónimo Ortega.

CAMPOMANES P. RODRÍGUEZ DE (1774), *Discurso sobre el fomento de la industria popular*, Madrid, A. Sancha (Ed. J. Reeder: Madrid, I. E. F., 1975).

CANGA J. (1833), *Elementos de la Ciencia de Hacienda*, Madrid, D. J. Palacios (Ed. F. Estapé: Madrid, I. E. F.-Ministerio de Hacienda).

— (1834), *Diccionario de Hacienda con aplicación a España*, Madrid, Marcelino Calero y Portocarrero (Ed. Madrid, I. E. F., 1968).

— (1840), *Suplemento del Diccionario de Hacienda con aplicación a España*, Madrid, Viuda de Calero (Ed. J. Fontana: Madrid, I. E. F., 1980).

CARLI G. R. (1784-1794), *Delle opere del Signor Commendatore Don Gianrinaldo Conte Carli*, vol. I, Milano, Imperial Monisterio di S. Ambrogio Maggiore.

COLMEIRO M. (1842), "Introducción" to J. Droz, *Economía Política, o principios de la ciencia de las riquezas*, Madrid, Viuda de Calleja e hijos.

— (1845), *Tratado elemental de Economía Política ecléctica*, Madrid, Viuda e hijos de Antonio Calleja.

CORRAL B. del (1864), *Examen crítico del Tratado de la usura, escrito por el Abate Marco Mastrofini*, Palencia, Imprenta y librería de Peralta y Menéndez.

DANVILA B. J. (1779), *Lecciones de Economía Civil, ó de el Comercio*, Madrid, J. Ibarra.

Filangieri G. (1780), "Delle leggi politiche ed economiche", vol. II of *La Scienza della Legislazione* (Ed. P. Villari: Firenze, Felice Le Monnier, 1864).

FORONDA V. de (1789-1794), *Cartas sobre los asuntos más exquisitos de la Economía*

Política y sobre las Leyes Criminales, Madrid, Manuel González (Ed. J. M. Barrenechea: Vitoria, Gobierno Vasco, 1994).
— (1801), *Cartas sobre la policía*, Madrid, Benito Cano (Ed. J. M. Barrenechea: Vitoria, Ararteko, 1998).
GALIANI F. (1770), *Dialogues sur le commerce des bleds* (Ed. F. Nicolini: Milano, Ricciardi, 1959).
GÁNDARA M. A. DE LA (1811), *Apuntes sobre el bien y el mal de España*, Valencia, Estebe (Ed. J. Macías: Madrid, I. E. F., 1988).
GENERÉS M. D. (1793), *Reflexiones políticas y económicas sobre la población, agricultura, artes, fábricas y comercio del Reyno de Aragón*, Madrid, Viuda e hijo de Marín (Ed. E. Lluch-A. Sánchez: Zaragoza, Gobierno de Aragón, 1996).
GENOVESI A. (1765), *Lezioni di commercio, ossia di Economia Civile* (Ed. P. Custodi: *Scrittori classici italiani di economia politica*, Milano, De Stefanis, vols. VII-VIII).
JOVELLANOS G. M. de (1795), *Informe de la Sociedad Económica de esta Corte al Real y Supremo Consejo de Castilla en el Expediente de Ley Agraria*, Madrid, Sancha (Ed. C. Nocedal: *Obras publicadas e inéditas*, B. A. E., Madrid, Rivadeneyra, 1858-1859, II, 79-138).
MORA, J. J. de (1843), *De la libertad del comercio*, Sevilla, Establecimiento tipográfico.
NORMANTE L. (1784), *Discurso sobre la utilidad de los conocimientos económico-políticos y la necesidad de su estudio metódico*, Zaragoza, Blas de Miedes (Ed. A. Peiró: Zaragoza, D. G. A., 1984).
— (1785), *Proposiciones de Economía civil y Comercio*, Zaragoza, Blas de Miedes (Ed. A. Peiró: Zaragoza, D. G. A., 1984).
PASO N. (1841), *Elementos de Economía Política*, Granada, Benavides.
PAULA F. (1792), *Reflexiones económico-políticas*, Madrid, Benito Cano.
SEMPERE J. (1788), *Historia del Luxo, y de las leyes suntuarias de España*, Madrid, Imprenta Real.
SISTERNES M. (1786), *Idea de la Ley Agraria española*, Valencia, Benito Monfort (Ed. V. Llombart: Barcelona, Alta Fuya, 1993).
Società economica (1791), *Atti della Real Società economica di Firenze ossia de' Georgofili*, vol. I, Firenze, A. G. Pagani e Compagni.
TORRENTE M. (1835), *Revista General de la Economía Política*, Habana, Jordán.
VALLE E. M. del (1842), *Curso de Economía Política,* Madrid, Colegio Nacional de Sordomudos.
Verri P. (1771), *Meditazioni sulla economia politica*, in *Biblioteca dell'economista*, ser. I, vol. III, Torino, 1852, 545-648.

III. Secondary Sources

AGUILAR F. (1981-1995), *Bibliografía de autores españoles del siglo XVIII*, Madrid, C. S. I. C. e Instituto Miguel de Cervantes.
ALMENAR S. (1976), "Agrarismo y librecambio en la crisis del antiguo régimen", *Información Comercial Española*, 517, september, 58-81.
— (1980): "Estudio preliminar" to A. Flórez Estrada: *Curso de Economía Política* (1828), Madrid, I. E. F.
ASTIGARRAGA J. (1990), *Pensamiento económico y reforma ilustrada de la Real Sociedad*

Bascongada de los Amigos del País, Doctoral Thesis, San Sebastián, University of Deusto.
— (1997), "Victorián de Villava, traductor de Gaetano Filangieri", *Cuadernos Aragoneses de Economía*, 7-1, 171-186.
— (1998), "Necker y Jovellanos: un "área *neckeriana*" en el *Informe de Ley Agraria*", *Revista de Historia Económica*, XVI-2, 559-570.
— (at press), "Necker en España (1780-1800)", *Revista de Economía Aplicada*.
BARRENECHEA J. M. (1984), *Valentín de Foronda, reformador y economista ilustrado*, Vitoria, Diputación Foral de Alava.
- (1994), "Estudio preliminar" to V. de Foronda (1789-1794).
- (1998), "Estudio preliminar" to V. de Foronda (1801).
BARUCCI P. (1965), *Il pensiero economico di Melchiorre Gioia*, Milano, A. Giuffrè.
BIANCHINI M. (1982), *Alle origini della scienza economica*, Parma, Studium.
— (1989), "Some fundamental aspects of Italian Eighteenth-Century economic thought", in D. A. Walker (ed.): *Perspectives on the History of Economic Thought (I)*, E. Elgar, 53-67.
CABRILLO F. (1978), "Traducciones al español de libros de Economía Política (1808-1880)", *Moneda y Crédito*, 147, december, 71-103.
CARDOSO J. L., LLUCH E. (1999), "Las teorías económicas contempladas a través de una óptica nacional", in E. Fuentes (ed.): *Economía y economistas españoles*, vol. I, Barcelona, Galaxia Gutemberg-Círculo de Lectores, 477-484.
CERVERA P. (1998), "Las *Lecciones de Economía civil ó de el Comercio* de B. J. Danvila y Villarrasa", *Cuadernos Aragoneses de Economía*, 8-1, 143-162.
COTTA S. (1954), *Gaetano Filangieri e il problema della legge*, Torino, G. Giappichelli.
CHIARAMONTE J. C. (1964), "Gli illuministi napoletani nel Río de la Plata", *Rivista storica italiana*, LXXVI-I, 114-132.
— (1979), *Pensamiento económico de la Ilustración*, Caracas, Ayacucho.
DI BATTISTA F. (1983), *L'emergenza ottocentesca dell'Economia politica a Napoli*, Bari.
— (1990), *Dalla tradizione genovesiana agli economisti liberali*, Bari, Cacucci.
FINOIA M. (1995), "La popolazione negli economisti napoletani del Settecento", in A. Roncaglia (ed.): *Alle origini del pensiero economico in Italia (I)*, Bologna, Il Mulino, 59-72.
— (1996), "L'idea di sviluppo tra le generazioni", in A. Quadrio (ed.): *Alle origini del pensiero economico in Italia (II)*, Bologna, Il Mulino, 105-119.
FERNÁNDEZ F., SCHWARTZ P. (1978), "El 'Ensayo' de José Alonso Ortiz. Monetarismo *smithiano* en la España de los vales reales", in A. Otazu (ed.): *Dinero y crédito (siglos XVI al XIX)*, Madrid, 393-435.
GIOLI G. (1972), *Gli albori dello smithianesismo in Italia*, Firenze, Facoltà di Economia e commercio.
— (1988), "La nascita e l'affermazione dell'insegnamento dell'economia politica in Italia: continuità e discontinuità (1750-1900)", in M. Augello, M. Bianchini, G. Gioli, P. Roggi (eds.), *Le cattedre di economia politica in Italia*, Milano, F. Angeli, 385-410.
GONDRA L. R. (1927), *Las ideas económicas de Manuel Belgrano*, Buenos Aires.
GRICE-HUTCHINSON M. (1978), *El pensamiento económico en España, 1177-1740*, Barcelona, Crítica, 1982.
GUASTI N. (1996), *Uztáriz, Forbonnais e la "Théorica y Práctica de comercio y de marina". Prime ricerche*, Tesi di laurea, Università degli Studi di Firenze, Facoltà di Lettere e Filosofia.

— (1998), "Forbonnais e Uztáriz: le ragioni di una traduzione", *Cuadernos Aragoneses de Economía*, 8-1, 125-141

HUTCHISON T. (1988), *Before Adam Smith*, Oxford, Basil Blackwell.

IRACI L. (1967), *Momenti del pensiero economico*, Roma, M. Bulzoni.

LLOMBART V. (1992), *Campomanes, economista y político de Carlos III*, Madrid, Alianza.

— (1996), "El *Informe de Ley Agraria* y su autor en la Historia del Pensamiento Económico", in A. GARCÍA y J. SANZ (eds.): *Reformas y políticas agrarias en la historia de España*, Madrid, Ministerio de Agricultura, Pesca y Alimentación, 105-159.

— (at press), "El pensamiento económico de la Ilustración en España (1730-1812)", in E. FUENTES (ed.): *Economía y economistas españoles*, vol. III.

LLUCH E. (1973), *El pensament econòmic a Catalunya (1760-1840)*, Barcelona, Edicions 62.

- (1999), *Las Españas vencidas del siglo XVIII*, Barcelona, Crítica.

LLUCH E., ALMENAR S. (1992), "Difusión e influencia de los economistas clásicos en España (1776-1870)", in *Actas do Encontro Ibérico sobre História do Pensamiento Económico*, Lisboa, CISEP, 91-155.

LLUCH E., ARGEMÍ Ll. (1985), *Agronomía y fisiocracia en España (1750-1820)*, Valencia, Alfons el Magnànim.

LLUCH E., SÁNCHEZ A. (1996), "Estudio preliminar" to M.D. Generés (1793).

MARTÍN M. (1989), "La institucionalización de los estudios de Economía Política en la Universidad española (1784-1857)", "Estudio preliminar" to Valle Santoro: *Elementos de Economía Política* (1829), Madrid. I. E. F.

MESTRE A. (1976), *Despotismo e Ilustración en España*, Esplugues, Ariel.

NUCCIO O. (1971), *Economisti e riformisti meridionali nel '700*, Roma, Bizarri.

PARISI D. (1984), *Il pensiero economico classico in Italia (1750-1860)*, Milano, Università Cattolica del Sacro Cuore.

PERROTTA C. (1982), "Il "lusso" negli economisti italiani del Settecento", in R. Faucci (ed.): *Gli italiani e Bentham*, Milano, F. Angeli, vol. I, 171-189.

— (1985), "Il contributo di Genovesi alla teoria illuminista dello sviluppo", in A. RONCAGLIA (ed.): *Alle origini del pensiero economico in Italia (I)*, Bologna, Il Mulino, 73-96.

PII E. (1985), *Antonio Genovesi*, Leo S. Olschki.

PORTA P.L. (1993), "A Note on Italian Economics in Early Nineteenth Century from Restoration to Risorgimento", *History of Economic Ideas*, 1, 43-70.

— (1995), "La concezione dello sviluppo economico nei *Dialoghi sul commercio dei grani* di Ferdinando Galiani", in A. RONCAGLIA (ed.): *Alle origini del pensiero economico in Italia (I)*, Bologna, Il Mulino, 59-72.

REEDER J. (1973), "Bibliografía de traducciones, al castellano y catalán, durante el siglo XVIII, de obras de pensamiento económico", *Moneda y Crédito*, 126, septembre, 57-71.

ROMANI R. (1994), *L'Economia politica del Risorgimento italiano*, Torino. Bollati Boringhieri.

SCHUMPETER J.A. (1954), *History of Economic Analysis*, London, G. Allen y Unwin (Spanish trans.: Barcelona, Ariel, 1971).

SMITH R. S. (1968), "English Economic Thought in Spain, 1776-1848", in C. D. W. Godwin et. al. (eds.): *The Transfer of Ideas: Historical Essays*, Durham N. C., 106-137.

— (1957), "La *Riqueza de las Naciones* en España e Hispanoamérica, 1780-1830", *Revista de Economía Política*, VIII-3, sep.-dec., 1215-1253.

— (1971), "Spanish Mercantilism: A Hardy Perennial", *Southern Economic Journal*, XXXVIII, july, 1-11.

USOZ J. (1996), *Pensamiento económico y reformismo ilustrado en Aragón*, 1760-1800, Doctoral Thesis, Zaragoza, University of Zaragoza.

— (1997), "Antonio Arteta y Miguel Dámaso Generés: la industria en el marco de una propuesta de desarrollo para Aragón", in *Industrialización en España: entusiasmos, desencantos y rechazos*, Madrid, Civitas, 121-138.

VENTURI F. (1973-4), *Spagna ed Italia nel secolo dei Lumi*. Corso di Storia Moderna, a[nno] a[ccademico] 1973-1974, Torino, Tirrenia (s. d.).

— (1957), "Illuminismo italiano e Illuminismo europeo", in M. FUBINI (ed.): *La cultura illuministica in Italia*, Torino, Radio Italiana.

— (1958), *Illuministi italiani. Riformatori lombardi, piemontesi e toscani*, Milano-Napoli, R. Ricciardi.

– (1962), "Economisti e riformatori spagnoli e italiani del '700", *Rivista Storica italiana*, LXXIV, 532-561 (Spanish trans.: F. Estapé (ed.): *Textos olvidados*, Madrid, I. E. F., 1973, 203-252).

— (1969-1984), *Settecento riformatore*, Torino (5 vols).

The Spread of Italian Economic Thought in Spain 1850-1945: from Historicism to Corporatism[1]

Juan Zabalza Arbizu
University of Alicante

The Spanish Enlightenment during the second half of the 18th Century and, later on, the Spanish Liberalism at the beginning of the 19th Century, were both greatly influenced by Italian economists, particularly from Naples, such as Filangieri, Galiani, and Genovesi, and, during the latter period, by the Milanese Verri. By the middle of the 19th Century, however, there were hardly any traces left of this distant but powerful influence. During the 19th Century, several generations of Italian economists adopted the Classical doctrine from Britain and France, and apart from a few exceptions like Melchiorre Gioja, the Spanish economists generally preferred the original source of such ideas, as Astigarraga points out in this volume. Therefore, it can be argued that the spread of Italian economic thought in Spain was greatest during the "splendor years" of Italian Economics. This idea is supported by recent works that defend the hypothesis of an interaction between the evolution of Economics abroad and the circulation of economic ideas in Spain throughout the period from 1750 to 1850 (Lluch and Almenar 1992; Estapé 1990: 124).

The interaction concluded during the second half of the 19th Century, a period of profound decadence for Economics in Spain (Estapé 1990). Olascoaga, a contemporary observer, deplores the isolation of Economic Science in Spain from foreign influences, especially from 1870 onwards, and in particular from marginalism and historicism (Olascoaga 1896: 7-10). In 1914, the restoration of Economic Science in Italy, led by Messedaglia, Cossa and Ferrara, moved the country nearer to the level of other countries in which Economics was much more advanced (Schumpeter 1985: 935). In Spain, however, this process was hardly known and only the Italian historicists arose any interest among their Spanish counterparts.

At the beginning of the 20th Century, the modernisation of Economic Studies in Spain, led by Francisco Bernis, and especially by Antonio Flores de Lemus, ended with the phase of decadence and isolation and it allowed the introduction of economic thought from abroad (Estapé 1990: 192). The affluence of economic

[1] I am indebted to Salvador Almenar (University of Valencia), Carlos Bastien (Technical University of Lisbon) and Piero Bini (University of Macerata) for their insightful comments to previous versions of this paper. I wish to express my gratitude to Antonio Magliulo (University of Florence) for his continuous support.

ideas from Italy to Spain is mainly manifested in the topics of Public Finance, Economic Statistics and Agricultural Economics. The intensity of this flow increased, reaching its peak during the thirties. In 1936, it suddenly stopped because of the outbreak of the Spanish Civil War. This event, however, paved the way for the advent of the Italian corporatist doctrine in Spain.

1. The "Italian Channel" for the Introduction of the Historicist Heterodoxy

Although the success of Say's *Traité,* between 1804 and 1838, coexisted with the diffusion of ideas from Bentham, Malthus, Ricardo and Sismondi, the wide acceptance of his doctrine, which characterised the spread of the Classical School in Spain[2], cannot be questioned. In spite of Say's widespread acceptance, the Enlightenment tradition persisted and the most renown Spanish economists of the 19th Century were nurtured on both of these doctrines: Flórez Estrada, Canga Argüelles, and Jaumeandreu among others (Lluch and Almenar 1992). During the forties, the decline of Say's influence coincides with the recognition of their French disciples, Blanqui and Rossi, who were gradually replaced by the "optimist" version, represented by Bastiat, Coquelin and the "Guillaumin group". Indeed, the free-trader group, known as "the economist school", was, doctrinally speaking, indebted to the French "optimist" movement. During the 1868 liberal revolution, the free-trader group, and especially its leader, Laureano Figuerola, held strategic positions in the Public Administration. He promoted the reforms included in the group's economic program, especially the widely debated Arancel Figuerola (1869) – Figuerola Duty – (Cabrillo 1991; Costas 1988). Indeed, the economic debate focused on the Protection vs. Free-Trade disputes and superseded any interest in analytical questions (Lluch and Almenar 1992)[3]. On the protectionist side, the Catalonian economists were, doctrinally speaking, heirs of Eudald Jaumeandreu's prohibicionism, who had occupied the Chair of Political Economy in the Junta de Comercio de Barcelona – Chamber of Commerce of Barcelona – in the 1830's and 40's (Lluch 1973: 303-332). The Catalonian group was clearly inferior in number and in analytical importance, but unlike the free-trader group,

---

[2] There are five different Spanish editions of the Traité and three translations abroad: Bordeaux (1821), Paris (1836) and México (1814). Lluch and Almenar (1992).

[3] Figuerola and Luis María Pastor led the free-trade group formed by the "old" professors Colmeiro and Madrazo and the "youngsters" Carballo, Bona, Pelayo, Rodríguez, Carreras, Moret and Echegaray. All of them shared a common doctrine and promoted the creation of institutions like La Sociedad de Economía Política – Society of Political Economy – and La Asociación para la Reforma del Arancel de Aduanas – The Customs Duty Reformation Association – and periodicals such as La Gaceta Economista – The Economists' Gazette –, La Tribuna de los Economistas – The Economists' Tribune – and El Economista – The Economist –. These initiatives were copies of their French counterparts.

it showed a remarkable "influence" from German and Italian historicists, mainly Luzzatti and Forti, as well as some "impact" from the socialists of the Chair, Lampertico and Cusumano (Artal 1991: 252-293). The Italians' established intellectual authority was employed as an argument for the inductive character of the Political Economy methodology and to reveal the erroneous interpretation of Smith by the Spanish free-traders in their efforts to defend free trade at any cost, and to reject protectionism (Artal 1991: 252-293)[4].

In 1874, the Restoration of the monarchy put an end to the Liberal Republican period and permitted the formation of a protectionist group around the politician and intellectual Cánovas del Castillo, who then abolished the principles of Figuerola Duty and all legal traces of free-trade (Serrano 1987)[5]. From the Economic Science standpoint, the decadence was quickened in 1875 by the margination and, in some cases, the suspension of professors who were politically committed during the liberalist period (Azcárate 1967). Despite the deep obscurity that enveloped the discipline of Economics in Spain during the last quarter of the 19th Century, there was a slight renewal of the flow of economic ideas from Italy around 1887, which coincided with the publishing in Spanish of two of Cossa's works: *Elementos de Economía Política – Elements of Political Economy* – and *Guía para el estudio de la Economía Política – A Guide for the Study of Political Economy* –, both translated by Jorge María Ledesma, Professor of Political Economy at the University of Valladolid. Although the translator's original aim was to use them for educational purposes, they were taken as references by professional economists for more than a quarter of century, as the main works of the period reveal. The success of both text-books was remarkable and *Elementos* was re-edited in 1886, 1892 and 1893. *Principios de Economía Financiera – Principles of Public Finance* – was also edited in 1893, and was the only foreign work on Public Finance that was translated into Spanish during the last quarter of the 19th Century[6]. Gerolamo Boccardo's *Historia de la Industria, del Comercio y de la*

---

[4] The ephemeral periodical, *El Foment de la Producció Nacional -The Promotion of National Production-* (1869-1879), is the most outstanding example of the promotion of the Italian historicist ideas. It was owned by the El Foment de la Producció Nacional, organisation formed by small manufacturers and industrialists, but not by the great Catalonian bourgeoisie. Its editorial views reflected the most intransigent protectionism. Its editors read the *Giornale degli Economisti* and reflected the views of the Italian historicists, and especially those of the Giornale's editor, Luigi Luzzati, whose publications arrived through Alberto Morelli. In fact, Luzzati's experiments in promoting cooperation and mutualism, such as the Banca Popolare, were well known. The principal aim of the bank was to provide credit to small commerce, industry and artisans, which probably aroused admiration among the Catalonian editors. Artal (1991: 230, 252-293) and Parisi (1998: 123-124).

[5] After the Republican "Sexenio Revolucionario" – Revolutionary Six-year period –, the Monarchic Restoration in 1874 was characterised by the system called "turno pacífico" – pacific shift –, consisting in the agreement to take Government in turn among the two monarchic parties, the Moderate and the Conservative ones. The Primo de Rivera's Dictatorship established in 1923, finished with the "turno pacífico" system, although the Monarchy was preserved. On the 31st April 1931, the proclamation of the democratic II Republic ended with the Monarchic institution. The continuous confrontations between the "Right" and the "Left" led into the Civil War in 1936, giving way to General Franco's Dictatorship.

[6] The Guía was re-edited in 1892 as *Introducción al Estudio de la Economía Política – Introduction to the Study of Political Economy –*.

Economía Política – History of Industry, Commerce and Political Economy – was translated by Lorenzo Benito, Professor of Commercial Law at the University of Barcelona, who regarded the Italian as a classical economist and a defender of the Free-trade doctrine (Benito S.a.; Romani 1994: 192-194)[7].

In general, the Italian historicists were the most influential of the Italian economists in Spain, and their ideas were introduced in two different ways: the above-mentioned Catalonian protectionist group, and the classical critics. The classical critics embraced a wide range of reformist groups: the so-called Krausists, the catholics and the heirs of Classical orthodoxy, who reduced the radicalism of the "optimists" and gradually replaced it with the moderate liberal doctrine advocated by Baudrillart, Leroy-Beaulie and Maurice Block (Serrano 1997: 252). They all defended the introduction of corrective measures on the "laissez-faire" system and they had a peculiar background, as they had been rather isolated from the evolution of Economics abroad[8].

This new perspective on social issues led the Krausists to introduce a variety of approaches that were quite different from those proposed by the French, such as Italian historicism[9]. During the Restoration of the Monarchy, Gumersindo de Azcárate took over the leadership of the group of the Krausist economists, and there is no doubt about the strategic role he played in the spread of economic ideas that were being adopted from abroad. His work *Estudios Económicos y Sociales – Economics and Social Studies* – (1876) afforded the Spanish economists the knowledge of a wide range of authors such as the Italian Sbarbaro and Minghetti[10]. Azcárate declares himself closed to moderate liberalism's concern for social issues, advocated by Braudillart, Dameth, and the Italian Minghetti. Minghetti's work *Des rapports de l'économie politique avec la morale et le droit*, attached**,** in a conflict situation, the undisputable priority of Ethics over Economics in case of a hypothetical conflict (Malo 1998: 269). Some years later, in 1893, Azcárate stressed Lampertico's differentiation between "social" laws and "socialist" ones, and used it to deduce social laws from the natural evolution of Law and not from

[7] Boccardo's positivism and his admiration for Spencer were remarkable. Both circumstances might be related to the role played by this book in the introduction of that current of thought in Spain. Boccardo's work was published at La España Moderna collection, one of the ways in which European ideas were introduced into Spanish culture and intellectual life. From the Economics point of view, Ingram's *History of Political Economy* and Marshall's *Principles* were the most important translations of the collection.

[8] In fact, this pluralism and the tempered character of the Spanish reformism became evident in the social institutions promoted to remove the social instability arose from the industrialisation: La Comisión de Reformas Sociales – The Social Reforms Commission, 1883 –, El Instituto de Reformas Sociales – The Social Reforms Institute, 1902 – and the Instituto Nacional de Previsión – The National Welfare Institute –. Palacio Morena (1985).

[9] The Krausist economists of the Restoration period were influenced by the more recent works of Ahrens, Krause's Belgian pupil, who added an economic dimension to the doctrine. Actually, there are two different interpretations of Spanish Krausism. Malo supports Krausism's moderate liberalism roots while Velarde places them closer to the German socialists of the Chair.

[10] Quotes from Sbarbaro and Minghetti are numerous in authors like Santa María de Paredes, Botella, Bernis and Buylla. Malo (1998: 315, 330, 282-283).

socialist ideology, as the Italian Civil Law School did (Malo 1998: 497-498). Álvarez Buylla, professor at the University of Oviedo, used to quote the Italian authors through Azcárate's influential work. In his speech at the opening of the Academic Year 1879-80, he pointed out the differences between the moderate character of the Krausists and the radicalism of the German socialist of the Chair. The latter's ideas were taken from Cusumano's work *Le Scuole economiche della Germania* and a great part of this work was literally plagiarised by Álvarez Buylla in his dissertation (Malo 1998: 281-282)[11]. Piernas Hurtado, the third Krausist economist during the Restoration, shows the most extended knowledge of Italian economic literature, from Economic Statistics to Public Finance (Piernas 1895; 1897: 14-18 y 71). Despite his preference for the German Public Finance School, he takes Cossa's *Principles* as a model (Piernas 1891: 20, 45, 58 y 60).

The Italian historicists, however, were not imitated exclusively by the Krausists. Melchor Salvá, who was probably the last of the Spanish Classical economists, was not evidently a socialist of the Chair, but he accepted their methodology, with which he was familiar through the works of Cusumano (Salvá 1880: 56-64). Some orthodox classical economists also sought arguments among the Italians to justify moderate government intervention. The most remarkable example of these was the veteran "optimist" Carreras y González. As Azcárate did, Carreras turned to Minghetti's authority in 1880 to define the rules of government intervention in the economy. In line with Minghetti, Carreras also outlined the intervention boundaries that exceeded the traditional restrictions established by Smith. Nevertheless, Carreras did not go as far as Azcárate and tried to tone down Minghetti's interventionism through Opzoomer's ideas (Malo 309-310). Finally, Olózaga's handbook, which contained numerous references to Italian economists of all tendencies and which was structured along Ciccone's definition of Political Economy, was indeed notoriously successful (Olózaga 1885 13-14; 25-26)[12]. The liberal economist Francesco Ferrara, however, who has proven to be far superior to the Italian historicists, was absolutely ignored during the entire period. This might be partly due to the strong influence exerted by Bastiat (of whom Ferrara was a declared disciple), on the Spanish "economist school" (Faucci 1995: 20).

Apart from the influence of Italian historicism on a variety of Spanish groups, we must emphasise the remarkable role played by the Italian language, during the end of the 19th Century and the beginning of the 20th. Italian was a valuable tool for introducing the economic ideas from abroad, into Spain and Latin America (Olascoaga 1896: 33; Gay 1906: IX)[13]. Pomba's publisher entrusted Gerolamo

[11] Cusumano was the most germanophile of the Italian historicists. Parisi (1998: 120).

[12] Olózaga's handbook is based on the notes taken by Olózaga himself and Fermín Castaño on the Salvá's dissertations in the Chair of the University of Madrid. The wide popularity of the economic history text *The Decline of the Slavery on* West *Civilisation* by Ciccone provoked the Spanish translation in 1913.

[13] Olascoaga underlines the strong relationship between Italian and Spanish lawyers. Olascoaga (1896: 32-33).

Boccardo to run the "terza serie" from Biblioteca dell'Economista. Boccardo's lack of doctrinal definition is evident from the wide range of translations, embracing from Walras and Jevon to Roscher, Schäffle, Schömberg, Scherer, Wagner and German historicists (Finoia 1980: 687). The publications of the Biblioteca dell'Economista in general, and the Italian versions of the German authors in particular, were widely quoted in the treatises of Buylla, Olózaga, Piernas and Salvá, and the collection was available in the libraries of the main Political Economy chairs in the Law Faculties of the time.

Summing up, the reception of Italian and German historicist ideas is characterised by the moderation of the original doctrine which made it possible to be used by a wide range of economists, including the liberal moderates at the close of the century, to justify an intermediate position and a moderate interventionism with regard to social issues. Finally, the reception of the Italian economists in Spain during the end of the century is characterised by the almost absolute ignorance of the great Italian theorists, but this issue has to be explained in a wider frame, the general ignorance of marginalism[14].

2. The First Third of the 20th Century. From the "Social Issue" to Applied Fields.

Although the references to the Italian historicists had not yet disappeared from works written by Spanish economists, the dawn of the new century witnessed a spreading of the Italian influence on other topics such as Applied Economics and the Social Issue. The increased number of translations, the contributions to journals and the influence of Italian ideas on Spanish specialists in general, is noteworthy. Furthermore, this new spread of the Italian socio-economic thought developed within an intellectual climate that was tending towards the "internationalisation" of Spanish culture, in an effort to overcome its traditional "casticismo" (Abellán 1989: 66-69)[15].

[14] There is no ample explanation for the general ignorance of marginalism in Spain. However some elements such as the location of the Political Economy Chairs at Law Faculties that were administered mainly by intellectuals who had been brought up on legal principles, the absence of theoretical debate, and the great doctrinal dependence on France, a country in which theoretical knowledge was kept in the background, helps to shed some light on the issue. Martín Rodríguez (1989), Malo (1998: 380) and Serrano (1997).

[15] The term "casticismo" was used by a great number of Spanish intellectuals at the beginning of the 20th century to define, sarcastically, the insularity of Spanish culture and science. Miguel de Unamuno, the Spanish philosopher and writer, wrote many articles on this subject, which he expressed in his book *En torno al Casticismo -About 'Casticismo'-*.

2.1. The "Social Issue"

At the beginning of the 20th Century, there was a remarkable Italian influence on Spanish Catholic reformism. The major boost came from the publication of the Pope's encyclical "*Rerum Novarum*", which promoted the translation and transmission of works on "social issues" written by Catholic economists, such as Le Play or Pesch, and in 1907, *Orientaciones Sociales en los Inicios del Siglo XX – Social Orientations at the Beginning of the 20th Century* – by Giuseppe Toniolo who enjoyed a close relationship with the most famous Catholic authors from Spain. With regard to Economics, however, the translation of the *Tratado de Economía Social – Treatise on Social Economics* – (1911) was indeed relevant. Its translator, Amando Castroviejo, professor of Political Economy and Public Finance at the University of Santiago de Compostela, conferred the task of counteracting the prevailing materialistic and positivist texts, abounding at Spanish universities, to Toniolo's book (Castroviejo 1911). In particular, Castroviejo states that Toniolo's *Treatise* overcame the classical and the historicist handbooks because it introduced an ethical dimension into Economics. The translation, therefore, merely responded to the new demands outlined by Catholic social reformism. The promotion of the Toniolo's texts, was probably not limited to Catholic circles, but rather, as Castroviejo hoped, extended to the universities, as there was a predominance of Catholics in faculty Chairs. It is well known that José María Zumalacárregui, Professor of Political Economy at the University of Valencia and the first Spanish economist to explicitly give up historicism and embrace the neo-classical "deductive economy", had also been influenced by Toniolo (Naharro Mora 1942: 42). There are other two translations of Italian authors at the beginning of the century, Achiles Loria's *Problemas sociales contemporáneos* – Contemporary Social Problems – (1904), and *La población y el sistema social – Population and Social System* – written by Francesco Saverio Nitti. The latter book was dedicated to Loria and displayed the powerful influence of Spencer's organicists ideas and was therefore a channel for the introduction of positivism into Spain (Barbagallo 1984: 45-46). Nitti became well-known in Spain after publishing *El Socialismo Católico – Catholic Socialism* – (1894), which was translated by the reformists Buylla and Dorado Montero who were closely linked to Krausism. In fact, Nitti's moderate stance on government intervention in social issues, inspired by Bismarck's Germany and intellectually promoted by Schäffle, Wagner, Brentano and others, unquestionably encouraged the Krausist translators (Barbagallo 1984: 26-28). The publication of *El Socialismo Católico* produced a negative reaction from the social catholics, since they considered Nitti's view excessively interventionist and too close to socialism (Montero 1983: 105-107).

At the same time, Spain's agricultural backwardness, the prevalence of indirect taxation, the indirect land ownership system and the large estates in the South, contributed to the spread of Henry George's ideas, mainly among engineers and notaries public, rallied around the Spanish League for the Single Tax, conceived by Antonio Albendín in 1911 (Robledo 1993; Martín Uriz 1985). But their internal disagreements and the failure to carry out legal reforms, dissipated the original enthusiasm of the group. Baldomero Argente was the driving force behind the recovery of Georgism around the 1930s and became its principal advocate. Between 1912 and 1914, he translated the Californian journalist's main works, and *Las bases económicas de la realidad – The Economic Bases of Reality – by* Loria in 1931, the same year that the Second Spanish Republic was proclaimed. Its publication preceded the approval of the Agrarian Reformation Law in 1932, which tried to temper the economic and social problems of Spanish agriculture, through the introduction, among other things, of some restrictions to land ownership. These measures obeyed an intensive reformist process which was being promoted by the first governments of the Second Republic (Malefakis 1980). Undoubtedly, Loria's translation should be seen within this reformist framework. It is remarkable that Pascual Carrión, who was quite close to Georgism in his youth and was one of the main members of the Technical Comission created by the government to study the 1932 Agrarian Reform, was now reading Loria's book (Robledo 1993: 115-116; García Delgado 1974: 17). Some years earlier, another influential agrarian reformist, the Aragonese Joaquín Costa, used *La Proprietà Fondiaria e la Questione Sociale* (1897) to summarise the doctrine on agrarian collectivism, which was, according to Costa, the only way to solve the agrarian problems in Spain (Costa 1915). However, Argente outlined the prevention caused by the radicalism of Loria's doctrine and its political consequences on the reformist circle[16]. Outside this strict agrarian circle, the well-known philosopher and writer Miguel de Unamuno was indebted to Loria, and during his socialist period he studied Economics, among other things, with the aid of Loria's books. Indeed, *Analisi della proprieta capitalista* (1889) was quoted and commented in several passages of his works, as well as *The costituzione economica odierna* (1899)[17].

2.2. *Agricultural Economics, Public Finance and Economic Statistics*

During the first part of the 20th Century, marginalism and in general theoretical works were still ignored, as a result of the inheritance from the 19th Century and the peculiar "modernisation" of Economic Science in Spain. Among the Italians,

---

[16] In fact, the translation of the books in which Loria dealt with typical land issues, such as *La propietà della terra e la questione sociale*, seemed more appropriate, but they proved to be far too radical for the Spanish reformists.

[17] Unamuno's quotations show that he had a better knowledge of Loria and Nitti than Marx. In addition to Loria's works, other Italian author's works stand out in his bibliography, such as *Saggi in torno alla concezione materiallistica della Storia,* and *In memoriam del Manifesto dei communisti* (1985) by Antonio Labriola, and *Manuel d'économie politique* by Vilfredo Pareto. Ribas (1981).

only Barones's *Principios de Economía Política -Principles of Political Economy-* was belatedly translated in 1942 as a text for teaching Economics. The Spanish version of Pantaleoni's *Principios de Economía Pura – Principles of Pure Economics* – was simultaneously edited in Buenos Aires and Madrid, in 1918, as a replacement of Gide's handbook in Argentine. The merit for the translation, however, belongs to the South American country. The translation of Pareto'*s Manual de Economía Política,* published in 1945 to provide a text-book on Economic Theory, was also an Argentinean translation[18].

There is a significant exception to this poor performance, however, in the mathematician Olegario Fernández Baños, who was influenced by the Italian mathematician Enriques, whom he visited in Bologna before becoming interested in Economics. Fernández Baños evolved from Analytical Geometry to Econometrics, and became the first Spanish economist to take part in an Econometric Society Conference. During this evolution, Baños discovered the dynamic nature of Economics and its importance for the future of science. He tried to reflect this idea in *Nociones fundamentales de Economía Matemática – Fundamental Notions of Mathematical Economics* – (1925), which was strongly influenced by Amoroso's *Lezioni di Economia Matematica* (Velarde 1990). Fernández Baños' indebtedness to Amoroso increased in both *Dinamismo de los Precios y Carestía de la Vida – Dynamism of Prices and Scarcity of Life – (1*928) and *Función de la Banca en un Complejo Integral – The Role of the Banking System in an Integral Economic System* – (1936). In the first of these works, Chapter II was dedicated to money matters. It seems to have been based on the formula that Amoroso proposed as an alternative to Fisher's monetary equation (Amoroso 1921: 73-165; Fernández Baños 1928: 49-66). The latter publication presents his theory of the business cycle, which was based on the theories by Wagemann, Hayek, Fisher, Pigou, Keynes, Frisch and finally Amoroso (Fernández Baños 1936: 31-39). Amoroso's debt was partially repaid in 1928 and 1929 with the translation and publication of two of Amoroso's articles in the *Revista Nacional de Economía*[19]. The Italian authors were undoubtedly an intellectual source for Fernández Baños. He was the only Spanish economist that quoted from Sraffa's 1926 article in the *Giornale degli Economisti* which he used to read regularly, together with *Annali di Economia* and *Metron,* and he often employed the expression "ofemility" in his works (Fernández Baños 1928).

The particular problems of the Spanish economy at the time, however, and the debates about the possible strategies for overcoming them, forced the Spanish

[18] Recently some notes taken by Carlos Orduña de Zarauz in 1928 at the Civil Engineers Special School in Madrid have been discovered. They reveal the use of expressions such as "ofemility" and suggest another channel for the introduction of marginalism and Pareto's ideas into Spain. Fuentes Quintana (1999: 243).

[19] The translation as well as the publication of the article entitled "Savings Supply" by Umberto Ricci in the *Revista Nacional de Economía* were Fernández Baños' initiative.

economist to seek solutions from abroad. A significant spread of the Italian economic thought can be observed in monographs, articles and book reviews published in Spanish periodicals. The influence of the Italian economists is clearly manifested in three subjects: Agricultural Economics, Statistical Economics and Public Finance. The intensity of this spread increased during the first part of the century and continued up to the middle of the 30's when it was diminished by the outbreak of the Civil War.

During the first half of the century, the Spanish agrarian tradition was improved by publication of empirical studies carried out by Antonio Flores de Lemus, who learned the inductive methodology from the German neo-historicists during his visit to Tübingen and Berlin (Velarde 1961: 12). Employing this methodology Flores tried to identify the "fundamental trends" in Spanish agriculture[20]. One of Flores' disciples, Manuel de Torres, had received a grant to study at the Colegio San Clemente de los Españoles in Bologna, in the mid-1920's[21]. On returning to Valencia, he became intellectually and politically involved in the defence of Valencian agriculture, which had specialised in the export of fruit and vegetables. In 1930, his first published work on agricultural economics was clearly inspired by Flores de Lemus, but after 1934 some adjustments are seen in his methodology, with the introduction of marginalist tools in his analyses, principally the "cost of opportunity" and the General Equilibrium framework. Zumalacárregui's teachings in Valencia were partly responsible for this change. However, its particular application in Spanish agriculture had its roots in the Italian agrarian economists (Zabalza 1995). Particularly remarkable was Arrigo Serpieri's influence on Torres' work, not only in a theoretical sense but also ideologically and conceptually. For both economists the agrarian progress was conditioned upon the development of share-cropping – the Italian "mezzadria" and the Spanish "aparcería" –, since it guaranteed both agrarian development and social stability (Zabalza 1998). Their concept of agrarian activity was quite similar and Torres continuously repeated Serpieri's expression "modo di vita" – way of life – which embraced the agrarian-urban dichotomy (that replaced the proletarian-capitalist dialectic through the national looking-glass) and the ideological preference for agrarian life and customs. Serpieri however, was not Torres's only source on the matter. Einaudi's work was also a good reference for portraying sharecropping as a way of promoting private initiative and social order in agriculture. Moreover, he frequently used Einaudi's

[20] The expression "fundamental trends" refers to the development laws on Spanish agriculture. Flores de Lemus' statistical skills led him to join the Board of Directors at Metron, the Italian statistics review.

[21] In the 20's Serpieri, Tassinari, Brizzi, Dragoni, and Medici worked in Bologna at the Institute of Agricultural Economics, just when this branch of the science was evolving into an independent subject. There is no evidence, however, of any contact having been made between Torres and the Institute's researchers during his visit to Bologna where he worked on his "tesi di laurea" on Inheritance Tax. But in Spain the group was indeed known, thanks to the information received from Juan Beneyto Pérez, who also obtained a grant to study in Bologna. Di Sandro (1995) and Beneyto (1929).

rhetoric to counteract sociological arguments that demanded social measures, rather than economic ones, to solve the agricultural problems of the time (Faucci 1985; Zabalza 1998).

In the 1930's, the agrarian engineer José Vergara Doncel, unlike other engineers and technical experts, was very interested in agricultural economics. In 1935, Vergara, who was concerned with the agrarian deflation and the policy of raising prices, published an article in the *"Revista Nacional de Economía"*, entitled *"Los Precios de los Productos Agrícolas, según el Profesor Dragoni" – The Prices of Agricultural Products, According to Professor Dragoni –*, which preceded Vergara's translation of Chapter 21 of Dragoni's *Economia Agraria – Agricultural Economics* – (Vergara 1935). Dragoni's book, which covered almost all agrarian issues, contributed to the great leap forward that took place in science of Agricultural Economics (Di Sandro 1995). In fact, Vergara's main intention was to provide the Spanish economic literature with a handbook that introduced an economic dimension to agrarian issues, but in spite of the advanced announcement of its imminent publication, the book was never printed, partly because of the outbreak of the Civil War.

The influence of the Italian demographer and statistician Corrado Gini, in Spain, was first due to a personal determination of Josep A. Vandellós to promote him. Vandellós went to Padova on a grant from the Barcelona Popular City Hall and during the 1924-1925 Academic Year, he worked in the Laboratorio di Statistica which was promoted by Corrado Gini. In all aspects, Vandellós was one of Gini's devout disciples[22]. In his most outstanding publication, *"Catalunya, Poble Decadent" – Catalonia, a Decadent People* – (1935), he applied Gini's demographic hypotheses developed in *Nascita, Evoluzione e Morte delle Nazione* (1930), to Catalonia's peculiar situation[23]. In the field of Economic Statistics research, Vandellós' most important contribution was his *Estimació de la Riquesa i la Renda de la Peninsula Iberica –Wealth and Income Estimation in the Iberian Peninsula* –, which he wrote in Padova under Gini's supervision. This work was taken as a reference for subsequent Income and Wealth estimations done in Spain

---

[22] Vandellós' professional career was practically directed by Gini. In 1925, he published an article La Richesse et le Revenu de la Peninsule Iberique, in *Metron*, which was, in fact, an appendix to Gini's research theme, *A Comparison of Wealth and National Income in Several Important Countries (Italy, France, Belgium, the U.K. and the USA), before and after the War.* In 1929, Gini supported Vandellós in his bid for admission to *The Hague Statistics International Institute.* In 1932, upon Gini's request, he was elected as member of the *Comitato Italiano per lo Studio dei Problemi della Popolazione*. Vandellós took Italy as a model to measure Catalonia's economic and demographic performance: *Butlleti del'Institut d'Investigacions Economiques* (Indice del Movimiento Economico Italiano) and *Servei Central d'Estadistica de la Generalitat* (Istituto Centrale di Statistica). Furthermore, the professional relationship between the two researchers was permanent. Zumalacárregui, who was also a member of the *Comitato Italiano per lo Studio dei Problemi della Popolazione,* would most likely have had some sort of relationship with Gini and Fernández Baños also frequently used the procedures designed by Gini. Nadal (1985: 21) and Pascual (1985: 151).

[23] Jordi Nadal suggests that Spengler's *The Decline of the West* influenced the writing of *Catalunya, Poble Decadent*, through a route that passed through Korherr, Mussolini and Corrado Gini. Nadal (1985).

(Pascual 1985: 188). Gini's influence lived on after the Civil War ended without any help from Vandellós who had fled to Venezuela. Before he fled, however, he translated Gini's *Curso de estadística – Course of Statistics* (1935), which was quite remarkable, in the context of Spanish literature, as there was a complete lack of translations from abroad during the 1930's. In fact, Gini's handbook only competed with those of the popular Schott and the more technical Mills (Fernández Baños 1948).

The Italian Public Finance School was responsible for the most intensive flow of economic ideas from Italy. In contrast to other national traditions in Public Finance, it was also the most widely spread since three of the six foreign books translated in the first forty years of the century were Italian. In 1907, Flora's *Manual de Ciencia de la Hacienda – The Handbook of Public Finance* – provides Spanish literature on economics with the first comprehensive handbook on Public Finance, replacing the previous one by Cossa, and complementing the existing treatises stipulated in Spanish legislation – Bernis, Ballesteros and Rodríguez Mata. The lack of comprehensive treatises on Public Finance, the tempered liberalism implied by its texts, and above all, the *Manual*'s educational aspects, with its clear and lively literary style, were some of the reasons for the Spanish edition, as pointed out by the translator Vicente Gay[24] (Gay 1906: XIX-XXIII).

Although Flora was not an outstanding author, the *Manual*'s characteristics referred to above, helped the book to enjoy three editions[25]. The 1918 edition, translated by the journalist Luis Víctor Paret, seems to have much the same aims as that of 1907. However, in the preface of the 1918 edition, Paret highlights the utility of the *Manual* as an updated reference for experts in Public Finance seeking solutions to the specific problems of Spain. Paret referred specifically to the economic and financial problems caused by the First World War. Neutrality had brought economic prosperity, and Santiago Alba, Public Finance Minister, tried to introduce an extraordinary tax on profits into the Spanish Tax System. The proposal, which was obviously controversial, caused a heated debate and strong opposition from the affected groups (Cabrera, Comín 1989; Paret 1918).

In 1927, Paret's initiative promoted the third edition of the *Manual*, which was published in the middle of the Income Tax debate. The debate came to a head when the Finance Minister José Calvo Sotelo appointment of a advisory Commission to study the possible introduction of a system of personal taxation in Spain. The Commission's Report advised against the reform because of the many deficiencies that existed within the administrative system, which was long adapted to the

[24] Gay, who was a disciple of Flores de Lemus and a declared follower of the members of the German "realistic" school (Bücher, Schmoller, Wagner and Neumann), showed a great knowledge of the Italian economic literature, from the statistician Benini to Nazzani, from Ferrara and Cossa to Einaudi. Gay (1923).

[25] The publication in 1907 of two articles on *Complementary Capital Gains Tax* in the *Revista de Economía y Hacienda",* and five other articles, published six years later, on the same subject, highlight this success.

collection of indirect taxes. It nevertheless recommended reform to the Spanish Tax System to prepare it for the future introduction of a personal taxation system. Fuentes Quintana refers to this slow and hidden reform process as the "Noiseless Tax System Reform" (Fuentes Quintana 1976). Paret, who did not agree with the Commission's conclusions, used the *Revista Nacional de Economía* to defend his proposal for a progressive Income Tax System and used arguments taken from Flora's *Manual* to support it (Paret 1927).

But Flora's *Manual* proved inadequate for the requirements of a number of Public Finance experts, some of whom had been inspired by Flores de Lemus. In the "Introduction" to *Principios de Economía Financiera – Principles of Public Finance* – (1934)[26], by Viti de Marco, the translator Pío Ballesteros expressed the need for a handbook like Viti's that could relate Public Finance rules to reality, as Flores de Lemus had done, and it displaced the old text-books, including Flora's *Manual (B*allesteros, 1934). More than a general debate over the prospects of State intervention, the translation, as some of Ballestero's comments suggest, attempted principally to instigate a debate on the specific issue of the introduction of personal taxation in Spain. Even Ballesteros, who was an authority on Italian Public Finance literature, seems to have been influenced by Viti di Marco when he defines the concept of public necessity and supports the concept of the state as a "cooperative production factor" whose basic role is to provide public services to the community and satisfy their collective needs (Ballesteros 1940)[27].

The Income Tax debate in Spain adopted one of the traditional subjects in the Italian School of Public Finance: double taxation on savings (Buchanan 1980). In 1932, the Finance Minister of the II Republic, Jaume Carner, promoted the reform that had been outlined several years before in the Income Tax Commission. This legal reform, known as the Carner Law, triggered a strong reaction from Manuel de Torres, who on graduating from Bologna University, presented a *Thesis* on Inheritance Tax. Torres was well versed in the Italian economic literature on Public Finance and his profound knowledge of the Rignano's theory on progressive Inheritance Tax, which had proven to be quite successful outside of Italy, was remarkable (Torres 1926, Buchanan 1980). His thesis supervisor's identity remains unknown, but it would most likely had been someone like Arcangeli or Flora, although he himself had mentioned his personal relationship with Luigi Einaudi (González 1990). Torres often visited him at the Laboratorio di Economia Politica di Torino and the *Corso di Scienza della Finanza, Il Problema della Finanza Post-bellica,* and *Osservazione critiche intorno alla Teoría dell'Ammortamento*

[26] Pío Ballesteros translated the German edition from 1932 (De Viti De Marco, A., *Grundlehren der Finanzwirtschaft*, J.C.B. Mohr (Paul Siebeck), Tubingen 1932).

[27] Julio Tejero coincides with Ballesteros in remarking the particularities of Viti de Marco's *Principios* in contrast with the old handbooks on Public Finance. However, on its aseptic book review of Viti de Marco's *Principios* on *Economía Española,* Tejero interpreted the Viti's Principles as an adaptation of the Sax ideas in Italy. Tejero (1934) and Fausto (1995).

dell'Imposta were well quoted throughout his Thesis. Torres' criticism of Giolitti's Inheritance Law's of 1920, which reflects Einaudi's thought, attributed such a fierceness to tax collection that proved highly detrimental to private property, tax justice and national wealth. Just as Einaudi had expressed, the "justice" principle still had priority over the "economic efficiency" principle (Torres 1927, Meacci 1987). Some years later, the *Comentario – Commentary* – to the Carner Law reflects ideas expressed in the *Corso di Finanza Pubblica* (1926) such as double international taxation, the distinction between "residents" and "non-residents", and embraced Einaudi's thoughts on the alterations proposed in *Contributo alla ricerca dell'Ottima Imposta* (1929) as it assumed the primacy of the "economic efficiency" principle over the "justice" principle, in an effort to defend the "Exemption on Savings" theory[28] (Torres 1933). But Einaudi's influence goes much deeper, and Torres' criticism of the Carner Law reflects his conviction that competition played an important role in economic progress. According to Torres, it is by providing incentives to those who better exploit their capabilities that societies move towards material and moral progress. As in Einaudi, any form of restriction on competition, such as monopolies or trade unions, violates this principle (Zabalza 1998a; Forte 1962: 31). From a historical standpoint, Fuentes Quintana attributes several common features to the Tax System of the Latin countries: indirect taxation, real taxation, tax on average income and the calculation of the taxable by means of the outwards signs instead of the contributor's declaration. He referred to this common system as "The Latin Tributary Style", whose renewer, according to Fuentes, was the Italian Luigi Einaudi (Fuentes Quintana 1978). From this point of view, Torres' opposition to the introduction of a personal Income Tax in Spain reflects his belief in the existence of a "Mediterranean" tributary tradition, whose deepest theoretical roots would be found in Italy (Zabalza 1998a).

The spread of Einaudi's doctrine in Spain did not stop at Torres, but seems to have extended during the first third of the 20th Century, principally from the publication of the *Corso di Scienza della Finanza* in 1926, as the works on Public Finance by several Spanish authors demonstrate (Ballesteros, 1940). Something similar happened with *Principes de Science des finances* by Nitti, known mainly through his French version. No mention is made, however, of the more recent Argentine edition, which was published in 1931 when Nitti's work had already fallen into obscurity (Forte 1980).

The period closes in 1935 with a symbolic edition of the *Principios de Política, Derecho y Ciencia de la Hacienda – Principles of Politics, Law and Public*

[28] Einaudi's doctrine embraces the taxation on average income as the "modus operandi" of the savings exemption, the distinction between average and effective income, the use of the cadastre as the best approach to get the exemption on savings in agriculture, the dichotomy of ordinary and extraordinary income and the determination of the taxable income from outward signs. These issues are systematically used in the *Comentario* on the Carner Law. However, some of them were developed by Torres following D'Albergo. Steve (1974: 101-111), Zabalza (1998) and D'Albergo (1931).

Finance – by Benvenuto Griziotti and translated by Enrique Rodríguez Mata, Professor of Economics and Public Finance at the University of Zaragoza and Flores de Lemus' disciple. Some years later, Ballesteros states that the most characteristic feature of the Italian School of Public Finance of the 20th Century is the building of discipline on a base that was more political than economic (Ballesteros 1940). This idea is clearly underlined in the "Introduction" by Griziotti, as he chooses an approach founded on the simultaneous consideration of "political orientation, legal basis, economic content and scientific organisation" (Griziotti 1935). This undoubtedly summarises the interest shown by Spanish economists for the Italian literature. In spite of the more abstract and universal Anglo-Saxon literature, Italian Public Finance was developed in a wider manner, closer to the Spanish needs for reform. In fact, this helps to explain the primacy of the Italian Public Finance School in Spain.

Another channel for the propagation of Italian economic thought within Spain was through the specialised periodicals, among which, the above-mentioned *Revista de Economía y Hacienda* showed interest in topics related to Public Economy[29], while the *Revista Nacional de Economía* was the channel chosen by the advocates of "integral protectionism" and focused on the monetary problems and the consequences of the First World War on the economy[30]. From the beginning of the 1930s, however, the *Revista Nacional de Economía* became scientifically pluralist and allowed contributions from a wide range of economists, not just those who were linked to economic nationalism. Around 1935, the book reviews and the news about new publications focused considerably more on Italy than any other country. The conscientious spread seems to be thanks to José Vergara who probably discovered the Italian tradition through his keen interest in Agricultural Economics. It was precisely in the *Revista Nacional de Economía* that he introduced the Dragoni book and published the Chapter 21 previously referred to. Vergara's interest in Italian economic literature led him to translate the remarkable *Los Movimientos Anormales del Capital* (1936) – *The Abnormal Transfers of Capital* – (1936 by Marco Fanno, published four years before its American edition. The outbreak of the Spanish Civil War hindered this propagation until 1939, although in the post-war 40's, as a contemporary economist pointed out, the intellectual competitiveness had increased as a result of the influx of the literature on the theory of Business Cycle coming from the Anglo-Saxon world (Paredes 1941: 344).

---

[29] In 1909, in addition to the seven Flora's articles, two other articles were published: "La municipalización de los servicios en Inglaterra y en Estados Unidos" – "The transfer of the services to the City Halls in England and the USA" – by Caviati and "La circulación y los bancos" – "The circulation and the banks" – by Luzzati.

[30] In 1916, the *Revista Nacional de Economía* summarises one of Pantaleoni's lectures and published "The economic consequences of the War" by Loria. In 1918, the works "Does it exists the international trade during war world?" by Porri and "The Gold Standard monetary system" by Loria were published. In 1919, the latter was reedited on *Revista de Economía y Hacienda.*

A detailed study of the spread of Italian economic thought within Spain, therefore, calls for an evaluation of the importance of translated Italian handbooks on Political Economy used for educational purposes. Unfortunately, given the lack of knowledge of the institutional framework and the academic circles within which the discipline was developed, it becomes difficult to arrive at any solid conclusions on the issue. The first of the translated handbooks, *Lecciones de Economía Política* – Lessons on Political Economy – by Murray, was edited in 1915, in a Sociology collection. There is no doubt about the tremendous success of Camilo Supino's *Principios de Economía Política – Principles of Political Economy –*. After its first translation in 1920, the handbook was edited at least four more times up to 1931 being translated by Flores de Lemus' pupil, Álvarez Cienfuegos. In fact, the use of the *Principios* among others books, as a starting point for discussions celebrated by Flores de Lemus with their disciples is remarkable. Such an event probably helps to explain the success of *Principios* by Supino in Spain (Velarde 1990: 103-104). Its strictly theoretical content, sticks anachronistically to the English Classical School doctrine, although it also included contributions from critics from the German historicist movement and, particularly, from the Austrian marginalist school, which is truly relevant considering the general ignorance that abounded with regard to marginalism (Supino 1928: 5).

3. The Corporatism

Just when the modernisation of the Economics discipline in Spain was beginning to consolidate itself, the Spanish Civil War broke out and effectively eliminated any prospects for the future evolution of the science (Velarde 1986). The groups around Flores de Lemus in Madrid, José María Zumalacárregui in Valencia (principally Manuel de Torres and José Castañeda), and the Servicio de Estudios del Banco de España – Research Centre of the Bank of Spain – lead by Olegario Fernández Baños, disbanded. Its members were dispersed, either in exile or in the new institutions founded at the end of the Civil War, and periodicals like the *Revista Nacional de Economía* and *Economía Española* disappeared entirely. The post-war period witnessed the introduction of the economic doctrine of corporatism, in both, its academic and its popular versions. The role played by the Italian economists in this process was considerable.

Despite the signing, in 1926, of a treaty of friendship and arbitration between the Spanish Dictator Primo de Rivera and Mussolini, it was not until the second Spanish Republic and the approval of the fascist Law on Corporations, in 1934, that the Corporatist economic doctrine was introduced from Italy. Curiously, the newly-founded National-Sindicalist Spanish Party – Falange Española – which, in certain aspects, was quite similar to other European fascist parties, though it had its differences, prevented the introduction of Corporatism into Spain. Some of the reasons were probably its vague ideology and the absence of any relationships with its Italian and German counterparts (Payne 1986: 46). The first news about Italian corporatism arrived to Spain indirectly, through *Los Fundamentos Económicos del Fascismo -The Economic Foundations of Fascism-* (1934) by Paul Einzig, who was fascinated by the economic changes that had taken place in Italy since 1934. The book, which includes the *Carta del Lavoro* in an Appendix, was positively received by Manuel de Torres, who had already expressed his enthusiasm for certain aspects of the Italian Corporatist doctrine and practice even before the Civil War began (Torres 1935). Torres particularly advocated the introduction of the national dimension into Economics and defended a new State structure, with a more open attitude towards government intervention. Despite Torres was well versed in this subject since his period in Bologna in the mid-1920s, the works of Serpieri were probably what mainly led him to the corporatist literature known as the "terza via". He shared with them an epistemological standpoint which combined the national dimension with the neo-classical economic methods and tools (Zabalza 1998; Zagari 1982)[31]. In Fernández Baños' works as well, there are certain elements that relate easily to moderate corporatism. He observes the effects of the conflicts between capital and labour on the economic cycle and the reduction of such conflicts through the promotion of harmony among the social classes (Fernández Baños 1928: 29-30; 1939).

Once the Civil War had broken out, all publishing activity, except for nationalist propaganda, was severely reduced. In 1937, the newly-launched magazine *Nueva Economía Nacional – New National Economy –*, linked to the Falange, published the *Carta del Lavoro* and several other articles explaining some of the economic concepts of Fascism. This fact coincided with the Italian suggestion to promote the *Carta del Trabajo – Letter of Work –*, which took the Italian *Carta del Lavoro* as model, in order to give a reformist appearance to "nationalist and Franquist" Spain (Payne 1986:173). The most outstanding publication, regarding Italian thought, was probably *Síntesis de Economía Corporativa – Synthesis of Corporatist Economics (*1937), by the lawyer Bartolomé Aragón. He attended a course on corporatism in Pisa, which was officiated by Spirito, Bottai and their circle. *Síntesis* undoubtedly represents Spirito's corporatist concept quite accurately, and was accepted by Aragón as the orthodox model. In fact, he promoted its translation in order to avoid misunderstandings of Corporatist doctrine in Spain (Aragón 1937).

At the end of the War, the victorious "nationalists" implemented an autarchic economic policy in Spain. In the circles close to the ministries with economic competences, composed mainly of technocrats with an engineering background,

[31] It is common in Torres' works to incorporate different influences, such as Einaudi and the corporatists. Zabalza (1998).

it was common to refer to anachronistic 19th Century sources – German Historicists, List or Carey – and the contemporary Romanian Manoïlescu, to justify the economic autarchy (Fuentes Irurozqui 1942; Paris Eguilaz 1938). The propagation of other minor Italian corporatist economic works was thanks to Ferrer Calbetó and Gay de Montellá, who were both close to the Catalonian bourgeoisie. At the beginning of the Civil War, the textile entrepreneur Felipe Ferrer Calbetó, exiled in Italy, became quite familiar with a group of professors and corporatist intellectuals, and on his return to Spain he promoted the translation of their works (Ferrer Calbetó 1992: 9)[32]. The lawyer Gay de Montellá, who had been interested in the economic relationships between Spain and Italy since his youth, justified an autarchic policy with arguments taken from the works of Giorgio Napolitano (Gay de Montellá 1923; 1940). He later translated the orthodox *Instituciones de Economía Corporativa* (1941), by Napolitano in an effort to "disseminate the concepts of the new economic doctrine among Spanish youth".

From the institutional and academic viewpoints, the reconstruction of the discipline, at the beginning, was channeled through the Economic Department at the heart of the Institute for Political Studies, which edited the *Revista de Estudios Políticos –The Journal of Political Studies-*, and the Sancho de Moncada Economic Institute, directed by the veteran José María Zumalacárregui, which published *Anales de Economía -Annals of Economics*. In June 1942, the periodical *Moneda y Crédito – Money and Credit* – was founded. It was financed by the private Bank of Urquijo[33]. These three periodicals, which published modern economic thought from abroad, will be used below as a guideline to trace the transmission of the Italian economic thought, mainly corporatist, during the early postwar years in Spain.

At the *Revista de Estudios Políticos,* the head of the Economic Department, José Vergara Doncel, resumed the propagation of Italian economic thought, as he had done before the Civil War from the *Revista Nacional de Economía*. However, the Italian literature shared the leading role with that of the Anglo-Saxons countries, the latter becoming more and more dominant as time went by, as is shown by bibliographic epigraphs[34]. From January 1941, in accordance with the ideology of the Political Economy Institute, Vergara focused on economic literature

---

[32] Several works were translated under Ferrer Calbetó's patronage: *El pensamiento económico de Benito Mussolini – Benito Mussolini's Economic Thought* – (1937) by Bertani, *La realidad económica* (1940) – *The Economic Reality*, by Mario Alberti, professor at Bocconi University, which includes a philosophic discussion defending a controlled economy, and the *Principios Generales del Orden Corporativo Fascista – General Principles of the Corporatist Fascistic Order* – (1942) by Biagi.

[33] The Faculty of Political and Economic Sciences, founded in 1943, was an important stage in the institutionalisation of Economics in Spain. Some of the most outstanding professors of the Faculty were transferred from the Sancho de Moncada Economic Institute and the Political Studies Institute. Velarde (1973: 55).

[34] During these first years the indexes from *Giornale degli Economisti e Annali di Economia*, *Rivista di Politica Economica, Rivista di Storia Economica, Rivista Internazionale di Scienze Sociali* and *Rivista Italiana di Scienze Economiche* were systematically published.

that had a corporatist slant (Sánchez Hormigo 1991: 78)[35]. In 1941, he translated the *Principios de Economía Política Corporativa – Principles of Corporatist Political Economy* – (1941) by Serpieri and wrote the book review in the *Revista de Estudios Políticos*. In the latter, Vergara expressed his agreement with the main concepts of the *Principles* and with the doctrine of the "terza via" group of economists like De Stefani and Amoroso (Vergara1941: 303). The Serpieri textbook became a guideline for understanding the doctrine behind the economic policies of the new totalitarian states, as Franco's Spain was. In fact, it was widely recommended and Professor Castañeda described it as "the best introduction available, not only for the student but also for the researcher in taking his first steps into the scientific knowledge of the economic life in modern totalitarian states" (Castañeda 1942: 56). Professor Castañeda, who was also a member of the Institute, seems to have been considerably influenced by Stackelberg and Hicks, as well as by Amoroso and Pareto in his *Lecciones de Teoría Económica – Lessons in Economic Theory* – (1946)[36].

The Spanish edition of *Principios de Economía Política – Principles of Political Economy* – (1942) by Enrico Barone is also Vergara's contribution, in an effort to provide Spanish economic literature with an academic handbook of pure economic theory (Vergara, 1942). Its anachronistic content opened a debate among the economists about the capacity of the book to achieve its pedagogic aim. *Principios* was interpreted in two different ways. On the one hand, Vergara and Sánchez Ramos stressed the priority of the "minimum cost of production" over any other goal, and particularly so over free competition, and avoiding Barone's interpretation as a liberal economist (Sánchez Ramos 1942; Vergara 1942: XXI)[37]. Vergara went even further and highlighted the Italian School's contributions, particularly the works of Amoroso, Pantaleoni and Barone, and stressed on its political closeness to fascism. On the other hand, the liberal Álvarez explicitly disagrees with Vergara's interpretation. Although Álvarez admitted the importance of the role played by the "minister of production" and the economic planning in Barone's work, he defended the foundation of the treatise on the principle of free competition (Álvarez 1942). Curiously enough, Álvarez, who was one of the most outstanding and active economists in the Political Economic Institute, became

---

[35] The Political Studies Institute was near to Falange Española. However, the group of economists of the Economic Department and their journal, the *Suplemento de Información Económica* published from 1943 onwards, were an oasis of intellectual freedom. During his period in Madrid (1943-1946), Stackelberg helped in the training of some of the Institute's economists, such as Álvarez, Castañeda, Paredes, Ullastres and Vergara. Harmes-Liedtke (1992: 561-562).

[36] Although it goes beyond the scope of this study, it is worth mentioning the remarkable role played by *Lecciones* in the training of successive generations of economists in Spain during the 50's and 60's. Almenar (2000: 198).

[37] The translation of *Principios* by Barone uses his last version from 1920-21, but it only contains the chapters included in the Volume II of the Italian edition in 1930 by Alberto di Stefani. Moreover, Vergara added Chapters IV and V included by Barone in the 1906's edition.

interested in Economics in the 20's, after reading Pareto's *Manuale* (Sánchez Hormigo1991: 45)

During 1942, reviews of four books by Italian economists who were mainly close to corporatism were also published *in Anales de Economía*[38]. The most outstanding members of the Sancho de Moncada Economics Institute, however, paid no attention to the Italian corporatists despite the totalitarian tendencies of some of them[39]. In fact, José María Zumalacárregui represented the neo-classical orthodoxy and some years later published an intellectual biography of Vilfredo Pareto to settle his debt with the Italian master (Zumalacárregui 1951)[40]. One of his pupils, the above-mentioned Manuel de Torres, adopted Keynesianism after the Civil War and through the direction of the Economic Collection of the Aguilar Press contributed to the spread of the new doctrine. As Torres' works and Aguilar's catalogue demonstrate, however, he adapted Keynesianism through the updating of his economic ideas, without renouncing, but rather, transforming the previous influences, including the Italian economists. In this vein, the most remarkable example was the publication of Einaudi's *Principios de Hacienda Pública – Principles of Public Finance* – (1946), which co-existed with the Keynesian works on Public Finance, also edited in the Aguilar Collection, that defended the budget deficit and a progressive Income Tax. In this particular case, the motivation of the translation was twofold, to settle his debt with the Italian master, and to expose Einaudi's re-interpretation within a Keynesian framework, as the "Preface" to *Principios* shows. Moreover, Torres implicitly argued, although not very convincingly, that Einaudi was in favour of public deficits and an active Public Finance policy (Torres 1946). Finally, the Italian edition of *Miti e paradossi della giustizia tributaria* (1940), by Einaudi, which included arguments in defence of the generalisation of the average-income as a taxation criterion, triggered strong criticism from Alberto Ullastres, a member of the Political Studies Institute (Ullastres 1943). Although Torres never replied to Ullastres, some years later he used some ideas taken from *Miti e paradossi*, and in the 50's, when Torres was promoting the introduction of Income Tax in the Spanish Tax System, he still defended the virtues of the tax average income, despite he admitted its technical impossibility (Torres 1968).

Zumalacárregui simultaneously headed the National Economic Council, which was the Economic Adviser Board of Franco's government. Some of the economists of the *Sancho de Moncada Economic Institute* were members at the Council and prepared the reports required by Spanish Government (Martínez Mesa 1997).

---

[38] The book reviews were from Serpieri, Graziadei, Fasiani and Vito works.

[39] Paris Eguilaz, for example, supported autarchy and was taught on Economics at Berlin by Wagemann in 1938.

[40] Zumalacárregui probably met Pareto during his stage on Lausanne at the beginning of the century, but there are not testimonies about it.

Two of the most ambitious projects promoted by the Council were the Annual Series of the "National Income", and the "National Wealth" estimate. The "National Income" Annual Series followed Simon Kuznets' procedures, whereas the "National Wealth" calculation, although not revealed, was inspired by the methodology used by Corrado Gini in *Ammontare e la composizione della ricchezza delle nazioni* (1914), a well-known work in Spain since Vandellós' Income Estimation in the 20's (Zabalza 1998). Gini was not only used in technical but also in ideological terms, as shown by the work published in 1943 in the *Revista Internacional de Sociología – International Sociology Review –*. In this work, he defended the so-called "Labour Economics" against "Bourgeois Economics", as a means to re-assess labour activity in the economy, as some thinkers close to the Falange did during the 40's (Gini 1943).

At first, *Moneda y Crédito* was a fluid channel for the spread of the Italian economic corporatism. José María Naharro was undoubtedly the driving force behind this promotion, and showed knowledge of the corporatist literature, probably more than any other Spanish economist of his day, with the possible exception of Vergara. Through "Acerca de la Teoría Económica Corporativa" – "On Corporatist Economic Theory" –, published in *Moneda y Crédito* as a book review on *Dall'economia finanziaria al corporativismo razionale* (1934), by Guido Menegazzi, Naharro provides Spanish readers with the first complete and commented outline of the Italian corporatist literature: from orthodox corporatists like Fovel, Carli or Arias, who replaced the "homo economicus" of the liberal economy with the so-called "homo corporativus", to the moderate wing represented by Amoroso, De Stefani o Vito (Naharro 1942; Cavalieri 1994). Later on, in other book reviews on *Economía Política Corporativa. Parte Generale* by Vito, and *Introduzione alla Política Económica* by Bresciani-Turroni, Naharro introduced the controversial issue on the division of power over economic policy between politicians and economists, which was also underlined by Vergara (Naharro 1943; 1943a). Despite Naharro's ambiguity, there was a general consensus on conferring the power of setting aims to the politicians and leaving the strictly technical analysis to the economists. The moderate Italian corporatists, like Vito and Serpieri, clearly contributed to this opinion (Faucci 1990; Zabalza 1998). At the same time, however, Navarro expressed some doubts about the approach of the "new economics", and gradually *Moneda y Crédito* paid more attention to the economic literature, coming from the Anglo-Saxon countries. But this is not exclusive of *Moneda y Crédito*. From 1945 onwards, on the one hand, the references to the Italian corporatists among the Spanish economists were manifestly reduced. On the other, the beginning of the internationalisation of Economics in Spain allowed the introduction of a vast economic literature from abroad diminishing the relative importance of the Italian works.

4. Summary and conclusions

After the slow decline of the presence of the Italian economists in Spain, the 70's of the 19th Century witnessed the beginning of the spread of the Italian economic thought, which gradually increases towards the decade of the 30's in the 20th Century. During the last quarter of the 19th Century, the Italian economists and the Italian language contributed to the introduction of economic ideas from abroad. The "terza serie" of the Biblioteca dell'economista, Cossa, and especially the Italian historicists led the transmission. However, despite some exceptions, the ideas of the Italian intermediaries, and in particular of the historicists, did not take solid roots in their Spanish counterparts. This was partly due to the liberal and moderate character of the critics of Classical orthodoxy in Spain, which was not very appropriate to the radicalism of the Italian historicists. With a few exceptions, the Spanish economists did not pay any attention to theoretical issues, and therefore during the last years of the 19th Century and the first part of the 20th Century, the theoretical works of the main Italian economists were almost unknown. This fact should be explained within a wider framework that investigate the general ignorance of marginalism in Spain and calls for further research.

At the beginning of the 20th Century, the modernisation of the Economic Studies, mainly promoted by Flores de Lemus gave an unequivocal practical direction to the discipline of Economics in Spain, which was clearly oriented towards the solution of the problems of the Spanish economy. In the first third of the 20th Century, the preference for the Italian tradition among Spanish economists was remarkable. The role played in such process by individuals such as, Torres and Vergara in Agricultural Economics, or Vandellós in Statistics, was particularly outstanding. A similar process occurs in the field of Public Finance. Despite the influence of the German School on the Spanish experts in Public Finance, a general spread of the Italian School ideas can be undoubtedly perceived. On the one hand, the Italians were considered by the Spanish as skilled as the Germans. On the other, the Spanish and Italian experts in Public Finance shared similar and common problems.

In the beginning of the 40's, the reception of corporatism, occurred in a political frame characterised by censorship and political repression. The nature of the corporatist economic literature coming from Italy was mainly orthodox. However, among professional economists, the preference for the moderate and more qualified branch of the economic corporatism represented by Amoroso, De Stefani, Del Vecchio, Serpieri, Vito and so on, was generalised. As happens in the international circulation of economic ideas, some aspects of the original doctrine are usually transformed and adapted to the particularities of the receptor countries (Cardoso and Lluch 1999: 86-87). The interest of the Spanish professional economists in the doctrine of Corporatism is partially explained, on the one hand, by the possibilities provided by the new doctrine for the intervention of the State in the economy, and on the other, by the introduction of a national perspective in the economic analysis. Nevertheless, corporatist ideas were not used in Spain to justify a corporation system as happened in Italy. This fact partially explains the lack of durability of the corporatist doctrine in Spain and gives way to the entrance of new doctrines such as Keynesianism at the beginning of the internationalisation of Economics in Spain.

To summarise, despite the lack of wider research on the introduction of economic ideas from abroad into Spain during the period analysed, the contribution of Italian Economic Thought to Spanish economic tradition is manifest. The forty translations of Italian economists between 1878 and 1946 denotes an intense flow of economic ideas from Italy. Although the main works were not always the most successful, in general, it can be argued that the works of the Italian economists were used by their Spanish colleagues as a valuable source to tackle the deep problems of economic development in Spain.

References

Abellán J.A. (1989), *Historia del pensamiento crítico español*, Madrid, Espasa-Calpe.

Almenar S. (2000), "The Development of Economic Studies and Research in Spain (1935-95)". In Coats (Ed.), *The Development of Economics in Western Europe since 1945*, London, Routledge.

Álvarez V.A. (1942), Book Review to Barone (1942). In *Revista de Estudios Políticos*, n. 7.

Amoroso L. (1921), *Lezioni di economia matematica*, Bologna, Zanichelli.

Aragón B. (1937), *Síntesis de Economía Corporativa*, Salamanca, Librería "La Facultad" de Germán García.

Artal F. (1991), *Pensament econòmic català 1840-1898: Del proteccionisme al regionalisme econòmic.* Unpublished PhD. Dissertation, University of Barcelona.

Azcárate P. (1967), *La cuestión universitaria*, Madrid, Tecnos.

Ballesteros P. (1934), "Al lector español". In Viti De Marco A., *Principios de Economía Financiera*, Madrid, Revista de Derecho Privado.

— (1940), *Manual de Ciencia de la Hacienda*, Madrid, Editorial Revista de Derecho Privado.

Barbagallo F. (1984), *Francesco Saverio Nitti*, Torino, UTET.

Barone E. (1942), *Principios de Economía Política*, Madrid, Revista de Derecho Privado.

Beneyto J. (1929), "Los problemas técnicos de la agricultura", *Revista Nacional de Economía*, Año XIV, n. 85, Tomo XXVIII, mayo-junio.

Benito, L. (S.a.), "Prólogo" to Boccardo, *Historia del Comercio de la Industria y de la Economía Política*, Madrid, La España Moderna.

Buchanan J. (1980), "La Scuola italiana di Finanza Pubblica". In Finoia M. (1980).

Cabrera M., Comín F. (1989), *Santiago Alba: un programa de reforma económica en la España del primer tercio del siglo XX*, Madrid, Instituto de Estudios Fiscales.

Cabrillo F. (1991), "Estudio preliminar". In Figuerola L., *Escritos económicos*, Madrid, IEF.

Cardoso J.L., Lluch E. (1999), "Economic Theories Seen through a National Looking-glass", *Book of Extended Summaries*, ESHET Conference, Valencia, pp. 86-89.

Castañeda J. (1942), Book Review to Barone (1942). In *Moneda y Crédito*, n. 3, diciembre, pp. 56-57.

Cavalieri D. (1994), "Il corporativismo nella storia del pensiero economico italiano: una rilettura critica", *Il Pensiero Economico Italiano*, II/2, pp. 7-49.

Castroviejo A. (1911), "Prólogo" to Toniolo (1911), *Tratado de Economía Social*, Ciencia y Acción. Estudios Sociales. Primera Serie. Madrid, Casa Editorial Saturnino Calleja Fernández. Tomos XVI y XVII.

Costa J. (1915), *Colectivismo agrario en España. Partes I y II. Doctrinas y hechos*, Madrid, Biblioteca Costa.

Costas A. (1988), *Apogeo del liberalismo en la "Gloriosa". La reforma económica en el Sexenio liberal (1868-1874)*, Siglo XXI Editores, Madrid.

D'Albergo E. (1931), *La crisi dell'imposta personale sul reddito*, Padova, Cedam.

Di Sandro G. (1995), *Gli economisti agrari italiani tra Otto e Novecento*, Bologna, CLUEB.

Estapé F. (1990), *Introducción a la historia del pensamiento económico. Una perspectiva española*, Madrid, Espasa Calpe.

Faucci R. (1985), *Einaudi*, Torino, UTET.

— (1990), "Il pensiero economico italiano fra le due guerre. Un'epoca di transizione? Le coordinate teorico-istituzionali del periodo", *Quaderni di Storia dell'economia politica* VIII/2-3, pp. 3-22.

— (1995), *L'economista scomodo. Vita e opere di Francesco Ferrara*, Palermo, Sellerio editore.

Fausto D. (1995), "I 'Principii di economia finanziaria' nella letteratura straniera". In Pedone A. (a cura di), *Antonio de Viti de Marco*, Bari, Laterza.

Fernández Baños O. (1928), *Dinamismo de los precios y carestía de la vida*, Madrid, Industrial Gráfica.

— (1936), *Función de la banca en un complejo integral*, Talleres Gráficos Marsiega.

— (1939), *Trabajo y Capital. Sus funciones en una economía nacional*, Madrid, Sobrinos de la sucesora de M. Minuesa de los Ríos.

— (1948), *Tratado de Estadística*, Madrid, CSIC.

Ferrer Calbetó F. (1992), *Pensamientos, opiniones y recuerdos (1957-1968)*, Arenys de Mar, Imprenta Santa María.

Finoia M. (1980), *Il pensiero economico italiano: 1850-1950*, Bologna, Cappelli.

Forte F. (1980), "Francesco Nitti". In Finoia (1980: 549-579).

Fuentes Irurozqui M. (1942), *Abastecimientos, tasas y racionamientos*, Madrid, Veritas 1942.

Fuentes Quintana E. (1976), "La ideología de la reforma tributaria silenciosa", *Hacienda Pública Española*, ns. 42-43, pp. 105-144.

— (1978), "El estilo tributario latino: Características generales y problemas para su reforma". In García Delgado J.L., Segura J. (Coord.), *Ciencia Social y Análisis Económico: estudios en homenaje al profesor Valentín Andrés Álvarez*, Madrid, Tecnos, pp. 195-279.

— (1999), "Ensayo introductorio". In Fuentes Quintana (dir.), *Economía y economistas españoles*, Tomo I, Barcelona, Galaxia Gutenberg-Círculo de Lectores, pp. 7-388.

García Delgado J.L. (1974), "Estudio preliminar". In Carrión P., *Estudios sobre la agricultura española (1919-1971)*, Madrid, Ediciones de la Revista de Trabajo.

Gay V. (1906), "Prólogo" to Flora F., *Ciencia de la Hacienda*, Madrid, Librería General de Victoriano Suárez.

— (1923), *Programa de Economía Política. Ensayo de sistematización didáctica*, Imprenta de O. Lozano.

Gay De Montellá R. (1923), *Italia y España. Sus afinidades culturales como base de su inteligencia política*, Imprenta Ortega, Barcelona.

— (1940), *Autarquía. Nuevas orientaciones de la economía*, Bosch, Barcelona.

Gini C. (1943), "Primeras líneas de una Economía Laboral", *Revista Internacional de Sociología*, II (2-3) abril-septiembre.

González M.J. (1990), "Prólogo" to Torres Martínez M., *Obra escogida*, FIES.

Griziotti B. (1935), *Principios de Política, Derecho y Ciencia de la Hacienda*, Madrid, Revista de Derecho Privado.

Harmes-Liedtke U. (1992), "Heinrich von Stackelberg y la economía española". In García Delgado J.L. (ed.) *Economía española, cultura y sociedad. Homenaje a Juan Velarde Fuertes ofrecido por la Universidad Complutense*, Madrid, Eudema, vol. II, pp. 553-71.

Lluch E. (1973), *El pensament econòmic a Catalunya (1760-1840)*, Barcelona, Edicions 62.

Lluch E., Almenar S. (1991), "Difusión e influencia de los economistas clásicos en

España (1776-1870)". In *Actas do Encontro Ibérico sobre História do Pensamento Económico*, Lisboa, CISEP, pp. 91-155.

MALEFAKIS E. (1980), *Reforma agraria y revolución campesina en la España del siglo XX*, Barcelona, Ariel.

MALO J.L. (1998), *Pensamiento económico y filosofía social en la España del siglo XIX. Liberalismo, krausismo y reformas sociales*. Unpublished PhD. Dissertation. University of Zaragoza.

MARTÍN RODRÍGUEZ M. (1989), "La institucionalización de los estudios de Economía Política en la Universidad española (1874-1857)", "Estudio Preliminar" to Valle Santoro (1829), *Elementos de Economía Política*, Madrid, IEF.

MARTÍN URIZ A.M. (1985), "Estudio preliminar" to *Henry George*, Madrid, Instituto de Estudios Agrarios, Pesqueros y Alimenticios.

MARTÍNEZ MESA J. (1997), *El Consejo de Economía Nacional*, Madrid, CES.

MEACCI F. (1988), The Principles of Capital in Luigi Einaudi's Work, *Giornale degli Economisti*, pp. 475-493.

MONTERO F. (1983), *El primer catolicismo social y la "Rerum Novarum" en España (1889-1902)*, Consejo Superior de Investigaciones Científicas, Madrid.

NADAL J. (1985), "Próleg" to Vandellós (1985), *Catalunya, poble decadent*, Barcelona, Ed. 62.

NAHARRO MORA J.M. (1942), "Acerca de la teoría económica corporativa", *Moneda y Crédito*, n. 3, diciembre.

— (1943), Book Review to Vito (1943), *Economia politica corporativa*, Parte Generale, Milano, Giuffré. In *Moneda y Crédito*, n. 5, junio.

— (1943a), Book Review to Bresciani Turroni (1942), *Introduzione alla politica economica*, Einaudi, Torino. In *Moneda y Crédito*, n. 6, septiembre.

OLASCOAGA R. de (1896), *Estado actual de los estudios económicos en España*, Librería de Victoriano Suárez, Madrid.

OLÓZAGA J.M. (1885), *Tratado de Economía Política*, Madrid, Imprenta de José Perales y Martínez.

PALACIO MORENA J.I. (1988), *La institucionalización de la reforma social en España (1883-1924). La Comisión y el Instituto de Reformas Sociales*, Ministerio de Trabajo y Seguridad Social.

PAREDES M. (1941), Book Review to Fanno M., *Los movimientos anormales del capital y las crisis*, Madrid, Revista de Derecho Privado 1936. In *Revista de Estudios Políticos*, Año I, n. 2, abril, pp. 244-346.

PARET L.V. (1918), "Prólogo" to Flora F., *Manual de Ciencia de la Hacienda*, Madrid, Victoriano Suárez.

— (1927), "El impuesto sobre rentas y ganancias", *Revista Nacional de Economía*, n. 71, pp. 43-63.

PARIS EGUILAZ H. (1938), *El Estado y la Economía. Política económica totalitaria*, Ediciones F.E. 1938.

PARISI D. (1998), *L'economia come scienza 'utile' e 'interessata'. Sapere tecnico e cultura economica a Milano tra Ottocento e Novecento*. In Porta P.L. (ed.), *Milano e la cultura economica nel XX secolo. I. Gli anni 1890-1920*, Milano, Franco Angeli.

PASCUAL J. (1985), "Annex". In Vandellós (1985), *Catalunya, poble decadent*, Barcelona, Ed. 62.

PAYNE S.G. (1986), *Falange: historia del fascismo español*, Sarpe, Madrid.

PIERNAS HURTADO J.M. (1891), *Tratado de Hacienda Pública y examen de la española*, 2 Tomos, Madrid, Tipografía de Manuel Ginés Hernández.
— (1895), *Principios elementales de la Ciencia Económica. Introducción al estudio de la Ciencia Económica*, Librería de Victoriano Suárez, Madrid.
— (1897), *Tratado elemental de estadistica*, Madrid, Libreria de D. Victoriano Suárez.
RIBAS P. (1981), *La introducción del marxismo en España (1869-1939)*, Madrid, Ediciones de la Torre.
ROBLEDO R. (1993), *Economistas y reformadores españoles. La cuestión agraria (1760-1935)*, Madrid, MAPA.
ROMANI R. (1994), *L'economia politica del Risorgimento italiano*, Torino, Bollati Boringhieri.
SALVÁ M. (1880), *Discursos leídos ante la Real Academia de Ciencias Políticas y Económicas, en la recepción pública de D. Melchor Salvá el martes 29 de junio de 1880*, Madrid, Imprenta de Alejandro Gómez Fuentenebro.
SÁNCHEZ HORMIGO A. (1991), *Valentín Andrés Álvarez*, Zaragoza, PUZ.
SÁNCHEZ RAMOS F. (1942), Book Review to Barone (1942). In *Anales de Economía*, Vol. II, n. 6, abril-junio.
SCHUMPETER J.A. (1985), *Historia del Análisis Económico*, Barcelona, Ariel.
SERRANO J.M. (1987), *El viraje proteccionista de la Restauración. la política comercial española, 1875-1895*, Madrid, Siglo XXI de España Editores.
— (1997), "Los estudios económicos en España a finales del XIX: historia de un estancamiento". In Bell G., Estruch A., *Industrialización en España: entusiasmos, desencantos y rechazos: ensayos en homenaje al profesor Fabián Estapé*, Madrid, Civitas.
STEVE (1974), "Luigi Einaudi e il concetto di reddito imponibile", *Annali della Fondazione Luigi Einaudi*, Torino, Vol. VIII, pp. 101-110.
SUPINO C. (1928), *Principios de Economía Política*, Madrid, Librería General de Victoriano Suárez.
TEJERO J. (1934), Book Review to Viti De Marco (1934), *Principios fundamentales de Economía Financiera*, Madrid, Editorial de Derecho Privado. In *Economía Española*, Año II, n. 19, julio, pp. 115-118.
TORRES M. DE (1927), *Studi sull'imposta di succesione*, Bologna, Tesi di Laurea.
— (1933), "Comentario a la ley Carner". In Beneyto and Torres, *El impuesto sobre la Renta. Historia, Derecho Comparado, técnica y legislación española vigente*, Bosch, Barcelona.
— (1935), "El liberalismo, el fascismo y la solución de la crisis económica mundial. Recortes con notas de dos lecturas", *Diario de Valencia,* 29 de marzo.
— (1946), "Introducción" to *Principios de Hacienda Pública*, Madrid, Aguilar.
— (1968), "Dictamen del profesor Torres". In Albiñana, *La Contribución General sobre la Renta en los años 1953-54*, Madrid, Revista de Economía Política, pp. 167-182.
ULLASTRES A. (1943), "La renta media como criterio para la imposición fiscal", *Suplemento de Información Económica. Revista de Estudios Políticos*, septiembre-octubre.
VELARDE J. (1961), *Flores de Lemus ante la economía española*, Madrid, Instituto de Estudios Políticos.
— (1986), "Las escuelas españolas de economía y el estropicio de la Guerra Civil", *Economistas*, n. 21, pp. 6-10.

— (1973), *Introducción a la historia del pensamiento económico español en el siglo XX*, Madrid, Editora Nacional.

— (1990), *Economistas españoles contemporáneos. Primeros maestros*, Madrid, Espasa-Calpe 1993.

VERGARA J. (1935), "Los precios de los productos agrícolas, según el profesor Carlo Dragoni", *Revista Nacional de Economía*, Año XX, n. 120, Tomo XLII, marzo-abril, pp. 171-178.

— (1941), Book Review of Serpieri, *Principios de Economía Corporativa, Revista de Estudios Políticos*, n. 2, pp. 303-305.

— (1942), "Introducción" to Barone (1942).

ZABALZA J. (1995), *El pensamiento económico-agrario valenciano del siglo XX: Manuel de Torres Martínez 1930-1936*, Alicante, Instituto Juan Gil-Albert.

— (1998) *El pensamiento económico de Manuel de Torres Martínez (1903-1960).* Unpublished PhD. Dissertation. University of Alicante.

— (1998a), "Manuel de Torres y la imposición personal sobre la renta: una alternativa teórica a la 'reforma tributaria silenciosa'", *Cuadernos Aragoneses de Economía.*

ZAGARI E. (1982), "Introduzione". In Perillo F.D., Zagari E. (1982), *La teoria economica del corporativismo*, Napoli, ESIC.

ZUMALACÁRREGUI J.M. (1951), *Vilfredo Pareto*, Madrid, CSIC.

The spread of Italian economic thought in Sweden 1750-1950

Lars Pålsson Syll and Bo Sandelin
Lund University and University of Gothenburg

Introduction

During the 20th century the Anglo-Saxon influence has made itself felt constantly in every area of economics. In the 18th and 19th centuries there was no such predominance of economic literature in English. French and German economists were still widely read in their own languages, not least in Scandinavia, where the French and German languages were taught as part of the upper class education, and the influence of French and German literature and culture at large could be seen everywhere.

In Sweden the Italian language has never enjoyed the same standing as those mentioned above. Few economists could read Italian – Wicksell and Lindahl at the beginning of this century being notable exceptions – which of course made the chances of being acquainted with and influenced by Italian economists writing in Italian very small. Some of the Italian economists wrote in French – e. g. Pareto – which probably gave them greater influence.

During the period prior to the marginalist revolution at the end of the 19th century it can hardly be said that Italian economics had any influence at all on Swedish economic thought. Of course one does find occasional references to Davanzati, Galiani and Beccaria – often in the field of doctrinal history – but this does not signify any real influence on Swedish economic thought comparable to the French, British or German influence. This is also confirmed by the acquisitions of Italian books by Swedish university libraries and the low number of Italian citations in Swedish doctoral theses in economics far into this century.

With the advent of marginalism and especially the writings of the Italian school of public finance, this changes. Most of the Italian works cited are on public finance and taxation, which reflects the early eminence of Italian economists working within this field of research. The linguistic barrier still prevented much communication and dissemination of Italian economic thought, but the Italian contributions to utility theory and public finance theory were noticed by some of the leading Swedish economists. Below we will give an account of the more prominent instances of this.

Before we look in detail at the most important Swedish economists influenced by Italian thought, we shall present a bibliographic overview. We shall find that the proportion of Italian books acquired by Swedish research libraries has fluctuated around one per cent. A similar result is found concerning citations of Italian works in Swedish doctoral theses, with Einaudi and Pantaleoni being the most cited authors publishing in Italy.

After the bibliographic overview, we shall consider the marginal utility theory and how Wicksell, Cassel and Myrdal looked upon Pareto. Finally, we shall discuss how Wicksell's and Lindahl's theory of public finance was influenced by Italian authors.

Italian books acquired by Swedish university libraries

We shall now look at some bibliometric variables which may give an indication of influences on Sweden from abroad. We shall compare the significance of Italy with the significance of other countries. First, we shall scrutinize acquisitions of foreign economics books by Swedish university libraries.[1]

Table 1. Foreign books on economics acquired by Swedish research libraries. Per cent by country of publication.

Period	Italy	France	Germany & Austria	GB	US	Other	Total
1886-87	0.0	19	60	7	2	12	100
1894-97	1.4	14	55	12	4	13	100
1903-07	0.2	15	50	15	9	11	100
1914-17	1.1	8	51	13	10	18	100
1924-27	1.2	5	37	19	17	20	100
1934-37	1.3	10	26	24	22	16	100
1944-47	0.4	11	4	19	42	24	100
1954-55	0.8	10	17	15	33	25	100

Table 1 shows the percentage distribution between different countries of publication for foreign economics books acquired during different periods of

[1] A few libraries in addition to the university libraries are included as well. The source consists of the Swedish accessions register for foreign books. For each year, or sometimes for a two-year period, each foreign book acquired is registered together with the libraries that have acquired it. Even if a book has been acquired by several libraries in one year (or, sometimes, in a two-year period), or by one library in multiple copies in one year (or, sometimes, in a two-year period), it still counts as one book in Table 1.

time. The Italian share is low, always below 2 per cent, for all the selected periods between 1886 and 1955. In 1886-87 not a single Italian book was bought, but in 1894-97, 15 Italian books were acquired, which corresponds to 1.4 per cent of the foreign books. This is the highest percentage found for any period. With one exception, the books in this period were acquired by the Nobel Library of the Swedish Academy. For the following periods, the ordinary university libraries and the library of the National Statistics Office are predominant among the receivers.

There is no clear tendency for the Italian share. It oscillates wildly, though this can be attributed to the fact that so few books are involved that a few books more or less have a large impact on the percentage. In total, for all the selected periods 73 books published in Italy are included. Almost all of these books are, of course, in the Italian language; the exceptions consist of four books in French, three in English and one in German.

As a comparison, we can look at the share of French books, which is much higher, amounting to almost 20 per cent in the 1880s and about 10 per cent in the 1950s. The difference between France and Italy can be attributed to the general cultural influence on Sweden and its effect on the knowledge of languages. During the whole period under consideration, French occupied a strong position in the Swedish school system and was normally studied by all pupils at the upper secondary level, while Italian was rarely studied. Thus, the ability to read Italian has been lacking, which of course has exerted a negative influence on the tendency to buy Italian books.

Which countries have contributed most to Swedish acquisitions? We find in Table 1 that in the beginning Germany and Austria dominated, delivering more than half the acquisitions. (Of these two countries Germany was clearly the more important; Austria attained at most 7 per cent, in 1886-87.) A clear decline came in the 1920s. It seems reasonable to ascribe this primarily to the consequences of the First World War. A second drastic decline of the German-Austrian share came in the 1940s, i.e. after the Nazi persecutions and the Second World War. This is hardly surprising. These events not only imposed restrictions on what could be published in Germany; many of its best economists had to leave the country and continue their work elsewhere, often in the USA. (Details are provided by Hagemann and Krohn (1992) and in Hagemann (1997).)

Replacing Germany, the USA advanced to first place among countries of publication of acquired books. This has, of course, some connection with the growth of academic economics in the USA, which will not be discussed in this paper. However, the improvement of communications between the end of the 19th century and the middle of the 20th century should also be mentioned. One of Germany's advantages to Swedish scholars – the comparatively short distance to Germany – had become less important by the middle of the 20th century. Consequently, it became easier than before for a variety of manifestations of American culture to gain a strong position in Sweden.

Our second bibliographic measure is citations in Swedish doctoral theses in economics. Table 2 shows the distribution between countries in which the works cited were published.[2]

Table 2. Country of origin for publications cited in Swedish doctoral theses in economics. Per cent.

Years	Italy	France	Sweden	Germany & Austria	GB	US	Scandinavia	Other	Total
1895-1909	1.2	4	38	30	14	9	4	1	100
1910-19	2.7	9	43	20	13	6	3	3	100
1920-29	0.5	4	17	34	23	18	3	1	100
1930-39	1.8	2	11	43	12	26	1	4	100
1940-49	0.1	1	72	2	6	17	2	0	100
1950-59	0.5	3	50	3	19	19	4	1	100

As in Table 1, the Italian numbers in Table 2 are modest and oscillating; the tendency is possibly declining. The marked oscillations are evidently a consequence of the low absolute number of Italian citations in a low total number of theses. Thus, the highest number, 2.7 per cent, is found for the period 1910-1919. In these years there were 21 citations of Italian works, of which 20 may be found in Erik Lindahl's thesis *Die Gerechtigkeit der Besteuerung*. Similarly, the 1.8 per cent in 1930-1939 are based on 20 citations, of which 12 are found in Erik Fornmark's *Skatteutjämningens problem* (The Problem of Tax Equalization), 5 in Tord Palander's *Beiträge zur Standortstheorie*, and 3 in Carsten Welinder's *Kommunala avgifter i de svenska städernas hushällning* (Charges as Part of the Revenues of Swedish Cities). The Italian citations in 1895-1909 occur in two theses, Knut Wicksell's *Zur Lehre von der Steuerincidenz* and Nils Stjernberg's *Till frågan om de s k rent ekonomiska kategorierna* (A Contribution to the Question of Purely Economic Categories).

The titles mentioned above allow us to make an additional observation. Most of the Italian works cited are found in theses on public finance and taxation. This

[2] "Year" refers to the year when the thesis was submitted, not when the publications cited were published. For 1895-1949, 38 of 39 theses are included, for 1950-59 a sample of 11 out of 16. If a thesis lacks a list of works cited, the references have been collected from the footnotes. In calculating the percentages for a given period, the publications cited in all the theses of that period are pooled. In the pooled list, on which the percentages for each period are based, a given publication is counted more than once if it is included in more than one thesis during that period.

is of course a reflection of the early eminence of Italian economists within this field, an eminence that would have been even more apparent if knowledge of the Italian language had been more widespread. Buchanan's (1983) words are worth quoting: "Now that the important early Swedish contributions on monetary and cycle theory have been made available, it may be asserted that the single most important national body of doctrine which remains largely unknown to and unappreciated by English-language economists is the Italian work in fiscal theory. The linguistic barrier has served effectively to prevent the dissemination of the Italian contribution in this area of applied economics, an area which has been an Italian speciality for at least a century."

With regard to countries other than Italy, the Swedish share is quite low in the 1920s and 1930s and high in the 1940s and 1950s. This is explained by the character of the theses. In the 1920s and 1930s there were several theses of a highly theoretical character with no or few references to Swedish reality, for instance the theses by Gunnar Myrdal, Bertil Ohlin, Gustaf Åkerman, Tord Palander and Erik Lundberg. For the 1940s and 1950s, in contrast, the Swedish share is very high, reflecting the fact that several theses with a substantial empirical content relating to the Swedish economy were submitted.

There is no continuous decline in the German and Austrian share, nor a continuous increase in the American share. In part, this is a consequence of the sharp fluctuations in the Swedish share, with the sum necessarily being 100. However, in both cases there is a clear difference between the early and late periods. An even more pronounced American dominance and small Swedish and German shares are found for the most recent periods, which are not shown in the table (see Sandelin, 2001).

Which Italian authors are cited? Table 3 shows those Italian authors who are cited at least twice in Swedish doctoral theses in economics between 1895 and 1949. Only cited works that are published in Italy are included,[3] which explains the absence of Pareto. There are two citations of Pareto in the data set, but neither of these has reference to his Italian publications and they are therefore not included in the table. Those citations refer to the French edition of his Manuel which is cited by Sundbom and Svennilson.[4]

[3] If the same publication is cited in two theses, it yields two citations. If two publications by the same author are cited in one thesis, they yield two citations.

[4] The way citations are collected probably implies an underestimation. Titles are registered if they are included in lists of works cited or in footnotes. However, especially in early theses, titles may be mentioned in the main text without reappearing in a footnote or in a list of works cited.

Table 3. Italian authors cited at least twice in Swedish doctoral theses in economics 1895-1949.

Cited author	Number of citations	In number of theses	Citing author(s)
L. Einaudi	5	2	E. Lindahl, E. Fornmark
M. Pantaleoni	5	3	K. Wicksell, N. Stjernberg, E. Lindahl
E. Barone	3	2	K. Wicksell, E. Lindahl
A. De Viti De Marco	3	3	E. Lindahl, C. Welinder, E. Fornmark
R. Murray	3	2	E. Lindahl, E. Fornmark
P. Bellemo	2	1	T. Palander
D. Berardi	2	2	E. Lindahl, N. Stjernberg
C.A. Conigliani	2	1	E. Lindahl
A. Graziani	2	2	E. Lindahl, E. Fornmark
U. Mazzola	2	2	E. Lindahl, E. Fornmark
A. Puviani	2	2	E. Lindahl, E. Fornmark
V. Tangorra	2	2	E. Lindahl, C. Welinder

Among the citing authors, the name of Erik Lindahl is especially frequent; eleven of the twelve Italians in the table are cited by him. As we have already indicated, this is a result of the strong Italian influence on the theory of public finance, which is the field of Lindahl's thesis Die Gerechtigkeit der Besteuerung. The same field of influence applies to the rest of the citing authors, with the possible exception of Nils Stjernberg.

In all, 33 citations of authors cited at least twice are included in Table 3. In addition to these authors, a number of authors were cited once in Swedish theses. They are (with the citing author in parenthesis): Arias (Ohlin), Cassola (Fornmark), Fanno (Fornmark), Gerbino (Ohlin), Loria (Palander), Macchiori (Palander), Marconcini (Palander), Masè-Dari (Lindahl), Morselli (Fornmark), Papi (Ohlin), Pugliese (Welinder), Scherma (Lindahl), Tivaroni (Fornmark), and Verri (Petander).

The marginal utility theory – Wicksell, Cassel and Myrdal on Pareto

Wicksell

With the advent of neoclassical economics much effort was devoted to attempts to formalize the stringent conditions for obtaining equilibrium and showing in what way the prices and quantities that obtained under free competition constituted some kind of social optimum.

The given equilibrium prices determine the income distribution, and, given individuals' preferences, the principle of diminishing marginal utility purportedly implies that a maximum of satisfaction is reached when each commodity's marginal utility is in relation to its price. In equilibrium the marginal utilities of the commodities are proportional to the given prices, and, since only one price can prevail in the market, this proportion has to be the same for all individuals on the market.

However, the fact that the equilibrium reached in free competition is an optimum for each individual – given prevailing prices and income distribution – was not considered by all economists to create a very strong case for a free market economy per se. It was impossible to prove that free trade and competition yielded a maximum of social utility. The gains made in exchange were not in themselves a manifestation of maximum social utility.

Knut Wicksell was one of those who criticized the idea of regarding the gain in utility arising from free competition as an absolute maximum. To Wicksell it was not worth criticizing the "pretentious sophism, lacking any scientific base" of a Bastiat or a Carey. But when propounders of the new theory – especially the Lausanne School of Walras and Pareto – overstepped the strict boundaries of science and used it in ascribing to the market economy properties it did not possess, Wicksell felt he had to react.

In 1897 Wicksell wrote a review of Pareto's *Cours d'économie politique* in which he criticized Pareto's treatment of the question of mutual gain in free exchange.[5] According to Wicksell, the equilibrium prices obtained under free competition did not prevent the trading subjects from concluding other, more profitable transactions. It is even possible, Wicksell thought, to show that the combined gain of all those involved in the case of free competition is the greatest only when certain definite conditions are fulfilled. Even if Pareto says that free competition must yield the greatest satisfaction of needs for everyone, once the prevailing distribution is accepted as a fact "there are cases where … the total gain of utility may be greater … [T]his applies to all enterprises for which the 'law of increasing returns' is valid" (Wicksell 1958 (1897), 144).

When the first edition of Wicksell's *Lectures on Political Economy* appeared in 1901 there was a whole chapter on "The Gains from Free Exchange." Wicksell gave the same mathematical proof of his point as he gave in the review of Pareto's *Cours*, summing up: "This condition of equal marginal utilities implies – approximately, but not exactly – a position of full economic equality, and in that case – though not otherwise – free competition would secure a maximum of satisfaction to all parties taken together to the exchange" (81).

[5] In "Grundriss einer elementaren Preislehre" (1899, p. 431) Cassel also criticizes Pareto's treatment in the Cours: "und so kommt es, dass es schliesslich gelingt, einen mathematischen Nimbus einem Optimismus zu verleihen, der der 'Harmonieekonomie' unangenehm nahe steht."

Wicksell comes back to the question in the section of the *Lectures* on the theory of production and distribution. In a discussion of the effects of an introduction of labour-saving agricultural machinery, he concludes his argument by stating that in equilibrium in this case, total production must "reach the maximum physically possible" (137). Here it may be appropriate to recall the problems of adding heterogeneous products that Barone discusses in *The Ministry of Production in the Collectivist State* (Hayek, 1935, 255-57). In a footnote to his review of Pareto's *Manuel* (Wicksell 1913, 169) Wicksell says: "Under more realistic conditions, where also prices are variable, it is only possible to formulate or demonstrate [the attainment of the greatest possible total of products] in rough outline, since it is impossible to make direct comparison of separate commodities or services. E. Barone seems to have overlooked this ... He states that under free competition the total income of the society is an exact maximum, although this can be precisely proved only with the simplifying assumptions [that we consider just the question of production, and disregard both distribution and the pricing of finished goods]."

Wicksell then goes on to show by means of an example that normally free competition is sufficient to ensure maximization of production, but that this maximization may presuppose a redistribution of the factors of production.

Wicksell renewed his critique of Pareto after the *Manuel d'économie politique* had appeared in 1909. After criticizing Pareto's proposed method of measuring marginal utility, he goes on to question his handling of the problem of *maximum d'ophélimité*. In order not to have his views confused with Walras's and to maintain the proposition that free competition gives the *maximum d'ophélimité*, Pareto now presents a "peculiar" definition of the concept. To Wicksell, however, the Paretian terminology amounts to nothing but a definition of free competition. Pareto's contention that different persons' utilities are non-comparable is questioned, since it would mean that there would be no "material basis for the idea of justice, whether in government or in social distribution" (Wicksell 1958 (1913), 168). Wicksell then goes on to state his view that, given some simplifying assumptions, free competition can only result in the greatest possible total of products. Not even a socialist society could do better even though it would ensure that the increased production improved the standard of all, and not just of a few. There was no trace of any consideration of this point in Pareto, who was instead "content to derive a more or less self-evident proposition" (170).

In the section on Pareto added to the third edition of the Lectures, Wicksell says that with Pareto's new definition it was obvious that this maximum would prevail under free competition. This was, however, not to say that free competition was satisfactory from a social point of view. Hence, even in its new guise, "Pareto's doctrine contributes nothing" (1934, 82).

With reference to Wicksell's critique of Pareto, Hla Myint (1948) says that Wicksell's criticism of free competition was inspired by his social sympathies, but unjustified with regard to Pareto, who abstracted from the unequal distribution of incomes "simply because it is not possible to formulate a scientific concept of subjective optimum which does not involve interpersonal comparisons of utility except on the basis of a given income distribution" (103).

The psychological level is touched upon again in Hennipman (1982), where Wicksell's critique of Pareto is said to show an uncharacteristic irritation which is "partly due to other than scientific causes, such as the sharp contrast between their ideological positions [and] a strong difference in temperament and style" (48). Wicksell's critique of Pareto may indeed seem somewhat perplexing, in view of Wicksell's own policy proposals on taxation in *Untersuchungen*. The principle of voluntary and unanimous consent advocated for budgetary decisions has a clear Paretian flavour, which is underlined even more strongly when Wicksell writes of "the advantage that one does not at all have to compare the subjective valuations of different persons, but only those of one and the same person" (Wicksell 1896, 164). Wicksell here considers comparisons of the first type "exceedingly difficult, strictly speaking impossible" to make. From the fact that Wicksell's theory of just taxation presupposes a just distribution of property and income, one might conclude that Wicksell's procedure is basically the same as Pareto's, for he too starts his discussion of the maximum ophelimity by assuming a given and just distribution. Wicksell's adverse reaction could be interpreted as a result of a more positive view of the possibility of making interpersonal utility comparisons after the publication of *Untersuchungen*, as shown above.

Wicksell's vacillation may show that to him the question did not concern the correctness of what in modern times are known as the two Fundamental Theorems of Welfare Economics. Wicksell would probably have shared the view of K. Arrow and F. Hahn (1971, 75) that their "informational requirements as stated are far beyond the possible." Since modern welfare economics is based to a large extent on the concept of Pareto optimality and ordinal utility, it has nothing (or very little) to say on the question of competitive equilibrium being a social optimum.

In a more positive vein, Wicksell does quote Pareto's *Cours d'économie politique*, Vol. I, in *Interest and Prices* (16) when discussing the question of how to measure the purchasing power of money. Although he finds that Pareto's *ophelimité élémentaire indirecte de l'or* perhaps fails to accord with ordinary usage, he nevertheless considers that such a definition of the value of money "ought fundamentally to be the least open to theoretical objection."[6]

[6] In the same book Wicksell also comments on Luzzatti's *Prezzi ideali e prezzi effetivi* (1892), but finds his critique of the quantity theory "fantastic and confused" (50). In the end Luzzatti's reasoning becomes so loose "that it is impossible to tell whether by the value of money he means its value in exchange with commodities, or its subjective value, varying from individual to individual" (50). In Lectures (II, p. 144) Wicksell mentions Davanzati as one of the first to hold the quantity theory of money. Also in Lectures (I, 101) he mentions Barone's "Studi sulla Distribuzione" (Giornale degli Economisti, 1896) as a parallel attempt – "elegant but unfortunately unfinished" – to his own of combining Walras's and Bähm-Bawerk's theories into a unified marginalist general equilibrium theory.

Cassel

As is well known, Gustav Cassel was a harsh critic of marginal utility theory. At the beginning of this century he was not alone in his criticism; there were many others, including some Italian neoclassical economists, who also criticized utility theory. Most of them, and their followers, however, restricted themselves to questioning only certain aspects of the theory, such as cardinality or the possibility of making interpersonal comparisons of utility, without any notion of discarding the theory in its entirety. This also goes for Antonelli (1886) and Pareto (1906).

Cournot's assessment (1838) had been more drastic. He refused to even consider utility, implying that market evaluations as shown by prices were quite sufficient in determining demand functions. Cassel, together with Boninsegni (1902) and Barone (1908), was the first of the modern economists to advocate and follow Cournot's more radical approach.

Claims have been made that the revealed preference approach is no more than a variant of Cassel's approach. Such a claim was put forward by Wold, who distinguished three main lines in the development of demand theory (1943, 85-6): 1) the demand function approach, "introduced by Cournot and Walras, and successfully developed by Cassel"; 2) the indifference surface approach, "established by Pareto and prefigured by Edgeworth and Fisher"; and 3) the marginal substitution theory, "mentioned as an alternative already by Fisher and Pareto, and worked out in detail by Evans, Hicks and Allen."

Schumpeter, however, was of the opinion that the Italians had made a greater contribution than Cassel (1067): "[Boninsegni and Barone] realized, of course, the necessity of restrictive assumptions about consumers' behavior from which the properties of demand functions would follow. This distinguishes their views from G. Cassel's, who simply advocated the scrapping of everything behind demand functions to make these the ultimate data."

Myrdal

During the period from 1925 to 1933 – when he still considered himself a 'centrist-theoretician' and a 'pure economic theorist' – Gunnar Myrdal wanted to apply to economic doctrines an 'immanent method' of criticism. His main interest was in criticizing received economic theory that had preserved structures of normative speculation built upon the concepts of utility and welfare.

Gunnar Myrdal started to write his classic *The Political Element in the Development of Economic Theory* ([1930] 1953) with the intention of criticizing harmony economics and laissez-faire dogmas. Already in his dissertation *Price Formation and Economic Change* (1927), Myrdal had subjected the utility theory of value to extensive criticism.

The point of departure for marginal utility theory was that value was determined by utility, rather than the cost of production. What Myrdal considers especially dubious in marginal utility theory is its value theory and its aprioristic tendency. The exchange theory embedded in marginal utility theory is nevertheless regarded by Myrdal as an indispensable foundation of economic theory. As an example, Myrdal takes Fisher's and Pareto's analysis of the value problem. By separating the economic problem from the psychological – by distinguishing between 'pleasure' and 'desire' – they show in fact how a true theory of value becomes empty. The economic problem is reduced to a problem of choice. This only shows how firmly the marginal utility theory is rooted in the utilitarian psychological truism that everyone acts as he wants. From this truism, according to Myrdal, all psychological deductions become either tautological circumlocutions of self-evident facts, or simply false.

In a letter to Cassel on January 18, 1930, Myrdal told Cassel: "To finally refute [marginal utility theorists] you have to show that they do not give any more real explanation than you do with your price formation theory. The old marginal utility theory has to be criticized with the argument that its basic psychology in itself is wrong … The new theory of choice (I. Fisher, Pareto, and others) has to be criticized with the argument that their whole theory (contrary to the old marginal utility theory) is a pure circle."

A second approach – the behaviorist interpretation of choice (theory of choice) – purports to abandon hedonism and its search for a psychological explanation of behaviour, but essentially expresses the same hedonistic view. To Myrdal it leads only to empty mathematical scholasticism, since "logical procedure never yields more than what is fed into it" (98). It only produces new terms for old hedonistic ideas, without any significant change of content. This kind of "logical acrobatics" introduces no empirical element but only revolves in circles. Instead of trying to elaborate on the subjective theory of value it ought, in Myrdal's view, to abandon it completely, as Cournot and Cassel had done. Pareto is criticized for his failure to refrain from "social value theories".

The theory of public finance

The Swedish school of public finance held a strong position at the beginning of the 20th century. On the basis of Walras's general equilibrium theory and the Austrian marginal utility theory, Knut Wicksell and his pupil Erik Lindahl made a penetrating and far-reaching attempt to justify fiscal policies with the help of marginalist economic theory. They argued for the benefit principle of taxation – seen as just since it meant that public expenditures and taxes had to be unanimously approved – which they thought should replace the old principle of payment according to ability to pay. As precursors of their theory – alongside Sax and von

Wieser – there stood some well-known Italian economists to whom both Wicksell and Lindahl also made extensive reference.

The guiding principles of the taxation system that Wicksell and Lindahl laid the grounds for were optimality and linkage. A person's benefits from public goods should be linked to his payments for public goods and produce a Pareto optimal outcome. The question the Wicksell-Lindahl tax scheme answers is how the government can find a way to ensure that each and every person's share of taxes is linked to his marginal benefit. The "trick" is to adjust the tax shares until every person agrees on the desired quantities and qualities of public goods. The Lindahl equilibrium gives an optimal level of public goods, but has a drawback: it relies on the information that the individuals give on their demand schedules for public goods. Here we have a free-rider problem. The opportunistic individual can conceal his true preferences and end up consuming a lot of public goods while paying little. The problem of demand revelation is the drawback that prevents the Wicksell-Lindahl tax scheme from being ideal. On the other hand, even later attempts in this field have shown that the ideal solution does not exist. All tax schemes have some more or less serious flaws.

In *Finanztheoretische Untersuchungen* (Jena 1897), Wicksell begins his discussion of how fiscal policies can be justified rationally by noting that this is basically an ethical question. Most of the book, however, is concerned with how to analyze the character of public goods and how to provide for them from a marginalist economic point of view.

Wicksell quotes Barone's "Sul trattamento di quistioni dynamiche" (*Giornale degli Economisti*, November 1894) when discussing how to incorporate issues of tax incidence into the general equilibrium system that according to Wicksell had to be the right frame of analysis (p. iv). On the problem of taxes on monopoly profits he also gives credit to Pantaleoni's contribution, alongside those of Marshall and Edgeworth (p. v; see also *Lectures* I, p. 93).

The Italian economist discussed at greatest length by Wicksell in *Finanztheoretische Untersuchungen* is, however, Mazzola. Wicksell, who had a good knowledge of the Italian language and was well acquainted with Italian economic literature, devotes five pages to a discussion of Mazzola's work on public goods theory. Even though Wicksell does not find Mazzola's attempt at specifying the grounds for the price of public goods totally satisfactory, he is partly influenced by it and says "it contains a core of truth" (101). Wicksell, however, objects to Mazzola's reasoning that it was self-evident that the prices and the marginal utilities of public goods had to be equal. In his opinion, this view "mit den Ergebnissen der Erfahrung verträgt sich … schlecht" (99). To Wicksell the equality was nothing one could take for granted, but was rather a problem seeking a solution. To the individual the utility and marginal utility of the public goods is dependent on how much all the other citizens are prepared to pay and only in a very small degree on his own willingness to pay. This free-rider problem shows that the extent of the provision of public goods does not depend on the individual, but on "aller Mitglieder der

Gesamtheit" (101). The equality of marginal utility and the price of public goods is therefore not the work of individual actors but rather a result of negotiation between the individual and all other individuals. How these negotiations are to take place and what they will look like Mazzola does not say.

In his account of the development of the modern theory of public finance in *Die Gerechtigkeit der Besteuerung* (1919), Lindahl – who also had a good knowledge of the Italian language – holds De Viti de Marco and Sax to be the two economists who simultaneously and independently of each other made the first attempts at using marginal utility theory to give a causal explanation of the public economy.[7] This new view had an especially fertile influence in Italy, where the problems of public finance have always been at the forefront of economic debate. As the most important contributions, Lindahl mentions those of Mazzola ("I dati scientifici della finanza pubblica", 1890) and Conigliani ("Studi di teoria finanziara" and "Le leggi scientifiche della finanza" 1894). Other Italian contributors discussed by Lindahl are Barone, Loria, Puviani, Einaudi and Tangorra. Even though they did not contribute directly to Lindahl's positive solution of the pricing and financing of public goods, he acknowledges them as having made substantial analytical contributions towards the development of the general frame of analysis in the modern theory of public finance.

[7] Lindahl also mentions Pantaleoni's "Contributo alla teoria del riparto delle spese publicche" (1883) as the first general interpretation of public finance as a "value phenomenon". However, the later attempt by Pantaleoni and his followers to subordinate the problem of taxation to the concept of "political price" does not appeal to Lindahl.

REFERENCES

ANTONELLI G. (1886), *Sulla teoria matematica della economia politica*. Pisa: Nella Tipografia del Folchetto.

ARROW K. and FRANK H. (1971), *General Competitive Analysis*. Amsterdam: North Holland.

BARONE E. (1908), "Il Ministro della produzione." *Giornale degli Economisti* 37 (August, October): 267-293, 391-414. Translated as "The Ministry of Production in the Collectivist State" in F. Hayek, *Collectivist Economic Planning*, 1938. London: Routledge & Kegan Paul.

BONINSEGNI P. (1902), "I Fondamenti dell'economia pura." *Giornale degli Economisti* 31 (February): 15-28.

BUCHANAN J. (1983), "'La scienza delle finanze': The Italian Tradition in Fiscal Theory". In Peter Groenewegen and Joseph Halevi (eds.), *Altro Polo - Italien Economics Past and Present*. Sidney: Frederick May Foundation for Italian Studies, University of Sidney.

CASSEL G. (1899), "Grundriss einer elementaren Preislehre." *Zeitschrift für die gesamte Staatswissenschaft* 55.3: 395-458.

— (1902), "Der Ausgangspunkt der theoretischen Ökonomie." *Zeitschrift für die gesamte Staatswissenschaft* 58.4: 668-698.

— (1903), "Det sociala värdets problem." (The problem of social value) *Ekonomisk tidskrift* 5:258-280.

— (1918), *Theoretische Sozialökonomie*. Leipzig: Scholl.

— (1932), *The Theory of Social Economy*. London: E Benn. Translation of (1918) by S.L. Barron. Reprinted 1967.

COURNOT A. (1838), *Recherches sur les principes mathématiques de la théorie des richesses*. Paris. Translated by N. T. Bacon 1897 as *Researches into the Mathematical Principles of the Theory of Wealth*. New York: The Macmillan Company.

HAGEMANN H. (ed.) (1997), *Zur deutschsprachigen wirtschaftswissenschaftlichen Emigration nach 1933*. Marburg: Metropolis-Verlag.

HAGEMANN H. and KROHN C.-D. (1992), *Die Emigration deutschsprachiger Wirtschaftswissenschaflter nach 1933*, 2nd ed. Diskussionsbeiträge aus dem Institut für Volkswirtschaftslehre (520). Stuttgart: Universität Hohenheim.

HENNIPMAN P. (1982), "Wicksell and Pareto: their relationship in the theory of public finance." *History of Political Economy* 14.1: 37-64.

MYINT H. (1948), *Theories of Welfare Economics*. London: Longmans, Green and Co.

MYRDAL G. (1927), *Prisbildningsproblemet och föränderligheten* (Price Formation and Economic Change). Uppsala: Almqvist & Wiksell.

— (1930b), Letter to Cassel, January 18 1930. In Gustav Cassel, Brevsamling 17, Kungliga Biblioteket, Stockholm.

— (1953), *The Political Element in the Development of Economic Theory*. Translation from the revised German edition of (1930) by P. Streeten. London: Routledge & Kegan Paul.

— (1965), *Interest and Prices*. New York: A. M. Kelley.

PARETO V. (1896-97), *Cours d'économie politique*. 2 volumes. Lausanne.

— (1906), *Manuale di economia politica con una introduzione alla scienza sociale*. Milan. Revised 1909 as *Manuel d'économie politique*. Paris.

—, Translated by Ann Schwier 1971 from the French edition as *Manual of Political Economy*. New York: Augustus M. Kelley Publishers.

SANDELIN B. (2001), "The De-Germanization of Swedish Economics", *History of Political Economy* (forthcoming).

SCHUMPETER J. (1954), *History of Economic Analysis*. New York: Oxford University Press.

WICKSELL K. (1893). *Über Wert, Kapital und Rente nach den neueren nationalökonomischen Theorien*. Jena. Translated by S. H. Frowein 1954 as *Value, Capital and Rent*. London: George Allen & Unwin Ltd.

— (1895), *Zur Lehre von der Steuerincidenz*. Uppsala. Doctoral dissertation, later incorporated as Part One of (Wicksell 1896).

— (1896), *Finanztheoretische Untersuchungen nebst Darstellung und Kritik des Steuersystems Schwedens*. Jena.

— (1897), "V. Pareto, *Cours d'économie politique*." *Zeitschrift für Volkswirtschaft, Sozialpolitik und Verwaltung* 6:159-66. Translated into English as "Vilfredo Pareto's *Cours d'économie politique*" and included in (Wicksell 1958, 141-58).

— (1901), *Föreläsningar i nationalekonomi: Första delen: Teoretisk Nationalekonomi*. Lund: Berlingska Boktryckeriet. Second edition 1911. Third Swedish edition of 1928 was translated by E. Classen 1934 as Lectures on Political Economy, I. London: George Routledge and Sons, Ltd.

— (1913), "Vilfredo Pareto, *Manuel d'économie politique*." *Zeitschrift für Volkswirtschaft, Sozialpolitik und Verwaltung* 22:132-51. Translated into English as "Vilfredo Pareto's *Manuel d'économie politique*" in (Wicksell 1958, 159-75).

— (1919), "Principerna för en rättvis beskattning" (The Principles of Just Taxation). Unpublished manuscript in The Wicksell Archives at Lund University Library.

— (1958), *Selected Papers in Economic Theory*, edited by E. Lindahl. London: Allen and Unwin.

— (1962), "A New Principle of Just Taxation." Translation of part II of *Finanztheoretische Untersuchungen*, in R. Musgrave and A. Peacock, *Classics in the Theory of Public Finance*. London: The Macmillan Company.

WOLD H. (1943), "A Synthesis of Pure Demand Analysis. Part I." *Skandinavisk Aktuarietidskrift* 26:85-118.

The spread of Italian economic thought in the United States, 1750-1850*

Daniela Parisi
Università Cattolica del Sacro Cuore, Milano

1. The relationship between economists from the two continents during the 18th and 19th century: general remarks

1.1. Two traditions within classicism

The knowledge and circulation of Italian economic thought in the United States between the 18th and 19th century falls within the wider frame of the relationships existing between those who dealt in economics and studied the economic phenomena in that period in the whole of the Western world.

The subject calls for some preliminary considerations which are the grounds of this research.

First of all, even though the historical period under examination deals with two distant and utterly different realities, there is one basic characteristic they have in common: the fact that they both fall within the frame of classicism.

The time span we are considering is the one usually referred to as the classical period of economic science: the period of the first attempts at a systematic construction of economic thought, followed by its development, circulation and decline; the period going from the last decades of the 18th century to the first half of the 19th century when debates on theory and economic policy gave way to a set of principles which were to lay the foundations of economic science to the point of becoming "real mind categories".[1]

Economic historiography tends to consider Francesco Ferrara as the leading figure in Italy's intricate scenario of classical economic thought.

The same applies to Henry Charles Carey – though with due specifications – if we consider the development of economic thought in North America in the period going from the first reflections by the intellectuals of the colonies during the second half of the 18th century to the middle of the 19th century.

If we want to tackle the topic of the relationship existing between the economic thought coming out of Italy and the one set forth for discussion in North America,

* I wish to thank Mr. Eugene Santoro (USIS, Milan) and Mr. Joseph Puccio (Library of Congress - Washington, DC) for allowing me to consult the requested material and for having guided me in consulting it at the Library of Congress - Washington, DC.

[1] This expression is used in Bobbio, 1981, pp. 215-216.

we could certainly centre this study on the relationship between Ferrara and Carey. It is a very interesting research because their relationship as scholars in economics was complex, it underwent changes over the years and was rich in controversial ideas and even profound misunderstandings.

One of the paragraphs of this short overview makes specific reference to their connections and to how Ferrara drew Carey to Italy, thus confirming his presence as Ricardo's opponent within the classical frame. However, the relationship between the Italian and North American ideas on economic phenomena cannot be restricted to the couple Ferrara/Carey.

Ferrara searched for Carey, he wrote to him and made this contact in the mid 1800, which is the end of the time period I have been asked to analyse; but this fact says very little about the actual knowledge of Ferrara and of Italian economic thought in North America.

These two economists were undoubtedly the most important ones in their respective scientific circles and the only ones who made a contact on the theoretical debate on economics between the "Italian" and North American tradition. On the other hand I would deem it incorrect from a historical point of view to restrict to these two personalities the reciprocal knowledge of two very different scientific and cultural backgrounds: the relationship between the two cannot exhaust the hundred year long hard and eventful progress which lead to this contact, no doubt the most mature in the history of economic thought.

Between the 18th and 19th centuries the development of economics in the Italian peninsula did not follow a straight path and did not lead to a "school", a uniform Italian economic thought, which was to have Francesco Ferrara as its leading figure in the 1850s.

The same was true in North America where in the same period there was not a unique line of economic thought, and where a different position on the development of economics was formed around every main centre in the States of the Union.[2]

In substance, therefore, the topic of the relationship between Italian and North American economic thought runs the risk of being dealt with superficially, and simplified, unless it is reformulated in the sense of a quest for the position held by the two different traditions within the wide frame of classical thought.

This is the only possible way to approach the knowledge of the two realities, both with their localisms and their cosmopolite tensions; but it is also possible to approach the knowledge of the links and inter-connections within classicism, a long period in the history of economic thought where different specific cultural and scientific sensitivities arose in answer to the questions generated by the fast and deep changes in the world and the circulation of works by the Classics.

---

[2] This diversification is evident in William Barber's collection on American economists and Universities before the 20th century (Barber, 1988).

This kind of research would give answers also to questions on what was the connective tissue between the different groups of economists who brought the scientific debate to maturity in each area in Europe through exchanges and connections between the reflections made in different circles in England, Spain, France, Germany and even America.

If the Western world's economic thought between the 18th and 19th Century is made up of backgrounds and levels matched with complex relationships between localisms, nationalities and continental features, within an overall reconstruction, the specific weft of relations between Italy and North America would then emerge; it would therefore also be possible to account for the two realities in the relations between Northern American and Italian economic thought, the knowledge of American economics in Italy and the knowledge of Italian thought in North America.

Therefore, it is within this wide context that the few data resulting from this specific research take on peculiar meaning; so that this small opening onto this limited portion of reality can contribute to the common work of historians, thus revealing the complexity of history where also all the exchanges for the construction and maturity of systems of ideas hold their place.[3]

In brief, relations between Italian and North American economic thought between the 18th and 19th centuries are part of the history of the complex development of economic thought in the Western world, which also include specific events connected to the transmission of ideas.

1.2. Problems relevant to the circulation of knowledge and the use of language

The second reflection is about the fact that works on economics written in the Italian speaking area were and continued to be little-known by the English speaking public of scholars, particularly in North America. Even Thomas Jefferson, who praised Italy in many ways, in 1787, at the end of his well known *Journey from Paris into the Southern Part of France and Northern of Italy* , was quite decided in saying that it was pointless for American youths to learn Italian: French would be of much greater use to examine closely one's roots.[4]

Though Italian was, and still is, little promoted as a foreign language[5], on the other hand it is evident that intellectuals and scientists from the different areas of

---

[3] I believe that what Antonio Allocati says about the work of economists can apply even more to historians when he writes that "Every thinker's valid contribution is always to be found in partial researches and results " because probably, quoting Claudio Magris, "each entirety offers itself to the laughter of the gods" (A. Allocati, 1990, pp. XXV-XXVI).

[4] Jefferson, 1997. This call to American youth sounds quite peculiar, as himself, Franklin and Madison all knew Italian and kept Italian books in their libraries (Tortarolo, 1986).

[5] There are, of course, important exceptions to what is being said here; for example, think of the vocabulary of musical language.

the Italian peninsula were capable of talking science in Italian and French, many in German, and quite a few may have also been able to converse in Latin correctly but, at least up to the 20th Century, they did not bother to write and publish their works directly in English.[6] This accounts for the fact that, although some Italians are today remembered as influential economists, very few are their scientific contributions present in the catalogues of North American libraries and collections.[7]

Only recently have the English translations of some indispensable resources for the historical reconstruction of economic thought made their appearance.

Some translations can be included among the sources of the history of the formation of economic science only in a broad sense.[8] Others are precisely identifiable as scientific contributions on economics: this is the case of the parts of the works by Antonio Serra and Ferdinando Galiani translated in Monroe's book (1924)[9] of the articles published in the *International Economic Papers* between 1951 and 1967, by the International Economic Association[10]; this is the case also of some classics of the theory of public finance grouped in the collection by Richard A. Musgrave and Alan T. Peacock in 1958[11]; the three recent volumes of *Italian Economic Papers*[12]; of some particular initiatives, among which the *First Principles of Public Finance* by Antonio de Viti De Marco (1936), the *Trattato analitico dei contrabbandi* by Cesare Beccaria (1968),[13] *On Money* by Ferdinando Galiani (1977), the *Reflections on*

---

[6] Among English editions of works by Italian authors published between the end of the 19th century and the beginning of the 20th by British and North American publishers, the following are worthy of a mention (only as examples and without any claim to being complete): the two versions of the manual by Luigi Cossa (1880, 1893) and the five editions (between 1899 and 1920) of Achille Loria's *The Economic Foundations of Society* (Ottaviano,1981; Allocati, 1990); later, over the years, the headings by Ugo Rabbeno and Ulisse Gobbi in the various editions of the "Palgrave Dictionary of Political Economy" and, later, of the "Encyclopaedia of the Social Sciences"; well known books, articles (by Einaudi, Loria, Sraffa, Tajani) and reviews in scientific periodicals (mentioned in other researches to which this essay makes reference); a few decades later, directly in the American edition, the volumes by Attilio Da Empoli (Chicago, 1931) and Marco Fanno (Minneapolis, 1939). On the considerable Loria's success in the Usa, see: Faucci and Perri, 1995, pp. 154-155.

[7] Baldassarri and Ciocca in their introductory notes to the issues of the "Rivista di politica economica" (1997) where they collect the essays forming the *Roots of the Italian School of Economics and Finance from Ferrara to Einaudi,* also state that many works found it difficult to circulate on the International scene because they were published in Italian.

[8] Among these *The New Science of Giambattista Vico* (1948), *The Science of Legislation - Abstracts and Summaries* by G. Filangeri (1976), *On Crimes and Punishments* by C. Beccaria (1963; three copies in Italian of this book were brought to Virgina around 1775 by Mazzei, see Tortarolo, 1986, p. 42), *The Mind and Society. A Treatise on General Sociology* by V. Pareto (1935). About Beccaria in St. Louis see Curti, 1964, p. 40.

[9] By Monroe, (1924, p. 144) the *Breve Trattato* by Serra (1613) "had no influence and attracted little attention among his contemporaries".

[10] These are contributions by economists published in Italian between 1900 and 1962. The complete list is available in the volume by Pasinetti , 1998, pp.387-390.

[11] Mazzola, *The Formation of the Prices of Public Goods*, in Musgrave and Peacock, 1958, pp. 37-37; Montemartini, *The Fundamental Principles of a Pure Theory of Public Finance*, in Id., pp. 137-151; Barone, *On Public Needs*, in Id., pp. 165-167.

[12] Published in 1992, 1993 and 1996, L.L. Pasinetti (editor) (On behalf of Società Italiana degli Economisti, Il Mulino-Oxford University Press).

[13] By Beccaria, the anonymous translation of *A Discourse on Public crime and Commerce* (1769), too.

Political Economy-1771 by Pietro Verri (1986), *Pure Economics* (1898) and some short essays by Maffeo Pantaleoni (1991)[14], are all worth mentioning.[15]

Finally, I believe it is right and proper to remember that during a seminar organised by "The Liberty Fund" on *Liberty and Progress in the early XIXth Century Italian Economic Thought* (1991), the translation of essays by Gian Domenico Romagnosi, Melchiorre Gioia, Francesco Fuoco and Carlo Cattaneo, were made available, though only intended for private circulation.

These publications give us a more complete picture of the development of economic science in time; they partly dispel the lack of knowledge of a relevant part of economic thought and reduce the widespread belief that entire traditions or even single theories do not belong to the history of science or are of no use for the maturing of thought.

They put the main lines of thought, those theories that lead the scientific competition, alongside the intuitions, the questions and reasoning of economists who are certainly to blame for not being at all able to circulate their knowledge: they did not realise that scientific results, the fruit of serious and rigorous individual effort, must also flow into the main stream of thought and skilfully find their place in scientific competition.

Since as early as the first half of the 18th century the English language has certainly been an important means, or rather the pre-condition, to guarantee this position within the international economic debate. No sooner was the use of a common idiom for scientific intercourse abandoned, than the knowledge of other languages beside one's own appeared to be the essential means to pass on and share knowledge. Economics, for instance, becomes a scientific subject when scholars stop using Latin in universities and start stressing the national peculiarities in the development of scientific thought: only then do economists start considering the need of either translating their works or of using an intermediary language which would make their writings known abroad and include them in the debate.

It can be validly assumed that in the 19th century a publication in English would certainly find its place on the shelves of European and North American libraries and then gradually increase its circulation in the other continents in the course of the following century. It was much easier to find a scientific publication by an Italian author in the library of a German or French intellectual. In particular

---

[14] *Observations on the properties of a political price system* e *The Concept of Justice:a Polyseme*, in Bellanca, 1991.

[15] Some texts translated from Italian are included in the Web Page *Archive for the History of Economic Thought*. (Beccaria, *A Discourse on Public Economy*; Botero, *A Treatise Concerning the Causes of the Magnificency and Greatness of Cities*, translated by Robert Peterson, 1606; Croce, *Historical Materialism and the Economics of Karl Marx*, translated by C.M. Meredith, Introd. by A.D. Lindsay, 1914; Davanzati, *A Discourse upon Coins,*Transl. By Toland 1696, Printed by J.D. for Awnsham and John Churchil, at the Black Swan in Pater-Noster-Row; Labriola Antonio, *Essays on the Materialist Conception of History*, transl. by Ch. H. Kerr, Chicago, Ch. H. Kerr Co-operative, 1908).

in the United States the main carrier is undoubtedly the English language, especially if we are to credit the quotations made by Antonello Gerbi which rule out the possibility that publications in French could be regarded as "importable goods" on the American market.[16]

There is no doubt as to the fact that Italian presence in international debate on economic theory is part of a picture where the prominence of certain topics and general lines went together and was favoured by specific historical situations and by a certain methodological conception of history.

Concomitant factors of a different nature meant that for a long time Italian economists were not acknowledged a 'useful' role in the construction of the "gelid succession of theorems". Only these, – it was believed – accumulated the knowledge which generated those theorisings that are regarded as still valid today.[17]

The absence of a great part of Italian economic literature is due to different interests in the field of economics. History tells us that the questions and the approaches to research also have distinctive local features, which bring about the phenomenon which historiography deals with in terms of 'national styles', 'local variants' of the thought that is developed outside historicity, territoriality and the protagonists' actual corporeality.[18]

On the other hand it was also undoubtedly a problem connected to the diversity of social and cultural contexts. The language used by Italian intellectuals did not coincide with the language used by the economists acknowledged by the prevailing historiography on the international market; scientific contributions in economics written in Italian were not translated into English; the circles chosen for debate (academies and journals, before Universities) were not popular with English speaking economists.[19]

2. The first exchanges of notions on economics through the initiatives of scholars and academies.

The circulation of economic thought from Europe to North America occurred as from the 18th Century through such a variety of channels and continuous currents of opinion that historians tend to admit that also in the 19th century the American theoretical debates took shape mainly depending on the ways and times required for the circulation of the classics.

[16] Gerbi, 1955, p. 297.

[17] The debate over these topics has been the subject of interventions by Giacomo Becattini, 1990 and 1998.

[18] Researches on "national styles" in the past fifteen years have been quite numerous. See for example the most recent surveys on Naples and Milan in the volumes edited by Roncaglia, 1995 and by Quadrio-Curzio, 1996, published on behalf of the Società Italiana degli Economisti. The included bibliography helps to broaden the picture on the sources.

[19] One of the first to take part in them was probably Buchanan who was in Italy in 1955-1956.

This means that a network connecting intellectuals from both continents was soon developed as a result of the knowledge of specialised press and personal meetings, both official and unofficial, as well as the activities of scientific associations. This enabled participation in the debates on economics.

Cultural exchange between the United States, France and England dates back to the traditional bonds of nationality[20]; exchange with German speaking economists starts in the years 1820-30: it becomes ever more deep-rooted and develops without pause throughout the century.[21]

As far as the overseas acquaintance with the works by Italian thinkers is concerned, there is no doubt as to the great interest aroused by Latin classics and many Italian authors in the 18th century. The roots of the political and constitutional debate on emancipation and republicanism can be traced in that Neo-Roman theory of liberty, the republican "libertas" of the Romans, intended as the absence of forms of domination, to which Philip Pettit[22] and Quentin Skinner have recently drawn attention.[23]

The debate centered on the link between the freedom of individuals – intended as non-interference or non slavery – and democracy in a political system; it was essentially a political debate rooted on the "Roman" understanding of Republic, resumed by Machiavelli, and afterwards by English constitutionalists and Montesquieu; this line, later shared by American constitutionalists, does not refer to and link up with the field of economic research, though it was a very topical subject in the 18th century.[24]

North American culture was very much concerned with these classical roots when it referred to Italy. Moreover, before the beginning of what is known as the "century of emigration" which saw Italians as protagonists and the start of complex

---

[20] On the means of circulation of French economic thought, which among other things find in the parallel revolutionary aspirations fertile possibility of development, see in particular Rosengarten, 1907; Spurlin, 1984; Mott and Zinke, 1987. In addition to this, it should be mentioned that in the first half of the 19th century J.B. Say's work was a university text book in as many as 14 universities.

For the connection with English thought we must refer to the knowledge of the works of the Scottish moral philosophers, W. Petty and J. Steuart, and, naturally, A.Smith, and in the 19th century to the Malthus-Ricardian rent theory, up to the adoption of the *Principles* of J.S.Mill as the most widely used text book for the teaching of political economy at university level.

[21] In the first half of the 19th century Friedrich List and Francis Lieber are fundamental in helping to understand these links. References to this situation for Italian readers are included in Parisi, 1990a.

See the recent work by Carlson, 1999.

[22] Pettit, 1997. On this American idea of liberty, its meanings, the pre-conditions that make it possible and the limits to the enjoyment of rights, see Elliott and Cownie, 1975; Foner, 2000.

[23] Skinner, 1998. Einaudi is currently preparing the publication of the Italian edition.

[24] It may be interesting to point out that the editions of the *Encyclopaedia Britannica* at the beginning of the 19th century – the 1810, 1817 and 1823 editions – include only two system theorists that can be connected to the Italian tradition, Nicolò Machiavelli and Ludovico Antonio Muratori. The Edinburgh edition was certainly to be found in the libraries of American intellectuals, alongside the *Enciclopédie*, before Americans were offered their own encyclopaedia through an autochthonous initiative (infra, note 82).

financial, commercial, political and cultural exchanges,[25] we can easily trace North American interest in Italy, and especially Italian art. In short, foreigners came to Italy mainly for its art, its climate, its natural beauties and to plunge into its historical wealth, where everyone could trace part of their roots.

As an article in *The Italian Race* reads, Italians have contributed more than others "to the enlightenment of the world and the march of civilisation" and Italy is the "mother of civilisation, of art and of science.... She has given to the world Marcus Aurelius, Dante, Columbus, John Cabot, Leonardo De Vinci, Galileo and in more recent times Volta, Galvani, Garibaldi, Verdi and Marconi... One of the marvels of human history is this extraordinary race that for two thousand years has blessed the world with a succession of geniuses, musicians, authors, creations of inspiration and advancement from which all other people have benefited". The said article was published by the editor of the "National Geographic Magazine" in January 1918.[26]

The same applies to the science of governing: all national systems are considered to be indebted to the Roman tradition both as far as the organisation of government and the juridical system are concerned.

But when it comes to drawing the general outlines of the links between economists, things become a little more complex since there is no intellectual tradition to refer to where scholars in economics of the Italies of the time have views in common with those shared by American intellectuals.[27]

The problem can be dealt with by fathoming the biographies, the collections of letters, the catalogues of libraries and, especially at the beginning, the accounts of the activities of scientific societies. Science historians are aware of the fundamental role played by Academies and Societies from the 18th Century even for the development of an autonomous "public economics" and an autonomous "economics of agriculture" and how important it became for an Italian from then onwards to support the programmes of foreign scientific Societies.[28]

The fact that contacts between Americans and Italians were fragmentary and due more to the will of some individuals than to a tissue of continuative relations accounts for the fact that it is even more difficult to find documents on such reciprocal acquaintance.

In the United States the knowledge of Italy is widened through this channel as well: the American Philosophical Society, founded in Philadelphia

---

[25] The subject of *The Italian Contribution to American Democracy* is interestingly analysed in a Ph.D. thesis published in Boston in 1921, and drawn up by Mariano: the theme is the "americanization", the "synthetization" between natives and Americans of Italian origin. The study clearly shows that very few Italian "scholars" – as far as the proportion of Italians of various generations making contributions – took part in the melting pot phenomenon.

[26] The article is mentioned in Mariano, 1921.

[27] An essential bibliography when analyzing this aspect is constituted by the essays by Pace, 1946, and 1950.

[28] The classical historiography on this subject constitutes the corpus of the secondary sources on which also the researches on primary sources collected in the volumes edited by M. Augello e M. Guidi, 2000b, are based.

in 1769[29], has Italian scientists too among its members and resolves to keep in touch with the main academies in Bologna, Turin, Florence, Milan, Modena and Naples. Academies brought together important and illustrious figures as they were the expression of the different interests present on the territory: scientists, philosophers, artists, poets, men of letter, and inventors had session or plenary assemblies to give an authoritative voice to their involvement, whether professional, public or private, in the problems relevant to the social and institutional tissue; they intended to give their contribution towards the improvement of society as a whole also by making advances in technical and scientific knowledge.

Apparently, the closest connections were with the Neapolitan school of naturalists, with the Grand Duchy of Tuscany and the Royal Academy of Science of Turin. Topics relating to nature, such as "animal and vegetable physics", the characteristics of the soil, maps, the whole natural produce, the conditions of agricultural production and breeding, the diseases of plants and animals, vaccines, cultivation techniques, the transformation and circulation of products (inland navigation and road network), might be listed as the elements which contributed to awaken the interest in economic research in the two environments on both sides of the Ocean.[30]

These topics seem to arouse great interest in many academies; it is quite evident how these were not areas for debate on theoretical themes around which political economists were defining their scientific discourse[31] in the second part of the 18th Century, but rather areas lying along the path gradually leading to the realisation that a special branch of science could be constructed around economy.

As revealed by recent studies, a relevant part of economic topics discussed in societies and academies up until the first half of the 19th century was concerned with economic policy, rural economics, social economics, moral economics, etc.

The above topics do not exhaust the reading of the overall history of economic thought, although it is clear that "the importance of economic discourse in social debates is increasing and tends to go beyond the practical ends to which power would like to restrict it. Its core can be found in the qualifier 'political' that is becoming its distinctive mark".[32]

This phenomenon "regards not only political economy in its more general aspects, but also agronomy, which often goes beyond experimentation and the

---

[29] Franklin became president in January 1770, Jefferson in 1809, Wistar in 1815 and Du Ponceau in 1830. On the main features of the Italo-American relationships through the American Philosophical Society, see *Fabbroni Papers* and *Mazzei Collection* (Tortarolo, 1986).

[30] In 1770, for example, an extensive essay on the cultivation of the Chianti vines and their adaptability to Virginia, Maryland and North Carolina was published and included an approximately one hundred long list of imported plants, including some from Sicily, the Alps and the Apennines.

[31] Naturally, "great" does not mean "exclusive"; let us just consider the importance that topics such as public administration and philosophy had in Italy, or constitutional issues had in North America.

[32] Augello and Guidi, 2000a, p. XIII. (The translation of these excerpts is by the author of this essay).

spreading of farming techniques and becomes what Beccaria defines as "political agriculture": from the reflection on the break up of the feudal system and on the privatisation of mortmain, extensive and intensive cultivation, on tax regulations for landed property, on the latifundium and métayer system, on rural education, and finally – the connection with political economy – on the equilibrium between agriculture and manufacture and on the alternative between free trade and protectionism"; so that, even "when reflection on rural economy appears in its most technical side, ..., the most fascinating themes regard the expediency of innovations and cultivation experiments, the pedagogical and moralizing role or the landowner, ... the efficient organisation of the farm." [33]

Starting from the second and third decades of the 19th century progress and civilization are beginning to be regarded as a natural process which takes place in the market and which needs, alongside the expertise in private management, some kind of "institutional construction"; the State is responsible for it, and is assigned infrastructural tasks in order to combine the development of economy with the development of society on the various levels, education, associations, promotion of science and technology, of social security and moral growth.[34]

The two central figures in the general scenario of the relations between these academic sides are Filippo Mazzei and Luigi Castiglioni; the former from Florence and the latter from Milan their perseverance in keeping in touch with the United States, is witnessed in the reports on the activities of the American academy.

Mazzei – "the venturesome Florentine "[35] – was particularly well-known for his presence in the constitutional debate, for his "unwavering attachment to the United States cause", for his friendship with Franklin first, then with Adams, Madison, Monroe, and finally with Jefferson[36], which lead to the strengthening of the party of free trade and of close business relations with France. As regards the Italian peninsula, he tried to transplant olive trees, vines, mulberry-growing and silkworm breeding to Virginia.

However, this is where he also introduces books: among these are "Davanzati's translation"[37], and the Livorno and Lucca editions of the *Enciclopédie* by Diderot,

---

[33] Ibidem. The essay mentioned constitutes the introduction to the aforementioned volume (Augello and Guidi, 2000b); therefore the remarks it contains are in a way taken from the rich contents of the analyses undertaken by historians in their single studies on Italian Academies.

[34] Ibidem, p. XXVII and pp. XXXIII ff.

[35] This is the way he is defined by A. Gerbi, pp. 290 ff. Starting in the Forties the *Early Proceedings of the American Philosophical Society* will show that Giuseppe Ceva Grimaldi - a leading figure for his responsibilities in government, his studies on the economic conditions and his proposals for the improvement of economy in the Kingdom of Naples, and President of the Regia accademia delle Scienze di Napoli - and Bernardo Quaranta were members of the Society, too.

[36] Giovanni Fabbroni also exchanged letters with Jefferson. The first professor of Foreign Languages to teach at the William and Mary College of Williamsburg, Carlo Bellini, came from Tuscany. (Tortarolo, chapter 2)

[37] This is a work by Bernardo Davanzati, the author of essays on different topics, including: the *Coltivazione toscana delle viti e d'alcuni arbori* (1579*), Notizia de' Cambi*(1581), collections of *Orazioni, Rime*, the *Zibaldone* and the famous *Lezione della Moneta* (1558). The latter was translated into English by John Toland (*A Discourse upon Coins*, London 1696).

the Proceedings of various Italian academies. Some references and some obvious paraphrase of excerpts from the *Meditazioni sull'economia politica* by Pietro Verri have also been found; they are included in the *Récherches historiques et politiques sur les Etats-Unis de l'Amérique Septentrionale*, published in French by Mazzei in 1788.[38]

Castiglioni,[39] was a botanist, a translator of agronomic works, a member of the *Philosophical Society* since 1786, he also attended the meeting in December of that year, the author of a journal on his *Trip in the United States of North America.*[40] He, like Mazzei, was convinced by the common features of climate and nature in the two hemispheres, in North America he looked for food, medical and ornamental plants to acclimatize in Lombardy; furthermore, he was the expression of the Lombards' permanent interest in the United States: Paolo Andreani and Carlo Amoretti, president of the Patriotic Society in Milan (Società Patriottica di Milano), the sender of a set of books to Philadelphia[41], were also members of the first overseas Academy.

An interesting exception to this scenario where naturalistic interests prevail[42], is a study on demographic growth presented in Philadelphia in 1791. These are a number of *Observations on the Probabilities of the Duration of Human Life and the Progress of Population in the United States of America*, posted by William Barton and read on March 18th 1791.[43]

What we would like to point out is that the data used for the study are relative to the populations of Naples and Turin.

The author sets out from the axiom that a numerous population gives contributes greatly to the wealth and the power of a State and that progressive growth in population is at the same time the cause and effect of wealth. He points

---

[38] Mazzei's arguments contained in the fourth chapter of the *Recherches* on the freedom of trade have an "hardly fortuitous analogy" with statements Verri made in the fourth chapter of his *Meditazioni*. (Tortarolo, chapter 4). The *Recherches* also include two essays by Condorcet and one by Turgot, totalling 243 pages. (Gerbi, p.294; Tortarolo, chapter 4)

[39] He was Pietro Verri's nephew and later married his sister; he is a member of the Società patriottica e dell'Istituto Lombardo and becomes the director of the Stamperia Reale in 1807 as well as President of the Accademia di Belle Arti; he is appointed senator.

[40] The diary (*Viaggio negli Stati Uniti dell'America Settentrionale*) is published in Milan in 1790, and translated into German in 1793. Castiglioni is remembered in Lombardy, among other things, also as the man who introduced the false acacia (robinia), that has now become quite common in the area.

[41] An outline on this subject can be found in the essays by Brianta, Rotondi and Parisi in Augello and Guidi, 2000b.

[42] There is evidence that in the 18th century volumes on botany and astronomy arrived from Italy as a result of exchanges with Academies; there is also evidence that the famous text on trigonometry by Antonio Cagnoli was purchased there. It is the *Trigonometria piana e sferica* published in Italian by Cagnoli in Paris in 1782, translated into French (1788), reprinted in Bologna in 1804 (French translation, 1808). Cagnoli is famous for the observatories he built in Paris in 1782 and in Verona in 1785; from 1798 he taught mathematics in Modena's Military Academy and publishes numerous works on astronomy, including a catalogue of stars and an essay on conical sections.

[43] Probably William Paul Crillon Barton, president of the Philadelphia Medical Society, and the author of studies on medicine and botany, published by Carey of Philadelphia.

out that if this is the case then the United States are privileged as far as the possibility of nurturing national vigour is concerned: marriages, the "source of population" should be encouraged.

Scientists found a "statistical-mathematical means" enabling to calculate the growth in population on the basis of data on births and deaths in parish records. These ratios for the calculation of demographic growth were used for England, France, the Swiss Vaud and for a few cities, such as Berlin, Copenhagen and Amsterdam. Barton suggests that the same tools should be applied to data regarding the United States, whilst bearing in mind that in this area the data on births and deaths relevant to the Indian and Black portion of the population are not in the books.[44]

However, on the basis of data on 14 English cities the author shows that on average each marriage 'produces' 4.75 children and that in Paris – according to Buffon – the average is equal to 4.36 births per marriage. Another method for calculation is used by Séjour, Condorcet and La Place: by setting out from the average births per year throughout the French kingdom and by multiplying this result by 25.5 the total population is obtained.

Barton concludes that the empirical confirmation of these calculations can be found in the two cases of Naples (1769) and Turin (1767 e 1768). Many scholars deal with the problem of population in these two cities – as well as in Milan, Mantua, Florence[45] and Rome –: some of them under a political perspective, others in a theoretical perspective by dwelling upon the laws that regulate the relation between subsistence and population, others with a substantially 'agnostic' attitude.[46]

In the first half of the 19th Century the most active among Mediterranean interlocutors seems to be Charles Lucien Bonaparte, prince of Canino, and the author of studies on ornithology, who in 1824 became a member of the *Philosophical Society* and who was to become its official representative during the seventh Congress of the Italian Scientists Association to be held in Naples in September 1846.

[44] The debate that was taking place in the same period between Richard Price and Arthur Young at the Philosophical Society of London on whether to use the number of houses or the number of families as a basis for population estimates is well known. See Glass, 1973, mentioned in Collison Black, 1987; Bertolino, 1926.

[45] In the second half of the century "… the academicians turned to the study of those disciplines upon which the salvation of Tuscany now seemed to depend… to bring their knowledge to bear upon 'the greater argument' which 'concern directly the common happiness and good of mankind' "(Cochrane, 1961, p. 220).

[46] This distinction between different ways of tackling the problem of population is proposed by Demarco, 1987.

3. Italian economists included in the scientific literature circulating in the United States

In the first part of the 19th Century the chances to become acquainted with the thought of Italian economists increase. The *American Society* receives a growing number of works in Italian, as well as Italian dictionaries: it is mainly the case of naturalistic studies but, among other works, in 1834 it is also possible to find the 1826 Neapolitan edition of the *Principi* by Gianbattista Vico, and in 1840 the historical research by Gian Francesco Galeani Napione on the "first discoverer of the New World" (1808 e 1809) and the *Statistica dell'Italia* by Luigi Serristori, published in Florence only the year before.

It would be quite realistic to say that towards the mid-19th century the first historical reconstructions of economic thought, the works by John Ramsey McCulloch in 1845 and by Travers Twiss in 1847 start to circulate in English. In the former, *The Literature of Political Economy,* the Italian works listed come from the *Raccolta Custodi*,[47] while in the latter, *View of the Progress of Political Economy in Europe since the Sixteenth Century*, there is an entire lecture dedicated to the Italian debate on monetary disorder.

American intellectuals were acquainted with the encyclopaedias published in Europe: the Lucca and Livorno editions of the *Enciclopédie,* and the various editions of the *Encyclopaedia Britannica*, were authoritative sources of knowledge; the definitive circulation of the *Encyclopaedia Britannica* in the American continent took place in the last decade of the 19th Century, when the first American version was published.[48]

Until 1823 the only Italian economist analysed in the *Encyclopaedia Britannica* is Ludovico Antonio Muratori. Five are included in the *Supplement* to the fourth, fifth and sixth edition in 1824, namely: Cesare Beccaria, Gaetano Filangeri[49], Paolo Frisi, Ferdinando Galiani, Antonio Genovesi. On top of these also Beccaria and Galiani are included again in the edition written between 1830 and 1842 under the heading *Political Economy*; furthermore, reference is made to Pietro Verri in the explanation of Phisiocracy for his *Meditazioni*, and to Salustio Antonio Bandini, for his analysis of commerce in the *Discorso Economico*.

The descriptions are written using French, English and also Italian sources directly. The following dictionaries are mentioned: the *Biographie Universelle* by Guillon (1816), the *Biographical Dictionary* by Chalmers (1814), the *General Biography* by Aikin (1815); the collection of *Scrittori Classici Italiani di Economia Politica* and a few writings: the *Correspondance par le Baron Grimm*, the 1797

[47] McCulloch's *Outlines of Political Economy* circulated in the John McVickar edition (New York 1825); Mc Vickar was Professor at Columbia College until 1857.

[48] See, infra, no. 82.

[49] The first two volumes of his *The Science of Legislation* were published in London in 1806.

new edition "of Morellet's French translation of the *Treatise on Crimes and Punishment*", the *Meditazioni* and the *Memorie del signor dom Paolo Frisi* (Milan, 1787) by Pietro Verri, the *Discourse preliminaire* by Say[50], the *Elogj d'illustri Italiani* (1786-1789) by Angelo Fabroni, mentioning Paolo Frisi in the index.

It may be that towards the mid-19th century both the *Storia della Economia Pubblica in Italia, ossia Epilogo critico degli Economisti Italiani* by Giuseppe Pecchio (Lugano, 1829), probably in its 1930 French edition by Leonard Gallois and the *Scienza del ben vivere sociale e della economia degli Stati - Parte storica e di preliminare* by Lodovico Bianchini (Palermo, 1845), included in the Kress catalogue, were known.

The real novelty is the first Encyclopaedia by an American publisher: the *Encyclopaedia Americana. A Popular Dictionary of Arts, Sciences, Literature, History, Politics and Biography brought down to the Present Time, Including a Copious Collection of Original Articles in American Biography*. Francis Lieber is the editor, aided by E. Wigglesworth and T.G. Bradford, and it is published between 1829 and 1833 by Carey and Lea of Philadelphia.[51]

In order to understand the atmosphere in which this publication is conceived, we must at least remember that in the course of these few decades North American economists draw closer on one hand to the line of classicism represented by Jean Baptiste Say which tends to stress the subjective sides of the economic act and the vision of the phenomena as an "equilibrium system", on the other to the setting out of German "economic romanticism".

The 1821 Boston edition (Wells and Lily) of the English translation of Say's work[52] and the fourteen later editions, are single events which reveal the original maturing of economic thought in North America in this first part of the 19th century.[53]

This episode is part of a scenario where other events that give a distinctive character to the overall picture on economic thought fit in. Among these, the 1817 publication of Say's *Catechism of Political Economy* on the part of Carey in Philadelphia, who a few years later will publish the American edition of the writings by Alexis de Tocqueville; also in 1817, the publication of the *Treatise on Political Economy* by Antoine Destutt de Tracy on the part of Milligan in Georgetown D.C.; the close relations between Destutt de Tracy, Jefferson, and the University of Virginia, where in1825 Say's *Treatise* is adopted, as, on the other hand, will happen later in Harvard University in Cambridge, in Yale as from 1827 and in Brown University in

[50] A long quotation of Galiani is taken from here (E.B., VII ed., 1842, p. 274).

[51] Since 1831 (Volume V) T.G. Bradford was added to Wiggleworth. Blanchard becomes a member of the Philapelphia publishers in 1835. Vol. IX to XII are published in1832; vol. XIII in 1833; volume XIV is edited by Henry Vethake in 1847.

[52] It is in fact a re-edition of the English translation published in London that same year, with additional notes by C.C. Biddle.

[53] Parretti, 1983.

1828-1829; the critical notes by Biddle on Ricardo; the meetings between Say and Alexander Everett and Jacob Newton Cardozo; the unexpected flop of the works by Ricardo, Malthus and James Mill, allowing for a few exceptions.[54]

In this context the American pride for the acquired independence clearly emerges; the identity of the American nation is sought for not with reference to its European roots any longer, but rather around an "original" vision of the world.[55] From the point of view of political economy this new attitude leads the different political groups on the American scene to converge on the famous "Compromise of Revenue Tariff" of 1833.[56]

The two figures who can be considered pioneers from this particular point of view are Francis Lieber and Friedrich List.[57] The latter, who arrived in the United States in 1825, proves he can express in an effective and brilliant way the ideas of the circle of Philadelphia protectionists, a reference point also for the publisher Carey, where in 1827 List publishes his *Outlines of American Political Economy*.[58]

It is in this kind of environment that the *Encyclopaedia Americana* comes to light. This latter is actually based on the seventh edition of the *Allgemeine Deutsche Real-Encyklopaedie fur die Gebildeten Stande German Conversation-Lexicon*, published in Lipsia by Brockhaus between 1827 and 1829.

This source proves to be particularly useful to place "American" thought within the scenario of political economy, since Francis Lieber much extended the descriptions under the headings of political economy, a discipline whose "definition ... has been a subject of some discussion... (...) ...has had his stages of progress, and some of its professors consider it now to be placed upon as firm a basis, and reduced to a system of rules as completely demonstrated, as that of astronomy since the time of Newton; while others consider the present state of political economy as far below a full development and demonstration of its principles...".[59]

---

[54] On the subject, see Teilhac, 1936; the essay by Whitaker, in Barber, 1988, pp. 15-41.

Clearly, just as not all economists were anti-Ricardians, there were economists who were against Say's approach. For each of the themes mentioned here, refer to the author's essay (Parisi, 1990a) which is intentionally 'vitiated' by the language employed (Italian): this was used precisely with the intention of widening the knowledge of North American thought (from intellectual history, to the history of economic thought and of the connected debates on political economy) in Italy, as this was almost totally ignored by Italian historiography.

[55] The analysis of the unique features of the intellectual life of the inhabitants of the North American continent is the central topic of the fundamental works by Wolff, 1944 and by Curti, 1964.

Pace, in the essays mentioned, writes that while in the age of Franklin relations with Europe are on an equal basis, from Jefferson onwards Europe is looked upon with the interest of an antiquarian and in the 19th century the first proud detachment from the origins takes place.

[56] It is the compromise on tariffs, sought by a diverse group of politicians and intellectuals and strengthened around a laissez-faire conception, in the sense of the defence of the individual's safety and property.

[57] Historiography is particularly exhaustive on the subject. See analysis and reference in Parisi, 1990a, par. 2.2.

[58] Galbraith, 1988 mentions the group of List and Carey in one of the chapters on "The Great Classical Tradition", undertitled "Around the margins" (pp. 89-102).

[59] *Political Economy*, E.A., vol. X, 1835, pp. 217-224.

Of particular interest the headings: Americanism, Capital, Consumption and, obviously, Political Economy, Smith, Ricardo e Say.

The author seems to be totally absorbed by two objectives: first of all the mission of contrasting some fundamental definitions given by the major economists (Smith, Ricardo, McCulloch, Say): their attitude towards abstract speculation, their "mystical, solemn, and somewhat pompous air", their conception of capital as stock, the doctrines of free trade and natural rate of wages, the rent theory; secondly, to state the centrality of the conception of "productive faculties and means" – intended as the combination of the "capacity and resources for producing things that have an exchangeable value" and that make the improvement of their institutions viable – and of the role of demand.[60]

The only Italian economist mentioned under the heading Political Economy is Antonio Genovesi: he appears, with his two volumes of the *Lezioni di Commercio ossia d'Economia civile* (Bassano, 1769), in the list of the "principal writers on political economy", as far as the mercantile system is concerned.

Beccaria and Carli are included in the second volume, Fabbroni, Filangeri and Galiani in the fifth, Gioja in the fourteenth. Among these authors, Filangeri is referred to as an expert in legislation and Beccaria as an expert in criminal law, author of numerous essays on different topics and member of the circle *Il Caffè*, together with "Visconti, Verri and others". Therefore the number of economists around whom an autonomous heading of the dictionary was constructed is four.

As for "Carli, Giovanni Rinaldo", his relevance is due to his position as president of the Consiglio delle Finanze (Council of Revenues) in Milan: on the other hand it is precisely on account of this that he was already known in the United States, for his remarks made in the *Lettere Americane* of 1777-1778 on the subject of the form of Austrian government in the Ducate of Milan under Marie Therese and Joseph II, and for the parallelism he made between this experience and the philanthropic and paternalistic despotism of ancient Incas. Here he is also remembered as an expert in astronomy and naval science.[61]

Giovanni Fabbroni is referred to as an Italian philosopher "who distinguished himself for his attention to political economy, agriculture and physical science", secretary of the Accademia dei Georgofili and member of the Società Italiana delle Scienze.

"Galiani, Ferdinand" is remembered for his "celebrated work" *Trattato della Moneta* of 1750 and for his *Dialogues*, where he expresses himself against the policy of free export of grains, in controversy with the French school.

The biographical notes of Melchiorre Gioia are taken from a text by Silvio Pellico, probably the review in four parts of *Del Merito e delle Ricompense. Trattato*

---

[60] E.A., vol. V, pp. 217-224.

[61] It is worthwhile reminding the reader that Italian interest for the American continent includes South America, though this area does not have bearings with economics as a science but rather with "contour" disciplines, which I believe have in any case accompanied the process of individuating a specific field for the study of economic phenomena. With reference to this, the second part of the debate taking place in the new world is particularly noteworthy: among the main figures also Carli with his *Lettres Américaines*, Boston [ma Parigi], 1788. Isidoro Bianchi donates the second edition of this book (Cremona, 1781-83) to Franklin. (Gerbi, cit.)

storico e filosofico di Melchiorre Gioia, autore del nuovo prospetto delle scienze economiche which appeared in the first volume of *Il Conciliatore*, in 1818.

Finally, under "Verri, Alexander", "Peter Verri" is also mentioned, who published "several valuable works… on political economy and legislation…".

Francis Lieber is the editor of the encyclopaedia, greatly influenced by the original German source, though there are some differences that are worth mentioning in this paper.

The headword *Nationalokonomie, politische Okonomie ober Staatwirtschaftslehre* (vol. VII, p. 688) is much shorter than the one dedicated in America to *Political Economy*; as for the Italian situation, in addition to Genovesi, the author dedicates a few lines to the *Trattato delle cause che possono far abbondare li regni d'oro e d'argento, dove non son miniere* (1613) by Antonio Serra; finally, the bibliography includes the *Storia dell'economia pubblica* by Pecchio.

Among the headings of single authors Alessandro Verri is not included (therefore Pietro is not mentioned, either) and the part dedicated to the economic contents of the work by Giovanni Fabbroni and Gaetano Filangeri is irrelevant. Many works by Galiani (who is mistakenly referred to as Fernando) are mentioned, and more precisely the unpublished letters with his French contemporaries; Carli's *Delle Monete* is also mentioned.

Henry Charles Carey is the son of the publisher of the American version of the *Encyclopaedia*.[62] He is responsible until the middle of the Thirties for the selection of books for publication; later, after he retires from business, starting from 1835, he concentrates exclusively on research and on his activity as a publicist, and becomes a reference point for the scientific world and for the political debate in the United States.

Carey is considered by historians as the emblem of the particular form taken on by 'economic liberism' for the greater part of the 19th century in the United States, where, right from the days of the Constitution, the principle of personal freedom tried to find some sort of mediation with national feeling and the promotion of general welfare and regulation of commerce. Many elements account for his reputation as the leader of an intellectual movement active towards the middle of the century: the size of his eclectic production of paperwork, the ability with which he set up his network of contacts with the international scientific circles and the particular attention in the training of his group of students.

Francesco Ferrara addressed a letter to him from Turin on December 15th 1851:[63] "I want to know all that was written in America about your method on

---

[62] For the main bibliography on the Careys and their circle see Green, 1985; Carey-Baird, 1885; Morrison, 1965, 1968, 1986; Wills, 1925; Barber, 1988; Eiselen, 1932; Phinney, 1918; and others.

[63] The letter is kept at the "Edward Carey Gardiner Collection" in the archives of the "Historical Society of Pennsylvania". For an analysis of the correspondence between 1851 and 1854, see Parisi, 1990b, Ferrara must have been struck by the interest shown in Carey by John Stuart Mill in his *Principles of Political Economy* del 1848.

rent", he wrote. He also asked him to "skim through the booklet" he was sending him, "my introduction to Bastiat's Harmonies, and let me have your remarks, so that I can use them in my preface to your Principii".[64]

On May 20th 1853 he sends him the volume of the Biblioteca dell'Economista with the translation of his *Principii*. The parcel contains a letter where Ferrara renews "the compliments I believe you deserve", confirming that his "theories are taken in the greatest consideration in Italy at the moment and are greatly favoured" and that he considers "new and fertile the perspective under which you placed the theories on Rent and on the Distribution of Wealth". In his reply Carey thanks his colleague whom he believes to master the subject.

This scientific relationship is built upon exchanges of letters and on writings by Carey translated by Ferrara[65], but especially on the famous *Prefazioni* to the *Biblioteca dell'Economista* that Ferrara used to spread his vision and his interpretation of the economic phenomena and of "Americanism in economics" across Europe and North America.[66]

The relationship between Carey and Ferrara is made of analogies and differences. There are clear differences in method and in the definition of economics: the science of wealth and utility for Ferrara, and the science of society (often unclearly defined) for Carey; they also hold distant positions with reference to the debate on the system of tariffs.

The relationship is also built on a deep consonance about some theoretical ties. They came together in trying to give an answer to the eternal issue of the value of commodities which would indicate the origin of the economic act in the subject performing that same act; because everywhere it is "demand that originates supply" as the individual finds the utilities for the satisfaction of his needs in specific commodities and resolves to procure himself those commodities through exchanges where expected utility and cost are in equilibrium.

In short, Ferrara in the first place makes his edition of the work of Bastiat, published in1851,[67] known in North America; and therefore the controversy on the conception of utility, a topic he will resume in 1856 in the introductory notes to the volume where he translates the work of John Rae[68] and in 1873 with reference to the *Manual of Political Economy* (New York, 1853) by Peshine Smith.[69]

---

[64] The translation of these paraghraphs from the Italian letters are by the author of this essay.

[65] Some aspects of this story emerge from studies which have already been published (1989, 1990a, 1990b) and by the previously unpublished text, presented and made available for private circulation only at the Seminar held at the University of Parma in September 1994 as part of the research project on the "national styles" of political economy; I was asked to analyse the development of the two streams of thought within the classical framework.

[66] Historiography is rich in studies on mainly specific aspects of Ferrara's economic analysis, also analysed in the biographical book by Faucci, 1995.

[67] B.E., 1-XII, 1851.

[68] B.E., 1-XI, 1856.

[69] B.E., 1-IX, 1873, p. 927.

Ferrara's interest in Carey probably depends upon the reputation the American author enjoyed in Italy for his opposition to Ricardo's rent theory. Several moments of Ferrara's life prove this: his course at University in 1851-52 dedicated to the distribution theory, the publication of Carey's work and a number of documents on the *Questione della priorità fra Federico Bastiat e H.C.Carey* in the *Biblioteca dell'Economista* in 1853[70], on the *Sunto della scienza economica* by Cherbuliez in 1864[71] and, again, in 1873[72], on *Lezione VIII* on rent by Rossi and the *Ordinamento dell'Industria* (1848) where Banfield – "great inventor" with reference to the issue of value and "importer of continental and American feelings and ideas" – resumes the terms of the controversy between Ricardo and Carey.[73]

This criticism of Ricardo and Ricardians, expressed by Carey, and later by Bastiat, but already formulated by Say, Fontenay, Banfield, and only partially by Rossi, are stimulated in Ferrara by Mill's *Principles*.[74] This same criticism is shared and explained to students in Italy and in other University classes in that same period.[75]

In my opinion the relationship between these two economists gives relevance to the critical reflection on some 'classical' theoretical ties, a reflection brings to the foreground some contributions that are typical of traditions other than the Anglo-Saxon one.

For the Americans this coincides with the maturing of contacts with German speaking economists: this constitutes a distinctive feature of the period we are examining, but in particular it brings about future developments for economic science in the United States.

---

[70] B.E., I- XIII, 1853. On the link between these lectures and the study on distribution theory which Ferrara was undertaking in that period, see Barucci and Asso, 1986.

[71] B.E., 1-X, 1864. The volume includes part of the *Corso di economia politica* by M. Chevalier; in the introduction to the volume, Ferrara makes reference to the "strange rent theory", which Ricardo "held on to" (p. LXXXVII). Cherbuliez (Paris, 1862) in the chapter *Della Rendita* mentions the "third school" - namely Carey, Bastiat and Banfield.

[72] B.E., I-IX, 1873.

[73] I have made a contribution on the positions of mid-19th century economists with reference to Carey at the Annual Meeting of the History of Economics Society held in Richmond, Va, June 1989; the paper is included in the collection of the proceedings of the meeting and its Italian translation can be found in Riss, 1989.

[74] Ferrara at the same time studies the role of "Mr Rae" and "Opedyke" (see Parisi, 1990b).

My analysis of the relationship between Ferrara and Carey (1989) fits in well with the precious notes by the editors of the previously mentioned *Lezioni di economia politica* by Ferrara.

[75] See Francesco Corbani's lectures from the course of Social Economics in the University of Siena in 1852-1853. In the second part of the first volume, paragraph 105, he analyses Carey, Bastiat, Rossi, Banfield and mentions Ferrara. Information may have been taken from the work of Antoine-Elysée Cherbuliez, *Riche ou pauvre, exposition des acuses et des affets de la distribution actuelle des richesses sociales*, Paris 1840, which he mentions.

4. Final remarks

If we consider the data resulting from my research on the acquaintance with the economic thought of Italian economists in the United States in strictly quantitative terms, these would seem to be rather poor. My studies are not complete and do not exhaust all consultable sources, therefore results descend from the tracks that were followed. By exploring in different directions, archives and libraries,[76] other contributions may surely give a better picture.

If money, taxation and agriculture were the three topics which early economic literature converged upon in the former colonies of America[77], we must come to the conclusion that direct contacts with Italian figures, eclectic and versatile Italians, took place mainly with reference to the exchange of knowledge on the third group of subjects. For scholars and travellers of the 18th and 19th century the description and study of nature was undoubtedly a way of becoming acquainted with the physical structure and the natural component of the economic system, but the ground on which these contacts took place – a central role was played in this respect by the Academies – was quite distant from the field of political economy.

As from the 18th century, intellectuals started to exchange paperwork, including a few Italian books on economics; in addition to this, in importing knowledge from Europe through economic literature in English, French and German, Americans came across names of Italian economists and formed a very general idea of their role in political economy.

Generally speaking, Italy in the 19th century remains an interesting region as far as art is concerned, a peninsula worth visiting, notwithstanding a few "great inconveniences", as indicated by the American Encyclopaedia under the headword *Italy*.

Many Italian scientists are considered to be authoritative in the fields of physics, astronomy, mathematics and biology; a few experts of the new scientific discipline of economics would seem to emerge from these fields where "Italian" science has undoubtedly made history: Beccaria, Galiani, Verri, Genovesi, Carli, Fabbroni, Gioia.

Some of them are remembered for contributions embracing law, administration and economics.

On the other hand, very little knowledge was imported from Italy, whether directly or indirectly, with reference to one of the great "American" topics: I am referring to the reflection on money.[78] The sources I consulted prove that the

---

[76] A track to follow could be to examine the historical catalogues of the first Universities; or a research focussing on Lorenzo Da Ponte, the famous importer of books from Latin countries.

[77] I do not believe this idea is contrasted by historians, right from the classical essay by Seligman, 1927.

[78] Money is a set of questions "debated among scholars for centuries", including the time when American government was facing the problem of "financing its war of independence" (Rolnick, in Madison, 1997).

works by Davanzati and Galiani were known, as well as, collectively, the authors included in the Custodi Collection, which I never found mentioned for contributions on money.

The lack of references in the sources I consulted which surprised me the most is relative to the following authors: Antonio Serra, Gasparo Scaruffi and Geminiano Montanari. The former, who appeared in the *German Conversation-Lexicon* and who was expunged by Lieber in his editing of the *Encyclopaedia Americana*, will enter economic literature in English around the middle of the 19th century thanks to the manuals by Twiss and Pierson and later on, with reference to the United States in particular, due to the translations of the Cossa's works and to the ninth edition of the *Encyclopaedia Britannica*.[79]

Scaruffi, will be mentioned in American publications for his *Alitinonfo* starting from the second half of the 19th Century by Ingram (1888), Cohn (1894), Monroe (1923 and 1924), Gobbi (1934) and Schumpeter (1954); he is included in the *Kress Library of Business and Economics-Catalogue 1818-1848* and his work was micropublished in 1974.

Montanari is still mentioned in chronologies and dictionaries mainly as an astronomer and mathematician. Before Haney (1911), Monroe (1923 and 1924) and Schumpeter have regarded him as a money theorist[80], Hanna Robie Sewall, in 1901, included him in her history of value theory, in the paragraph called *Conception of exchange value as dependent upon wants. Davanzati, Montanari, Barbon.* She understood the depth of his definition of money as the measure of wants and passions; this conception enables to regard the amount of money one is willing to spend for a commodity as the measure of the want for that commodity: wants, in other words, measure the value of things, and the money one is willing to spend conforms to this.

The case of these three authors is very interesting in a historical perspective: they dealt with an issue that was of topical interest at the time and that nowadays we know was aptly studied by economists belonging to the Italian tradition. Their absence was due to factors not necessarily connected to their intrinsic scientific value. It shows on one hand the scarce visibility outside the limited boundaries of their milieu of many thinkers of the past belonging to what were considered to be lesser traditions, and on the other of the persistence of cultural stereotypes which influence the way the biography of well-known scientists is perceived.

It must also be noted that Gianrinaldo Carli and Giovanni Fabbroni are both known and mentioned in the United States, but that there is no trace of their works on money.[81]

---

[79] See, infra, no. 82.

[80] Monroe (1924) in particular defines him the first to clearly formulate the quantitative theory and to deal with it extensively.

[81] I am referring to: G. Carli, *Nuove osservazioni sulla riforma della moneta* (1770) and to: G. Fabbroni, *Lega, valore e proporzione reciproca delle monete* (1786) and to *Lettera circa il sistema monetario napoletano (*1794). We find also Gian Battista Vasco in Schumpeter (1954), Theocaris (1961), and Baumol and Goldfeld (1968).

In the specific case of Serra, Scaruffi and Montanari, I believe the translation of Cossa's works played a fundamental role in making them known and in letting their works circulate.[82] In any case, some absences constitute "historical events" in their own right.

There is a final remark I would like to make, though very briefly: all information resulting from this research, but in particular each of the investigations which were necessary in order to bring each of the data to light has contributed to historical knowledge in two ways, at least. First of all, it forced me and my reader to concentrate on aspects and constitutive moments of Italian and American economic thought between the 18th and 19th century, where these data come from; secondly it contributed to the knowledge of these scientific contexts included in the general frame where they are situated and developed. We could therefore conclude with a proposal for a reflection upon a point of fact: data of little importance from a quantitative point of view, such as those emerging from this research, do not always imply, indicate or correspond to qualitative irrelevance of the historical facts which these data help to focus and highlight.

---

[82] Parisi, 1988.

The effects of the circulation of Serra through Cossa in my opinion have been greater than through the work by Custodi.

If the circulation of an author's ideas is connected also to the knowledge of it outside the restrictive boundaries of a nation, it is undoubtedly true that the change regarding Serra's contribution takes place when the manuals by Twiss (London, 1847) and Pierson (Amsterdam, 1866) are published, but even more when an extensive analysis is made by Macmillan publishers with the *Guide* (London) and the *Introduction* (London-New York) by Luigi Cossa (1880 and 1893). In the same years Serra is also featured in the Encyclopaedia Britannica (ed. 1875-1889, vol. 19, p. 357).

It should be noted here that the ninth edition of the "Encyclopaedia Britannica", edited between 1875 and 1889 was on sale also on the American market, through an authorised edition (Charles Scribner's Sons), which sold 45,000 copies; publications in the United States were not protected by copyright control and this led to the presence on the American market of different 'versions' of the "Encyclopaedia". (see: E. B., 1963, vol. 8, p. 376). Many Italian economists are included in the volumes of this ninth edition: Bandini, Genovesi, Galiani, Beccaria, Verri, Carli e Filangeri, Mengotti, Ortes, Serra, Vasco, Gioja (under *Political Economy*, grouped in the Italian section and subdivided according to periodi); the description is backed by a bibliography including Cossa, 1876 e 1878 (English translation, 1880), Pecchio, 1829.

Main Bibliographical References

Allgemeine Deutsche Real-Encyklopaedie fur die Gebildeten Stande German Conversation-Lexicon, 1827-1829, Leipzig, Brockhaus.

Allocati A. edited by (1990), *Carteggio Loria-Graziani (1888-1943)*, Ministero per i Beni Culturali e Ambientali - Pubblicazioni degli Archivi di Stato - Fonti XI, Roma.

American Philosophical Society for the Promotion of Useful Knowledge (Compiled by One of the Secretaries, from the Manuscript Minutes of its Meetings from 1744 to 1838), 1884, *Early Proceedings*, Philadelphia, Press of McCalla & Stavely.

American Philosophical Society, 1838/39/40-1886, *Proceedings*, voll. I-XXIII, Philadelphia.

American Philosophical Society, 1969, *Early Transactions*, Published in the American Magazine during 1769. Reprinted in facsim. With a Commemorative Essay by a member of the Society, Philadelphia.

Asso P.F., Barucci P. and Ganci M. (ed.) (1990), *Francesco Ferrara e il suo tempo*, Bancaria editrice, Roma.

Augello M.M. and Guidi M.E.L. (ed.) (2000a), *Associazionismo economico e diffusione dell'economia politica nell'Italia dell'Ottocento - Dalle società economico-agrarie alle associazioni di economisti*, F. Angeli, Milano, 2 volls.

Augello M.M. and Guidi M.E.L. (2000b), *Da dotti a economisti. Associazioni, accademie e affermazione della scienza economica nell'Italia dell'Ottocento*, in Id., 2000a.

Baldassarri M. and Ciocca P. (ed.) (1997), *Radici della scuola italiana di economia e finanza da Ferrara (1857) a Einaudi (1944)*, "Rivista di politica economica", June-July.

Barber W. (1988), *Breaking the Academic Mould*, Wesleyan Univ. Press, Middletown, Conn.

Barucci P. and Asso P.F. (1986), *Nota introduttiva*, in F. Ferrara, *Lezioni di economia politica - Parte prima - Corso per l'anno accademico 1856-57*, Roma (coll. F.F., *Opere Complete*, vol. XI).

Barucci P. and Carpenter K. (compiled by) (1985), *Italian Economic Literature in the Kress Library 1475-1850*, Boston-Baker Library for Business Administration-Kress Library of Business and Economics (in Collaboration with A. Calcagni Abrami and R. Reinstein Rogers), Banco di Roma.

Baumol W.J. and Goldfeld S.M. (1968), *Precursors in Mathematical Economics: An Anthology,* London School of Economics and Political Science, London.

Becattini G. (1990), P*er una critica dell'economia contemporanea: alcune considerazioni e una proposta*, in Id., *Il pensiero economico: temi, problemi e scuole*, coll. "Biblioteca dell'Economista", VIII Series, Third Section, Vol. III, Utet, Torino.

Becattini G. (1998), in "Il Sole-24 Ore", November 15th, n. 314, p. 30.

Beccaria C. (1963), *On Crimes and Punishments*, by H. Paolucci, The Bobbs-Merrill Company, Indianapolis.

Beccaria C. (1968), *Tentativo analitico sui contrabbandi (Il Caffè, vol. I, 1764) - An Attempt at the Analysis of Smuggling*, in Baumol and Goldfeld, pp. 147-149.

Bellanca N. (1991), edited by and Introduction, *The Liberalist Political Economy of Maffeo Pantaleoni*, in "Economists' Archives", 2, Supplement to "Storia del Pensiero economico", 22.

Bertolino A. (1926), *Il problema della popolazione nel pensiero di G. Filangieri e le sue relazioni con le correnti intellettuali del secolo XVIII*, in "Studi senesi", XV, fasc. 2.

Bergin Th. G. and Fisch M.H. (1948), by *The New Science of Giambattista Vico*, Cornell

University Press, Ithaca and London (1961; revised 1968; The John Hopkins University Press, 1976).

BERTOLINO A. (1926), *Il problema della popolazione nel pensiero di G. Filangieri e le sue relazioni con le correnti intellettuali del secolo XVIII*, in "Studi senesi", vol. XV, fasc. 2.

BOBBIO N. (1981), *La teoria dello Stato e del potere*, in Id., *Max Weber e l'analisi del mondo moderno*, Torino, Einaudi.

BRIANTA D. (2000), *Il dibattito economico-agrario nelle accademie lombarde tra Sette e Ottocento*, in M.M. Augello and M. Guidi, 2000, pp. 3-38.

BUXBAUM M.H. (1987), *Critical Essays on Benjamin Franklin*, G.K. Hall and Co., Boston.

CARLSON B. (1999), *Wagner's Legacy in America: Re-Opening Farnam's Inquiry*, in "Journal of the History of Economic Thought", Sept., pp. 289-310.

COCHRANE E.W. (1961), *Tradition and Enlightenment in the Tuscan Academies 1690-1800*, The University of Chicago Press.

COLLISON BLACK R.D. (1987), *La teoria della popolazione prima di Malthus in Inghilterra ed in Irlanda*, in G. Gioli (1987), pp. 47-69.

CORBANI F. (1853), *Economia sociale. Compendio e guida degli studenti nel pubblico Studio di Siena pel corso accademico dell'anno 1852-1853*, Landi e Alessandri.

COSSA L. (1876), *Guida allo studio dell'economia politica*, Hoepli, Milano.

COSSA L. (1878), *Saggi di economia politica*, Milano, Hoepli.

COSSA L. (1880), *Guide to the Study of Political Economy*, Transl. From the 2nd Italian Edition, With a Preface by W.S. Jevons, London, Macmillan and Co.

COSSA L. (1893), *An Introduction to the Study of Political Economy*, Revised by the Author and Translated from the Italian by Louis Dyer, Macmillan, London-New York.

COSSA L. (1893), *Taxation; its Principles and Methods,* Translated from the "Scienza delle Finanze", with an Introduction and Notes by Horace White, together with a Compilation of the State Tax System of New York and Pennsylvania, New York and London, Putnam's Son.

CURTI M. (1964), *The Growth of American Thought*, Harper and Row, New York-Evanston and London. (Third Ed.; Fisrt Ed. 1943; Second Ed. 1951)

DA EMPOLI A. (1931), *Theory of Economic Equilibrium*, Chicago Ill., Christiano and Catenacci Publ. Co.

DEMARCO D. (1987), *Le dottrine della popolazione in occidente prima di Malthus*, in Gioli, cit., pp. 18-46.

DE VITI DE MARCO A. (1936), *First Principles of Public Finance*, by E. Pavlo Marget, Jonathan Cape, London.

ELLIOTT J.E. and COWNIE J. (1975), *Competing Philosophy in American Political Economics*, Goodyear Publ. Co., Inc., Pacific Palisades, California.

Encyclopaedia Americana. A Popular Dictionary of Arts, Sciences, Literature, History, Politics and Biography brought doen to the Present Time, Including a Copious Collection of Original Articles in American Biography, edited by Francis Lieber, con l'assistenza di E. Wigglesworth e T.G. Bradford, volls I-XIII (1829-1833), vol. XIV (by H. Vethake, 1947), Carey and (and Blanchard, 1835), Philadelphia.

Enyclopaedia Britannica, 1810 (IV Ed.); 1817 (V Ed.); 1823 (VI Ed. and 1824 Suppl.); 1842 (VII Ed.); 1853-1860 (VIII Ed.); 1963 (Inc. Ed. William Benton)

FANNO M. (1939), *Normal and Abnormal International Capital Transfers*, The University of Minnesota Press, Minneapolis; Milford, Oxford University Press, London.

FAUCCI R. (1995), *L'economista scomodo. Vita e opere di Francesco Ferrara*, Sellerio editore, Palermo.

FAUCCI R. (2000), *L'economia politica in Italia. Dal Cinquecento ai nostri giorni*, Utet, Torino.

FAUCCI R. and PERRI S. (1995), *Socialism and Marginalism in Italy 1890-1910*, in I. Steedman, *Socialism and Marginalism in Economics 1870-1930*, Routledge, London and New York, pp. 116-169.

FERRARA F. (ed.), *Biblioteca dell'Economista*, 1851, Pomba e Comp. Editori Librai, Torino, 1-XII; 1853, 1-XIII; 1856, Stamperia dell'Unione Tipografica Editrice, Torino, 1-XI; 1864, 1-X; 1873, Unione Tipografica editrice torinese, 1-IX.

FILANGERI G. (1976), *The Science of Legislation - Abstracts and Summaries*, in "American Philosophical Society - Transactions", vol. 66.

FOA B. (1949), *Monetary Reconstruction in Italy*, Washington D.C.-Carnegie Endowment for Peace, Kibngs Crown Press, New York.

FONER E. (2000), *Storia della libertà americana*, Donzelli, Roma.

GALBRAITH J.K. (1988), *Economics in Perspective*, Houghton Mifflin Co., Boston.

GALIANI F., *Money (1613)*, in Monroe, 1924, pp. 279-308.

GALIANI F. (1977), *On Money*, Dept. of Economics, by Peter Toscano, The University of Chicago Press.

GERBI A. (1955) (I ed.), *La disputa del nuovo mondo. Storia di una polemica 1750-1900*, Milano,-Napoli, Ricciardi. (II ed., 1983, Ricciardi, Napoli)

GIOLI G. (ed.) (1987), *Le dottrine della popolazione prima di Malthus*, F. Angeli, Milano.

HAY R., *Archive of the History of Economic Thought*, McMaster University, Ca., http://socserv2.socsci.mcmaster.ca

International Economic Association, *International Economic Papers*, 1951-1967, Macmillan, London-New York, voll. 12.

JEFFERSON T. (1997), *Viaggio nel Sud della Francia e nel Nord dell'Italia*, con *Introduzione* di M. Sioli, Ibis, Como-Pavia (*Memorandums taken on a Journey from Paris into the Southern Parts of France and Northern of Italy, in the Year 1797*).

Kress Library of Business and Economics - Catalogue 1818-1848, 1940-1967, Boston, Baker Library, Harvard Graduate School of Business Administration.

MADISON J. (1997), *Money (Observation written posterior to the circular Address of Congress in Sept. 1779, and prior to their Act of March 1780)*, in "Quarterly Review", Fall, pp. 3-7, With an Introduction by Arthur J. Rolnick (*In This Issue)*, pp. 1-2.

MARIANO J.H. (1921), *The Italian Contribution to American Democracy*, Department of Economics - School of Business and Civic Administration - College of the City of New York, Boston (Ph D. Thesis).

MAZZEI F. (1788), *Recherches historiques et politiques sur les Etats-Unis de l'Amerique Septentrionale...*, A Colle, et se trouve a Paris, chez Froullé.

MCCULLOCH J.R. (1964), *The Literature of Political Economy*, (London 1845), Reprints of Economic Classics, Kelley, New York 1964.

MONROE A.E. (1924), *Early Economic Thought. Selection from Economic Literature prior to Adam Smith*, Harvard Univesity Press, Cambridge.

MOTT T. and ZINKE G.W. (1987), *Benjamin Franklin Economic Thought*, in M.H. Buxbaum, 1987.

MUSGRAVE R.A. and PEACOCK A.T. (1958), *Classics in the Theory of Public Finance*, Macmillan, London.

OTTAVIANO C. (1981), *Quando l'Italia esportava idee. La diffusione degli scritti di Loria fra gli intellettuali americani*, in "Annali della Fondazione Einaudi", pp. 281-321.

PACE A. (1946), *The American Philosophical Society and Italy*, in "Proceedings of the Am. Phil. Soc.", vol. 90, pp. 387-421.

PACE A. (1950), *Benjamin Franklin and Italy since the Eighteenth Century*, in "Am. Phil. Soc. – Library Bulletin", pp. 242-250.

PANTALEONI M. (1898), *Pure Economics*, Translated by T. Boston Bruce, London-New York (New York, Kelley and Millman, Reprint, 1957).

PARETO V. (1935), *The Mind and Society. A Treatise on General Sociology*, Dover Publ., New York.

PARISI D. (1988), *Scaruffi e Montanari. La presenza di due scienziati emiliani nella storiografia nordamericana*, in A.V., *Economisti italiani tra sedicesimo e diciottesimo secolo*, Mucchi ed., Modena, pp. 101-115.

PARISI D. (1989), *L'American System of Political Economy e la storiografia economica dell'Otto-Novecento: da Francesco Ferrara a John Kenneth Galbraith*, in "Rivista Internazionale di Scienze Sociali", 3-4, pp. 487-497.

PARISI D. (1990a), *Nascita e sviluppo dell'American System of Political Economy. Il pensiero economico nordamericano tra Sette e Ottocento*, in "Rivista internazionale di scienze sociali", 4, pp. 547-581.

PARISI D. (1990b), *Francesco Ferrara e l'economia politica nordamericana*, in P.F. Asso, P. Barucci and M. Ganci, 1990, pp. 189-204.

PARISI D. (2000), *L'Istituto lombardo di scienze e lettere nel periodo post-unitario*, in Augello and Guidi, ed., pp. 3-37.

PARRETTI S. (1983), *L'economia politica americana tra Say e Ricardo*, in "Storia del pensiero economico", 11, pp. 3-7.

PASINETTI L.L. (ed.) (1992, 1993, 1998), *Italian Economic Papers*, vol. I, II, III, Il Mulino-Oxford University Press.

PECCHIO G. (1829), *Storia dell'Economia pubblica in Italia, ossia Epilogo critico degli Economisti italiani*, Lugano.

PETTIT P. (1997), *Republicanism: A Theory of Freedom and Government*, Oxford University Press (trad. it., 2000, *Il repubblicanesimo. Una teoria della libertà e del governo*, Feltrinelli, Milano).

QUADRIO-CURZIO A. (ed.) (1996), *Economia e istituzioni. Il paradigma lombardo tra il secolo XVIII e XIX*, Il Mulino, Bologna.

RONCAGLIA A. (ed.) (1995), *Moneta e sviluppo negli economisti napoletani dei secoli XVII-XVIII*, Il Mulino, Bologna.

ROSENGARTEN J.G. (1907), *The Early French Members of the American Philosophical Society*, in "Proceedings of the Am. Phil. Soc.", n. 46, pp. 87-97.

ROTONDI C. (2000), "Re*ndere facili le verità utili". Dalla Società patriottica all'Istituto lombardo (1776-1859)*, in Augello and Guidi, 2000b, pp. 39-62.

SCHUMPETER J.A. (1954), *The History of Economic Analysis,* Oxford University Press, New York.

SELIGMAN E.R.A. (1927), *The Early Teaching of Economics in the United States*, in J.H. Hollander, ed., *Economic Essays contributed in honor of John Bates Clark*, Macmillan, New York, pp. 283-320.

SELIGMAN E.R.A. (1944), *Economists*, in "Cambridge History of American Literature", New York, (I ed. 1917), Book III: Part III, Chapter XXIV, pp. 425-443.

SERRA A., *A Brief Treatise on the Causes which can make Gold and Silver Plentiful in Kingdoms where there are no mines*, in Monroe, 1924, pp. 143-168.

SEWALL H.R. (1901), *The theory of value before Adam Smith*, Publication of the American Economic Association, Third Series, vol. II, n. 3, August.

SKINNER Q. (1998), *Liberty before Liberalism*, Cambridge University Press.

SPURLIN P.M. (1984), *The French Enlightenment in America*, Univ. of Georgia Press, Athens.

TEILHAC E. (1936), *Pioneers of American Economic Thought in the Nineteenth Century*, transl. from French by E.A.J. Johnson, Macmillan, New York.

TEOCHARIS R.D. (1961), *Early Development in Mathematical Economics*, St. Martin's Press, New York.

TORTAROLO E. (1986), *Illuminismo e rivoluzioni. Biografia politica di Filippo Mazzei*, F. Angeli, Milano.

TWISS T. (1847), *View of the Progress of Political Economy in Europe since the Sixteenth Century,* London.

VASCO G.B., *Saggio politico della moneta (1772) - Vasco's Footnote [rate of exchange between gold and silver]*, in Baumol and Goldfeld, 1968, pp. 249-252.

VERRI P. (1986), *Reflections on Political Ecoonmy - 1771*, by B. McGilvray and P. Groenewegen, Department of Economics, Sidney.

WHITAKER J.K. (1988), *Early Flowering in the Old Dominion: Political Economy at the College of William and Mary and the University of Virginia*, in Barber, 1988, pp. 15-41.

WOLFF S.L. (1944), *Scholars*, in "Cambridge History of American Literature", New York - Cambridge (I ed. 1917), Book III: Part III, chapter XXV, pp. 444-491.

Receptiveness, knowledge and influence
The spread of Italian economic thought in the United States (1890-1940)*

Pier Francesco Asso and Luca Fiorito
University of Palermo and University of Siena

> When a given body of information passes the national frontiers it acquires a new complexion, a new national, cultural physiognomy
> *Thorstein Veblen*

1. Introduction

The object of this chapter is to describe whether and to what extent Italian economic thought reached a significant degree of diffusion and influence in the United States, between the advent of marginalism and the interwar years.

When this research project was started, we noticed that the existing literature had not produced a clear verdict on the relevance and reputation of Italian economists in the US. On the one hand we knew, from Schumpeter, that in the interwar years Vilfredo Pareto enjoyed a limited vogue in the U.S., particularly after the American edition of his *Treatise on Sociology* had been published [Schumpeter, 1949 and 1954, 859]. In more general terms, from the reading of Joseph Dorfman's encyclopaedic enterprise, we had learnt that, after 1890, American and European economic thought became so closely connected that one could speak of "a strong interrelationship and mutual influence" [Dorfman 1947-1959, IV, 164]. Also from a quantitative point of view, recent work by Goodwin and Meardon drew again our attention to the circumstance that Terence Hutchison made familiar almost 50 years ago, namely that in the United States, "the century opened with a strikingly high level of internationalization based mainly on the sense of dependency felt by American economists on authorities overseas and on the need they had to obtain

* We acknowledge our gratitude for permission to quote from manuscripts in their possession to the following institutions: the University of Chicago Library (Simons papers), the Columbia University Archives (Mitchell Papers, Moore Papers, Seligman papers), the Harvard University Archives (Parsons papers, Schumpeter papers, Taussig Papers), the Princeton University Archives (Viner Papers).

Writing this paper has been facilitated through correspondence and conversation with Piero Barucci, Edward J. Nell, Warren J. Samuels, Ernesto Screpanti who, as usual, are not in any way implicated in the final outcome. We also received useful comments on specific points by Luigino Bruni and Italo Magnani. Also in this case the usual disclaimers apply. Finally, this paper is part of a wider research project on the reception of Italian economics in the United States (see Asso-Fiorito 2001). Both authors are responsible for: the research of materials (published and unpublished); the formal structure of the essay; its main conclusions. However P.F. Asso materially wrote §§2 and 3 while L. Fiorito wrote §4.

advice on a wide range of policies for a rapidly growing and industrializing nation" [Goodwin - Meardon 1998, 313].

However, on the other hand, we had in mind what the doyen of American economists, Francis Amasa Walker, had solemnly stated in his Presidential Address before the American Economic Association, when he denounced the lack "of vital communications with the economic thinkers of Europe" [Walker 1889, 322]. As far as Italian economics was concerned, we also had more vivid recollections of Bob Coats' several inquiries into the Continental transmission of economic ideas towards the U.S. Nowhere did they mention the possibility of a significant Italian connection, even though US economists "were receptive not only of German teachings; they also adopted Austrian marginalism and English neoclassical economics" [Coats 1992, 408]. Therefore, as far as the Italian case was concerned, Dorfman's emphasis seemed to be quite misplaced: as a matter of fact, no Italian economist deserved to be mentioned in his 5 volume work, apart from a passing reference to Pareto's law of income distribution.

At the end of our work we feel confident enough to say – with no fear of exaggeration – that the picture looks quite different and that our anticipations were wrong. From different sources – published and unpublished – we managed to collect a good deal of evidence which shows that the knowledge of Italian economic thought was particularly widespread and not limited to the leading figures. More significantly, theories, concepts and tools which Italian economists had elaborated were rather influential in stimulating a restricted but qualified cluster of research projects which were launched by US economists between the two centuries.

The wealth of materials on the interrelationship between Italian and American economic thought has prevented us from telling our story in a single paper. Therefore, in a parallel work [Asso - Fiorito 2001], we will be dealing with our subject in somewhat greater detail, while the main results are summarised here. The interested reader is, therefore, kindly requested to refer to the other work for further elaborations and a rich archival appendix.

2. The environment

More than with other kinds of historical inquiries, all speculations on how economic ideas are spread from one place to another, from one culture to another, or from one community of scholars to another, must necessarily be closely related to the environment. To make the process of transmission a valuable subject of research, one must first of all measure the receptiveness of a national context (*the United States*) to the dissemination of ideas coming from external sources (*the Italian economists*) over a specific number of decades (*1890-1940*).

Were US economists, as a whole, well disposed to reading or learning what was coming from abroad or did they show any preconceived tendency towards insularity or cultural autarchy? Did they bear as a group the burden of any subjective or objective constraint which prevented them from communicating and integrating? Were the strands of research they thought worth cultivating more or less open to external influences and mutual exchanges? What did they do to increase the rate of international mobility of economic ideas?

Of course this paper does not claim to answer all these questions. Nevertheless, we find confirmation that, as a potential receiver, the United States represented an ideal cultural milieu for accepting or rejecting economic ideas coming from the Continent. As Bob Coats and William J. Barber, among others, have taught us, ever since the late institutionalization of American economic thought the search for a new national identity or, to put it more bluntly, the struggle to escape from British cultural subjugation, strongly dominated the US economist's agenda[1]. As a consequence, many of them began to have frequent contacts with Continental European writers and institutions. It is another well-known story that their "grand tours" of Europe became a common and very influential experience for the shaping of American economic thought from the 1880s onwards[2].

Consequently, most American economists felt that all possible barriers which hindered regular communication with European thinkers were worth breaking down. Linguistic barriers, first of all, needed to be surmounted, but so did all those obstacles which retarded the exchange of doctrinal, editorial, legislative and empirical information on the working of the economic system. It may be noted in this respect that, with the possible exception of Jacob Viner, all leading figures of American economic thought of this age were able to read Italian books. Their libraries as well as those of the academic institutions they used to work for, regularly received Italy's leading scientific journals and publications. Most of them kept in touch with their colleagues overseas, exchanging letters and information on policy issues and legislation. On both sides of the Atlantic the process of transmission was also eased by the growing availability in the means of publication, which significantly increased the speed of penetration of foreign ideas. In this respect one result of our research has been to show how many articles were commissioned and accepted for publication by the *Journal of Political Economy*, the *Political Science Quarterly*, or the *Quarterly Journal of Economics*. Italian economists submitted articles on comparative economic matters, such as railway tariffs, taxation, the working of municipalities or public utilities as well as on matters of pure theory. [see Asso-Fiorito 2001, ch.3]

Indeed Dorfman was right when he talked of *mutual* influence and integration. Among Continental economists a widely shared opinion was that establishing fresh intellectual relations with the growing number of "young turks" coming from the other side of the Atlantic, could become a fruitful and productive opportunity. It was

[1] Coats [1992; 1998]. Barber [1998].

[2] Between 1820 and 1920 nearly 9000 Americans went to study at German Universities. See Carlson [1999].

Leon Walras himself, just to mention one example, who in November 1895 encouraged Major Enrico Barone, at the time in desperate need of an academic tenure, to make an attempt with Columbia University; being aware, as Walras put it, that "I know from experience that having the English against us brings to our side the Americans who are generally well disposed in our favour" [Jaffé 1965, 38]. Barone's hopes for a new appointment were frustrated, and apparently John Bates Clark played no little role in cutting down, with his veto, the "marginal" rate of Italian emigration. However, more than arguing – as William Jaffé did some time ago – what would have become of American economics had Barone succeeded in coming to the United States[3], in this essay we have chosen a more positive and descriptive approach.

Briefly, in what did this potentially strong appeal for what Europeans and, in particular, Italian economists were doing, consist?

First of all we need to specify that our reconstruction is limited to the two communities of *professional* economists. Indeed one could trace important signs of influence which economists belonging to one national group had on *non*-economists of the other national group; conversely, other cases could be found where the line of transmission of ideas goes the other way around, i.e., from *non*-economists to economists. We could just mention, on the one hand, the deep impact which Achille Loria's theories of free land had on Jackson Turner and American general historians or, on the other, the influences which the political writings of Giuseppe Mazzini had on the shaping of John Commons' institutional economics. Both these lines of research, which have already attracted some attention[4], have been deliberately left out of our picture.

Apart from this methodological caveat, one first element for potential connections can be traced in what has been called the US economists' methodological *pluralism*. A second element has been found in their strong favour for cultural *pragmatism*.

The evolution of American economic thought until 1940 can be – and has been – described as a search for pluralism: the willingness to get rid of British cultural hegemony took the shape of a rich proliferation of different methods and alternative research projects. Some of them were still directed by neoclassical authors who embraced a strict Marshallian creed; but others saw the emergence of applied economists, mathematical economists, institutional economists. Moreover, many instances could be mentioned where economists felt the growing responsibility to embody in the prevailing, orthodox approach such new dynamic and potentially disturbing phenomena as those coming from the daily observation of the economic system: primarily, the modern corporation; its new methods for

[3] As Jaffé put it: "Had either Harvard or Columbia found a place for Barone at that time, his theoretical work which - according to Schumpeter - was never properly appreciated in Italy might have found new scope. And economic theory in America might earlier have been enriched from abroad." Barone's episode is also recanted in Dorfman [1955].

[4] Ottaviano [1981]; Leathers - Raines [1991].

large scale investments and long productive cycles; the growing complexity of new legal organizations; the presence of "big" market players, powerful cartels, and influential institutions with their wake of real and financial innovations; the explosion of mass immigration and urbanization. Thus, the picture of American economics as divided into two homegeneous and antithetic blocs formed by neoclassical economists and institutionalists does not hold – as few contemporaries and many later observers have already noted[5]. Eclectism, heterogeneity and catholicity of interests were, above all, elements that could be found within the two blocs, rather than between them.

Now, much the same thing can be said to have happened in Italy at the same time[6]. The *methodenstreit* of the 1870s, which had similarly divided the profession into two radically opposed camps, might not have reached the peaks of the Austro-German debate, but nonetheless had nowhere left impressed the mark of blind dogmatism which had elsewhere characterised the triumph and consolidation of marginalism. Such figures as Maffeo Pantaleoni, Luigi Einaudi, Vilfredo Pareto, Marco Fanno or Costantino Bresciani Turroni had shown that with the new methods of economic inquiry the economist was not necessarily bound to produce barren abstractions or artificial speculations in pure theory. As a consequence, the Italian tradition in such fields as public finance, economic dynamics, applied statistics, monetary theory, and economic sociology was, as we shall see below, highly regarded and widely read.

We also mentioned "pragmatism." With growing intensity – which became a real boom during and after World War I – the call for "action" in the field of public policy became widely heard within the economics profession. American economists of different beliefs, training and education showed no hesitation in following Irving Fisher's outcry to become an "economist in public service" [Fisher 1919][7]. The demand coming from markets and authorities, both domestic and international, for a new breed of economic experts in monetary, fiscal and policy affairs was particularly appealing, and the US economics profession reacted very promptly. Also a variegated troop of "amateur" economists happily jumped on the bandwagon, while the foundation of research institutes received public and private support. As the American leader of the Psychological School, Frank Fetter, observed as early as 1925, Fisher's appeal had not been left unheard: "The war

---

[5] For one recent example, see the various essays in Morgan - Rutherford [1998]. Among contemporaries see Patten [1924] who, in an essay on the Development of American Economic thought, observed with pride how "economic pluralism has won over economic monism."

[6] Writing about the consequences of the long struggle between marginalism and the historical school in Italy, Cavalieri and Faucci stated that "even the founders of 'pure economics' in Italy, Vilfredo Pareto and Maffeo Pantaleoni, felt that a merely theoretical approach to economics risked proving insufficient to grasp the entirety of economic phenomena. Pure economics was thus held to be a first approximation, necessary but by no means sufficient, to understanding the actual course of the economy, whose full investigation called for a multi-disciplinary approach" (see Cavalieri – Faucci [1994]).

[7] This was the title of his 1918 Presidential Address before the American Economic Association.

period of 1917-1924 greatly increased the appreciation of economics in the public service. No other economic discipline gained more in popular esteem. The effects appeared in many ways. Businessmen who had seen the work of economists during the war paid them the sincere flattery of outbidding the universities and opening economic research departments. Various governmental departments retained economists who had been given leave of absence from college duties during the war and created new positions for them as economic advisers" [Fetter 1925, 15].[8]

In so doing, US economists were particularly eager to learn from other national contexts, where economists had shown the same, pronounced disposition for militant campaigns, social reforms, institutional engineering, fact finding and manipulation. They also looked with envy and admiration at those countries which had for a long time asked for the economists' services, generously granting them appointments in the highest quarters of the public administration. And again, in both cases, Italy had an established tradition of militant economics of the sort that, with different tastes and purposes, Seligman, Taussig, Fisher or Wesley Mitchell were trying to design and implement for their own homeland.

Let us give just two examples of the deep appreciation which American economists showed for what their Italian colleagues were doing: at the beginning of our period, we may quote the words with which the *Journal of Political Economy* hailed Pantaleoni's campaigns against the degeneration of the moral fabric of Italian society after a new wave of banking scandals and the new surge for colonial militarism: "readers are familiar," it said in an editorial note of 1895, "with the uncompromising manner in which Professor Pantaleoni has maintained the fight against corruption in governmental affairs and against unsound measures of legislation" [Journal of Political Economy 1895, 86].

In the second half of our period, and particularly in the completely different circumstances of the 1930s, Italian economists achieved a strong reputation for their capacity to construct statistical instruments and indices for a "neutral" verification of what was being preached at a more theoretical level or implemented in different political environments. Connections with Italy on applied statistics were started at the turn of the century by Columbia's Henry L. Moore with his treatment of Pareto's early methods for the construction of demand curves [Moore 1908; 1914; 1929]. After he spent a sabbatical year in Rome, Moore's research efforts were also directed toward the construction of time series and correlation methods. Moore followed, as George Stigler has already shown, the route traced by Bresciani Turroni and Rodolfo Benini and agreed with their methods to go "beyond Pareto" in the construction of demand curves [Stigler 1965]. In the 1930s cooperation on

[8] In the same address, Fetter summarized as follows the different attitude towards theory between American and English economists: "In England it never has been customary as in America to disparage the systematic economics of the schools as 'mere theory' and therefore worthless, while really English political economy has continued to be more doctrinaire and old-fashionably abstract than with us" [Fetter 1925, 13].

these subjects was more fully enhanced by the development of the so-called Econometric Society Movement. Despite the hard times, Italian economists actively participated in the development of the new trend of quantitative economics as well as contributing notably to the first issues of *Econometrica.*

Therefore, we could say that pluralism and pragmatism were the two main "endogeneous" ingredients which helped the construction of stable professional relations between Italian and US economists after 1890. Let us examine this more deeply and see how about Italian economic culture actually spread through the United States.

3. The network

In order to measure and assess the transmission of Italian economic thought in a highly receptive environment we have followed two procedures: first of all, inspired by the suggestions of J. J. Spengler [1970] and, more recently, Bob Coats and David Colander [1988], we decided to reconstruct the complex and interdependent network of communications between the two groups of economists. In so doing, we attached great importance to the quantitative side of our story, searching for articles, book reviews, text books, lecture notes, citations, letters, and so forth. We hoped we could thus illuminate the contour lines of the network and answer a number of questions, which are mainly related to the "sociology of knowledge." Then we decided it was time to shift our attention from "knowledge" to "influence": we thus tried to verify whether and in what particular cases the process of dissemination had succeeded in producing new developments in theoretical or applied economics. Our attention was essentially focussed on what we believed were the most important "case studies" where the influence of Italian economic thought on US economists was more clear and profound. While this paragraph summarises the results of the "sociological" network of knowledge, the following is devoted to the second part of our story, namely the degree of influence which Pantaleoni, Pareto and De Viti de Marco had on American economic thought.

Let us start first of all with the quantitative side of this phenomenon. In trying to show how ideas were transmitted, we have drawn extensively from a number of different sources: book reviews; articles written by Italian economists which were published in US economics journals; quotations of Italian economists which we found in a selection of treatises, monographs or articles written by US economists; letters and other miscellaneous materials (lecture notes, unfinished papers, unpublished comments on Italian books etc.) which are available in US economists' archives. While, again, a more scrupulous description is made in our parallel work [Asso-Fiorito 2001] – which also makes available the most interesting pieces of unpublished material – the main results of this inquiry can be summarised as follows.

The number of book reviews is quite impressive (see Table I). If we merely look at the four leading economics journals (*Journal of Political Economy*, *Political Science Quarterly*, *Quarterly Journal of Economics*, *American Economic Review*, whose first year of publication was 1911), between 1890 and 1940 more than 350 books written by Italian economists received recognition and critical comment. Of course, book reviews cannot be treated as a homogeneous bloc: some of them were long and critical; others were merely intended to provide basic information to potential readers. They were also very unevenly distributed according to the editorial policy of each journal. At any rate, from our table, it emerges that first the *Political Science Quarterly* (under the editorial thrust of Edwin R. A. Seligman) and then the *American Economic Review* were the two most prolific tribunes for learning about what Italian economists were doing. Both the *Journal of Political Economy* and particularly the *Quarterly Journal of Economics* give somewhat more disappointing results, but this is only true in relative terms: in fact, Chicago and Harvard shared the editorial decision to publish a much smaller number of "review-articles," irrespective of the author's nationality[9]. On the other hand, whenever a book was reviewed, both the *Journal* and the *Quarterly* stand out for their extremely accurate presentation which often provoked heated debate. This, as we shall see, was the case of Henry Simons' *JPE* hypercritical review of De Viti De Marco's *Principles of public finance*.

Table I

Journal	Number of Book Reviews
AER (1911 - 1945)	199
JPE (1892 - 1945)	79
PSQ (1886 - 1945)	70
QJE (1886 - 1945)	4
Total	352

In Table two all book reviews have been further disaggregated according to their subjects. Our data show that four subjects seem to have been preferred and taken into consideration for book reviews: general theory (here included works on the history of Italian economic thought); economic history; public finance and taxation; and particularly after World War I, books on monetary policy, stabilization and reform. Most interestingly, relatively smaller attention was given to books on agriculture, statistics and international trade.

[9] Quite interestingly, the *Quarterly Journal of Economics*'s editor, Frank Taussig, published several reviews of Italian authors in the *Political Science Quarterly*.

Table II

Subjects	Number of Book Reviews
Accounting, Business Methods, Investments and the Exchanges	4
Agriculture, Mining, Forestry and Fisheries	5
Capital and Capitalistic Organization	9
Economic History and Geography	63
General Works, Theory and Its History	81
Insurance and Pensions	2
Labor and Labor Organizations	5
Manufacturing Industries	8
Money, Prices, Credit and Banking	48
Pauperism, Charities and Relief Measures	1
Population and Migration	14
Public Finance, Taxation and Tariff	52
Social Problems and Reform	9
Socialism and Cooperative Enterprises	20
Statistics and Its Methods	19
Trade, Commerce and Commercial Crises	11
Transportation and Communication	1

US book reviews on Italian economists are also interesting because they tell us something about the reviewers themselves. In this respect, up until the end of the century, methodological issues generally attracted the reviewer's attention. The specific contents of the book under review – from Rabbeno's *American commercial policy* to De Viti's *La funzione della banca* – were generally disposed of in few paragraphs, while the author's performance is measured by means of his methodological preferences, his technical skills, and his capacity to embrace or criticise the new orthodoxy[10]. Hints at the methodological controversy between the historical and the neoclassical schools are often quoted and the publication of Pantaleoni's and Pareto's works was no exception to this rule. On the one hand, according to one reviewer, Pantaleoni's refusal to definitely discard the classical heritage "was a serious blemish upon a brilliant and valuable work" [Sherwood 1898, 548]. While his revival of the wage fund theory had led him to a "classical" synthesis, American economists generally saw it as a typical methodological counter-revolution. On the other hand, Pareto's *Cours* was hailed by some as one of the most convincing proof of the triumph of mathematical methods in economics. As another reviewer wrote in the *Journal of Political Economy*, "the

[10] See Hill [1896], Willis [1898] and Young [1913].

topics selected for mathematical treatment are well chosen, and the author has been no less discriminating to what he has omitted than in what he has included" [Merrit 1898, 351].

Still in relation to methodological issues, it is worth mentioning that some of the reviews show the clear influence of Veblen's "evolutionary" criticism of received economic doctrines [Veblen 1898]. This is the case, for instance, of the two reviews by L. Ardzrooni to Loria's *Le bases économiques de la justice internationale* and *The Economic Synthesis* both published by *The Journal of Political Economy* [Ardzrooni 1913; 1914]. Here Ardzrooni, a former student of Veblen at the University of Missouri, found Loria's research project inconsistent with "the modifications which the conception of evolution has undergone within the last half of century and especially since the late development of the science of heredity" [Ardzrooni 1914, 702]. This inconsistency, he continued in purely Veblenian terminology, arose from the contrast between the unteleological concept of natural selection and the teleological Marxian process of the class struggle, on which the Italian thinker had based his own theory of the origin and development of capitalistic institutions. "Judged by its fundamental hypotheses as well as by its method" – this was Ardzrooni's conclusion – "*The Economic Synthesis* seems to hold forth scant reassurance to the science with which it deals, though it is a result of a laudable ambition and an amazing erudition. Substantially, it stands as a nicely arranged system of logic constructed by passing through the crucible of Hegelian classical economics, tempered by the Marxian categories of 'exploitation,' 'surplus value,' and 'class struggle'" [Ardzrooni 1914, 704].

Conversely, in the interwar years, methodological issues almost disappear, while U.S. reviewers reveal a marked preference for books on policy, public finance, and the restoration of the international monetary system. The pragmatic character acquired by American economics as a consequence of the War now becomes the best yardstick by which books for review are chosen and commented. As a consequence, books written by Italian economists are constantly compared to the prevailing needs of the American economy: from Einaudi's conception of taxable income to Rignano's proposal to employ the proceeds of the inheritance tax for broad macroeconomic purposes, the temptation for "plug and play" what the Italian economists were doing seems to have been widely practised[11]. Apart from Minnesota's Arthur Marget, little attention is given to the economics of Fascism, while Italian corporativism is unanimously dismissed by neoclassical economists as a blend "of the most extreme utterances of the German Historical School, American Institutionalism, the Universalism of Othmar Spann, and, in general, of all those movements which lie to one side of the main stream of traditional economic doctrines" [Marget 1935]. In this respect, we have noticed with some

[11] See Blakey [1925] and Leland [1925].

surprise the almost complete lack of influence that Italian economists had on American Institutionalists, despite the vivid interest that some Italian corporativists showed for the works of Veblen, Mitchell and particularly John Maurice Clark[12]. Generally speaking, for American economists, the banner of corporativism was just another aberration imposed by a coercive political power upon accomodating University professors: a cult that the real exponents of the Italian neoclassical tradition would never have practised[13]. Again it was Arthur Marget who rethorically (and quite ironically) wondered "if Pareto were alive today, would the head of the Italian government permit him to be badgered into abandoning forever the traditional corpus of economic theory, which he had helped to create, in favour of the 'Corporative economics' of professor Gino Arias?" [Marget 1935, 417][14].

Besides book reviews, the exchange of correspondence seems to have been another widely used channel of communication and integration. Our archival research – which benefitted from the consultation of the personal collection of papers of Seligman, Fisher, the two Clarks, Mitchell, Taussig, Viner, Moore, Simons, Knight, and Schumpeter – managed to bring to light around 500 pieces with and about Italian economists – mostly correspondence.

A closer scrutiny shows that letters did not generally deal with conventional affairs or purely personal matters: for both American and Italian economists correspondence was an important vehicle to exchange information at various stages of their professional activities. Most letters dealt with bibliographical, statistical or legislative matters. Letters were also a means to advance proposals for publication; to exchange books and reviews in times of political and economic strains; to exchange views on political developments, international relations, jobs opportunities and other academic matters of various nature; to exchange judgements on other economists, new ideas or policy proposals. Undoubtedly, the Seligman collection stands out for its richness and interest: ever since the 1880s

---

[12] For instance, John Maurice Clark pioneering study on *The Economics of Overhead Costs* was translated and abridged into Italian: "Studi sull'Economia dei Costi Costanti," abridged and translated by G. Demaria and A. Piana, Nuova Collana di Economisti, Stranieri e Italiani, edited by Giuseppe Bottai and Celestino Arena, Vol. 5: *Dinamica Economica*, Torino: UTET, 1932, pp. 183-417.

[13] Among Italian economists who had emigrated in the 1930s, George Tesoro published several critical reviews on Italian corporativism. One of these dealt with Fontana Russo's essay on war economics. According to Tesoro, the book was "biased and superficial [...] descriptive, factual, and always political, that is, fascistic" [Tesoro, 435]. For the benefit of the American readers, Tesoro observed that all responsible Italian economists who still lived in their native land had different views on the economic performance of the Totalitarian government in the last decade: "it should be pointed out that the picture of fascist Italy at war as presented by Dr. Fontana is at variance with their contribution on this subject. A recent symposium by leading Italian economists expresses clear criticism of totalitarian economic policies and theories. This criticism may explain why the fascist government suppressed only a few months ago the oldest and most authoritative Italian economic magazine, *Il Giornale degli Economisti*, which thus shared the fate of another once glorious Italian journal, *La Riforma Sociale*. It strikingly demonstrates that leading Italian economists, unlike Fontana Russo, are still devoted to the cause of objective research and scientific freedom" [Tesoro 1943, 437].

[14] As Schumpeter [1949] put it, US economists often wondered whether, had they lived longer, Pareto, Pantaleoni, Barone – who all died between 1923 and 1924 – would have maintained their benevolent and cooperative attitude toward Fascism. And Marget was just another case.

Seligman regularly exchanged correspondence with many Italian economists, from the Head of the Italian Census, Luigi Bodio, to the young Pantaleoni, from Achille Loria to Vilfredo Pareto, from Ugo Rabbeno to other exponents of the Italian historical school. He continued to do so until his very last days.

While a selection of Seligman's most relevant correspondence is published in our parallel work [Asso - Fiorito 2001], we mention here just one example that allows us to illustrate the importance of these epistolary exchanges. It refers to an episode which followed Seligman's publication of his *The Shifting and Incidence of Taxation*. In the chapter dedicated to the contribution by the so-called "Mathematical school," Seligman praised Pantaleoni's *Teoria della Traslazione dei Tributi* [1882] as the study which contained, on the whole, "the best existing treatment of incidence as a matter of pure theory" [Seligman 1892, 208]. However, Seligman complained that "[w]hile there is a great deal of acute and original thought in the monograph, the work suffers from the fact that its doctrine of incidence is largely based upon economic theories which are open to question." [Seligman 1892, 207][15]. Pantaleoni wrote a letter to Seligman where he frankly admitted the cogency of his remarks. This passage is an admirable example of close friendship and intellectual honesty: "I really am not astonished to hear (or see) you say that you don't agree with several doctrines expounded in my Traslazione. I myself don't agree with myself! I was very young when I wrote it and would have not written it if had not been obliged to write it to get a living. I knew nothing of Walras then, or of Menger, and nothing of the admirable papers of Marshall, and had not made then some mathematical studies which I later felt necessary. If I had time to write the subject over again, I believe, I could do it differently. A few curves settle a great many things."[16]

In the following editions of the *Shifting and Incidence of Taxation*, Seligman left his criticism of Pantaleoni unaltered. Nevertheless, as a sign of loyalty towards his Italian colleague, he decided to inform the reader that "it may, in fact, be affirmed that some of the doctrines upheld in the work no longer represent the views of the author," explicitly referring, in a footnote, to his private correspondence with Pantaleoni: "In answer to a letter from the present writer stating that he did not agree with several of the doctrines laid down in the work, Professor Pantaleoni intimated that his present view differ in some respect from those expressed in the book." [Seligman 1927, 208, n 1][17].

At least in quantitative terms, our reconstruction of the network of knowledge produced somewhat more disappointing results after we examined a broad sample

[15] For a detailed and insightful discussion of Seligman's criticism of Pantaleoni see Magnani [1995].

[16] Pantaleoni to Seligman, March 31st 1891. Seligman Papers, Rare Books and Manuscript Library, Columbia University.

[17] Analysis of correspondence also allowed us to reveal what Italian Economists thought of their Italian colleagues. See for example what Einaudi wrote to Irving Fisher on the Italian school of public finance. The letter is published in Asso - Fiorito [2001].

of treatises, books and articles. Italian economists are hardly ever quoted in the avalanche of textbooks which US economists sent to the publishers between 1881 and 1920. In the interwar years we have been unable to extract a single quotation of an Italian economist from a list of 45 textbooks in economics.[18] The only significant exceptions are, in this respect, Davenport and, again, Seligman. The former, in his critical reflections on the value of Austrian economics, discussed Pantaleoni's approach to hedonism and the cardinal measurement of utility. The latter, revealed ever since the 1880s a very extensive appreciation and knowledge of Italian economics which he strengthened during his 1894 sabbatical staying at the University of Rome[19]: in his *Principles,* Seligman critically reviewed some authors of Italian modern treatises in economics, from Augusto Graziani and Maffeo Pantaleoni to such minor figures as Camillo Supino or Ulisse Gobbi; while his still unpublished courses on public finance[20], and the recently published course on the history of economic thought devoted a more significant attention to the Italian heritage and the achievements of Loria, Cossa and the Italian historical school[21].

Among the treatises, one further exception which deserves a brief mention, is Haney's *History of economic thought* [Haney 1911], where a whole chapter is devoted to the development of Italian economics. Published in 1911, Haney's can be considered as the first modern American textbook in the history of economics. In his account, Haney, once a student of Ely at Wisconsin, does not give a very good performance in terms of originality, scholarship, and thoroughness. His only sources of inspirations seem to have been Rabbeno's and Loria's articles on the more recent trends of Italian economic thought which had been published two decades before in the *Political Science Quarterly* and in Philadelphia's *Annals of the American Academy of Political and Social Sciences* [Rabbeno, 1891; Loria 1891]. As a result, the Italian school of public finance and the more theoretical achievements of Italian marginalist writers were hardly mentioned in Haney's book. On the contrary, Italian exponents of the Historical school gained the highlights and also such minor figures as Nazzani, Cusumano, Messedaglia and Lampertico were presented to the American student for their capacity to provide new life and versatility to the German-bred movement. Pantaleoni and the new

---

[18] The complete set of textbooks is quoted in Asso - Fiorito [2001]. See also Ise [1932].

[19] Around the turn of the century, Taussig, Fisher and Moore were other cases of American economists choosing Italian universities for their sabbatical leaves.

[20] "Italy has produced a very large number of very good first-class writers in public finance. Nitti, who is now hiding in Switzerland, wrote Science of Finance, which was soon translated into French, Einaudi has written a large number of books on special topics. He contributed a great many essays during the war to Corriere della Sera. Graziani is a fine thinker, a first-class mind who has published a five-volume work on the principles of public finance. It is illustrated, interesting, and up-to date" [Fiorito-Johnson-Samuels forthcoming].

[21] In a letter to Henry Moore [Jaffé 1965, III, 1605], dated Nov. 27, 1905, Leon Walras wrote that while Seligman had devoted a section of his History of Economics course to "some recent development," Pareto and Fisher were both excluded.

wave of Marginalist writers were only reminded for their "wide readings" and their ability "to soften and harmonize" the teachings of the various schools. On the more constructive side, Haney uncritically offered a blunt judgement on Pantaleoni, Pareto and their followers: "it remains true that [...] their original contributions to the progress of economic science has been slight" [Haney 1911, 845].

We just said that the Italian followers of the Historical school were mainly responsible for introducing Italian economic thought in the United States. We have also mentioned Rabbeno's 1891 and Loria's 1891 articles. In times of deep, internecine struggles within the economics profession, both authors indirectly warned their American colleagues that, in Italy, the historical method had never been more alive. In their view, all attempts to "bury" it or "purify" it with new quantitative techniques had been unproductive or, what was worse, were inevitably leading to barren abstractions. Pantaleoni was the main target of Rabbeno's critical presentation. His method was dangerous, his terminology obscure, his real contribution to the theory of value was just an exercise to express "old ideas in new words" [Rabbeno 1891]. Loria showed a greater clemency for Pantaleoni: he praised his early essays on the incidence and the shifting of taxation ("a brilliant exposition")[22], but nevertheless dismissed his *Pure Economics* as a passive reproduction of otherwise wellknown (classical) theories. Compared to Pantaleoni, the obscure and little-known Nazzani gained a prominent place in Loria's article. In Loria's prophetic words, Nazzani's appearance "in the scientific arena must be considered as indicating the commencement of a new era for Italian economic thought" [Loria 1891].

Quite interestingly, American marginalists showed little sympathy for this description of Italian economic thought and wrote words of disapproval particularly against Rabbeno's article. Irving Fisher reacted very promptly, and in his doctoral dissertation [Fisher 1892] reassessed those Italian economists who had decided "to draw off thought for a time to pure theory" [Fisher 1892, 128][23]. Pantaleoni, however, did not reply to Rabbeno's and Loria's attacks. At least he decided not to do so in the short run or, for what mattered, in the same American journals which had hosted their pieces. This conclusion holds true also for other major figures of Italian economics: in general, Italian neoclassical economists refused all proposals for publication in US professional journals in order to make their ideas more widely known. The overall picture gives only 5 articles until 1914, besides Rabbeno's and Loria's. They became 28 in the interwar years, mainly because the

[22] In his private correspondence with Seligman Rabbeno heavily dismissed the originality of the Italian school in public finance: "our literature in finance is very scarce, and we have much to learn from the foreign treatises." Rabbeno to Seligman, February 22nd, 1890. Seligman Papers, Rare Books and Manuscript Library, Columbia University.

[23] Fisher's comments were primarily directed against Rabbeno, since he acknowledged that he was not yet "acquainted with Pantaleoni's book, nor with any Italian author." The first Italian edition of Pantaleoni's *Principi* had been published in 1889.

number of US professional reviews greatly increased and *Econometrica* took the leading share.

Indeed, even before the turn of the century Pantaleoni and Pareto, above all, had both received invitations to write and present their own theories in a concise form to the American audience. Why they always refused to do so is a matter for speculation and even the correspondence of those days is of little use in this respect. Quite likely, at least as far as Pareto is concerned, the rather cool way with which Fisher, the elder Clark and other American "mathematical" economists had reacted to the publication of his 1896 *Cours* may have had a part in his refusal to participate more fully in the heated *JPE* debate on utility and marginal productivity, as many other Continental writers were doing. In his review of Pareto's *Cours*, Fisher wrote that its corrections to the Walrasian system were insignificant and not original. An interpretation that, quite interestingly, the young Paul Samuelson totally agreed with when he set out to write his seminal paper on revealed preferences[24]. While Pareto's ability with the mathematical method was undisputed[25], Fisher objected that the Italian economist had made too extensive a use of it, making its universal adoption a more difficult task: "the book would have been more efficient in destroying the prejudice against mathematical analysis if the writer had rigorously abstained from mathematical language except where really helpful [...] such overfondness for mathematical machinery strengthens the impression [...] that it is capable only of grinding out truisms" [Fisher, 1896a, 325]. According to Fisher, Pareto's *Cours* had also analytical weaknesses, particularly in his confused treatment of utility and indifference curves. Pareto, Fisher argued, was wrongly obsessed with the problem of measurement, and in his writings utility had become just another methaphisical category, of the kind which hindered the real understanding of economic phenomena. In the end, Fisher restricted the original parts of the *Cours* to the reconstruction of statistical series and to Pareto's promising attempts to go beyond economics and find useful connections with other branches of the social sciences, namely history, sociology or statistics[26].

Pareto decided to reply to Fisher's criticisms only in his personal correspondence. What mainly bothered the Italian economist – as it also emerges from a letter to Pantaleoni – was that Fisher had charged him with asserting that

---

[24] As Samuelson later recalled in a letter to William Jaffé of intellectual reminiscences: "personally I never cared much for Henry Schultz's 1929 JPE article. Nor have I admired the Pareto improvements on Clark - Wicksteed - Barone - Wicksell and Walras [...]. I believe Pareto muddled the waters in trying to be too realistic at this first stage of approximation [universal constant returns to scale]. At a second stage of approximation we can introduce increasing returns, limitational factors, and joint products. I doubt that Pareto ever succeeded in doing this properly." Samuelson to Jaffé, July 1st, 1964. Viner Papers, Princeton University Library.

[25] Another champion of American neoclassical economics, Frank Knight, acknowledged the originality of both Pareto and Pantaleoni. In his doctoral dissertation on *Risk, Uncertainty and Profit* [Knight 1921, 6], he wrote that Vilfredo Pareto "is now the most prominent exponent of the mathematical method," while "among 'literary' pure theorists, Wicksteed, Schumpeter and Pantaleoni stand out."

[26] In the same year, Fisher published an article on the *Economic Journal* [Fisher 1896b] where he disagreed with Pareto's treatment of capital goods as presented in the *Cours* [Fisher 1896b, 531].

total utility could not exist when the utility of each commodity was a function of the quantities of other commodities. In his rejoinder Pareto showed to his American colleague, by quoting verbatim from the *Cours*, that he by no means denied the possibility of the existence of a total utility function in the case under discussion. What he had affirmed was simply that such a function could not exist unless some formal requirements were met. Quite honestly, Pareto attributed Fisher's misreading to his lack of familiarity with the French language: "Je vous prie de croire que je connais assez le calcul intégral pour ne pas tomber en une erreur aussi grossière. J'ai dit, ce qui est fort different, «Cette function Φ existe toujours quand ϕ_a est seulement fonction de x_a, ϕ_b de x_b... *Elle peut ne pas exister quand* ϕ_a, ϕ_b... sont fonctions de toutes le quantités x_a, x_b»...(*Peut ne pas exister* ne se traduit pas en anglais par *cannot exist*. Peut être vous avez confondu: *peut ne pas exister* avec *ne peut pas exister*. Ce sont deux sens entièrement différents)" [Pareto 1962, III, 410; emphases in original].

The point raised (mistakenly) by Fisher represented a secondary aspect of the more general problem of integrability conditions, namely, the requirement that there is a utility function from which a demand function or a system of demand functions derives.[27] As convincingly argued by Mirowski [1989, 228-231], neither Fisher nor Pareto seemed to have, at that time, fully perceived the analytical implications of the absence of integrability – possible non existence of such quantity as total utility and path dependence of equilibrium – although the American economist explicitly acknowledged such a possibility in his 1892 *Mathematical Investigations* [Fisher 1892, 119].

To our knowledge, the first accurate discussion of the problem of integrability by an American writer made its appearance in Edwin B. Wilson's review of Pareto's *Manuel d'Economie Politique* [Wilson 1912]. Here, the author – a Harvard mathematician – pointed out in formal terms that, with three or more commodities, it might not be possible to proceed from a scale of preferences to a utility function.

In this connection, Wilson discusses, quoting from Pareto's treatment of the subject in the *Manuel*, the case in which the consumption of certain amounts of the various goods may yield very different increments of pleasure according to the order in which they are consumed. In Wilson's opinion, however, Pareto's reference to a menu is exceedingly liable to cause confusion because, while the order of consumption which is in question in the problem of integrability is merely a

[27] Since the great relevance attached by Mirowski to the integrability conditions for the history of neoclassical economic thought, it is worth describing them in greater detail. In the standard utility maximization problem, demands x(p, m) are generated by the maximization of a utility function U(x) with parametric prices and money income. The integrability problem reverses the process, so that the utility function is "recovered" through "integration" of the demand function. Integrability concerns two questions: what properties of given demand relations "guarantee the existence of a 'generating' utility function..., i.e., of a utility function that is maximized, subject to budget, by these demand relations;" and given the existence of such a function, "how the utility function can be 'recovered' (determined) from the knowledge of the demand relations" [Hurvicz 1971, 176: emphases in original].

"conceptual order," the order of consumption which is involved in the example discussed by Pareto is a "time order" which "either has nothing to do with the other order or has some very fundamental and subtle and neglected relation to the whole question of utility" [Wilson 1912, 468]. Wilson continues his discussion by suggesting two possible solutions to the difficulties implied by the consideration of the time element into the determination of equilibrium. Suppose first that we could integrate the equation and thus obtain an index of pleasure. He then argues that this index ought to apply either a) to a given instant (and to contain the time as a parameter owing to the fact that at different times the price ratios and the integrating factor are different), or b) to an interval of time, as a day or a year, during which conditions were supposed to remain the same (in this case the time would not enter at all).

According to Wilson, Fisher in his *Mathematical Investigations*, distinctly took the latter point of view: "[t]his is the time average way of obtaining definite results" [Wilson 1912, 468-69]. Conversely, Pareto in the *Manuel* adopted the first position by considering the homo oeconomicus as an idealized individual free from inconsistent behavior: "[t]his is the ensemble average way of getting definitiveness" [Wilson 1912, 469]. In neither case, however, does the time enter into the determination of equilibrium or of the path followed to attain the point of maximum utility – unless, he warns the reader, "the whole analogy with mechanics and thermodynamics is to break down at a vital point" [Wilson 1912, 469]. As a consequence, this is Wilson's conclusion with regard to Pareto's "menu" example, "[t]he difference in the increase of pleasure which a person would experience in eating his dinner in inverse as opposed to direct order cannot, we believe, be logically taken into account, and we are inclined to think that the whole discussion of the order of integration, a point that naturally occurs to the mathematician, *can be thrown out of court by the economist*" [Wilson 912, 469; emphasis added][28]. In spite of Wilson's invitation to dismiss it, the problem of integrability continued to attract the attention of many economists until when, in the forties, Hicks in *Value and Capital* [Hicks 1946], as well as Samuelson in the *Foundations* [Samuelson 1947], presented the now familiar result that utility maximization — subject, of course, to the budget constraint — implies the symmetry and negative semidefiniteness of the Slutsky-Hicks substitution term matrix.

At the beginning of the new century American economists tried to establish closer connections with the other leading figure of Italian marginalism, Maffeo Pantaleoni. However, also in his case, he was not particularly receptive to US economists' invitations: despite his deep friendship with Seligman, Pantaleoni did not even contribute to, or participate in, a 1909 symposium which the American

[28] The Chicago economist Henry Schultz acknowledged Wilson's point that "too much attention has been attached in utility analysis to the problem of the order of consumption [...]. This problem has little or no significance in an economy dominated by routines" [Schultz 1938, 13].

Economic Association organised on his behalf. In the 25 year old history of the Association, Pantaleoni would have become the first European economist to have achieved this recognition. On that occasion, with three papers presented by John Bates Clark [1910], Frank Fetter [1910], and Simon Patten [1910], US economists decided to pay a tribute to Pantaleoni's seminal contributions to economic dynamics. Fetter used the occasion to draw comparisons between Italian and US economic traditions in this field and recalled how, ever since the works of Carey, the latter were well equipped to deal with the forces of progress, cumulative change and systemic instability. Pantaleoni's paper brought fresh evidence that something was changing in European economic thought: dynamic influences were "more general and far reaching and are profoundly affecting the societies of Europe and the thought of European economists" [Fetter 1910]. John Bates Clark was definitely more praiseworthy and talked of the "enormous gains" which the recent studies of Pantaleoni had meant for the profession: Pantaleoni had shown that, without borrowing from history, sociology or other cognate disciplines belonging to the "non-economic zone," the economist could master such difficult topics as firm concentrations, economies of scale, or permanent changes in the economic structure. Pantaleoni's approach was, according to Clark, systematic and purposeful. Patten agreed and explicitly acknowledged Pantaleoni's role in "helping to free his own mind and the minds of his readers from the influence of traditional themes" [Patten 1910 and 1924]. Indeed, we may argue that John Maurice Clark may have been just one of them. In fact, despite the fact that the Italian economist is nowhere quoted in Clark's essays on the theories of overhead costs [Clark 1923] one could find many connections between his later studies and Pantaleoni's treatment of the growth of fixed capital outlays and their role in the generation of dynamic instability[29].

With the discussion of Pareto's utility function and Pantaleoni's essays on dynamics we believe that we are already moving from "the network of knowledge" to the more restricted "network of influence." Let us, however, draw one final, general conclusion on the transmission of economic knowledge. As we have already observed, we need to stress in more specific words that Columbia's Edwin Seligman was the man most responsible for bringing Italian economists to the attention of the American public and the economics profession at large.

In 1886 Seligman wrote that "it may be said with truth that in no country in the world with the exception of Germany, is there such a numerous and able set of economic writers as in modern Italy" [Seligman 1886]. Certainly, in those days, Seligman had in mind especially Achille Loria and his followers: Loria's stadial model of economic development based on the gradual appropriation of free land was a fascinating idea for an American, indeed much more so than anything

[29] On Clark and Pantaleoni, see Sylos Labini [1995].

which had been produced in Great Britain during the heyday of classical economics. In fact, it was again Seligman who involved Loria and his friend Rabbeno in the preparation of the two essays (which he edited and translated) on the recent developments of Italian economic thought.

But Seligman also had in mind the first and much lesser known writings of the Italian school of public finance. That Italian economists had generally embraced marginalism was a fact that Seligman had praised since 1886, as emerges from his favourable comment on the new series of the *Giornale degli Economisti*. Referring to the recent foundation of economics journals in the US, Seligman wrote "that both Italians and Americans should have found occasion to inaugurate economic journals of a strictly scientific character and should at the same time take ample notice of each other is certainly a matter of congratulation and augurs well for the future of our science" [Seligman, 1886, 703]. In the following decades, Seligman became an ardent admirer of the Italian attitude towards marginalism and its main sponsor within the US economics profession: the generation of Pantaleoni, De Viti, Einaudi and Pareto had helped to refine new theoretical developments without losing contact from all the problems that both history and contemporary events were constantly creating for the economic analyst. As he wrote in his entry on "Financial literature" for the *Handbuch der Finanzwissenschaft*, "it could be generally said that modern Italian literature regarding public finance is superior to all other European countries as to versatility of talents, erudition and abundance of suggestions" [Seligman 1929 quoted in Rocca 1929, 141].

4. The influence

In his 1901 review of Jannaccone's book on production costs, Wesley Mitchell emphasized that "of late Italian economists have been giving us a long series of elaborate monographs upon theoretical subjects of fundamental importance and great difficulty." [Mitchell 1901, 460] If one looks at American economics literature between 1890 and 1940, the most frequently quoted cases are Pantaleoni's and Einaudi's works on taxation, Graziani's works on machineries, Loria's on the stages of capitalism, Fanno's on banking and colonization, Bresciani Turroni on the German inflation and the transfer mechanism, Jannaccone on the monetary approach of the balance of payments. Also empirical and statistical inquiries were widely considered as the Chief of the American Census, Francis Amasa Walker, had acknowledged ever since his first, controversial book on the wages question [Walker, 1876].

In general, one could say that the qualities which American economists found in Italian economics were often restricted to their prodigious knowledge of economic literature, i.e. to the setting of new standards of cosmopolitan scholarship and intellectual receptiveness. From Pantaleoni to Loria, "erudition" seems to have been the main innovation which Italian economic thought had managed to produce. In fact, at a more analytical level, the picture we get is rather different. Italian economists, so their American colleagues argued, could not be associated in any way with specific advances in economic theory, conceptualization or policy proposals. Again we may borrow from Mitchell's review of Jannaccone and argue that what the Columbia economist wrote could be taken as representative of American economists' opinion: "one sometimes gets the impression that originality is a virtue less esteemed among the modern Italian economists than erudition. Apparently they are less intent upon contributing new ideas to the discussion than upon furnishing their students with an Encyclopaedic digest of English, German, French, and American opinion, past and present, which shall restate in diluted form currently accepted doctrine upon all possible topics" [Mitchell 1901, 460].

In this paragraph we intend to show whether and to what extent this lack of doctrinal novelty in the Italian literature is a conclusion that American economists widely shared. Our analysis will be restricted to the most celebrated cases of Pantaleoni, Pareto, and De Viti de Marco.

Indeed, if we again refer to Mitchell's authority, Pantaleoni's *Principi* was the most celebrated case where one could typically talk of "erudition without originality." Most American economists agreed with this verdict. Of course there were formal differences, particularly if we compare neoclassicals with institutionalists. Fisher, among the former, exalted Pantaleoni's virtues for clarity and synthesis. Writing about Pantaleoni's *Principles*, Fisher observed: "we do not know where else in English can be found so compact and excellent an epitome of modern economic theory" [Fisher 1898, 123]. As to Henry Moore, he generally agreed with Fisher, and praised Pantaleoni for being among the first scholars to have attached "permanent importance to Marshall's early graphical essays" [Moore 1926, 587]. Moore was never sympathetic with partial equilibrium approach. However, he underlined the important influence which Pantaleoni's little book had exerted on Pareto and therefore on the more general development of economics as a science: Pantaleoni was "the inspiring friend who indirectly gave new vigor to economic theory, by inducing Pareto to seek the goal that lay buried in the complex research of Leon Walras" [Moore 1926, 587]. Among neoclassical economists, the American Marshallian, Frank Taussig, did not completely share the same feelings with Fisher and Moore. Quite to the contrary, Taussig thought that Pantaleoni had exaggerated the merits of precursors (i.e. Gossen) while overlooking the contributions of later writers of the same school [Taussig 1896, 302].

Not surprisingly, however, more open criticism came from the institutionalist camp. A pupil of Commons, the labour economist E.B. Andrews, expressed strong reservations for Pantaleoni's search for a "classical synthesis" of the same kind that Marshall was trying to achieve. In comparative terms, Pantaleoni's *Principi* was of little value as a textbook, while his treatment of wages and distribution was utterly inadequate. In his review for the *Political Science Quarterly*, Andrews reached the conclusion that Pantaleoni was "very old school, ranking in this respect more nearly with Leroy Beaulieu and the editor of the *Journal des Economistes*, than with any other economist of note now living" [Andrews 1891, 741-742]. Among American institutionalists Mitchell wrote the final and very influential words, if one can almost literally find them reproduced in Schumpeter's *History of Economic Analysis*: while Pantaleoni tried unsuccessfully to base economic theory on a hedonistic foundation, in his *Principi* – thus Mitchell argued – there was nothing "of striking originality, but the work of an ingenious and learned man who knows thoroughly and seeks to reproduce and harmonize classical political economy with the works of Thunen, Jevons, Walras and Marshall [...]. Little that is new aside from the eclectic fashion in which doctrines from many different sources are fitted together" [Mitchell 1949, 821].

More or less devastating as these critical remarks were, we may wonder what remained of Pantaleoni in American economic thought? We have already briefly referred to the fact that Pantaleoni's reputation as an original thinker was mainly built after he published his 1909 essay on dynamic instability. Here we must turn our attention to methodology and public finance. Fisher embraced without reservation his activities as a militant economist. In many ways Pantaleoni could be taken as a model for the economics profession in the new century. Fisher informed his readers that Pantaleoni genuinely possessed the qualities that all economists should have: "he is a well equipped and efficient teacher, writer, editor and reformer" [Fisher 1898, 123]. And it is not surprising that when Fisher first met Mussolini to gain the Italian government's official sponsorship to implement his plans for monetary stabilization, the Yale economist introduced himself as "an old friend of Pantaleoni" [Asso 1994]. As far as public finance was concerned, ever since the 1880s Seligman acknowledged and subsequently stressed in more than one occasion that Pantaleoni was the first modern economist who had studied the problems of incidence and the shifting of taxation. While ignoring Cournot's pioneering contribution, Pantaleoni had managed to give pride of place to a much neglected subject, showing how financial phenomena needed to be treated also as a matter of pure theory. Indeed Seligman was rather critical of the kind of theory the young Pantaleoni was using, particularly when analysing how taxation affects the "laws" of income distribution; but nevertheless Seligman thought that with his 1882 monograph the Italian economist had broken new ground and influenced the production of new research [Seligman 1892; 1895].

As to Vilfredo Pareto, we have already talked about the scant fortune enjoyed by his *Magnus Opus* in the United States and the contrasting opinions with which American economists welcomed the use he made of the mathematical method. Nonetheless this section is dedicated to the analysis of Pareto's influence in the United States both as economist and as a sociologist. Our study has revealed that, at least until the end of the thirties, Pareto's economic ideas had a direct impact on two distinct research programs, namely, the quantitative investigations into the distribution of income, and the statistical estimation of neoclassical demand curves.

As far as the first kind of studies is concerned, the attention of American economists was mainly attracted by the famous Pareto's law, that is the empirical regularity in the distribution of income over different historical periods that the Italian economist discovered and presented in his *Cours*. According to Henry Moore, who reviewed the work in *The Annals of the American Academy of Political and Social Science* [Moore 1897], "the study of the distribution of wealth is probably the most original and suggestive part of the work." Pareto depicted the distribution of incomes by plotting the numbers of incomes above certain amounts against the respective amounts, employing logarithmic scales on both axes. As originally formulated, the law stated that the plotted points would take the form of a straight line with a certain slope. The line would be straight and the slope would be the same, he held, in all countries and at all times.

In order to understand Pareto's proposition correctly it is useful to recall that when the individual incomes are distributed according to either of the two principal forms which Pareto's Law assumes, the average income X is given by the following relations: $X=\alpha h/(\alpha-1)$ and $X=(\alpha h+a)/(\alpha-1)$, where h represents the lowest income. In connection with the above formulae, Pareto provided two theorems. According to the first theorem the minimum income h will vary directly with the average income, provided the degree of inequality among individual incomes does not vary or, to put it in formal terms, when α and a do not vary. Alternatively, holding minimum income constant, an increase in the average income implies a reduction in α and hence in inequality. In other words, Pareto affirmed that the only way for the lower classes to escape poverty was through an increase of the overall level of production.

In looking for a rationale for such empirical regularity, Pareto excluded both the role of chance and the influence of the institutional structure of society[30], affirming that the distribution of income depended primarily on human nature. However, as Persky [1992, 184] correctly pointed out, Pareto did not clearly specify the meaning of this assertion. In some instances he argued that the distribution of incomes was determined by the underlying distribution of human abilities. At some other places, Pareto provided instead a "political" interpretation of "his" law, suggesting that "those who won the struggle for society's reward would have a tendency to accept a certain share (as measured by its distribution) rather than fighting without end" [Persky 1992, 184].

The first attempt to verify the validity of Pareto's law was made in 1909 by the Harvard statistician Warren M. Persons, who tested the law in connection to the distribution of real estate property in France and Great Britain. The conclusions

[30] "These results are very remarkable. It is absolutely impossible to admit that they are due only to chance. There is most certainly a cause, which produces the tendency of incomes to arrange themselves according to a certain curve. The form of this curve seems to depend only tenuously upon different economic conditions of the countries considered, since the effects are very nearly the same for the countries whose economic conditions are as different as those of England, of Ireland, of Germany, of the Italian cities, and even of Peru" [Pareto 1895-1897 II, 312].

reached by Persons were by no means encouraging: "the accuracy of Pareto's first approximation – he wrote – is apparent and not actual. Pareto's method is not to be relied upon in comparisons where the difference in the amount of variability is not great" [Persons 1919].

Hints at Pareto's theory of income distribution can also be found in a 1917 essay by Allyn Young, published in the *American Economic Review*. Here the author, commenting on the recent statistical findings on the concentration of wealth in the United States, discussed Pareto's index of inequality of the distribution of income. According to the interpretation offered by the Italian economist in his *Cours* [vol. II, 320, note], such measure was based on the expressed assumption that when the number of persons with incomes of less than a given size increases as compared with the number of persons with higher incomes, the inequality of income distribution diminishes. Young did not contest the underlying assumption of Pareto's index. As he explicitly admitted, once a definite income range is given, with small incomes more numerous than large incomes, the hypothesis was generally consistent with the common idea of the meaning of equality in distribution. However, Pareto was mistaken in interpreting the relation between his index and the definition of inequality. As Young put it: "[...] so far as I know, it has not been noticed even by his critics that Pareto, brillant mathematician as he is, made a curious slip in interpreting the relation of his index to his definition of inequality. *His index does not increase as he supposed, with what he deemed inequality in the distribution of incomes, but decreases*. It can be used, as Benini and Bresciani have used it, in this inverted fashion. At best [...] is a poor index being merely a rough measure of the evenness with which income receivers are distributed through the income range. It gives no simple and definite standard of comparison" [Young 1917, 149: emphasis added][31].

As a matter of fact, the "inverted fashion" in which both Benini and Bresciani used Pareto's index was the correct one. In his remarks, Young had not realized that the alleged slip made by Pareto was actually a printer's error which substituted an "increase in inequality" for a "decrease in inequality" in a crucial passage. It should be noted, however, that in a footnote Pareto correctly concluded that in terms of his own definition of inequality lower values of α were associated with a reduction in inequality (see discussion by Persky [1992, 185 n5]).

Apart from Persons' and Young's, the most devastating attack on the validity of Pareto's law was brought about a few years later by Frederic Macaulay and the

[31] Young also expressed strong reservation on the value of the index that the Italian statistician Corrado Gini had suggested as a substitute for Pareto's. According to Young, this index, which takes into account the sum of the differences between each income and every other income, "[m]ay be interpreted as a summary arithmetical expression of the degree of concentration denoted by the Lorenz graph. So, finally, with all these measures, such as the average deviation, probable error, and standard deviation, which indicate in a general way the extent to which incomes as a whole differ from the average income. The significant thing is that all of these ways of expressing the degree of inequality in the distribution of wealth use as a standard or reference of comparison an absolutely equal and uniform distribution" [Young 1917, 149-50].

team of researchers who worked at the newly established National Bureau of Economic Research under the supervision of Edwin Gay and Wesley Clair Mitchell. In their published study *Income in the United States 1909-1919* a whole chapter was dedicated to the testing of Pareto's law in the United States. Drawing upon the impressive amount of data series then available at the NBER the research showed that, at least for the American case, Pareto's law did not hold true: "the tails of the distributions on a double log scale are not linear. The straight lines do not show even approximately constant slopes from year to year or between country and country. The tails are not of the same shape from year to year or between country and country." In terms of policy advocating the criticism to Pareto's conception of an "invariable" law of distribution was even more devastating: "Pareto's conclusion that economic welfare can be increased only through increased production is based upon erroneous premises. The income curve is not constant in slope. Internal movements suggest the possibility of important changes in distribution" [Macaulay 1922, 344]. At a more technical level, Macaulay contested Pareto's methodology on the grounds that the process of using logarithmic scales on both axes had the effect of greatly compressing the data with the implied result of concealing irregularities.

During the thirties Pareto's law received a new wave of attention by American scholars (see especially Leven [1934]; Crum [1935]; Johnson [1935; 1937]; Tucker [1938], Snyder [1940], Davis [(1941) 1963]). Such a resurgence of interest was probably related to the rising tide of econometric studies in the United States during those years and, possibly, as a side effect of the publication of the English translation of Pareto's *Trattato di Sociologia Generale* (see below)[32].

Several of these studies tended, in general, to confirm the findings of earlier critical investigations, rejecting the hypothesis that incomes, in different places and epochs, were approximately distributed in accordance with an invariable law. For instance, in a comprehensive investigation over the distribution of income in the United States for the years 1863-1935, Rufus Tucker showed that concentration of income had a pro-cyclical tendency: it increased in the upward phase of the business cycle and decreased in the downward phase. This was mainly due "to the fact that the rising phase is characterized and perhaps caused by rising profits, and concentration is mainly the result of large profits." For this reason, Tucker concluded, concentration of incomes in times of peace is "usually a sign of increasing national income, rising wages, and more employment" [Tucker 1938, 587]. A much more cautious comment was put forward by a Federal Reserve Bank economist, Norris O. Johnson. Although admitting that the phenomena of linearity and constancy of slope observed by Pareto should not have been called a "law," Johnson concluded that discarding it completely would involve "the sacrifice

[32] Quite interestingly, in fact, *Econometrica* itself reviewed the English edition of Pareto's *Treatise*.

both of a most valuable piece of analytical machinery and of the general conclusions to which its application leads" [Johnson, 1937, 26][33].

Other authors did not share Johnson's caution and rather than limiting themselves to verify the logical consistency or empirical validity of Pareto's law, enthusiastically explored its moral and political, as well as heuristic, implications. This is, for example, the case of Harold T. Davis and Carl Snyder[34]. Particularly for Snyder Pareto's law provided an illuminating precedent for the formal construction of index numbers which could ideally represent other aspects of the economic system.

Harold T. Davis was among the leading figures of the so-called "econometric movement" of the late thirties and early forties. He co-founded *Econometrica* and participated, since its beginning, to the activities of the Cowles Commission for Research in Economics. In his monograph on *The Analysis of Economic Time Series* [(1941) 1963], he devoted a whole chapter to the inquiry into the possible political effects of an abnormal deviation of Pareto's index from its assumed normal value of 1.5[35]. Although admitting the lack of reliable statistical data for those national economies which had been disrupted by revolution and civil wars, Davis ventured that "it is not unreasonable to suppose that disturbances in the Pareto index and the concentration ratio may be accompanied by economic and political disturbances" [Davis (1941) 1963, 434]. In support of his thesis, he provided several examples, mainly inferred from historical sources. According to Davis both the French and the Russian revolutions "were [...] aggravated, if not actually caused, by an undue concentration of wealth and income." Not satisfied by this incursion into history, Davis went further, arguing that even the American Civil War was largely a result of disturbances in the natural distribution of incomes. "The distribution of slave holdings in this region [the Southern States] – he wrote – was approximately Paretian and hence a large disturbance was caused in the concentration ratio when the slaves were freed. It is not unreasonable to suppose that the slow economic recovery of the south, when compared with that of the north, was not so much due to the fact that the North was victorious as to this

---

[33] According to the mathematical economist, L. Crum, the recent wave of articles on Pareto's law confirmed the findings of pre-war critical investigations. Again, Pareto's formal representation of income distribution had not passed the test of reality: "the direction of the line of best fit changes considerably over time; and its variation appear systematically associated with the economic cycle, rather than random. The line is not a good fit, even within the tax range, since several years show a well marked curvature of a fairly uniform type. Tests of other fitted curves than a straight line yield somewhat closer fit within the tax range, but no case was found in which the fit was of the sort appearing to warrant extrapolation. Examination of distribution for specific sources of incomes reveals such disparities for specific sources of income that, in view of the variable structure of combined income, the likelihood of a general law of distribution applying to combined income appears remote" [Crum 1935, 130].

[34] We became aware of Snyder's interest on Pareto's law from the insightful remarks in Persky [1992]. Therefore, the spirit of our discussion above, as well as the specific passages quoted, draw heavily on Persky.

[35] It was Pareto that observed that the values of the parameter (the absolute value of the slope of the distribution line) clustered around 1.5. See Persky [1992] for more details.

dislocation of the concentration parameter" [Davis (1941) 1963, 435]. Davis concluded that Pareto's law represented a *necessary* condition of any stable economic state; necessary in the sense that rapid changes in the concentration ratio can easily trigger changes both in the sphere of production and labor. "If these changes are too rapid or too extended – this was Davis' final remark – then violent political repercussions may be expected" [Davis (1941) 1963, 440].

Carl Snyder is another author who, with his remarks on Pareto, exemplifies the doctrinal structure of the brand of political conservatorism that was emerging in those years in the United States, partially as a reaction to the New Deal experience. Snyder had been for more than a decade the Head of the Statistics Department at the Federal Reserve Board of New York. A close adviser of Governor Strong on monetary policy and credit control, Snyder had published important articles on the leading economics journals on monetary stabilization, index numbers, and the formal construction of the general CPI. Being, as Schumpeter put it in a letter to Marget, "a collector of statistics without reference to theory, as our friend [...] Macaulay (is) doing,"[36] Snyder joined Davis in his enthusiastic endorsement of Pareto's law, considering it as a "general expression for practically every kind of highly specialized ability." In his opinion, the empirical regularity discovered by the Italian economist "is destined to take its place as one of the great generalizations of human knowledge," since it reflected the economic manifestations of our inability to create "by legislation or any fanciful law [...] a Newton, a Shakespeare or an Edison" [Snyder 1940, 61; quoted in Persky 1992, 189-90]. From this premise, Snyder reached the conclusion that any attempt to redistribute away from this natural distribution of human abilities would result in "the ruthless destruction of civilization by these barbarian hordes" [Snyder 1940, 418; quoted in Persky 1992, 190]. Snyder's enthusiasm for Pareto's law led him to formulate an invariable law of production which ruled out the existence of cycles in the economic activity. His statistical effort to reproduce a "steady rate of increase in total production" was sneered by many economists, and particularly by those who were taking great pains in trying to explain the acute phases of business cycles. Schumpeter and Gottfried Haberler were just two of them and, quite interestingly, in their private correspondence, the former assimilated Snyder's index to Pareto's alpha. According to Schumpeter these were the two most striking examples "of unexplained invariants in economic life [...] These things point to the presence of very constant relations between a few fundamental quantities and to the possibility of expressing them by very simple factual hypothesis"[37]. They were – as Schumpeter might have added – two further examples of a "Ricardian

[36] Schumpeter to Marget, 28 December 1928. Jospeh A. Schumpeter papers, Harvard University Archives, Pusey Library.

[37] Schumpeter to Haberler, 20 March 1933. Jospeh A. Schumpeter papers, Harvard University Archives, Pusey Library.

vice" in the history of economic analysis which the rigorous scholar ought to discard outrightly.

Turning our attention to neoclassical demand theory we note that the impact of Pareto's contribution on American scholars was much more of a constructive nature. The call for a "statistical complement of pure economics" was launched as early as in 1908 by Henry Moore in a paper published in the *Quarterly Journal of Economics*. What Moore had in mind, when he spoke of "pure economics" was the economics of Walras and the improvement made upon it by Pareto. If Moore played the role of the "proselytizer," to borrow Philip Mirowski's vivid expression [Mirowski 1990], it was the Chicago economist Henry Schultz – a former student of Moore at Columbia – who put his efforts on the new quantitative research agenda[38].

Taking as a starting point Pareto's mathematical refinement of Walras – which he preferred to Fisher's[39] – Schultz produced a series of econometric studies which aimed to reveal the microfoundations of the estimated demand functions[40]. Schultz's major contribution was *The Theory and Measurement of Demand* which appeared in 1938, the very same year of his sudden death in a car accident. As D. Wade Hands and Philip Mirowski have acutely pointed out the book turned out to be essentially a swan song for Walrasian empirical economics: "Schultz bravely reported the empirical debate in detail, and then produced a litany of excuses that things had not worked out as he hoped" [Hands-Mirowski 1998, 264]. Apart from Schultz's failure to test empirically Pareto's demand functions, two more "revolutionary" events contributed to the decline of the research program started by Moore. First of all, the advent of Keynesianism and the consequent shift of emphasis towards the "macro" analysis of aggregate demand. Secondly, the publication, again in 1938, of Samuelson's pathbreaking contribution on "revealed preferences." Here, the rising star of American economics intended to move "beyond" Pareto in emancipating economics from psychological assumptions, and presented his own version of demand theory "freed from any vestigial traces of the utility concept" [Samuelson 1938, 71].

We now proceed to a brief discussion of the diffusion of Pareto's sociology in the United States. Compared to other studies on the subject[41], our analysis has an exclusive focus on the interwar years and on the role played by the Harvard sociologist Talcott Parsons. While an undergraduate at Amherst, Parsons studied under Clarence Ayres and Walton H. Hamilton who introduced him to the

---

[38] See also on these issues Hands and Mirowski [1998].

[39] In comparing the two authors Schultz observed that their fundamental contribution was the introduction of indifference curves and the related use of index functions. Both concepts allowed the discarding of a subjective theory of value and could be defined "in terms of operations which have a clear observable measurable basis" [Schultz 1938, 13]. While very similar to Pareto's theory of choice, he concluded, Fisher's version of indifference curves "did not develop the implication of his theory as fully and as thoroughly as did Pareto" [Schultz 1938, 13].

[40] Schultz [1928; 1933;1938].

[41] See Lopreato–Rusher [1983] and Lane [1978].

institutionalist critique of neoclassical economic theory. In this connection, it is interesting to note that Parsons considered Pareto's contribution to sociology as a "way out" from the methodological disputes in which institutionalists and neoclassicists were engaged at that time. As he wrote in his review of the American edition of the *Trattato di sociologia* [Pareto 1935]: "Pareto's experience has a peculiar relevance to the current methodological controversies in American economics between "orthodox" and "institutionalist" schools. For he took a way out of the situation underlying the controversy which is not very widely accepted, at least in any systematic, methodological, self-conscious form, but which is in my opinion exceedingly fruitful" [Parsons 1935, 501]. More specifically, Parsons' appreciated Pareto's idea of residues and derivations and their classification in groups and classes. Such taxonomy of human motivations had the advantage of providing an explanation for both the intentional and deliberative aspects of human behavior, avoiding the kind of psychological determinism – "psychologism" in Parsons own expression –, which marked Veblen's theory of instincts. Perhaps the most interesting comment by Parson is to be found in an unpublished fragment, dated 1934, in which the Harvard sociologist called for the construction of a "new institutionalism, based on an enlightened and mutually respectful cooperation between the best and methodologically most sophisticated of the orthodox economic theory, and the newer sociological theory of such men as Pareto, Durkheim and Max Weber, and their successors. In the understanding of concrete economic activities neither can get on without the other."[42]

Parsons' outcry for the "construction" of a new institutionalism grounded on the sociological approach of the continental tradition remained an isolated case within the institutionalist community. To our knowledge, as far as the Italian thinker is concerned, none of the leading figures of the movement made use of Pareto's analysis of human behavior and his name never appears in the most influential institutionalist treatises of the thirties. Even Wesley Clair Mitchell, who had dedicated a chapter to the Italian economist in his *Types of Economic Theory* [Mitchell 1949], did not seem to appreciate Pareto's sociological enterprise as we evinced from a brief note in his diaries: "Finished reading Pareto's *Mind and Society* (4 volumes). I had begun it earnest on July 16th. Rather disappointed on the whole."[43]

Two other authors who tried to build on Pareto's sociology were J. Harvey Rogers and Henry Moore. Rogers, a student of Fisher who had spent some time in Lausanne studying under Pareto, recommended a fusion of some aspects of Veblenian and Deweyan social theories with Pareto's scheme of non-logical human actions. As he wrote in 1928, almost all that had passed for social sciences

---

[42] Parsons T. 1934. "Institutionalism," Talcott Parsons Collection, Harvard University.

[43] Mitchell's Diary, August 4th, 1935. Mitchell Papers, Rare Books and Manuscript Library, Columbia University.

"will be cast aside by future generations as mainly rationalizing: Dewey reached this conclusion in regard to philosophy; Veblen [...] to traditional political economy; and now comes an Italian sociologist, Vilfredo Pareto, who in his huge *Treatise on general sociology* devoted hundreds of pages to substantiating a similar thesis affecting all the social sciences" [Rogers 1928 quoted in Dorfman 1947-1959, IV, 143]. Rogers, also for his premature death, did not translate his project of a constructive synthesis of Pareto with American pragmatism into any published work. He nevertheless played an important role in promoting Pareto's sociological ideas in the United States as supervisor of the English translation of the *Trattato*.

We have already encountered Moore as the pioneer of empirical studies based on Pareto's demand functions. Interestingly, after the publication of his major work, *Synthetic Economics*, Moore decided to abandon his studies on statistical economics and turned his attention to sociology. Evidence that the shift in Moore's research interests was mainly due to the appearance of Pareto's *Treatise* on sociology has emerged from our archival research at Columbia. In 1924 Moore filled many notebooks with his personal remarks on Pareto's theory of residues, and, still in the same year, he began to write a paper entitled "Fascism: a Sociological Interpretation." Moreover, as reported by Mirowski [1990], after his retirement from Columbia University Moore embarked upon a book, to be titled *The Good Life in a Progressive Society*, which was intended to serve as a sociological complement of his work on quantitative economics. Moore never concluded this final project but from the portions of the original manuscript that can be found at the Columbia University archive it is not difficult to individuate in Pareto the source of inspiration of Moore's final venture into sociology.

The last case study we discuss in this paper is related to the appearance in 1936 of the English translation of De Viti's *Prinicipii di Economia Finanziaria*. At that time both the book and its author had acquired an international reputation as it emerges from both published and unpublished evidence. In 1932 the German translation of the *Principii* had been welcomed in England by its reviewer, LSE's Frederick Benham, as "probably the best treatise on the theory of public finance ... [a book] comparable to the *Principles* of Marshall," while in 1935 Frank Taussig, in replying to a letter of Gaetano Salvemini, who had inquired about the possibility of an English translation of the book, asserted: "[...] I know about De Viti de Marco's book and have no doubt it is a thorough and scholarly performance [...]. I shall be glad to have a look at it again and consider whether any success is likely if an English translation is proposed to an English or American publisher."[44]

As the English edition of the *Principii* appeared in print (with the title of *First Principles of Public Finance*), Chicago's Henry Simons – the father,

[44] Taussig to Salvemini, February 15th, 1935. Taussig Papers, Pusey Memorial Library, Harvard University.

together with Frank Knight of the "first" Chicago school – was assigned to write an extensive review article for the *Journal of Political Economy*. The review, though phrased in an elegant style, was extremely negative [Simons 1937]. Simons started expressing his resentment towards the critics "who induced him to search in this treatise for the profound analysis and penetrating insights which it does not contain" – here, the implicit reference is to Benham's review – and continued affirming that De Viti's *Principles* "may be regarded as a model for the kind of writing which has made our own literature of public finance a disgrace in economics and a means for stultifying those who pursue the usual routines of academic speculation." Discussing in more detail the contents of the book, Simons attacked De Viti for his incautious use of economic terminology to describe different institutional orders (the distinction between co-operative and monopolistic state), for his criticism of progressive tax rates, and for his treatment of the problem of incidence and shifting of taxation. The only point on which Simons declared to agree with De Viti concerned his condemn of Mill's notion of double taxation of saving. He nevertheless, also in this case, found the discussion of the subject by the Italian economist both confused and unsatisfactory.

Textual scrutiny of De Viti's *Treatise* shows that, Simons' criticisms were substantially misplaced. For instance, as far as the criterion of direct taxation is concerned, Simons interpreted De Viti's objections to progressive taxation, on the ground that it inhibits capital accumulation, as an implicit support of proportionality: "At all events strict proportionality is held up as the proper norm in taxation." As it has been showed by Fausto [1995], what De Viti had in mind was actually a combination of the two systems – progressive taxation up to medium incomes and to be realized by a program of fiscal exemptions, proportionality for higher incomes – so that the proposal contained in his book reduces itself to a mild form of progressiveness which would guarantee, at the same time, both greater accumulation and a more equal redistribution of income.

The correspondence between Arthur Marget – a personal friend of De Viti and the husband of Edith Marget, the translator of the *Principles* – and Henry Simons, allowed us to reveal another aspect of Simons' critique which appears to be, at best, misdirected. In a passage of his review article the Chicago economist criticized De Viti for having endorsed all the "crudities" of the older doctrines of the incidence of taxation, by quoting with approval "an especially bad passage from Seligman." For "crudities" Simons meant the conception of the tax as an increase in the cost of production that the producer must necessarily compensate by an increase in the price of the product and, therefore, by transferring the burden of the tribute to the final consumer. In his epistolary rejoinder to Simons, Marget decided to turn his attention on this specific point. "I should suggest" – he wrote – "that you read again the part of De Viti in which there appears the quotation from Seligman. You say that he quotes this passage with approval. If you read De Viti again you will discover that he not only disapproves of that passage most emphatically, but bases his whole discussion of incidence on his disagreement."[45] Careful reading of De Viti's chapter on incidence shows the validity of Marget's remark. Nowhere in his treatise the Italian economist seems to abandon his own version of the "benefit" doctrine in order to agree with the position held by Seligman. According to De Viti the State is an agent who participates to the production process with its own services. The tax is therefore seen not as a burden to escape or to shift, but rather as the price paid by the producer to the State in exchange of those services. All this implies that whether the tax is to be considered in terms of a loss for the producer depends only on the contribution to the economic efficiency brought by the services provided by the state. In De Viti's own words: "[I]t is necessary to discuss the problem on the most general hypothesis that the substitution of public enterprise for private enterprise results in advantages for the taxpayers. But even if the contrary hypothesis is adopted, it will always have to be admitted that it is not the tax paid by the producer that decides, but the nature of the public service produced and the degree to which each individual enterprise can in fact make use of these services. [...]. To sum up: the cost of production may have been increased, left as it was, or diminished by an increase in taxes." [De Viti De Marco 1936, 151]

As a concluding remark, it seems to us that Simons' critique of De Viti reflects a more profound difference between the two authors, a difference that involves two distinct approaches to public economics and which probably caused Simon's misreading of De Viti's *Principles*. In De Viti's intentions the *Principles* should have served as a theoretical framework in order to reconcile Public finance with the underlying principles of orthodox economic theory. This is the reason why in the first sections of the book he insisted extensively on the analogy between political and economic phenomena by constructing the ideal types of the co-operative State (where individuals demand "public goods" produced by the State which operates according to the laws of competition) as opposed to the monopolistic State (where the State fixes both the price and the quantity of services to be sold in the market). The book itself was not intended to be an apology for fiscal reform but rather as a tool for the modern analyst in public finance who wanted to conjugate theoretical rigor and analysis of different institutional settings.

The starting point of Simon's speculation on public finance was completely different. Simons' economic ideas represented a synthesis of liberalism with social and economic reformism. Indeed, much of Simons' work clearly indicates his skepticism toward both the night watchman State and State collectivism. It was his faith in the market which led him to reject Keynesian anti cyclical policy agenda (at least in the version vulgarized by Hansen). But, at the same time, it was his diffidence towards a more radical approach to laissez faire which made him seek for fiscal reform as a necessary means in order to achieve freedom and equality of

[45] Marget to Simons, November 20th, 1937. Department of Special Collections, University of Chicago Library.

opportunities – the values which he considered the prerequisites for the fair working of the market institution. As it has been recently remarked by one biographer, "Simons' view had a distinctly populist flavour that is absent from those more recently associated with Chicago economics [...]. He favoured use of Government power to reduce the size of large firms and labor unions. Where such losses would lead to unacceptable losses of efficiency (e.g. natural monopolies) Simons favoured outright public ownership, in sharp contrast to more recent Chicago statements on the matter. Simons emphatically supported progressive income taxation to promote a more egalitarian distribution of income. Finally he proposed a requirement of 100% reserves against demand deposits and restriction of FRB discretion in monetary policy in favour of fixed rules designed to stabilize the price level" [Reder 1987, 425-16].

In conclusion, Simons' reading of De Viti appears to be both superficial and biased. But we can find also another reason that could account, apart from Simons' review, for the scant fortune enjoyed by De Viti's *Principles* in the US, namely, the nature of the book itself. In fact, the *Principles* were neither a textbook (at least in the American meaning of the term) suitable for graduate teaching, nor a monograph or a general survey on the state of Italian literature on Public finance capable to attract the attention of the American scholar who was looking for insights on the concrete problems of the time. In this connection it is interesting to note that in his famous lectures on public finance at Columbia, E. R. A. Seligman decided to ignore De Viti's *Principles* but included several chapters from Graziani's five volumes treatise in his suggested reading list.

5. Conclusions

In this paper three main channels of integration have been explored in order to reconstruct the pattern of diffusion of Italian economic thought in the United States between 1890 and 1940. First we have examined the degree of openness which American economics guaranteed to the importation of Italian economic ideas. We have found in this respect that the American market constituted an ideal environment for efficient interactions and that most barriers to cultural exchanges were gradually relaxed. Italian economists were often invited to present their research to the American public, while different sorts of academic connections were established and developed. Moreover the fact that the two groups shared common preferences for a pluralistic and pragmatic approach to economics stimulated a real wealth of contacts and scientific initiatives.

Secondly, we have briefly sketched the peculiarities of this network of knowledge. Using different sources, we showed that American economists had an enviable awareness of what their Italian colleagues were doing in both theoretical and applied fields. Throughout these five decades, the number of book reviews published by the leading American journals is impressive as well as the amount of correspondence and other exchanges on specific aspects of contemporary economic life and research. Quite significantly, this network of knowledge was not biassed by such partisan presentations as the ones provided by Rabbeno and Loria at the beginning of our period. Their attempt to demolish the Italian contribution to marginalism or public finance produced no great damage, and leading American economists never seemed to follow their suggestions.

Thirdly, we have analyzed the degree of influence which Italian economists managed to exert on their American colleagues. Strong Italian connections were established on applied statistics, and particularly on the discussion of alternative methods for the derivation of demand curves. Fisher, Moore, and Schultz, were among those who looked with interest at the Italian mathematical school, and critically examined its contributions to general equilibrium theory and market structures. The early debate on the integrability conditions represent another interesting – albeit quite isolated – case of successful diffusion and knowledge of Italian economics. The active participation of Italian economists to the Econometric Society Movement is another result which goes in the same direction.

In terms of influence, however, our research gives mixed results. On the one hand, Italian economic thought is often depicted as being old-fashioned and surpassed by more modern professional standards. As Wesley Mitchell put it in his characterization, what was coming from Italy could be classified as "erudition without originality," as systematic but backward-looking, as useful but not innovative. Such critical judgements we have found to be quite widely shared within American economists. It is quite likely that they became responsible for the many "missed opportunities" which in the end diminished the rate of scientific influence. Pantaleoni's early reception, particularly for his studies on dynamics, is probably the most important case; but also the demolition of De Viti's *Principles of Public Finance* or the surprising neglect of Barone's works on value and distribution were two further casualties of this prevailing interpretation.

Pareto, however, remains an important exception: his writings were quite influential, his method was highly praised, while some of his analytical tools were made the object of further technical refinement and inductive verification. Also Pareto's sociology had a favorable impact on American studies, both for its new categories and the methodological implications of his message.

References

ANDREWS E.B. (1891), "Review of M. Pantaleoni, *Principi di economia pura*", *Political Science Quarterly*, Vol. VI, pp. 741-42.

ARDZROONI L. (1913), "Review of *Les bases économiques de la justice internationale*, par Achille Loria", *Journal of Political Economy*, Vol. 22, p. 169.

ARDZROONI L. (1914), "Review of *The Economic Synthesis*, by Achille Loria", *Journal of Political Economy*, Vol. 23, pp. 702-4.

ASSO P.F. (1994), "The economist as preacher: the correspondence between Irving Fisher and Benito Mussolini and other letters on the Fisher plan", *Research in the History of Economic Thought and Methodology*, Archival supplement, 4.

ASSO P.F. and FIORITO L. (2001), *Dalla periferia al nuovo mondo. La diffusione del pensiero economico italiano negli Stati Uniti*. Roma, Ente Einaudi.

BARBER W.J. (1998), "Remarks on 'America-ness' in American economic thought", in Rutherford (1998).

BENHAM F. (1934), "*Principii di economia finanziaria*. A. De Viti De Marco (Einaudi, Torino, 1934) – *Grundlebren der Finanzwwirtschaft*. A. De Viti de Marco (J.C.B. Mobor: Tübingen, 1932)", *Economica*, pp. 364-67.

BENSON L. (1950), "Achille Loria's influence on American economic thought", *Agricultural History*, 24, October.

BLAKEY R.G. (1925), "Review of *The Social Significance of the Inheritance Tax* by Eugenio Rignano", *American Economic Review*.

BRESCIANI-TURRONI C. (1910), "Di un indice misuratore della disuguaglianza nella distribuzione della ricchezza", in *Studi in Onore di B. Brugi*, Palermo.

BRESCIANI-TURRONI C. (1939), "Annual Survey of Statistical Data: Pareto's Law and the index of Inequality of Incomes", *Econometrica*, Vol. 7, pp. 107-33.

CARLSON B. (1999), "Wagner's legacy in America: reopening Farnam's inquiry", *Journal of the History of Economic Thought*, 3, pp. 289-310.

CAVALIERI D. and FAUCCI R. (1994), "Italian-style pluralism in economics", *History of Economic Ideas*, 3, pp. 63-98.

CHAZEL F. (1997), "L'entrée de Pareto dans la sociologie américaine et son appropriation sélective par T. Parsons e George Homans", in Bouvier A. (ed.), *Pareto aujourd'hui*, Paris: PUF, pp. 129-152.

CLARK J.B. (1910), "The Phenomena of Economic Dynamics. Discussion", *American Economic Association Quarterly*, pp. 122-35.

CLARK J.M. (1923), *Studies in the Economics of Overhead Costs*, Chicago: University of Chicago Press.

COATS A.W. (1992), "Economics in the United States, 1920-1970", in *On the History of Economic Thought: British and American Economic Essays*, vol. 1, London, Routledge, pp. 407-455.

COATS A.W. (1998), "What is American about American economics", in Rutherford (1998).

COATS A.W. and COLANDER D. (eds.) (1988), *The Spread of Economic Ideas*, Cambridge University Press.

CRUM W.L. (1935), "Individual Shares in the National Income", *Review of Economic and Statistics*, Vol. 7, pp. 116-130.

DAVIS H. (1963), *The Analysis of Economic Time Series*. The Principia Press of Trinity

University, Originally published as monograph N. 6 of the Cowles Commisssion for Research in Economics, 1941.
De Viti De Marco A. (1936), *First Principles in Public Finance*, London: Jonathan Cape.
Dorfman J. (1947-1959), *The American Mind in the Economic Civilization*, 5 vols., New York, Viking.
Dorfman J. (1955), "The Role of German Historical School in American Economic Thought", *American Economic Review*, May.
Fausto D. (1955), "I *Principi di economia finanziaria* nella letteratura straniera", in A. Pedone (a cura di), *Antonio De Viti de Marco*, Bari, Laterza.
Fetter F. (1910), "The Phenomena of Economic Dynamics. Discussion", *American Economic Association Quarterly*, pp. 122-35.
Fetter F. (1925), "The Economist and the Public", *American Economic Review*, Vol. 15, pp. 13-26
Fiorito L., Johnson M. and Samuels W.S. Forthcoming. "Edwin R. A. Seligman Lecture Notes in Public Finance: 1927-1928", *Research in the History of Economic Though and Methodology*, Archival Supplement.
Fisher I. (1892), *Mathematical Investigations in the Theory of Value and Prices*, New Haven, Yale University Press.
Fisher I. (1896a), "Book notices. *Cours d'Economie Politique* and *La courbe de la repartition de la richesse*", *Yale Review*, 5, pp. 325-328.
Fisher I. (1896b), "What is Capital?", *Economic Journal*, Vol. VI, pp. 509-534.
Fisher I. (1898), "Review of M. Pantaleoni, *Pure Economics*", *Annals of the American Academy of Political and Social Sciences*, Vol. 10, pp. 122-125.
Fisher I. (1919), "Economists in the Public Service", *American Economic Review*, Vol. 9 (supplement), pp. 5-21.
Goodwin C.D. and Meardon S. (1998), "The International Dimension of American Economics", in Rutherford (1998).
Hands D.W. and Mirowski P. (1988), "A Paradox of Budgets: The Postwar Stabilization of American Neoclassical Demand Theory". In Morgan Rutherford (eds.), pp. 260-292.
Haney L.H. (1911), *History of Economic Thought*, New York: Macmillan.
Hicks J.R. (1946), *Value and Capital*, Oxford: Clarendon Pres.
Hill W. (1896), "Review of *The American Commercial Policy*, Three Historical Essays by Ugo Rabbeno", *Journal of Political Economy*, p. 255.
Hurvicz L. (1971), "On the Problem of Integrability of Demand Functions", in Chipman J.S., Hurvicz L., Richter M.K., Sonneschein H.F. (eds.), *Preferences, Utility, and Demand*, New York: Harcourt Brace Jovanovich, 1971, pp. 174-214.
Ise J. (1932), "Recent Textbooks in Economics", *Quarterly Journal of Economics*, 46 (2), pp. 385-397.
Jaffé W. (ed.) (1965), *Correspondence of Leon Walras and Related Papers*, 3 vols., Amsterdam: North Holland Publishing Company.
Johnson N.O. (1935), "The Brookings Report on Inequality in Income Distribution," *Quarterly Journal of Economics*, Vol. 52, pp. 718-24.
Johnson N.O. (1937), "The Pareto Law," *Review of Economics and Statistics*, Vol. 9, pp. 20-26.
Journal of Political Economy (1895), "Editorial note: Professor Pantaleoni. Appointment to the University of Naples", *Journal of Political Economy*, Vol. 4, pp. 85-86.
Knight F.H. (1921), *Risk, Uncertainty and Profit*, New York: Houghton, Mifflin.

LANE J. (1978), "Pareto's English Language Critics: a Reassessment of British and American Interpretations of *A Treatise on General Sociology*, *Revue Européenne des Sciences Sociales*," 16, 43, pp. 105-129.

LEATHERS C.G. and RAINES P. (1991), "The Italian Influence of John R. Commons' *Institutional Economics*", *Rivista Internazionale di Scienze Economiche e Commerciali*, vol. 38, pp. 543-558.

LELAND S.E. (1925), "Review of *The Social Significance of the Inheritance Tax* by Eugenio Rignano", *Journal of Political Economy*, 407.

LEVEN M. (1934), *America's Capacity to Consume*, Washington: The Brookings Institution.

LOPREATO J. and RUSHER S. (1983), "Vilfredo Pareto's Influence on USA Sociology", *Revue Européenne des Sciences Sociales*, 21, pp. 69-122.

LORIA A. (1891), "Economics in Italy," *Annals of the American Academy of Political and Social Sciences*, Vol. 3, pp. 59-80.

MACAULAY F.R. (1922), "Pareto's Law and the General Problem of Mathematical Describing the Frequency of Distribution of Income," in Mitchell W.C. (ed.), *Income in the United States*, New York: National Bureau of Economic Research.

MAGNANI I. (1995), "Il Marginalismo ed il ruolo dello Stato nel Sistema Economico", *Rivista di Politica Economica*, marzo, pp. 49-98.

MARGET A.W. (1935), "Review of *Lezioni di Economia Generale e Corporativa* by Giuseppe Ugo Papi", *Quarterly Journal of Economics*, pp. 137-38.

MERRIT F. (1898), "Review of *Cours d'Économie Politique* Par Wilfredo Pareto", *Journal of Political Economy*, 351.

MIROWSKI P. (1989), *More Heat than Light*, New York: Cambridge University Press.

MIROWSKI P. (1990), "Problems in the Paternity of Econometrics: Henry Ludwell Moore", *History of Political Economy* (22), pp. 587-609.

MITCHELL W.C. (1901), "Review of Pasquale Jannaccone's *Il Costo di Produzione*", *Journal of Political Economy*, Vol. 9, pp. 460-464.

MITCHELL W.C. (1949), *Types of Economic Theory*, ed. by J. Dorfman, 2 vols., New York: Kelley Publishers.

MOORE H.L. (1897), "Review of Pareto's *Cours d'économie politique*," *Annals of the American Academy of Political and Social Sciences*, Vol. 9, pp. 444-47.

MOORE H.L. (1908), "The Statistical Complement of Pure Economics," *Quarterly Journal of Economics*, 23, pp. 388-408.

MOORE H.L. (1914), *Economic Cycles. Their Laws and Cause*.

MOORE H.L. (1926), "Pantaleoni's Problem in the Oscillation of Prices", *Quarterly Journal of Political Economy,* XL, 4, August, pp. 586-593.

MOORE H.L. (1929), *Synthetic Economics*, New York: MacMillan.

MORGAN M.S. and RUTHERFORD M. (eds.) (1998), *From Interwar Pluralism to Postwar Neoclassicism*, Durham: Duke University Press.

OTTAVIANO C. (1981), "Quando l'Italia esportava idee. La diffusione degli scritti di Achille Loria fra gli intellettuali americani", *Annali della Fondazione Einaudi*, vol. XV, pp. 281-321.

PARETO V. (1896) (1965), "La Courbe de la Ripartition de la Richesse". In Busino G. (ed.), *Oevres Completes de Vilfredo Pareto*, vol. III, *Ecrits sur la Courbe de la Ripartition de la Richesse*, 1-15. Geneva: Libraire Droz.

PARETO V. (1895-1897), *Cours d'Économie Politique*. In Bousquet G.H and Busino G. (eds.), *Oevres Completes de Vilfredo Pareto*, vol. I. Geneva: Libraire Droz, 1964.

PARETO V. (1906) (1971), *Manual of Political Economy*, translated by Ann Schwier. New York: Augustus M. Kelley, a translation of the 1927 French edition, from the 1906 *Manuale di Economia Politica*.
PARETO V. (1935) (1963), *The Mind and Society: A Treatise on General Sociology*, translated by Andrew Bongiorno and Arthur Livingston. New York: Dover Publications, a reprint of the 1935 translation of the 1916 *Trattato di Sociologia Generale*.
PARETO V. (1962), *Lettere a Maffeo Pantaleoni: 1890-1923*, edited by G. De Rosa, 3 vols., Roma: Edizioni di Storia e Letteratura.
PARSONS T. (1935), "Review of the *Mind and Society* by Wilfredo Pareto", *American Economic Review*, pp. 501-506.
PATTEN S.N. (1910), "The Phenomena of Economic Dynamics. Discussion," *American Economic Association Quarterly*, pp. 122-35.
PATTEN S.N. (1924), *Essays in Economic Theory*. Edited by R.G. Tugwell with an introduction by H.R. Seager, New York: Knopf.
PERSKY J. (1992), "Retrospectives: Pareto's Law", *Journal of Economic Perspectives*, Vol. 6, pp. 181-192.
PERSONS W.M. (1909), "The Distribution of Wealth and Income", *Quarterly Journal of Economics*, Vol. 23.
REDER M.W. (1987), "Chicago School", in *The New Palgrave Dictionary of Economics*, London: Macmillan, pp. 413-418.
RABBENO U. (1891), "The Present Condition of Political Economy in Italy", *Political Science Quarterly*, June.
ROCCA G. (1929), "Review of *Pricipes des Sciences des Finances*, par Francesco Nitti", *Journal of Political Economy*, 141.
ROGERS J.H. (1928), "Vilfredo Pareto: The Mathematician of the Social Sciences", in *Proceedings of the International Mathematical Conference, Toronto*: Toronto University Press.
RUTHERFORD M. (ed.) (1998), *The Economic Mind in America: Essays in the History of American Economics*, London and New York: Routledge.
SAMUELSON P. (1938), "A Note on the Pure Theory of Consumer Behavior", *Economica* (5), pp. 61-71.
SAMUELSON P. (1947). *Foundations of Economic Analysis*, Cambridge, Mass.: Harvard University Press.
SCHULTZ H. (1928), *Statistical Laws of Demand and Supply*, Chicago: University of Chicago Press.
SCHULTZ H. (1933), "A Comparison of Different Elasticities of Demand Obtained by Different Methods", *Econometrica* (1), pp. 274-301.
SCHULTZ H. (1938), *The Theory and Measurement of Demand*, Chicago: University of Chicago Press.
SCHUMPETER J.A. (1949), "Vilfredo Pareto", *Quarterly Journal of Economics*.
SCHUMPETER J.A. (1954), *History of Economic Analysis*, Oxford: Oxford University Press.
SELIGMAN E.R.A. (1886), "Review of *Giornale degli Economisti*," *Political Science Quarterly*, pp. 703-704.
SELIGMAN E.R.A. (1892), *On the Shifting and Incidence of Taxation*, Baltimore: Guggenheimer.
SELIGMAN E.R.A. (1895), *Essays in Taxation*, New York: MacMillan.
SELIGMAN E.R.A. (1927), *On the Shifting and Incidence of Taxation*, 5th edition, New York: Columbia University Press.

SHERWOOD S. (1898), "Review of *Pure Economics* by Professor Maffeo Pantaleoni", *Journal of Political Economy*, pp. 547-48.

SIMONS H.C. (1937), "Review of *First Principles of Public Finance* by Antonio De Viti De Marco", *Journal of Political Economy*, pp. 712-17.

SNYDER C. (1940), *Capitalism the Creator*. New York: Macmillan.

SPENGLER J.J. (1970), "Notes on the International Transmission of Economic Ideas", *History of Political Economy*, Spring.

STIGLER G. (1965), "Statistical Studies in the History of Economic Thought", in *Essays in the History of Economics*,

SYLOS LABINI P. (1995), "Idee sulla dinamica economica", *Rivista di politica economica*, marzo, pp. 197-204.

TAUSSIG F. (1896), *Theory of Wages*, New York: MacMillan.

TUCKER R.S. (1938), "The Distribution of Income among Income Taxpayers in the United States," *Quarterly Journal of Economics*, pp. 547-587.

TESORO G.A. (1943), "Review of *Preparazione e Condotta Economica della Guerra* by L. Fontana Russo," *American Economic Review*, Vol. 33, pp. 435-37.

VEBLEN T. (1898), "Why is Economics not an Evolutionary Science," *Quarterly Journal of Economics*, Vol. 12, pp. 373-97. Reprinted in Veblen [1919].

VEBLEN T. (1919), *The Place of Science in Modern Civilization and Other Essays*, New York: Huebsch.

WALKER F.A. (1876), *The Wages Question*, New York: Macmillan.

WALKER F.A. (1889), "Recent progress of political economy in the United States," in publications of the American Economic Association, vol. IV. Reprinted in F.A. Walker, *Discussions in Economics and Statistics*, ed. by D.R. Dewey, New York, 1899.

WILLIS H.P. (1898), "Review of *La Funzione della Banca* by A. De Viti De Marco", *Journal of Political Economy*, 432.

WILSON E.B. (1912), "Mathematical Economics: *Manuel d'Economie Politique*", *Bullettin of the American Mathematical Society*, Vol. 18, pp. 462-74.

YOUNG A. (1913), "Review of *Intorno al concetto di Reddito Imponibile e di un Sistema di Imposte sul Reddito Consumato* by Luigi Einaudi," *American Economic Review*, 679.

YOUNG A.A. (1917), "Do the Statistics of the Concentration of Wealth in the United States Mean What They are Commonly Assumed to Mean?" *American Economic Review*, Vol. VII, pp. 145-156.

List of contributors

PIER FRANCESCO ASSO, is Associate Professor of History of Economic Thought at the University of Palermo, Italy. Author of several contributions on the history of Italian economic thought, the history of XXc economic thought and the history of banking. He wrote numerous essays on the History of the Bank of Italy and the history of Italian monetary policy. He is chief editor of the Complete works of Francesco Ferrara.

JESUS ASTIGARRAGA is Professor in the Departamento de Estructura e Historia Económica y Economía Pública at the University of Zaragoza (Spain). He has written numerous books and articles on the History of Economic Thought in Spain, especially in the eighteenth century. In his latest book, about to be published, he looks at the institutions, reforms and economic thought in the Bask country during the Enlightenment.

LUIGINO BRUNI is Research Fellow of Economics at the University of Milan - Bicocca, and teaches History of Economics at Bocconi University, Milan. He has published with Elgar *Vilfredo Pareto and the birth of modern microeconomics* (2001), and several papers especially on Italian economic thought.

JOSÉ LUÍS CARDOSO is professor of economics at the Technical University of Lisbon, Portugal. He has published several articles and books on the history of economic thought in Portugal (*O Pensamento Económico em Portugal nos Finais do Século XVIII*, Lisboa: Estampa, 1989; *Pensar a Economia em Portugal: Digressões Históricas*, Lisboa: Difel, 1997; *Dicionário Histórico de Economistas Portugueses*, Lisboa: Temas & Debates, 2001). He is co-editor of *A History of Portuguese Economic Thought* (London: Routledge, 1998), general editor of the series *Classics of Portuguese Economic Thought* (30 volumes published between 1990 and 1998) and co-editor of *The European Journal of the History of Economic Thought.*

LUCA FIORITO is Research Fellow of Economics at the University of Siena and doctoral candidate at the New School for Social Research, New York City. He has published several articles on the history of North American economic thought with particular regard to the history of institutional economics. He is the editor of unpublished works by W. C. Mitchell and E.R.A. Seligman.

CHRISTIAN GEHRKE, is Associate Professor of Economics, University of Graz. Assistant Editor of *Metroeconomica*. Has published several contributions on economic theory and on the history of economic thought in books and journals, including *Economic Systems*

Research, *European Journal of the History of Economic Thought*, *Metroeconomica*, *Review of Political Economy*, and *Structural Change and Economic Dynamics*.

HARALD HAGEMANN, is Professor of Economic Theory at the University of Hohenheim, Stuttgart, Germany. His main areas of research are Growth, Structural Change, New Technologies and Employment and the History of Economic Thought, where recent work has focused on the emigration of German-speaking economists after 1933 and the development of business-cycle theory. He has been the Theodor Heuss Professor 1999-2000 at the New School for Social Research in New York and a Visiting Professor at the Universities of Bologna, Cambridge, Linz and Nice. He is a managing editor of *Structural Change and Economic Dynamics* and a member of the Editorial Board of the *European Journal of the History of Economic Thought*.

HEINZ D. KURZ, is Full Professor of Economics and Chairman of the Department of Economics, University of Graz. Managing editor of "Metroeconomica" and of the "European Journal of the History of Economic Thought". Author or editor of several books, including "Theory of Production" (together with Neri Salvadori), CUP 1995 (paperback 1997), and "Critical Essays on Piero Sraffa's Legacy in Economics", CUP 2000; and author of numerous articles in journals, including, *Cambridge Journal of Economics*, *Economica*, *European Journal of Political Economy*, *Journal of Political Economy*, *History of Political Economy*, *Kyklos*, *Metroeconomica*, *Oxford Economic Papers*, *Revue d'Economie Politique* and *Studi Economici*.

ANDRÉ LEGRIS is Professor of Economics at the University of Nice-Sophia Antipolis. He is a member of the LATAPSES, a CNRS research group. His works are devoted to classical and marginalist economic analysis and to Italian economic thought. Among others, he has published articles on Italian economists in the Inter war period in "Il pensiero economico italiano", in "Oeconomia" and in the "Revue économique", on Galiani and Quesnay in "Il pensiero economico italiano".

FIORENZO MORNATI, is Research Fellow in the Centre Walras-Pareto at the University of Lausanne. His main research interests are the intellectual biography of Pareto and the history of the Paretian branch of the Lausanne school of economics. He wrote a book on *Pasquale Boninsegni e la Scuola di Losanna* (1999) and he is the scientific editor of 31st volume of Pareto's *Oeuvres Complètes* (2001).

LARS PÅLSSON SYLL, PhD in economic history (1991), PhD in economics (1997), both at Lund University, Sweden. He is currently Senior Lecturer at University of Jönköping, Sweden, where he teaches economics, philosophy and social theory. He has published extensively on the history of economic theory and economic methodology, with special emphasis on heterodox theories, structural analysis, and critical realism.

DANIELA PARISI is professor at the Catholic University of the Sacred Heart in Milano. She now teaches History of Economic Thought in the Faculty of Economics and in the Faculty of Arts and Humanities (Degree Course Philosophy). She has been carrying out researches on several topics in the field of Italian economic thought in the frame of the global history of economic theory and thinking. She has published a number of books and articles, including *Il pensiero economico classico in Italia* (1984), *Nascita e sviluppo dell'American System of Political Economy* (1990), *Internazionalità della scienza economica lombarda* (1996), *Keynesian elements in a Long-term Analysis: the Views of Two Influential Pre- and Postwar Italian Economists* (1999), *Preclassical Economic Thought: Profitable Commerce and Formal Constraints in the Economic Studies of the Young Pietro Verri* (1999), *About the Dissemination of Ideas in HET: the Case of German Economists and their Reception in Italy* (1999).

TIZIANO RAFFAELLI is Associate Professor of History of Economic Thought, Università di Cagliari. He has recently published *La Ricchezza delle Nazioni. Introduzione alla lettura* (Carocci 2001) and, with P. Barrotta, *Epistemologia ed economia* (UTET Libreria 1998). He is now writing a book on *Marshall's Evolutionary Economics* (Routledge, 2002)

MATTHIAS RÖSCH, is a PhD student at the University of Hohenheim, Stuttgart, Germany, where he completed his diploma in economics in 1999. He made postgraduate studies at the University of Bologna in 2000 and currently writes his doctoral thesis on investment wage schemes.

BO SANDELIN, Professor of economics at the University of Gothenburg, Sweden, where he presently teaches macroeconomics and the history of thought and methodology. His early research interests dealt with capital and investment theory, the economics of housing and the economics of crime. In the last decades he contributed on topics in the history of economic thought, especially Wicksellian economics and the internationalization of economics.

JUAN ZABALZA teaches History of Economic Thought in the Department of Applied Economic Analysis at the University of Alicante. He is author of several articles and books focused on Spanish Economic Thought in the Twentieth Century.

Finito di stampare in Firenze
presso la tipografia editrice Polistampa
Ottobre 2001